D0259144

THE FUTURE OF THE UK MOTOR INDUSTRY

An economic and financial analysis of the UK motor industry
against a rapidly changing background for
European and worldwide motor manufacturers

THE FUTURE OF THE UK MOTOR INDUSTRY

by

Krish Bhaskar
Professor of Accountancy and Finance
University of East Anglia

With contributions from
Garel Rhys, Senior Lecturer, University College, Cardiff

KOGAN PAGE

First published 1979
Copyright © Krish Bhaskar 1979

ISBN: 0 85038 259 9

Published by Kogan Page Ltd, 120 Pentonville Road, London N1 on behalf of Poland Street Publications Ltd. Printed by Ennisfield Ltd, 372 Old Street, London EC1V 9LT

iv

To my parents

CONTENTS

PREFACE

This book is a broadly based attempt to cover the entire motor industry. Cars and commercial vehicles obviously spring to mind in connection with the motor industry, but there are other segments of the industry which are significant in the context of the UK economy. Such areas include the components industry and the retail motor industry. Therefore, I have specifically attempted to include an analysis of these sectors in the book. The book is divided into five sections. Section 1 provides an introduction and overview of the motor industry. Section 2 is by far the largest section and deals exclusively with cars. The justification for providing a long section on cars is that it is the most unhealthy section in the UK motor industry. Section 3 deals with the commercial vehicle sector of the UK motor industry, including trailer manufacturers. Section 4 deals with other aspects of the motor industry, including the components industry, which supplies the motor vehicle manufacturers. This section also deals with marketing aspects of the motor industry, including distribution systems and the problems facing motor retailers. Finally, Section 5 provides a conclusion with some tentative policy recommendations and a brief analysis of the proposed Chrysler-Peugeot-Citroen link-up, news of which came too late to incorporate in the main body of the text.

Although the motor industry has become synonymous with cars, this sector does not command more resources than the commercial vehicle, components, other motor products and distribution sectors in total. Unfortunately it is the car sector which is in most serious difficulties and, like a disease, may spread to the other sectors of the motor industry. In recent years a great deal of attention has been lavished on this particular industry and each event that has occurred has been closely scrutinised by the media. Why? Obviously, cars and commercial vehicles have acquired a position of central importance as one of the principal means of transport and communication in the modern world. Those who own cars and spend a certain amount of time and a large proportion of their income in acquiring and maintaining them are naturally interested in the workings of an industry which provides what they consider to be an indispensible commodity. Quite apart from the opportunities the car provides for social pleasure (driving as an end in itself or as a means of access to social activities which would otherwise be unavailable) the public are aware of the economic importance of the dual functions of car ownership and production. On the one hand the motor vehicle carries a large part of the working population to and from work, thus enabling them to be productive in their own spheres; on the other hand, the motor industry itself commands an important infrastructure, requiring labour, (directly or indirectly employing up to 10 per cent of the UK labour force), components and raw materials and involving a vast range of industries and services. The motor industry has also been a major contributor to the UK Balance of Payments. But this may not continue.

The demise of the UK motor industry will seriously effect the economy. However, there can be no doubt that there is some room for cautious optimism but such optimism is critically dependent on supportive and interventionist UK government actions. Having been used to government support, the motor industry is now hooked on it, and the withdrawal symptoms, should this support not be forthcoming, could be disastrous. Where it will all end is, of course, a question that is ultimately in the hands of the government. Thus, precise forecasting of future developments is impossible. The broad indications contained in this book are at best a guess – albeit an informed one.

Inevitably, when dealing with any subject matter that constantly changes, much re-writing has been necessary in order to ensure that the book is kept abreast of the rapidly changing events within the motor industry. No doubt that by the time this book is published, recent events will have overtaken some aspects of the motor industry.

Many people have warned me against writing this book, claiming that things changed too quickly to be frozen in print. They were, and still are, correct. Not only has the book been continuously revised but the possibility of the Peugeot-Citroen takeover of Chrysler's European operations caught me, and the book, on the hop. Fortunately, the future in the short run, of Chrysler's UK plants may not be significantly changed. The longer run is analysed separately in a hastily written Chapter 17.

In 1975, a team of researchers, spearheaded by myself, completed a giant research project entitled "Alternatives Open to the UK Motor Industry : An Analysis and Evaluation". The team included Alan Armstrong, Martin Slater, Garel Rhys, Andy Friedman, Glyn Barker, Tim Mawby and others. This book stems from that project. Of the original team, only Garel Rhys has directly contributed to the current volume, although some of the original material supplied by Alan Armstrong (demand for cars), Martin Slater (economies of scale) and others have inevitably been indirectly incorporated. Garel Rhys provided two draft chapters on the commercial vehicle industry, which have been rewritten and, with additional material from myself, expanded into the three chapters. Garel and I disagreed initially on the prospects for the future of the UK commercial vehicle industry. Garel's optimism and my doubts have been integrated in the section to provide an agreed conclusion of cautious optimism. Garel also provided a draft Chapter 13, on the components industry, and again I felt it necessary to temper some of the optimism by the addition of an addendum. Although Garel has provided invaluable assistance in many of the remaining chapters, the responsibility for errors and omissions must remain mine. In particular, I alone must bear the burden of incorrect or inadequately analysed conclusions.

The project would not have been possible without the research grant kindly offered by the JRSST Charitable Trust. I also offer my grateful thanks for a contribution from Price Waterhouse & Co. Grateful thanks must be given to Anne Beech, who has sorted most of my and Garel Rhys' writings into English. Many of the forecasts and projects in the book have been produced by a maze of computer models. My thanks go to Mike Lowcock for his computing assistance. Thanks must also go to Val Harvey, Fenella McCann, Kate Davies, Mark Denton and Iris Horwood for typing and other assistance. My special thanks also to Richard Wainwright, Duncan Lewis, Lord Chitnis and Evelyn Hill. I would also like to thank Ron Sewell, Mike Binney, Mike Crossfield and Roberta McElhinney. In a project of this sort, it is of vital necessity to have contacts in the motor industry. I thank all of them; many of the ideas in the book are attributable to them.

Many people have provided me with confidential information and every endeavour has been made not to break that confidence. If however, some piece of information has been provided by another source with no strings attached, then I have regarded the information as non-confidential. One plea that I would like to make fairly strongly; UK data seems to be clothed in secrecy. Why? Reasons for commercial confidentiality is the usual response. Yet most European companies all provide a vast amount of so called confidential information such as detailed production and export information in their annual accounts. I do not see why the UK should be any different.

Finally, my special thanks to Renee Thomson and John Mason for all the production processes involved prior to the printing of the book.

Krish Bhaskar
University of East Anglia

SECTION ONE

INTRODUCTION and OVERVIEW

CHAPTER 1

INTRODUCTION

The UK motor industry must be seen in the context of the world motor industry. Canada and the US — with a market demand in excess of 17 million vehicles — manage to support only three major manufacturers: General Motors (GM), Ford and Chrysler. American Motors and Volkswagen operate with a very much smaller capacity. The story is similar in Japan, with a smaller but rapidly expanding market of around 4 million vehicles dominated by two major concerns, Toyota and Nissan (Datsun). The market in Europe, however, began as a collection of smaller, national markets, although since World War Two there has been a systematic tendency for Western Europe to evolve as a single integrated market. Although Japanese or North American conditions are not yet exactly duplicated in Western Europe, the similarities are now striking, with one important exception. Whereas West European demand now runs at a level of roughly 11 million to 12 million vehicles, there are no fewer than 14 major car manufacturers[1] working to meet that demand, with many more commercial vehicle (CV) producers. In comparison with other advanced motor markets in the World, the West European market must be described as highly fragmented and urgently in need of some rationalisation.

To add to the problem, Western Europe is also facing a series of crises. On the export front, European producers have faced a serious challenge in the traditional markets (e.g. the US) from the Japanese, while import penetration within the West European market has also risen, partly as a result of Japanese efforts. The Japanese, however, are not the only newer producer to pose a potential threat to Western Europe. Latin America, the Communist Bloc, Korea and others all have burgeoning car industries and would all be eager to fill any vacuum should the Japanese challenge disappear. The motor industry in the UK and Western Europe entered the decade of the 1970s facing some major structural problems, although in the early 1970s the gravity of the situation was partly obscured by the generally high levels of demand for vehicles. European firms found that their plants were operating at or near to full capacity. Peak demand was brought to an abrupt halt by the oil crisis and a world wide recession, during which demand for new cars fell dramatically. The motor industry, which has typically been characterised by high break-even points, was forced to take drastic action to avoid complete insolvency. Only the fittest were apparently equipped to survive: in the US, Chrysler and American Motors both found themselves in acute financial difficulty; in Europe, weaker firms merged with stronger ones; and in the UK, the government intervened to bail out two major manufacturers, British Leyland (BL) and Chrysler UK. Elsewhere in Europe, Renault, Peugeot-Citroen, Alfa-Romeo, Volvo, Volkswagen and BMW have all received government aid in varying degrees.

Since then, the UK press have had a somewhat hysterical field day, maintaining a constant newspaper vigil on BL and Chrysler and eagerly reporting on anything even remotely untoward. Of the two, the Chrysler rescue has gone more smoothly, partly because the operation was designed as a measure of

1. Reduced to 13 if the Chrysler-Peugeot-Citroen merger goes through — see Chapter 17.

3

short-term relief and partly because government liability has been limited to a maximum of £163 million. Chrysler's longer-term problems are discussed subsequently in Section 2. The BL rescue, on the other hand, involved major long-term changes in the company policy, structure and approach, and was inevitably more expensive. Reaction to the £2.8 billion salvage was adverse, although expenditures of that sort are modest by car manufacturers' standards: Daimler Benz, for example, is spending £1.3 billion on its car divisions between 1977–80, while GM has allocated a $15 billion research budget for 1976–80. Many other European firms moreover, were in a similarly troubled position, having to contend with poor productivity, labour difficulties, ineffective quality control, an unreliable product, public disquiet and political antipathy to the long-term financial liabilities involved. Why, then, did the BL rescue meet with such a hostile reception?

THE CAUSE FOR ALARM

The UK motor industry comprises four major manufacturers, three of which are owned by US multinationals (Ford, Chrysler and Vauxhall [GM]). There are in addition a number of smaller producers, some of whom are significant, notably ERF, Foden, Rolls-Royce, Lotus, etc. Not surprisingly, the smaller producers have had a troubled history. More unexpectedly, the four major manufacturers have also all experienced difficulties. Ford, the least hard hit of the four, has been bedevilled with labour relations crises, while both GM and Chrysler have reported losses on their UK subsidiaries for a number of years. BL's chronic problems were – and are – legendary. All four firms would have been in trouble with or without the 1973-4 world recession, and in each case – although details vary – the problems were essentially structural.

BL failed to reorganise and rationalise after the British Motor Holdings Ltd merger with Leyland in 1968. Chrysler UK and Vauxhall operated as completely separate entities in a rather stagnant UK market, a weakness that could have been avoided by fuller integration with their various European counterparts to form a single European Company. Ford, who alone was quick to realise the advantages that might accrue from European integration, reaped the benefit of massive economies of scale in doing so – the extent of which is considered in the following chapters. These tangible difficulties to some extent obscured the rather alarmingly high incidence of industrial unrest apparently endemic in the UK motor industry.

RECENT EVENTS

Although the problems encountered in 1974-5 should have been foreseen, they were not. Instead, there was widespread optimism. It was generally assumed that entering the EEC would boost sales, virtually as a matter of course. When it failed to happen, the pundits were quick to offer advice in the form of a number of major government/official reports – the Ryder Report, the CPRS Report[1] and the two reports from the Expenditure Committee – and scholars, economists, theorists and academics poured forth their various offerings, which are referred to in this chapter.

1 *The Future of the British Car Industry,* The Central Policy Review Staff, HMSO, 1975.

THE BL RESCUE – THE RYDER REPORT

Committed to some form of help to BL, the government called in Sir Don Ryder (later Lord Ryder) to conduct an 'overall assessment' of BL's present position and future strategy. The Ryder team was appointed on 18 December 1974 and completed its report by March 1975.

The Ryder Report, *British Leyland: The Next Decade* (HMSO, 1975) established a future for BL: 'vehicle production is the kind of indusry which ought to remain an essential part of the UK's economic base. . . BL should remain a major vehicle producer, although this means that urgent action must be taken to remedy the weaknesses which at present prevent it from competing effectively in world markets' (Ryder, para. 13, p.3). Ryder formulated a strategy whereby the company remained in the specialist and volume car market and in the CV sector. The Report recommended that BL eliminate competition between models within the same sector and reduce the number of different body shells, engines, transmissions, etc. The West European market was designated as the major growth area for sales of BL products, encouraging CV sales in certain developing markets, i.e. Iran, Nigeria and Turkey. One of the main features of the Report was the new capital expenditure programme of £2 billion (in money terms) with an additional £750 million (in money terms) required for working capital. Capital expenditure on this scale was central to the Ryder thesis:

> The most serious feature of BL's production facilities is, however, that a large proportion of the plant and machinery is old, outdated and inefficient (para. 28, p.6).

> This record of underinvestment is the main reason for the low productivity of BL's work force compared with say Fiat or Volkswagen (para 8.11, p.29).

In simple terms, the Ryder plan envisaged a unified model policy, an integrated car division and expansion of the CV sector. In response to internal pressures, the Jaguar division retained its own engineering facilities. Further, detailed discussion of the Ryder strategy appears in later chapters.

Having produced the Ryder Report, Ryder himself was then asked to oversee the implementation of the strategy he had recommended through the NEB. The wisdom of such an arrangement was questionable. To begin with, the volume of finance required almost overwhelmed the NEB, which had been created primarily to function as a shareholder in profitable concerns and was ill-equipped to mount a full scale rescue operation. Ryder's own chairmanship of the Ryder Report Committee made any deviation by the NEB from the Report's recommendations unlikely or at least difficult.

The Report itself had been roundly criticised in the press and in subsequent political debate. The fourteenth Report of the Expenditure Committee, Trade and Industry Sub-Committee, *The Motor Vehicle Industry* (HMSO, 1975) which was published four months after the Ryder Report, in the summer of 1975, provoked a renewed public debate on the wisdom or efficacy of the Ryder plan.

THE EXPENDITURE COMMITTEE

In view of the possibility of large sums of public money being involved, the Trade and Industry Sub-committee of the Expenditure Committee[1] decided to conduct its own investigation into the UK Motor Vehicle industry. During the course of the Committee's investigations it became clear that BL was in particular difficulty. The scope of the enquiry was therefore broadened to encompass the whole of the motor industry, in the course of which the Committee heard 3,264 submissions, interviewed more than 100 witnesses and received 91 items of written evidence, all of which provided substantial documentation on the motor industry. The final report lacks the sharpness of the CPRS document or the heavily abridged Ryder Report, consisting of an evaluation of the evidence received and a critique of the Ryder Report, together with a detailed summation and analysis of further problems to be anticipated and acted upon. The report takes account of increasing government involvement in the motor industry, to which end there are a number of specific recommendations (see Table 1.1). The strengths and weaknesses of the motor industry are identified and the Ryder Report itself is criticised. The Expenditure Committee expressed strong reservations about the amount of money to be used under the Ryder Plan and the way in which the money was to be used, concluding that 'resources on a huge scale have been committed without sufficient examination of the aims, mechanics and desirability of such a step.' (p. 128)

Clearly some of the comments in the Expenditure Committee report were overtly political in nature:

> It is certainly significant that the Ryder Report proposes with such confidence so sweeping a solution to the problems of BL. Given the scale of funds involved in this solution, we have noted with even greater interest the speed with which the Government accepted the Report's main conclusions. (p.94)

Other criticisms were more substantive and to a large degree have been corroborated by subsequent events. The report, for example, was critical of the lack of organisational safeguards which it felt was a 'major weakness of the proposed structure'.

> We are of the opinion that Ryder has put too much of the onus on the compatibility of personalities rather than on the correctness of the structure. This is inherently dangerous. (p. 96)

On the question of model policy, the Expenditure Committee noted:

> We see no reason to believe that the number of basic models envisaged for BL will allow it to compete effectively in as wide a range as Ryder recommends. (p. 98)

1.   Ibid.

TABLE 1.1

Summary of Expenditure Committee's Recommendations

1. A detailed industry-wide study of the problems of achieving correct manning levels is urgently needed (Paragraph 107).

2. The Government should make clear the implications for other major motor manufacturers of selective assistance to British Leyland (Paragraph 118).

3. We attach fundamental importance to the establishment of firm criteria for the expenditure of public money in selective assistance to industry, and to adherence to those criteria (Paragraph 149).

4. We fail to see how a firm can avoid becoming a "permanent pensioner" if it is not viable, and we wish to see a resolution of the apparent conflict in the Department of Industry's approach to selective assistance for industry to which we draw attention in Paragraph 153.

5. It is essential that the Department of Industry's provision of staff at Headquarters and in the Regions should be adequate for the surveillance and detailed knowledge of an industry of the size and significance of motor manufacturing (Paragraph 157).

6. Greater attention needs to be given to the whole question of consumer preference (Paragraph 168).

7. The development of more extensive lay-off schemes for plants which are particularly vulnerable to external disputes would be helpful (Paragraph 205).

8. There is the strongest possible case for ensuring that the tax payer gets fair return on his involuntary investment in British Leyland (Paragraph 219).

9. Given that to a remarkable degree the Ryder report endorses the type if not the scale of the changes which B.L.M.C. themselves were planning to make, it appears that the team accepted the concept study too readily as part of a detailed plan of action. A firm's concept study based on "a fairly free availability of cash" is unlikely to have rigid economy as its central theme, and it is rigid economy and high cost-effectiveness which should be two of the criteria for the expenditure of public money, not to mention commercial survival (Paragraph 235).

10. The Ryder report has put too much of the onus on the compatibility of personalities within British Leyland rather than on the correctness of the Corporation's structure, and this is inherently dangerous (Paragraph 238).

7

(Table 1.1 continued)

---

11. We note that the decision not to retain the services of Mr. Barber followed from the Government's adoption of the Ryder recommendations on structure, which Mr. Barber judged unsuitable and to the shortcomings of which we draw attention (Paragraph 239).

12. We see no reason to believe that the number of basic models envisaged for B.L.M.C. will allow it to compete effectively in as wide a range as the Ryder report recommends (Paragraph 243).

13. We do not believe that "withholding the next tranche" of money for B.L.M.C. is a practical possibility. If it were carried out, it could well ensure the squandering of the sums already expended. The threat of a sanction which cannot be used is no threat (Paragraphs 258-259).

14. The fundamental conflict between the mutually incompatible desires for local management responsibility in the field of wage bargaining and a universal wage structure must be emphasised even if it cannot be resolved (Paragraph 261).

15. We are concerned that the arguments for and against completely independent truck and bus, quality car and mass-produced car companies should not have been made to the House; we have no evidence that they have been examined seriously at all (Paragraph 264).

16. We do not wish to see the only way of correcting a fundamental mistake in the Ryder report turning out to be payment from public funds (Paragraph 266).

17. The indications seem to be that the U.K. motor industry must shed capacity or increase its share of the European market (Paragraph 288).

18. We feel that the House will want to give close attention to the extent to which Government assistance to British Leyland may subsidise the company's operations (Paragraph 291).

19. The Chief Executive of British Leyland will need to be strong enough to resist interference, particularly in the context of close Government involvement (Paragraph 293).

Source: Fourteenth Report from the Expenditure Committee, *The Motor Vehicle Industry.* pp. 144-5.

The Expenditure Committee also pinpointed certain weaknesses in the control aspects of the Ryder Report. For example:

> The Department of Industry did not make sufficiently clear the definitions of responsibility as between the Department and the NEB and the lack of a clear distinction could make the monitoring of BL's progress less effective. (p. 104)

The Ryder Report expected to force union compliance with its recommendations by withholding successive franchises of Government money required by BL for investment, a policy which the Expenditure Committee rightly criticised: 'To carry out the threatened withholding of a tranche could well ensure the squandering of the sums already expended.' (p. 105)

Neither the Government nor the Ryder Committee had shown any willingness to evaluate possible alternatives to the Ryder Report, a reluctance which did not escape the Expenditure Committee:

> We are concerned that the arguments for and against completely independent truck and bus, quality car, and mass-produced car companies should not have been made to the House. Indeed, we have no evidence that they have been seriously examined at all. (P 107)

Although certain aspects of the Ryder plan have been (and presumably will be in the future) changed, the Ryder plan is still important. The Ryder strategy was based on the concepts of BL management. Therefore there are many parts of the plan which may still be relevant. We therefore do expound at considerable length on exactly what the plan entails later in the book.

UNIVERSITY OF BRISTOL REPORT

The University of Bristol Report,[1] entitled 'Alternatives Open to the UK Motor Industry', published in September 1975, attempted to analyse and to evaluate the various alternatives open to the industry. Although the Report was lengthy, it was completed in a very short time; at least some of the conclusions were perhaps arrived at a little too quickly. One of the main points to emerge from the Report was that although the Ryder Report had certain weaknesses, the plan embodied in the report was basically sound, suggesting that if the plan's recommendations were adopted, BL could expect to generate profits when the market was reasonably healthy. If conditions were less than favourable, however, due to production losses or a depressed demand, then BL would make a loss, possibly requiring further government aid, principally for the car division. As will be seen later, the main problem has not been so much with the Ryder plans as such, but with their implementation.

In more general terms, the Bristol Report concurred with the Expenditure Committee Report in suggesting that Chrysler UK — like BL — would soon run into difficulties. That, at least, was shown to be correct.

1. See Preface.

9

THE CHRYSLER RESCUE AND THE CPRS REPORT

In the autumn of 1975 the Government was faced with a choice between the threatened collapse of Chrysler UK or the offer of some form of state aid or takeover. The events leading up to the £163 million rescue operation are described in some detail in Young & Hood's *Chrysler UK — A Corporation in Transition.*[1]

At the time of the crisis the Government had already commissioned the Central Policy Review Staff (henceforth CPRS) to carry out a survey of the British car industry. The CPRS[2] report was prepared with the help of McKinsey, (the international firm of consultants) in order to provide an independent view of the motor industry in the UK, but the Report's conclusions, independent or not, were an embarrassment to the Government, which found itself announcing the terms of the Chrysler salvage operation only hours after publication of a Government-sponsored report recommending quite the opposite course of action! The CPRS survey, for example, when discussing the thorny issue of UK capacity, observed: 'It is clear, therefore, that if the [British Car] Industry is to become viable there is no alternative but to cut capacity by at least 400,000 units' (p. 134). With Chrysler UK on the verge of collapse, this would have been a golden opportunity to implement this recommendation. In fact quite the reverse occurred, the rescuers unwittingly increased the Chrysler capacity by 18 per cent for cars[3] as the Government was forced to admit[4].

The CPRS conclusions were probably rejected partly in order to maintain existing levels of employment, especially in Scotland and, partly to buttress the balance of payments. In fact, the £163 million cost of the Chrysler scheme represents remarkably good value given that it saves at least 20,000 jobs in Chrysler alone and possibly double that number in the ancillary trades.

The CPRS report in its published form was virtually unabridged and — without the coverage of the Expenditure Committee's Report — it was brief, to the point, well-written and beautifully presented. It recognised many of the problems already noted in both the Ryder Report and the Expenditure Commitee's Report: poor distribution networks abroad, inappropriate model mix, quality control difficulties, poor delivery record, unsatisfactory industrial relations, under-investment and finally the destabilising effects of government fiscal policy. Where the CPRS report deviated most radically from the conclusions of the Ryder Report was on the question of the effect of capital expenditure: 'Even where it is possible to measure the effect of under-investment on productivity, the results demonstrate that inadequate capital equipment is only a minor cause of low productivity' (CPRS, para. 85, p.87). The main CPRS contention was that low productivity was due to over-manning, slower work-pace and poor maintenance rather than old, outdated and inefficient capital equipment. Much was made in the Report of poor productivity:

1. S. Young and N. Hood, *Chrysler UK — A Corporation in Transition* (New York: Praeger 1977).
2. *The Future of the British Car Industry* Central Policy Review Staff, HMSO, 1975.
3. Eighth Report from the Expenditure Committee, Trade and Industry Sub-committee Public Expenditure on Chrysler UK, 1976, pp. 99 – 100.
4. Public Expenditure on Chrysler UK, Government's reply to the Eighth Report from the Expenditure Committee, 1977, para. 37, p 14.

There is not the slightest chance of Britain retaining a volume car industry at anything like its present size if present shopfloor attitudes persist. Present 'trench warfare' attitudes of management and labour will not serve in the assembly industries of 20th century Western Europe. The British car industry's approach to quality of workmanship, to new working practices, to continuity of production and manning levels is so out of date that it cannot survive. Workers and management must see the danger and adapt rapidly or go under. They must not be persuaded otherwise by politically motivated militants (p. xiv).

The CPRS Report also conducted a series of experiments comparing UK productivity with comparable plants in Western Europe, concluding that:

> with the same power at his elbow and doing the same job as his continental counterpart, a British car assembly worker produces only half as much output per shift (CPRS Report, p. v).

The main disagreement between the CPRS Report and the Expenditure Committee's report concerned the controversy over the significance of capital investment and *inter alia* the contribution of labour relations in its broadest sense to the appalling level of UK productivity. The Expenditure Committee, agreeing with Ryder, insisted that 'inadequate investment and the lower productivity of old plant have been the greatest contributors to poor profitability of the mass-production car side of the industry' (Expenditure Committee, p. 34). Although the CPRS conceded that old plant was a problem, they determined that other problems were more important: 'To improve productivity, investment alone is not enough. The basic problem is attitudes – attitudes of both management and labour'[1] (p. v). The main conclusions of the CPRS report are shown in Table 1.2.

TABLE 1.2

Main Conclusions by the CPRS on the Future of the British Car Industry

1. The prospect is one of very tough competition in the Western European car industry for at least the next decade.

2. The British car industry has serious competitive weaknesses. There are too many manufacturers with too many models, too many plants and too much capacity. These are the responsibility of management.

3. Other severe weaknesses are poor quality, bad labour relations, unsatisfactory delivery record, low productivity and too much manpower. With the same power at his elbow and doing the same job as his continental

---

1. This is a simplifcation of the issues involved. For example the Expenditure Committee made the same observations before publication of the CPRS Report *(The Motor Vehicle Industry* 1975, para 97, p. 39). The main debate from the technical standpoint was over the main explanatory variable or the explanatory power of that variable.

TABLE 1.2 (cont.)

counterpart, a British car assembly worker produces only half as much output per shift. It is not too late to correct these weaknesses. They basically arise on the shopfloor and it is on the shopfloor that they must be corrected.

4. If the weaknesses are not corrected, employment could fall by 275,000 by 1985 and the balance of trade in cars deteriorate by over £1 billion a year at 1975 prices. The most optimistic prospect is a United Kingdom industry volume of 1.9 million in 1985. The volume is bound to be lower in the years between. 1.9 million in 1985 will only be reached if, in the years immediately ahead, productivity sharply improves (and therefore manning levels are reduced). Without a reduction in the labour force in the short term there is no prospect of large scale employment long term.

5. To improve productivity investment alone is not enough. The basic problem is attitudes of both management and labour. The future of the industry lies in its own hands and in no one else's, but the Government now owns half the industry and cannot avoid the responsibility of leadership. The Government must:

(a) Declare its determination to do all in its power to achieve a viable, substantial, internationally competitive and unsubsidised car industry in the 1980s.

(b) Sponsor a programme designed to achieve the fundamental changes in attitude throughout the industry required for improving productivity, quality and continuity of production.

(c) Recognise the need to rationalise plants and reduce assembly capacity and to ensure that this reduction takes place with the least possible adverse effects on the general level of employment.

(d) Stabilise the domestic market for cars in particular by stabilising fiscal policy towards the industry. Study alternative means of restraining Japanese imports against the possibility that the coming talks with the Japanese should not prove satisfactory.

(e) Take action in British Leyland (BL) to bring about the changes which the CPRS has shown are necessary throughout the industry. Make the provision of capital to BL dependent on achieving *specified* improvements in productivity, quality and continuity of production. Consider future requests for financial assistance from other car manufacturing firms in the light of the CPRS Report.

SECOND EXPENDITURE COMMITTEE REPORT[1]

The Eighth Report of the Expenditure Committee in 1975-6, 'Public Expenditures on Chrysler UK Ltd',[2] was on the whole far less critical of Government action than its predecessor in that it endorsed the Chrysler rescue, with a single proviso: 'It could be argued that the Government concluded the right agreement for the wrong reasons' (p. 133). All in all, the committee was pleased with Chrysler UK's progress, which it described as 'encouraging' (p. 133), but the Committee also noted that the future was not uniformly rosy:

> a profitable operating position must not be confused with long-term viability. (Chrysler UK must be able not only to show profits but to be able to generate sufficient funds after 1979 to finance a continuing model programme as well as repaying their loan.) We do not think that Chrysler UK will be able to generate such funds. It might then be suggested to the Government that since with the help of the Chrysler Corporation (the US parent company) the loans could be repaid or a new model programme financed, but not both, the loans might be funded into equity. Should such a situation arise, the Government ought not to be unprepared. If the funds available to Chrysler UK are inadequate and if Chrysler Corporation are unwilling to help, then the thrice-postponed collapse of the company (1964, 1967 and 1975) might occur (p. 133).

Both Young and Hood[3] and the Expenditure Committee recognise that long-term viability is critically dependent on the successful integration of Chrysler UK with Chrysler's operation in Europe. Young and Hood comment:

> The rescue itself could be defended as a laudable attempt to maintain a motor industry in the UK. However, with Chrysler, as with Leyland, it was wrong to put public money at risk with so few guarantees. . . since the Government probably has a breathing space before the next recession and the next bout of industrial collapse, there is time to remedy the situation (p. 312).

CONTENTIOUS ISSUES

Although all of the reports mentioned agree that low productivity is a principal cause of the weakness of the UK motor industry, there is a fundamental disagreement between the reports on how to increase productivity. Is capital investment likely to succeed or not? The productivity targets aimed for in turn affect levels of employment in the motor industry. Apart from capital investment and employment, decisions must be made on (i) model policy and reliability, (ii) the degree of commonality of parts between models, (iii) number of plants and (iv) distribution and dealer network policy.

Although the Ryder Report has presumably made clear recommendations in these areas, most of the recommendations have remained confidential. The

1. On matters concerning the Motor Industry.
2. Eighth Report from the Expenditure Committee, Trade and Industry Sub-Committee, *Public Expenditure on Chrysler UK Ltd* (HMSO, 1975-6).
3. Young and Hood, *Chrysler UK, ibid.*

Expenditure Committee, the CPRS and a number of other reports may have given the BL management a greater degree of freedom than Ryder. Certainly, Chrysler, Ford and Vauxhall all face similar decisions, although they must also decide on the degree of European (and indeed global) integration between parent company and subsidiaries.

The issues are far from clear-cut. Ford, who has been front-runner in integrating its European operation, has chosen to expand production facilities in Spain rather than concentrate all operations in one area. GM (Vauxhall in the UK, Opel in Germany) and Chrysler have both adopted a more unified 'European' approach. The contentious issues for BL are both more fundamental and more costly in nature. There are a greater number of jobs at stake, for example, and any change in BL's position would have a much greater impact on the balance of payments. For Ford, Chrysler UK and Vauxhall, UK model policy hinges on worldwide model policy and production decisions made elsewhere. There are no such constraints on BL. For the company, the new Chairman, for the government and the NEB the immediate future will involve many decisions based on a multitude of factors and informed by a plethora of contradictory advice.

From the point of view of the private individual, BL's problems in its car division seem bizarre. Cars which are not selling well can be produced, whilst 'high demand' cars always seem to run into supply difficulties. We do attempt to explain why such situations arise. What is not dealt with at great length here is the reason for the industry's poor industrial relations situation. That it exists cannot be ignored and we believe that many planning exercises in the past have been guilty of under-estimating the impact of a troubled industrial relations environment on the planned UK supply of vehicles.

There are, however, other contentious issues. Since World War II, the UK motor industry has become more concentrated, culminating in the formation of BL in 1968. The Ryder plan carried the implementation of the concentration movement one stage further. However, the appointment of Michael Edwardes as Chairman of BL in 1977 brought a partial reversal of the process for the first time. Such a move brought howls of protest *and* support. An analysis of the pros and cons of such a move is subsequently made. However, one myth concerning BL ought to be dispelled. Poor industrial relations, considerable press and media comment and BL's declining share of the UK car market have all led to the general feeling that BL is a sinking albatross. Although this may be true of the car divisions, there are other segments of BL which are profitable. The CV division and the Special Products division have been commercially viable. Whether they will continue to be so is analysed subsequently in the book. One rather incongruous division set up by the Ryder plan was an international marketing/sales division. Despite considerable adverse comment, the division has been remarkably successful, increasing exports of BL's products: whilst on the domestic front car sales have plummeted, BL's International division has seemingly performed a miracle of actually increasing exports. Table 1.3 provides a breakdown of the various divisions for 1977. Nevertheless, even if BL Cars is in serious difficulty, precedents set elsewhere indicate that it is too early to write off its future. A remarkable transformation was achieved by Volkswagen during the early 1970s. The key to the revitalised

Volkswagen was a new model programme as well as management and productivity changes. The same formula for change could well apply to the ailing British Company.

TABLE 1.3

BL's Profitability Record in 1977 Net Profit Before Tax

	Half Year	Full Year
	£m	£m
Cars	-15.7	-32
Truck and Bus	21.2	27
Special Products	7.1	8
TOTAL	12.6	3

The good performance of BL's Truck and Bus and Special Products divisions are masked by the cars division losses. Nevertheless, at an early stage in the book, this introduces a note of optimism for some segments of the industry.

GOVERNMENT TO BLAME

Finally, there is one clearly uncontentious point which the reader ought to bear in mind. In the final analysis, the Government has to bail out the UK motor industry of its current mess. Some observers are even beginning to feel sympathetic towards the Government with yet another ailing industry to support. Such sympathy is misplaced because it has been successive and consistent Government action which is primarily to blame for the poor state of the industry as a whole. There are several major reasons. First, the car has always been treated as a luxury item. The Labour Party, for example, has always had a doctrinaire dislike for the "luxury" symbolised by a car and the fact that cars are *private* as opposed to *public* goods. Equally, the Conservatives have done little systematically to promote the industry. Secondly, all governments have found it useful to conduct the demand management of the economy through demand for consumer durables and particularly demand for motor vehicles. This has led to very large swings in the demand for motor vehicles which in the 1950s and 1960s created cyclical employment in the industry and helped to stoke the inherent insecurity of the labour force. The resulting insecurity partly explains the horrendous industrial relations and trench warfare attitudes identified by the CPRS Report. Thirdly, such inconsistent government interference has had another effect. The UK motor industry has always been characterised by long lead times and high break-even points which make it difficult for the industry to react to external changes. Yet, as one manager of BL International is reputed to have said:

15

> In the period 1960-70, the initial growth period of the European and Japanese industries, the terms on which cars could be purchased — the rates of purchase tax and the conditions of credit payment — were altered on average every ten months. . . Solely because of selective intervention on the part of the Government, the UK motor industry faced a period of seven year's decline and stagnation immediately following a period in which demand had leaped over 60% in three years. All this at a time when all its competitors experienced continuous and generally rapid growth in their domestic markets. *(Financial Times,* 13 September 1977).

So not too much sympathy must be lavished on UK governments in general; in fact, it is fitting that they should now be lumbered with a problem of their own creation. One can only hope through the experience with the motor and other industries that the government will not again adopt such a short-sighted approach to industry — especially that which is still in private hands. The Ford strike in the Autumn of 1978 is a classic example. Left to their own devices both Ford and their labour force could probably reach an agreement. However the direct intervention of the UK government via the 5 per cent limit on pay rises has once again hit one of the UK motor industry's healthiest areas.

THE STRUCTURE OF THE BOOK

This book attempts to evaluate the industry and to suggest some of the possible remedies. It will also sift the available evidence — and provide new evidence — to aid the public at large and the decision-makers to choose between the conflicting arguments which already cloud the debate and which are likely to confuse the issue even further in years to come. In this respect, the book is essentially forward-looking, although we have also tried to draw together a set of assumptions common to all of the various reports, on which we have based a forecast of the probable trends in the UK motor industry.

Section 1 provides a brief overview of that industry, together with a more detailed discussion of some of the reports already mentioned in this chapter. Section 2 deals exclusively with the car industry, while Section 3 discusses the commercial vehicle sector. Section 4 considers other aspects of the industry, including the components industry, marketing considerations and retailing. Section 5 acts as a conclusion.

Although many of the contentious issues are further discussed in the various sections during the remainder of the book, Chapter 4 in particular attempts to examine them from a general standpoint.

The possible purchase by Peugeot-Citroen of Chrysler's European operations came too late to incorporate in Sections 1—4. Chapter 17 deals with this proposed merger.

CHAPTER 2

HISTORICAL CONTEXT, THEORETICAL CONSIDERATIONS AND INTERNATIONAL PERSPECTIVES

HISTORICAL CONTEXT

Car production was established on a relatively modest commercial scale in the UK by the turn of the century. By 1911, an American-owned company (Ford UK) had introduced mass-production techniques at its Old Trafford factory and by 1914, using parts imported duty free from the US, the company was assembling 6,000 cars a year and through highly competitive pricing had captured the major share of the UK market.

The First World War, however, worked to the advantage of Ford's British competitors in the domestic market. The imposition of high import duties had an adverse effect on Ford's price competitiveness, while at the same time the demands of war work gave British companies greater experience of flow-line mass production techniques, enabling them to streamline manufacturing methods and increase efficiency. This led, in turn, to an increased output in the immediate post war period. By now, British firms (principally Morris, the new market leader and Austin) were in a position to exploit economies of scale and lower both costs and prices while increasing volume. By 1929, Morris has carved out a 35 per cent market share, followed by Austin with a 25.6 per cent share and Singer with 15 per cent. The number of smaller independent manufacturers, however, had dropped dramatically – from 96 in 1922 to fewer than 40 in 1931. Ford's share of the market had fallen to 39.9 per cent.

In the late 1920s and throughout the 1930s the situation changed yet again. It is generally accepted that although Morris and Austin did not surrender the lion's share of the market, they were not successful in exploiting their lead. Both companies needed more flexible management structures and new plant and they were both failing to exploit the emergence of a new market – for a 'medium-sized' car. Ford, meanwhile, had established the first integrated plant at Dagenham in 1931, marking the start of a successful marketing offensive with the introduction of the Ford 8. Vauxhall (acquired by GM in 1925) developed a more aggressive approach in the same period and began to increase its market share. While relative and absolute production of both Morris and Austin cars declined, Ford, Standard (who also met the demand for a medium-sized car with the introduction of 9 and 10 h.p. models), Rootes and Vauxhall increased output; by 1939 these six companies accounted for 90 per cent of the mass market.

The Second World War brought heavy investment in the motor industry, enabling the larger firms to re-equip on a massive scale and vastly increase productive capacity, so that in the post war period they were well prepared to supply an apparently limitless demand for new cars world wide. Seventy per cent of total production was exported (with the blessing and frequently the active encouragment, of the government), while potential home sales (adversely affected in the short term by tight credit controls, limitations of hire purchase, escalating petrol costs and material shortages) were left largely unexploited. In the rush to realise short-term export profits, scant attention was paid to other aspects of the industry — industrial relations, for example, and the marketing and service infra-structures of the companies concerned. This oversight was to have harmful repercussions in later years, as customers became increasingly dissatisfied with the unreliability of British cars (and the non-existent after-sales service they frequently needed); the labour force were later to demonstrate an increasing unwillingness to co-operate with managements.

The decade of the 1950s saw further changes in the structure of the car industry, as demand conditions were re-established and major manufacturers outside the UK regained their foothold in world markets. Within the UK, Ford, resuming production at Dagenham, once again posed a serious threat to Austin and Morris and in 1952 the two companies formed the defensive alliance of BMC, in an attempt to beat off Ford's potentially serious rivalry. Car output rose appreciably (from 0.5 million in 1950 to 1.8 million per annum in 1960) due to a substantial increase in capacity. As output increased, profits grew — but not uniformly. BMC, for example, were evidently unable to create suitable economies of scale. Whereas in 1956 Ford realised a net profit of £45 per vehicle, BMC could only make £35. By 1961, the gap had widened: Ford made £53 per vehicle, whereas BMC could only show £6.50 as profit per car! This, in itself, is a striking illustration of the problems that, by the early 1960s, beset the UK car industry in general — and BMC in particular. The company seemed to be obsessed with capacity expansion at the expense of capacity renewal, producing a wide range of models without improving and updating plant and equipment. This, coupled with BMC's inadequate provisions for depreciation (50 per cent lower than Ford's), led to high production costs — further complicated by under pricing.

In the early 1960s there was a fresh assault on the increasingly important medium-sized car market — particularly from the two American firms, Vauxhall and Ford. With the Viva and the Cortina respectively, both companies challenged the BMC 1100 and the Rootes Minx. Rootes, moreover, miscalculated the strength of the small car market, gearing the Linwood plant to Imp production just as the market retracted. The company was saved only by the increased participation of yet another American firm — Chrysler.

Difficulties in the domestic car market were compounded by an increasing vulnerability in export markets, due partly to the problems of sterling in 1964-7, to an over-dependence on one or two traditional markets at the expense of a global export drive and (one, at least, of the many early chickens coming home to roost) the major export disadvantage of poor marketing and after-sales service.

The UK car industry experienced a series of rapid (and sometimes dramatic) changes in the period from 1965 to 1968. Leyland (LMC), for example, had bought-out an ailing Standard Triumph in 1961, thus becoming one of the major car manufacturers. The company had gone on to acquire Aveling Barford (manufacturers of construction equipment) and Rover, moving Triumph up market and away from the centre of competition. LMC merged with (or took over, as many would have it) BMH (itself the product of a defensive merger between BMC and Jaguar) in 1968 to form BLMC. Elsewhere, Chrysler, despite increasing (and eventually total) participation in Rootes, failed to make the company profitable and Vauxhall, after an initial success with the Viva, similarly failed to record a profit in successive years. BLMC's losses, of course, are part of history. The succession of defensive and offensive mergers had a profound effect on the UK car industry, leaving only one major car manufacturer *not* in foreign ownership and with only one (foreign-owned) company — Ford — showing anything like an acceptable profitability.

In this section we have merely sketched the barest chronology of events. In subsequent chapters we will examine the reasons for these moves in greater detail and explore the consequences of the historical jigsaw that has created the mid-1970s (lack of) status quo.

THEORETICAL CONSIDERATIONS

Before outlining the current state of the UK motor industry and evaluating the various alternatives open to it, a few theoretical considerations must be given.

Economies of Scale

There are two principal ways in which the average costs of producing vehicles vary with the level of output and it is important to make a clear distinction between them. First, if a factory with given machinery and staffing levels is producing fewer cars than it is designed for, then obviously the fixed overheads must be spread over a smaller volume, resulting in higher unit costs. This variation is essentially a short-run phenomenon and must not be confused with the second variation — long-run economies of scale. In this latter case, the management (starting more or less from scratch) can decide on the best size of factory and best type of machinery to install; for the moment, we are more concerned with estimating the way unit costs vary with the *designed* output of the various types and scales of plant available — in other words, considering what sort of output the producer should set out to achieve in order to benefit from maximum economies of scale. Once that has been decided and plant built with the necessary productive capacity, only then does it become susceptible to the short-run variations in unit cost caused by actual production falling below the levels for which the plant was designed.

For example, in Figure 2.1 two cost curves relating to two factors of different optimal sizes are given. If output is only at level x, then the smaller factory has lower costs.

Another important factor is that many of the fixed costs are in fact initial ('one-off') costs associated with a particular model (e.g. design and development, special tools required, etc.) which are incurred only once in the 'lifetime' of a model and must be spread over the total lifetime model output.

Production Processes in the Motor Industry

The operations normally carried out within a large 'integrated' car plant can be divided into four areas. First, there are the foundry operations, where the engine and transmission components are cast, usually in grey iron or aluminium.

FIGURE 2.1

Costs and Optimal Plant Sizes

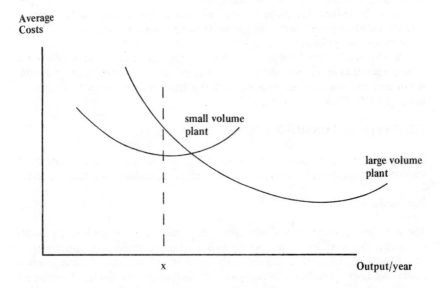

During the machining operation, the rough castings are machined to the tolerances required, culminating in the assembly of complete engines, gear-boxes and axles. The body panels of the car are pressed or stamped from sheet steel using massive presses fitted with the appropriate dies. These three processes precede the assembly operations: the pressed body panels are fitted together in jigs and welded (body assembly); the complete body is then painted and moves onto the trim and final assembly lines, where interior and exterior fittings are added and the mechanical units (engine, gearbox, axle) are installed. At the end of the line, the car is given a short test drive and then driven off to await delivery. All the assembly operations (body and final assembly) are carried out on a moving production line (see Figure 2.2).

In most cases, car firms work a two-shift, 16-hour day, five days a week and output per year figures are quoted on this basis. Three-shift working would give better utilisation of facilities in theory, but in continuous flow production processes it is necessary to have off-shift maintenance time — and the greater flexibility in being able to work overtime in periods of high demand is convenient.

At each of the four stages, specific economies of scale particular to the operation in question can be achieved and these we now examine.

Foundry Work

Although the available evidence varies, it is widely thought that using modern flow-line techniques there are economies of scale to be achieved in producing up to between one and two million engines a year.

Engine and Transmission Machining

For the manufacturer, a reasonable range of engine types and capacities is an important (and desirable) factor. There appears to be a minimum requirement of about 250,000 units per year of one basic engine type. There are further advantages to be gained from higher outputs or by grouping two or more different engine lines in one plant. As a manufacturer will want to cover the full range of engine capacities, he will require two or three basic engines, which will entail a plant capable of producing between 500,000 to one million engines overall per year. Because the costs of design and development are large and the investment in specialised tools to produce it equally so, the usual practice is to spread this cost over as long a lifetime as possible. The manufacture of gearboxes and axles is similar to that of engines, with perhaps marginally significant economies to be achieved.

Stamping

Presses are arranged in lines and sheet steel is passed down a line of presses; the required form is produced by a series of blows from different dies. Rate of output and the total lifetime output of a particular model are again both important variables. The process is capital intensive, involving three items of capital expenditure which must be spread as thinly as possible over each car — the presses, very expensive but with a long life (20 years) and not specific to any particular model; the dies, less expensive and with a shorter life, but specific to the model; and, finally, the design and development costs of the body (obviously model-specific).

Ideally, each press should operate continually with the same dies, as die-changing is expensive and time-consuming. However, at the rate that presses currently in use are capable of working, this would require a volume of nearly 2.5 million identical units per year; die-changing, therefore, is inevitable. The optimal length of press runs between die changes is determined by trading off the costs of more frequent die changes against the costs of holding the greater stocks of finished panels entailed by longer runs. Few manufacturers achieve even 50 per cent utilisation of their presses and die utilisation must be much lower, which means that the cost per car off the presses and dies is twice as high as it could be. It is obvious that large economies from better press-scheduling could be obtained from greater volume. Our conclusion would be that there are significant economies to be gained right up to the output of 2 million identical cars per year.

Assembly

Assembly operations are probably least susceptible to significant economies of scale. The work is labour-intensive, with many workers only requiring screwdrivers or spanners. There are some large automatic pieces of equipment — such as the multi-welders performing several welds simultaneously on some large sub-assemblies — but most welding is still done by hand. In many factories, painting is also done by hand, although fully automatic processes are available.

21

FIGURE 2.2

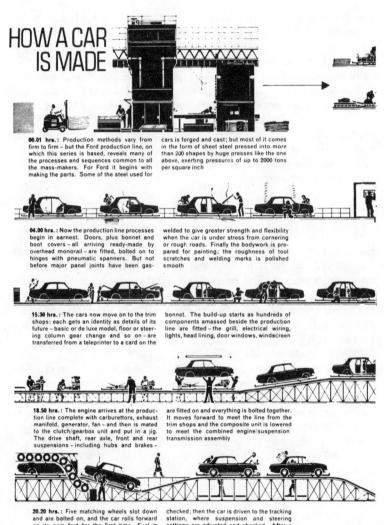

HOW A CAR IS MADE

00.01 hrs.: Production methods vary from firm to firm – but the Ford production line, on which this series is based, reveals many of the processes and sequences common to all the mass-makers. For Ford it begins with making the parts. Some of the steel used for cars is forged and cast; but most of it comes in the form of sheet steel pressed into more than 200 shapes by huge presses like the one above, exerting pressures of up to 2000 tons per square inch

04.00 hrs.: Now the production line processes begin in earnest. Doors, plus bonnet and boot covers – all arriving ready-made by overhead monorail – are fitted, bolted on to hinges with pneumatic spanners. But not before major panel joints have been gas-welded to give greater strength and flexibility when the car is under stress from cornering or rough roads. Finally the bodywork is prepared for painting; the roughness of tool scratches and welding marks is polished smooth

15.30 hrs.: The cars now move on to the trim shops: each gets an identity as details of its future – basic or de luxe model, floor or steering column gear change and so on – are transferred from a teleprinter to a card on the bonnet. The build-up starts as hundreds of components amassed beside the production line are fitted – the grill, electrical wiring, lights, head lining, door windows, windscreen

18.50 hrs.: The engine arrives at the production line complete with carburettors, exhaust manifold, generator, fan – and then is mated to the clutch/gearbox unit and put in a jig. The drive shaft, rear axle, front and rear suspensions – including hubs and brakes – are fitted on and everything is bolted together. It moves forward to meet the line from the trim shops and the composite unit is lowered to meet the combined engine/suspension transmission assembly

20.20 hrs.: Five matching wheels slot down and are bolted on, and the car rolls forward on its own feet for the first time. Fuel is added to the tank and the car at last springs to life. Seats are the last item to be added to the interior. The engine idles as it is checked; then the car is driven to the tracking station, where suspension and steering settings are adjusted and checked. After a final examination of the trim the car is passed (or rejected) before it goes on to the roller testing station

The most expensive item, however, is the transfer line (or track) itself. Scope for further automation exists, but at current European volumes and wage levels, the cost advantage of such machines is doubtful, particularly in the UK.

The optimum speed of an assembly line is determined principally by two factors: the capacity of the large automatic machines and the efficient use of workers along the line. Each worker stands at a particular point along the line, with the necessary tools and stocks of components performing one or more jobs on each car as it passes. To increase output the line must move faster and

courtesy
THE SUNDAY TIMES

03.00 hrs.: The pressings are carried by fork lift trucks to the pre-production line workshops – and in separate processes the building of the superstructure and underbody begins. First, small sub-assemblies are put together by spot welding. Then these are fitted into jigs, which hold the pieces in place as they are fed into automatic welders; from these the major superstructure and underbody units emerge complete. At the upper level in our diagram, the men are tack-welding together the roof, sides and scuttl. of the car; at the lower level the underbody is taking shape. Finally the superstructure and underbody come together, the wings are fitted and the whole unit is welded together. At one stage the car is inverted in a roll-over jig for stitch-welding to take place

09.00 hrs.: Before the paint is put on the car gets a complete washing, inside and out; all joints are covered with a sealer and gas welds painted over. Then the underbody is dipped waist-high in an epoxy resin bath which gives an anti-corrosive finish to metal and seals the drainage channels. Priming coats are sprayed on by hand – a red primer first, and, before it is dry, a grey primer. The cars pass through a gas-fired oven for 40 minutes, then each body is wet-sanded with demineralised water and dried. Now three top colour coats are sprayed on; beside the line a teleprinter taps out the colour or colour combination for each car based on an analysis of orders from dealers and overseas distributors which has already been completed. Drying takes an hour as the cars move slowly through a steam-heated oven

16.40 hrs.: Into the car, too, go the horns, battery, brake fluid reservoirs, steering column, radiator and pipes – all under-the-bonnet parts. The instrument panel is fitted, and from it sprout the lengths of bright coloured wiring and tubes which will soon be connected to the engine. Finally a few more externals are put on – chrome fittings, door handles and catches

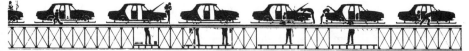

19.20 hrs.: The nearly completed car now moves along a raised line. Above are fitted the rear-view mirror, wipers and interior trim; the radiator is filled and hydraulic fluid fed into the brake and clutch systems. Underneath everything is connected up – oil, petrol and brake pipes, steering, pedals – and a gear lever is added. The laying of carpets and mats almost completes the trim

22.00 hrs.: The car is driven on the rollers – testing the engine, transmission, steering, brakes and lights. If declared safe, it goes for a brief road test. After this comes the water test; the car is sprayed with 36 streams of water at 50 lb. per square inch pressure – a total of 400 gallons bombarded in four minutes – to check for leaks. Dried down, it has its final check; then it's parked in the trade lines to await the delivery driver and the trip to market

either each worker must do his set tasks faster or the number of tasks per worker reduced and additional workers brought in. The latter alternative requires a longer line and more space and uses up stocks of components faster, requiring either larger stocks or quicker replenishment. Reducing the number of tasks per worker increases efficiency: time is saved by fewer tool changes, picking up fewer components, etc., and, through repetition, the worker becomes exceedingly proficient. As speed increases, however, he must spend more time moving between cars and this, together with the cost of extra components and space, places limitations on the maximum speed.

Most writers are in agreement that the optimum rate of production for assembly is 200,000 to 300,000 cars per year, corresponding to an hourly rate of 60-80 cars. Although some UK and Japanese plants have higher rates these are probably impracticable given European attitudes to production line work. Although the US practice is to have one long fast-moving track, the majority of British manufacturers seem to prefer two slower lines, which probably does carry some cost penalty.

Other Economies

Thus far, we have dealt only with technical economies of scale at plant level, but there are other areas in which economies can be achieved, mainly concerned with spreading central business overheads. There are always slight economies to be gained in specialisation of management function but the major administrative problem even in small motor companies is the avoidance of diseconomies of bureaucracy rather than the attainment of further economies.

A more important function in which there are economies of scale to be achieved is in product development and design. Specialisation in different aspects of design has always been fruitful. Faced with a plethora of safety regulations changing from day to day and from one country to the next, it is important to assign specialist responsibilities in the various fields to ensure that one's cars remain saleable in as many markets as possible. A large design staff can prove expensive but it is really the key to achieving all possible economies of scale, as the demand potentials of most models fall below the ideals for least-cost production and good design can offset this disadvantage to some extent by standardisation of components between models. With skilful adaptation, engines, gearboxes, suspensions, trimmings, pressings, etc. can all be used to a greater or lesser extent in different models but it takes a concerted design effort to achieve this level of standardisation. Most equipment used in the car industry is specific to a particular model. A firm which is in a position to change models frequently is better able to gain the cost-saving advantages of new technology.

Diseconomies of Scale

Economies of scale, brought about by an increase in size, carry with them potential diseconomies of scale. Simply because of the sheer number of people involved, there is the possibility of loss of effective control. Greater automation and increasingly specialised equipment could prove insufficiently flexible in an industry increasingly vulnerable to considerable fluctuation in demand and the consequent risk. And, finally, size brings with it even greater barriers to effective management/worker communications. These are not inevitable penalties (consider, for example, the experience of large American corporations already operating on a larger scale) but they must be taken into consideration. We return to consider diseconomies of scale later in the chapter.

Overall

It would appear that the possibilities of achieving economies of scale are never really exhausted in the car industry. Larger scale, up to 2 million identical units per year for example, will always confer some advantage, but the most significant advantages are to be gained at lower scales. There is widespread agreement that individual models should be produced at levels exceeding 200,000 per year and that, ideally, a firm should have an overall output of not less than 1 million cars per year. Individual engine types should also be produced at rates of at least 300,000 per year, so that a firm with an output of 1 million overall could cover the whole capacity range with three types (see Table 2.1).

TABLE 2.1

Estimates of Minimum Efficiency Scale
Thousand units p.a.

	Casting	Machining	Stamping	Assembly	Overall	
						Complete
					1 Model	Model Range
Pratten[a]	1,000	250	500	300	500	1,000
Rhys[b]	200	1,000	2,000	400	–	2,000
White[c]	small	260	400	200	400	800
University of	1,000-2,000	400-1,000	500+	200-400	200	1,000
Bristol Motor Industry						with small
Research Group (for European Conditions)						economies
						thereafter

a. C.F. Pratten, *Economies of Scale in Manufacturing Industries*, 1971
b. D.G. Rhys, *The Motor Industry: An Economic Survey*, 1972
c. L.J. White, *The Automobile Industry Since 1945*, 1971

A firm operating at this sort of level would be too large to fit on one site and operations would have to be split between several sites. Body assembly, paint, trim and final assembly on a particular model should be carried out together because of the high costs involved in transporting assembled bodies. Transport of unassembled panels is less expensive and the location of the pressing plant is therefore less crucial. Engines and powertrain components are easier and cheaper to transport and the production technology involved is also very different, so there is no particular need to have these plants on the assembly sites. The same would apply to gearbox and axle production. Other, small components produced internally may have their own plants or be integrated with others of a similar nature, depending on circumstances.

It is difficult to quantify the cost penalties of operating on a smaller scale, but, as an example, the cost of producing only 250,000 units per year over a four or five year model life has been estimated at between 6 and 20 per cent –

a very considerable difference in cost. The cost penalties of producing a model range over a similar period become progressively steeper with levels of less than 100,000 units per year. As Adam Smith said a long time ago: 'The division of labour is limited by the extent of the market'. Thus, the extent to which economies of scale can be used in the executive and luxury segments of the market are limited, though Daimler Benz no doubt benefits from its model runs of greater than 100,000 quality cars per year. A reasonable volume for a car classed in the executive market segment (see Chapter 3) is around 100,000 to 200,000, whilst similar economies of scale for a luxury car are upwards of 30,000 to 50,000.

The model mix of a firm can also be important. For example:

> In order to retain customers' loyalty, mass producers need a range of vehicles as buyers graduate from mini-to-light-to-medium-to-large cars. As well as a minimum of four mass-produced vehicles, an executive saloon is needed to tap the profitable market made up of more affluent corporate or individual customers. Therefore, attempts to over-rationalise to give the potentiality of lower unit costs, may mean that such costs are not realised as customers turn to more appropriate cars made by other firms. (D.G.Rhys, 'European Mass-producing Car Makers and Minimum Efficient Scale: A Note', *Journal of Industrial Economics,* June 1977)

This explains why many of the mass producing firms have been moving 'up-market'. A similar argument can be made for a full coverage of the commercial vehicle market.

Organisational Structure and Decentralisation

Following from this it would appear that the Ryder strategy of one integrated company is correct. However, the existence of technical economies of scale is one thing but the administrative organisational set-up can be argued to be quite another. At one time, it was popular[1] to argue that because of administrative and control problems, there were clear limits to the size with which firms could grow. However, more recently, good arguments[2] have been given to counter this limit to firm size. In particular, it can be argued that by decentralisation and adopting appropriate control devices, firms may offset these costs of growth. One possibility open to most firms is to change the organisational structure of the firm in order to minimise the 'control loss' inherent in large firms. Consequently, the type of organisational form is now an important variable which may allow new discretionary opportunities to become opened up to management.

1. See, for example, E.T. Penrose, *The Theory of the Growth of the Firm* (Oxford:Basil Blackwell, 1959).
2. See, for example, O.E. Williamson, *Corporate Control and Business Behaviour* (Englewood Cliffs; Prentice-Hall, 1970).

There are two standard organisational forms within an enterprise: the centralised unitary form of organisation (U-form) and the multi-division form (M-form).

Organisation form influences goal formation and the effectiveness of internal control devices. Expansion of a U-form organisation takes the form of amplification. Simon's concept of 'bounded rationality'[1] explains why this will lead to the introduction of additional hierarchical levels of management, with a consequent increase in information transmission across these levels. 'Simple control loss' varies directly with the volume of information transferred; 'compound control loss' involves, in addition, communication bias. 'Decoupling' (shortening the transmission network) provides only temporary relief from this problem. Cumulative control losses of these types eventually limit growth of the firm when they are no longer declining in relation to market transactions costs, of which they are the internal equivalent. Expansion of the U-form organisation meets the capacity problem at top management level by adding the heads of functional divisions (i.e. operational executives) to the management team. Direction of the enterprise (the strategic decision-making process) becomes the joint responsibility of the managers (the entrepreneurs. . .) who have been used to taking an overall view and those (the managers. . .) who have taken a partisan view. Members of the latter group are likely to continue using opportunities for discretion to advance their own individual and functional interests, subject to certain constraints (the degree of imperfection of product and capital markets — competition in the latter being only a partial substitute for lack of competition in the former). As a result, the goals of the enterprise and of the augmented top management group may now diverge, the new members of the group may pursue subgoals (e.g. have an interest in introducing organisational slack). Further loss of control may occur through communication biassing.

The M-form organisation, which evolved in the US in the 1920s as an adaptive response to the inherent weaknesses of the U-form organisation, has as its distinguishing feature the recognition of quasi-autonomous 'natural decision units'. Multidivisionalisation is substituted in the expansion strategy for functional amplification. On the available evidence, significant advantages appear to have stemmed from this organisational innovation: control loss is minimised through a strong concentration of staff advisory and auditing (performance checks) functions centrally; the number of hierarchical levels, information flow and the size of the internal communication network are all reduced, and the 'psychological commitment' of the strategic decision-makers is more closely identified with the pursuit of enterprise goals.

From: *Management Accounting: A Conceptual Approach*, by L.R. Amey and D.A. Egginton, Longman Business Series, 1973, p387-388.

---

1.   H.A. Simon, *Models of Man* (New York: John Wiley, 1957).

Thus the advantages of the M-form are in allowing a better control system which is richer in the coverage and monitoring of both internal and external changes within the company – i.e. consistent with Michael Edwardes' now infamous statement 'A tree that a man can put his arms around'. Any variances between observed results and internal performance standards (variances which have tended to be large for BL in the recent past) can be more easily analysed into firstly deficiencies of control and secondly failure of the environment to conform to management's expectations. In the context of BL, Michael Edwardes' structure is an attempt to limit the administrative and control problems inherent in a U-form organisation. In theory, there may be no consequent loss of technical economies of scale. However, there have been a number of specific criticisms with regard to BL's move towards decentralisation; these are discussed in Chapter 7.

Importance to the UK Economy

Car manufacturers do not exist in a vacuum. They are part of a complex inter-dependent network of raw material suppliers, components manufacturers, the producers themselves and their dealer networks. Factors affecting one part of this inter-linked network have repercussions in every other part. If prices of raw materials, for example, are higher on average in the UK than elsewhere, then the UK manufacturer (and his dealers) will be at a competitive disadvantage and sales will be adversely affected. 'Weakness in any one link will soon prejudice any strengths in the others. A bad distribution system will make it difficult to sell cars, even if the manufacturer is efficient; poor performance by manufacturers soon destroys any advantages there may be from different component manufacture' (CPRS, p. 5).

Not only are these interdependent functions important to each other – taken as a whole, they are of 'central significance' to the British economy. It has been estimated that the 'total job significance of motor manufacturing, selling, repair and maintenance, before applying a multiplier, is of the order of 1.3 million, about 5 per cent of the total national workforce' (CPRS, p. 9).[1] In some areas – the West Midlands, for example – the motor industry accounts for 16 per cent of total local employment. In Coventry, Birmingham, Glasgow, Liverpool,[2] and Oxford(all cities where car manufacturers employ over 7,000 people on one site) any significant reduction in the workforce would increase unemployment in the affected area substantially.

Between 1971 and 1973, the motor industry accounted for roughly 6 per cent of total investment in plant, machinery and vehicles by the manufacturing sector of British industry. In a report published in 1968 (*Effects of Government Policy on the Motor Industry,* NEDO, 1968 – more recent figures are not available, but the CPRS report concluded that the situation has not changed greatly) it was calculated that the industry as a whole (manufacturers, component suppliers, etc.) accounted for 10.6 per cent of total industrial output.

1. Original source was Fourteenth Report of the Expenditure Committee, Trade and Industry Sub-Committee, *The Motor Vehicle Industry,* 1975.
2. Prior to the closure of BL's Speke plant.

In 1974, the industry exported more than £1,300 million worth of goods and has a 'positive trade balance of nearly £700 million . . . of which cars only accounted for £65 million'.

TABLE 2.2

British Car Industry Imports and Exports

(At constant 1970 prices)

	1970	1971	1972	1973	1974	1975	1976	1977	% change 1970-7
1. Built-up car exports[a]	228	226	168	157	145	173	215	221[d]	-3
2. Knocked-down car exports[b]	100	114	105	100	95	92	85	86[d]	-14
3. Total car exports[c] (1)+(2)	328	340	273	257	240	265	299	307[d]	-6
4. Car imports (all built up)	85	158	255	281	190	282	419	540[d]	+535
5. Balance of trade in cars	243	182	18	-24	50	-17	-120	-233[d]	-196

a.   Derives from the value in 1970 and index of number of vehicles exported.

b.   Unit value index derived from SMMT data for assembled and unassembled vehicles to take account of different levels of local content throughout the years.

c.   Price indices for export and import units for transport equipment from DTI (Monthly Digest of Statistics).

d.   Estimated

Source: CPRS Report and SMMT

The car industry's contribution to the balance of payments has exhibited a depressing long run trend. The reason for this deterioration in the early 1970s was partly lack of capacity. Recent years have shown that capacity is not the problem but that there are other deeper structural problems.

It is important to bear this in mind when considering any radical alterations to the motor industry, as the role it plays is evidently of some importance to the strengths of the British economy.

International Perspectives

Just as the motor vehicle manufacturer in the UK does not function in splendid isolation so the UK industry is part of an increasingly international and multi-national network. Since 1940, there has been an enormous increase in production world-wide (see Figure 2.3). Correspondingly, the worldwide trade in cars as a percentage of all cars produced has steadily increased from 9 per cent in 1950 to 30 per cent in 1970.

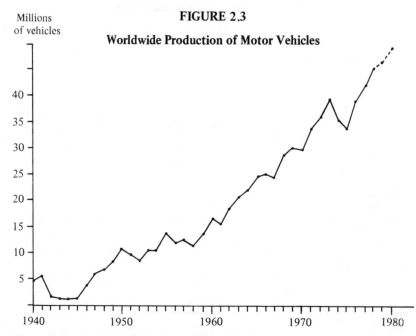

Millions of vehicles

FIGURE 2.3

Worldwide Production of Motor Vehicles

The multinational ramifications of the industry began with the expansion of the three major US corporations (Ford, GM and Chrysler) into Europe, to counteract a slackening of demand in the domestic US market. European and Japanese producers then began assembling vehicles in Commonwealth and Third World countries, in an attempt to overcome tariff barriers and other limitations to trade. Both developments have increased international competitiveness but have not yet radically altered the balance : the three major car producing blocs are still Europe (with Britain accounting for 15 per cent of total production in the area), North America and Japan, hotly pursued by the Communist Bloc, South America and the Middle East. Despite markets of similar size, Western Europe has traditionally produced more vehicles[1] than North America (as shown in Figure 2.4). (Canadian production is only around 1.5 million.) The US was, however, hit during the recent depression, whilst the Communist Bloc and Japan were less effected. In export terms, however, Japan clearly dominates, having effectively ousted Europe's traditional place as top exporter to the lucrative North American market.

1. In value terms, North America still leads.

FIGURE 2.4

World car production

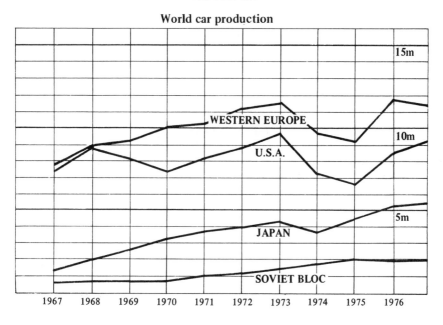

FIGURE 2.5

World commercial vehicle production

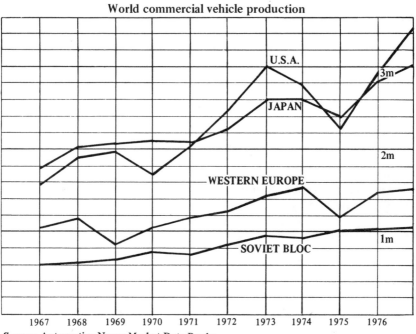

Source: Automotive News: Market Data Books

The story with CVs, as shown in Figure 2.5, is entirely different, with Japan challenging the US and the Soviet Bloc close to Western European production levels. But this story must be carefully interpreted. Japanese vehicles are much smaller than European or US vehicles. Moreover, the growth in the US market during recent years has been in the market for smaller recreational vehicles. In terms of exports, Japan clearly dominates the world with Western Europe a very long way behind.

Britain In The World Context

In Table 2.3, the 1973 figures (a year of high demand) are shown for car and CV parks (the number of vehicles in use), new registrations and productions by major area. Although the car industry is one of the best-documented industries in the world, not all world statistics are in agreement. For 1973, estimates of the total world figures obtained from different authorities vary by as much as 2 per cent.

The European Scene

The British motor industry must be considered in the context of the European motor industry, of which it is a part. The EEC will eventually eliminate any remaining tariff barriers, and three of the four major UK vehicle producers are subsidiaries of American corporations, who also have manufacturing capacity elsewhere in Europe. Moreover, the European manufacturers are producing an increasingly similar product, irrespective of the remaining national boundaries, so that European competition for the traditional British export markets is likely to increase.

The European industry consists of 14 firms chasing a market of some 10 million cars with a total capacity of approximately 15 million cars. Of the 14 firms, 9 are in the volume car market:

BL (UK, Belgium)
GM (Opel, West Germany, Belgium; Vauxhall, UK)
Renault (France)
Peugeot-Citroen (France)
Ford (West Germany, UK, Belgium, Spain)
Fiat (Italy)
Seat (Spain)
Chrysler (France, UK, Spain)
VW (West Germany)

Eight were historically in the specialist car market:

BL (Rover, Triumph, Jaguar)   BMW
Peugeot-Citroen   Volvo
Fiat (Lancia)   Saab
Daimler-Benz
Alfa-Romeo

TABLE 2.3
Worldwide Parks, Registration and Production

	Parks in 1976		New Registration				Production			
	CARS millions	CVS millions	CARS millions		CVS millions		CARS millions		CVS millions	
			1973	1976	1973	1976	1973	1976	1973	1976
NORTH AMERICA	115.4	28.6	12.4	10.7	3.3	3.4	10.9	9.7	3.4	3.4
WESTERN EUROPE (INC. UK)	88.1	10.3	9.8	9.5	1.1	1.1	10.5	11.7	1.4	1.6
AUSTRALASIA	6.7	1.7	.5	.5	.1	.2	.4	.4	.1	.1
SOUTH & CENTRAL AMERICA	12.7	4.6	1.3	1.5	.4	.5	1.0	1.4	.3	.4
COMMUNIST BLOC	10.1	7.2	1.0	1.3	.8	.9	1.6	1.9	.9	1.0
JAPAN	17.2	10.3	2.9	2.5	2.0	1.7	4.5	5.0	2.6	2.8
OTHER AREAS	9.9	7.4	1.5	.3	.6	1.5	1.1	.5	.2	.3
	260.1	68.4	29.3	29	8.3	9.3	30.0	30.6	8.9	9.2
U.K.	13.8	2.0	1.7	1.3	.3	.2	1.7	1.3	.4	.4

Many of the so-called volume manufacturers are trying to move up-market with some of their top models (e.g. VW using its Audi division). The possible Chrysler-Peugeot-Citroen merger may reduce the number of volume manufacturers to 13 firms.

The fourteen European firms must be contrasted with the US total of four firms satisfying a market very similar in size. This comparison could yield the conclusion that there are too many producers in Europe, and that numbers should be reduced to, say, three main producers. European governments, however, are anxious to preserve the autonomy of their nation's industry, and would presumably oppose attempts at multinational integration. Whatever the outcome, the next decade could mean either a period of dramatic change in the structure of the European car industry or a period of intense competition between existing companies (some of whom operate on massive government subsidies) — or both!

There are also many major CV producers:

Company	*Owned by*
Bedford	GM
BL	Government Agency (NEB)
Chrysler	Peugeot-Citroen?
Daimler Benz	
ERF	
Foden	
Ford	
Iveco	Fiat Group (80%)
MAN	MAN Engineering Group
Pegaso	Government Agency
Saviem-Berliet	Renault
Scania	Saab
Seddon-Atkinson	International Harvester
Volvo	(partly by Norwegian interests?)
Daf	$1/3$ by International Harvester
	$1/3$ by Dutch Government
	$1/3$ by Van Dorne family

Defensive mergers in the CV market to obtain economies of scale are leading to a much more integrated structure in Europe — for example the 'Club of Four' merger to produce medium weight CVs. See Appendix 17.2 for production statistics of both cars and CVs by the major European manufacturers.

American Subsidiaries

Until the recent crisis, both GM and Ford left their subsidiaries to operate more or less independently. Ford, however, began to rationalise both its model range and production facilities in the late 1960s. The company has always tried to restrict the production of its various engine ranges to one per location. Now both Chrysler and GM have been forced to follow Ford's example, seeking to reduce costs either by introducing a common European model policy, or by fully rationalising production facilities throughout Europe. Neither company

TABLE 2.4

Car Production

	1977 Million	1976 Million	1973 Million
NORTH AMERICA			
American Motors	.2	.3	.4
Chrysler	1.5	1.6	1.8
Ford	2.9	2.4	2.9
GM	5.5	5.4	5.7
EUROPE **Chrysler**	10.1	9.7	10.8
UK[a]	.17	.15	.27
France	.48	.48	.56
Spain	.08	.08	.09
	.73	.71	.91
Peugeot Citroen & Chrysler (Europe)[b]			
UK	.17	.15	.27
France	1.82	1.75	1.76
Spain	.21	.19	.14
	2.20	2.09	2.17
Ford			
UK[a]	.41	.38	.45
Belgium	.29	.28	.27
West Germany	.54	.49	.46
Spain	.21	.02	-
	1.45	1.17	1.17
GM			
UK	.09	.11	.13
Belgium } West Germany }	.92	.92	.87
	1.01	1.03	1.00
BL	.65	.69	.88

a. Figures supplied here are those of the SMMT. Both Ford and GM would argue that their production was higher; the higher figure would include some knock down kits which the SMMT would not count as one whole unit. A countable unit is usually any set of parts which is greater than 50 per cent of the value of the complete vehicle.

b. Includes an element of double-counting (see Chapter 17 and Appendix 17.2)

have yet achieved this objective: GM will probably produce 'concept' cars using similar powertrain and with more or less the same body shape, whereas Chrysler were until recently planning on producing front wheel drive models in France, and rear wheel drive versions of the same model in the UK.

The production figures for 1973 and 1976 show that, aggregating the European operations, all three of the multinationals have a viable production volume and can achieve economies of scale. GM has amalgamated its Belgian and West German operations. Chrysler continues to run its French and British operations as separate entities, although the two share a common design centre at Whitley in the UK; the Spanish Chrysler operation is too small to achieve much other than supply the Spanish market with Simca products from France, although the larger Chrysler cars are now being assembled in Spain. Ford have also begun operations in Spain, which will presumably confer marketing advantages but which is, in effect, a move away from rationalisation, as establishing the necessary infrastructure will involve Ford in high initial costs.

Size and Relationship to Economies of Scale

Cars

Working on the principle that one million units is the minimum output at which a company can expect to achieve economies of scale, and that maximum economies of scale can be achieved (assuming a suitable organisation within the

TABLE 2.5

	Estimated Capacity (1976–80) Cars and Car-based Vans	No. of Basic Models (planned)	Potential Output per Model (thousands)	Planned Output per Basic Engine (thousands)
Chrysler	1,000,000	3/4	250 – 350	220 – 270
British Leyland	1,200,000	4/5	240 – 300	185 – 260
GM	1,550,000	4/5	310 – 388	420
Renault	1,550,000	8	194	800
Peugeot-Citroen	1,650,000	7	236	425
Ford	1,650,000	5	350	570
Volkswagen	1,800,000	5	360	610
Fiat	1,850,000	6	308	650

Source: D.G. Rhys, 'European Mass-producing Car Makers and Minimum Efficient Scale: A Note', *Journal of Industrial Economics,* June 1977.

company) at levels of 2 or more million units, it is possible to assess the European car producers. Remembering that 1973 production was universally high — probably near to capacity — it is possible to estimate the economies to be gained in each company. Ford, VW, Renault and Fiat are all clearly within a cost competitive volume area (see Table 2.5). Citroen and Peugeot will be, if they rationalise production. GM and Chrysler — if both of them integrate effectively — should just come within the lower limits. Although BL's maximum production (in 1972) was only 916,000, the company could benefit from economies of scale if volume was only slightly increased, although the company at present is not taking advantage of possible economies already available to it and will have to rationalise production further. The same could apply to both GM and Chrysler.

The other producers (BMW, Daimler Benz, Alfa-Romeo, and Volvo-Saab) are smaller specialist or quality producers who in their present form are not operating as volume car producers. It is not inconceivable, however, that there will be further mergers, possibly involving some of the 'specialist' producers. The 1970s have already seen mergers involving Fiat (Lancia), Volvo (Daf) and Peugeot (Citroen).

As far as CVs are concerned, scale is less crucial in the heavier categories. The heavy CV sector places quality rather than quantity at a premium. Although production of car-derived vans is similar to car manufacture (for obvious reasons). Within the light, medium to medium heavy range, say from 3 tons to 24 tons, the importance of scale economies reappears.

CONCLUSION

Three of the four major firms in the UK are multinational companies, and, with the exception of Ford, there is insufficient demand in the UK alone to enable these companies to survive. In the aggressive and competitive years ahead, increasing pressure will be placed on the control of costs; because of this, scale will become all important, and production by the multinationals in the UK will become inextricably involved in European operations, to the extent that the UK plants may concentrate on assembly of components and parts imported from the continent or, alternatively, may manufacture components for assembly abroad. Whatever the outcome, a decentralised car division for BL does not necessarily imply an economies of scale penalty. New discretionary opportunities may be opened up to management, which together with greater control and faster feedback of blossoming problems might conceivably provide the missing ingredient which BL has lacked in the post Ryder years. This is not to say that the Ryder plan was wrong: conceptually a company the size of BL is not large within a worldwide definition. But local management expertise, often lacking any formal training or of mediocre ability, made what is acceptable in worldwide terms unacceptable in the micro conditions prevailing within the UK motor industry.

38

CHAPTER 3

OVERVIEW OF WHOLE INDUSTRY

In this chapter we intend to provide a broad outline of the workings of the four major UK manufacturers; in doing so, we hope to explain why three, at least, of the four producers concerned, are apparently unable to sustain a viable enterprise without massive infusions of aid from either US parent companies or the UK government. Although this chapter is biased towards cars it does have a generality over the whole industry.

PLANTS

It is first of all necessary to provide a brief 'geography' of the various production and assembly facilities within each company.

Chrysler
Operations at Chrysler UK and Vauxhall are roughly similar in scale, and although Chrysler's recent (and much publicised) difficulties were thought to have led to a reduction in capacity, the reverse was the truth.[1] However, Chrysler UK is now probably the smallest of the four major producers, with major plants at Linwood (primarily assembly), Stoke (powertrain), Ryton (assembly only) and Dublin (assembly only).

Vauxhall
Vauxhall, the third largest in size of the Big Four has plants at Ellesmere Port (car assembly and other facilities), Luton (car and commercial vehicle assembly) and Dunstable (commercial vehicle assembly only). With no foundry operation of its own, however, Vauxhall buys in the components and materials required for powertrain and axle production.

Ford
Although Vauxhall has substantial *capacity* for the production of commercial vehicles, Ford (with CV plants at Langley, Basildon, Southampton) actually produce more CV units (mainly of the smaller variety), in addition to possessing far greater car assembly and powertrain production facilities, with major car assembly plants at Halewood (specialising in gearbox assembly) and Dagenham (engine assembly). More than the other major manufacturers, Ford produces some of its own components — such as spark plugs and some of the electrical components required. The older and more cramped foundry at Dagenham may be a candidate for closure.

British Leyland
Within a UK context alone British Leyland is, still at the moment, the largest of the Big Four. Most of the assembly work on the volume range is carried out at Cowley and Longbridge, using panels supplied from Swindon and Castle

---

1. See Chapter 1, p. 10.

Bromwich and various parts and components – such as engines, petrol tanks, exhausts, radiators, seat frames, suspensions and gearboxes – manufactured in a series of smaller plants. The Triumph range is assembled primarily at Speke Hall/Woodend[1] and Canley (which is currently destined to become a centre for BL components manufacturing rather than an assembly facility), while the main Rover plants are at Coventry and Solihull (the latter recently expanded and modernised at a cost of £90 million in 1975/6, in order to produce the new Rover range). Jaguar engines are manufactured at Sandy Lane and the cars are assembled at Browns Lane, although Jaguar itself has no paint or body building plant (relying, as with Rover, for its bodies from Castle Bromwich).

In addition to volume car production, BL encompasses a more success-ful CV division (principally at the Leyland, Bathgate, AEC and Albion plants), Special Products (the Coventry Climax, for example), components and foundry operations.

EMPLOYMENT

As we have already noted very briefly (see Chapter 2, pp. 28–9), the motor manufacturing industry, as an employer, is of 'central significance' to the British economy. Expenditure Committee figures for total employment in the UK motor industry are given below:

	1973/4 '000s	1977/8 '000s
Direct Manufacture (as defined by Minimum List Heading 381)	510	485
Other supply and component sectors	325	300
Vehicle selling, repair and maintenance	450	400
	1,285	1,185

Source: Fourth Report from the Expenditure Committee for 1974-5 Session, *The Motor Vehicle Industry,* August 1975, and author's estimate for 1977/8 figure.

Table 3.1 gives the 1973 (an all time high) and 1977 (an all time low) employment figures for the four major manufacturers, together with some European comparisons. Chrysler UK experienced the greatest drop in numbers employed (as a percentage of previous levels), whilst loss of jobs at BL is accounted for primarily by a reduction of the work force within the car division, falling from a peak of about 130,000 (for the UK) to a low of 115,000 in Autumn 1975. However, under Alex Park's and Derek Whittaker's ambitious plans for BL, employment was expanded and by late 1977 there were once again around 130,000 employees in BL's car division. Under Michael Edwardes' new plans, the car division in 1978 is again shedding labour to form a unit employing just under 120,000 people.

1. Prior to the closure of the Speke plant.

TABLE 3.1
Number of Employees
'000s

	1973	1977
Domestic Employment		
BL	171	172
Ford (UK)	66	73
Chrysler (UK)	31	23
GM (Vauxhall/Bedford)	34	33[a]
VW	161	133
Daimler-Benz	134	138
Fiat	201	267
Renault	98	101[a]
Peugeot-Citroen	135[a]	157
Worldwide Employment		
BL	204	195
VW	215	192
Daimler-Benz	156	169
Fiat	201	342
Peugeot-Citroen	151[a]	185
Ford (Europe)	129[a]	146[a]

Component Manufacturers
The following companies, Dunlop, GKN, Lucas, Pilkingtons Associated Engineering and the Chloride Group employ over 250,000 people; the majority of which are engaged on the automotive side.

a. Although not all employees are engaged in the automotive side, most are, approximately over 50 per cent.

Variations in total employment figures, such as these, reflect variations and uncertainties in market demand which the motor industry has been confronted with in recent years. A 'stop-go' economic environment, and the decision taken by successive governments to control aggregate demand by placing severe restrictions on car demand — and then lifting them, as conditions 'improved' — have had serious consequences for the motor industry as a whole, forcing the introduction of a three day week (a frequent occurrence in the 1950s and currently — in the 1970s — in operation at Chrysler UK's Linwood plant), lay offs and redundancies. With the introduction of statutory minimum redundancy payments, employers are finding it increasingly difficult to dispose of workers for whom, due to a slackening of demand, there is no work. Natural wastage and voluntary redundancy are cheaper alternatives, but it must be remembered that, having once reduced the size of the labour force, managements will think more than twice before enlarging it again, when faced with the prospect of yet another massive bill for redundancy payments, should the market weaken once more. This explains why actual two-shift capacity is less than the maximum theoretical two-shift capacity.

MODELS

The CPRS report suggested some rather unsatisfactory market divisions, when discussing model ranges, by proposing seven major segments — mini, small, medium, large, executive, luxury and sports. The first four divisions — mini, small, medium and large — were differentiated principally by external dimensions and engine size. Executive cars were seen as distinct from large cars by virtue of higher prices, superior fittings and marginally better performance, whilst luxury cars, in turn, were larger and more expensive than executive models. Sports cars, differentiated by body type, were placed in an entirely separate category. These divisions produced some strange results. The Range Rover, for example, appeared in the same category as the Jaguar, whilst the VW Sirocco, rather surprisingly, was placed alongside the Ford Granada in the large car segment! The Fiat 126 and 127, meanwhile, both appeared in the mini segment. However recent clever marketing by West European manufacturers has managed to produce models which span both the large and executive markets. Such development may mark the end of separate large and executive marketing segments.[1]

Any attempt to categorise a particular model in terms of the arbitrary divisions produced by any scheme will lead to inconsistencies and disagreements. We feel that the CPRS divisions could be improved by subdividing the CPRS segments to arrive at a total of ten major categories. This would give seven basic saloon requirements — mini, small (e.g. Vauxhall Chevette), small/medium (e.g. Vauxhall Cavalier), large, executive and luxury. Sporting saloons are further divided into four main categories, i.e. slow coupes, fast coupes, sports cars as such (differentiated by body shape) and ultra luxurious sports cars or coupes (e.g. Ferrari), leaving one additional category for 'special' models not easily incorporated elsewhere. This, we feel, overcomes some of the inadequacies of the proposed CPRS classification, whilst at the same time giving a more accurate 'overview' of the pattern of various model ranges from one company to the next, revealing both correspondences and discrepancies more clearly.

In evaluating the UK model range, the CPRS report identified two main problem areas — product range and product quality. As far as product range is concerned, four sources of competitive weakness were singled out for comment:

(i)   unbalanced range;
(ii)   poor 'packaging', providing less car for the money than

1.   This is further discussed in Chapter 14.

foreign competitors;[1]
(iii)   outdated product;
(iv)   the erosion of price advantages since early 1973.[2]

In our view, the criticism that the range is unbalanced is not valid, with the (possible) exception of the small car segment, which during the oil crisis, has been a major growth segment. In some cases, manufacturers have been slow to meet this growth in demand with either new models or improvements to existing small car models. The criticism of poor packaging is true in substance for some ranges, but ignores the fact that manufacturers have identified the fault and are making considerable efforts to rectify it (for example, in the case of British Leyland, the Allegro 2 and Marina 2, and the upgrading of the Clubman engine from 1000cc to 1100cc). In the executive segment, the new Rover compares favourably with its European rivals in terms of interior size, luggage capacity, design and 'refinement' in general.

The most serious criticism, and the one most difficult to refute, is that substantial parts of the range are unsuccessful.[3] The Mini,[4] for example, is now twenty years old, and other volume cars, together with some of the specialist models, are ageing fast.[5] Although the French car industry has experienced similar problems in marketing 'old' models, particularly at the lower end of the market, the position has been much improved with the introduction of at least some new models (e.g. the Citroen CX, the Renault R5 and R30 and the Peugeot 604). Ford and GM are both introducing a new range of models which compare favourably with the activities of Datsun, Fiat and VW, all of whom have introduced a range of new models recently.

The final criticism — that of relative price disadvantage — we leave for fuller discussion in Sections 2 and 3.

The second major problem identified by the CPRS report was that of product quality. In terms of product reliability and quality, there is considerable evidence to suggest that the performance of the UK manufacturers in this respect compares unfavourably with that of their French, German, Swedish and Japanese counterparts. If this is indeed the case, then it is a major liability, for poor quality in a new car quickly creates customer dissatisfaction and, more seriously, carries with it a financial penalty for the hapless buyer, in terms of transport costs to and from the garage, the cost of breakdowns of hiring a replacement car, possible loss of earnings, etc. A reputation for poor quality is particularly serious, in this respect, in the

1.   Product 'packaging' includes price, service requirements, performance/handling/ road holding, fuel economy, dimensions, engine size, interior finish and comfort, instrumentation and controls, seating, and additional refinements.

2.   CPRS Report, p.67, para. 12.

3.   For example, the Marina and Allegro, (both before the versions 2).

4.   A pre-publication comment noted that the Mini is now perhaps in a market segment of its own — it still consistently outsells the Fiestas.

5.   But the new Rovers 3500, 2600, 2300 have replaced the old range and cover the former Rover/Triumph model overlap.

TABLE 3.2
Car Model Policy

	Mini	Small (Super-Mini)	Light	Medium	Large	Executive	Luxury	Sporting Saloons & Coupe 1	2	Specials
UK										
BL: Current	Mini		Allegro	Maxi Marina	Princess ← Rover		Jaguar	Dolomite Midget MGB TR7 Stag	XJS	Range Rover
: Future		New Mini (LC8)	LC10	? Dolomite	Princess Replacement range	Rover	Jaguar range	?	?	Range Rover Road Rover
Chrysler		Sunbeam	Avenger Horizon	Hunter Alpine	180/2 litre			Borgheera		Matra Rancho
Ford: Current		Fiesta	Escort	Cortina →	Granada →			Capri Granada/ Cortina coupe		
Vauxhall		S car	T car (Chevette) Viva	Cavalier	Victor Victor replacement →	Senator		Cavalier coupe	Monza	

(The arrow indicates that the model attempts to cover more than one segment)

TABLE 3.2 (cont.)

	Mini	Small (Super-Mini)	Light	Medium	Large	Executive	Luxury	Sporting Saloons & Coupe 1	2	Specials
FRANCE										
Simca (Chrysler)		1000	1100	1301/1501	180/2 litre[a]					
Citroen	2CV Dyane	Ami 6 LN ↓	Visa	GS		CX ↙				
Peugeot		104	304	305	504	604		Gordini		
Renault	R4	R5	R6 R14	R12 R18	R16 R20	R30		R15/17		
GERMANY										
VW-Audi		Polo 50 Audi 50	Golf	Passat Audi 80	Audi 100 } ← Avant			Sirocco 100s		
BMW			1602	Series 3		Series 5	Series 7		Series 6	
Ford (See under UK)										
Mercedes				170?	200	S Series	600		SL	Four Wheel Drive[b]
Opel		S Car	Kadett	Ascona	Rekord	Commodore	Senator Monza	Manta	Monza	
ITALY										
Fiat/Lancia Alfa-Romeo	126	127	Ritmo Alfa-Sud	131	132	Gamma Alfetta		X1/9 Alfa-Sud Alfetta Giuletta	Gamma	Ferrari

(The arrow indicates that the model attempts to cover more than one segment)

a Spain only   b In collaboration with Steyr, Daimler Puch production will take place in Austria.

45

effect it has had on the large, executive and luxury end of the market —
formerly one of the strongest areas in the UK model range, in particular for
British Leyland. As the CPRS report comments: 'The poor reputation of
British cars will have to be corrected as a matter of urgency, because a
reputation for poor quality and workmanship materially influences consumer decisions, especially abroad.'

All of the British manufacturers have taken steps to absolve their poor
performance by providing greater warranty cover. BL has gone to the extreme
of offering AA and AA Relay membership, and what amounts to a subsidised
insurance scheme covering the second year; while this does offset some, at
least, of the direct costs incurred by the consumer as a result of poor quality,
it is woefully inadequate in dealing with the annoyance aspect of the problem
or the remainder of the consumer's out of pocket expenses. Locking the stable
door after the horse has bolted is not the answer. There is no alternative but to
admit the problem and solve it head on by improving quality, which can not
be done by handing out insurance and warranty sops piecemeal.[1]

The picture for the CV product range is hearteningly different. In terms
of segment classification, five basic market segments can be isolated: car
derivative vans, panel vans and trucks (e.g. Ford Transit), mass-produced light
weight chassis trucks (which can be further subdivided into four weight divisions), medium weight volume trucks and heavy CVs (premium built trucks
and quality made heavy trucks). Comparing total output from all UK manufacturers, it can be seen that no other country can compete with an equally
comprehensive range. The Japanese producers have almost as broad a range,
but offer no real competition at the heavy end of the market. France and
Germany (excluding the 'Club of Four') lack competitive models in the middle
of the range. Scandinavia is competitive only at the heavier end, and Italy
has gaps across the specturm. Despite defensive mergers (i.e. the 'Club of
Four') British producers operate from a position of strength, [2] although recent
CV model developments in Europe might reduce that strength.

DISTRIBUTION SYSTEMS

A competitive product range with a reputation for high quality will not improve a producer's market share if it is not backed by an effective distribution
system and a strong dealer network.

The most important single change in the composition of the UK dealer
network in recent years has been the increase in the number of dealers handling imported cars. This situation has been largely brought about by a series of
'rationalisations' undertaken by the major British manufacturers during the
period 1968 to 1976, during which time nearly 7,000 dealers were 'disenfranchised'. Some of them were able to switch from one British manufacturer

---

1. A pre-publication comment noted that Ministry of Defence 05–21 and related Quality
   programmes are being introduced as well as better supplier Quality procedures.
2. Except in the heavyweight category where UK firms are only now catching up with the
   rest of Europe – See Section 3.

TABLE 3.3

	Car Derivative	Panel Van/Truck	Mass Produced Light Weight Chassis				Quantity Made "Medium Weight" Trucks 12–32 tons	Heavy CVs	
			3½–6 tons	6 tons–16	16–22 tons	22 tons+		Quantity Made "Heavy Trucks" 12–32+ tons	Premium Built 12–40+ tons
BLMC	Mini Marina Land-Rover	Sherpa EA Land-Rover	FG	Terrier-Boxer-Mastiff series			Chieftain-Clydesdale Reiver series	Lynx-Bison-Buffalo series Mercury-Marshall-Mammoth Major series	Routeman Marathon Crusader
Bedford	HA	CF	TJ	TK	TK	TK	TM	TM	
Chrysler		PB	Walk-Thru	Commando	Commando		Dodge 500	11382	
Ford	Escort	Transit	A Series	D Series	D Series	D Series		Trans-continental	
Reliant	Robin								
Foden								"High Volume"	Various models

47

TABLE 3.3 (cont.)

	Car Derivative	Panel Van/Truck	Mass Produced Light Weight Chassis 3½–6 tons	6 tons–16	16–22 tons	22 tons+	Quantity Made "Medium Weight" Trucks 12–32 tons	Heavy CVs Quantity Made "Heavy Trucks" 12–32+ tons	Premium Built 12–40+ tons
Seddon-Atkinson							Seddon 200 13+ tonnes	Seddon 400 28+ tonnes	Atkinson 400 range: 28–38 ton
ERF								Various ERF	Various ERF
Dennis									Specials
Shelvoke and Drewry									Specials
Ford (Holland)								Trans-continental	
Chrysler (Spain)		Panel series					K range		11382
Ford (Germany) Escort	Escort	Transit							
Opel	Rekord	Blitz	Blitz						

TABLĖ 3.3 (cont.)

	Car Derivative	Panel Van/ Truck	Mass Produced Light Weight Chassis				Quantity Made "Medium Weight" Trucks 12–32 tons	Heavy CVs	
			3½–6 tons	6 tons–16	16–22 tons	22 tons+		Quantity Made "Heavy Trucks" 12–32+ tons	Premium Built 12–40+ tons
VW		Transporter	4 ton VW. MAN VW-LT	VW-MAN					
Daimler-Benz		L206 1–2 ton	L608 L306	L750	Medium Series			LPK Series LS Series AK Series	LPS Series
MAN			'Saviem'-type	VW-MAN			MAN 12 tonnes+	MAN-F type	FT Series
IVECO (FIAT) Fiat - OM	Auto-bianchi	850 T 241	NC OM55	NC OM75			NP	619	
Magirus-Deutz			'Club of Four'	'Club of Four'			P	D Series	D Series
Unic							Unic.	Unic V8	
Renault-SAVIEM	R4	Renault Estafette	Saviem	'Club of Four'				'MAN' type Berliet	'MAN' type Berliet

TABLE 3.3 (cont.)

| | Car Derivative | Panel Van/Truck | Mass Produced Light Weight Chassis | | | | Quantity Made "Medium Weight" Trucks | Heavy CVs | |
			3½–6 tons	6 tons–16	16–22 tons	22 tons+	12–32 tons	Quantity Made "Heavy Trucks" 12–32+ tons	Premium Built 12–40+ tons
Citroen-Peugeot	AMI8 AKL 404/204	Citeoen HY J7							
Simca	1100								
DAF	44			'Club of Four'			F Series		
Volvo			F.83	'Club of Four'			F10	F12	
Scania								L50 L80	L140
Mitsubishi	X	X	Canter	T	T	T	T900	W	
Hino	X	X	KL300	KL300	KL300	KL300	KL300	X	
Isuzu	X	X	Elf	Forward	TX	SP2	X	X	
Nissan	X	X	X	X		X	X	X	

TABLE 3.3 (cont.)

| | Car Derivative | Panel Van/Truck | Mass Produced Light Weight Chassis | | | | Quantity Made "Medium Weight" Trucks | Heavy CVs | |
| | | | 3½–6 tons | 6 tons–16 | 16–22 tons | 22 tons+ | | Quantity Made "Heavy Trucks" | Premium Built |
							12–32 tons	12–32+ tons	12–40+ tons
Toyota	X	X	X						
Saurer-Berna								DM	DV
Sisu		K	K				V		R142 M162
Pegaso							1068A/1	2011/50	
Steyr							690	790 990	1490 1890

to another, some abandoned the motor trade altogether, but available figures[1] suggest that the majority of those who continued in the trade were able to obtain import franchises from foreign competitors all too anxious to increase their penetration of the UK market. As the CPRS noted : 'rationalisation by the British manufacturers of their dealer networks in the early 1970s helped importers to build up their distribution systems'.

The fact that importers now account for something like 40 per cent of total dealer outlets has a direct effect on the overall sales pattern. Given that the standard assessment of the competitive strength of the various dealer networks is measured in terms of average sales per outlet, and that on this basis there is rather less variation between the leading importers and domestic manufacturers than between individual domestic manufacturers, it seems reasonable to expect that something approaching 40 per cent of total sales will be of imported cars. Such a level of import penetration is way above the average for the Common Market. If this does not occur, then the dealer network will change to reflect the market situation.

The performance of British manufacturers through the distribution networks overseas is good, taking the car industry as a whole, although there are one or two significant weaknesses in the British Leyland network which in the US market are partly the result of problems in maintaining the levels of supply and quality (where, despite a successful drive to improve representation, BL sales per dealer lagged far behind their closest import competitors) and in Europe partly the result of poor coverage, where supply problems have bedevilled attempts to attract or retain good dealers.

EUROPEAN ORGANISATION

As a result of changes in the European organisation of their respective US parent companies, three of the four major UK producers — Ford GM and Chrysler — are not using productive capacity to produce and assemble cars in Britain for export to Europe. Rather, the reverse is true. GM are marketing some Asconas and Mantas[2] assembled at their Antwerp plant (using German parts), while Chrysler are importing some Alpines and 180/2 litre models from France at the moment and started to assemble Alpines in the UK at their Ryton plant from French produced KD kits late in 1976. Ford is currently importing some of the Ghia models and the RS Escort models from Germany; the engine for the new Ford Fiesta is to be manufactured in Spain, and a number of other parts will be imported from Spain and Germany. Unless Chrysler and GM reverse this trend, by manufacturing more components elsewhere and assembling more cars in the UK, they will not be making full

---

1.   Quoted in CPRS, Chap. 3, P.71.
2.   Sold at Cavaliers and Cavalier coupes, although UK production of these models began in 1977.

52

TABLE 3.4

British Distribution Networks by Manufacturer
(1977)

	CARS		CVs	
	Sales per [a] Dealer [b]	Average No. Dealers	Sales per Dealer	Average No. Dealers
Ford	302	1,260	97	305
Datsun	234	380		
GM (Vauxhall/Bedford)	221	624	75	216
Fiat	197	353	40	29
Renault	151	381	10	23
VW	148	346		
Chrysler[c]	148	612	53	96
BL	143	2,250	50	279
Citroen	115	228		
Peugeot	113	201		
Volvo	101	218	97	29
Toyota	100	269		
Lada/Moskvitch	83	148		
GM (Opel)	82	210		
Honda	80	250		
Mercedes-Benz	74	95	82	37
Alfa Romeo	72	130		
BMW	62	146		
Mazda (Toyo Kogyo)	60	261		
Skoda	37	270		
Colt (Mitsubishi)	31	222		
Saab-Scania	25	188	37	24
Polski-Fiat	19	80		
Seddon Atkinson			88	35
Magirus Deutz			24	27
MAN			20	24
DAF			62	23
Foden			57	20

a. Includes car-derived vans
b. Based on the average level of dealers in 1977 and 1977 United Kingdom registrations.
c. Includes Simca sales of cars includijng light vans which are in only 477 outlets.

Source: Sewell Profit Information Unit, Franchise Networks

use of their UK productive capacity, and therefore not benefitting from the economies of scale which could be gained. Ford, for example, have attempted to mitigate their problem by announcing a major investment programme in the UK to source engines from South Wales. This rather depressing picture is more or less reversed in the case of commercial vehicles, where all three of the US subsidiaries manufacture in the UK for export to Europe (be it complete vehicles or major components).

CAPACITY

The CPRS report and the Expenditure Committee report failed to agree in their estimates of total car production capacity in the UK (the Expenditure Committee placing the figure at 2½ million units per year, while the CPRS report arrived at a somewhat lower figure), but both figures suggest that total capacity is in excess of 2 million units annually,[1] with the CPRS report indicating that break-even point was reached in the UK at about 1.8 million cars.

Figures for total CV capacity are more difficult to arrive at, as the product mix is more diversified. It *is* certain, however, that BL has the largest capacity, followed by Ford and GM, with Chrysler, the smallest of the four, bringing up the rear.

Figures for potential productive capacity (together with actual capacity estimates using existing machinery and labour measures) shown in Table 3.6 indicate the probable result of changes and improvements in plant and machinery and plant organisation. For example, although BL's productive capacity in the Volume division currently stands at only 850,000 per year, with the introduction of new machinery at its Longbridge plant it could be facilitised to much higher production levels, giving an overall car total for Solihull, Longbridge, Cowley and other plants of 1.2 to 1.3 million.[2]

1. Perhaps a revised 'best guess' at the current easily achievable car capacity is: Chrysler 320,000; Vauxhall 350,000; Ford 650,000; BL say 1,000,000 allowing for the closure of various plants) – thereby making a total capacity of 2.3 million. With current industrial relations an achievable maximum output is probably around 1.8 – 2.0 million cars per year.
2. See Chapter 7.

TABLE 3.5

Major Car Manufacturers' Utilisation of European Assembly Capacity

Volume Car Manufacturers	1974 Profit After Tax a (£ m.)	2-shift Capacity (i)	Units ('000) Production in best Year (II)	Production in 1974 Actual (iii)	% Capacity Utilisation (1974)
BL (including Belgium)	- 6.7	1,190	916	738	62
Chrysler (United Kingdom/France)	- 25.8	900	780	647	72
Fiat	- 13.7	1,850	1,850	1,206	65
General Motors (Vauxhall/Opel)	- 20.8	1,400	1,116	715	51
Peugeot/Citroen	- 85.4	1,570	1,263	1,127	72
Renault	- 21.1	1,500	1,174	1,174	78
Volkswagen (including Audi-NSU)	-168.7	1,800	2,032	1,436	80

a. Before extraordinary items.

Source: CPRS Report, p.52 with modifications
(N.B. More up to date profit figures are provided in Table 3.9)

TABLE 3.6

	Actual Capacity^c (Estimated in 1977)	Maximum Planned Car Capacity on a Two-shift Basis in 1976/7^a		Best Global Year 1972	Record Production	
		'000s	(Potential)	'000s	Output (Class) '000s	Year of Occurrence
Austin-Morris	720	850	(850)	698	720	1964
Jaguar	30	45	(50)	24½	31½	1971
Triumph ^d	100	190	(100)^e	138	144	1968
Rover (inc. new Solihull factory)	140	60	(200)	56	56	1972
BL TOTAL	990	1,145	(1,200)	916	951	
Ford (UK)	450	550^b	(650)	547	553	1968
Chrysler	200	300	(365)	264	28½	1971
Vauxhall	150	365	(440)	184	245	1968
	1,790	2,525		1,911	2,031	

a. Expenditure Committee's definition Table 8, p. 22.
b. Assembly capacity; powertrain capacity is higher.
c. Using current machinery and labour resources.
d. Possibly no capacity; part of Triumph (Speke plant in Liverpool) is already scheduled for closure and future rationalisation plans may well see Canley transformed into a component plant.
e. Assumes closure of Speke.

Note: The difference between the three sets of capacity figures are as follows. The maximum potential car capacity on a two-shift basis is what may be achieved if all plants are brought up to their peak two-shift level of production. In order to achieve this maximum, a small amount of additional capital investment would be necessary to remove certain bottlenecks. Maximum planned car capacity was that estimated by the Expenditure Committee which presumably takes into account the existence of the bottle-necks. The actual capacity figures are based on the assembly lines which were in operation in 1977 and the speed with which a particular shift operated and the number of shifts in operation.

PRODUCTION

Production figures for the major UK car manufacturers are given in Table 3.7, although it should be remembered that statistical compilations of this sort are beset by definitional problems. The SMMT, for example, includes as a countable unit all built up cars; any KD[1] units that are over 50 per cent in value are counted as one production unit, but units of less than 50 per cent are totally excluded from the figures.

TABLE 3.7

UK Car Production[a]

	1972 '000's	1973 '000's	1974 '000's	1975 '000's	1976 '000's	1977 '000's
BRITISH LEYLAND						
Austin Morris	698	672	561	450	511	501
Specialist cars [b] (inc. some Land Rovers)	219	203	179	155	177	150
TOTAL	916	876	740	605	688	651
CHRYSLER UK [c]	264	265	262	227	145	169
FORD (UK) [d]	547	453	384	330	383	407
VAUXHALL	184	138	137	99	109	93
TOTAL [e]	1,921	1,747	1,523	1,267	1,333	1,328

a. This table uses the SMMT definition of production: one unit equals either a BU unit or a KD unit if greater than 50 per cent of the value of a BU Unit.
b. Includes Land Rover station wagons (13,000; 11,000; 10,000 and 14,000 for 1972-1975 respectively).
c. Includes, for 1975, about 120,000 KD kits for Iran.
d. Does not include powertrain production exported.
e. Total includes production by smaller manufacturers.

1. KD stands for Knock Down. CKD is often referred to as a countable kit − a kit which would be 'counted' in the production figures as one car (usually defined as being a kit with greater than 50 per cent of the value of the total car).

Lower production levels in 1975 and 1974 were partly caused by a corresponding gap in demand. The low 1973 production figure, however, must be attributed to other factors, for demand was then running at its pre-oil crisis peak. CV production figures (see Table 3.8) have remained at a more constant level during the period in question, partly because demand far outstripped supply in the early 1970s.

TABLE 3.8

UK Commercial Vehicle Production[a]

	1972 '000's	1973 '000's	1974 '000's	1975 '000's	1976 '000's	1977 '000's
BRITISH LEYLAND						
Austin Morris	64	57	53	53	51	60
Land-Rovers[b]	39	36	35	39	36	30
Leyland Vehicles	37	43	38	40	33	30
	140	137	126	133	120	120
CHRYSLER	24	26	25	19	14	16
FORD	144	137	131	129	141	148
VAUXHALL	91	107	112	91½	86	92
SEDDON-ATKINSON	3	4	4	3	3	3
ERF	2	2	2	2	2	3
FODEN	1	2	2	1	2	2
OTHERS	2	1	1	2	2	3
	408	417	403	380	372	386

a.   SMMT definition (see previous table)
b.   Remaining Land-Rovers (which are not included under cars)

FINANCIAL PERFORMANCE

The profitability of the British car industry has been dangerously low for a number of years. Table 3.9 gives pre-tax profit and loss figures for the four years from 1970 to 1974. During that time British Leyland recorded small profits (and even they disappeared entirely in 1975). Vauxhall has recorded pre-tax losses since 1969, with the single exception of 1971, when a pre-tax profit of £1.8 million was reached (although in 1976, the loss of £1.7 million was almost break-even). Apart from two fairly healthy years in 1964 and 1965, profits have otherwise been small. Chrysler has consistently made either small profits or losses, although since 1975 Chysler has reported much larger losses. Ford, with the exception of a substantial pre-tax loss recorded in 1971, is the only one of the major competitors to have consistently shown substantial pre-tax profits. Moreover, even British Leyland's extremely modest profits fail to give an accurate picture of the company's position, for if British Leyland had made the same provision for replacement of machinery and plant as its rivals, the company would have recorded heavy losses. Furthermore total BL profits did not equal the sum of the best year of the individual parts (before the formation of BL in 1968) even in money terms until 1976 – in real terms their profits have been nowhere near achieved.

From 1970 to 1973 only Ford and BL managed to earn a return on capital employed that was higher than the bank lending rate during that period, and in that time, Ford was the only one of the four companies 'able to finance capital expenditure from retained profits plus depreciation' (CPRS Report, p.63).

Put quite simply, these dismal figures merely underline the fact that the British motor car producers were simply not making enough money to carry on without help.[1] All of the recent changes in the industry – the NEB take-over of BL, and British Government aid for the Chrysler operation – are the direct result of poor financial performance in each case, for which there are three main reasons: loss of market position; failure to achieve production targets; and an uncompetitive cost structure.

Loss of market position is widely attributed to product quality problems, product range problems and distribution difficulties (the latter exacerbated by the failure to produce enough cars to meet the estimated demand, in many cases leaving distributors with nothing to sell). These factors have already been considered in greater detail elsewhere (see pp.42-52). There are in turn three principal reasons for the failure to meet production targets: industrial disputes within the industry; shortage of materials (caused by the effects of labour disputes in the supply industries, or by poor internal or external management); mechanical breakdowns, which according to the CPRS Report, resulted in 'the loss of about twice as many production hours in the UK as on the continent'. And, finally, a combination of factors are generally considered to be the cause of the uncompetitive cost structure : poor productivity; over-manning; a fragmented industry structure with too many plants; too many models and too many powertrain ranges competing for the same market segment; and, finally, an emphasis on engineering sophistication at the expense of cost burdens. We shall examine each of these charges in turn.

PRODUCTIVITY

Although productivity figures have been included here, it should be remembered that straightforward comparisons are less revealing than they might at first appear to be. Within any one range, for example, particular models (e.g. heavy CVs) take longer to produce than others, and product-ivity figures are further biased by the inclusion of a number of 'bought out' components as a percentage of the total raw materials used. What is striking, however, in country by country comparisons, is the much higher productivity figures for both the US and Japan – which are nearly twice as high as the figures for their European counterparts (see Tables 3.10 and 3.11).

1. UK Car manufacturers are not alone. Alfa Romeo are estimated to have made an operating loss of in excess of £90 million in 1976 (i.e. £450 loss for each car produced). The Alfa-Sud plant alone had losses of in excess of £200 million.

TABLE 3.9

Profitability of European Manufacturers

Trend of Unit Sales and Revenue				Actual Competitive Sales Returns		
Sales Revenue				Return on Sales After Local Taxes		
	1974	1975 (in $millions)	1976		1972 %	1973 %
British Leyland	3.7	4.1	5.2[a]	British Leyland	1.6	1.7
Vauxhall	0.8	0.9	0.9	Vauxhall	(Loss)	(Loss)
Chrysler UK	0.7	0.8	0.6	Chrysler	0.5	1.3
Ford of Britain	2.2	2.5	2.9	Ford of Britain	3.5	3.6
Ford Europe	4.0	4.8	5.7	Ford Europe		
VW/Audi	6.6	7.7	8.5	VW/Audi	1.3	2.0
Opel	1.9	2.5	3.5	Opel	5.5	5.5
Daimler-Benz	5.3	6.6	7.3	Daimler-Benz	2.5	2.1
BMW	1.1	1.5	1.9	BMW	3.5	3.6
Ford of Germany	1.9	2.6	3.4	Ford of Germany	2.8	4.2
Renault	3.4	4.3	5.4	Renault	0.5	0.4
Peugeot/Citroen	4.5	6.6	7.3	Peugeot/Citroen	2.3	2.1
Chrysler France	1.0	1.3	1.7	Chrysler France	2.0	2.9
Fiat	4.4	4.9	4.6	Fiat	0.8	—
Volvo	2.4	3.3	3.6	Volvo	2.2	2.6
Saab-Scania	1.5	1.9	2.1	Saab-Scania	2.1	2.3

a.   For period September 1975 to December 1976.

The CPRS Report found evidence to suggest that 'on average the man hours required in Britain to assemble the same, or a similar, car are almost double those on the continent' (CPRS Report, p. 81). It was felt that there were four reasons for this: slow work pace (50 per cent slower, according to one CPRS experiment); shortage of materials (to which was attributed up to 40 per cent of total production stoppages); the high incidence of quality faults, requiring additional rectification time; and, finally, poor maintenance. We would dispute the CPRS findings in this respect, however, on the grounds that the

TABLE 3.9 (cont.)

1974 %	1975 %	1976 %	The European Automotive Industry – Operating Results Profits(Losses) Before Taxes	1974	1975 (in $ millions)	1976
(Loss)	(Loss)	1.5[a]	British Leyland	5	168	127 [a]
(Loss)	(Loss)	(Loss)	Vauxhall	(42)	(28)	(3)
(Loss)	(Loss)	(Loss)	Chrysler UK	(42)	(78)	(76)
0.2	0.6	3.6	Ford of Britain	18	25	218
(Loss)	1.4	5.1	Ford Europe	(21)	(130)	(556)
(Loss)	(Loss)	4.7	VW/Audi	(197)	99	593
0.1	.8	8.7	Opel	23	54	450
1.9	1.9	2.3	Daimler-Benz	377	522	741
1.5	2.0	2.7	BMW	26	65	133
(Loss)	4.5	7.4	Ford of Germany	(73)	147	362
0.2	(Loss)	2.4	Renault	8	(129)	142
(Loss)	0.8	4.1	Peugeot/Citroen	(118)	84	608
(Loss)	(Loss)	2.6	Chrysler France	(11)	(25)	58
–	–	1.7	Fiat	57	5	153
0.9	0.1	0.4	Volvo	43	20	40
2.0	1.6	1.7	Saab-Scania	48	53	71

experiments performed to estimate the effect of each one of these factors on the variable concerned were not sufficiently controlled. Continental and UK plants are not directly comparable; the UK plants are older, less spacious and not as well planned as their European counterparts, and this, in turn, is a direct result of the failure to invest capital in new plant and equipment throughout the UK motor industry. As this is an important point, we will go on to consider it in greater detail.

With Ford as the honourable exception, Chrysler, Vauxhall and BL have the

TABLE 3.10
(From the CPRS Report)
Vehicles Produced Employee/Year[a]

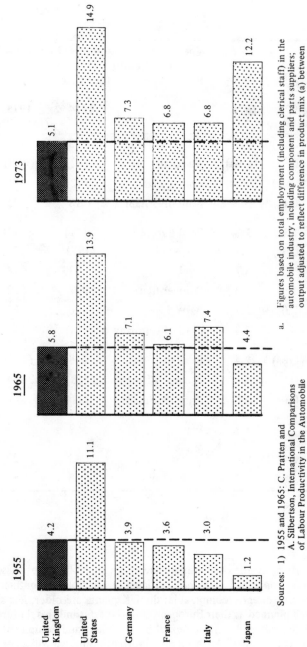

	1955	1965	1973
United Kingdom	4.2	5.8	5.1
United States	11.1	13.9	14.9
Germany	3.9	7.1	7.3
France	3.6	6.1	6.8
Italy	3.0	7.4	6.8
Japan	1.2	4.4	12.2

Sources: 1) 1955 and 1965: C. Pratten and A. Silbertson, International Comparisons of Labour Productivity in the Automobile Industry, 1950-1965 August 1967
2) 1973: CPRS estimates using 1973 SMMT VdA, and national employment statistics to update Pratten and Silbertson's original analysis.

a. Figures based on total employment (including clerical staff) in the automobile industry, including component and parts suppliers; output adjusted to reflect difference in product mix (a) between cars, and (b) between cars and CVs (trucks, vans, buses). Does not take into account differences between countries in the relative proportion of component imports/exports.

TABLE 3.11

Employees and Productivity

(a)	Unit Sales per Employee			
Company Data	1973	1974	1975	1976
BL	5.7	4.9	4.5	5.0
Ford UK[a]	9.5	8.6	8.0	9.5
Chrysler UK	11.7	10.3	9.8	7.8
Vauxhall	7.6	7.6	7.5	8.0
Renault	14.5	15.4	15.3	14.2
Peugeot	12.4	12.3	11.1	12.4
Mercedes	4.3	4.4	3.7	3.8
VW	10.6	10.1	13.8	14.2
Opel	14.8	12.9	14.3	15.3
Volvo	5.6	4.9	4.9	5.2
Fiat	6.7	7.3	7.2	6.4
Ford (worldwide)	12.6	11.6	11.3	12.2
Chrysler (worldwide)	12.5	10.8	11.4	12.8
GM (worldwide)	10.7	9.1	9.7	11.5

a. Using SMMT production figures which excludes non-countable KD units, the productivity figures are around 1.3 units lower. Using the SMMT figure for 1976 gives a productivity of 7.7.

dubious distinction of appearing at the bottom of the table (see Table 3.12 (a)).

Although Chrysler's Ryton and Linwood plants are relatively new, little has been done to them in the last six years. The plant at Stoke is very much older and more antiquated, and the Ford plant at Dagenham has been severely criticised for its lack of new equipment. BL's analysis of plant in use (see Table 3.12 (b)) shows clearly just how old a substantial portion of their equipment is. [1]

Capital Investment

The capital investment within the UK motor industry has been abysmally low. Working from the Annual Accounts for 1970 to 1973, we derived the figures for capital expenditure that (for the UK) bore little resemblance to those contained in the CPRS Report — these are shown in Table 3.12 (a).

1. Confirmation on this point comes from the Expenditure Committee *(Public Expenditure on Chrysler UK Ltd.)*. In fact the CPRS admitted that BL had an investment problem and that they had not visited Chrysler UK. Consequently over 50% of UK car making capacity had an investment problem and this was not incorporated in the evidence which the CPRS had amassed to tone-down the effect of this deficit of capital per man on value-added per man.

TABLE 3.11 (cont.)

(b) Employees in BL by Division

British Leyland Data up to 1974, estimates thereafter.

Number of Employees '000s	1970	1971	1972	1973	1974	1975	1976	1977	1978
Austin Morris	88	81	80	85	84	79	81		
Jaguar	} 42	10	9	10	10	9	} 10	135	125
Rover-Triumph		30	34	34	34	30	33		
Trucks & Buses	29	28	25	26	28	28	27	28	28
Special Products	13	13	13	13	13	12	} 12	14	14
Prestcold	4	3	3	3	3	3	3		
Others	–	–	–	1	2	2	2	2	2
TOTAL	176	169	164	171	173	164	168	179	169

Source: Annual Reports and other sources.

64

TABLE 3.11 (cont.)

(c)

Productivity in BL by Division

Productivity in units	1970	1971	1972	1973	1974	1975	1976	1977	1978
Austin Morris (including allowance for car derived vans)	7.6	9.2	9.6	8.6	7.3	6.9	7.7	NA	NA
Jaguar	5.0	3.2	2.7	2.8	3.6	2.2	2.4		
Rover-Triumph (including allowance for car derived vans)		7.1	6.9	6.2	5.2	4.9	5.6		
Trucks and Bus Division	2.0	1.8	1.5	1.6	1.3	1.5	1.2	1.5	1.8
All cars, car derived vans, and Land Rovers	6.9	8.0	8.2	7.5	6.4	5.9	6.3	5.4	6.7

Source: Annual Reports of British Leyland Productivity figures are authors' estimates.

65

TABLE 3.12

Capital Expenditure, 1970-73

(a)   (at December 1973 exchange rates)

£ Million		Number of Vehicles Sold 1973 (000)
Volkswagen	+1,041	2,281
Fiat	575	1,620
Daimler Benz	490	509
Nissan Datsun	414	1,915
Toyota	407	2,383
Renault	336	1,410
Opel	257	847
Volvo	239	269
British Leyland [a]	222	1,161
Ford-Werke	209	732
Ford (UK)	190	674
Citroen	165	677
Peugeot	162	754
BMW	138	214
British Leyland [b]	127	1,161
Simca	69	576
Vauxhall	61	259
Chrysler (UK)	30	362

Source: Annual Accounts and CPRS Report
a.   Annual Accounts
b.   As per Ryder Report (i.e. excluding: tools, acquired companies and regional grants)

Older plant is frequently incapable of producing work of acceptable quality, which in turn means that rectification work must be carried out. Breakdowns are more frequent, leading to stoppages during and between shifts (which, due to the cramped lay-out of British plants, can bring the entire plant to a stand-still while repairs are carried out). More maintenance staff are required to keep the equipment operating (up to 78 per cent more, according to the CPRS Report). Older machines are usually incapable of working as fast as newer ones, and often require more men to operate them, leading to higher manning levels and slower working. And, finally, plant lay-out itself can affect productivity, through lack of space or costly misuse of existing space. All of which affects the entire production process and, indeed, the morale of men who are obliged to work in far from perfect conditions.

TABLE 3.12

(b)   Age Analysis of Plant in Use by BL at 30th September 1974

Year of Acquisition to 30th September	Cost £m	Accumulated Depreciation £m	Net Book Value £m
1974	53	3	50
1973	49	15	34
1972	20	7	13
1971	28	13	15
1970	21	13	7
	171	52	119
1969	20	15	5
1968	28	23	5
1967	21	19	2
1962 – 1966	78	78	–
1957 – 1961	112	112	–
1952 – 1956	17	17	–
Pre 1952	2	2	–
	449	318	131

In face the table understates the proportion of old plant since in today's prices the cost of the plant acquired many years ago would be much higher.

Source: Ryder Report.

Too Many Models

In brief, the UK car industry (with the exception of Ford) produces too many different models[1] in insufficiently large quantities, carrying far too heavy a

1.   Interestingly enough under cross examination by the Expenditure Committee, Sir Kenneth Berrill revealed the enormous political pressure he and CPRS were under; for having unequivocably called in the CPRS Report, for the elimination of assembly capacity (i.e. the weakest car manufacturer which at that point in time was Chrysler UK), Sir Kenneth Berrill modified his position from 'too many manufacturers who happen to have too many models' to 'too many manufacturers with too many models' (Para. 58, Public Expenditure on Chrysler UK). Such a statement is clearly at odds with the reduction in assembly capacity advocated in the CPRS Report and Sir Kenneth Berrill's own admission that any manufacturer needed a full model range.

TABLE 3.13

Analysis of Lost Production October and November 1974

Quality faults	
Facility changes	
Programme changes	18%
Absenteeism	
Industrial Disputes	
Internal	15%
External	4%
	19%
TOTAL LOST PRODUCTION	37%

Source: Ryder Report.

cost penalty in terms of costs associated with a particular model (e.g. advertising cost, capital investment for model replacements, etc.) without reaping the benefits of economies of scale. German companies, for example, manufacture 15 engine ranges in comparison to the 26 engine ranges produced in the UK.

Too Many Plants

Just as there are too many model ranges for the UK car industry to function profitably, so too there are too many plants in relation to the number of cars produced. The fragmented structure of the industry increases the costs of overheads incurred on a plant by plant basis (rent, rates, power, heat and light, senior and middle management, communications and transport) and leads to a considerable duplication of effort. Moreover, less than a third of the existing plants in the UK are large enough to derive maximum benefit from economies of scale at the levels we have suggested. The structure at present is costly, cumbersome and wasteful.

The CPRS Report produced an interesting illustration of the effects of too many products and plants syndrome although this problem is mainly caused by BL – this is shown in Figure 3.1.

TABLE 3.14

Production of main saloon models by Company, 1976

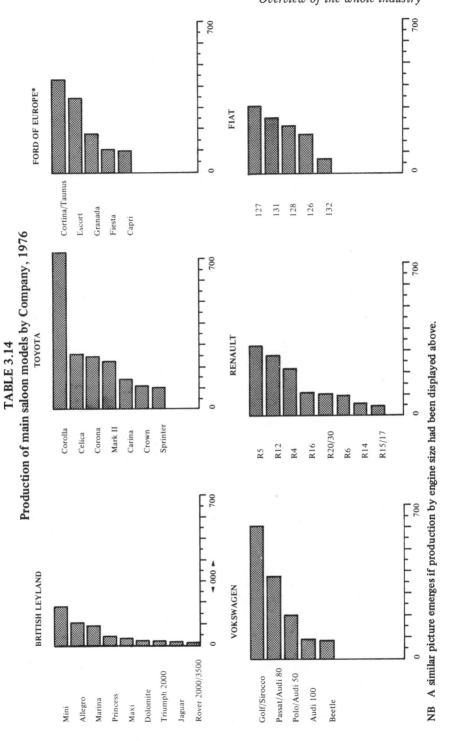

NB A similar picture emerges if production by engine size had been displayed above.

FIGURE 3.1

Illustration of the Effects of Failure to Rationalise Product Range and Plants

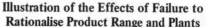

Source: CPRS Report

Labour Disputes

Table 3.15 provides a mass of detailed evidence relating to the extent of labour disputes in the motor industry and the causes of these disputes.

TABLE 3.15

(a)   **Numbers of Vehicles Lost due to Internal Labour Disputes**

1,000's

	1972	1973	1974
BL (estimated)	149	157	131
CHRYSLER	31	76	22
FORD	28	129	89
VAUXHALL	4	24	3

Source: Minutes of evidence from Expenditure Committee and author's estimates.

70

TABLE 3.15 (cont.)

(b)

Causes of Lost Production
UK Motor Vehicle Manufacturers
(%)

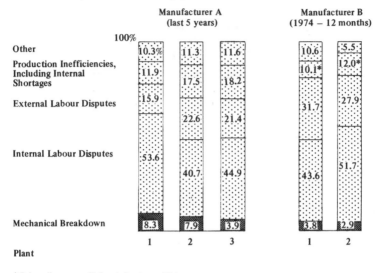

| | Manufacturer A (last 5 years) | Manufacturer B (1974 – 12 months) |

* Primarily mass relief and shortage of labour

Source: CPRS Report

TABLE 3.15 (cont.)

(c) **Days Lost in the United Kingdom through Industrial Action**

Man Days Lost per 1,000 Workers

	United Kingdom Motor Industry	All United Kingdom Manufacturing Industry and Services
1969	3,100	305
1970	2,150	485
1971	6,150	600
1972	2,750	1,100
1973	4,100	325
1974	3,550	650
1975	1,800	275
1976	1,750	150
1977	5,798	450

Source: Employment Gazette

71

TABLE 3.15 (cont.)

(d) Comparison of Incidence of Disputes in Car Plants in the Same Company (1974)

	Internal Disputes (Number)	Number of Employees ('000)	Days Lost ('000)	Days Lost per Employee	Type of Plant
CUK					
Linwood	324	5.6	62	14.7	Assembly/Powertrain/ Stamping
Ryton	112	3.6	81	22.5	Assembly
Stoke	49	4.5	29	6.5	Powertrain
BL					
Longbridge	172	15.9	828	52.1	Assembly/Powertrain

Source: CPRS Report

(e) Causes of Industrial Disputes (1974)

Cause	Proportion of Disputes		Share of Days Lost	
	Ford (%)	BL (%)	Ford (%)	BL (%)
Wage demands	11	20	52	62
Workload, manning levels	30 [a]	40	3	28
Conditions of work	15	6	1	—
Political action	7	0	4	1
Other	37	34	40	9
Number of disputes	629	696		
Days lost per worker	10.2	10.0		

a May include some disputes over wage structures.

Source: CPRS Report

Absenteeism[1] and high labour turnover are not unusually high in the British motor industry — absenteeism, for example, runs at a daily average of about 5 per cent, in comparison with 15-20 per cent in Italy and 25 per cent in Holland. Labour disputes and stoppages, however, are an extremely serious problem. A stoppage of any sort is particularly severe in 'flow-line' car assembly since disruption at any point in the line can halt production completely and lead to lay-offs at other stages. To quote a telling example : for every hour lost by a man on strike in 1974, BL lost between two and three additional hours as 'a result of consequential lay-offs' (CPRS Report, p.99). A CPRS survey concluded that the problem was industry-wide, that disputes seemed to occur in larger plants more frequently than smaller (and then more often on the assembly line than in the stamping, foundry or powertrain plants) and that wages were the single most important cause of industrial disputes. The report went on to suggest that there were six main causes of disputes. To begin with, it appears that the 'uncertain operating environment', together with 'objective evidence of the declining competitive position of the British car industry' has led to a lack of confidence on the part of the workforce in the ability of the industry to tackle the problems confronting it with any degree of success. There is, moreover, a long history of disagreement and dispute, with both management and labour citing examples of agreements dishonoured and acts of bad faith. Past experience of difficulties has created the present feeling of mutual distrust and suspicion, and attempts at negotiation are made even more difficult by cumbersome and rather unsatisfactory lines of communication from management via trade unions and shop stewards to the work force. As the CPRS Report expressed it:

> this not only leads to misunderstanding, confusion and mistrust, but also creates a more fundamental problem. Management is unable to communicate clearly and convincingly to its workforce the true competitive state of the British industry. Consequently, the workforce does not accept the urgency and the scale of improvements required, but rather sees management's efforts, for example, to reduce manning levels as an attempt to boost profits at the expense of the workforce. (CPRS, Chap. 3, p.102)

The introduction of measured day work (MDW) at BL and Chrysler has also been suggested as another major cause of disputes, even though the system has been operating successfully at Ford and Vauxhall for a number of years. It is apparent, however that it is a difficult system to administer effectively, and that a great deal of research into manning levels and output standards is required before MDW is put into operation — which it seems was not the case at either BL or Chrysler, where it is generally agreed the system has led to overmanning (and consequent disputes), a decrease in productivity (due to the removal of any incentive) and has made heavy demands on foremen in many cases ill-equipped to cope with unfamiliar pressures. The topic of piece rates and incentive schemes is returned to in the conclusion as well as being discussed in passing in the remaining sections of the book.

1. It was this that forced Volvo and Saab to introduce their novel production techniques — see Chapter 4.

Perhaps the most conspicuous disputes within the motor industry are those over wages. In this respect, the CPRS suggested that the vast number of separate pay settlements negotiated each year (BL, for example, negotiates over 200 separate settlements a year) gives rise to far greater opportunities for disagreement and dispute over pay differentials than would be the case if (as happens at Ford and Vauxhall) wages negotiations were conducted at a national level.

The final problem noted by the CPRS in their analysis of labour disputes was the fragmentation of the union structure itself within the motor industry. Unlike the USA or Japan, where one union represents the interests of all workers in the car industry, British workers can choose from a bewildering selection of 17 unions. Disagreements on policy and rivalries over recruitment and demarcation between the unions must inevitably cause trouble. Within such a disparate system, there can be no industry wide bargaining as is found, for example in the US.

Before completing the overview of the motor industry, a short summary of the organisational changes to BL will be given. These changes are crucial to the understanding of subsequent events at BL.

BL's REORGANISATIONS

The Ryder Report split BL into four separate divisions: Leyland cars, Leyland Truck and Bus, Special Products and an International division which provided a single centralised marketing and sales division for all exports of BL's products. In Michael Edwardes' reorganisation of February 1978, the International division was shorn of responsibility for exports. Instead it would only manage certain subsidiaries and trade investments abroad. In addition, a new company, BL Cars, would be formed as an umbrella organisation with three main subsidiary companies: Austin Morris, with responsibility for volume cars; Jaguar Rover Triumph, embracing specialist models; and BL components, with responsibility for parts, foundry operations, the SU/Butec business and the body operations (formerly the Pressed Steel Fisher organisation). It is unclear whether the Jaguar Rover Triumph operations will be further broken up to form three separate sub-subsidiaries, Rover Triumph cars, Jaguar cars and Land Rovers; or whether the single subsidiary will in the fullness of time split to form separate companies under the single umbrella organisation of BL Cars.[1] The organisational chart shown in Figure 3.2 (c) is only the first stage of an evolving process. As Michael Edwardes is reported to have said: 'We will give ourselves the whole of 1978 to allow the organisation to evolve'.[2] Even after 1978, the umbrella structure of BL Cars allows sufficient room for manoeuvre. One issue still to be finally settled is exactly what will become a centralised function for BL Cars and what will be split up under the separate profit centres of the subsidiaries. Some long-term[3] product planning

1. A pre-publication commented that the point of BL cars is that it is a legal entity – not an organisational function and the influence of BL Cars on the three car companies Austin – Morris, Jaguar Rover Triumph and BL components, will be very restricted. (See Chapters 4 and 7 for a further analysis of the Jaguar Rover Triumph split.)
2. *Financial Times,* 2 February 1978.
3. Projects between 5 and 15 years away.

74

FIGURE 3.2

Recent Organisational Charts for BL

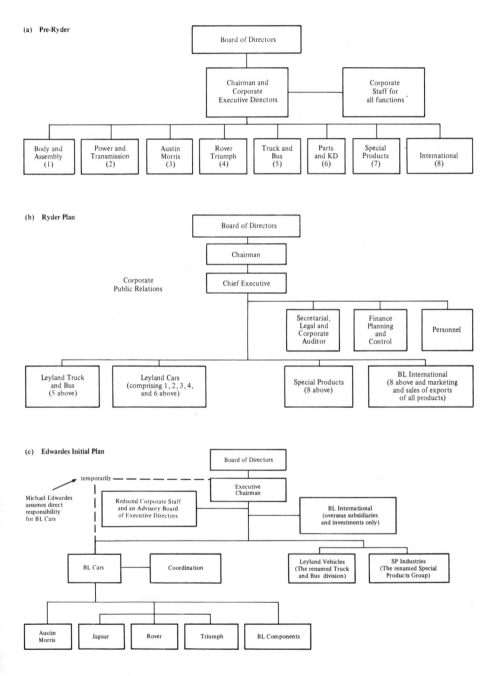

(a) Pre-Ryder

Board of Directors

Chairman and Corporate Executive Directors — Corporate Staff for all functions

| Body and Assembly (1) | Power and Transmission (2) | Austin Morris (3) | Rover Triumph (4) | Truck and Bus (5) | Parts and KD (6) | Special Products (7) | International (8) |

(b) Ryder Plan

Board of Directors

Chairman

Corporate Public Relations — Chief Executive

Secretarial, Legal and Corporate Auditor — Finance Planning and Control — Personnel

| Leyland Truck and Bus (5 above) | Leyland Cars (comprising 1, 2, 3, 4, and 6 above) | Special Products (8 above) | BL International (8 above and marketing and sales of exports of all products) |

(c) Edwardes Initial Plan

Board of Directors

temporarily

Michael Edwardes assumes direct responsibility for BL Cars

Executive Chairman

Reduced Corporate Staff and an Advisory Board of Executive Directors

BL International (overseas subsidiaries and investments only)

BL Cars — Coordination

Leyland Vehicles (The renamed Truck and Bus division)

SP Industries (The renamed Special Products Group)

| Austin Morris | Jaguar | Rover | Triumph | BL Components |

75

and engineering development would continue to be centralised. Similarly, a central unit of focus under BL cars will be maintained for labour relations – this makes sense after the effort made to introduce synchronised bargaining dates and a common wages policy throughout the car divisions.

Exactly what other functions will be centralised remain to be seen. Whilst data processing and certain finance functions are certain to remain centralised, the Edwardes' plan seems to indicate that marketing and sales worldwide might be decentralised to each of BL Cars' subsidiaries.

CONCLUSION

In this chapter an attempt has been made to overview the problems of the UK motor industry. In Section 2, further material is provided in relation to cars, whilst Section 3 deals with commercial vehicles. The components industry has not been dealt with and is left until Section 4. Before analysing each part of the motor industry in further detail, we provide some of the assumptions which form the basis of the analysis in the remaining sections of the book. Chapter 17 in Section 5 deals with the proposed Chrysler and Peugeot-Citroen merger. However much of the information in earlier sections relates to the existing Chrysler UK plants and is still relevant.

CHAPTER 4

FALLACIES, CONTROVERSIES AND ASSUMPTIONS

INTRODUCTION

This chapter deals with a number of assumptions upon which the remainder of the book is based. In this chapter, some fallacies are discussed, and a number of contentious issues are reappraised before the economic scene is set by a number of background assumptions. To begin with, two popular theories are discredited : the first concerns the feasibility of introducing 'unit working' (the Swedish solution to job dissatisfaction problems on the assembly line) to the UK; the second advocates the transfer of UK production facilities to a less developed country with lower labour costs. The regional problem of whether the UK motor vehicle manufacturing industry should be concentrated in certain locations is also discussed. The contentious issue of the production and organisational forms of BL are analysed. The question of whether the UK should be in the volume car business is discussed in abstract. Finally, before enumerating a list of background assumptions, the causes of low productivity are further explored; the CPRS and Expenditure Committee reports were seen in Chapter 1 to have disagreed on this issue.

UNIT WORKING

Unit working is an arrangement whereby small groups of workers are involved in problem-solving and production work at a number of different stages in the manufacturing process. Demarcation is minimal, thus allowing all members of the group to engage in the tasks that the group as a whole decide upon, with the aim of increasing job satisfaction through stimulating the workers' interest and involvement and by encouraging worker interaction. When problems arise the workers involved are encouraged to discuss them freely and arrive at their own solutions. In the more conventional assembly-line or conveyor-belt process, workers are restricted to the performance of a single relatively simple task, such as spot welding the joints of a car sub-frame, which makes few demands on the worker and can quickly become routine and monotonous. Job satisfaction in assembly line work is low.[1] Workers find it hard to identify their task with the finished product, while employers suffer from a rapid labour turnover and a lowering of standards as the work is performed with little care or concern.

In theory, unit working could be the answer to the motor manufacturer's prayer, by increasing worker involvement and enhancing job satisfaction, which should in turn improve quality and reduce absenteeism. It has been introduced to a limited extent in a number of industries in Sweden where production line methods were previously used. Saab, for example, opened a new engine assembly division in 1971-2 based almost entirely on unit working, while Volvo's newly opened car assembly plant has also adopted the unit

1.   A different type of robotic assembly line is discussed in Chapter 7, page 200.

working approach[1] Elsewhere, Fiat have also experimented with the unit working technique. In all three cases, however, unit working accounts for only a small proportion of total production. None of the manufacturers concerned have extended unit working to other production areas and none of them have incorporated unit working in their more recent plant developments — an omission which should give UK manufacturers pause for thought.

In many respects, the unit working method has no particular relevance to conditions in the UK motor industry. It is usually adopted in the final stages of car, engine or component assembly; the plant and equipment needed in many of the pre-assembly stages, such as steel pressing or paint spraying, would make the duplication of equipment required for unit working an impractical and prohibitively expensive proposition. Moreover, some allowance must be made for important differences in the composition of output from the Swedish and UK car industries. Volvo (excepting its newly-acquired Daf plant) and Saab both produce a limited range of low-volume high-cost cars, whereas the UK firms manufacture a wide range of high-volume relatively low-cost models. While unit working might be appropriate for low production volumes, it carries a significant cost penalty at·higher volumes because of the unavoidable duplication of essential machinery and equipment and the costly distribution of components to each of the unit working stations. Falling productivity has also been noted following the introduction of unit working, which makes unit working even less attractive[2] The cost of duplicating machinery is sufficient to limit the application of unit working to assembly operations only, while the need to carry additional stocks of components and parts further increases the cost penalty. Manufacturers might be forgiven for thinking that lower training costs and a marginal improvement in quality were inadequate compensations. All the evidence points to a net cost penalty high enough to outweigh the reduced incidence of industrial unrest or any other slight improvement in labour relations which the introduction of unit working might bring about. If the UK is to become internationally competitive, it cannot afford to introduce unit working.

Admittedly, unit working and a more peaceable industrial relations climate would be preferable to a continuation of assembly line working and a further deterioration in labour relations — but both are inferior to assembly line working *and* an improvement in labour relations, an enviable state of affairs which many of the European manufacturers have been able to sustain, although it has so far eluded their UK counterparts.

One final point must be made: unit working can only be successful if the workers involved are able to interact. If interaction becomes difficult — through disagreement over the allocation of 'worst' or 'less desirable' jobs, for example — the system breaks down, and the problems of job monotony are replaced by equally counter-productive intra-unit disputes.

1. At the beginning of the 1970's, Volvo's worker absenteeism was roughly 14 per cent, with an annual labour turnover of between 30—40 per cent.
2. In the region of 10 per cent lower productivity has been experienced by Volvo.

PRODUCTION IN LESS-DEVELOPED COUNTRIES

When industrial relations disputes become a regular, almost daily feature of the UK car industry, exasperated commentators frequently suggest that car production ought to be transferred lock, stock and barrel to a less developed country, e.g. Tunisia or Turkey, where labour is relatively cheaper and presumably more conscientious. The proposal is not a completely facetious one, but it is not particularly practical either. First, the car market in a less developed country is based on the demand for a very much more basic, utilitarian model than the standard, relatively luxurious volume car produced for the UK market. If cars for the UK were to be produced in a less developed country (LDC), production there would have to cater for two completely different types of car – one for the domestic LDC market and one for the export market. This sort of fragmentation of output would reduce the economies of scale and consequently increase costs.

There are other, equally compelling reasons for discounting the 'total relocation' argument. For a car to be truly competitive (i.e. as cheap as possible) it must be made with cheap components. Components can only be manufactured cheaply at an advanced stage of industrialisation, for without a sophisticated industrial infrastructure, the network of facilities required will simply not exist. In their absence, components must be imported – but at a higher cost. To this must be added the associated cost penalty (between 1 and 5 per cent) of transporting the finished car to the market for which it has been produced – in this case, the UK. A car plant, wherever it is located, cannot exist in splendid isolation. Apart from the plant itself and the components it processes, it may be necessary to construct housing estates, roads, schools, hospitals and community centres (as in Spain). Workers have to be trained, or retrained, and lack of expertise – especially in the initial stages – could have an adverse affect on productivity. There is ample evidence to suggest that this was the case with the new Alfa-Romeo factory near Naples, which among other difficulties ran into problems with a labour force unfamiliar with assembly line work.[1] Finally, labour costs account for, at most, only 30 per cent of the total cost of a volume car. Direct labour costs could be as low as 8–10 per cent. Any savings in labour costs could very easily vanish in the welter of increased cost penalties incurred elsewhere, or at least until the industry has achieved a certain level of sophistication – by which time, the relative labour cost advantage might have disappeared completely.

THE REGIONAL FALLACY

One fallacy which has gained popular support is that the car industry is wedded to its current location. Ford by announcing that their new £250 million engine

---

1. One of these problems was that Alfa-Romeo were not allowed to hire the people of their choice but were forced to choose lower calibre people for political reasons. Publicly Alfa-Romeo has blamed the lack of industrial aptitude by workers who have come from a predominantly agricultural environment.

plant will be sited in Waterton Cross, Bridgend has demonstrated that this is not so. This new engine plant will make the new front wheel drive Escort engine for the whole of Europe. The Dagenham engine plant on the other hand is to have reduced and/or changed capacity.[1] Certainly some of the spare capacity will be taken up by CV engine production. Some redundancies will, however, be inevitable. The foundry in Dagenham will also probably be a casualty in this rearrangement of its production facilities.

It is rumoured that of the twenty-five odd European sites put forward, the top four locations were all in South Wales (Bridgend, Llantrisant, Cardiff and the coastal plain below Ebbw Vale). There were many reasons why South Wales came out top. The fact that there is a big pool of labour (in 1977 unemployment was running at 8 per cent) which is relatively skilled (Ford estimates that some 40 per cent of the available labour in the region is skilled) and excellent communications are all important. Nevertheless such factors do not seem to outweigh Henry Ford II's critical statement in 1971 – 'I could not in good conscience recommend to my board any new capital expenditure in Britain'. In truth this statement was directed at the assembly plants. Industrial relations on the component manufacturing side of Ford's have always been very much better than on the assembly side. In any case, the new factory – which will only employ 2,500 people and probably turn out 500,000 (plus) engines per year – will be highly automated. (Dagenham may have to shed some labour from its engine plant which currently employs around 5,500.)

Coupled with this is the short-term effect of a depreciated sterling and an appreciated Deutschmark. Even in Spain Ford has been faced with 30 per cent wage demands. Most importantly the Government must have welcomed the possibility of new employment which could counteract the increased redundancy within the steel industry. Hence not only will Ford get a regional grant in the form of a 20 per cent investment grant, it will also receive funds under Section 7 of the Industry Act. Selective grants in the aid of regional policy may be made. Usually this means another £1 for each £1 of regional assistance – i.e. another 20 per cent grant. Add to this the fact that the land is owned by the Welsh Development Agency and will probably be given to Ford on a rent-free basis, and the capital investment commitment by Ford is nearly halved. The EEC will also provide a retraining grant for the redundant steel workers who may be employed by Ford. British Rail with its high speed link will also probably pay for all the appropriate sidings, etc. All in all, Ford's commitment may be less than half of the total of £250 millions.[2]

Similarly it is quite feasible for BL to partially move one of its production centres to South Wales. Other less central areas with almost equally good communications are the North East and North West – these are also possibilities. Surprisingly the cost of putting up a new greenfield site is not markedly different from re-equipping an old BL plant.

1.   The Dagenham engine plant is to switch production to diesel engines whose demand is something of an unknown quantity.
2.   The actual Government contribution for the £180 million Bridgend plant and the £130 million being spent on Halewood is £148 million; made up of a £75 million interest relief grant under the 1972 Industry Act's selective regional incentives, and £73 million in automatic regional development grants paid in assisted areas.

Later on in the book, an important argument is made for developing more smaller assembly plants for BL's car operations. Hence, Ford's decision to move to a plant in Bridgend is important in dispelling the fears of those who point to Chrysler's Linwood plant as being a failure in terms of moving out of traditional car producing areas. The Linwood plant has always suffered from Chrysler's lack of success. Time and again Chrysler has threatened successive governments with the closure of Linwood unless additional funds were forthcoming. Consequently 'trench' warfare has been a feature of the Linwood plant. There are many plants which have been moved to new areas and which are working relatively smoothly; for example, BL's plants at Llanelli (components) in South Wales and Bathgate (light CVs) in Scotland. Liverpool, on the other hand, has had a poor record. Ford's Halewood plant, BL's Speke plant and, to a lesser extent, Vauxhall's Ellesmere Port plant, have all had industrial relations problems. However, we believe that BL could successfully establish viable assembly plants in South Wales and the North East which would operate at substantially higher productivity levels than some of its traditional plants.

PRODUCTION AND ORGANISATIONAL FORMS FOR THE CAR INDUSTRY

Although in Chapter 2 it was noted that from a theoretical point of view there were economies of scale up to two million units, the optimum production plan involved the splitting up of the overall capacity into a number of units. The optimal split would be as shown in Figure 4.1 with 1 pressing plant, 2 powertrain plants and 8 assembly plants. Translating this again from a theoretical standpoint for a firm producing around 1 million vehicles per year, maximum economies could be achieved if there were:

1 pressing plant

2 powertrain plants

and 4 to 5 assembly plants

A schematic representation of this plan is shown in Figure 4.2. However, in the interests of reducing the risk from single sourcing, dual sourcing of body pressings from two pressing plants may be advisable to hedge against industrial unrest.

Each plant would only employ a maximum of 10,000 employees. One of the advantages of having relatively small plants is that from the theoretical angle, no one plant would dominate the employment prospects of a particular town. Unfortunately, Chrysler does dominate Linwood's employment. But there are many counter examples where a firm employs 10,000 or less and whose proportion of the area's total employment is thus low. If a firm dominates the employment prospects within an area, it is, in effect a monopsonist. To counter this, labour will organise itself so that a bilateral monopoly will result. Hence a suitable setting for trench warfare between management and organised

FIGURE 4.1

Organisation and Scale Economies in Car Production

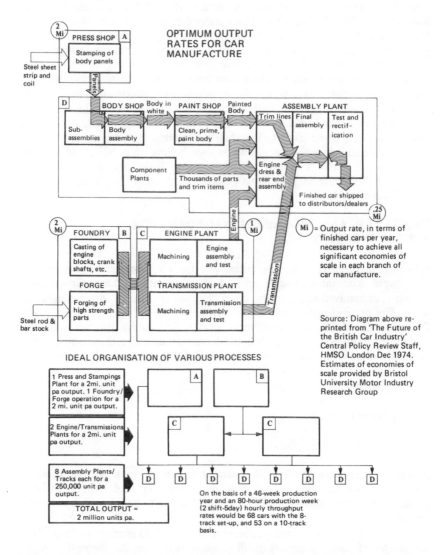

Source: Diagram above reprinted from 'The Future of the British Car Industry' Central Policy Review Staff, HMSO London Dec 1974. Estimates of economies of scale provided by Bristol University Motor Industry Research Group

labour. If the firm does not dominate an area's employment prospects, market forces can either operate or be argued to operate (e.g. XYZ Ltd down the road pays £a for this job, etc.). Similarly, neither management nor labour are under such pressure since both have alternatives (i.e. change jobs or hire new labour) which do not exist in the bilateral monopoly situation.

Even if one adopts the ideal plan, some form of management must be superimposed on the physical plant. In Chapter 2, the M-form (divisional)

FIGURE 4.2

Possible Ideal Plant Mix
for BL with Different Organisational Forms

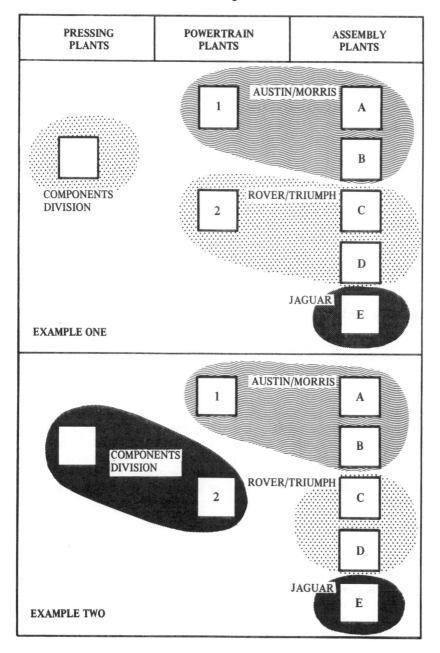

and the U-form (centralised) organisational forms were compared. The physical layout of the plants in the ideal plan is obviously suited by the centralised and functional U-form type of organisation. Is it possible to fit the ideal into a divisional structure? Briefly, the answer is yes. Each division must be in charge of its own sales and marketing decision. The production facilities attached to each M-form division could take a variety of forms. For example, there could be a separate and autonomous components division in charge of certain components which would supply the independent assembly/marketing divisions. Assuming there is only one pressing plant, the possibilities for the divisional split could be:

(1) By assembly plant only; the powertrain and assembly plants form a separate division or divisions. Note that under this scheme there could be up to 8 autonomous divisions — each one operating on a plant level.

(2) By assembly plant and powertrain plant; the pressing plant forms a separate division; this would not, however, rule out the possibility of each division using powertrain components produced by other divisions. Note that under this scheme only two assembly divisions and one components division is possible.

(3) A mixture of (1) and (2) is possible where some divisions only have an assembly plant whilst others also have a powertrain plant.

(4) Where one division also operates the pressing plant and supplies the other divisions with either body pressings or even complete bodies.

With two pressing plants a slightly larger set of possibilities could be envisaged. The above examples are illustrative of the range of options providing the necessary degree of flexibility to cope with most situations. In Figure 4.2, sample schemes for BL's divisions are provided as illustrative examples.

From the design and engineering point of view, each division would be in charge of its own products. However, in order to ensure that the maximum economies of scale are present, a centralised design centre would co-ordinate plans and ensure that where feasible and where there is no 'marketing loss', a common component should be utilised rather than design a new one for each division. In addition certain components, where there may be a corporate-wide requirement, would be sponsored by the centralised design and engineering centre.

THE VOLUME CAR QUESTION

A fundamental issue which could be raised is whether volume car production should be the kind of industry the UK and BL should be in. With relatively expensive labour, Western manufacturers cannot compete with some of the newer low labour cost producers once their industries have reached sufficient size to reap economies of scale. Similarly, and this includes the UK market, there is only a relatively small market segment which demands the cheap basic cars usually produced by an emerging nation. (The Japanese are in a transition from emergent producer to the ranks of the mature producers.) Consequently, Western manufacturers are forced to concentrate on the more specialised higher priced, greater performance and more luxurious cars. In order to minimise the threat of competition from the newer producers, the emphasis must be on maintaining a technological advantage. In this way to talk of volume cars *per se* is a misnomer; for technological development will be used to compete with even the Japanese.

A second avenue of approach to the volume car question is whether we can compete with Ford, Renault, Volkswagen, Nissan or Toyota. Since BL's total capacity and therefore its technical economies of scale are below that of its rivals, the answer must be no. But this is not to say that BL cannot produce cars which sell in large volumes. What it must do is to develop the majority of its products where there are marketing gaps or where price as a selling factor is less important[1] — i.e. the specialist car. Both BMW and Daimler Benz now produce specialist cars in greater numbers than many of our volume cars, as can be seen in Table 4.1.

CAUSE OF LOW PRODUCTIVITY

As discussed in Chapter 1, the extent to which capital investment is to blame for the ills now facing the UK motor industry is a contentious issue. To summarise the debate we have extracts from the Ryder Report:

> The most serious feature of BL's production facilities is, however, that a large proportion of the plant and machinery is old and dated and inefficient. (p.6)

and

> This record of under-investment is the main reason for the low productivity of BL's work force compared with, say, Fiat or Volkswagen. (p.29)

From the Expenditure Committee:

> . . .inadequate investment and the lower productivity of old plant have been the greatest contributors to poor profitability of the mass-production car side of the industry. (p.34)

The CPRS, however, rejected this argument:

> Even where it is possible to measure the effect of under-investment on productivity, the results demonstrate that inadequate capital equipment is only a minor cause of low productivity. (p.87)

1. See Chapter 14 for an elaboration of this point.

TABLE 4.1

BL's Car Production Compared with Other Specialist Producers for 1976

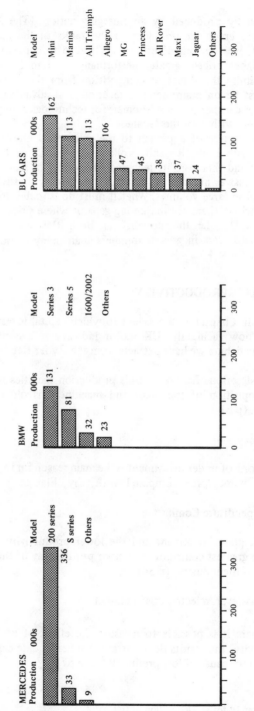

The CPRS found that over-manning, a slower work pace (including the effects of strikes) and poor maintenance were responsible for BL's low productivity. Whilst on average continental car firms paid 50% more than British firms for labour costs per employee in assembly, for nearly all cases examined, the CPRS concluded that the lower output per employee more than offset the cost advantage. This conclusion was based on experiments comparing man-hours required to assemble identical or similar cars and powertrains in the UK and the Continent. However, it has been clearly established [1] that experiments were not completely reliable. Industrial relations, component shortages, plant layout and other parameters were not held constant, as should have been the case in a controlled scientific experiment.

One of the problems in making any comparisons is the so-called production rhythm of a particular plant. Car plants consist of complicated inter-related production processes. Most operations require parts from a previous operation. It is invalid to make comparisons using a single line without looking at the remainder of the equipment which supplies the line. The speed at which a line can operate will depend on the whole production process. Such a complex process as car manufacture, relying on thousands of different components, achieves a production rhythm. To replace any one machine or assembly section will not appreciably alter this rhythm. Significant changes in the rhythm could only be brought about by substantial investment.

The Expenditure Committee using the information contained in Table 4.2 conducted a statistical analysis of the value added per man and the fixed assets per man. They concluded that there was a close relationship between value added and fixed assets per man — about 66 per cent of the difference in value added per man could be 'explained' statistically by different levels of fixed assets per man. [2] However, other explanatory variables are significant and there may be no causal relationship between value added and fixed assets per man.

Equally it is clearly wrong to blame worn out machinery and under-investment for the low productivity of 5 vehicles per employee per year that was achieved by BL in 1977. As Michael Edwardes has pointed out, Solihull's new Rover plant had suffered the worst production and quality problems in the whole company, despite £90 million investment in a new and up-to-date

1. 'A Critique of the Report on The British Car Industry by the Central Policy Review Staff', by A.L. Friedman and K.N. Bhaskar, Minutes of Evidence to the Expenditure Committee, 1976.

2. 'Regression analysis gives the following relationship between value added per man (Y_1) and the independent variable fixed assets per employee (X_1):—

$$Y_1 = 897 + 1.203 X_1$$

Standard errors   (837.17) (0.25)

+ Statistics   (1.07) (4.79)

$$R^2 = 0.657$$

It should of course, be borne in mind that these are cross-section data, not a time series; the T statistic of 4.79 shows that the relationship is not a chance result.' Expenditure Committee, *The Motor Vehicle Industry*, 1975, p.36.

TABLE 4.2

Relationship between Value Added per Man and Fixed Assets per Man

(1974)	Value Added per Man	Gross Output per Man	Fixed Assets per Man
GM (US)	£8,600	£17,495	£4,346
Ford (US)	£7,966	£19,905	£5,602
Opel	£5,875	£14,747	£3,612
Daimler Benz	£5,207	£12,672	£2,694
Volvo	£4,886	£14,790	£4,662
Ford Germany	£4,883	£14,186	£3,608
Volkswagen	£4,767	£11,087	£3,632
Saab	£4,637	£19,972	£3,141
Renault	£4,133	£12,928	£2,396
Ford (UK)	£3,901	£11,397	£2,657
Chrysler (UK)	£2,765	£ 9,968	£1,456
Vauxhall	£2,560	£ 7,975	£1,356
Fiat	£2,259	£ 8,142	£3,160
BLMC	£2,129	£ 6,539	£ 920

Source: Expenditure Committee, *The Motor Vehicle Industry*, 1975, p.36

Note that for BLMC the Value Added to Fixed Assets per man ratio is one of the highest, indicating that the company was extremely efficient in using its fixed assets. Unfortunately this type of efficiency is not necessarily relevant in a high labour cost economy.

plant.[1] The lesson is that capital investment alone does not necessarily get results.

Taking into account both the CPRS Report and the Expenditure Committee, BL's low productivity can only be improved to comparable European levels if a substantial amount of capital investment is undertaken and if the trench warfare approach abandoned.

In summary, therefore, both the CPRS and the Expenditure Committee are correct. To improve only industrial relations would not make a viable BL. A brand new BL with a labour force torn by industrial strife is equally unacceptable. However, in the interim between now and the installation of new capital investment, productivity can only be improved by better attitudes on

---

1. In his 1 February 1978 speech.

the shopfloor.[1]

The reader may wonder why there is a need for capital investment at all? There are three major reasons: newer machines are faster, cheaper and can be consistently more accurate. The first two reasons are primarily concerned with price, whilst the third reason effects reliability. However, an increase in productivity has employment implications.

EMPLOYMENT

One of the depressing conclusions that emerges from an examination of the motor industry is that direct employment prospects do not look particularly good. Either segments of the industry will be allowed to collapse, or the industry will have to become more competitive through increased productivity. If the increased productivity does not go hand in hand with a commensurate increase in sales, then direct employment by the UK motor manufacturers, and BL in particular, must fall. Figure 4.3 assumes that BL's car production will be around 1 million units and a graph of employment is traced for alternative levels of productivity. For comparison purposes, the actual employment figures in cars are shown for a number of years. The minimum competitive position is probably around a productivity figure of 12. Taking into account many of the specialist vehicles an argument could be made for a marginally lower competitive productivity figure. However, it is clear that somewhere between 30,000 to 60,000 jobs[2] will have to be shed if the industry is to produce 1 million cars economically. This, in turn, raises some fundamental assumptions about the type of society the UK is moving into. If there is a continual run down of employment in many sectors, then a depressing scenario of high unemployment emerges. On the other hand, new industries may emerge to take up the slack.

AMOUNT OF CAPITAL EXPENDITURE

Another popular fallacy which exists is that the planned Ryder capital expenditures for BL are high. In relation to other Western manufacturers, Ryder's planned £2.8 billion is not only reasonable but on the low side. For example, the planned expenditure on cars alone is only £1.6 billion over eight years. Yet Daimler Benz plan to spend £1.3 billion over three years (on cars alone). Table 4.3 provides other comparative data — past and present. Thus Ryder type expenditures within the motor industry are modest. By virtue of inflation they are now almost certainly an underestimate of BL's requirements — unless BL can internally generate the necessary funds.

1. ' "Investment by itself means nothing". Success will not be achieved without using efficiently the additional productive capacity created by additional investment.' Fourteenth Report of the Expenditure Committee, *The Motor Vehicle Industry*, 1975, p.39.
2. Citroen's 50,000 workers can consistently make over 800,000 cars whilst BL's 130,000 odd car employees produced less than 800,000 vehicles in both 1976 and 1977.

FIGURE 4.3

Alternative Employment and Productivity Levels to Produce 1 Million Cars a Year

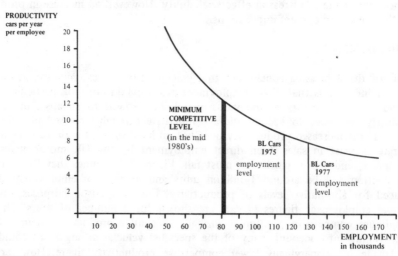

BACKGROUND ASSUMPTIONS

We now move on to analyse some of the economic factors which may affect the motor industry in the UK and in Western Europe as a whole. Obviously, any set of assumptions is open to criticism, although it seems probable that some, at least, of the assumptions discussed below are realistic. Most of the assumptions we have outlined apply to the European car industry. As three of the major UK manufacturers are directly concerned with general European conditions, this 'European' approach is neither accidental nor inappropriate.

Demand Assumptions

One important assumption throughout this book is that there will be no fundamental change in transport; people, for example, will replace cars with cars. In other words, there will be no viable alternative to the existing pattern of use of the motor vehicle notwithstanding the impending threat of an energy crisis. The planning horizon of this book is 1990 and it seemed that the above assumptions were appropriate during this time span.

However, from 1990 onwards, the UK must begin to have a growing awareness of the problems lurking around the corner when the North Sea oil reserves have been depleted. Although it may be considered deplorable that little research is being conducted into alternative forms of transport, it is argued later on in this chapter that the technological developments will make the motor vehicle more efficient in its use of fuel and enable a variety of alternative fuels to be developed.

TABLE 4.3

(a) Planned Capital Investments by Motor Manufacturers

	£ billion	Period
BL	2.8	1975-1982
Daimler-Benz (cars only)	1.3	1977-1980
Opel	1.4	1978-1982
Ford (US)	4.5	1977-1980
GM (US)	8.0	1977-1980
VW	1.2	1978-1980
Renault	4.1	1978-1982
Peugeot-Citroen	4.0	1978-1982
BMW	.8	1978-1983

(b) Capital Investment Record (in £ million)

	1970	1971	1972	1973	1974	1975	1976	1977
GM (worldwide)	971	645	782	907	1,101	1,107	1,357	2,026
Ford (worldwide)	446	408	491	641	393	505	620	n/a
Chrysler (worldwide)	177	98	143	271	199	190	n/a	402
BL	67	50	42	67	108	92	114	149
Ford UK	68	49	32	42	52	52	56	81
Vauxhall	21	19	6	13	26	9[a]	25[a]	25[a]
Chrysler UK	18	4	3	5	1	7	14	18
VW	107	107	98	102	327	165	229	445
Opel	47	61	42	61	68	n/a	n/a	n/a
Renault	101	89	86	84	117	226	n/a	n/a
BMW	42	34	63	63	40	42	n/a	n/a
Daimler-Benz	191	189	152	138	180	223	186	238
Peugeot Citroen							204	351

a. Estimates

The Economy

In general, inflation ran at a higher rate in the 1970's than either the 1960's or the 1950's and although only a fool would care to rush in with anything as categorical as a prediction, there are several good reasons for supposing that higher levels of inflation (say 10 per cent — 25+ per cent are going to be with us for some time to come. Table 4.4 compares inflation rates since 1960.

TABLE 4.4

Inflation Rates for Selected Countries (%)

	1960–9	1970-7
UK	3.3	13.7
France	3.7	9.0
Germany	2.5	5.6
Italy	3.9	13.2
Sweden	3;8	8.4
US	2.3	6.6
Australia	2.4	11.0
Japan	5.3	10.6

One of the main reasons for a higher rate of inflation is the excess demand for commodities over their available supply, and again, there are grounds for assuming that demand will continue to outstrip supply, as the lower and middle income sectors in advanced countries demand parity and as the less developed countries (especially the resource-rich ones) move towards increasing economic prosperity. The population explosion could also accelerate demand; and demand can be expected to grow in the public sector to implement massive welfare programmes.

Economic Growth

The current rates of economic growth in advanced countries will in all probability be slower than hitherto. Governments will take stronger action to curtail inflation and there could very well be a move away from growth objectives in themselves, reflecting a growing concern for the environment and the quality of life. The continuing growth in demand in the less developed countries could create a world capital shortage which might reduce investment and restrict growth in the advanced economies. Rising primary commodity costs would force resource-poor countries to allocate a higher proportion of their wealth for the purchase of these commodities. If productivity stagnates or rises more slowly than in the past, as many think it might, then the rate of growth in real incomes will also be affected, since rising productivity is an essential precondition for economic growth. Finally advanced economies dependent on imported resources may move to restrain imports as the cost of raw materials rises. Import controls of this sort would also inhibit growth. Table 4.5 shows the relative decline in the rate of growth since 1963.

Trade

In the last 30 years there has been a steady move towards liberalisation of trade and capital flows among the advanced nations, but the process could be reversed, as resource-poor countries try and protect themselves by limiting the import of certain commodities and thus safeguarding their own balance of

TABLE 4.5

Growth Rates for Some Selected Countries (%)

	1950-70	1963-73
UK	2.5	2.3
France	5.1	5.0
West Germany	6.3	4.0
Italy	5.4	4.2
Sweden	4.0	2.4
US	3.6	2.5
Canada	4.5	3.5
Japan	9.6	9.6

Source: World Bank (1975)

payments. Alternatively, the suppliers may attempt to form cartels, in order to force prices up through monopoly bargaining. Trade unions could adopt an increasingly nationalistic attitude towards direct foreign investment by advanced countries, while less developed countries may seek more effective protection for their own newly-established industries and could limit imports of foreign-made consumer durables in an attempt to improve or strengthen their balance of payments position.

Labour

Possible labour trends are even more problematic than economic ones, and often more contradictory. On the one hand, worker dissatisfaction could increase, particularly amongst semi-skilled assembly-line workers, causing problems in advanced countries. On the other hand, workers could become more concerned with the fruits of their labour than the labour itself, which would mean higher labour costs in real terms. Further moves could be made towards a shorter working week and increased leisure time, especially in the more advanced countries, but it will be increasingly difficult to regard labour as a viable unit of production, making it almost impossible to hire or fire workers in accordance with the vagaries of a fluctuating trade cycle. As workers come to expect greater job protection, so too will they demand a more participatory role in industrial management.

In the past West European countries employed migrant labour in an effort to overcome industrial relations difficulties, but in West Germany in particular the influx of 'guest workers' created a new and equally intractable set of social problems. Currently, many firms have adopted a policy of southwards migration, moving factories to areas where there is a pool of surplus cheap labour, but as we have already suggested, relocating in this way has its own associated problems: cheap labour quickly learns to follow the labour trends in more advanced countries.

Summary of Background Assumptions

The economic environment of the future is not likely to be a comfortable one: higher inflation rates, lower growth, the possibility of trade restrictions, a shorter working week coupled with increased worker participation in management and growing dissatisfaction with assembly line work all point to a bleak future, but the problems should not be overstated. The factors we have mentioned will not all occur simultaneously − it may be a decade or more before some of the trends discussed make any impact. Contrary to popular opinion, the UK economy is remarkably buoyant, and in the past has adjusted quickly to changing circumstances. Although the standard of living will rise at a much slower rate than hitherto, there is plenty of evidence to support the view that further improvements are possible.

The West European Market

The trends we have been discussing above will certainly have a direct effect on the market. Increased leisure, for example, will create new demands. In the US, for example, there has already been a marked increase in demand for recreational vehicles and the European market can expect a similar growth in new patterns of demand, albeit on a more limited scale. As some of the major European markets approach saturation, we can expect to see motor manufacturers diversifying their product range and developing new products. Following the lead of the US market, Europe must expect rising import penetration and greater variation in demand, as market trends reflect the upwards or downwards movement of the business cycle, swinging to smaller cars in periods of depression. At the other extreme, there could be a growth in demand for more luxurious cars equipped with a range of optional extras, such as automatic transmission, power steering, air-conditioning, etc. There could be a greater frequency of model changes, although in this single respect in particular Europe is unlikely to follow the North American lead.

Urban congestion and other environmental and consumer preoccupations could also have a marginal affect on demand. Government controls on car ownership and use may extend to limitations on fuel consumption in an attempt to control balance of payments deficits following an increase in the relative price of oil. Growth in demand for increasingly specialised vehicles could dampen demand for the all-purpose family saloon: in congested cities for example, an electrically operated 'urban car' could become a reality. In general terms, demand is likely to show far more cyclical fluctuation as the market nears saturation and demand consists almost entirely of the inherently unstable replacement demand rather than *new* demand.

Relations within Europe and with the World

The European market is already developing a much more consolidated character. Intra-market trade has been increasing and will probably continue to grow, although further unrestricted growth could be affected by the emergence of a nationalist attitude towards car production and the motor industry in general. Moreover, further growth within the market will not be uniform. A number of European countries (i.e. Spain, Portugal, Turkey, Greece) are still at the development stage and can expect higher growth rates than the West European average as they attempt to catch up. At the moment, Western Europe as a whole is a net exporter, although again this position could very easily change. By 1975 net exports had already fallen to only 1 million cars, reflecting an increase in import penetration and the erosion of traditional West European export markets, both the result of Japanese activity. Even newer producers (in Latin America, the Communist Bloc and the Middle East) could pose a further threat to the net export position of the Europeans.

Government Involvement

Government intervention will certainly increase, in a number of ways, following the move in most advanced industrial democracies towards a greater degree of central planning to control economic growth targets, implementation measures, resource availability, industrial training and employment strategies, investment policies, overall consumption targets, etc. Governments can act either to control supply (through measures affecting taxation, monopoly, location, pollution and conservation or trade restrictions) or to control demand (through controls on ownership, driver licensing, the regulation of vehicle use, public investment or economic incentives).

We have already suggested that rising commodity prices may provoke deficits. Rising import penetration could lead to similar measures, but trade difficulties are not the only cause for government concern. National governments will face growing pressure to control inflation and maintain employment through more rigorous domestic policies, particularly in the use of such policies to control the availability of finance (i.e. indirect monetary controls) and hence curb or stimulate demand.

Direct Intervention

The motor industry has assumed a position of central importance in most West European economies, with makes it particularly susceptible to government intervention to counter inflation, combat regional unemployment, control business cycles and adapt the industry to the economic targets established by the indicative planning process. Governments could exercise direct control either as a lender of last resort (as in the case of BL and Chrysler UK), whereby ownership could pass into the public sphere or through planned expansion of state ownership in the critical industries. In general, European governments can be expected to encourage further consolidation within the industry, and government subsidies could be forthcoming in an endeavour to speed up the rate of technological change and innovation.

Design Controls

The three main government objectives in the control of vehicle design concern safety, the regulation of exhaust emission and improvements — i.e. reductions in fuel consumption. As things stand at the moment, Japan and the US exercise far more stringent design controls than Western Europe and it is possible that West European governments may seek to control fuel consumption, in particular, through measures intended to restrict use rather than alter design specifications. Exhaust emission and safety control measures, however, could be increased to counter the cost of any further rise in accidents.

Superimposed on these three aspects of control over vehicle design is the question of harmonising regulations between the various member governments of the EEC — a topic which will be considered separately.

Consumer Controls

We have already noted the various ways in which governments can control demand for and use of motor vehicles. In the past, controls have usually operated to encourage vehicle ownership and use, but this pattern could change as government priorities alter, and greater emphasis is placed on policies to combat congestion (particularly urban congestion) through the provision of alternatives to the private car or through a policy of decentralisation. Moreover, the public sector can be expected to assume even greater responsibility for the myriad of controls and regulations on the supply and demand of motor vehicles — even in the UK, where, anomalously, the public sector is both a principal supplier and the largest individual consumer of motor vehicles.

Technological Developments

We have argued that the relatively high economic status which Western Europe presently enjoys can only be justified in the future by the increasing reliance on advanced technology. As existing technology has changed very little in the last decade or so, and is now widely adopted throughout the world, technological change will only come about through a greatly accelerated programme of research and development, concentrating principally on four main areas: propulsion systems; vehicle design; new materials; and new components.

Figure 4.4 gives a morphology of the existing heat engine, currently the most common type of propulsion system and generally thought capable of further refinements and improvements. An alternative to the heat engine system is the regenerated stored energy system, usually based on an electrical battery and a spinning flywheel. At the moment the prototype electric cars which have thus far been developed on the basis of this system are of only limited usefulness due to their relatively short distance capabilities, but the development of hybrid systems combining elements of heat and stored energy propulsion are more promising.

Further work on improvements to vehicle design will concentrate on the development of more effective safety devices and improvements in the aerodynamic properties and transmission mechanisms, although opinions differ on whether or not model lives will be extended (through less design obsolescence) or shortened (by excessive competition between manufacturers producing similar models). Fuel consumption will be improved through the use of lighter or thinner gauge materials in the construction of the car body — particularly

FIGURE 4.4
Morphology of Heat Engines

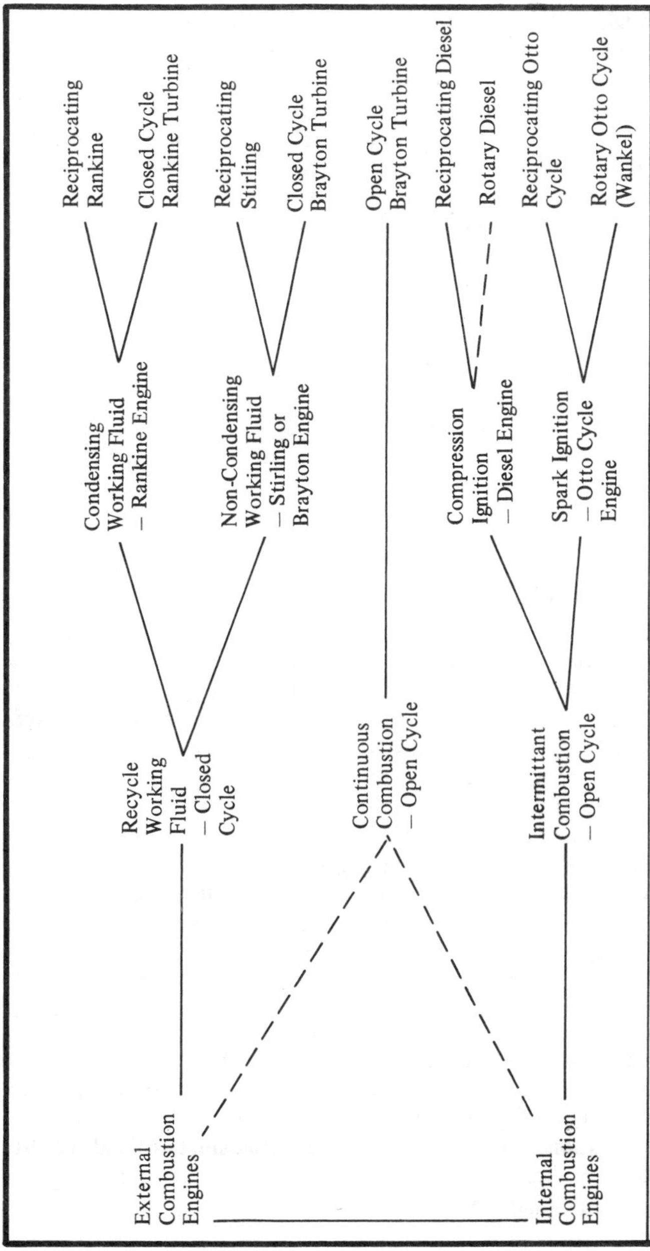

NB Rankine Engine – Sometimes likened to a steam engine
Brayton Engine – Gas turbine either open (as in jet) or closed whereby a gaseous fluid is continuously circulated
Stirling Engine – similar to Rankine but working fluid does not undergo a change – uses dry gases such as Helium or Hydrogen

Source: Adapted From *The World Automotive Industry to 1995*, Business International.

aluminium, plastics and ceramics. Components will feature a much wider use of electronic and computer systems as they gradually supplant the more familiar mechanical systems, while the manufacturing processes themselves will have to adapt not only to changing materials but also to the exigencies of a shorter working week and the need to alleviate the tedium of assembly line working through wider use of automation. Judging from the direction several manufacturers are taking at the moment, easier and cheaper maintenance per mile will also be used to offset higher fuel costs.

It seems likely that the pace of technological development will be more rapid in the future, especially as the scope for change and innovation is far greater now than it ever has been. The availability (or lack) of capital to fund these developments would appear to be the only major restraint, although it is an important one. If the motor manufacturers are unable (or unwilling) to finance the necessary research and development, a number of non-related industrial giants would be more than happy to step into the breach and reap the profit reward.

Problems for the West European Manufacturers

The problems facing West European producers apply with equal force for the UK, although in some respect they could be considered as more acute in the UK (see Table 4.7).

Fuel Supplies

Western Europe as a whole is faced with an acute fuel supply problem, even though the UK, at least, is buffered by supplies of North Sea oil — at least until the end of the twentieth century. The fact remains, however, that oil is a depleting resource; it will eventually run out. Other countries are producing alternative fuels, such as synthetic oil extracted from shale or coal or even methanol. The availability of North Sea oil, however, means that the UK plans for developing alternative energy sources may be somewhat delayed. Oil will continue to be the principal source of motor vehicle fuel in the UK for some time to come, particularly as UK oil prices are at the moment extremely low (see Table 4.6). It might be argued that cheap petrol is simply another symptom of UK poverty, but it could just as easily be the case that the existence of North Sea oil has allowed politicians a degree of confidence in pricing petrol.

CONCLUSION

For the mature countries — and this includes the UK — the future holds many problems. From now on the motor industry and the consumer will have to accept the consequences of relatively higher running costs of automotive products, higher inflation, and growing labour dissatisfaction and unrest. Slower growth and poorer financial prospects will create a much more aggressive and uncertain climate in the motor industry.

TABLE 4.6

Fuel Prices in mid-1977 in US Dollars

Fuel Prices in mid-1977	per US Gallon
UK	1.19
West Germany	1.48
France	1.75
Italy	2.12
Spain	1.78
Belgium	1.66
Netherlands	1.64
Average for Western Europe	1.61
US	.63

TABLE 4.7
Problems Facing the European Manufacturer

Problem	Explanation
— Increased import penetration and reduced exports	— Competition from Japanese plus other newer producers.
— Increased competitive pressure	— Excess capacity in Europe plus above
— Labour problems	— Higher wages, more leisure time, etc.
— Insufficient scale to compete effectively	— A comparison with the US motor industry would lead to the conclusion that there should be only 3 or 4 European manufacturers serving the European Market which is of similar size to the North American market.
— Government controls	— Ultimate effect will be costly.
— Lower level of automation compared with Japanese or US rivals	— Higher costs in Europe.
— New technology	— Again, high capital expenditure required.

SECTION TWO

CARS

INTRODUCTION TO SECTION TWO

This is the first of the remaining sections of the book which concentrates on a particular aspect of the UK motor industry. Section 2 deals with cars and is the largest section, partly because it has been the worst hit in recent times and partly because it is the most important sector in terms of employment implications, balances of payments, capital investment, etc. In 1978, the UK car industry employed around 200,000 workers. The constant talk about the possibility of redundancies is proof enough that this section of the industry has suffered from ill health. Will it recover? This question is analysed in the next five chapters. Chapter 5 deals with demand for cars; Chapter 6 discusses supply considerations; Chapter 7 deals with British Leyland exclusively; Chapter 8 brings together the supply and demand considerations to look at the future of UK car production; and Chapter 9 discusses the numerous small manufacturers that have, with mixed fortunes, concentrated on specialist and luxury cars.

We do have some policy recommendations in this area but they are explored more fully in the conclusion. In this section it is argued that Ford will remain strong, whilst GM will convert its Vauxhall car plants into assembly operations of its Opel subsidiary in order to integrate its European car operations. News of the proposed merger between Chrysler and Peugeot-Citroen came too late to include an analysis for Chrysler UK's plants under new management. This chapter does however place grave doubts about Chrysler's long-term solution without this merger. Chapter 17 explores the link-up more fully. BL Cars should benefit from having been integrated as one large company. Unfortunately, the Ryder Plan was too ambitious and overestimated managerial and other resources. By and large we agree with the new plan for BL, in which a more divisionalised approach (M-form organisation) is envisaged. We provide a different plan with regard to production and plants; we are also anxious to maximise the commonality of components where possible, thereby gaining most of the technical economies of scale.

103

CHAPTER 5

DEMAND

INTRODUCTION

The UK motor industry has several important constituent marketing areas for its products, the most important of which, naturally, is the domestic UK market. The UK, however, is to a large extent already an integral part of Europe by virtue of its participation in the EEC, and the European marketing area is of increasing importance: two thirds of all the cars imported into the UK are European in origin, and in turn, nearly half of our total car exports are sent to Europe. North America is next in importance, followed by Asia, Africa and Oceania.

DEMAND FOR CARS IN THE UK

We begin with an examination of the pattern of demand in the domestic market. It is worth remembering that most of the observations and assumptions made in relation to this market apply with equal force in both the North American and European areas.

Background to UK Demand

Following a period of rapid growth during the 1950s and 1960s, the demand for cars in the last decade has followed a series of very different trends. Demand peaked at 1.2 million cars in 1964, then stabilised at the relatively low level of 1.0 − 1.1 million per year for the next six years, restrained by the generally slow growth in the British economy and by the continued use of hire purchase regulations as an economic management tool. The repercussions for the motor industry during this period were serious : firms operated well below optimal capacity and new investment was discouraged.

The removal of hire purchase restrictions in July 1971 provoked a sharp increase in demand; new registrations rose to 1.7 million in 1972 (50 per cent higher than the 1970 level),[1] remaining high until the oil crisis in the autumn of 1973. The resulting economic recession in 1974, together with the sharp rise in the cost of petrol, reduced demand to 1.27 million cars in that year, with a further drop in 1975.

Before considering the likely pattern of future demand in the UK, two distinctive features of the UK market should be noted. To begin with, it is helpful to distinguish between replacement demand and new demand. Until the mid 1960s most of the growth in demand was the result of new demand, as the total stock of cars increased with the spread of car ownership. In 1960-64, replacement demand constituted about 28 per cent of total annual demand. As the growth in car ownership slowed down, new demand became

1. This phenomenal increase was too sharp for UK manufacturers to adjust production. The consequence was that imports were 'sucked in' .

less important, and by 1970-74 two thirds of total demand was replacement demand. The other notable aspect of demand in the UK is that a significant proportion of that demand is non-private, i.e. fleet sales to businesses and hire companies (which account for around 40 per cent of total demand), or more indirectly to employees who receive some sort of financial assistance in the purchase and/or running of their cars.

TABLE 5.1

Manufacturers Exports of Cars ('000)

	1970	1971	1972	1973	1974	1975	1976	1977
EXPORTS								
Europe								
EFTA	124	111	84	54	51	35	46	38
EEC	228	229	237	255	190	164	211	246
Other	19	20	11	13	9	6	13	16
TOTAL	371	360	332	322	250	205	270	300
America								
North	99	138	89	73	87	77	90	69
Other	32	37	31	24	16	10	12	15
TOTAL	131	175	120	97	103	86	102	84
Asia	62	59	63	95	121	171	104	138
Africa	71	57	45	58	28	25	10	35[a]
Oceania	98	83	75	52	61	48	59	33
Other	7	8	6	6	6	0	3	1
WORLD TOTAL	740	742	641	629	568	534	548	591
UK SALES	923	1,038	1,253	1,206	1,269	1,194	1,286	1,324

a. Increase mainly due to Ford's increased exports to South Africa.

Source: SMMT

Future Demand Influences

Forecasting the demand for cars (or any other consumer durable) is never an

FIGURE 5.1
Registrations, Stock and Scrapping UK Cars 1953-77

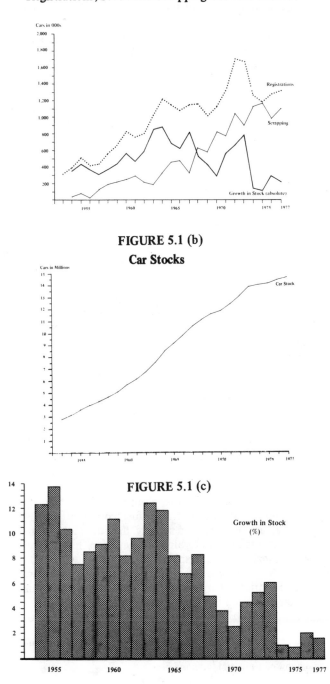

FIGURE 5.1 (b)
Car Stocks

FIGURE 5.1 (c)

easy exercise; replacement purchases are postponable, and any attempt to forecast the growth of new demand requires an estimate of the saturation level of ownership.[1] This postponability of the purchase of consumer durables leaves manufacturers open to the risk of extreme demand fluctuations. Cars being one of the largest purchases in monetary terms are particularly susceptible to financial constraints and credit restrictions. And at the moment, any attempt at a reasonable forecast can not afford to ignore the likely consequences of a continued rise in the price of petrol, and the length and breadth of the current economic recession.

To forecast total demand in 1980 and 1985, several factors must be taken into consideration, and certain assumptions made about each one of them. They are : growth in the economy; developments and changes in the design of car engines; environmental factors; petrol price; the price elasticity of demand; and, finally, the price of new cars.

(i) Growth in the Economy

At the present time the UK economy is recovering from the worst recession in its post war history, but for the purposes of this discussion we must assume that appropriate policies will be found and that the economy will eventually recover by 1979-80, thereafter returning to what has been regarded as a normal pattern of growth of GDP in the region of 2 to 3 per cent per annum. It is probable that North Sea oil will permit slightly faster growth, but since the timing and magnitude of the gains to be derived from this source are uncertain, it will be given minimal prominence in our assessment, though it will not be completely ignored.

(ii) Car Engine Design

Although it seems likely that the internal combustion engine will remain the most widely used source of power, alternative sources should not be completely discounted. Some alternatives — for example, the metallic gas turbine engine — can be dismissed fairly easily because of their higher fuel consumption. The Wankel engine, however, although handicapped by an additional 20 per cent fuel consumption, may become more popular because of its superiority to the spark ignition engine in weight and size, the fact that it requires fewer parts and is therefore cheaper to manufacture. Diesel and Stirling engines, both with considerable fuel consumption advantages, are costly to produce, although it seems likely that diesel engines will become more popular. The ceramic gas turbine engine offers fuel consumption on a par with conventional internal combustion engines, but its use may be restricted to heavy CVs, as it operates most effeciently when producing very high power output.[2] Stratified charge engines (which both Honda and Ford have shown some interest in) are basically a variation on the standard internal combustion engine.

1. Evidence from the US (post oil crisis) indicates that there may be no such thing as saturation levels.
2. eg. Several hundred to several thousand bhp

If the price of petrol remains of central importance, then it is probable that the emphasis would be on the development of a lighter car, with better aerodynamics, and an engine modified to achieve lower levels of fuel consumption with little if any significant reduction in performance. It is unlikely that the electric car, once hailed as the saviour of the motorist and the environment, will in fact pose a serious threat in the short or medium term future. As the CPRS report noted :

The widespread introduction of electric vehicles will not be achieved by the year 2000 unless work on the development of suitable batteries is started now, and it could take significantly longer if unexpected hazards are encountered. (CPRS report to Energy Conservation, July 1974)

(iii) Environmental Factors

The environmentalist lobby has increased in strength in recent years, directing the main force of its argument against private motoring, on the grounds that public transport is a more efficient use of resources, and that pollution from cars should be more stringently controlled.

Although we express sympathy with these arguments, it would seem that, in the short term at least, neither factor will significantly inhibit car demand. Considering public transport, for example, it is certain that the cost of improving existing resources or developing and operating alternative forms of transport would be unacceptably high, and the likely benefits disproportionately small, producing overall reduction in mileage rather than a reduction in the number of cars on the road. Politically (and practically) speaking, public transport costs are a sensitive area.[1] To be effective, any moves made in this respect would impose severe restrictions on private motoring, and it is doubtful whether any government would welcome the opportunity to introduce them in present circumstances. In the same way, legislation to control exhaust emission levels could expect to encounter strong opposition from both manufacturers and unions, and, indeed, from consumers, as such controls would undoubtedly increase the cost of the car and petrol consumption. In the longer term, the environmentalist argument will almost certainly prove effective, but for the period under discussion – however regrettable one might feel this to be – it is unlikely to make any impact on levels of demand.[2]

(iv) Petrol Prices

The price of petrol obviously has an effect on the amount of petrol people feel they can afford to buy, and consequently, the amount of motoring they do. Two assumptions must be made in this respect : how much the price of

1. Public transport costs revised commensurately during the oil crisis. The index (1970= 100) for all operators offering stage service fares is:
   1965–66   1970–100   1973–119   1976–219
2. See Chapter 4, section on Background Assumptions.

petrol is likely to rise, and the effect such a rise would have on demand. There is no strong evidence to suggest that there will be no further increase in the *relative* price of oil, and that, in keeping with current OPEC policy, any future rise in oil prices will be a straightforward reflection of any increase in the price of manufactured goods imported by the oil producing countries. If anything, a relative fall in price is possible, in view of the surplus capacity in oil producing countries and the need to increase the volume of production and earnings in some of the poorer producing countries. Moreover, in the case of the UK, should the domestic rate of inflation exceed the global rate, this too would tend towards a reduction in the relative price of oil. On balance, it seems safer to assume that there will be no significant change in the price of oil relative to prevailing price levels in the UK — although increased running costs may occur for 'other' reasons, e.g. high servicing costs.

But what of the increases already introduced? Will they have a permanently depressing effect on demand, or will demand return to its original level as consumers adjust to the increase? There are three reasons for supposing that the long term effect of price increases will not greatly alter the level of demand, namely (i) the fact that the cost of petrol is only part of the total cost of car ownership; (ii) that improvements in engine design will greatly enhance their efficiency; and (iii) that the car plays an important part in modern life.

Although the cost of petrol has been the subject of much recent debate, when allowance is made for other necessary costs (such as insurance, maintenance, depreciation, etc.), petrol costs account for only 30 per cent of total cost. There are, obviously, exceptions to this figure, but in the average case, assuming a rise in petrol of 10 per cent, the increase in the total annual motoring bill would amount to no more than 3 or 4 per cent. Similarly, an increase of 25 per cent in petrol prices would add less than 10 per cent to the total annual mileage, or an improvement in mpg of 5 per cent, coupled with a 10 per cent reduction in total annual mileage would leave total outlay unchanged. However, if incomes and all other prices *also* rose by 25 per cent, the same increase in the price of petrol would probably have no effect on consumer behaviour — demand would be unaffected. Moreover, refinements in engine design, one of the three factors mentioned, will eventually improve petrol consumption. Better overall car design, coupled with increased engine efficiency will mean smaller-engined cars offering levels of accommodation and performance previously associated with much larger cars, which could change the pattern, but not the level of demand.

(v) Price Elasticity of Demand for Cars

Changes in the price of motoring may force individuals to use alternative forms of transport to the car. Most estimates put the price elasticity of demand with respect to motoring costs at somewhere between -0.2 and -1.5 in the long run and considerably higher in the short run. Taking the lower figure of 0.2, this means that for every 10 per cent rise in petrol prices, consumption falls by only 2 per cent. Other running costs such as parking meters and maintenance costs have a similar effect.

(vi) Price of New Cars

One factor which has been responsible for depressing demand is the rise in the price of new cars relative to other commodities. Table 5.2 shows that between January 1974 and December 1976 car prices had virtually doubled whilst the retail price index had increased only by 65.8 per cent and that for (male manual) wage rates by 74.0 per cent. Despite this increase in the relative price of cars, the demand for cars has not decreased by as much as one would have expected. This is partly because the car market itself has adapted. A company car for many people now forms part of their 'take-home' pay, and in this way the incomes freeze of the last few years can be circumvented. In the early 1970s the business car[1] market was less than 40 per cent and this has now risen to between 50 to 70 per cent. Business car sales will not, however, maintain this new high share of the market. Future recovery of the market must be in the area of the purely private buyer. This, of course, does not necessarily preclude the growth of the business market consistent with the growth of the UK economy and any long term trends. Nevertheless car demand is highly elastic [2] with respect to price, and an expansion in demand requires the real cost of cars to fall.

TABLE 5.2

Relative Price Rise of New Cars

	Retail Prices 15 Jan. 1974 = 100	Index of average earnings: all employees Jan. 1974 = 100	Car List Prices, Jan. 1974 = 100			
			Ford	BL	Chrysler (UK)	Vauxhall
Jan. '74	100.0	100.0	100.0	100.0	100.0	100.0
Jan. '75	119.9	133.6	140.2	136.6	140.7	139.2
Jan. '76	147.9	161.2	162.2	171.6	169.1	170.7
Dec. '76	168.0	178.9	187.8	198.9	197.6	197.3
Feb. '77	174.1	181.0	202.3	211.8	210.4	208.3
June '77	183.6	187.6	216.9	225.6	225.1	221.8

1. Business car market in its broader sense – i.e. non-private market as well as the fleet car market. A discussion of this market is returned to on p.115.
2. See for example, 'Price, quality and advertising competition: econometric investigation of the UK car market', *Economica, 1971*.

The final factor likely to affect demand is the central importance of the motor car in modern life. It provides an attractive (and in many cases essential) alternative to increasingly unsatisfactory public transport systems, and on balance, most car users would consider that the advantages of ownership far outweigh the costs involved and the disadvantages. An increase in the price of petrol will undoubtedly affect the 'marginal' car owner, but the vast majority of private car owners, if faced with an income restraint, are more likely to reduce annual mileage, switch to a smaller car or economise elsewhere, before foregoing car ownership. By way of illustration, in an experiment involving a number of large companies in West Germany, the cost of public transport was dramatically cut (with the help of a DM 1 million subsidy) for a period of eight months. During that time, only 13 per cent of the 10,000 workers involved in the experiment switched to using public transport; when the experiment ended, all but 2 per cent reverted to their private cars, giving us their reasons for doing so: – the need to save time, the discomfort of public transport and the inconvenience of following timetables.

Taking all of these factors into consideration, it seems reasonable to conclude that the oil crisis (and the associated recession) will delay the further growth of car ownership, but that by 1978-80 demand will have stabilised at a pre-oil crisis level. Growth in ownership will be slower, but as saturation levels are approached, this is to be expected. The net effect of the oil crisis could mean only that the levels of ownership previously forecast for 1981 will not now be reached until 1985.

This conclusion is reinforced by experiences in Western Europe. France, West Germany, Netherlands, Denmark and other countries had peak new registrations in 1976, demonstrating that demand had recovered, albeit still below trend growth, from the oil crisis.

In Chapter 14, further marketing considerations are analysed. In particular, the effect of advertising, distribution policies and other factors on the sales of cars are discussed. Another trend that must be discussed concerns the stability of the UK market. Reference has already been made to the fact that the non-private car market has now increased to around 70 per cent of this market. One beneficial effect this has had on the market during the recent depression is that new car registrations dropped by less than the European norm consistent with the decline in global economic activity. Once an individual is hooked as a business buyer, he is unlikely to return to being a 'private' buyer unless marginal income tax rates drop significantly. This ratchet effect is therefore beneficial to the UK car market; it makes demand less prone to fluctuations and it provides a resilience that defies increases in the real cost of buying and maintaining cars.

FORECAST OF DEMAND

Many of the forecasts used in the car industry are based on econometric forecasting models explaining demand in terms of five factors : income per head (or GDP); the price of a new car and running costs relative to the price of other goods; hire purchase limitations, or the cost and availability of alternative finance; total number of cars in use; changes in the size of the car-driving population. But, as the CPRS report noted, 'to use relationships based on past experience to forecast future levels of new registrations assumes that the effect of different explanatory variables ... will be much the same in the future as it was in the past'.[1] The effects of the oil crisis, high rates of inflation and a worldwide economic recession are all likely to have an effect on demand, but, with virtually no experience in assessing the extent of the impact (i.e. a new and uncharted part of the demand curve may be relevant), any forecasts are 'subject to wide margins of error'. With this in mind, it seemed more appropriate to assess existing forecasts, rather than propose a new one. For example, it is known that the rate of growth of the total stock of cars (i.e. new demand) has fallen steadily in recent years – from an average growth rate of 10.5 per cent in 1953-8 dropping to an annual rate of 4.5 per cent in 1968-73 (see Table 5.3). It seems reasonable to assume that this rate of growth will slow down even further, say to between 2 and 3 per cent p.a. between 1975 and 1985.

Replacement demand, on the other hand, is more difficult to forecast, as it depends on the 'life expectancy' of a car. If petrol price increases result in significantly reduced annual mileages, the life of a car could be prolonged. On the other hand, higher maintenance costs as the car grew older, together with more stringent safety regulations and testing could reduce the average car life. The net effect of these factors may not be significant. Another approach in estimating replacement demand is to extrapolate the scrappage rate, i.e. scrapping expressed as a percentage of the current stock. The problem with this approach is in interpreting the ratio in a meaningful way when the total stock is growing. Further, even with a constant life and unchanged scrapping policy, this ratio will tend to vary with the present (and past) rate of growth of stock. It seems more appropriate to relate the number of vehicles scrapped in any year, t, to registrations in year t–L, where L is the average life. Table 5.3 shows scrapping and registrations 10 years earlier; as both series are subject to considerable cyclical movement they are both shown as five year moving averages.[2]

This method can be used to estimate scrapping and thus replacement demand in 1980 and 1985. Assuming that there is no marked change in average car life replacement in 1980 is likely to be 1.26 million, and 1.36 million in 1985. If we now bring together these estimates of the two demand categories, we are in a position to comment on other available forecasts.

It can be seen that most other forecasts fall within the range of these tentative calculations with the exception of the low Fiat figure for 1980, and the high figure forecast by Business International for 1985. Interestingly enough, the Ryder, BL and CPRS forecasts all lie in the middle of our suggested range. From this it would seem that an acceptable range of demand would lie between 1.55 – 1.7 million for 1980, and 1.7 – 2.0 million for 1985. These forecasts assume a trend growth. An economic depression could undermine new demand and could cause the postponement of some of the replace-

1. *The Future of The British Car Industry;* ibid
2. 'This has shown a stable, although very gradual, downwards trend from 13 years in 1965 to 11 years in 1974, a rate of decrease of 0.2 years per annum.'
    Evidence submitted to Select Committee Enquiry on Chrysler UK, by D.M.N. Starkie

TABLE 5.3

Relationship Between Scrapping

and Past Registrations

(Five year moving average)

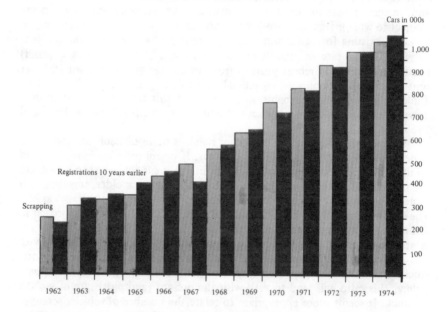

*Scrapping = New registration less increase in UK licensed stock.

ment demand. This deferred new demand and postponed replacement demand could be released in boom periods in which it would be added to normal replacement and new demand. Thus the total new registrations figure could be much higher than the trend figure.

The projection for 1990 incorporates a wider set of assumptions with a resulting index range of projected demand. The replacement demand range depends on the car stock in 1980. New demand for cars depends on the many other factors already discussed. The range indicated in Table 5.4 embodies an optimistic and pessimistic view of those factors. In view of the current propensity to be optimistic in forecasting, unless North Sea oil radically changes the structure of UK society, it is probably safer to err on the side of pessimism.

IMPORTS

Having estimated demand, it is of crucial importance to the UK car industry to determine how much of that demand will be supplied by foreign manufacturers. The import share increased dramatically after 1970, reaching an all time high in excess of 50% of new car registrations during periods of 1978. Allowing for the fact that business sales [1] account for between 50 – 70 per cent [2] of total demand and that business buyers are far more loyal to the UK manufacturers, then import sales to the private market now represent between 60 – 80 per cent of the private market. Of the non-private business, the fleet market business is even less highly penetrated than the non-fleet market.[3] Tariff reductions and the competitive weakness of the UK manufacturers around 1970 helped foreign manufacturers to increase their share of the UK market. UK producers were unable to increase production sufficiently (or overcome the subsequent supply difficulties) to meet the sudden upsurge in demand following the removal of hire purchase restrictions in 1971, which again worked to the advantage of foreign manufacturers. The fact that UK firms have had surplus capacity since 1973 seems to have had no effect on import penetration. The import share also increased in 1976 and in 1977. Japanese and European manufacturers – also carrying surplus capacity – have been eager to sell in foreign markets, even at less than full cost. Allowing for transport and other import costs, together with the depreciation of sterling, it is doubtful whether many of the cars imported into the UK earn much of a profit for their suppliers, but, always providing that sales revenue exceeds direct costs, this policy of 'dumping' makes sense at a time of surplus capacity, in that it makes some contribution to overheads and has the additional advantage (in the case of new producers) of gaining a foothold in the market.

Figure 5.3 shows the recent increase in import penetration. However, the continued rise in 1977 must be interpreted by the events described in Chapter 2. Namely, a continued integration of operations by the US multinationals, with tied imports and, in the case of Ford, exports. Once European and even a degree of worldwide integration has been completed by Chrysler and GM, we may (and this is discussed in Chapter 6) see both Chrysler and GM exporting US made cars to West Europe. At the moment it seems more reasonable to regard import penetration as consisting of all imports excluding Ford – whose integrated policy includes exports at the price of some imports. Three sets of figures for import penetration are shown in Figure 5.3. It can be seen that import penetration, excluding the tied imports of all US multinationals, has not deteriorated very much since 1973. More worrying is the decline in 1977 which, like that in 1972 and 1973, may be attributed to a failure in supply of UK made cars rather than a definitive statement of preference. The import penetration may be as much as 10 per cent lower should all four major companies switch production so as to satisfy all UK sales by UK produced vehicles. However, European integration implies increased imports as well as increased exports. GM's switch of some Cavaliers to UK production will help. However, despite spare capacity at Ryton, Chrysler still import a few Alpines from France. Both GM and Chrysler must utilise their UK productive capacity to a

---

1. Of which strict fleet sales take about one third of the business market.
2. This range reflects the difficulty of defining what is meant by the business buyer. Company representatives' cars obviously belong in the fleet market. But what about the self-employed (e.g. doctors) and the semi self-employed? This is referred to here as the non-fleet part of the business market.
3. Between 10-20 per cent of the fleet market and rising.

FIGURE 5.2

United Kingdom New Car Registrations

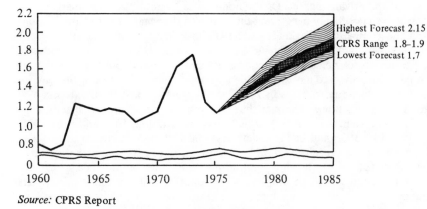

Source: CPRS Report

TABLE 5.4
Some Forecasts of UK New Car Registrations
(million units)

(a) Our forecast	1980	1985	1990
Car stock	15.4 −16.1	17.0 −18.7	18.0 −19.0
New demand	.30− .47	.33− .54	1 − .4
Replacement demand	1.26	1.36	1.6
Total demand	1.56− 1.73	1.69− 1.90	1.7 2.1

(b) Other forecasts (and date of forecast)			
CPRS Estimates (1975	1.55− 1.65	1.8 − 1.9	
Ryder and BL (1975)	1.6	1.7+	
EFP (1974)	−	1.7	
Eurofinance (Euroeconomics) (1975-6)	1.55	1.73− 1.85	
Business International (1976)	−	2.15	
SMMT (1975)	1.7	2.0	
Predicasts (1975)	1.8	2.1	
Fiat (1975)	1.45	−	
Chrysler UK (1976)	1.55	1.8	
Other Manufacturers			
(a) (1975)	1.64	1.97	
(b) (1975)	1.7	1.9	
Forecast used in later analysis	1.55− 1.7	1.7 − 1.9	1.7 − 2.1

greater extent, if the policy of European integration is to have a beneficial effect on the UK economy. We return to this topic in the next chapter.

The failure of manufacturers to meet production targets affected, for ex-

FIGURE 5.3

Import Penetration as a Percentage of Total Market

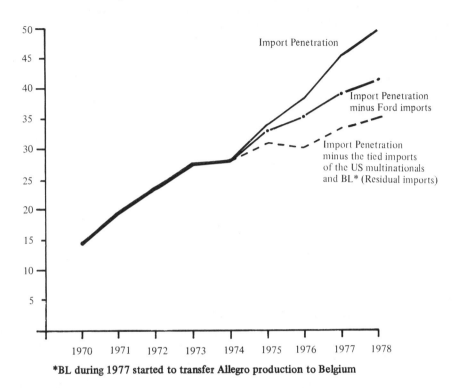

*BL during 1977 started to transfer Allegro production to Belgium

ample, BL, Ford and Chrysler in 1977. This aspect of the failure of supply to meet demand is considered separately in later chapters in this section. On the question of demand it is impossible to calculate what the level of import penetration would have been had UK supply kept pace with UK demand. There are, however, a number of factors to take into consideration. There seems to be a ratchet effect. Once a foreign manufacturer establishes a distribution system, it is difficult to dissuade dealers from selling their products. Meanwhile, the number of dealers selling UK products has drastically declined (see Chapter 4). Another factor which concerns BL and, to a lesser extent, GM and Chrysler, is the lack of competitiveness of models in certain market segments. Certainly, in 1973, 1974 and 1975 the four US manufacturers were caught with models which were approaching the end of their model life. This has not been remedied. BL's problem is one of out-dated model design and lack of competitive marketing (see Chapter 13). Furthermore, attitudes to foreign cars have changed, and this has certainly had an effect on sales. There is an increasing tendency to regard them as more reliable and of a higher quality (see *Which?* and *AA* reliability reports) and, rightly or wrongly, this has influenced prospective buyers, despite the fact that foreign cars in general are

117

known to be more expensive to service and repair.[1] Consumers have also found that the ranges offered by foreign manufacturers (particularly in the mini and small/medium segment) correspond more closely to their requirements. British manufacturers have been slow off the mark in recognising the growth in demand for a smaller-engined car.

TABLE 5.5
Sales by Engine Size

	up to 1200cc	%	1200 – 1800cc	%	1800 – 2500cc	%	2500cc plus	%	TOTAL
1966	574	53.9%	371	34.8%	66	6.2%	54	5.1%	1065
1972	382	23.0%	970	58.4%	238	14.3%	72	4.3%	1662
1973	352	21.4%	958	58.2%	258	15.7%	78	4.7%	1646
1974	305	24.7%	677	54.9%	188	15.2%	64	5.2%	1234
1975	334	28.6%	629	53.9%	154	13.2%	50	4.3%	1167
1976	328	26.1%	691	55.0%	180	14.3%	57	4.5%	1256
1977									

Source: Department of the Environment

TABLE 5.6 (a)

Car Market Segments: UK Demand for Small Cars[a]

	Share of UK Market	Import Penetration of Total Market	Import Penetration of Small Car Market Segment[b]
	%	%	%
1969	45.9	10.5	10.4
1970	45.9	14.3	14.5
1971	43.3	19.3	18.9
1972	37.5	23.5	29.3
1973	38.6	27.4	35.7
1974	45.9	27.9	31.4
1975	49.5	33.2	36.4
1976	46.7	38.0	38.1
1977	44.7	45.4	43.8

a. Small cars include the following models: (BL) Mini, 1100/1300, Allegro; (Chrysler) Avenger, Sunbeam, Imp, Simca 1000, 1100; (Citroen) Ami, Dyane/CV6; (DAF); (Datsun) Cherry, Sunny; (Fiat) 127, 128, 133; (Opel) Kadett; (Ford); Fiesta, Escort; (Honda); (Lada); (Mazda); (Peugeot) 104, 204, 304; (Polski Fiat); (Renault) R4, R5, R6, R8/10; (Toyota) 100c, Corolla, Camina; (VW) Beetle, Golf, Polo; (Wartburg), (Vauxhall); Chevette.
b. Includes tied imports by UK multinationals and BL.
1. This is a protection which is increasingly going to become less of one as spare parts are manufactured in volume by UK component manufacturers.

TABLE 5.6 (b)

Size of Car Market Segments

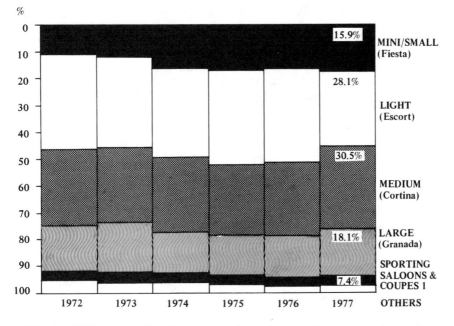

Prior to 1973 the trend had been very clearly towards larger engined cars, and the British ranges still reflected this preference, although the trend towards smaller cars which developed immediately after the oil crisis appears to have been reversed. In 1974, however, the market had begun to change : cars with an engine capacity of less than 1200 cc. accounted for 25 per cent of total sales. In 1975, imported small/medium cars accounted for 18 per cent of total registrations, with the Datsun Cherry and Sunny, the Toyota 1000 and Corolla, the Simca 1000 and 1100, the Renault 6, the Skoda and the VW Golf all selling well throughout 1975-6. Only with the introduction of the Vauxhall Chevette, the new Ford Escort/Popular and the Fiesta, and the Chrysler Sunbeam, were UK manufacturers able to compete in this segment. It may well have been a matter of luck or local market conditions rather than astute judgement that foreign manufacturers were producing so many small cars just as demand for them increased so enormously. Be that as it may, the fact that they *were* doing so, and that British manufacturers were not, helps to explain the fact that imported cars increased their share of this part of the market from 19 per cent in 1971 to over 50 per cent in 1978.

To sum up: foreign manufacturers are offering competitive cars with a reputation for reliability and quality that British cars do not have. They have proved more adept at satisfying the requirements of a post-oil crisis shift in consumer taste, and they do not seem to have encountered the supply problems which continue to bedevil UK producers.

119

FUTURE IMPORT PENETRATION AND THE DOMESTIC MARKET

Will this trend continue? In the next few years — and until demand recovers — all the major producing countries will have surplus capacity; the temptation to continue dumping in foreign markets will thus remain strong. Looking ahead to about 1980, when demand may have caught up with existing world capacity, both in developed countries and in developing countries where it is, in effect, already happening. With every new installation, output will exceed demand, which in turn means that European and Japanese producers will continue to sell cheaply in export markets. This means that, for the next decade at least, we could be assured of a steady supply of relatively inexpensive (and therefore attractive) foreign cars. The Japanese will continue to offer cheap basic cars (albeit becoming increasingly sophisticated)[1] whilst the Western European manufacturers may attempt to market their cars increasingly on technical sophistication.

Because of the high service and repair costs associated with foreign cars, this influx should have little effect on business sales but the future import penetration of the private sales market is more difficult to assess. Price is obviously an important factor, but so also is the poor reputation of British cars for quality and reliability. As imported cars age (by mid-1975, 50 per cent of imported cars were less than 2½ years old), they will require more repairs; will their owners feel that the higher costs involved are a severe penalty (severe enough to discourage them from buying another foreign car when the time comes for replacement) or will they feel that although their repairs are more expensive they have required fewer of them? If buyers continue to believe (notwithstanding the higher cost of servicing and repair) that imported cars are better in value in this respect because they are better made than their UK equivalent, imports are likely to remain high.

Furthermore, will UK manufacturers be in a position to offer the *type* of car people want? Assuming that the demand switches back to a medium size car, BL in particular will have to work very heard to convince potential buyers that existing models meet their requirements. UK manufacturers will also have to strengthen their competitive position, in order to overcome their present weakness. As we have seen, it is virtually certain that foreign manufacturers will place continuing pressure on the UK market, and that UK producers will have to work hard simply to maintain their position, let alone improve it. The CPRS Report felt that it was 'unrealistic . . . to expect that the import share of the British car market can consistently be cut back to below 28 per cent'. Moreover, 'import penetration . . . could reach 45 per cent if the competitive weaknesses are not corrected'. The competitive weaknesses have not been corrected and import penetration — partly due to tied contracts — has exceeded 50 per cent. As it is import penetration in the private market has now reached 60 – 70 per cent. If imported cars were in a position to capture a significant share of the fleet market, their present penetration, which accounts for the majority of private sales, could well account for far more than the CPRS figures of 45 per cent of the total market. There are clear signs that the

1. A second generation of technically improved cars is expected shortly.

fleet buyer is now flirting with the possibility of switching to importers. This increase in import penetration is principally due to the failure of BL and Chrysler to maintain market share.

The distribution network already established by foreign manufacturers makes it unlikely, in fact, that the import market share will fall even to 28 per cent. The share is rising and will continue to rise as strikes disrupt UK production. What is of more importance than the import penetration figure is the possible market share position of all four major UK manufacturers. Whether the market share will be satisfied by UK production will be discussed subsequently. Figure 5.4 shows the UK market shares of the four major manufacturers. Significantly, whilst both Ford and GM have made a recovery, Chrysler and BL have not. Although Chrysler now has a set of new models on tap, BL's new models (apart from the new Mini) are some way away. The situation by 1980 is described below. Ford can be confidently expected to maintain its usual position of holding between 24 – 28 per cent of the market. GM, with its model policy still as yet incomplete, will desperately try to maintain its 10 per cent share and may even increase this to 12 per cent. Chrysler has probably reached its low point and will probably start to increase its market share – but not by much. BL's 'new Mini', whatever form that may take, and one or two minor offerings, is all BL can offer to stop the rot before 1980. Therefore, BL's market share will probably be in the range 22 – 27 per cent. Although as will be argued in Chapter 8, it is equally possible that this may fall to the 14 per cent to 22 per cent range – partly due to policy decisions by the UK Government, BL and the US multinationals.

FIGURE 5.4

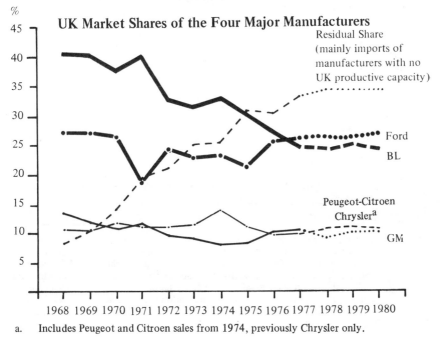

UK Market Shares of the Four Major Manufacturers

a. Includes Peugeot and Citroen sales from 1974, previously Chrysler only.

Of course, it is unlikely that Ford, GM and Chrysler will all simultaneously do well, since in the fleet car market they are competing among themselves and with BL. Similarly, it is unlikely that the bottom of the forecast market share range will be achieved by all firms. The residual market share supplied by non-UK manufacturers is therefore likely to be in the range 30-40 per cent.

Assuming that BL remains intact and is financed by the Government, its new models will be on stream by 1985. This should stop the further deterioration of BL's market share which will reach an all-time low around the 1980-85 period. Assuming that Chrysler too remains in the UK, then its market share should remain around its 1980 level — but its share would begin to exhibit a declining trend. Ford and GM should maintain their 1980 levels, though with some loss of sales because of a revitalised Leyland model range. The residual market share will have a slightly lower range of around 30-33 per cent.

In analysing how well BL's new models will do there are three factors to take into account. First, will BL be able to produce competitive new models? Secondly, will BL's new models (if successful) erode the market share of the US multinationals or will they erode the importers' share (i.e. the residual market share). Thirdly, will all the US multinationals still be UK producers? We now examine the third question. The residual share could only rise over the 40 per cent level if either Chrysler or Vauxhall (the weakest of the four major producers) virtually ceased UK production on anything approaching a volume

TABLE 5.7

	All UK Manufacturers remain in the UK	One Manufacturer ceases production in the UK	Two Manufacturers cease production in the UK
The Big Four			
Fleet sales	660	585	510
Private sales	380	350	320
	1,040	935	830
Others (i.e. Importers)			
Fleet sales	60	135	210
Private sales	500	530	560
	560 (35%)	665 (41.6%)	770 (48%)
UK Market	1,600	1,600	1,600

Note: Non private car market assumed to be 45 per cent of total market (low by current standards but may be realistic during the 1980's once private buyers can afford to re-enter the market). Only 25 per cent of the fleet car market would change their manufacturer if it left the UK. However, 50 per cent of the private market would switch brands to remain loyal to British production. Both of the smaller manufacturers are assumed to have 10 per cent market penetration of the UK, of which 62½ per cent is made up by the fleet market and the remaining 37½ per cent by the private market.

car level. If both companies close their car operations in the UK, the residual share could (by definition) reach 50 per cent or more. Whether or not this could happen in either case (although Chrysler's position, by virtue of the Iran order, is ostensibly more secure than Vauxhall's — until 1980, at least) is a matter of conjecture. If both companies continue to function as major car companies, the residual share will probably not increase to much above 37 per cent. On the darker side of the picture, however, if *both* Chrysler and Vauxhall cease production in the UK, the residual share could very easily approach, or even exceed, 50 per cent. If Vauxhall moves out of the UK, some of its fleet customers would probably continue to buy *imported* Vauxhalls, were such cars available. This transferrence of brand loyalty could also apply to private car buyers whose resistance to 'foreign cars' could thus be overcome. A hypothetical example in Table 5.7 illustrates this phenomenon.

Assumptions

In constructing various scenarios we have assumed (i) that to begin with the import share is 35 per cent; (ii) that the fleet car market comprises 45 per cent of the total market; (iii) that Chrysler and Vauxhall will each have a 10 per cent share of the UK market (comprising 62½ per cent fleet sales, and the remainder private sales). If either (or both) of the two companies move out, it is assumed that only 25 per cent of their fleet customers would change to another manufacturer, but that 50 per cent of their private sales would switch to one of the remaining British producers. From this it can be seen that were one UK manufacturer to cease production in the UK, the residual import share would rise to 41.6 per cent. Scenario 2 — with two UK manufacturers ceasing UK operations — gives a residual import share of 48 per cent. Although the methodology is suspect (in its assumptions) the example serves to illustrate the *possible* consequences of two not inconceivable outcomes, although it is unlikely that both Chrysler *and* Vauxhall will leave the UK. Indeed Chrysler needs its UK capacity to remain a viable size for Europe as a whole.[1] The alternative is for Chrysler to be producing below the minimum efficient scale in a competitive market. Chapter 17 discusses the link-up with Peugeot Citroen.

Our own subjective estimates of probable long-term (1985-90) outcomes are as follows:

Residual Import Share Range %[2]	Probability Estimate
under 25	0
25–30	.05
30–35	.30
35–40	.40
40–50	.20
over 50	.05

1. It is argued in Chapter 17 that Peugeot-Citroen-Chrysler does not however need its UK capacity to achieve maximum economies of scale.
2. These import shares include imports by Peugeot-Citroen.

Whether it is likely for GM or Chrysler to withdraw from the UK market is discussed in the next chapter. This still begs the question of whether BL's new models will be competitive and whether an increased market share will occur primarily at the expense of the other UK manufacturers or at the expense of the residual share (the importers).

The extent to which the current tide of increasing import penetration can be stopped depends not only on the European production policies of the US multinationals, but also on the competitiveness of their and BL's products. It was unfortunate, as mentioned in Chapter 3, that all four companies' models were in phase during the 1973/4 beginning of the depression. By in phase we mean that all the companies had old models which should be replaced. This combined with the lack of financial reserves for the UK could not have made for a strong justification for a more aggressive model policy. The question of the future model policy of manufacturers is discussed in the next two chapters. We therefore defer a final judgement on import penetration until after then.

What *could* affect market shares is the rather disturbing increase in import penetration in the luxury car market, traditionally an area in which British car manufacturers have shown considerable strength, and where a gap in market coverage was allowed to develop as the Rover and Triumph 2000 models became outdated.

WESTERN EUROPE (EXCLUDING THE UK)

Having considered the forecasts for demand in the UK, we will now examine the West European market as a whole, excluding the UK.

Demand in the area rose very rapidly in the 1960s, from 2.8 million in 1960 to 8.1 million in 1973. It was during this period that the mass market

TABLE 5.8
Some Forecasts of Western Europe (Excl. UK)

	Year of Forecast	New Car Registrations 1980	1985
Ryder Report	1975	9	10
Euro Finance	1975/6	8.4	9.6–10.5
EFP	1974	–	7.5
SMMT	1975	9.0	10.2
BL	1975	8.8	9.8
Predicasts	1975/6	11.2	12.6
Business International	1976	–	8+
Fiat	1975	9.2	–
Other Manufacturers (a)	1975	9.46	11
(b)	1975	7.9	–
Chrysler	1976	8.48	
Forecast used in later analysis		9	10

NB: *The 1977 new car registrations were 8.6 million cars*

1. 9.9 million including the UK.

FIGURE 5.5
Western Europe
New Car Registrations in Millions

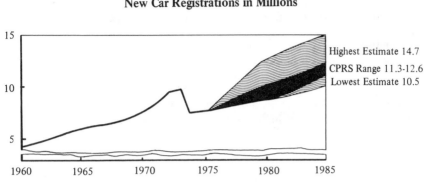

Source: CPRS Report

was more or less created, in many European countries, and the total car stock was increased at an average annual rate of nearly 12 per cent. New registrations peaked at 8.1 million in 1973. Thereafter, the effect of higher oil prices and the associated recession reduced demand to 7 million in 1974 and to about 6 million in 1975. By 1977, the 1973 peak had been exceeded with a record of around 8.6 million[1] (thus making some of the forecasts in Table 5.8 rather pessimistic).

Even before the oil crisis, however, the rate of growth of the car stock was in decline as replacement demand increased in importance relative to new demand. Fluctuations in demand in Europe should correspond to the pattern suggested for the UK though perhaps slightly less so: a setback of approximately two or three years growth of ownership and demand as consumers adjust to the increase in the price of petrol. As in the UK, it is unlikely that high petrol prices will have any significant long-term effect on demand, although it may increase the demand for small and small/medium cars, and place greater emphasis on improvements in engine design to achieve lower fuel consumption. In support of this argument, it is interesting to note that, although petrol prices were much higher in France, Italy and Germany than in the UK during the 1960s, car ownership in the former countries remained unaffected, although demand concentrated on smaller, more economical cars. This reinforces the suggestion that demand in both the UK and Western Europe should not be adversely affected in the longer term by higher petrol prices; both markets will absorb petrol prices provided that they are not in excess of the general rate of inflation.

Of the demand forecasts available for Western European demand[1] in 1980 and 1985, both Ryder and SMMT suggest a level of 9 million cars (excluding the UK); Eurofinance proposes a more cautious figure at 8.4 million. As the level of registrations was high in the early 1970s, it is reasonable to expect a correspondingly high level of replacement demand of at least 7 million in 1980. Past figures (and comparisons with the US) indicate that the total car stock

1. Western European demand excluding the UK.

125

will be increasing by at least 2.5 per cent annually, and possibly at three per cent or more, implying a new demand of at least 2 million. Total demand (both new and replacement) is unlikely to be below 9 million. Two other forecasts – by EFP and Business International – are based on unreasonably pessimistic assumptions and can be ignored.

By 1985, most forecasts suggest a demand level of 10 million or more. Replacement demand will probably remain at the 1980 level, as new registrations in the period 1973-77 will be no higher than in 1968, and these are the cars that will be due for replacement in 1985 and 1980 respectively. Assuming a growth in total stock (which will by then be approaching 100 million cars) of about three per cent per annum, the forecasts of total annual demand of 10 million are reasonable.

The crucial factor, however, is not simply the size of the market, but the market share that British firms can expect to obtain. The UK share of the Western European market has dropped from 5.2 per cent in 1970 to 2.9 per cent in 1976; in that year 268,000 cars (including unassembled vehicles) were exported to Europe, with BL models accounting for the lion's share of 185,000 (equivalent to 2.2 per cent of the total market). The BL exports fall into three categories of roughly equal importance: Minis assembled by Innocenti in Italy, Minis, Allegros (for assembly in Belgium) and some Marinas; and direct exports of assembled vehicles to all countries. With European integration of Ford, GM and Chrysler, one may expect exports of cars by these firms to become more significant. However, the UK is currently the second largest exporter *within* Europe of cars exported to areas *outside* Western Europe (see Table 5.9). We now turn our attention to these areas.

TABLE 5.9

Exports outside Western Europe for 1976 (in '000s)

Belgium	France	Italy	Sweden	UK	West Germany
18	298	165	63	314	541

NORTH AMERICA

A major market to consider is North America – a feature of which is the captive market for BL sports cars. An alternative and perhaps more correct viewpoint is that BL is captive to the US market – it affords the volume sales which allows BL to produce specialty cars economically (although the TR7 is rumoured to be a loss maker). BL sales there have recorded an impressive increase over their 1973 level despite a major slump in total demand in both the US and Canadian markets, with exports running at just under 100,000 cars.

Total North American demand is unlikely to exceed its 1973 peak of 12.3 million before 1980, and will probably hover around the 13 million mark by 1985. However, the UK share of the market is so small, and its production so specialised, that forecasts of total demand have little direct bearing on UK sales

in the region – although UK firms could do much to conserve their reputation for a quality product. Only two developments could affect the British
performance in North America: the introduction of additional pollution and
safety controls, and the possibility that European manufacturers might establish assembly operations on the North American continent. At the same
time, the American Ford, GM and Chrysler corporations are all planning to
market a 'European' style car of their own in the US. It therefore seems
unlikely that apart from BL and specialist firms there will be very much scope
for further growth in export sales to the US.

A reasonable assumption is 100,000 units in 1980 and 1985 for the
specialist BL cars.

TABLE 5.10

Some Forecasts of North American New Car
Registrations (Million Units)

	1980	1985
Ryder Report	12.8	13.0
Eurofinance	11.3	13.1
EFP	–	10.7
Fiat	11.5	–
Business International	–	13.1
Forecast of UK exports to North America	.1	.1

THE REST OF THE WORLD

In 1976, the UK exported 265,000 cars to markets in other parts of the world.
Over the next ten years, car demand in the Middle East, Latin America and
parts of Africa and Asia will undoubtedly grow rapidly, but forecasting the
'takeoff' into mass car ownership in any of these areas is difficult. Two points
must be considered: the extent to which world supply exceeds demand, and
the growth of supply capacity in those areas which are at present either non-
producers or who manufacture on an insignificant scale.

Japan

The Japanese market is second only to the US in size, and yet foreign manufacturers account for less than 2 per cent of the total market. As the CPRS
Report noted, at first sight there appears to be no compelling reason for this
unimpressive record. At 6.4 per cent, the tariff on cars is in fact lower than the
EEC rate. Imports, furthermore, now face no other tax discrimination. Although
the emission controls are stringent, their application to import models has been
successively delayed and when they are eventually implemented they will
probably be in force in Europe anyway. Restrictions on foreign capital investment in the motor industry have been lifted, and the Japanese themselves have
demonstrated, by their success in Europe, that the distance between the two
areas presents no overwhelming handicap. This at least is the situation at

present, but in fairness to foreign manufacturers it must be said that until recently the Japanese market was highly protected. (Although it has been argued that continued use of non tariff barriers still affords the Japanese a measure of protection.) During the open period of protection, Japanese producers were able to establish a comprehensive distribution network, and it would now be very difficult to persuade existing dealers that there was any advantage to be gained by switching to imported models. The alternative − investing capital in creating new dealerships − would probably be too costly and present too many difficulties in staffing, etc. Ford have overcome the problem by distributing their range through the Honda network − an arrangement only made possible because of the complementarity of the two ranges. There is little likelihood that similar marketing agreements could be negotiated by other European manufacturers.

There should be some growth of imports to Japan, but volumes will probably be small, one source (the Japanese Industrial Structure Council), suggesting that they would not exceed 100,000 units by 1980 (3 per cent of the passenger car market) and 170,000 by 1985. As the CPRS report concludes: 'The competitiveness of the Japanese manufacturers suggests that the only real potential for increased sales lies in cars which are not in direct competition with the Japanese volume cars and that can justify premium prices.' The development by the US of its smaller models might have an adverse effect on the Japanese, and might be sold in Europe in large quantities.

Other Markets

In theory, the former Commonwealth countries (Australia, New Zealand, South Africa), Latin America, Eastern Europe, the Middle East, Nigeria, South-East Asia and the Indian subcontinent should all represent potential growth markets for European car exports, although in practice most of the countries mentioned are anxious to protect their own car industries and have imposed, or are in the process of imposing, severe limitations on imports. In Brazil, for example, high tariffs protect the local car industry, and similar tariffs apply to commercial vehicles. In Nigeria, cars with an engine capacity of less than 200 cc can only enter the country under licence; larger cars face heavy tariffs, rising to 100 per cent in the case of cars with a capacity of over 2750 cc. Poland has virtually prohibited the import of Western cars, and imports into Spain are limited by a global quota amounting to about £10 million for built up cars and £2.5 million for parts, accessories and components.

Where European manufacturers have been successful in exporting cars in kit form, local governments are increasingly anxious to see an increase in local content. Chrysler, for example, in exporting KD[1] Hunters to Iran, planned to increase the local content to 45 to 50 per cent in 1977. It now appears that the Iran National Industrial Manufacturing Company (INIM), expects to achieve 60-70 per cent local content during the 1980s. European manufacturers will have to expect similar problems whenever they export to countries

---

1. KD stands for knock down kits of cars.

TABLE 5.11

Import Restrictions in Major Third World Markets[a]

| MARKET | MARKET CHARACTERISTICS | | | LIMITATION ON IMPORTS | | |
	New Registrations (000)	Estimated Population (million)	European Exports (000)	Restrictions on BU Imports	Discriminatory Tariff on BU Imports	Local Content Rules for Assembly
Spain	570	34.4	41.6	Yes	Yes	Yes
Brazil	460	96.0	1.3	Yes	Yes	Yes
Australia	460	12.9	41.0	Yes	Yes	Yes
Mexico	250	51.7	33.5	Yes	Yes	Yes
South Africa	230	21.1	97.3	Yes	Yes	Yes
Argentina	225	23.7	5.2	Yes	Yes	Yes
New Zealand	100	2.7	37.3	No	Yes	No
Iran	100	31.0	54.5	Yes	Yes	No
Nigeria	100	66.0	17.7	Yes	Yes	Yes
Philippines	20	39.0	5.7	Yes	Yes	Yes
Indonesia	15	119.2	7.0	Yes	Yes	Yes
Total			342.2	= 50.6% of exports outside Europe and North America		

Source: CPRS Report: *The Future of the British Car Industry*, HMSO, 1975

a.   As in the early 1970s

129

which are determined to develop domestic car production.

Finally, competition — between developed countries and between established producers and newcomers — will make further export penetration of Third World countries increasingly difficult. Of the established producers, the Japanese present the most serious threat. Countries such as Iran, South Korea and countries in South America, anxious to build up their own production capacity, offer lower labour costs and often an impressive array of concessions and incentives that could persuade manufacturers to move operations out of Europe — as is already beginning to happen in Brazil.

These problems are common to all European producers. British manufacturers, however, experience additional difficulties peculiar to the UK car industry and its export market. UK exports, for example, are in particularly vulnerable markets. Australia, New Zealand and South Africa, which now account for 20 per cent of UK export sales, are all in process of establishing their own car industry and are also subject to heavy pressure from the Japanese producers. The future of the Chrysler market in Iran is uncertain. As three of the four major UK firms are American owned by corporations already operating in Third World countries, the potential for exporting even components to those areas is severely limited. BL, moreover, has had little success in establishing overseas operations.

In the late 1960s and early 1970s Western Europe was a major exporter, particularly to North America. Japanese cars have not only eroded the European share of the North American market, but have also affected a significant and growing import penetration into Western Europe itself! This fact, coupled with the threat of cheap Communist Bloc imports *and* declining world exports means that the Western European producers could lose their present positive balance of trade in cars. The worst predictions forecast a reduction in exports of approximately 1.3 million units by 1980, with a corresponding increase in imports of 1.2 million, leaving a positive balance of trade in cars of only 100,000 units.

EXPORT POTENTIAL

As we have seen, the UK car industry has not maintained its position in the major growth markets (Western Europe, USA) and it has lost its market share in the traditional export strongholds (Australia, *et al.*) as a result of the activities of local producers and through increased competition from Western Europe and from the Japanese producers. Unless the multinationals use UK capacity to supply continental and overseas markets — or the Japanese prove more receptive to imports — there would seem to be few opportunities for the UK industry to improve its position greatly. Some gains can still be made — by BL in North America, and by an updated BL range in Western Europe — provided that problems affecting quality, distribution and delivery can be overcome.

European Market Share

If the three multinationals (Ford, GM, Chrysler) are to gain maximum benefit

TABLE 5.12

European Car Exports and Imports
(million cars)

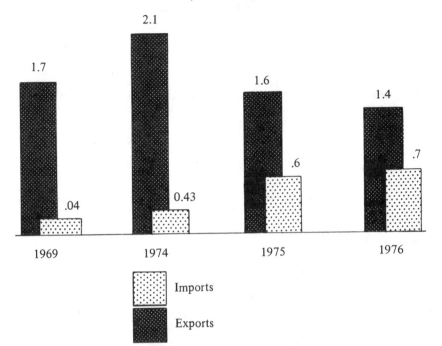

Imports

Exports

from economies of scale, their European operations must become more fully integrated and capacity in the UK, in particular, will have to be increased — either to manufacture parts and components for export to assembly plants in Europe, or to assemble components produced on the Continent. Either way, exports of components, knocked down or built up units must increase. Ford have always operated in this way and will probably continue to do so. Chrysler and GM — if they wish to make full use of their capacity in the UK and elsewhere — will have to follow Ford's example, and organise their operations on a European scale, making more efficient use of their UK plants, and, despite the rather serious drawback of a poor industrial relations record, gaining maximum benefit from the relatively inexpensive labour costs in the UK and the existence of a strong components manufacturing industry in this country.

If we assume that all three multinationals do make more efficient use of their UK productive capacity, this could result in exports of around 100,000 units p.a. for both Chrysler and Vauxhall, with a further 200,000 units from Ford, making a total of 400,000 export units p.a. from the multinationals alone. If 75 per cent of this were to go to Europe, this would represent a 3 per cent share of the total European market, although not all of the units would be built up. The main marketing thrust of fully assembled cars for export to Europe must however come from BL. If suitable successors for the

131

Mini and medium car ranges can be found (and assuming that the new Rover, Triumph and Princess fulfil marketing expectations), BL should be in a position to improve its current share (185,000 units in 1976) of the European market. The multinationals and BL combined should be able to improve the total market share by between 4 and 6 per cent by 1980, possibly more by 1985.

Rest of the World Market Share

The UK cannot realistically expect to export large numbers of cars to the remainder of the world markets in 1980. Limited sales will still be made in Asia (Formosa, Iran, Israel, Malaysia, the Philippines, Singapore, Thailand, etc.), Africa (Kenya, Nigeria and South Africa), and to Oceania (principally to New Zealand); there is a (limited) potential for increased sales of specialised cars to the Communist Bloc and the Middle East. All in all, 150,000 export units a year in 1980 would not seem too low a figure — although even that could be hard to achieve. If Chrysler were to use the UK as an export base, however, this figure could rise to 200,000 units, and the removal of protective tariffs in the newer producing countries (who by 1985 might wish to increase their own export potential) could boost the total even further — possibly to around 250,000 units a year.

Manufacturers Export Performance

Figures for export performance in 1974 and 1975 are shown in Table 5.13. Our projection for future sales assumed that all four UK producers will increase sales to Europe (over their 1977/8 levels), that BL will increase exports to the US and that Chrysler's Iran contract will have ended by 1985. In Table 5.14, the full model by model export breakdown is given for 1975.

CONCLUSION

The demand estimates for UK production proposed here may seem high, but we consider that the mood of recent demand estimates has been over-pessimistic — possibly reflecting the current recession. Taking UK demand for example: at least 1.2 million cars will have to be replaced by 1980. The cost of petrol, car prices and the retail price index have all doubled in the last four years. In real terms, petrol is no more expensive now than it has ever been in relative terms. However, the real price of cars has risen. Until real wages catch up, demand is unlikely to exceed its former peak in 1973. Once the car buying public have accepted this, and as soon as there are signs of a genuine economic recovery, demand will strengthen and should surpass its previous level. We now turn our attention to whether there will be any significant increase in productive capacity.

TABLE 5.13

Car Exports by Manufacturers (000's)

	Europe	America	Asia and Middle East	Africa	Oceania	Total
1974						
BL	159	68½	12	20½	28	309
FORD	36	36	30	5	12	92
CHRYSLER	33	4	78	2	14	133
VAUXHALL	40	1	2	2	13	58
	268	110	122	30	67	590
1975						
BL	125	76	5	12	17	237
FORD	43	4	28	9	20	105
CHRYSLER	18	3	137	3	8	171
VAUXHALL	18	0	0	0	3	21
	205	86	171	25	48	538
1976						
BL	185	91	5	8	10	310
FORD	42	4	25	1	27	102
CHRYSLER	18	5	73	1	5	100
VAUXHALL	22	0	0	0	7	30
	268	102	104	10	59	548

NB. 0 indicates less than 500 units and difference between columns sums and columns totals indicates exports by "others".

TABLE 5.14
UK Čar Manufacturers Export Figures Broken Down into Model/Area Split
1975 ('000s)

	Europe	America	Asia and Middle East	Africa	Oceania	Total
BL Cars						
Mini	66	3	2	4	3	79
Maxi	3	0	0	0	2	5
18 –22	2	0	0	0	0	2
Allegro	28	0	0	0	2	31
Marina	9	7	1	4	2	23
MG	1	30	0	0	0	31
Triumph Sports	4	30	0	0	1	35
Other Triumph	2	0	0	0	6	8
Rover Saloons	1	0	0	0	0	2
Range Rover	4	1	2	2	1	9
Jaguar	4	5	1	1	1	12
	125	76	5	12	17	237
Ford						
Escort	30	1	12	1	13	57
Cortina	11	2	16	1	7	37
Capri	2	0	0	0	0	2
Granada	1	0	0	7	0	8
	43	4	28	9	20	105
Chrysler						
Hunter	4	2	110	0	4	121
Avenger	14	1	27	3	4	50
	18	3	137	3	8	171
Vauxhall						
Viva	9	0	0	0	2	12
Victor	1	0	0	0	0	1
Chevette	7	0	0	0	0	7
	17	0	0	0	2	19

NB   0 indicates less than 500 units and column and row totals may not add up due to rounding errors.

CHAPTER 6

THE UK CAR MANUFACTURERS

INTRODUCTION

In the previous chapter demand considerations were analysed. This chapter begins to concentrate on the corollary: given the assumptions in Chapter 5, how is that demand to be satisfied? First a brief historical word. UK car production increased more or less steadily until the mid 1960s. Since then car production has stagnated, and has now developed two detrimental reputations; one for strike proneness and the other for poor durability, quality and reliability. The reasons for the stagnation are many fold. During the late 1940s and 1950s, the UK car manufacturers were able to sell everything they produced regardless of quality or price. One interpretation would be that an attitude of complacency set in during this period of excess demand. However, as discussed in Chapter 1, successive governments practised demand management of the UK economy primarily through 'luxury' consumer durables. With no sustained increase in domestic car demand coupled with surplus capacity in the 1960s, UK car manufacturers did not expand. The cutbacks that occurred in 1951, 1952, 1956, 1961, 1965, 1967 and 1969 all had employment implications. As discussed in Section 1, the lack of a stable job environment has helped to cause the industrial relations problems. One way

FIGURE 6.1

Production in '000s

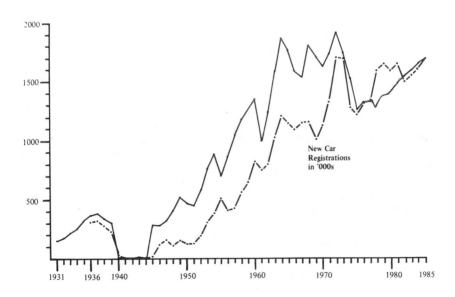

135

out of the lack of a stable domestic demand is the development of an export market. But because of the inherent faults in the UK industry which were outlined in Chapter 3, growth of exports did not occur.

It must be said at the outset that the UK is only a part of one of the three major motor industry 'territories' (North America, Western Europe and Japan). Nor is it, at the moment, a particularly bright star even within the West European galaxy. With some 15 per cent of West European capacity and a rather smaller share of actual European production, the UK motor industry is not a high flyer in the ranks of the European car industry. Of the four major UK producers, only one — BL — is in British hands.

THE EUROPEAN CONCEPT

Not even an excess of nationalist sentiment could now persuade the four major UK producers that the UK market exists in splendid isolation. Car sales in the UK have been low in comparison with, say, West Germany and the UK market has exhibited very little growth potential in recent years. Manufacturers must now conduct their marketing operations on a pan-European scale, and there are sound reasons for extending this 'continental' approach to the production side. By rationalising, spreading and expanding capacity throughout Europe, it may be possible to achieve even greater economies of scale. (See Appendix 17.2 for details of European manufacturers' production.)

Table 6.1 lists the top fifty best-selling models in world markets, excluding models produced in North America. If we discount models produced for domestic UK consumption only (i.e. Vauxhall Viva, Victor, the Chrysler Avenger), then it is apparent that the most profitable European and Japanese companies can claim impressive sales and production totals, in excess of 300,000 units per annum of the most popular models. Model runs in the UK, however, have until recently been abysmally low; only Ford could claim to be any exception to the otherwise depressing rule. Now, both GM and Chrysler have started to integrate their UK production on a European wide basis, the results of which should improve the UK (associated) position in the model production league. The reorganisation of BL's production facilities could also extend production runs of certain models. Production of the new Mini, for example, should be in the region of 400,000 units per year, compared with around 225,000 unit run for the original Mini.[1]

Why is a 'European' approach so important for an understanding of the UK motor industry? Table 6.2 shows the extent to which the UK manufacturers tried to 'spread' their production facilities across Europe; given the unexpectedly buoyant post-oil crisis car demand in West Germany, France, the Netherlands, Belgium and Sweden, it is hardly surprising that the US multinationals should temporarily forsake the UK and look elsewhere for growth. Italy and the UK, meanwhile, share a common fate. Both are small and are currently rather less buoyant markets.

THE US MULTINATIONALS

Of the three US multinationals operating in the UK, Ford has shown a far

1.   Under Michael Edwardes a reduced productive capacity is envisaged.

more progressive approach to the problems of rationalising its policy position on a European basis. In the US market, Ford cannot realistically expect to overtake GM, in the forseeable future, and the company has therefore devoted greater attention to the growth potential of the European market, where it is pursuing a deliberately expansionist strategy. To date, Ford has clearly out-stripped GM in Europe; the company has one of the largest car manufacturing capacities in the area, and will soon be market leader, although this possibility will be discussed in greater detail later. Ford's growth objectives have been at the expense of profits, since by and large GM is still more profitable, despite massive losses on the UK Vauxhall operation. Chrysler, in third place behind GM and Ford, has also tried to diversify plant locations, but the company has been constrained by low capacity (a maximum of one million units in the whole of Europe) and by the need to conserve resources to meet substantial (and unavoidable) capital expenditure commitments in future in order to make the company competitive. Chrysler's position has certainly been affected by the company's choice of location. The Chrysler Simca division has been reasonably profitable, but Chrysler (UK) has suffered from the weakness of the UK market. Chrysler's sales in France have experienced the negative effects of a nationalist backlash, with French buyers tending to prefer a Peugeot-Citroen or a Renault to a multinational hybrid.[1]

In simple terms, then, Ford leads the multinational field in Europe al-though it concedes higher profitability to GM's Open division. Chrysler — already weakened in the domestic US market — seems poised to suffer a similar fate in the European market. We will now examine each of the multi-nationals more closely. One of the most significant questions, given the in-creased growth in the European market, is where the two leading US multi-nationals, Ford and GM will install increased capacity to meet the projected increase in demand.[2]

Ford

In the early 1970s Ford covered the light, medium and large car market seg-ments with a model line up consisting of the Escort, the Cortina, the Granada and the Capri, of which the Cortina accounted for the bulk of sales. Overall, Ford did have a particularly high technical reputation, and their models were often criticised for poor road-holding. In the mid-seventies the company decided to venture into small-car production with the Fiesta. Ford had made little impact on the Spanish, French and Italian markets, and it was hoped that the Fiesta would provide an opportunity to establish a strong marketing base in these and other areas, in line with the company's growth objectives.

Some observers feel that in the longer term Ford will base production on a three model line up (Fiesta, Escort and Cortina) offering two different wheelbase lengths of their large car. Interestingly, the newest Cortina and Granada models are similar and incorporate a number of identical body panels

1. Hence Chrysler has been the most European of the multinationals with front wheel drive Simca models.
2. As discussed in the previous chapter.

(e.g. floor sections). Other commentators feel that a four-model line up in-

TABLE 6.1

Top 50 Best-selling Models in World Market excluding North America

Rank	Make	Model	1976	1975
1.	Toyota	Corolla	816,897	648,965
2.	Datsun	Sunny	541,838	531,430
3.	Volkswagen	Golf	528,876	419,620
4.	Ford	Taunus/Cortina	435,044	321,890
5.	Renault	R-5	408,856	299,609
6.	Renault	R-12	397,713	368,412
7.	Ford	Escort	397,163	372,161
8.	Honda	Civic	390,522	328,107
9.	Volkswagen	Beetle	339,960	379,500
10.	Toyota	Corona	326,244	317,243
11.	Opel	Kadett	312,573	244,051
12.	Fiat	127	306,062	307,042
13.	Opel	Ascona	286,808	167,726
14.	Peugeot	504	274,000	241,753
15.	Fiat	131	251,291	204,000
16.	Simca	1307/1308	241,430	46,708
17.	Citroen	GS	231,927	215,970
18.	Volkswagen	Passat	229,294	196,779
19.	Renault	R-4	229,291	233,185
20.	Toyota	Celica	223,631	139,193
21.	Fiat	128	213,643	221,024
22.	Datsun	Bluebird	213,643	196,273
23.	Simca	1100	203,400	216,794
24.	Nissan	Cherry	197,064	188,480
25.	British Leyland	Mini	190,000	167,527
26.	Opel	Rekord	181,924	168,719
27.	Nissan	Violet	180,763	169,495
28.	Fiat	126	175,655	166,270
29.	Volvo	240	175,000	180,000
30.	Mercedes-Benz	W-123	172,000	0
31.	Ford	Granada	168,048	141,253
32.	Toyota	Carina	167,122	149,983
33.	Peugeot	104	155,560	114,534
34.	Audi	80	150,390	118,030
35.	Nissan	Skyline	148,013	162,923
36.	Volkswagen	Polo	143,677	74,180
37.	Peugeot	304	137,087	93,286
38.	Citroen	2 CV	134,396	117,914
39.	Citroen	Dyane	118,871	123,532
40.	Opel	Manta	117,666	57,866
41.	Renault	R-6	116,064	137,373
42.	Toyota	Sprinter	114,273	136,367
43.	Austin/Morris	Marina	113,000	109,832
44.	Citroen	CX	112,339	96,778
45.	Ford	Fiesta	109,838	0
46.	Renault	R-16	107,745	120,452
47.	Austin	Allegro	106,000	98,000
48.	Toyota	Crown	105,605	129,155
49.	Ford	Capri	103,573	100,050
50.	Honda	Accord	94,973	0

Source: Automobile International, Market Data Survey 1977.

corporating the Granada is more likely. The existing Capri segment is a much smaller specialist market, but if necessary a Capri-type car could be developed as a variation on one of the four principal models.[1] It has been argued that the specialist Capri market will decline as consumers adopt a more ultilitarian approach to car ownership, but this is no more or less plausible than the counter argument that specialist segments of this sort are ripe for further expansion. Obviously their ideal strategy is to maximise the profit potential at the minimum unique investment in the model series. Either way, Ford will be reluctant to retain the Capri as a completely autonomous model and will probably follow GM in developing it as a variation on one of the existing basic models.

The story behind the Fiesta development programme is also illustrative of Ford's worldwide policy. The US market has in the past exhibited sluggish growth. Consequently during the oil crisis, some capital investment programmes had to be cut. Ford chose to drop its US model developments during the mid 1980s in favour of the $1 billion Fiesta and facelifts to its European models (costing around $100 million in total). In giving Europe preference, Ford are in a better position to gain a larger share of an expanding market. Nevertheless although the Fiesta programme has with hindsight proved correct in terms of maintaining market share, the decision to build the plant in Spain has not yet been vindicated.

Ford's integrated production policy is reviewed almost continually. Table 6.3 illustrates the major relocation policy changes that the company has made or is expected to make in 1978-79, and outlines a number of possible policy changes which could be decided upon in the slightly longer term. Ford Assembly plants are relatively large (200,000+ capacity) which means that they are not always restricted to the production of only one model. To achieve a least-cost position (excluding the cost of transport to the point of sale), Ford periodically reviews production in order to maximise plant utilisation and minimise costs. One example should illustrate this process. Ford noticed a falling off in Escort sales in 1977 at a time when interest was growing in the new Granada. Ford therefore decided to transfer part of the low-series Capri production to Halewood, releasing spare capacity at Cologne for production of the Granada. In actual fact this move never occurred for other reasons (e.g. poor productivity at Halewood) but it illustrates the decision-making process. At the moment, the Fiesta is produced in three different locations, but if, for example, Granada sales exceed expectations, the high-series Capri production could be moved from Cologne to the Ford plant at Saarlouis and Fiesta production in Spain stepped up. Once the initial marketing thrust is completed, Ford may revert to a dual-sourcing operation. If the Valencia plant expands to full production capacity (400,000 units), Spain could act as the sole source of Fiesta output until Ford is able to renegotiate its commitment to export two thirds of the Spanish run. Further revisions in model policy will switch production of the new Granada, Cortina and Capri series to plants at Dagenham, Ghenk and Cologne, in such a way as to minimise costs.

1.   As in the case of the Opel Ascona – Manta series, and Vauxhall Cavalier Coupe series. The new US developed Mustang/Capri may be imported into Europe either as an alternative or as a complement.

TABLE 6.2
Extent of Multinationalisation as at 1973
with Guesstimate of Two-Shift Car Assembly Capacity

Manufacturer	UK	West Germany	France	Belgium	Italy	Spain
British Leyland	Longbridge (350,000) Cowley (400,000) Rover/Triumph plants (250,000) Jaguar (35,000)	—	—	Seneffe (60,000)	Innocenti (60,000)	Authi (60,000)
Ford	Halewood (250,000) Dagenham (300,000)	Cologne (400,000) Saarlouis (250,000)	automatic gearbox & components at Bordeaux	Ghenk (250,000)	—	Projected for 1976 Valencia (250,000) but with engine capacity 500,000
GM	Luton (150,000) Ellesmere Port (200,000)	Russelheim (325,000)	—	Bochum (310,000) Antwerp (275,000)	—	—
Chrysler	Linwood (200,000) Ryton (200,000) Dublin (20,000)	—	Poissy (500,000)	—	—	Madrid (100,000)

TABLE 6.3

Example of Ford's Integrated Production Policy

	1978 (actual)	Early 1980s A (example of possible future policies)	B
Fiesta	Dagenham, Saarlouis and Valencia	Valencia Dagenham	Valencia (capacity increased)
Escort/Erica[a]	Halewood and Saarlouis high series, Saarlouis only	Halewood and Saarlouis	Halewood and Saarlouis
Cortina/Taunus	Dagenham and Ghenk	Dagenham and Ghenk	Dagenham and Ghenk
Capri	Cologne	Cologne	Dagenham
Granada	Cologne	Cologne	Cologne

a. Now front wheel drive car designed to be a modern replacement for the Escort, although a revised Escort body with a hatchback variant will be brought out before the Erica – which is due out in 1981.

141

One thing is certain — with the Fiesta launch, Ford have shown their determination to change their European image. The cheap, basic Ford will be gradually replaced by a more sophisticated car offering advanced engineering[1] and modest maintenance costs (an increasingly important consideration). The next series of Escorts will be front-wheel drive and technically up to date; with the emphasis on design that enables a component to function efficiently and reliably. There is a strong suggestion that Ford will continue to exploit the component manufacturing field on a similarly multinational basis.

Logically this would indicate that Ford continued to produce its larger cars in West Germany, its small/medium cars in the UK (Escort and Cortina) and its smallest range (Fiesta) in Spain. However poor productivity by the UK labour force coupled with poor workmanship may modify the ideal. The UK, for example, may find itself producing only the low and medium series model (as it currently does with the Escort) whilst the high series models are produced where there is a greater chance of higher workmanship. Superimposed upon this strategy is Ford's treasured policy of multi-sourcing — being able to assemble (and produce) most components from at least two separate sources. As European production becomes more integrated and as trade union links strengthen within the EEC, strikes may spread across frontiers and therefore annihilate some of the advantages of multi-sourcing. Until then, and partly because of optimally sized assembly plants of only around 200,000 to 400,000 units a year Ford will always attempt to assemble their principle models in at least two centres. The UK, for example, will always produce the Escort and the Cortina. West Germany will always produce the largest car plus some of the higher series Escorts. Valencia will always produce the Fiesta. In Table 6.3, Capri production is shown to be transferred to Dagenham whilst high series Fiesta production is transferred to Valencia. Alternatives to increasing capacity in Valencia are discussed below.

Within the UK, the shift of engine capacity from Dagenham to Bridgend in South Wales does not improve the efficiency of cramped assembly operations elsewhere. It is unlikely that the Dagenham assembly plant will be expanded. Capacity at Halewood is also unlikely to be increased as there are no particular bottlenecks: rather than doubling up facilities at Halewood, Ford would prefer to increase production elsewhere or build a new assembly plant in countries where no assembly facilities exist.

Possible areas for new plants are; France, Italy, North Africa, Balkans, Egypt and the Communist Bloc. Although some years ago France would have been considered a high priority for possible expansion, the market has adopted a more protectionist attitude including economic nationalism. Italy despite being a low labour cost area suffers from the French syndrome and has similar industrial relations problems to the UK. Whilst a good argument can be made for using the cheap labour areas of North Africa and the Balkans, experience from Spain militates against this. The advantage of building capacity in low labour cost countries is to install cheaper labour intensive assembly processes. However at the new Spanish plant, Ford choose to install the same high technology plant as found elsewhere in Europe. Why? The answer is that only

---

1.   Or at least engineering that is not noticeably less modern than its principal competitors.

one set of engineers is required if the same technology is used throughout Europe. If two distinct production processes are required this would involve two engineering teams, the training of management in two skills, etc. These costs presumably outweighed the benefits from using more labour intensive processes coupled with cheaper labour.

The Communist Bloc solution may permit Ford simply to sell the technology and leave someone else to iron out all the problems, in exchange for a possible share of the output. However such a strategy is a high risk one as Fiat found out, since the Communist countries may start to compete in the same markets alongside the supplier of the technology using identical – or slightly outdated – models. Another problem concerns the quality of workmanship of products manufactured or assembled behind the Iron Curtain.

Where does this leave the UK? For Ford, the UK must be ranked as a low labour cost area. Yet it is a country which is used to supporting high technology manufacturing with an appropriately well developed infra-structure. In addition Ford has established itself as market leader and is planning to push its sales to 30 per cent or even the magical Ryder figure of 33 per cent. Despite being an ambitious target, this would represent around 600,000 cars with a market size of 1.8 million. Such output is in practice well beyond the scope of existing UK plants even allowing for the import of all Granada and Capris. In addition substantial Government funds are available in the form of regional investment grants and the usual capital allowances.

There are however two weaknesses with UK plants. First, production is unlikely to exceed 70 per cent of capacity owing to low productivity.[1] In fact at the Halewood plant, productivity is significantly worse than the older Dagenham plant. Ford's management have made a whole series of experiments of the Halewood plant to try to increase production. Two examples are the variation of manning levels and the wholesale import of German management teams; neither were the least bit successful. Ford is now implementing a $250 million investment plan aimed at improving working conditions, however it must be said that the prognosis is not good. Why it may be asked did Ford take the risk of installing new engine capacity at Bridgend? The answer is that engine plants are essentially a more automated process, and in any case the Welsh productivity record has been relatively good.

The second weakness peculiar to the UK is the reputation of UK made cars in the durability, quality and reliability respects. Table 6.4 shows the order of magnitude of the penalty involved in assembling a UK car as opposed to German or Belgian assembly. Unfortunately, whether deserved or not (and Table 6.4 demonstrates that for Ford it is), the reputation of a UK produced car is poor. Although Ford may feel confident that they can improve quality, there may always be a gap between UK and German produced vehicles, since the quality of German produced cars is also improving.

The argument for increased UK capacity would be strengthened if a newer level of automation at the assembly stage was introduced, which further minimised the operator dependency of machines. The attitude of Ford's UK workforce can be contrasted with that of the Japanese. Groups of workers in

1. A combination of strikes, over-manning, slow work practices and frequent breaks from the assembly line.

Japan have been rumoured to form quality control groups in their spare time and issue quality demands to the workforce. Some commentators would argue that the difference in attitude was partly due to the 'responsible autonomy' attitude given to the Japanese workforce which is in contrast to the 'direct control' regime which typifies Ford's employee relationships.[1]

The above two weaknesses are not peculiar to Ford but have also been experienced by the other two US multinationals.

TABLE 6.4
Comparison of the Reliability of UK and Non UK Made Cars

	UK Produced Cars per 100 cars	German Produced Cars per 100 Cars
Fiesta		
Owner reported problems in 1977	242	142
Escort		
Owner reported problems in 1977	256	125
Repair rates in 1976/7	525	287
Taunus/Cortina		
Owner reported problems in 1977	250	266*
Repair rates in 1976/77	551	365*

* Assembled in Belgium

General Motors

GM (Europe) is something of an enigma. The GM Opel division in Belgium and West Germany is fully integrated, with an approximate annual car production capacity of 350,000 at the West German Russelheim plant, and 325,000 and 300,000 respectively at the Belgian Bochum and Antwerp plants. Vauxhall, however, is a completely separate entity, although GM's CV operations have been integrated for some time.

This apparent contradiction is a result of GM's inflexible approach to policy and planning. In the US, GM has been able to maximise economies of scale and still retain five partly autonomous car divisions, within which there is a certain flexibility, permitting skilled but often minor variations and a certain amount of 'customising' to distinguish one model range from another. The system works reasonably well in the US, but it may not necessarily be the most appropriate response to market conditions in Europe. GM, however, have decided that a similar approach can be usefully and profitably employed elsewhere. Rather than develop common identical models, a common 'concept' is evolved which can then be tailored to market a slightly different product and/or to suit local market conditions. This semi-autonomous divisional

1.   A.L. Friedman, *Industry and Labour: Class Struggle at Work and Monopoly Capitalism.* Macmillan, London, 1977.

structure explains why Opel and Vauxhall have been allowed to go their own separate ways. GM have never insisted on maximum economies of scale world wide: national frontiers and defined markets have acted as impenetrable barrriers to integration. Now, however, the company appears to be changing tack, and considering Western Europe as a single unified market rather than a series of smaller, national markets. Vauxhall's poor performance and Ford's newly agressive growth-orientated approach may have led GM to re-evaluate its European operations.

GM had three major options on the car manufacturing side: (i) to follow Ford into a high-growth area (e.g. Spain); (ii) to increase European capacity by expanding the Vauxhall operation and establishing a major powertrain factory in the UK; or (iii) to concentrate on expansion of existing West German and Belgian plants; using Vauxhall to source the UK and certain export markets more or less as an Opel subsidiary.

GM's attempt to break into the Spanish market by purchasing BL's Authi plants (option (i)) was thwarted by the Spanish Government's veto. Of the two remaining options, GM seem to have decided on the final option – to expand the Opel division, probably at the expense of any further major expansion of car production in the UK. The reasons for this choice are not yet clear, but they probably involve a number of considerations, namely: the political climate in the UK; the possible decline in productivity of the UK labour force; the UK's low potential growth rate; and finally, the fact that in any event, GM's major markets are primarily in the Benelux Countries, West Germany and to a lesser extent Italy.[1]

Opel, then, has now emerged as the dominant car producer, and Vauxhall the major CV producer. In a way, this development is perfectly logical. GM's particular strength has always lain in the more profitable medium and large car segments, for which Germany represents the largest market in Europe.

GM's integration, however, will not be as complete as Ford's. Opel and Vauxhall will continue to pursue different marketing strategies (see Chapter 14) using separate and in some cases quite distinct distribution networks. The device of minor styling variations will still be employed to differentiate one range from another.

At this point, it might be helpful to consider the profitability of the large car segment in greater detail. In general, the *size* of a car has little effect on the design and distribution costs on the fixed overheads. Nor do labour costs vary significantly from one (small) car to another (larger) one – although a more luxurious model will need extra labour to fit additional materials at the trimming stage. The main cost difference is accounted for in materials, although the price increase in the large car segment covers not only the additional cost of materials but also a higher profit margin. By concentrating on the medium and large car segments, GM has always been able to generate healthy profits. In recent years, however, GM's model policy has been metamorphosed. First, the company has developed a wider model spread, starting with the Chevette/Kadett at the lower end of the market and moving through

1.   Under GM's Bedford brandname.

the Cavalier/Ascona/Manta range and the Rekord/Carlton range to the up-market Commodore/Diplomat range at the executive end of the spectrum. The Chevette/Kadett series is now part of the world wide concept car — the T car — incorporating minor styling variations on a similar design theme. The same concept also applies to the Cavalier/Ascona/Manta series, in which the Cavalier is basically an Ascona body with a Manta front, and the Manta is more or less identical to the Cavalier coupe.[1] The medium and large car ranges will shortly be rationalised on a similar world wide concept basis, although US produced models may not be greatly affected.

The introduction of the concept car allows GM to market a rather more all-encompassing model range than Ford. With the soon to be released 'S'[2] car, GM will have a complete five-model strategy, with one model for each segment:

Segment	Model
small	'S' Car
light	Chevette/Kadett ('T' car)
small/medium	Cavalier/Ascona
medium +	Rekord/Carlton, Commodore
large	Senator/Royale
specialist	Cavalier Coupe/Manta
	(derived from small/medium segments)
	and Monza (derived from the large segments)

GM may develop one model with two different wheelbases and minor styling differences, thus covering two market segments.

GM's production policy has again been affected by the company's 'divisional' approach. Vauxhall, for example, simply cannot afford at the moment to implement all of the changes required by the parent company's new world wide model strategy. Although Vauxhall have been reluctant to discuss the matter, it is known that the new Chevette was partly sourced from Belgium and West Germany.[3] Only the powertrain was certainly manufactured wholly in the UK. Similarly, the Cavalier was initially produced in Bochum. Some production has now been transferred to the UK, which suggests that GM has completed the process of integrating European production, although as we have already suggested integration will never be quite as thorough as the Ford arrangement, since GM models are tailored for individual markets and are not necessarily identical. In future, smaller models will probably be produced in the UK, with production of larger models confined almost exclusively to the Opel division in West Germany. Final details of GM's plan have not yet been finalised, although news has filtered through of a £1.3 billion Opel expansion programme. Much depends on the state of the UK car market and the discontentment of the labour force. Vauxhall still has a strong marketing

---

1. Similarly the Vauxhall Carlton is basically a Rekord with a 'droop snoot' nose and with a family resemblance to the Chevette and Cavalier. The Royale has only minor styling differences.
2. Codenamed the XP903.
3. Import content of the Chevettes has been reduced to 12½ per cent.

advantage in some of the former colonial territories and elsewhere, an advantage which GM are reluctant to discard and which could persuade the parent company to retain some independent car manufacturing activity in the UK.

GM therefore has a clear choice in its UK production policy. Vauxhall plants are running below their theoretical capacity of around 365,000 cars per year. First, GM can reduce its UK assembly capacity to be consistent with supplying the UK market. In this instance GM will probably choose to expand its existing production facilities and may choose to build new assembly facilities in Yugoslavia, Greece, Turkey or Spain. Secondly, GM can rely on increased utilisation of its UK plants to supply the European market in general. Sourcing of body panels and powertrain units may however come from both Belgium and Germany. Both policies have their attractions. The increased utilisation of existing facilities in Belgium and Germany means that production is more concentrated and that transport costs are minimal. At the moment GM are hedging their bets with no clear decision either way. Once UK plants are manufacturing a model range which is being produced on a European wide (or indeed worldwide) basis, then the UK could in theory make good production shortfalls elsewhere. However as with Ford there are two major obstacles in so doing; low productivity leading to poor plant utilisation and the poor reputation of British made cars in respect of durability, quality and reliability. It therefore seems doubtful whether spare UK production and assembly facilities will prevent the modest expansion of existing facilities outside the UK.

With the introduction of the Carlton and Royale as Vauxhall equivalents of Opel's Rekord and Senator (but with minor styling differences) GM seems to have made a firmer commitment to Vauxhall being a subsidiary of Opel. Although the Carlton is to be produced in the UK, the Royale will always be sourced from outside the UK. The extent of styling differences (particularly the Carlton) and the common styling theme of the Vauxhall range does enable GM's UK subsidiary to supply cars to a broader market than just the UK.

Chrysler

An analysis of the proposed Peugeot-Citroen takeover of Chrysler is provided in Chapter 17. There is unfortunately a certain amount of material in this section which is now out-of-date. An example of this can be seen in the arguments that led to the long run conclusion that Chrysler's chances of survival, on current form, were slim. Nevertheless there is much that is still relevant in the short run, since Peugeot does not take full control until 1981 and the task of integrating Chrysler into the rest of the group will, in any case, extend into a number of years.

Of all the US companies, Chrysler has suffered the most. The main factors which are responsible for this are partly its unfortunate locational strategy, partly the lack of financial strength of its US parent company, and partly because Chrysler was late in its move to Europe and therefore had to be content with what was available. Chrysler's main plants are in France and the UK. The UK has been a poor market, whilst the French market has had a much smaller medium and large car market segment (the latter has in any case been dominated by Citroen and Peugeot). The implication being that the large profits earned in West Germany by the higher mark-up from medium and large cars has not been available to Chrysler.

After the near withdrawal of Chrysler from the UK — which resulted in the £165 million package deal with the UK Government — Chrysler has been systematically integrating its European operations.

Chrysler seemed set on a course midway between the Ford and GM model and production policies. Some models, such as the Alpine (C6) were to have been established as a European wide car. Other models would have been UK or French oriented: with France as the European/technically sophisticated producer, whilst the original plans would have established the UK as the more basic producer servicing the export markets in less developed countries. This pattern has already been established with a new small car. The UK produces the conventional rear wheel drive Sunbeam, whilst the French company produces the more sophisticated Horizon (with front wheel drive). This policy has however now been modified because of the difficulty in selling cars to developing countries; in particular the renewal of the Iran National order may have run into problems. Moreover the new light car that was planned for 1979/80 as a replacement for the Avenger may not be necessary as the Horizon is virtually an Avenger replacement.

The reorganisation of Chrysler (UK) Ltd saw the introduction of a new UK production policy established at a lower overall level of productivity. Ryton (with a much larger capacity) was facilitised to assemble Alpines from French kits at the rate of 40,000 a year. Linwood on the other hand concentrated on the new Sunbeam and the older Avenger. The powertrain plant at Stoke-on-Trent is still kept reasonably busy with the Iran order; but has now been adapted to produce some of the Alpine components.

Before the cancellation of the new light (rear wheel drive) car to be built at Linwood, Chrysler was committed to marketing a daunting list of models in Europe. These include:

Model	Country of Production
Simca 1000 replacement	France
C2/Horizon	France & Spain
C2/Horizon	US with a VW engine
424/Sunbeam	UK
C4[1]	France and/or UK
New light car to be introduced in 1979	UK (but now cancelled)[2]
C6/Alpine/1303/6	France and UK
180/2 litre to be replaced by C9	Now Spain but perhaps UK or France in the future.

1. A possible model somewhere between the Horizon and the Alpine.
2. This model formed part of the agreement with the UK Government.

The new C2 rivals the Escort or more accurately the VW's front wheel drive Golf, whilst the new C9 should re-establish Chrysler's presence in the large car market. The new Simca 1000 (which will be revitalised in the early 1980's) should be a front wheel drive rival to Ford's Fiesta. The announcement in 1977 that Iran National was to add a Peugeot derived model to its range may have been the death blow for the Avenger replacement, although other factors (discussed later) obviously took their toll. Instead a saloon variant of the hatchback C2 (Horizon)[1] or another front wheel drive model will be produced in Ryton — which is now destined to become the front wheel drive producer in the UK. Table 6.5 provides a rough outline of probable Chrysler production.

TABLE 6.5

Chrysler's Production Policy

| | UK | | France | Spain |
	Linwood	Ryton	Poissy	Madrid
Capacity (millions)	0.2	0.2	0.5	0.1
Models				
1977	Sunbeam Avenger Hunter *	Alpine (C6)	Simca 1000-1500 range 1303/4 (C6) Horizon (C2)	180 and 2 litre
early 1980s	Sunbeam ?	Alpine (C6) C2 or C6	Simca 1000 C2, C4, C6	C2, C9

* Assembly now takes place in Dublin, though sourcing is from Linwood and Stoke.

Although the proposed switch of the Avenger replacement to Ryton due to take place early in 1979 marks a fundamental shift in emphasis from the rescue negotiated with the Government, the move has merit. First, Ryton is operating way below capacity levels. Second, Ryton is now used to producing front wheel drive cars. Thirdly, the poor productivity record of Linwood may have featured in the decision making process. In which case, the surplus capacity problem is simply switched to Linwood unless Sunbeam sales manage to soak up the spare capacity.

A more rational short-term production policy may be to shift C2/Horizon assembly to Ryton, transferring all C6/Alpine production to Poissy. Linwood would then concentrate on producing rear wheel drive Sunbeams and Avengers.

1. This car, instead of being the promised Avenger replacement will be the more logical development of producing a four-door plus conventional boot version of the C2/ Horizon along the VW Gold/Derby lines.

Given that Chrysler has mored towards this scheme one may ask how does this change in policy affect Linwood? Table 6.5 shows that in the longer term, with Ryton concentrating on front wheel drive production, Linwood has basically only one product – the Sunbeam. Even this product has a low targeted production[1] – perhaps consistent with the realisation that this model cannot compete with the new breed of Super-Minis. It is still possible that the decision to cancel the new light car will be reversed. This, together with the existing rear wheel drive Sunbeam and Hunter would provide a revitalised model range for exporting to less developed countries. However, if these exports do not occur then one more logical development would be to develop the Simca 1000 (front wheel drive) replacement. Such a model could possibly be a smaller Sunbeam with front wheel drive. This model (call it C1), the C2, perhaps a C4[2], the C6 and the C9 provides a sensible model policy. (The Sunbeam should be dropped).[3] Further economies could be gained by ensuring that two or three engine ranges covered the entire model range. The C9 might also be sourced with a Chrysler US range of engines. The engine range that may be fitted to other models might even be produced in the US or Europe thereby supplying both the US and European versions of, say, the C2 at a considerable cost advantage (although transport costs reduce this advantage). In this model policy, the UK plants might produce the smaller models, whilst France produced the C6, and a more successful larger car (C9). This would leave room for dual sourcing of either the C1,[4] C2, or some other model depending on demand conditions. France was, in this strategy, chosen to produce the larger cars since it can easily supply the German markets where there is a significant large car segment. In this way Chrysler could play the Ford game and become completely integrated. However such a strategy seems remote at the present.

Returning to the question of the possible effects of this switch to Linwood, it can be seen that Chrysler appear to be treating Linwood almost as expendable – its success depending on possible export orders to less developed countries. Why has Linwood been left out in the cold? Although higher transport costs undoubtedly have played a role, the principal reason must be laid at the door of industrial relations problems. Falling productivity, and a hostile and undisciplined labour force may have persuaded Chrysler that Linwood at best is marginal, at worst a liability.[5]

Some observers believe that Chrysler UK are convinced that the company is firmly established towards profitable levels. The reason for this belief lies in the apparent reorganisation of the company which is supposedly organised on a European wide basis. Earlier in Chapter 1 doubts both from Young and Hood[6] and the Expenditure Committee were expressed as to the long run via-

1. Around 30,000 to 70,000 units per annum.
2. A possible model midway between the Horizon and the C6.
3. Old fashioned engineering combined with closeness to the Horizon are the principal reasons.
4. Simca 1000 replacement.
5. It has been rumoured that there have been attempts by union leaders to encourage the labour force to work conscientiously which have been met with indifference. In the first two weeks of June production was 68 per cent of target and the target itself was below capacity.
6. *Chrysler UK: A Corporation in Transition,* by S. Young and N. Hood, Praeger, 1977.

bility of the company. Young and Hood felt that the European integration had not occurred on a sufficiently thorough basis.

The problems associated with the Chrysler strategy must be considered in greater detail. First, whilst some attempt has been made to integrate operations, this process is far from complete. There even seems to be a certain reluctance by the French division to treat UK assembly plants as part of their operations. Both these points are illustrated in an analysis of the Poissy and Ryton operations. For example Poissy (in 1978) will be operating at near capacity with the new C2 (Horizon), the C6, (1303/4), and the existing Simca range. Yet Ryton which has only been facilitised for 40,000 odd units has significant spare capacity. Poissy might claim that it has insufficient machining and pressing capacity. However, taking into account the machining and pressing capacity in the UK (Stoke-on-Trent and Linwood), there would be ample capacity to supply a much larger volume at Ryton. The failure to integrate production is further emphasised by the fact that the C2 (Horizon), C6, and the planned C4 and C9 are very much French/Spanish models. Apart from small scale Alpine (C6) assembly facilities at Ryton, and some component manufacture at Stoke, no other integration has taken place. Of course it could be argued that the replacement for the Avenger (should it prove to be a separate model) might be built entirely in the UK, thus providing a degree of integration. However, it is doubtful whether the French company would be happy in seeing one model completely sourced from the UK.

Thus a major problem for Chrysler Europe is that, despite the theoretical existence of a central management structure for its European operations, in practice it seems sadly lacking. Even more startling are the press rumours of Chrysler being engaged in serious negotiations to build an assembly plant in Austria with a capacity of 100,000 cars per year – whilst spare capacity in Chrysler's UK plants exceeds 100,000 cars. To some extent, this implies that the UK production facilities have been written off; although from the European context, an assembly plant in Austria would strengthen the company. However, the Austrian plans are still only rumours.

A third criticism concerns the model strategy of Chrysler. The line up neither has the succinctness of Ford's range (Fiesta, Cortina, Granada) nor does it have the marketing strength of GM's slight styling differences. Instead it has a built in duplicity (see Table 6.6) – at least for the short run. For example the Avenger and the C2 (Horizon) are to a certain extent covering the same market segment, although the Avenger is of a more conventional engineering design. This criticism merges into the fourth criticism, which concerns economies of scale. The Sunbeam will be produced in the UK at rates somewhere between 30,000 to 70,000 a year. Reference to Table 6.1 demonstrates that this rate of production is low for a volume car – in fact too low to achieve significant economies of scale. This criticism might however be partially answered by pointing out that the Sunbeam shares common components with the Avenger and in this way achieves economies of scale. Nevertheless the combined production of the Avenger and the Sunbeam do not compare with either GM's Kadett/Chevette or Ford's Escort or Fiesta range. Both Young and Hood and the Expenditure Committee reiterate the economies of scale argument. Hence:

Because Chrysler will be smaller than most other European mass producers even when it is integrated it must reduce the number of major items (such as powertrains, axles and body shells) much more drastically than Ford or GM, and source them from single plants. For example, the UK and French operations could make two cars each of a four-model integrated range, and one engine could be manufactured entirely at Stoke, and another at Poissy. Only this sort of right integration will overcome the problem of scale, which, in comparative European terms, will not have been banished entirely. (The Expenditure Committee on Chrysler UK Ltd, paragraph 240, p. 112)

Since the 1975 crisis at Chrysler UK, some headway has been made. Despite the aforementioned criticisms, Chrysler has developed some surprisingly competitive products − the final model of which will be launched in the early 1980s. By this time it is hoped that Chrysler UK should be generating modest profits[1] and Chrysler France should be making healthy profits. However, the extent of Chrysler France's profitability is limited by Renault's strategy (which is one of non-profit making). In Chapter 1 we discussed the Expenditure Committee's attitude; either a new model programme can be financed or the rescue loans can be repaid to the UK Government − but not both. It is in the post-1979 era that GM and Ford will be at their most aggressive with a new range of models; both companies will be drawing upon profits created from the lucrative West German market.

Young and Hood[2] argue that there is sufficient time to remedy the position before the next recession. They argue that it is naive of the Government to recommend that no money should be forthcoming for Chrysler after 1980, pointing out that should the 1975 circumstances arise again, then similar decisions would probably be taken. They recommend that a new and much more detailed agreement, incorporating binding commitments on operational issues and including a planned programme leading to complete integration by the mid-1980s should be negotiated in return for further financial support.

However, Young and Hood's conclusion, that given this reorganisation there is every opportunity for long run viability, is questionable. To be sure there is a greater chance of long run viability, but that is different from saying that long run viability is guaranteed. The structural problems facing Chrysler are two-fold. First, the US parent company itself has spare capacity and is not as profitable as GM or Ford. The parent company does not, for example, have sufficient profits to continue to finance a new model programme in Europe. (Although Europe and the US may, as with the C2/Horizon, share common models.) Secondly, within Europe, Chrysler is locationally at a disadvantage compared with its US rivals. Chrysler has no productive capacity in the lucrative West German market. Its best market, the French market, is

1. Chrysler UK's loss of £22 million in 1977 and the fact that Linwood is still in a mess indicate that modest profits are by no means guaranteed.
2. Op cit.

TABLE 6.6

Chrysler's Model Line-Up in 1978

	CHRYSLER					VW
	Horizon C2	Avenger	Sunbeam 424	Simca 1100	Alpine C6	VW Golf
Wheelbase in inches	99.2	98	95	99.2	102.5	94.5
Length in inches	159.8	161.4	150.8	156	167	146.5
Width in inches	66.2	62.6	63.1	62.3	66	63.5
Height in inches	55.5	55.3	54.9	57	54.7	55.3

Note the similarity in size between the Horizon, Avenger and Simca 1100. The 1975 rescue plant "committed" Chrysler to replacing the Avenger with a new Avenger.

renowned for its love of technical superiority. Therefore Chrysler's products have had to be technically sophisticated, thereby incurring a cost penalty, to remain competitive within this market. The UK market has been one of slow growth and UK production has been marred by poor labour relations. In the final analysis, Chrysler's survival depends on the competitiveness of its products, and there are some question marks over Chrysler's model policy notwithstanding the recent development of some highly competitive models. Where does this leave Chrysler UK? By the mid 1980s, Chrysler's model range will again need revitalising. Both Ford and GM will have launched a very competitive new range of vehicles. Several other European manufacturers will have introduced new models. It is likely that the UK Government will forego repayment of their loans to Chrysler UK, thereby allowing Chrysler, sufficient finance to regenerate new models. However, a recession or a model which is not successful could land Chrysler in another financial crisis. Long run viability would be assured if Chrysler could guarantee substantial exports of its planned rear wheel drive models (the Sunbeam and the abortive Avenger replacement and, perhaps at sometime in the future, a revitalised Hunter). This would ensure that UK capacity was filled. However, such export orders are not assured and may very well go to a company offering a more technically sophisticated car. In the absence of such orders it would appear that rear wheel drive cars may not find a large market within Europe. In this event long run problems can be foreseen for Chrysler UK. The only other alternative would be to rationalise the model range for four or at the maximum five non-competing models which would be single sourced for some models and only dual sourced for models with annual sales of greater than 250,000 odd units. French, Spanish and UK plants would be organised as with Ford in order to minimise overall costs. Full integration would, of course, require additional capital investment of around £100 or £200 million.

At the moment the Iranian order runs until 1980. The conditions for long run viability of Chrysler UK in conclusion are therefore either the continuation of part of the Iranian contract, or the supplying of another country with rear wheel drive cars, or the full integration of UK, French and Spanish plants with a unified European or worldwide range. Chrysler's management must be aware of these conditions and it is unlikely that no action will be taken. However because of financial constraints it is possible that any action will be taken too late. Iran National, the Iranian motor vehicle manufacturer has already signed a contract with Peugeot which does not read well for Chrysler. Thus although long run viability of Chrysler UK is a real possibility, there can be no guarantees. It will only be after 1980 that the imponderables will become sufficiently clear to make a more accurate assessment.

As it happens action was taken and when Chrysler UK looked as if it might break-even or make a profit (for the first time in a number of years), Chrysler's US management decided to attempt to sell the European operation lock, stock and barrel. As pointed out at the beginning of this section, there is very little that can be changed in the short-run, and therefore much of the previous analysis may still be relevant. Questions such as whether the takeover will be beneficial to the UK are deferred until Chapter 17. For the healthy parts of Chrysler's European company, this merger is clearly beneficial. Surgery on the gangrenous parts will inevitably have unpleasant consequences for the UK.

British Leyland – the Only Non-Multinational

If anything British Leyland's policy vis-a-vis Europe has been the complete reverse of the US multinationals. BL now has only one non-UK plant, at Seneffe in Belgium, having disposed of the Italian company Innocenti[1] (which was sold to the state agency GEPI) and the Authi plant (to Seat). Although there were obviously good short-term reasons for closing down both plants (e.g. labour problems, insufficient capacity to meet the assembly requirements of the European factories, lack of a competitive model strategy) the closures were not necessarily in the best long-term interests of the company. BL was the *only* multinational with a toe-hold (however tenuous) in Italy, which could have given the company a strong marketing advantage. Conditions in Spain were rather different. With Ford, Renault, Chrysler and Seat all chasing a small albeit expanding market, BL may have been correct in deciding that the competition was too fierce and that the returns might diminish rapidly.

In the immediate future, BL's Seneffe assembly plant will be completely integrated with the UK operations and could become a one-model car plant rather than assembling a range of models. Capacity is expected to be increased to over 100,000 vehicles per year, which will cost BL about £25 million.

---

1. The contract to supply kits remains – but for how long?

MARKET SHARES AND MODEL POLICY

Once production has been integrated to maximise economies of scale, the market share becomes critical – not on a country by country basis, but for Western Europe as a whole. Figure 6.2 gives the Western European market shares for each of the major manufacturers. Renault, Fiat, Peugeot-Citroen, Ford, VW and GM between them are all fighting for a share somewhere between 7 and 14 per cent of the total market. If the proposed Chrysler/Peugeot –Citroen merger comes off then the new group with an 18 per cent market share effortlessly overtakes Ford and breaks away as the clear leader in an otherwise tightly bunched pack.

FIGURE 6.2

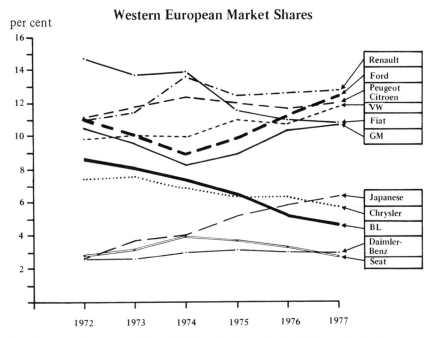

per cent   **Western European Market Shares**

In Chapter 3 some of the CPRS criticisms of the UK car industry were discussed, but an additional comment can be made from an examination of the European market shares. In 1973 – that is, before the real impact of the oil crisis was felt – BL, Ford and GM all lost part of their respective market shares, and Chrysler were quick to follow their lead. What is the explanation for this curious coincidence? Unfortunately, all of the UK car manufacturers had reached the point at which most of their model range was in need of renewal. Since the 1973 slump, Vauxhall has launched the Chevette, the Cavalier and a Victor replacement, while Ford has brought in the Fiesta and new versions of the Escort, the Cortina and the Granada. Chrysler introduced a modified Avenger, Sunbeam and the new Alpine. Only British Leyland has yet to revitalise its model range: the 'new' Mini is due in 1979-80 and the

155

LC10 medium car series should be in production by 1983.

GM and Ford have substantially increased their European market shares as a result of their new model launches, although British Leyland, and to some extent Chrysler, have yet to put their major new model policy programmes into effect. Thus the poor performance of the UK in terms of a deteriorating balance of trade in cars may be attributed to model policy of both British Leyland and the multinationals.

It is interesting to note that Ford's increase in market share, with the exception of the Fiesta, were minor enhancements involving no new power-train, platform, new materials or package developments. It seems that stylistic obsolescence is important within a European context.

Ford, GM and possibly Chrysler are probably now locked in to some sort of phased model policy to avoid giving any one manufacturer a competitive advantage. Although annual model changes are unlikely, severe competition might create a tacit agreement on a policy of simultaneous model changes. If British Leyland had been in a stronger position, the model phase problem which arose in 1973 might not have been so acute, but the fact remains that existing BL models are either outdated or uncompetitive (certainly in a pan-European context).

MARKET SEGMENTS

We have already discussed the relative size of various market segments. Table 6.7 gives the size of these segments for Western Europe as a whole and for the UK, France and West Germany. While the French market is clearly dominated by the small car, the West German market evidently favours a larger car. The most popular car in the UK at the moment is the 'light' model of the Escort type. Overall, the medium and large car segments dominate the West European market. As these models are also the most profitable units to produce in volume, it will be in this area that the fiercest competition will be encountered, particularly between the three US multinationals.

One factor that is likely to change in future years is the extent to which the US multinationals emanate the highly profitable strategy of Daimler Benz. Figure 6.3 illustrates how the specialist car/taxi image of the company combined with a strong CV model line-up has bred the most profitable European company. The US multinationals will surely try to latch on to the relevant market segments which have allowed the Mercedes brand name to have a high mark-up. If this occurs even on a minor scale, then the US multinationals will in effect be moving up market. The repricing of the latest Ford Granada illustrates that sales can actually increase with a price rise, although the face-lift can be argued to have 'differentiated' the product. Nevertheless the Granada has moved upmarket and one can expect all the US multinationals to continue to say that the most of the US multinationals business will be in the medium priced cars, although part of the product range will attempt to cream off the Mercedes type profits.

FIGURE 6.3

Total Automotive Profits Before Taxes
(in millions of US dollars)

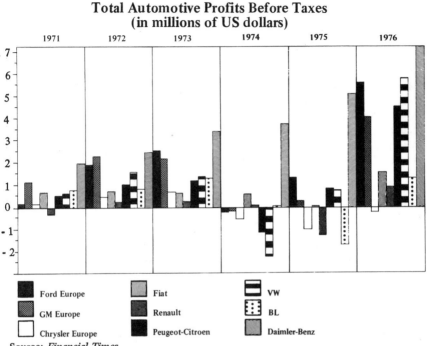

Source: *Financial Times.*
Note: These figures differ marginally from those in Table 3.9.

CONCLUSIONS

The US multinationals will undoubtedly battle for dominance in the large and medium car segments which account for over 50 per cent of the French and West German markets, although they represent only 45 per cent of the UK market. The UK has a much larger light car segment, the largest in Europe, which means that products specifically tailored for the UK market (e.g. Escort/ Chevette) will not find as large a market elsewhere. To accommodate these variations most of the US multinationals have introduced slight product differences. The Chevette, for example, is marketed as a more compact car than the Escort, while the Cavalier is slightly smaller than the Cortina. If we take the European market as a whole, competition will be fiercest in the light, small and medium car segments. Old marketing images will be transformed and European production will be more fully integrated and equipped to meet the demands of particular markets. Ford and GM will concentrate on the West German market, while Chrysler focuses on the French market. BL — with no plant in either of these markets — will have to avoid direct conflict with the multinationals if it is to have any chance of success. It is Chrysler's misfortune that the locations it chose (rather late in the game) were not particularly good ones. The combined strengths of Peugeot-Citroen and Renault present a formidable

157

TABLE 6.7

Market Segments

	1972	1973	1974	1975	1976	1977
Western Europe						
Market Size						
(million)	9.2	9.3	8.1	8.3	9.4	9.9
Mini to Small (%)	21.2	22.6	28.3	25.6	25.1	27.5[a]
Light (%)	27.9	26.8	25.3	26.0	23.4	21.6[a]
Medium (%)	22.0[a]	23.0[a]	22.8	23.1	26.0	25.6[a]
Large (%)	20.0[a]	27.0[a]	15.5	17.2	18.1	17.9[a]
UK						
Market Size						
(million)	1.6	1.7	1.3	1.2	1.3	1.3
Mini to Small (%)	10.6	11.5	15.0	15.7	15.0	16.7
Light (%)	35.0	33.0	32.3	24.7	32.5	28.8
Medium (%)	28.5	28.5	27.7	26.4	29.2	29.6
Large (%)	17.0	18.2	16.4	15.5	11.5	17.7
West Germany						
Market Size						
(million)	2.1	2.0	1.7	2.1	2.3	2.5
Mini to Large (%)	9.8	9.8	11.8	12.8	12.9	15.3
Light (%)	26.6	26.4	27.2	26.5	22.8	19.7
Medium (%)	18.7	24.0	24.6	23.6	27.3	26.6
Large (%)	32.8	26.7	21.8	23.3	24.2	25.8
France						
Market Size						
(million)	1.6	1.8	1.5	1.5	1.9	1.9
Mini to Small (%)	26.8	29.1	39.9	36.3	33.0	37.0[a]
Light (%)	19.4	18.5	15.7	15.3	12.8	10.5[a]
Medium (%)	31.2	30.3	25.8	27.0	31.2	31.5[a]
Large (%)	16.8	16.4	14.7	18.6	20.1	18.6[a]

[a]Estimates

Note: Difference between the sum of the columns and 100 is accounted for by the executive, luxury and speciality segments.

competitive obstacle within the French market which Chrysler — with the best will in the world — will find difficult, if not impossible, to overcome.

Further discussion of British Leyland is left until the next chapter. For the multinationals who have provided the focus for this chapter, one must express a guarded optimism. Ford — industrial relations problems apart — appears to be going from strength to strength, which bodes well for the UK, as a substantial proportion of the company's West European production is based here. Assuming that the readjustments at Vauxhall are now complete, one can hope that the company will follow in the more impressive footsteps of its German cousin. The switch may mean a smaller car component work force but it could also mean more work and greater job security for assembly workers. What the UK division of General Motors has lost in terms of car production it has gained in an expanded CV operation. Chrysler's recovery, meanwhile, whilst initially impressive may have been a false start. Although in the short term, the company seems to be in a much more competitive position; despite a continuing shortage of funds it has managed to reorganise itself on a new strategy in record time though this reorganisation has not gone far enough.

Manufacturer's reactions are discussed at greater length in Chapter 8, in which an attempt is made to match demand and supply considerations. In the course of that discussion, Chrysler's recovery is seen as only a short-term phenomenon, but despite a possible failure in this one respect, the prospects for all UK based multinationals are good in the short run. The future for British Leyland is unfortunately a very different story. The future of Chrysler's UK plants is returned to in Chapter 17.

CHAPTER 7

BRITISH LEYLAND

INTRODUCTION

The appointment of Michael Edwardes as the new chairman and his subsequent reorganisation was met with dismay by the author for two reasons. First, a rewrite was necessary. Secondly, Edwardes actually carried out changes and proposals which were advocated in this chapter — with one or two exceptions. Having had our limelight stolen, this chapter concentrates on the analysis of Edwardes' plans and possible alternatives open to BL in the future. Two points must be made at the outset. First, there is no way BL can hope to catch up on its original targets and Edwardes has made this clear. Second, there will be a political problem in reducing the BL Cars workforce from its current level of 130,000 plus to 60,000 to 90,000[1] employees required to produce its planned output. It is to be also hoped that BL Cars will, in the future, be dealt with in the context of an overall industrial strategy. We start with recent history from which it is very evident that decisions were made on different criteria.

Recent History

By Summer 1977 the first phase of the Ryder plan for British Leyland had been implemented, although not without serious delays. The original plan called for a series of moratoriums on capital investment, making further infusions of government money conditional on improvements in productivity (implying fewer production losses as a result of industrial action). Productivity did not improve and there were delays in making further grants available as a result. Further, the implementation programme envisaged by the Ryder Report may have been too ambitious. Certainly, the report was over confident in its estimate of the engineering and managerial resources available and falsely assumed that government ownership would lead to an improvement in industrial relations.

The most serious interruption occurred in February-March 1977 when the toolmakers went on strike to try to establish differentials — which had been prohibited during Phase II of the Labour Government's incomes policy. The strike was concluded in a further round of negotiations, but the Prime Minister and Varley, the Secretary of State for Industry, joined the Leyland management[2] and the NEB in issuing a final ultimatum to the recalcitrant Leyland toolmakers, a group whose strike record until then had been exemplary. At the same time, the NEB decided to undertake a thorough review of Leyland's operations, although that decision was not a direct result of the toolmaker's strike. The issue now was whether continued support for the Leyland group

1. That is a productivity level of 9 to 14 cars per year per man. The latter figure seems high now but may become the European norm in the 1980s and 1990s. *It should be made clear that these are the authors estimates and not those of BL.*
2. As it was then called.

could be justified in view of its failure to improve its performance or implement the recommendations of the Ryder Report. The review was undertaken by BL itself, with two NEB observers. Leyland's findings were completed by the end of April, the NEB submitted an interim report to the Department of Industry in early May, and Varley outlined his proposals in the House of Commons on 26 May 1977. The NEB report reiterated the findings of the Ryder Report, stressing that if the conditions set out in that report – notably a substantial improvement in productivity and industrial relations – could be achieved then it would still be in the best interests of both BL and the country as a whole to retain the group as a producer of Volume and Specialist cars. The NEB report recommended that a final decision on future BL car production strategy should be deferred pending the results of work on a revised corporate plan for BL designed to place industrial relations in BL on a surer footing. The report also concluded that the Mini replacement programme had a vital part to play in re-establishing BL as a volume car producer, and the NEB was authorised to allow work on the programme to resume as soon as tangible progress had been made towards improvements in industrial relations.

The NEB was accorded more direct control over the future direction of BL policy following the Lib-Lab pact in July 1977,[1] when the next £100m tranche was granted. Subsequently further production problems, partly caused by industrial relations problems in component suppliers, have necessitated the borrowing of £50m out of the £100m allocated, in order to finance current operations.

However, the final decision on the future strategy of BL was never taken. Events once again conspired against the company. By Autumn 1977 urgent action was clearly necessary in order to prevent a further deterioration in market share coupled with increases in strike losses.[2] The necessary action finally resolved itself in the form of the new Chairman, Michael Edwardes, who was appointed in October 1977. In an effort to make BL more manageable a certain amount of decentralisation took place. A more modest Corporate Plan was then put together in February 1978 and both the NEB and the Lib-Lab overseers decided to support the plan and in effect issue BL with £450 million of equity. Further changes and new plans will inevitably be formulated for BL.

NEB

Very early on in its life the NEB was saddled with two large rescue operations – BL and Rolls Royce (1971) Ltd. At its inception, the NEB was instructed to invest as a major shareholder in small-to-medium size profitable enterprises, applying desirability to the UK as the criteria for any such investment. Yet BL and Rolls Royce were veritable giants whose immediate cash requirements absorbed virtually the entire NEB budget. The NEB has always indicated that it would be an irresponsible use of public funds to invest in projects with no long-run chance of viability, and it is therefore still possible that the NEB

1. The Liberals were keen to give the NEB more interference – free control over BL.
2. BL Cars budgeted output for 1977 was 950,000 vehicles, in actuality only 739,000 vehicles were produced.

would consider closing down BL cars or handing the operation over to the Department of Industry should the Board consider that the long-run viability of the car operation was unlikely. The fact that the NEB has not withdrawn from BL does not imply that they are unconcerned: it is simply too soon to pull out, the attitude being that BL cars must be given more breathing space and Michael Edwardes a fair chance before any far-reaching decisions are taken.[1] Although there will be a review in 1979 a major decision is not expected to be taken until 1980. If BL has not by then reached its more modest targets a fundamental rethink might be made.

Although the NEB is a multi-staged management structure, the board would find it impossible to manage BL directly. At the moment, BL Cars report to BL, which in turn reports to the NEB, who submit a final report to the Department of Industry. As a result, detailed managerial decisions are often debated on the floor of the House. The NEB sees itself as nearer to a finance house (although it *is* more than just a finance house) than an intrinsic part of BL's management structure. To the extent that the NEB has been instrumental in shaping the role it performs, it probably sees its function as one of setting longer-term parameters and monitoring progress towards the ultimate goal of achieving full commercial viability for BL.

In line with the recommendations of the Ryder Report (discussed below) and subsequent revisions the NEB is determined to establish BL as a competitive manufacturer and a commercial force to be reckoned with in Europe. Since Ryder's departure from the Board, and the appointment of Michael Edwardes as the new Chairman, there have been signs of a new approach to the problem of British Leyland, although the Ryder Report itself had provided the impetus for the massive reorganisation that has taken place since 1975 and which must form the basis of future plans.

The arrival of a new chairman for BL in October 1977, Michael Edwardes, meant a boost for BL. Edwardes made it plain at the start that he would not be tied by past policy decisions and that he would be taking a more active role in reorganising BL. At the same time, both the Government and the NEB have made it clear that it is up to management now to sort out its own problems. The closure of the Speke plant is a case in point; despite muted howls of protest, little sympathy was provided by either the media or the politicians. One of the reasons for this lack of sympathy is Speke's appalling record. For example although potentially the plant has a capacity of around 100,000[2], maximum output has never topped the 30,000 car figure. Low productivity is not the only problem experienced at Speke. Quality control problems also abound. US evidence tends to suggest that the TR7 has warranty claims several times greater than BL's worst competitor. Also one in every two cars had to have substantial warranty work. Manning levels are high, particularly on maintenance jobs where job descriptions are extremely narrow. Coupled to this the TR7 was not a successful model. If US regulations had gone to plan then open top cars would have been banned. As it was the older MGB,

1. Although the Department of Industry might be obliged by its political overseers to instruct the NEB either to retain Leyland cars under any circumstances or to assume direct responsibility for the management of the car operation.
2. In fairness to the Speke's labour force, they have never been set targets at that level.

163

Midget and Spitfire enjoyed continued success which cut into the potential market for TR7's.

A brief description of BL and an elaboration of what those problems were, is now provided.

DESCRIPTION IN EARLY 1978

In line with the Ryder plan, employment at the major Leyland plants fell from from nearly 130,000 employees to an all-time low of 116,000 towards the end of 1975, although it crept up again to approximately 135,000 by the end of 1977. Table 7.1 explains BL's present plant structure. Longbridge produces the Allegro and the Mini, assembling a number of units in KD form for export to the GEPI-controlled Innocenti plant in Italy and to BL's own assembly plant at Seneffe in Belgium. The Marina, Maxi, Princess and MG models are produced at Cowley, although final assembly of MG sports cars takes place at Abingdon. Rover uses its original Meteor works, taking only a small part of the available capacity, and the new £90 million plant, both at Solihull. Triumph plants have been replanned so that Triumph sports cars[1] are produced in Liverpool with production of all other models in the range centred at Canley. Jaguar cars are produced at Browns Lane in Coventry. In addition, there are two pressing plants at Swindon and Castle Bromwich, with pressing facilities at Liverpool and Cowley. Body-building operations can be carried out at Swindon, Cowley, Longbridge, Solihull, the Meteor works, Liverpool and Canley. Only the Jaguar plant at Browns Lane in Coventry has no facilities for body building.

As things stand, the Leyland plant arrangement is far from satisfactory. Many of the plants are working at only a fraction of the theoretical maximum two-shift capacity, and yet some models are still in short supply owing to Leyland's inflexible production conditions. It is almost impossible for Leyland to recover lost production or make good delays in production, and yet there is little doubt that the company currently has excess capacity.

Table 7.2 gives the production record by major assembly plant for the whole of Leyland, together with production by model for the various ranges. Both Longbridge and Cowley are working well below capacity, while the new Rover plant at Solihull has only one of its three assembly tracks working at full capacity following the closure of the Rover P6 series.[2] Liverpool too was working below full strength until the strike at Speke (September 1977 to February 1978) worsened an already poor situation. BL's performance in the domestic UK market has been disastrous; the company's market share has declined steadily. Many of the models in production are simply too old or too poorly designed (with the recent exception of the new Rover saloon and certain other models), or technologically obsolete. The BL product has acquired a reputation for unreliability. The decision to cut the number of retail outlets from some

1.   Plant number 1 produced TR7 and Dolomite pressings, whilst plant number 2 produced TR7s.
2.   Whilst this was true in 1977, all three assembly lines were in operation in 1978, and production was up by 100 per cent in early 1978.

TABLE 7.1

Leyland Cars Plants Details

Assembly Plants (Pedigree)	Estimated Number of Employees '000	Estimated Maximum Two-Shift Capacity '000	Models Produced	
Longbridge complex + adjacent works (Austin)	28	300-350	Mini,LC8 Allegro	
Cowley North and South Works (Morris)	23	350-400	Marina LC10 Maxi Princess MG	
Meteor Works (Rover)	8	100	Land-Rover Range Rover	
Solihull	8	160	Rover Saloon + sports models	
Canley & Tile Hill	10	100	Dolomite Spitfire	Production split is not as
Liverpool-Speke and Woodend Avenue (Triumph)	7	50-100	TR7 Spitfire	straight- forward as indicated here.
Browns Lane (Jaguar)	9	40	XJ6 - 12 XJS	
Drews Lane and Common Lane (BMC)	7	30	Vans	
Seneffe[a]	7	50-70	Allegro	
Total	107	About 1,200[b]		

a.   Allegro production has been transferred to Seneffe to make way for plant modernisation at Longbridge, where the new Mini will eventually be produced.
b.   Though capacity is actively being reduced in future plans.
N.B. TR7 production has been transferred to Canley with the closure of the Speke plant.

5,000 in 1968 to 2,000 coupled with slow delivery times for certain products
has not helped to re-establish BL's market share to its former levels.

TABLE 7.2
Leyland Cars Production by Major Assembly Plant in '000s

Plant	1972	1973	1974	1975	1976	1977	1985 Ryder Plan (Estimated Capacity)
(a) Cars and Land Rovers[a]							
Longbridge	439	302	233	254	286	285	400+
Cowley (+ Abingdon)	256	369	326	195	224	213	400+[b]
Meteor Works (including all Land-Rovers)	96	83	80	76	76	55	100+
Solihull (new plant)	–	–	–	–	included in above figure	23	150
Triumph	139	130	98	95	113	77	100
Browns Lane (Jaguar)	24	28	36	22	24	25	40
TOTAL	954	912	773	645	724	678	1,190+
(b) Commercial Vehicles[c]							
Car Derived Vans[d] (Cowley and Longbridge)	48	40	39	41	34	40	50
Drews Lane and Common Lane	17	18	14	11	17	20	20
(c) TOTAL VEHICLES	1,019	970	826	697	775	738	1,260+

a. 1977 Land Rover production was 51,305 compared with 1976 figure of 58,066
b. Capacity could be increased to 500,000 or 600,000
c. CVs produced by the car division only
d. Includes Taxis produced at Cowley (1977=2,629)
NB. Interim targets for 1980 probably envisaged about 500,000 vehicles for both the home and export markets.

Strikes have been as disastrous for Leyland as the loss of the domestic market share. Production losses as a result of either internal or external industrial disputes have been considerable (see Table 7.5 below). The Ryder plan hoped to improve industrial relations (and hence productivity) by giving BL car workers a greater say in the management of the company. In theory at least, industrial democracy would improve industrial relations; eventually production losses through internal strikes would virtually disappear. Production losses arising either from industrial disputes outside of BL or as a result of supply difficulties have diminished in importance in recent years. In 1976, for example, only 19 per cent of total lost production could be attributed to non-Leyland problems, and in the first six months this had fallen to less than 5 per cent. This compares to figures of between 25 per cent and 40 per cent in the early 1970s. After the toolmakers strike which almost closed BL Cars in February and March 1977, production losses from April to June of 1977 were in fact lower than in many previous three-monthly periods, low enough, in fact, to convince the NEB and the Government that the BL car division was at least capable of sustaining periods of industrial peace — but more of that later.

On the export front, BL Cars have achieved notable success due partly to the efforts of the International Division (which acted as a separate profit centre) and partly to the rapid devaluation of the pound, although current UK inflation will soon eradicate this temporary 'advantage'. Table 7.6 gives export figures for each of the BL car divisions from 1972 to the present; exports are currently nearing the 1972-3 levels and show every sign of remaining strong, but the economic climate is changing rapidly and it must not be assumed that BL's present export success will continue indefinitely.

INVESTMENT DELAYS

Until recently all Leyland investment projects over £5 million expenditure had to be referred to the NEB, while all projects requiring more than £25 million were referred to the Department of Industry. Within these limitations, however, it is important to remember that if a strike is severely crippling the company, any spare cash at hand may be used to finance existing operations rather than fund a new project. Nevertheless, BL's management have scrupulously observed the principle of cash conservation, arguing that as they are unable to predict how long any one strike will last, they are therefore reluctant to ask for more funds to finance current operations, as this would spark off a political row. To avoid that outcome, they have made every effort to save what cash they already have, often conducting their own investment moratoriums in addition to those already insisted upon by the NEB and the Department of Industry. In effect, BL have imposed their own 'freeze' and in doing so have affected both volume and quality car productions. There have been few improvements in either industrial relations or productivity, and as a matter of policy this has in turn created investment delays. The longer much-needed investment is delayed, the longer it will take for BL to become profitable — and any further time lag will involve additional government funds to prop up the company in the period of transition. Although the picture is a gloomy one, there is room for some optimism.

167

TABLE 7.3

	Production			Allocation for Export			Allocation for Home Market		
	1975	1976	1977	1975	1976	1977	1975	1976	1977
Cars									
Austin Morris									
Mini	167	179	190	79	106	120	88	73	70
Allegro	87	107	95	32	46	39	55	61	55
Marina	87	95	90	20	24	13	67	71	77
Princess	29	45	48	3	11	9	26	34	39
Maxi	35	37	32	5	6	3	30	31	29
MG	40	47	43	31	38	33	9	9	10
Obsolete Models	4	–	–	2	–	–	2	–	–
	448	508	498	172	231	217	276	277	281
Rover Triumph									
P6 (2000) + SD1	14	17	26[a]	2	2	8	12	15	18
Dolomite	34	36	26	5	2	2	29	34	24
2000/2500	18	17	8	6	7	5	12	10	3
Sports	43	60	43[b]	38	46	30	5	14	13
Total Rover Triumph (excluding Land-Rovers)	109	130	103	52	57	45	57	73	58
Jaguar	22	24	25	12	14	13	10	10	12
TOTAL CARS	579	664	626	236	301	275	343	363	351
Land-Rovers									
Range Rover	11	10	10	8	8	8	3	2	2
Land-Rovers (Cars)[c]	14	13	12	13	12	11	1	1	1
Land-Rovers (CVs)[d]	39	36	30	29	26	22	9	10	8
TOTAL LAND ROVERS	64	58	52	50	46	41	13	12	11
CVs (light)									
Car Derived Vans	41	34	38	9	13	12	32	21	26
Vans (Sherpa)	11	17	20	2	6	7	9	11	13
Taxi	2	3	3	–	–	–	2	3	3
TOTAL CVs	54	54	61	11	19	19	43	35	42
TOTAL VEHICLES	697	775	738	298	366	335	399	409	404
Jaguar Rover Triumph (excluding MG)	195	212	180	114	117	99	80	95	81

a. This includes 3,717 Rover P6 (2000s).
b. This is split into 17,716 Spitfires, 84 TR6s, 22,934 TR7s and 1,836 Stags.
c. Classified as cars – Land-Rover Station Wagons.
d. Classified as CVs – Other Land-Rovers.

QUALITY

Why is BL's quality so poor? Quality is a function of available resources, and at the moment BL do not have the resources – financial or otherwise – to improve the quality of their product rapidly. Quality undoubtedly suffers

TABLE 7.4

Market Share in % of the UK Market

	1975	1976	1977	1978
Mini	7.1	6.3	4.6	4.6
Allegro	5.3	4.2	4.2	3.9
Marina	6.6	5.5	5.0	5.2
Princess	2.4	2.5	2.3	2.3
Maxi	2.3	2.6	2.0	2.0
MG	0.8	0.7	0.7	0.8
Total Austin/Morris	*24.5*	*21.7*	*18.8*	*18.7*
Rover Saloons	1.3	0.8	1.3	2.0
Range Rover	0.2	0.2	0.1	0.1
Dolomite	2.5	2.3	1.9	1.4
2000/2500	1.0	0.8	0.5	0.1
TR7/Spitfire	0.2	0.5	1.0	0.3
Stag	0.2	0.2	0.1	0.1
Jaguar	1.0	0.8	0.7	0.8
Rover/Triumph & Jaguar	*6.4*	*5.6*	*5.6*	*4.8*
Sports	*1.2*	*1.3*	*1.8*	*1.7*
Specialist (Inc Sports & Princess)	*9.6*	*8.7*	*8.6*	*7.9*
TOTAL	30.9	27.4	24.33	23.48
UK Market ('000s)	1,194	1,285	1,324	1,592

from old machinery with poor tolerances, the lack of coherent standards and guidance and the absence of either suitable measuring equipment or the personnel to implement quality checks and rectify mistakes. Quality control procedures were finally established only in the Summer of 1977,[1] covering both design and manufacture. Quality improvements in product design are obviously not a matter of overnight transformation: the effect of the recent changes will not really be felt until the 1980s, although the new Mini will certainly benefit from greater attention to product design. Stronger links have now been forged between product design and manufacture. Much remains to be done, but at least the major problem areas have been identified. On the manufacturing side, poor machinery, inadequate quality control systems and frequent breaks in production have all taken their toll in the past. All in all, quality is still poor but should be vastly improved when the new quality control systems are fully implemented.[2]

OTHER PROBLEMS

BL's car division has obviously suffered from other managerial and technical problems. The new Solihull plant is a case in point, where the introduction

1. Although a Quality Index was set up in early 1976.
2. A pre publication comment pointed out that consistent production is also an important factor.

TABLE 7.5

Effect of Disputes

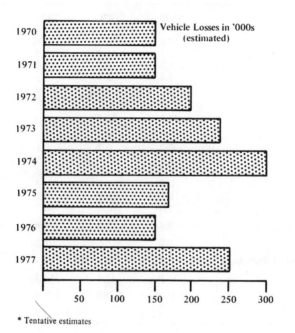

* Tentative estimates

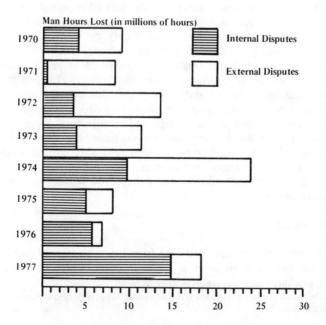

TABLE 7.6

BL Cars – Exports of Cars and Land Rovers in '000s

	1972	1973	1974	1975	1976	1977 estimated	1985a Ryder Plan estimated
Austin-Morris cars	292	274	242	172	206	217	385
Rover-Triumph cars	36	48	48	60	58	56	120
Jaguar cars	13	17	19	12	16	16	20
Land Rovers	37	34	33	43	39	40	50
Car derived Vans + Sherpa	11	10	11	11	16	20	25
TOTAL	389	383	353	298	335	349	600

a. Interim figures for 1980 would envisage only about 500,000 vehicles for 1980.

of manning and productivity standards, the problems of component supply and the creation of additional paint plant capacity at Castle Bromwich have all proceeded at a disappointingly slow pace. The problems to be dealt with at Solihull are the problems that will have to be resolved on a larger scale throughout BL, but this begs an important question. Is there enough time to overcome these difficulties, or will other factors and other decisions intervene before solutions have been found — despite Michael Edwardes rearguard action to save BL?

Managers and engineers are in short supply at BL. The engineering staff shortage in particular can be measured in terms of thousands of personnel rather than merely hundreds, and is nearing the point at which it becomes critical. In the past, the absence of a dynamic new model policy and the fragmentation of BL's engineering service meant that very few engineers were required. In any event, financial crises, low pay and poor working conditions made BL an unattractive proposition as an employer. BL's once legendary engineering strength has been grossly depleted, and it may not be restored to full strength much before the mid-1980s. Without a full complement of qualified engineering staff, BL will simply take longer to complete the vital preliminary work involved in the production of a new model. Elsewhere, the gestation process is usually in the region of three to four years. The same process at BL, however, could well take up to five or six years.

We conclude this section with the observation that although much remained to be done before the appointment of Michael Edwards, BL had at least made some of the right moves in some of the right directions. But it had not moved fast enough or far enough. To demonstrate this, a description of how far it was expected to go in the first place is now given.

THE RYDER PLAN

Since 1975, most of the detailed planning and nearly all of the major policy recommendations concerning BL's future have been based on the proposals embodied in the Ryder Report. It is virtually impossible to discuss BL Cars in any meaningful sense without reference to either the Ryder report or to the other published reports, and we will therefore devote this section to an analysis of all the published reports concerning Leyland. In reading between the lines, we hope to build up a detailed picture of the precise quantitive plans.

In its final form, the Ryder plan proposed the large scale injection of public funds to enable BL to carry out a massive capital investment programme (see Table 7.7), although there is now a great deal of evidence to suggest that the capital requirement was seriously under-estimated by a factor of between 20 and 50 per cent. In 1977,[1] for example, planned expenditure on the new Mini and other projects alone would have amounted to over £200 million, whereas the Ryder Report allowed for only £167 million. In addition to the capital investment programme, BL's working capital requirement is sizeable. In 1976, BL as a whole had to finance not only a £113 million capital

---

1. Without investment moratoriums.

investment programme, but also a £205 million increase in working capital. The Ryder Report envisaged an increase of working capital of some £260 million (1975 prices) over their eight year planning cycle which again would appear to be an under estimation.

TABLE 7.7

BL Cars: Capital Investment Programme as per Ryder (£, 000's)

	1975	1976	1977	1978	1979	1980	1981	1982	Total
1975 Prices	83	92	126	169	142	129	110	78	929
In inflated prices	83	106	167	249	249	262	255	204	1,575

Current estimates of total capital investment programme required to maintain Ryder plan = £2.0 billion in 1977 prices spread over 10 years.

Ryder's model policy for BL cars concentrated on plans for product rationalisation, which apparently consisted of a complete range of cars covering the Mini series and the medium, large, quality and luxury segments. Coupe or sports derivatives were planned for each segment. The entire range was to have been established by 1982, but subsequent delays suggest that 1985 would now be a more realistic date.

BL, meanwhile, had been actively considering a new model, the small quality saloon usually referred to as the SD2. This was to have been produced at the Solihull plant, but critics of the plan felt it might be wiser to abandon the idea for a completely new product unrelated to any other BL model range and concentrate instead on creating a carefully marketed product wholly based on the existing BL medium range.[1]

The future of the medium car range itself is by no means settled. BL's plan focused on a 3-model medium range with two saloon bodies and a coupe, but this 3-model plan was considered to have only marginal priority and has vanished in the welter of policy review changes.

The Ryder plan made a number of firm recommendations on the need to reorganise the BL Car engineering section, by bringing together on to one site all of the product planning, design, styling and vehicle engineering skills required for effective product development.[2] The Jaguar engineering department opposed the move and remained independent.

In line with the Ryder report, BL announced that assembly work at the Canley plant would cease; the complex would eventually switch to components manufacture. The plan envisaged other smaller plants such as Speke Hall (Liverpool) could be closed whilst a compensating increase in capacity could be made elsewhere.[3] It seems unlikely that BL's structure will alter

1. This decision was taken in 1975.
2. This was the £100 million Engineering Centre which would have employed 5,000 people under Spencer King's direction.
3. This has now been carried out.

greatly once Cowley and Longbridge have been established as the two major production centres. Some plants which have hitherto concentrated on production of volume cars may switch to quality car production.

The Ryder Report also emphasised the need not only for greater product rationalisation (at the time of the Report BL were producing 9 distinct car body types and 12 basic engines) but also for a much wider use of common components, suspensions and structures, without abandoning or jeapordising those market sectors where some vestige of a reputation for quality remained. If anything, the concern for a distinctive, competitive product should extend to all model ranges, while attempts should be made to lessen competition between different BL models within the same market segments. This emphasis on quality and distinction at the top and bottom ranges of the market conflicts with BL's own interest in developing the new 'basic' Mini and the company's general concern to develop a range of products for the lower end of the market. Although the Ryder Report also asserted that BL should be able to compete effectively in the production of volume cars, most of the evidence suggests that direct competition with either of the two rapidly-growing Japanese car giants (as suggested in the Ryder Report) would be disastrous for BL.

At the very beginning of the Ryder Report the committee noted that 'vehicle production is the kind of industry which ought to remain an essential part of the UK's economic base'. In its present form, it is certainly a major employer and it makes a substantial contribution to the balance of payments, but these two considerations alone are not enough to justify BL as a volume car producer when the indications are that it would function more efficiently in a different role. And even allowing for the Ryder Report's concern to maintain levels of employment, the measures proposed would have meant substantially fewer jobs unless the Ryder sales assumptions are realised (see Table 7.8). Many observers felt that the Ryder forecast for UK sales (33 per cent of the market as opposed to the existing 24 per cent) was unrealistically high and that export sales assumptions are similarly over optimistic.

Industrial Relations

The Ryder Report — even in its abridged form — had a great deal to say on the topic of industrial relations. The Ryder Report assumed that longer-term improvements in industrial relations would lead to improvements in productivity.

However, the interim objectives of the Ryder Report were quite modest: a substantial reduction in the number of collective bargaining units within BL and a common reduction in the number of renewal dates for wage settlements, coupled with an attempt at industrial democracy which was to be organised through a newly created structure of joint management councils, committees and conferences. Also postulated under the global heading of industrial relations was the ill-fated tranche concept; each new injection of Government finance at each stage would depend upon 'evidence of a contribution both by the workforce and the management to the reduction of industrial disputes and improved productivity' (p.42). BL's internal managerial targets in conjunction with both the NEB and the Department of Industry went far beyond

TABLE 7.8

Estimates of Vehicle Sales for Leyland Cars as per Ryder Plan

		1975	1976	Ryder Plan 1980	Ryder Plan 1985
1.	UK market for cars (millions)	1.19	1.29	1.6	1.7
2.	Market share %	30.9	27.4	33	33
3.	Home sales of cars '000s	369	352	528	561
4.	CV sales at home '000s[a] (incl. Land-Rovers)	53	46	60	65
5.	Western European market for cars (millions)	7.2	7.8	9	10+
6.	Market share %	1.7	2.0	3.5	4
7.	Car sales in Europe '000s	125	159	315	400+
8.	US car sales '000s	76	75	90	85
9.	Rest of the world car sales '000s	36	45	40	40
10.	Stock changed + statistical errors '000s	7	–	–	–
11.	Land Rovers exports '000s	43	39	50	50
12.	Car derived vans and Sherpa van exports '000s	11	17	23	25
13.	Total exports (7+8+9+10+11+12) in '000s	298	335	518	600
14.	Total sales (13+3+4) in '000s	720	733	1,106	1,226

a.   CVs produced by BL Car division

the interim proposals outlined in the Ryder Report. Building upon Ryder's interim objectives; a much greater move towards centralisation and unification was envisaged.

The principal recommendations were:

(i) Synchronisation of pay claims to a common review date for annual wage agreements;
(ii) Group-wide grade and pay structures and the adoption of parity in all Leyland car grades;
(iii) Centralised bargaining rather than plant bargaining;
(iv) The introduction of group-wide incentive schemes.

With hindsight these extended proposals may have been too ambitious; an intermediate step of plant bargaining may have been easier to implement. To date it has taken longer than originally planned to introduce the proposed reforms — although some progress has been made. Group-wide grade and pay structures and incentive schemes have been approved, but plans to synchronise pay claims seem to have been jeopardised by pay policy. Discussions on central-ised bargaining are continuing, although there is a split on the issue between those who accept that parity cannot be achieved without centralised bargaining and those who believe that traditional plant bargaining should continue. BL's security-of-earnings offer, guaranteeing earnings for three weeks during a lay-off has also been accepted by the unions in February 1978 after months of discussion.[1]

Whether enough tangible progress towards industrial relation reforms has been or will be made may be irrelevant. Although structural reforms of the sort discussed above may lessen the burden of separate negotiations and the need to relate one award to another, they may not solve the fundamental problem of low productivity caused by industrial action. Wage bargaining procedures have no effect on the scale of wage demands. Massive demands could still result in strikes, and production losses would still be inevitable. Improvements in management-worker relations could, however, improve the production flow and might also have a positive effect on product quality. Set against this is the possibility that even if the reform package is fully implemented, the reforms themselves could be the source of renewed conflict as different pressure groups resort to industrial action to achieve what they have failed to achieve around a negotiating table.

More recently, several other industrial relations problems have emerged. Rover employees at the new Solihull plant, have expressed reluctance to work night shifts.[2] Longbridge toolroom employees have criticised the newly installed robotic multi-welding machines, partly because they felt that the new worker-participation procedures have been used to force acceptance of technological change. In the past, introduction of radically new technology would have involved 'money-on-the-table' negotiations. With, say, £1½ billion[3] of capital investment still to be undertaken in BL Cars, the problems experienced at Longbridge (with the introduction of a new Mini) may be the tip of the iceberg. The principle of centralised bargaining has been sharply criticised by 14,000 skilled BL workers. If they are successful in forming an unofficial craft grouping with its own separate bargaining right there would be an avalanche of similar separatist units — the development so strongly resisted in the Ryder Plan and subsequently supported by Michael Edwardes.

Is the Ryder Report still relevant? The answer is broadly yes, but with some modifications. Michael Edwardes has already given broad support to the original Ryder Report, although there will obviously be changes in detail and a reduction in targets. This is hardly surprising; the Ryder Report consisted largely of the sum of ideas of the constituent components of the old BLMC. As such, it can be readily disaggregated back into its constituent components.

All in all, the Ryder Report has been much maligned. At the time of its writing, given the available evidence, it was a sensible, logical and perfectly justifiable strategy. It should have worked. What was wrong with it?

Critique of Ryder Plans

An attempt is made to list, on an objective basis, the reasons why the Ryder

1. But subject to a penalty clause against unofficial strikes.
2. The problem has now been overcome and all three assembly lines are working, albeit two of them at less than full capacity.
3. £1 billion to 1981 and a further £½ billion between 1982-4.

Plan failed. First, the sales assumptions were ambitious. This was due to a failure to recognise the new aggressive competition taking place on a world-wide scale rather than to poor forecasting of market sizes. Second, the Ryder plans incorrectly anticipated the effects of industrial action which has accounted for a significant percentage of lost production. To be sure the state takeover and the threat of withholding tranches of Government money was (incorrectly) predicted to improve industrial relations. Nevertheless, despite surplus capacity, BL's inflexible production conditions made it difficult to increase production temporarily to meet the backlog of orders arising from an industrial dispute. There is, however, a basic logical flaw to the withholding of Government money – a flaw which BL fell into. If a firm badly needs finance to reorganise itself and produce competitive products, then the longer the delay the worse the firm's position becomes. Repeated investment moratoriums simply had the effect of making the gap between BL and its competitors greater and hence the possibility of recovery more remote.

The failure to allow for production losses due to industrial action highlights another criticism of the Ryder plans, in that they failed to allow for the inherent risk in using single point estimates for the evaluations of various alternatives. Systematic sensitivity analysis, tracing the change in key variables over a wide range of assumptions could be used to overcome this problem. The Ryder plan was extremely sensitive to the small changes which have in the past pushed BL off course. Table 7.9 shows the results of a computer run evaluating one particular scenario, while Figure 7.1 uses the same computer run to illustrate sensitivity to changes in sales totals or production losses. The Ryder plan was not a safe one, nor was it cautious, but if BL could have met the targets and forecasts on which the plan was based, it could – for once – show a healthy profit.

If targets were not met, BL would have become only marginally profitable, sharing losses in some years and small profits in others. Further government finance – or even subsidy – would be *de rigueur* in the latter case.

A third avenue of criticism concerns the herculean task of actually implementing the Ryder Plan. The size and scope of the operations was basically underestimated by just about everyone involved. There were enormous problems of bringing together several separate units, each with their own brand of loyalty, into one organisational structure. Management were not only asked to run the company, they were also asked to plan future strategy, co-ordinate what were autonomous units, and conduct a general tidying up and administrative role. Even if the managerial ability had been there, it was a formidable undertaking.

However, the above criticisms were not apparently shared by the Government until it was very nearly too late.

FACTORS LEADING TO THE EDWARDES PLAN

Despite the toolmakers' strike which hit production badly in the first quarter of the year, both the NEB and the Department of Industry managed to convince the Government and the Liberals[1] in July 1977 that BL had improved

1. Owing to the Lib/Lab pact, the Liberals were consulted and agreed, with some reservations.

TABLE 7.9

Computer Simulation Run of BL Cars
modified Ryder Plan – Option 1[a]
(in 1977 prices)

Year	1977	1978	1979	1980	1981	1982
Physical data						
Actual achieved sales ('000s)	788	829	825	747	828	919
UK sales ('000s)	431	462	469	417	460	520
Export sales ('000s)	357	366	356	330	368	399
Production losses due to strike action ('000s)	250	67	67	61	67	74
Number of employees ('000s)	125	131	130	121	122	123
Financial summary						
Revenue £m	2,031	2,027	2,284	2,295	2,492	2,691
Raw material costs £m	1,148	1,244	1,282	1,282	1,399	1,516
Labour costs £m	519	544	537	501	506	511
Fuel, power, heat & oil £m	22	24	24	22	24	26
Bought in services £m	51	55	57	57	62	67
Warranty costs £m	58	61	60	55	61	68
Trading profit £m	233	279	324	377	441	502
Finance costs £m	55	75	101	122	135	140
Depreciation £m	27	63	95	107	139	140
Other overheads £m	130	133	139	144	152	160
Net profit before tax £m	21	8	12	4	14	61
Capital investment £m	135	235	260	220	215	165
Increase in working capital £m	51	101	85	54	35	38
New annual finance required £m	188	227	256	164	80	0[b]

a. Run in March 1977.
b. Repayment of loans to the tune of £16m could be made.

Note:
Allowance must be made for the fact that BL Cars now faces substantially reduced debt interest charges owing to the £450 million equity injection.

sufficiently to vote another £100 million tranche of money. In the event, only £50 million were taken up in September (although by Christmas BL was desperately in need of further finance, but Michael Edwardes has been able to acquire extra funds[1] without offering any new guarantees[2] although the poss-

1. Probably from the large banks; though at cheaper rates than those charged by the NEB.
2. *Financial Times,* 11 January 1978.

FIGURE 7.1

**SENSITIVITY ANALYSIS OF
COMPUTER SIMULATION MODEL IN 1982**

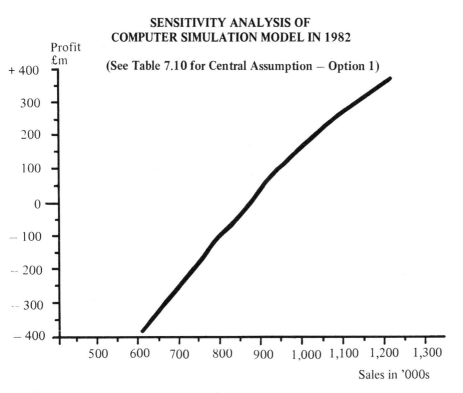

Profit £m

(See Table 7.10 for Central Assumption – Option 1)

Sales in '000s

ibility of being able to draw the £50 million voted by Parliament obviously acted as suitable collateral). However, the new-found confidence in BL during the Summer of 1977 was shortlived.

The factors which decided all parties concerned to take a tougher action towards the Autumn involved a culmination of events. First, market share had continued to fall despite an improvement in industrial production. Second, industrial peace had become more precarious. There were several threats of industrial unrest which could be disastrous. The toolroom workers[1] for example, were threatening industrial action. The Speke workers in Liverpool started their long strike in September 1977. The new Solihull plant was still at an appalling low level of productivity. Arguments were still raging about industrial relations reforms. Moreover, by Autumn 1977, it was apparent that despite a substantial increase[2] in employees in the car division, car production was actually lower in 1977 than 1976 – productivity had failed to increase! Thirdly, there was a growing disillusionment with the model policy and especially the new Mini. Fourthly, whilst there were long waiting queues for certain models, there were ample stocks of other models. Fifthly, there was an element of doubt about the ability of top management either to over-

1. Their 5-week old strike in February and March 1977 lost over 100,000 vehicles.
2. About 10,000 to 15,000 employees.

DATA FOR FIGURE 7.1

Sensitivity Analysis of Computer Simulation Model in 1982
(See Table 7.10 for Central Assumption – Option 1)

Sensitivity Analysed for			Resulting Affect on					
Sensitivity Level	Sales in '000s	% Change	Profit £m	Cash Flow £m	Outstanding Government loans £m	Export Revenue £m	Labour Force '000s	Productivity Output per man per year
1	612	-50%	-383	-428	2.9	.78	113	5.4
2	656	-40%	-319	-358	2.6	.83	115	5.7
3	707	-30%	-245	-286	2.3	.9	116	6.1
4	765	-20%	-159	-201	1.9	.97	118	6.5
5	799	-15%	-111	-153	1.7	1.01	119	6.7
6	835	-10%	-58	-102	1.5	1.06	121	6.9
7	875	-5%	-2	-46	1.2	1.11	122	7.2
8 Central Assumption	919	0	61	16	1.0	1.16	123	7.5
9	941	2.5	94	49	.9	1.19	124	7.6
10	964	5	124	78	.8	1.22	125	7.7
11	987	7.5	155	109	.7	1.25	125	7.9
12	1,010	10	181	135	.6	1.28	126	8.0
13	1,056	15	238	190	.5	1.34	128	8.3
14	1,101	20	274	180	.4	1.40	129	8.5
15	1,220	35	374	205	0	1.54	135	9.0

NB All values are in January 1977 terms.

come the existing problems or to provide the necessary innovative flair to create a new strategy. Figure 7.2 shows how production and productivity varied month by month in 1976 and for 1977. Finally, there was a question of financial failure.

180

FIGURE 7.2

Production and Productivity in BL Cars

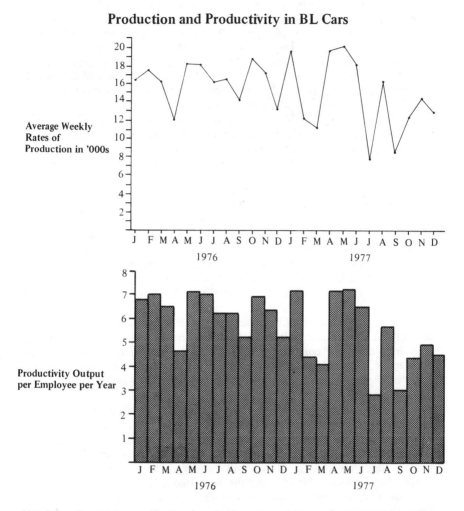

N.B. It is estimated that continuity of production using existing equipment would produce productivity levels of around 8 cars per year per employee.

From the finance angle 'the straw that broke the camel's back' was the payment of £50 million of government funds in September 1977 to cover the wage bill and other current costs — even though in July a larger sum of £100 million had been allocated for BL (and voted for) by Parliament. Although the Ryder plan foresaw BL internally generating £1.5 for every £1 provided by the state, this would clearly not be the case in the period 1975-80. In fact, the majority of the profit and internally generated cash flow would occur in 1981 and 1982. However, it is clear that the Ryder Report did not envisage the Government having to provide external finance to BL to bail out its current operations.

In the final analysis, it was probably a combination of dissatisfaction about BL's future plans and a lack of confidence in top and lower levels of management which persuaded the NEB and the Department of Industry to institute some changes. Plans were made to look for and appoint a new Chairman who would provide both a new approach and a more positive style of leadership. Michael Edwardes was chosen to replace Sir Richard Dobson as Chairman long before Dobson's taperecorded gaffe, although this misfortune must have affected the precise timing of the changeover.

Michael Edwardes thus became the new Chairman in October 1977. Soon he announced himself as Executive Chairman and started his reorganisation. In doing so, his plans, ideas and thoughts were systematically leaked[1] to the press, thereby providing a more open style of management and better public relations with the press and media.

THE EDWARDES PLAN

Michael Edwardes, when he announced his reorganisation on the 1 February 1978, highlighted the most pressing problems: loss of vehicles due to strike action (250,000 vehicles in 1977) and falling market shares against a rising market.[2] Edwardes' solution to the problem was to decentralise the car division – thus an alteration from the centralised (U-form) organisation to the M-form.[3]

According to the new Chairman, the centralised structure had not worked well in the time available; it had introduced remote management and excessively long chains of command led to poor performance. Too much time had been spent on merging the once independent companies. Instead, the reputation of the old marque names would be re-established and would form the basis of the new structure for cars.

As noted in Chapter 3, the planned structure is still in a state of flux and will be allowed to evolve gradually. At the moment, certain functions will be centralised: long term product planning and advanced engineering, personnel co-ordination of marketing and sales,[4] data processing and certain finance functions. Austin Morris will consist of the assembly facilities at Longbridge, Cowley, Abingdon and the associated powertrain and transmission factories that currently supply the volume car range. The Jaguar Rover Triumph company will have the assembly plants at Brown's Lane, the Meteor

---

1. '.... people are literally walking past our showrooms without a second look. Is it any wonder our dealers are worried and some are defecting to our competitors and strengthening the hold of imported cars in this country?' – *Financial Times*, 2 February 1978.
2. A pre-publication comment noted that there were several briefing meetings to combat the growing danger of a collapse in the confidence of the company by the public. Other similar meetings were held for national union officials and senior employee representatives.
3. See Chapter 2 for a further discussion of the theoretical concepts underpinning the various forms of organisation.
4. A pre-publication comment noted that it is franchise policy that is centralised, Austin Morris and JRT will have their own sales and marketing functions.

Works and the new plant at Solihull, Canley and the Liverpool plants. The BL Components company would rob Special Products of some of its products by taking over parts, foundry operations, the SU/Butec business and the body operations.[1] Already broad hints have been given for a separate subsidiary company (Land-Rover) to establish a four-wheel drive business[2] and a body building operation based on the old Pressed Steel Fisher company.[3] The range of possible development in structure is shown in Figure 7.3. Either a proliferation in true subsidiaries or a lengthening in the chain of command are the possible alternatives. Similarly, Jaguar and SU/Butec might become semi-autonomous companies. At the moment BL seems to be both expanding the span of the organisation and increasing the chain of command. No doubt the organisation will change quite a bit before an equilibrium is established with the new structure.

FIGURE 7.3

Possible Developments in Organisation of BL Cars

(a) Lengthening of span of command

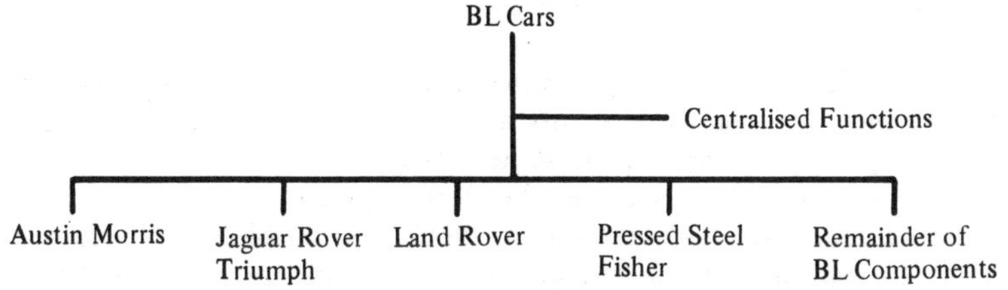

(b) Lengthening of chain of command

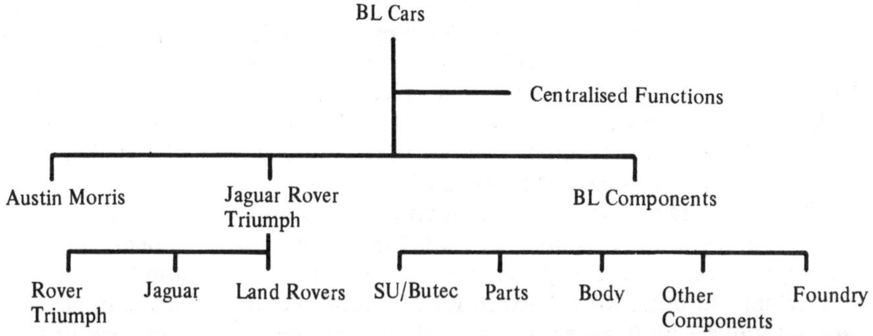

N.B.See footnote on previous page. BL have in effect chosen to lengthen the the chain of command.

1. A pre-publication comment pointed out that the components company has been formed out of the cars organisation – which already included four lines (they were switched from Special Products at the time of the Ryder reorganisation), SU/Butec and body build which were also part of Leyland cars before the Edwardes reorganisation scheme.
2. A pre-publication comment pointed out that within the car Jaguar Rover Triumph company there will be separate activities – Jaguar cars, Rover-Triumph and Land-Rover.
3. Pressed Steel Fisher is to be a separate organisation within BL components.

An earlier draft of this book recommended something akin to the Edwardes plan. The justification was as follows :

> To be frank, we consider it unrealistic to take an optimistic view of Leyland cars. The scale of the industrial relations problem, the lack of managerial and engineering resources and the sheer gap between Leyland and its competitors reduce optimism to an exercise in blinkered vision. Judging by Leyland's performance to date — and there have been many major changes — a continuing crisis of confidence would be well justified. We would, however, favour further attempts to exploit Leyland's present marketing advantages by splitting the firm into three (volume cars, specialist cars and a common components company). This would involve the loss of certain economies of scale, but this would be more than offset by the improvements in industrial relations and a more innovative management approach if the company were divided into a volume division, a specialist company and a components company supplying both specialist and volume concerns with certain components. It is not a particularly elegant solution, but shared components manufacture would at least curtail any loss of scale economies.

The actual split of BL Cars recognised the economies of scale argument at least in respect of the components and pressings. Powertrain production is still to be split. This may impose some cost penalties in the areas of possible overlap of the two divisions (i.e. the 1,800 to 2,600 cc power category). With experience and co-ordination it should be possible to overcome this problem by selling engines and gearboxes to each other — although such transfers may have marketing repercussions which could outweigh the economies of scale argument.

Michael Edwardes' plan to reduce employment by 12,500 in 1978 simply corrects a mistake that was made in 1976 when employment was expanded. The labour force, even after these cuts, is large by European standards — both Volkswagen and Renault produced around 1.3 million vehicles with less than 100,000 employees. Edwardes' plan envisages a production of 819,000 cars in 1978 by a labour force of around 120,000 employees.

The decentralised M-form organisation has often been called the profit centre concept. Such functions as marketing, product development, finance, engineering, component supply, etc., are made the responsibility of the smaller unit. In order for the executive of a profit centre to carry out his task satisfactorily he must be given many of the back-up services for each of the above functions. Consequently, there are several avenues of criticism for and against the decentralisation argument which are shown in Table 7.10. Ultimately decentralisation can only result in benefits so long as care is taken to maximise the economies of scale (or at least trade-off economies of scale with the benefits of decentralisation). The question of economies of scale has already been discussed; the conclusions being that the small loss in scale economies may be more than outweighed by the advantages of decentralisation. The ease of control, marketing advantages and the greater degree of flexibility are convincing arguments in favour of decentralisation.

184

TABLE 7.10
Arguments for and Against Decentralisation of BL Cars

FOR	AGAINST
1. Easier to control because management is closer to the ground and can more easily see the objectives they are aiming at.	1. Loss of economies of scale due to lower production runs.
2. BL's managers lack skill and experience to manage large structures.	2. The necessary duplication of certain functions costs more. Both Morris and Jaguar Rover Triumph will have their own marketing, engineering and product development staff.
3. Marketing advantages; customer loyalty to old marques.	3. The 'who makes what' question. Since none of the divisions are completely self-sufficient, there is the problem of which division makes particular items in order to gain scale economies. Such conflicts are easier to avoid in a centralised organisation.
4. Ease of identification of trouble spots in smaller units.	
5. BL's existing structure will still be amenable to split.	
6. Salesmen should be brought close to dealers and export customers.	
7. Management is closer to dealers and shop-floor — transmission loss within communications is reduced because of the short chain of command.	4. BL Cars has already begun to emerge as an integrated company. Some major component manufacture (e.g. powertrain) will now be split between the two subsidiaries. Spencer King's new £100m developing and testing centre may not now go ahead, although the longer run design function will still be centralised. Marketing has now been centralised for the UK and has been delegated to BL International for exports. The distribution network has been integrated.
8. Flexibility for both expansion and contraction.	
9. Separate companies introduce an element of competition.	
10. Loyalty of staff to traditional marques.	

The move towards smaller units is only one part of the Edwardes plan. A recent thread of his plan concerns managerial changes. His intention was to appoint management of a suitable calibre for the task in hand. Initially a very high priority was assigned to the task of trying to get the right management into the right jobs. Having accomplished this, management's attention was to be focused on the short run day-to-day problems. Consequently, such things as selling, production and quality control are all very much the concern of the new divisional management. Previously the old style management had been too preoccupied with the longer term (e.g. the LC10 medium saloon) to notice the very collapse of BL under their eyes. The Edwardes reasoning is clearcut. If domestic market share drops to below 21 to 23 per cent[1] then the dealer network might start to disintegrate. After 1980 new models starting with the new Mini will come on stream and help to increase market share. Therefore the critical period is 1978 and 1979. If management can prop up market share then BL's dealer network will survive until the 1980's and the new model programme.

Priority is therefore given to short run actions in the event that there is a conflict for resources between short run and long run.

COMPARISON OF THE EDWARDES PLAN WITH THE RYDER REPORT

Michael Edwardes' new plans recognised the two fundamental failings in BL's modified Ryder plans; the optimistic sales targets[2] and the underestimating of production losses due to strike action. Consequently the new plans included reduced sales targets (down to 25 per cent UK market share but not much change in exports) coupled with the splitting up of BL into more manageable units. The new plans, however, kept all the industrial relations reforms of centralised bargaining. The centralisation of engineering was partly retained, although, owing to the shortage of engineering resources, it is doubtful whether the new engineering centre will be broken up. Instead individual engineering centres may be added for the subsidiary companies, thus adding to BL's total engineering and product planning staff. The major change in decentralisation concerns the small production unit which now has control over its own sales worldwide.[3] Edwardes' model policy is vital to the revitalising of BL. BL must follow in Volkswagen's footsteps and make a successful comeback by introducing a new range of models. On the volume side, it has been announced that the old Mini will be retained. The new Mini, codenamed AD088 (and nicknamed the Mighty Mini) was to be larger, faster and quieter than the old Mini, with quite different driving characteristics. The AD088 was then scrapped in the formulation of BL's new corporate plan. Doubts about the competitiveness of the product are one possible reason for the cancellation. Another is that if both the old and the new Mini are to be produced in parallel, then neither model may be produced in sufficient quantities to make the model line viable. The current investment could be used to produce a new larger model which might even be a 'stretched new Mini' or a collapsed Allegro. This model may fall more into the VW Golf/Chrysler Sunbeam class. An advantage of this policy is that BL has no representation in this area and the Mighty Mini is unlikely to 'pinch' sales from the old Mini. In the end a stretched AD088 was decided upon and has been codenamed the LC8 (but is still termed the Mighty

1. i.e. around 300,000 to 350,000 cars a year on the UK market.
2. Ryder's original forecast had included a UK market share of 33 per cent. This had been revised down to 31 per cent in BL's Option 1, but was still too high.
3. Under the Ryder Plan, BL's International division had responsibility for all exports.

Mini). The new LC10[1] will continue to be a middle range car to be produced at Cowley. On the quality side, changes to Jaguar models will be made in order to build on its standards of performance, refinement, ride and handling. The highest priority, however, was to be given to the expansion of Land Rover and Range Rover production.[2]

In the interim, BL is thought to be planning a number of minor revisions to its model policy. The Princess is to have a new powertrain unit and a hatchback. The Marina is to be reskinned and its handling improved. The Allegro is to have a number of minor modifications including the provision of new powertrain units for some models. Emphasis will clearly be given to new models.

Michael Edwardes has also succeeded in changing the Ryder financial strategy. BL already received £200 million equity, plus in total another £150 million of loans (at commercial interest rates) from the NEB. Every time BL required finance, a submission had to be made to the NEB which then went to the Department of Industry, Cabinet, and finally to Parliament. According to the Ryder plans, the Government is still due to provide BL (all companies) a further £850 million which together with internally generated funds, would be sufficient to finance the capital investment programmes. Edwardes argued for and got an infusion of £450 million of new equity. The company's future needs will now only be reviewed annually and will not be subject to good behaviour by the unions. The arguments in favour of this were as follows. First, BL required the money at least one year ahead. Secondly, BL needed some freedom of manouevre in order to respond to market and other conditions. Thirdly, it releases BL's management from the pressure of justifying further Government finance every few months. Fourthly, the financial deterioration of the company, particularly by the cars division, in the last few years has so worsened the financial position that a fresh interest-free injection of money is urgently required.

Some casualties of Edwardes' new plans for BL will include some plants and some parts of the Ryder expansion and modernisation programme — such as the foundries. Although the Ryder Report was correct in identifying weaknesses in BL's foundries, subsequent events have left the UK with excess foundry capacity — so this too is a rational move.

PROBLEMS WITH THE EDWARDES PLAN

Obviously, the Ryder Report failed to find all the right answers. Will the Edwardes plan do better? Once the debate over decentralisation has passed, criticisms of the new plan for BL cars centres around model policy, industrial relations and economies of scale. Taking these in reverse order the loss of economies of scale through decentralisation has been discussed.[3] We can only wait and see whether this will result in a heavy cost penalty.

The problem with industrial relations concerns the reversal of the movement towards integration. However, for BL Cars, an integrated personnel

1. The LC10/11/12 series will probably be scrapped and a new medium car planned.
2. A policy urged by our 1975 report, 'Alternatives Open to UK Motor Industry'.
3. See Chapter 2.

function will be maintained, although inevitably there must be some duplication of functions in the separate subsidiary companies. Are there any advantages for industrial relations in decentralisation? T.N. Beckett[1], at an Expenditure Committee hearing said:

> . . .you do have to have large units to be economic; but having large units employing a large number of people does of course create this problem of communication and this feeling that they are not getting the type of personal attention that every person expects he has a right to.[2]

It is this sense of contact which may possibly bring an improvement in industrial relations through decentralisation.

BL's model policy can still be criticised on a number of grounds. The issue of the new Mighty Mini is a particularly contentious one. Critics feel that the new Mini will be marketed in competition with the Ford Fiesta, the Chrysler Sunbeam, VW's Golf and the Fiat 127. However much money BL pours into the development of the new Mighty Mini, it could be argued that this money would be better invested in updating the old Mini, which is sold in a completely different market segment and has met with little direct competition. There are similar model policy problems in the medium car segment. Much of the capacity at the Cowley and Longbridge plant is used to produce the Marina and Allegro ranges and yet the two models (the Marina in particular) are hardly competitive with the VW Golf, Passat, or the Audi 80. The new medium range models will not now be introduced before 1982-3 or even later, by which time the current medium range models will be in an even less competitive position. Some observers would prefer Leyland to abandon the new Mini programme altogether and concentrate instead on a crash development programme for the medium car range. This is reinforced by the fact that the small car market segment is only 30 per cent of the European market. Why not go for the remaining 70 per cent.

The solution may not be quite as simple as this suggests. Moreover, the fact that the existing Mini product is expensive to produce (a point conceded even by the Mini critics) is an argument in favour of radically improving and updating the product, in an effort to cut production costs. The Longbridge plant, which has been designated as the new Mini production plant, is now badly in need of modernisation and much of the expenditure on the new Mini can in fact be accounted for in renovation and modernisation of the plant and assembly lines. Most importantly, most of the design and engineering work on the old version new Mini[3] has already been completed and the engineering resources to develop the Mighty Mini will not be great. Even if the Mini project were abandoned altogether in favour of a new assault on the medium car range, BL would find it almost impossible to recruit the necessary engineering per-

1. Managing Director of Ford of Britain.
2. Question 906, Minutes of Evidence taken before the Trade and Industry Sub-Committee Volume 1, Fourteenth Report of the Expenditure Committee, *The Motor Vehicle Industry, 1975.*
3. The old version of the New Mini (ADO88) was to be slightly larger than the old Mini but smaller than most of the existing small car competitors.

188

sonnel from within the company. The extent to which plans for the medium car range could be brought forward is marginal at best, and even a revised schedule would involve a five year period before any new models could be introduced.

The only other totally new product, the SD2, was originally planned as a replacement for the Dolomite Series, but the project was cancelled in 1975. If the Mini was also abandoned it could be a savage blow to the morale of the planning and engineering divisions — an intangible consequence but not an insignificant one. More importantly, BL have decided to keep both the new and the old versions of the Mini in production, which would retain the marketing advantages of a wider market coverage but could lose some of the economies of scale. Common components may be used to maximise some scale economies, but these components may be out of date or expensive to produce.

Other criticisms concern not just the Mini model policy but the entire BL model policy embodied in the Ryder Plan. In manufacturing capacity terms, BL is a small company; it is even smaller in its volume car sector, and yet the Ryder proposals recommend a five-range model policy which is designed to compete directly with other major manufacturers. No specific policy revisions have yet been proposed which would reconcile the volume/quality dichotomy in the Ryder Plan and so the criticisms that could be made in this respect may not apply. Edwardes may be falling into the same trap as Ryder. The Ryder Plan, however, contained a more serious planning error in its plans for the four wheel drive Land-Rover. Prompt action in 1975 to expand Range Rover production and to modernise the Land-Rover might have saved and even increased the now much diminished Land-Rover market share. Action was not taken, and Land-Rover's world market share — naturally — fell sharply. Belatedly, this mistake has now been rectified and capacity is scheduled to rise from the current 1,300 per week to 1,600 per week in 1978. In the original Ryder Report, Land-Rover and Range Rover production was to have been expanded to 2,700 vehicles per week. BL Cars now plan to increase production to around 3,200 vehicles per week[1] (160,000 per year). The plan is sound, but it may have come too late. The Japanese, East European and North American producers have already entered the market and the new four-wheel drive vehicle designed jointly by Daimler-Benz (Mercedes) and Steyr-Daimler-Puch will pose a major threat to Land-Rover sales. The new vehicle is due to be launched in 1978 or 1979, and the Land-Rover is being equipped with the new V-8 Rover engine to meet the challenge.

Reports suggest that even before the Edwardes plan the recent BL review supported the expansion of Land Rover production to higher levels than those anticipated in the Ryder Plan. BL's management[2] were apparently so impressed by projections for the four-wheel drive vehicles that they have opted for the further growth in this segment in addition to the policy recommendations in the Ryder strategy. In the 1975 report entitled 'Alternatives Open to the UK Motor Industry', expansion of the Land Rover division was one of the principal recommendations and we welcome its adoption, however belated. We now turn

1.   Although the new more modest plan for BL may have deferred the final expansion stage to 3,200.
2.   Prior to Michael Edwardes' appointment.

our attention to what may happen in the future if BL Cars' performance fails to improve.

ALTERNATIVES

It is expedient to take a broader view in evaluating what other factors might be taken into consideration by the Government in reaching a decision on the future of BL Cars. Although BL itself, the Government and the NEB have more or less reaffirmed their support for the Edwardes plan, this is by no means a guarantee that present or future governments will adhere to this decision. Already, the outcome of the current reassessment of plans for the medium car range could alter the whole operation.

Obviously, the Ryder Report had not found all of the right answers – but what other plans, apart from Ryder, were available for consideration? And what are the alternatives as seen by BL, the NEB and the Government? Even Michael Edwardes has made it plain that he will not hesitate in taking drastic action in order to stop BL Cars' losses from continually mounting. What action might he take?

We begin with the published reports of BL's Spring 1977 review, undertaken in the aftermath of the toolroom-makers' strike.[1] BL itself was evidently not averse to considering alternatives to the Ryder plan at that time. We will now examine these alternatives,[2] as they provide a useful indicator of the avilable options open to BL. Alternative A concerned a modified Ryder Plan, while Alternative B called for a quality car operation only, involving a controlled withdrawal from the lower end of the market. Alternative C advocated specialist car production only, and rapid withdrawal of all models below the Princess, while Alternative D called for a complete range, but with production operating at a reduced level and less expensively. In all four cases, the quality end of BL's range was largely untouched. The options called for involve either the small car (Mini) or medium car segments. Most of the four options contained a number of variants, most of which are listed in Table 7.11 as Options 1 to 6, with Option 1 representing the large-capacity plan, Option 6 the small capacity plan. Options 1 to 4 involve a complete car range, Option 5 involves only a quality car range and Option 6, only a specialist car range. In order to simplify matters a little, the main features of each option are listed as follows:

Option 1 – modified Ryder Plan
Option 2 – middle car range dropped in favour of an upgraded Allegro
Option 3 – investment in vehicles at lower end of range curtailed
Option 4 – as Option 3, with Mini replacement abandoned in favour of modifications to existing car
Option 5 – controlled withdrawal from volume cars leaving a restricted medium range and with no Mini
Option 6 – concentration on specialist cars only, with rapid withdrawal from volume car segment.

1. In February and March, 1977.
2. It should be made clear that these are reconstructions, albeit close ones.

BL felt that Option 2 would place the company in a vulnerable position in the medium car market, while Option 3 — which has the same disadvantage — also has lower overall productivity. BL's management saw Option 4 — wherein the new Mini is abandoned in favour of a revamp of the existing Mini model — as one which would worsen the company's position even further and damage company morale at all levels. Leyland's preferred alternative was Option 1 which they felt provided the company with the chance to be financially viable and eventually capable of self-financing (and incidentally is the closest to the original Ryder Plan). Options 5 and 6 offered lower returns on sales and assets. The plant closures involved could provoke potentially damaging confrontation with the unions. Options 2 and 3 would be less expensive but the profits yielded would be too small to make the company viable.

The 1975 report, 'Alternatives Open to the UK Motor Industry', considered a wider set of alternatives: several variants of the Ryder Plan; several stages of minor and major rationalisation; various alternatives based on the quality of specialist cars only options; alternatives involving greenfield sites; options involving the merger of BL and Chrysler UK; separation of volume and car divisions; and alternatives involving the nationalisation of the entire industry. A summary of some of these alternatives is given in Table 7.12, showing the break-even production levels — although some of the assumptions behind the analysis are now out of date. The first three options have been more or less covered by the old BL review and the Edwardes plan covers the seventh option. It remains to be seen whether or not future governments will be prepared to evaluate the remaining alternatives. Some of them — e.g. the merger with Chrysler and total nationalisation — seem particularly unlikely in the present political and economic climate.

If at some future time, BL's Austin Morris division was allowed to collapse in its entirety, then this would have severe repercussions on the profitability of Jaguar Rover Triumph. At the moment, this specialist division makes substantially fewer than 300,000 vehicles — which is the break-even figure for this division. Higher component costs coupled with the loss of allocating unavoidable overheads over a larger volume are responsible for the change in the profitability. If a specialist car strategy is to work, it must be at volume levels sufficient to compete with Daimler Benz or BMW. Alternatively, the range of models within the division must be drastically reduced.

In analysing alternatives, however, the Government must consider profitability and long-term viability, the cost to the Government in terms of cash help, employment, the effect on the balance of payments and existing industrial relations objectives, of which employment and the balance of payments are likely to have a higher priority. Redundant BL employees are unlikely to find alternative employment which could have been a decisive factor in the Government's acceptance of BL's plans. Apart from the immediate political consequences of large-scale redundancies, the Government's transfer payments (social security benefits) could exceed the differential amount of money needed to prop up BL. For example, between Options 5 and 6 in Table 7.11, 20,000 jobs are saved at a cost of only £200 million, whereas social security payments for the same 20,000 workers would amount to £50 million a year and there may, of course, be more jobs lost in the comp-

TABLE 7.11 – Leyland's Options

Option Leyland's Code No	1 A Modified Ryder	2 A1 Variant of A	3 D Curtailment Investment in vehicles at lower end of range	4 D1 Variant of C	5 B Controlled withdrawal from Volume Cars	6 C Rapid withdrawal from Volume Cars
Description	This option is based on Leyland's original plans but takes into account recent developments and delays in capital expenditure.	The proposed new middle car would be dropped in favour of an upgraded Allegro.	Favours specialist cars but the Mini project would continue with less investment and lower productive capacity (and lower-productivity).	As per C but Mini replacement abandoned in favour of minor changes to existing car.	Favours specialist cars but would leave a restricted medium range with a quality car emphasis.	All energies concentrated on Specialist Cars with a quick withdrawal from volume cars.
Model Policy by mid-1980's	Complete range (all new).	Complete range using upgraded Allegro.	Complete range using upgraded Allegro and a slightly less new Mini.	Complete range using revamp of Mini and upgraded Allegro.	Restricted range from upgraded Allegro and Princess upwards. Emphasis on quality cars.	Specialist range from Princess upwards with perhaps a small BMW type SD2 in existence.
Plant Closures	Canley and perhaps Liverpool, redundancies elsewhere as increased and much needed mechanisation is introduced.	As per A	As per A not dependent on market above	As per A	Longbridge, Cowley North works, Liverpool and Canley.	Longbridge, Cowley South works, Liverpool Canley, Tile Hill, Castle Bromwich and Senifte.
estimates of* Employment by Leyland Cars	120,000	115,000	113,000 but dependent on market share	109,000	70,000	50,000
Estimated Capital Investment in £ million excluding working capital	1,200+	1,100+	1,000+	850+	700+	500+
Maximum two-shift capacity approx. in millions of units	1.4	1.3	1.1	1.0	.8	.5
Leyland sales* estimates (1985) in millions of units	1.2	less than A (e.g. around 1.0)	less than B (around .9)	less than C (around .8)	.7	.45
Profitability in* real terms	£150m.	less than A	marginal	Insufficient profits to fund its future.	£50m.–£100m.	£25m.–£50m.
Leyland's Estimates of Long Term Viability	Yes	Vulnerable	Possibly Unviable	Possibly Unviable	Unviable	Unviable

*   Computed by financial simulation model of British Leyland.

onents industry. Assuming that the job situation does not recover for a number of years, Option 6 would then be costlier than Option 5. The alternative which comes closest to meeting both the employment and the balance of payments criteria is, in fact, the modified Ryder Plan (Option 1).

Another possible alternative is to use BL's manufacturing capacity to manufacture cars under licence. A less severe form is to link with another manufacturer by means of a functional merger. Co-operation or collaboration may result in the spreading of design and/or production costs.[1] In the 1975 report, 'Alternatives Open to the UK Motor Industry', we encouraged the development of links with other European firms, on the grounds that this sort of arrangement would permit maximum economies of scale. BL has now set up a joint working party with Renault, which seems to be a move in the right direction, but it should not preclude further links with Japanese and even Communist Bloc producers. BL must not necessarily assume that it can stand alone in the face of rising international competition among multi-national giants. On the other hand the difficulties of joint mergers should not be underestimated and this topic is discussed further in the conclusion (Chapter 17).

We have already seen that Government acceptance of a modified Ryder Plan implies no sure future commitment, and there are several other factors which could influence future decisions on a further reaffirmation of the plan in its present form. A vocal minority in BL's work-force have clearly not been intimidated by Government threats to withhold support from the company and there is no guarantee that they will comply with any of the existing proposals. A new BL review may ask for more money than the Government is prepared to spend. If the cash is forthcoming the company have to be watched very closely to ensure that requests for additional aid were justified. The future is very much less certain than one might assume. The NEB or Michael Edwardes could eventually decide that BL has no chance of achieving long-run viability.

In any event, BL's new model policy will not be fully established until the mid-1980s, by which time BL's market shares in certain key sectors are bound to have deteriorated — particularly in the medium car sector. Many of the major European producers will be especially active in launching new models. Loss of market share will certainly damage BL's profitability. As BL borrows more money from the NEB, so its finance costs will increase (although the new equity injection has eased this burden, placing an additional charge on already meagre profits. In much the same way, depreciation charges will rise as capital investment proceeds. All of this indicates that BL may continue to turn in a loss before it can establish itself in the 1980s. If this is correct, and if the Edwardes plan produces no improvement, then the current decision will almost certainly prove to be only a temporary one. Public outcry and/or a change of government could bring about a re-evaluation in the not too distant future. Ryder's departure from the NEB board has already had some effect on the Board's approach. It would seem that decisions on BL's future are not simply a matter of objective fact. As personalities, political parties and priorities change, so too will BL change.

1.   e.g. Renault, Peugeot and Volvo jointly designed and produced the Douvrin range of engines.

RECOMMENDATIONS

Industrial relations, an uncompetitive car range, poor quality control and political uncertainty are perhaps the most acute problems which now confront BL. Long-term viability will in part depend on what the company can achieve in dealing with these problems. It is doubtful whether BL's volume car section could ever achieve viability on the current or planned scale of operations, although both BL and the NEB have made it clear that they no longer necessarily identify with the Ryder Plan. If BL can concentrate on its specialist car division (Jaguar, Rover and sports models) and launch an aggressive attack on the four-wheel drive market, then its potential profitability could be greatly improved, particularly if maximum economies of scale can be achieved through the use of common componentry. If this strategy were to succeed, BL would be identified primarily as a specialist car manufacturer, resembling a British Mercedes but retaining an interest in the Mini and volume car sectors. But if BL cannot solve its industrial relations and quality control difficulties, the uncertainty now expressed by management may well be justified. Our specific recommendations for BL therefore fall into several headings: model strategy, volume specialist mix, production and organisational plans, and finance.

(a) Model Strategy

In the short run, volume sales in Austin Morris have reached all time lows. Highest priority would therefore go to reskinning the Marina and improving its roadholding and handling. Attention would be given to making the Mini quieter, and a new faster version would be announced (i.e. shades of the old Mini Cooper S but at a sufficient mark up to cover costs). The Princess model might be offered with a hatchback option and a new powertrain. The TR7 could be offered in a soft-top version and the decision to cancel the Stag replacement (codenamed Lynx) should be reviewed. Although given the existence of an engineering bottleneck, it could be argued that all engineering efforts should be devoted to the bread and butter models rather than the slice of jam on top. The new Rover might be offered in a standard saloon version. However, this still leaves the Jaguar Rover Triumph division light on products. This would make it imperative that the now cancelled SD2 should be reintroduced as quickly as possible; or alternatively to reskin the Dolomite series.

In the medium term, Table 7.12 shows the planned model outlet which would include the Mighty Mini and might also include the reintroduction of the Jaguar E type or equivalent. The longer term also brings out an important dichotomy between the planned Ryder model policy and what we think might be better. The marketing concept underpinning this approach is for Jaguar Rover Triumph to pursue the Mercedes Line. But what of Austin Morris? Should this company concentrate on volume cars? Should it compete with the larger manufacturers? We think not. Austin Morris may also become more of a specialist manufacturer. For example, in the past the MG Sports cars produced by this division have always been successful (neither the Mini nor the Princess were intended to compete head on with its rivals). In the new organisation however, MG presumably is classified as Sports cars and therefore falls within

TABLE 7.12

Possible BL Car Model Policy

1979-1980	1981-1983	Mid 1980s onwards
AUSTIN MORRIS		
Mini	Mini	Mini?
	Mighty Mini (LC8)	Mighty Mini (LC8)
modified Allegro	Allegro	LC10
modified Marina	Marina	LC11?
modified Maxi	Maxi	
Princess 2	modified Princess	Princess replacement?
		CM(1)
		Sports range?
JAGUAR ROVER TRIUMPH		
modified Dolomite	SD2 (resurrected and developed)	Small saloon
Rover range	Rover range	Large saloon
modified Jaguar	Jaguar range	Jaguar range (Slant 6 engine)
modified MGB	MGB?	
TR7 range	TR7 range	Sports range
	Lynx[a] (cancelled)	
LAND ROVER		
Range Rover	Range Rover	Complete four-wheel
Land Rover	Road Rover	drive, utility and
	Land Rover	recreational range.

a. Although a TR8 may be developed using the TR7 body and the Rover engine range.

the Jaguar Rover Triumph/specialist division.

Austin Morris should move up-market *and* draw upon its previous sporting image. Marketing gaps should be exploited. The Mini is a good example. The Maxi, however, could be marketed as more of a utility/recreational vehicle. MGs are still one of the few convertible cars sold in the US and such a near monopoly position should be fully exploited in such an important market. There may be one or two models which would have to compete with larger manufacturers, simply in order to provide distribution networks with a complete range. Such vehicles could be made distinctive by the range of options, luxuriousness of trim or greater performance.

BL's strategy would be to produce some volume production models. But the strategy outlined here would temper any more production with a penchant for avoiding direct competition with the multinationals.

Our belief in the concept of the Land Rover may be reiterated. However, there is scope for a smaller and cheaper vehicle than the Range Rover. The Simca Rancho is an example of the marketing concept.[1] A car which is specifi-

1. Which is planned to be produced in about the same quantity as Maxi production.

cally designed to pull loads or go off the road but without the benefit of four-wheel drive would probably have a market size greater than the Maxi has at present. Based on the Maxi/small version of Range Rover, the car would be a beefed up, more rugged version with a higher ground clearance. Such a vehicle could be made to cover not only the utility uses but also the recreational vehicle market segment.

Some of the suggestions with regard to model strategy may be speculative. As commented in the previous chapter, the US multinationals may try to emulate Daimler Benz by moving part of their product range up-market. If this is so then the up-market Rover-type product may come under increasing competitive pressure. The maxim that "a Ford is a Ford" may take on an entirely new connotation.

(b) Multi-sourcing

BL Cars has made enormous progress in its ability to multi-source (i.e. have several supplying companies) for components supplied from external sources. There is still room for improvement. Components are now produced in an international market and BL Cars should have at least two suppliers for most components. This begs the question of whether internally produced components should be multi-sourced. It has been argued that in order to attain economies of scale, some components should be single sourced from a series of operations designed to maximise the economies of scale. Such an argument ignores the problem that industrial unrest in one plant could stop production at other plants throughout BL. Multi-sourcing may be financially feasible where the cost of industrial disruption outweighs any economies of scale. However, there will be some operations which are clearly only feasible at one site. What can be done to ensure a reliable and regular supply?

(c) Capacity

Availability of cars has been one of BL Cars' chronic problems — and there is no easy or cheap solution. Industrial peace could probably be obtained by buying off the labour force. The consequence would be higher manning levels, a slower work pace and no guarantee that future demands might not escalate beyond all reason. The net result would be higher labour costs and lower productivity, thereby imposing a severe cost penalty. The profitability gap between BL and the rest of the European producers would be that much greater.

What strategy then will secure a production of, say, one million cars if 300,000 of them are being lost through industrial strife? The answer is to plan to produce the target figure plus an allowance for the maximum number of cars expected to be lost through industrial relations problems. If p is the target level of production, s is the proportion of vehicles lost through internal industrial relations problems and a is actual production, then:

$$a = \frac{p}{(1 + s)}$$

In other words, for actual output to achieve the target figure, p, the planned production figure (p*) must be equal to:

$$p^* = a (1 + s)$$
$$= a + as$$
$$= \text{actual production} +$$
an allowance for cars lost through
industrial relations figures.

For example to achieve a 1 million production figure with a 30 per cent vehicle loss figure would require a planned production figure of 1.3 million.[1]

If production was unaffected, the extra cars would lead to a stock build-up. The opportunity cost or interest forgone would be high but necessary in order to create consumer confidence in the availability of BL cars.

(d) Size of Plant

Two factors that were mentioned in Chapter 4 are persuasive in postulating a move to smaller plant sizes. First, the communications argument that was mentioned by many of the leaders of the motor industry[2] is important. Even Michael Edwardes embraced this idea with his concept of a managerial unit which, like a tree, is small enough for management to put their arms around. Communications works both ways; the diffusion of decisions and orders made at the top and the feed-back of events and problems on the shop-floor back up to top management. A smaller managerial span of control and the reduced number of hierarchical levels are both important in advocating smaller plant sizes.

The second factor of importance in large plants is the impact such units may have on employment in a town or community. In Cahpter 4 it was argued that firms should not be the principal or only employer within a community; for the creation of an employing monopoly may lead to compensatory union activity in the creation of a bi-lateral monopoly. Whether the employer's decisions are fair or not is a question that cannot be tested by reference to market conditions — for there are no other comparable employers. Psychologically, employees may always suspect that the employer may be taking an unfair advantage of its monopolistic position and react accordingly.

These two factors taken together imply that the maximum plant size should be small — somewhere between 5,000 to 10,000, judging from the evidence provided in the Expenditure Committee[3] — and that the town or community should be sufficiently large to permit several plants of this size,[4] owned and run by different companies. Such a policy cannot ignore the economies of scale. In the 1975 report, 'Alternatives Open to the UK Motor Industry', we evaluated a cottage industry approach in which BL Cars

1. Note that this policy thus has the same effect of making BL a high cost firm. This point is further discussed in the conclusion.
2. In the Minutes of Evidence, Fourteenth Report of the Expenditure Committee, *The Motor Vehicle Industry*.
3. Op. cit.
4. Unlike Linwood, where Chrysler is the largest single employer.

is split into its existing plants but each plant produces a complete car (see Table 7.11). This alternative was hopelessly unprofitable, principally because of the lack of scale economies, but the continuity of production was considered to be the highest of all the alternatives. How then can we keep the industrial relations advantages of the cottage industry approach and yet take advantage of the scale economies which exist in the motor industry?

(e) Production and Plant Policy

This question can be answered by reference to the *ideal*[1] plant layout from the economies of scale point of view (outlined in Chapter 4) which was:

> 1 pressing plant
> 2 powertrain plants
> 4 or 5 assembly plants

Bearing in mind the risk from single sourcing and the existing plant structure of BL this may be modified to:

> 2 pressing plants
> 2 or 3 major powertrain plants
> and 1 minor plant
> 5 major assembly plants and several minor ones

The minor plants would cater for the Jaguar and some of the specialist plants, but this should not be conclusive. Because Jaguar models have always been produced in the Brown's Lane factory in Coventry, this does not necessarily mean that Jaguars should always be produced there in the future.

One possible way of implementing this plan is outlined below although the above plant policy can be translated into reality in a large number of ways — some of these alternatives are shown in Table 7.13. The two obvious candidates for pressing plants are Swindon and Castle Bromwich.[2] The powertrain centres are not so obvious. A major powertrain centre is now firmly established at Longbridge itself and around Longbridge (eg Coventry Engines). Longbridge is likely to remain a major producer of powertrains, but there may be insufficient capacity to support the volume envisaged in the original Ryder plans. (This may no longer be relevant). However one may still ask what other plants might become major powertrain centres. One possibility is Canley, which is scheduled for a change of use from assembly to component manufacture. It may also be advantageous to build a new greenfield site engine plant, as Ford are currently designing. (The smaller Jaguar engine plant at Sandy Lane might remain separate).[3] The major assembly plants of Cowley and Longbridge are too large to fit into the overall pattern, whilst Canley and Speke are too small.

1. See Chapter 4.
2. Although the Rover engine plants at Tysley and Woodcock Lane would be too small to be converted to major engine plants.
3. The Woodend pressing plant at Speke should be closed and production of pressings transferred elsewhere.

Ideally, plants would be in the 200,000 to 400,000 capacity range with a maximum plant employment of around 10,000 per plant.

Longbridge and Cowley would thus be transformed into assembly lines of reduced capacity. Solihull would remain as a major assembly plant although there may be a question mark on the older Meteor works. Jaguar's small assembly plant might remain. This leaves a deficit of at least two major assembly plants. Canley might be beefed up into a larger plant — although Speke is locationally better from the export point of view, being closer to the docks though presumably its poor record of productivity would have ruled Speke out even if it had not been decided to close the plant. Alternatively, two new greenfield site assembly plants could be built in development areas in South Wales and the North East — both should be preferably situated on the coast in order to facilitate export of models.

TABLE 7.13

Alternative Plant Functions

Assembly Plants (4 or 5 major plants + Browns Lane)	Powertrain (2 or 3 major plants)	Major Pressing Plants ** (2 plants)
	Cowley *	Swindon
upgraded Canley	Coventry Engines	Castle Bromwich
reduced Longbridge *	Canley	Greenfield site
reduced Cowley	Longbridge *	Cowley *
Solihull	Meteor Works	Longbridge *
Meteor Works	Greenfield site	
Greenfield site A	Cardiff	

* Cowley and Longbridge should either have only one function or a maximum of two.
** Llanelli could remain a minor pressing plant but the Speke pressing plant will probably be closed.

NB. Possible candidates for greenfield sites are South Wales or the North East; higher transport costs probably rule Scotland out.

This still leaves many smaller plants which are used for component manufacture. Where they are profitable, under the auspices of the BL Component company, they may remain. Some regrouping of the companies may be necessary for control reasons. In the above plan Cowley would, for example, serve as both an engine plant and an assembly plant. Longbridge may also follow suit, although to reduce the bi-lateral syndrome it was argued in (d) above that both Cowley and Longbridge are too large. As long as the management structure is sufficiently autonomous and isolated, it may be possible to operate on the basis of one powertrain and one assembly plant in the same factory — as in Ford's Dagenham plant.[1] Total capacity in this production plan would be in the theoretical region of 1.4 million cars — an increase of only 200,000 or

1. Although even Ford are effectively moving part of their engine plant to South Wales.

400,000 over BL's maximum theoretical capacity. This theory dovetails nicely into the additional capacity postulated under (c).

(f) Other Industrial Relations Questions

Loyalty of employees should be taken into account and rewarded. For example, the Abingdon plant has a good record in both industrial relations and productivity, and the reward could be continued employment despite being too small to fit into the overall plans of BL. This reward is of great importance, for to keep open a plant would indicate to other plants that loyalty paid off.

One theory gaining increasingly popular acceptance in Europe is that industrial peace may be attained through industrial democracy and worker participation. The Ryder plans for worker participation have not, however, had a significant effect on improving industrial relations. Nor can it be supposed that management by workers can necessarily secure the badly needed industrial peace. This is not to say it cannot help − for it can − but the evidence to date within BL is not encouraging. No great reliance should therefore be placed on achieving improved industrial relations through greater participation although without this participation the problem may get worse.

(g) Flexibility and Boredom

BL Cars must be unique in its reputation for falling market shares in its volume models yet having long delivery queues on some of its specialist models (e.g. Rover 3500 and Jaguar models) *and even* some volume models (e.g. Mini 1275 GT, MG models, etc.). Similarly, when industrial relations problems threaten production of product lines with particularly long waiting times, it may be useful to be able to switch production of this model (or component) to another plant − although this is a more contentious issue.

A second factor must be considered. There can be no doubt that boredom on the shop floor has led to 'inefficient and counter-productive' customs and practices. This problem is not peculiar to BL and is particularly prevalent at Ford's Halewood plant, where production in 1977 dropped to only 154,000 cars despite having a plant capacity of over 300,000 cars. In Chapter 4 it was argued that the Swedish concept of unit working was not the answer.[1] There is only one way to achieve an economic solution to a boring and repetitive process and that is to automate the process and use the labour force profitably in maintaining the equipment, and in trouble shooting. Such a solution obviously has employment implications whichever is preferred: no employment in the car manufacturing industry because of the uncompetitiveness of the industry, or, alternatively, some employment in a competitive industry. One level of automation is shown in the development of programmable robotic welding machines[2] in which the welding mechanism is positioned at the end of a mechanical arm which probes in and around the body shell to find the appropriate point. The Fiat machine tool company, COMAU,[3] has developed

1. Productivity was reduced by 10 per cent and absenteeism was still high.
2. e.g. Unimate.
3. The automatic trolley was developed in collaboration with a Swiss electronics company called Digitron.

an extension of these welding machines called the Robotgate system. This system involves the use of trollies (as opposed to the traditional assembly lines) which move automatically over the floor guided by a series of invisible magnetic tracks. The course which trollies take on the shop floor depends on the computer controlled instructions which they are given. The welding machines can be programmed to sense the particular model on the trolley and the appropriate welds can be made without human intervention.

Such techniques as these can even be extended to the traditional assembly line, as long as each work station with the robotic machine (a) knows the car it is working on and has the appropriate instructions and programme stored in a memory, and (b) receives the correct parts from a supplying transfer line. A central computer system would be required to co-ordinate all the work stations and the supplying transfer lines. As well as the central computer, each work station, robotic machine or automated trolley would have its own mini computer and memory to store the different instructions and operations required for a range of products.

The advantages of automation are several. First, the boredom of the remaining work force is lessened, and the character of the work will become more skilled and varied. The second advantage is the flexibility of production. Traditionally, each assembly line and supplying transfer lines contain much equipment which is fixed to only one type of vehicle. Each production line is geared to a particular model. In periods of low demand for that model the production line runs at below capacity. If demand is higher for the model than the capacity of the production line, then the excess demand cannot be switched to another line because it will not have the appropriate machinery. The new process allows a production line to take several models (with each product simply having a separate programme in the robotic machinery). The increased flexibility means that BL should be able to match the pattern of demand more closely than in the past. Moreover, deficiences in production due to industrial relations unrest may be made up by switching production to other plants, although such a policy may cause additional problems.

The third advantage of the new production system is that it will reduce capital expenditure in assembly plants (but not pressing or powertrain plants) by about 60-80 per cent. This is because it will not be necessary to radically alter the transfer lines and other fixed equipment which is specifically tied to certain models.[1] The computer controlled equipment, mechanical arms, trollies and other equipment could simply be reprogrammed and, if necessary adapted.

The reduction in employment is not as great as might be supposed. The mechanical parts of the equipment would need regular servicing. There would also be a new area of electronic maintenance. Each robotic piece of equipment may require a human monitor in case something went wrong or in case the repertoire of programmed instructions did not include the particular set of events which were found to occur. In addition, whenever a new model or operation is introduced, the computerised equipment will need reprogramming. This software development will require substantial manpower. Altogether,

1. 'Fiat calculates that about 70% of the total capacity of the system is attributed to the fixed components in it.' *Financial Times,* 2–10–78.

the consequential reduction of the labour force would only be of the order of magnitude of around 30-40 per cent,[1] although the nature of the work would change, and a substantial retraining programme may be necessary.

The computer part of the equipment would give an added boost to the UK computer industry (e.g. ICL, GEC, Ferranti and Systime).

(h) Finance

BL should be allowed to follow the example of Renault; the French Government merely guarantees loans made on the commercial market. With Michael Edwardes borrowing £50 million around Christmas 1977, and having successfully raised £450 million of equity from the NEB, there is every chance of additional finance being sought from commercial sources.

Of course, not all of these recommendations need to be carried out. However the capital cost of implementing the plans is not all that great. The internal multi sourcing of minor components would be around £200 million but its success may be doubtful once the unions begin to co-operate between the different plants. Higher stocks of raw materials, work-in-progress and finished goods stock could cost upwards of £500 million but an allowance was made for this within the Ryder Strategy. Additional capacity was already planned for in the Ryder report so the extra cost is minimal — say a maximum of 1 assembly plant and 1 powertrain plant—£400 million. The new smaller plants envisaged should not cost much more than the rebuilding, refurbishing and re-equipping of older plants. However, at worst an additional £100 to £200 million might be required for land, the development of the land and some basic buildings. The additional cost of all the above is therefore not great in relation to the planned Ryder expenditure. Capital expenditure would also occur in the development of the robotic equipment. Including the hardware and software development costs, the total sum could be in the region of £500 to £1,000 million, but there would be substantial savings in the future in the form of lower capital expenditures for introducing new models. Of course this argument could also apply to many of the other recommendations. Namely the improved performance of BL Cars would justify the capital expenditure.

CONCLUSION

In the next chapter, two different scenarios for BL are considered. One posits the maintenance of BL's share over the next few years until a new model range is announced in the early 1980s. A second scenario sees the continued slide of BL's market shares. In this scenario BL gradually withdraws from the volume market though it would always market some volume cars. This covers the dichotomy of whether BL will eventually win through to something approaching the Ryder plans, or whether it will compact to one of the lower volume alternatives considered in this chapter.

1. Our estimates of the reduction on competitive manning levels over competitive European manning levels. Since BL does not have competitive manning levels, the reduction in labour force is likely to be that much greater.

The ramifications of the proposed merger between Chrysler's European operations and Peugeot-Citreon might persuade BL to try and find a European partner with greater urgency. This question is returned to in Section 5.

CHAPTER 8

DEMAND AND SUPPLY IN THE UK

INTRODUCTION

In the last two chapters the demand and the supply of cars were considered in isolation. In this chapter the possible responses by the four major UK car manufacturers are analysed. These responses are interpreted as quantitative guesstimates of their likely production plans. A number of assumptions have been made. First and foremost it is assumed that BL will exist more or less in its current form and may have a modest increase in capacity in line with the Ryder proposals. A new range of small/medium cars will be introduced in the 1980s. However, it is assumed that BL will have moved more towards a specialist car producer. Chrysler UK will have survived and will run into no serious difficulties until the late 1980s. Although loss of market share might be compensated by the UK assembly of Japanese car kits, this has not been assumed, because Government and other resistance may be considerable. Despite the prospect of the proposed Peugeot-Citroen merger, the assumption about the Chrysler UK plants may still be valid.

Peugeot-Citroen sales are assumed to be part of residual imports in this chapter.

DEMAND

Table 8.1 shows the likely range of demand for UK products. The UK car market forecast was discussed in Chapter 5. The market shares of the four manufacturers were also discussed. Briefly BL loses market share before a full model programme has been launched by the middle 1980s. Even then to achieve a 27 per cent share in 1980 means that BL must make a remarkable recovery; perhaps by retaining the old Mini, introducing the New Mini (in an enlarged form) and releasing versions of SD2,[1] Lynx,[2] modified Allegro, re-skinned Marina, hatchback Princess, facelifted Dolomite, etc. Ford's range continues to be competitive with the changed emphasis on engineering being successfully implemented. GM maintains and slightly improves its position. Chrysler too is assumed to improve its position which by 1990 might either be just maintained or may, more likely, have begun to deteriorate.

Exports to Europe by the three US multinationals are inevitably linked to their production policy and are therefore tied, the price of tied exports being tied imports. Apart from Chrysler, non-tied exports by Ford are small, and by GM insignificant. Only BL's exports to Europe are essentially non-tied to production policy. Although even with BL, the Seneffe plant in Belgium will be brought into BL's operation in a more integrated way.[3] Of all the UK manufacturers, BL alone is poorly endowed with overseas production and assembly

1. Cancelled in 1975.
2. Cancelled in 1977.
3. And to make up deficiencies in demand by UK plants.

TABLE 8.1

New Registrations of Cars: Range of Demand Projections

Scenario One[a]
in million cars per year

	1980	1985	1990
UK market[b]	1.55 – 1.7	1.7 – 1.9	1.7 – 2.1
Market share in %			
BL	22–27	23–28	24–33
Ford	24–28	23–27	20–27
GM	9–12	9–12	8–12
Chrysler	7– 8	7– 8	3– 7
	63–75	63–75	55–79
UK sales			
BL	.341 – .459	.391 – .532	408 – .693
Ford	.372 – .476	.391 – .513	.340 – .567
GM	.140 – .204	.153 – .228	.136 – .252
Chrysler	.109 – .136	.119 – .152	.051 – .147
	.962–1.275	1.054–1.425	.935–1.659
Non-tied exports			
North American	.080 – .150	.080 – .175	.080 – .175
Asia + Africa	.050 – .150	.040 – .125	.020 – .075
Oceania	.050	.050	.050
BL's Exports			
to Europe	.150 – .250	.200 – .300	.200 – .450
	.330 – .600	.370 – .650	.330 – .730
Total demand	1.292–1.875	1.424–2.075	1.265–2.389

a. BL remains a volume car manufacturer
b. Assumes trend growth; recession or boom may take actual demand above or below forecast range.

plants. Thus BL has a clear motivation to export, whilst other manufacturers may simply use other productive facilities to maintain overseas market shares. Consequently the bulk of the non-tied exports are attributable to BL.

There are however a number of problems with the demand specification.

First, the demand range may not be attained due to supply difficulties. Second, if one considers either GM or Chrysler in isolation, it is quite conceivable that their market share could improve significantly. For example, if GM markets its new models (S car, new Chevette, new Cavalier, and a large car range) really aggressively within the UK, and adjusts its distribution network appropriately, then there is no reason why the GM market share should not be close to Ford's. Similarly Chrysler could also drastically increase its market share. Hence supposing the market share situation became:

Ford	25%
GM	20%
Chrysler	15%
BL	25%
Importers	35% (currently attained)

then 120 per cent of the market would be allocated. For GM and Chrysler to raise their market share means that some other manufacturers must lose market share. In order to increase market share, it is probable that both Chrysler and GM need to attract new dealers. It is also doubtful whether Ford will relinquish its position without a fight. BL would possibly maintain its market position by reducing prices. The Japanese importers are unlikely to lose much market share, and other West European manufacturers individually only account for a small proportion of the total market. GM and Chrysler will probably only be able to gain market share at the expense of Ford or most likely BL. Such an action has severe implications for GM and Chrysler. The UK Government would be unwilling to see its investment in BL disappear without some protective action and it is precisely this threat which may deter GM from taking such an aggressive stance.

In fact, this chapter considers a second set of assumptions (dubbed Scenario Two) in which BL loses domestic market share and where the US multinationals and particularly the importers can adopt a more aggressive stance, which even bite into Ford's UK market share. The distinction between this scenario and the previous set of assumptions embodied in Table 8.1 (dubbed Scenario One) are discussed subsequently. However, suffice it to say that Scenario Two may be brought about by industrial unrest within BL itself, through outdated and uncompetitive models, from Government action or from the combined 'natural' behaviour of the US multinationals and importers.

Table 8.2 shows the range of demand projections under Scenario Two. As can be seen the total demand for products in Scenario Two does not change very much despite a curtailment of non-tied exports. BL's retrenchment[1] in this scenario to more specialist car manufacturing does mean a slight lowering in the expectations of exports. However, most of the residual loss in demand is made up by increased US multinationals sales.

A disaster scenario can be envisaged either under Scenario One (Table 8.1) or Scenario Two (Table 8.2) by simply taking the lower end of the market share

1. The dealer network would therefore gradually adjust to the levels shown in Table 14.9.

TABLE 8.2

New Registrations of Cars: Range of Demand Projections

Scenario Two
(assuming gradual withdrawal of BL from volume cars)
in millions of cars

	1980	1985	1990
UK Market	1.55 – 1.7	1.7 – 1.9	1.7 – 2.1
Market shares in %			
BL	15–22	14–20	12–15
Ford	22–30	22–31	24–32
GM	10–13	10–13	10–14
Chrysler	7– 9	7– 9	3–10
	54–74	53–73	49–71
UK Sales			
BL	.233 – .373	.238 – .380	.204 – .315
Ford	.341 – .510	.374 – .589	.408 – .672
GM	.155 – .221	.170 – .247	.170 – .294
Chrysler	.109 – .153	.119 – .171	.051 – .210
	.838–1.257	.901– 1.387	.833 –1.491
Non-tied exports (as per Table 8.1 but curtailed top end)	.330 – .550	.370 – .580	.330 – .600
Total Demand	1.168–1.807	1.271 –1.967	1.163– 2.091

range for all the UK manufacturers. This would allow the residual manufacturers (i.e. non–BL, Chrysler, Ford or GM) to increase their market share
beyond the current level of around 35 per cent to 37 per cent in Scenario One
and to over 40 per cent in Scenario Two.

The distinctions between Scenario One and Two concern the behaviour of
BL, the expansion of Ford, the recovery of GM and/or Chrysler plus the
success of the residual importers. Scenario One assumes that BL will eventually
recover as a volume manufacturer. It also assumes that the success of the
residual importers will be stemmed and may even be reversed. In Scenario
Two BL does not maintain its market share in the volume car sector. The
residual importers steadily improve their position. Ford, GM and Chrysler
(together with the importers) take over the market share relinquished by BL.
Fleet car use goes primarily to the US multinationals, whilst private buyers
split between the importers and the US multinationals. However, by the late
1980s, GM may have launched a concerted attack on the specialist car market

TABLE 8.3
New Registrations of Cars – Central Forecasts
in million of cars

	Scenario One			Scenario Two		
	1980	1985	1990	1980	1985	1990
UK market	1.6	1.8	1.9	1.6	1.8	1.9
BL						
UK market	1.6	1.8	1.9	1.6	1.8	1.9
BL						
UK market share %	24	25	27	20	18	14
Exports	.316	.400	.500	.300	.350	.300
Total demand	.700	.850	1.013	.620	.674	.566
Ford[a]						
UK market share %	26	25	24	27½	28	29
Total demand	.420	.450	.460	.440	.504	.551
GM[a]						
UK market share %	10	10	10	10½	11	12
Total demand	.160	.180	.190	.168	.198	.228
Chrysler						
UK market share %	7½	7½	6½	8	8	8
Exports (non-Tied)	.075	.050	.025	.075	.050	.025
Total demand	.195	.185	.184	.203	.194	.177
Total demand	1.475	1.665	1.811	1.431	1.570	1.522
Residual importers market share in %	32.5	32.5	32.5	34	35	37

a.   Exports for Ford and GM are assumed to be insignificant.

segment within Europe, whilst BL may have had more success with some 'down-market' projects.

Although Table 8.2 provides illustrative figures of how BL's relinquished market share may be divided up, a word of caution is appropriate. The principal assumption is that Ford will gain most. The extra slack may equally go to an aggressive GM and Chrysler or even partly to importers. The reason for donating most of BL's share to Ford is simply indicative of Ford's current plans to take over 30–33 per cent of the UK market coupled with a national marketing policy.

CENTRAL DEMAND FORECAST

The ranges given in the two scenarios do not allow a sufficiently precise forecast of what might happen. In order to demonstrate the likely conditions prevailing, two single point estimates are provided as representative central forecasts under both scenarios. These central forecasts are shown in Table 8.3. The UK market size for both Scenarios is assumed to be the same — more or less the median of the range given in Chapter 5. In Scenario One, the forecasts assume that BL will re-establish its position towards the late 1980s capturing some 27 per cent of the UK market. In order to do this a crash model policy requiring over £2 billion of capital investment[1] in the car division alone will be necessary, together with a firm commitment from all political parties to support BL. In the period 1979-82 BL will be in the most difficult situation as its new model range will have not been introduced (in contrast to most of BL's competitors); given this situation and adverse publicity, political parties may find it increasingly difficult to provide continued support.

The GM, Ford and Chrysler market shares are very much interchangeable. A successful GM model and a poor Ford model may enable GM to grab market share from Ford. Similarly unless GM produces a model to compete with the Chrysler C2 (Horizon) and the Ford Fiesta, Chrysler may very well increase its market share at the expense of GM. However in the Scenario One central forecast embodied in Table 8.3, Ford maintains its current market share. GM maintains its position at around 11 per cent of the market. Chrysler recovers its position to 7½ per cent of the market but the problems of long term viability once again arise in the later 1980s causing market share to drop. The residual importers are then reduced to just less than one third of the market. No significant increase is made on the market despite intense European, Japanese and Communist Bloc competition. BL exports of the volume medium cars will be reduced in Scenario Two as compared with Scenario One. The same pessimistic view of Chrysler's exports (mainly to Iran) is taken under both Scenarios. Other exports are assumed to be insignificant (although it is not inconceivable that Ford would source the US market with Fiestas built in the UK).

SUPPLY CONSIDERATIONS

The three US multinationals given the above demand can attempt to supply it in a number of ways. Given sufficient available supply, for example, the UK demand could be met entirely from non-UK sources, although such an outcome is unlikely. But before analysing how the demand for UK cars could be supplied, it is necessary to calculate how much spare UK capacity there may be. In order to do this the total West European situation must be appraised. Current estimates of capacity vary. By 1980 the CPRS Report put capacity at just under 15 million cars. However, certain manufacturers (e.g. VW) are actually planning on phasing down their assembly capacity. Other manufacturers such as Fiat and Renault have never achieved production close to their

---

1. For the 1978-88 period.

capacity levels. Estimates of the 1980 maximum two-shift capacity (including modest expansion by BMW, Daimler Benz and GM) are provided in Table 8.4. If high demand conditions are expected to occur then further modest expansion may occur as shown in Table 8.4.

TABLE 8.4
Western Europe's Capacity
Estimated Maximum Two-Shift Capacity
in millions of cars

Non UK	1980	1985	1990
Alfa Romeo	.35	.35	.35
BMW	.35	.4	.5
Chrysler	.65	.65	.75
Daimler-Benz	.45	.5	.5
Fiat	1.6	1.6	1.6
Ford	1.0	1.3	1.5
GM	1.1	1.3	1.5
Peugeot-Citroen	1.5	1.55	1.6
Renault	1.4	1.5	1.55
Seat and Authi	.45	.65	.75
Volvo and Saab[a]	.5	.5	.5
VW	1.8	1.7	1.6
UK	11.15	12.0	12.7
BL	1.1	1.2	1.3
Chrysler	.35	.3	.3
Ford	.55	.6	.65
GM	.35	.35	.35
	2.35	2.45	2.6

a. That is what a merged company would achieve.

Table 8.5 attempts to estimate total spare capacity. By analysing the balance of trade for Western Europe, and the new registration of cars within Europe, a total range of demand for Western European cars can be derived. Total capacity estimates can then be compared against this demand in order to provide an estimate of excess capacity. This, for example, in 1976 measured around 3.0 million cars. However, maximum capacity is infrequently achieved. Some manufacturers would require extra labour if full capacity were to be achieved. For other manufacturers 80 per cent or 90 per cent of full capacity is achievable but it is becoming more difficult to increase production. In the UK for example, production plans are often interrupted by industrial action either in the manufacturing companies or their suppliers. Hence the theoretical maximum capacity figure is not a useful measure of available capacity. One figure that is used as a measure of practical capacity is 80 per cent of the theoretical maximum. Thus in Table 8.5 a 'practical capacity' is assessed more realistically at 80 per cent of the total. On this basis there is very little excess capacity. On the other hand by having a third shift or weekend working, the overall maximum capacity is probably achievable and could even be surpassed. By 1990 and even in 1985, the likely range of demand exceeds that of practical capacity. Of course such a shortfall may be made up by increased (i.e. sucked in) imports, or alternatively a new manufacturer (e.g. a Japanese manufacturer) might place an assembly plant within Europe. At the moment much of the excess European capacity is in the UK. Of the 3.6 million excess capacity of cars in 1976, around 1.3 million was attributable to the UK. This situation did not improve in 1977. Much of the UK excess capacity could not be utilised in the short-run (due in part to low productivity).

TABLE 8.5
Western Europe's Excess Capacity
in millions of cars

	1976	1977	1980 Low	High	1985 Low	High	1990 Low	High
1. Exports	1.4	1.5	1.0	1.7	0.9	1.7	0.9	1.6
2. Imports	0.7	.8	0.7	1.0	0.8	1.1	0.9	1.2
3. Balance of trade[a]	0.7	.7	0	1.0	−0.1	.6	−.3	0.7
4. New registrations	9.4	9.9	10.0	11.2	11.0	12.6	12.0	13.8
5. Total demand (3+4)	10.1	10.6	10.0	12.2	10.9	13.2	11.7	14.5
6. Maximum capacity	13.7	13.5	13.0	14.0	14.0	15.0	14.1	15.8
7. Practical capacity = 80% of 6	11.0	10.8	10.4	11.2	11.2	12.0	11.3	12.6
8. Excess maximum capacity (6−5)	3.6	2.9	3.0	1.8	3.1	1.8	2.4	1.3
9. Excess practical capacity (7−5)	.9	.2	.4	−1.0	0.2	−1.2	−0.4	−1.9

a. Estimate arrived at by a combination of 1 and 2; low forecast uses low exports and high imports, whilst high estimate uses low imports and high exports.

UK PRODUCTION FLOWS

Because there is unlikely to be much European spare capacity in the late 1980s, UK capacity will be used by all UK manufacturers who have sufficient finance to invest in an on-going model development programme. A larger question-mark must be placed on the intervening years between now and the late 1980s. Of particular interest is the extent of spare non-UK capacity for the three US multinationals. This is analysed within the framework of Table 8.6. An assessment is made of likely Western European sales. By reference to the central forecast of demand (Table 8.3), likely UK sales are deducted in order to form an impression of non-UK sales within Western Europe. This is compared with non-UK capacity within Western Europe in order to provide the possible range of deficit of demand over supply which may be made good by UK production. Added to this figure should be those exports to areas outside the UK. For Ford, their small car will be sourced in the US from Europe. So added to the deficit should be at least 100,000 to 200,000 extra cars a year. This means that Ford will have a substantial deficit that could be made good by the UK. GM is less likely to source US demand from European production. The possible GM deficit is therefore as shown in Table 8.6 plus 50,000 to 100,000 vehicles. For GM, the spare UK capacity only becomes significant if optimistic assumptions come true in 1980, or towards the mid and late 1980s. With Chrysler it is conceivable that some European demand will be sourced from the US. Thus the new C2 (Horizon) has been marketed in Europe as

TABLE 8.6

Non-UK Spare Capacity – Range Estimates
in millions of Cars

	1976	1977	1980	1985	1990
European demand (in million cars)	9.7	9.9	10–11.2	11–12.6	12–13.8
FORD					
European market share%	11.2	12.3	12–13	11–14	11–14
European sales	1.1	1.2	1.2–1.5	1.2–1.8	1.3–1.9
Less UK demand	0.3	0.3	0.4	0.4	0.4–0.5
Non-UK sales[a]	0.8	0.9	0.8–1.1	0.8–1.4	0.9–1.5
Non UK capacity[a]	0.8	1.0	1.0	1.0–1.3	1.0–1.7
Deficit in non-UK[a] supply[b]	0.008	-0.04	-0.2–+0.1	-0.2–+0.4	-0.1–+0.5
GM					
European market share%	10.3	10.0	11–12	10–13	10–13
European sales	1.0	1.0	1.1–1.3	1.1–1.6	1.2–1.8
Less UK demand	0.1	0.14	0.2	0.2–0.3	0.2–0.3
Non UK sales[a]	0.9	0.86	0.9–1.1	0.8–1.4	0.9–1.6
Non UK capacity[a]	1.0	1.0	1.0	1.0–1.3	1.0–1.5
Deficit in non-UK[a] supply[b]	-0.023	- 0.03	-0.1–+0.1	-0.2–+0.4	-0.1–+0.6
CHRYSLER					
European market share%	6.4	5.7	6.5–8	6.5–8	6–7.5
European sales	0.6	0.6	0.7–0.9	0.7–1.0	0.7–1.0
Less UK demand	0.1	0.1	0.1	0.1–0.2	0.1–0.2
Non-UK sales[a]	0.5	0.5	0.6–0.8	0.5–0.9	0.5–0.9
Non-UK capacity[a]	0.7	0.7	0.7	0.7	0.7–0.8
Deficit in non-UK[a] supply[b]	- 0.008	- 0.01	-0.1–+0.1	-0.2–+0.2	-0.2–+0.2

a. Non-UK defined as within Europe but excluding the UK
b. Extent to which UK production may be used to supply European and other sales. Negative figure implies net imports into the UK. The 1976 and 1977 figures are estimated 'actual' figures for net UK exports within Europe (but excluding non-European sales) by the US multinationals.

either the French built product or the US built product (with a VW engine). The deficit shown in Table 8.6 is probably a realistic assessment bearing in mind the non-European sourcing and some European exports. Taking the mid-point of the range, Chrysler will have no overall deficit. Only if Chrysler exceeds 7 per cent of the European market will there exist a deficit which may be made good by UK production or assembly.

The greatest possible deficit in non-UK supply within Europe could not be met by any of the US multinationals from existing UK capacity. The question must therefore be asked whether any of the US multinationals would be willing to expand their production and assembly facilities within the UK. Although Ford may expand component manufacture, and make it easier to achieve near capacity figures at Dagenham and Halewood. Spain and another country bordering on the Mediterranean were considered to be the likely beneficiaries of any expansion. However recently the UK must have once again become a serious candidate for expansion by Ford.[1] (We return to this topic in Section 5.) For GM it was argued in Chapter 6 that further concentration is probably unlikely, although the full capacity may for the first time be fully utilised. Similarly Chrysler's loyalty must surely be for its French subsidiary which has a greater chance of being self sustaining. Although some deficit may be made good by UK assembly, the Chrysler plan forsees UK capacity as being a buffer which may be exported to non-European and non-US markets. Possible expansion of Chrysler's Spanish facilities might occur in the late 1980s but this is doubtful as the small deficit could be met largely from UK and US sourcing, and Chrysler is unlikely to have spare finance for such investment plans.

However, as with the range of demand, many considerations may interfere with production plans. UK labour relations, and UK Government policy are two such factors. In order to tie down the likely range of such a supply deficit, central estimates are now discussed.

CENTRAL FORECAST OF EUROPEAN SUPPLY DEFICIT

Ford and GM in Table 8.7 have been forecast to achieve a central position in the likely European market share range given in Table 8.6. Both companies maintain their position in the late 1980s, whilst Chrysler is assumed to achieve an optimistic market share during the early 1980s, with some slip towards the late 1980s. The more optimistic Scenario Two is assumed to modify European market share of the US multinationals. In other words the market share range given in Table 8.6 assumed that Scenario One (a thriving BL) was relevant for the UK. Thus in Table 8.7 it can be seen that the estimate of non-UK European sales are identical under both scenarios.

Expansion of capacity is more problematic and only an estimate of practical achievable capacity has been assessed. A certain amount of expansion in GM's case, and possible rearrangement of facilities in Ford's case will be necessary if the 1980 practical capacity estimate is to be achieved. By 1985 Ford will have

---

1. The Ford strike in Autumn and the consequent Government action may modify this conclusion.

TABLE 8.7

Central Forecast of European Supply Deficit
(in millions of cars)

	Scenario One			Scenario Two		
	1980	1985	1990	1980	1985	1990
FORD						
European demand	1.3	1.5	1.7	1.32	1.55	1.79
Non-European demand	0.1	0.07	0.05	0.1	0.07	0.05
Total European sales	1.4	1.57	1.75	1.42	1.62	1.84
UK demand[a]	0.42	0.45	0.46	0.44	0.50	0.55
Non UK sales	0.98	1.12	1.29	0.98	1.12	1.29
Practical non-UK capacity	1.0	1.1	1.1–1.3	1.0	1.1	1.1–1.3
Deficit possibly made						
good by UK	0	0.02	0–+0.19	0	0.02	0–+0.19
(assuming no additional						
UK plant)						
GM						
European sales	1.2	1.4	1.5	1.21	1.42	1.54
UK demand[a]	0.16	0.18	0.19	0.17	0.20	0.23
Non-UK sales	1.04	1.22	1.31	1.0	1.22	1.31
Practical non-UK capacity	1	1.1–1.2	1.1–1.3	1	1.1–1.2	1.1–1.3
Deficit possibly made						
good by UK	0.04	0–+0.12	0–+0.21	0.04	0–+0.12	0–+0.21
CHRYSLER						
European sales	0.08	0.89	0.9	0.80	0.90	0.96
UK demand[a]	0.20	0.19	0.15	0.20	0.19	0.18
Non UK sales	0.60	0.70	0.75	0.60	0.70	0.78
Practical non-UK capacity	0.70	0.7–0.80	0.70	0.70	0.70	0.7–0.80
Deficit possibly made good						
by UK	0	0	0–+0.05	0	0	0–+0.08

[a]From Table 8.3

expanded its Valencia plant, built a small scale assembly plant elsewhere (but not in the UK), and may have built a new assembly plant in the UK. GM will have marginally expanded its Belgian and German plants and possibly might construct a small scale assembly plant in one of the developing markets (e.g. Spain). However such an expansion is far from sure. If the UK labour relations, quality of workmanship and component supply appear reasonable, the deficit of supply might be made up from the UK, although the poor UK reputation with respect to durability, quality and reliability mitigates against this. In either event the UK will probably be called upon to increase its supply of component manufacture in order partially to supply the additional GM and Ford assembly capacity.

With Chrysler the story by 1985 is no overall European deficit. Before the mid-1990s however, Chrysler could afford to supply some of the UK market from non-UK plants. In the event of Middle East sales being higher than anticipated this may have been useful. However Chrysler UK exports will probably be on the decline from 1980 onwards. It is therefore more likely that some sourcing from the French Poissy plant will be likely despite spare UK capacity. However, this would be fairly moderate and should not exceed 50,000 units or so.

By 1990 all three multinationals might once again increase capacity. For Chrysler an expansion of its Spanish or even its French plants is a possibility.[1] For GM the expansion might take the form of enlarging an assembly plant or building a new assembly plant depending on the assumptions made in 1985. For Ford, increased capacity may mean an expanded Valencia plant, a marginal increase in capacity at existing plants or the introduction of a small assembly plant in a new area. On the other hand the UK could, given spare UK capacity, supply most or all of this deficit. Whether the US multinationals choose to do this would in part depend on labour relations in the UK,[2] the reputation for the quality of UK workmanship, competitive labour costs and the available supply of UK components. The cost penalty of transporting cars from the UK to European locations need not rule out the UK from supplying a very large number of cars for any one company – the Japanese being a case in point. Additional capacity accounts for about 10 – 20 per cent of total car costs. It can be argued that anything less than this in transport costs favours the use of existing capacity. Poor industrial relations (which in turn has lead to poor productivity) combined with higher transport costs together dictate against the use of existing spare UK capacity in favour of additional installed capacity. Another supporting factor is the poor quality of UK work as perceived by the European marketplace.

SPARE UK CAPACITY

The second question to be raised is whether there would be any spare UK capacity to meet a European deficit in supply. Table 8.8 shows the range of UK demand, and gives a practical assessment of UK achievable capacity, which together yield the likely range of spare UK capacity. Although Ford has a theoretical capacity of 550,000 cars, the low UK productivity implies that even allowing for an improvement, practical UK capacity is unlikely to exceed 450,000. This is the assumed figure for 1980. By 1985 this will have risen to 600,000 and by 1990 further improvements will allow 650,000+ units to be produced. These increases may only be achievable by the building of a new assembly plant in the UK and this point is further discussed in Section 5.[3] The estimates of the possible European deficit is provided both

1. Although the takeover of Chrysler Europe by Peugeot-Citroen probably dictates expansion of Peugeot/Citroen plants at the expense of the Chrysler brandname.
2. Which have been appallingly poor; Ford's Halewood plant despite a capacity of 1,500 cars a day, produced less than half this figure in 1977.
3. Although the Government sanctions subsequent to the Ford strike in Autumn may modify this conclusion.

from the range estimates derived from Table 8.6 and the central assumptions forecast made in Table 8.7. From Table 8.8 it will be seen that no significant deficit will occur in the European supply until the late 1980s except perhaps for GM in the middle 1980s. Despite this and primarily because of power-train and other UK manufactured components, Ford will probably be a net importer of vehicles to Europe. In any case such a deficit would only be made good to the extent of 100,000 or so vehicles by any company. To source any greater number of cars from the UK would probably place an unacceptably high degree of risk from a country whose industrial relations record has become notorious, and whose quality of workmanship is poor. The UK may however, achieve the production of the maximum estimate of 200,000 vehicles because it may prove more economic to produce one model, at one plant than to incur the cost penalties of transporting cars across the Channel.

For Ford the central estimate of the likely trade balance between the UK and Europe is net imports of about 50,000 cars in 1980, a small positive balance in 1985 and larger net exports by 1990. For GM the early 1980s forsee small net exports which will be eradicated from the mid 1990s onwards by the addition of extra capacity elsewhere. For Chrysler the early 1980s, when European integration has not fully occurred and some models (e.g. C2 and C9) will be made in France or Spain, may see net imports into the UK. Later in the 1980s once the Iran order has died down to a trickle, the UK European supply situation will probably break even.

Of course a breakeven situation does not necessarily mean that no exports and imports take place — only that imports are balanced by exports. Greater European integration requires specialisation of production. This means that in any particular time period, one particular model may or may not be produced in the UK. This could cause the central estimates of the UK trade balance reproduced in Table 8.9 to deviate by as much as 100,000 cars either way. Also shown in Table 8.9 is the deficit range from Table 8.6 but truncated at the top end of the range by the maximum spare UK capacity given in Table 8.8. The central forecast thus shows a deteriorating situation at the turn of the decade but one which should improve during the 1980s

Although BL has not been mentioned as being a tied importer or exporter, BL's Belgium plant will probably not source UK models once BL has rebuilt its Longbridge plant, so that BL production which is supplied by UK produced kits has been lumped together with BL's UK production. Although when the New Mini is in production, the Belgian plant has sufficient capacity to produce the 'old' Mini in its desired quantities — up to 100,000 units a year In this instance BL would 'import' back to the UK 50,000 or so 'old Minis'.

Finally it is unlikely that all three US multinationals would simultaneously import significant numbers of cars. Bearing this factor in mind a maximum likely range for tied trade with Europe but excluding BL probably a net import situation although in theory a balance of plus or minus 200,000 cars may result in 1980; between 200,000 net imports to 300,000 net exports in 1985; and between 200,000 net imports to 400,000 net exports in 1990.

TABLE 8.8

Spare UK Capacity
(in millions of cars)

	1980	1985	1990
Ford			
UK demand	-0.4 – 0.5	0.4 – 0.5	0.4 – 0.6
Non European sales	0 – 0.1	0 – 0.1	0 – 0.1
Total	0.4 – 0.6	0.4 – 0.6	0.4 – 0.7
Practical UK capacity	0.45	0.6	0.65 – .7
Spare UK capacity	-0.15 –+0.05	0 –+0.2	-0.05 –+0.35
Possible European deficit (from Table 8.6)	-0.2 –+0.1	-0.2 –+0.4	-0.1 –+0.5
Central forecast deficit possibly made good by UK (from Table 8.7)	0	0.02	0 –+0.19
Central estimates of deficit made good by UK	-0.05	0.02	0.1
GM			
UK demand	0.2	0.2	0.1 – 0.3
Practical UK capacity	0.3	0.3	0.3
Spare UK capacity	0.1	0.1	0 –+0.2
Possible European deficit (from Table 8.6)	-0.1 –+0.1	-0.2 –+0.4	-0.1 –+0.6
Central forecast deficit possibly made good by UK (from Table 8.7)	0.04	0 –+0.12	0 –+0.21
Central estimate of deficit made good by UK	0	0.05	0
Chrysler			
UK demand	0.1	0.1 – 0.2	0.1 – 0.2
Non-European sales	0.1	0 – 0.1	0 – 0.1
Total	0.1 – 0.2	0.1 – 0.3	0.1 – 0.3
Practical UK capacity	0.3	0.3	0.3
Spare UK capacity	-0.1 –+0.2	+0.1 – +0.2	–+0.2
Possible European deficit	-0.1 –+0.1	-0.2 –+0.2	-0.2 –+0.2
Central forecast deficit possibly made good by UK (from Table 8.7)	0	0	0 –+0.05
Central estimate of estimate of deficit made good by UK	-0.03	0	0

TABLE 8.9

Estimates of UK Trade Balance with Europe for the US Multinationals
(in millions of cars)

	1976	1977 (estimated)	1980	1985	1990
Central estimate					
Ford	0.008	– 0.04	– 0.05	0.05	0.1
GM	– 0.023	– 0.03	0	0.05	0
Chrysler	– 0.008	– 0.01	– 0.03	0	0
	– 0.023	– 0.08	– 0.08	0.1	0.1
Possible range					
Ford			– 0.2–+0.1	– 0.2–+0.2	–0.1–+0.2
GM			– 0.1–+0.1	– 0.2–+0.1	–0.1–+0.2
Chrysler			– 0.1–+0.1	– 0.2–+0.2	–0.2–+0.2
			– 0.4–+0.3	– 0.6–+0.5	–0.4–+0.6
Maximum likely range for total industry			– 0.2–+0.2	– 0.2–+0.3	–0.2–+0.4

TOTAL UK CAR PRODUCTION

The CPRS Report produced the figures that are shown in Table 8.10 for estimates of UK car production. In Appendix 8.1 revised estimates are shown based on the methodology of working out the UK manufacturers market share, assessing the production policy of the three multinationals and calculating true export sales (mainly attributable to BL after Chrysler's Iran order has been completed). These figures are summarised in Table 8.11. Despite a more careful analysis of the UK situation, the original CPRS estimates stand out as being surprisingly good. The widest range provided in Table 8.11 is too wide to be of much use. The central forecast under either of the two scenarios falls within the original CPRS estimate. The difference between the two scenarios occurs in the composition of total UK output. Scenario One sees BL with a higher and a rising share of total UK output. Scenario Two predicts a lower and falling share of UK output, although it stabilises at some 40 per cent because of BL's export success. Scenario One veers on the side of optimism, whilst perhaps Scenario Two is too pessimistic. If events continue to conspire against BL, then its market share may drop more sharply than predicted (as it did in 1977 contrary to most observers' opinions), or alternatively a political decision may be made to scale down BL more quickly. Similarly the Ryder estimates for exports are not outrageous. Given the dealer network and a competitive model range now, then a 33 per cent market share would be possible. Unfortunately the BL dealer network has been drastically reduced (see Chapter 14) and the new model range is not expected until at least the early 1980s and is likely to be delayed until the middle of the 1980s. A significant improvement in market share is therefore not possible until the new model range has been developed. Even then BL will find it hard work to make up lost ground in the UK. However, and partly due to BL's now defunct International division, export sales of specialist cars could continue to be strong irrespective of what happens on the UK market. These conclusions and those embodied in Table 8.11 assume that proposed merger between Chrysler (Europe) and Peugeot-Citroen does not greatly affect production. If Peugeot-Citroen decide to close down the Linwood plant then total UK production would be reduced by a proportion of the Linwood production.

CONCLUSION

This chapter has attempted to make a realistic assessment of both the likely demand and supply considerations of the four major UK manufacturers. The estimates provided in this chapter are central forecasts. Boom conditions in the UK, and lack of supply in Europe might both increase UK production. However, in the absence of these factors UK production will only catch up on its peak of the early 1970s in the middle 1980s. From then on UK production should exceed 70 per cent of installed capacity and should be reasonably profitable. Question marks have already been raised about Chrysler and is further discussed in Chapter 17. The Peugeot-Citreon merger with Chrysler (Europe) has both some good and some bad points. BL at its level of sales in the late 1980s could be viable but may notwithstanding this, require Government finance or loans in times of depression.

Financial viability for either Ford or GM is assumed under the central forecasts given above. BL under either scenario will not be profitable until it has achieved a complete new car range in Scenario One or until (Scenario Two) it really has slimmed down to a specialist producer. Even in Scenario One – as was stated in the previous chapter – a severe recession or a prolonged strike may cause BL to seek aid. Chrysler's longer run profitability in the assumptions given above is doubtful since no new substantial export orders are gained. Survival may be assured through a rationalised model programme and a fully integrated production plan with perhaps some US sourcing. But the most pressing problem in the early 1980s will be a troubled BL.

TABLE 8.10

CPRS Estimates for Possible Outcomes for British Car Industry in 1985

	1980		1985	
	Worst case	Best case	Worst case	Best case
Sales in Britain				
New registrations (m)	1.55	1.65	1.8	1.9
Import share %	45	28	45	28
British produced sales (millions)	0.85	1.19	0.99	1.37
Exports to EEC/EFTA				
New registrations (m)	7.25	8.45	8.6	9.7
British share %	3	4	2.8	4.5
British produced sales (millions)	0.22	0.34	0.24	0.44
Exports to rest of world				
Exports to North America (m)	0.08	0.1	0.08	0.14
Exports to the rest of the world (millions)	0.14	0.19	0.14	0.19
Total British car production	1.29	1.82	1.45	2.14
Likely British production in 1985			from 0.7 to 1.95	

(depending on market shares in key markets by UK manufacturers)

Future Car Production Projections for the UK and BL under alternative assumptions

	1980		1985		1990	
	1.29 – 1.82		1.45 – 2.14			
	Scenario 1	Scenario 2	Scenario 1	Scenario 2	Scenario 1	Scenario 2
CPRS Estimates						
Chapter 8 Methodology						
Widest range[a]	0.91–2.18	0.77–2.11	0.84–2.58	0.67–2.47	0.87–3.04	0.76–2.74
Central forecast[a]	1.45	1.43	1.82	1.72	1.98	1.75
Range assuming zero tied balance of trade with Western Europe[a]	1.31–1.68	1.15–1.79	1.44–2.08	1.27–1.97	1.27–2.44	1.16–2.14
Range assuming central forecast of UK sales plus maximum tied import or export range (as given in Table 8.9)	1.33–1.73	1.31–1.71	1.51–2.02	1.42–1.92	1.68–2.28	1.45–2.05
Likely range of total British produced sales	1.3–1.6	1.2–1.5	1.55–2.0	1.4–1.9	1.45–2.15	1.4–2.0
BL Sales						
1) Central assumption						
UK sales	0.38	0.32	0.45	0.32	0.51	0.27
Exports	0.32	0.30	0.40	0.35	0.50	0.30
Total sales	0.70	0.62	0.85	0.67	1.01	0.57
2) Ryder Proposals (see Chapter 7)						
UK sales at 33% market share	0.53		0.59		0.63	
Exports	0.45		0.6		0.65	
Total sales	0.99		1.19		1.28	

a. detailed figures provided in Appendix 8.1.

APPENDIX 8.1
UK CAR PRODUCTION

	1974	1975	1976	1977	1980 Scenario One		1980 Scenario Two	
					Range	Central Forecast	Range	Central Forecast
UK Sales								
1. New registrations (millions)	1.27	1.19	1.29	1.32	1.55–1.7	1.6	1.55–1.7	1.6
2. Market share by four UK manufacturers %	74.27	68.84	69.28	66.5	63–75	67.5	54–74	66
3. UK sales	0.94	0.82	0.89	0.88	0.98–1.28	1.08	0.84–1.26	1.06
4. Tied imports	0.05	0.04	0.10	0.16				
5. Tied exports to EEC/EFTA	0.1	0.08	0.08	0.08				
6. Tied trade balance with Western Europe = 5 – 4	+0.05	+0.04	–0.02	–0.08	–0.04–+0.3	–0.08	–0.4–+0.3	–0.08
7. UK sales + tied trade balance = 3 + 6	0.99	0.86	0.87	0.8	0.58–1.58	1.0	0.44–1.56	.98
Exports (non tied)								
8. Europe (BL sales + non EEC/EFTA)	0.17	0.13	0.19	0.19	0.15–0.25	0.20	0.15–0.23	0.20
9. America	0.11	0.09	0.10	0.10	0.08–0.15	0.10	0.08–0.15	0.10
10. Rest of the world	0.22	0.24	0.17	0.16	0.10–0.20	0.15	0.10–0.17	0.15
11. Total exports (non-tied) = 8 + 9 + 10	0.50	0.46	0.46	0.45	0.33–0.60	0.45	0.33–0.55	0.45
12. Total British produced car sales = 7+11	1.50	1.32	1.33	1.25	0.91–2.18	1.45	0.77–2.11	1.43

APPENDIX 8.1 (cont.)

	1985 Scenario One		1985 Scenario Two		1990 Scenario One		1990 Scenario Two	
	Range	Central Forecast	Range	Central Forecast	Range	Central Forecast	Range	Central Forecast
1.	1.7–1.9	1.8	1.7–1.9	1.8	1.7–2.1	1.9	1.7–2.1	1.9
2.	63–75	67.5	53–73	65	55–79	67.5	49–71	63
3.	1.07–1.43	1.22	0.90–1.39	1.17	0.94–1.66	1.28	0.83–1.49	1.20
4.								
5.								
6.	−0.6–+0.5	0.1	−0.6–+0.5	0.1	−0.4–+0.6	0.1	−0.4–+0.6	0.1
7.	0.7–1.93	1.32	0.30–1.89	1.27	0.54–2.26	1.38	0.43–2.09	1.3
8.	0.20–0.30	0.25	0.20–0.28	0.23	0.20–0.45	0.39	0.20–0.35	0.25
9.	0.09–0.18	0.12	0.08–0.15	0.11	0.08–0.18	0.13	0.08–0.15	0.1
10.	0.09–0.18	0.13	0.09–0.15	0.11	0.05–0.15	0.08	0.05–0.15	0.1
11.	0.37–0.65	0.50	0.37–0.58	0.45	0.33–0.78	0.6	0.33–0.65	0.45
12.	0.84–2.58	1.82	0.67–2.47	1.72	0.87–3.04	1.98	0.76–2.74	1.75

CHAPTER 9

SMALLER MANUFACTURERS

INTRODUCTION

One of the most distinctive features of the West European motor industry is the number of specialist and/or smaller manufacturers. Curiously enough, although the UK market is now one of the smallest in Europe (in relation to population) it nevertheless has a surprisingly large number of small producers — more than any other country in Europe. Many of the once legendary West European names have now disappeared: the French firm of Facel Vega collapsed in the 1960s, and the great Italian producers — Ferrari, Maserati, Lamborghini, De Tomaso — have all run into difficulties. Ferrari's link with Fiat has provided financial backing and a degree of autonomy, while the Italian state-owned agency, GEPI, has now taken a controlling interest in Maserati and de Tomaso, but it remains to be seen whether Lamborghini can survive as an independent entity. In France, Matra-Simca is to some extent supported by Chrysler, while the Alpine company now has links with Renault. Porsche, the German sports car firm, with a total capacity of roughly 20,000 units, can no longer be considered as a small manufacturer, although the car itself is heavily dependent on the US market. Table 9.1 summarises production figures for most of the smaller car manufacturers in France, Italy and the UK. Although the UK has the highest number of independent firms, France has the largest production total, thanks largely to the success of the Matra Simca range. No other mature car market has any direct equivalent to this highly specialised car market. The Japanese product is aimed almost without exception at the volume car sector: although the US producers market two ultra-luxury products — the GM Cadillac and the Ford Lincoln — they are both relatively cheap in comparison with Rolls-Royce, which is a product at the luxury end of the West European specialist range.

What exactly does the term 'specialist' or small producer signify? Three main types of product traditionally associated with the smaller manufacturer can be identified: first, the quality car, made by a medium-sized firm, often a division or subsidiary of a larger firm; second, the luxury executive limousine or grand touring car; and finally, the more idiosyncratic 'sports' models, not necessarily extremely expensive but always eccentric or at least flamboyant in character. The quality car manufacturers must compete with the mass producers at the top end of the volume market, whereas the maker of an unashamedly luxury product is not obliged to make any concessions to competitive pricing, although the basic 'cost-plus' approach is now more often tempered by a cautious respect for a slight elasticity in demand even in the upper income brackets: wealthy, price-insensitive customers are not in unlimited supply (with the possible exception of Rolls-Royce customers). In the final category, the 'sports' model, manufacturers are again not directly involved in competition with the volume car producers as sales reflect the 'distinctive' quality of the product, modified by an awareness that the demand for such a product often arises in only the average (or slightly below average) income groups in the population, and that price must therefore be more carefully controlled. Many of the firms operating in this sector are precariously under-capitalised, because of this need to keep prices as low as possible and still manufacture an appealing non-mass-produced product.

The quality car producers must make a virtue of necessity, in claiming that the often inefficient (i.e. high-cost) techniques they are obliged to use, result in a conspicuously better product than anything manufactured by a volume car producer. It can however be argued that the real difference lies not in the actual quality of the product or the measurable advantages it has over a mass-produced rival, but in the skill with which it is marketed and the premium prices charged. In too many 'quality' cars, we suspect, the high price tag has more to do with inefficiency than with any inherent superiority it might claim to possess. However it is true that greater care may be taken in the assembly of the cars.

Keeping these three categories in mind, we turn now to a number of observations on the current state of affairs in European specialist small-scale car manufacture. To begin with the obvious: because of the specialist (and therefore in most cases limited) nature of the demand for their products, most of these smaller manufacturers operate at the periphery of the market. Their position is vulnerable, and they are all too liable to succumb to extreme financial and/or market pressures. The market they cater for is small and highly competitive: a mistake could be fatal, and lack of finance ruinous.

We have already noted that the demand for a distinctive product is not necessarily demand for a product manufactured in limited quantities. This applies particularly to demand for a quality car. Consumers can be (and have been) convinced that a volume car manufacturer is capable of producing a quality model to satisfy their particular needs. Quality, per se, is not a sole or even necessary condition of small-scale manufacture. This places further pressure on smaller manufacturers, particularly those in the quality rather than the luxury market. Moreover, specialist demand is highly regional in character, taking Europe as a whole. In Germany, specialist demand follows a functional approach where even sports cars are simply faster versions of the solid German family saloon, whereas Italian sports models have an unmistakably flamboyant, not to say romantic, image. In choosing a specialist model, the French are probably motivated more by a species of sporting jingoism and technical sophistication than anything else, whereas in the UK great emphasis is placed on tradition, prestige and 'quality'.

With a floundering domestic market, the smaller UK manufacturers have been forced to choose between launching (or expanding) an export sales drive or restricting production to receipt-of-order sales. Rolls-Royce, Morgan, Bristol and Panther all produce vehicles on receipt of a firm order only. Because of the nature of the products they manufacture, these firms are assured of a small but reasonably inelastic demand (although this by no means guarantees demand, as both Aston Martin and Lotus discovered to their cost). The demand from 'motoring enthusiasts' for a distinctive sports car (e.g. Morgan, Lotus)[1] is less

---

1.   Prior to their move to up-market sports cars in the 1970's.

TABLE 9.1

Production of Small Car Manufacturers

	1972	1973	1974	1975	1976	1977
UK						
Rolls-Royce	2,472	2,771	2,899	3,137	3,261	2,872
Reliant	2,053	2,405	2,167	1,395	3,247	2,377
Lotus	3,059	2,830	1,466	655	931	1,074
Jensen	1,817	5,120	5,556	1,928	272	–
TVR	388	388	421	132	333	366
Aston Martin	*	*	*	*	171	261
Morgan	*	*	*	382	401	396
Others	733	749	679	44	34	43
Total	10,522	14,263	13,188	7,673	8,650	7,389

* Indicates production is included in the 'others' figures

	1972	1973	1974	1975	1976	1977
ITALY						
Ferrari	1,843	1,772	1,436	1,337	1,427	1,798
Iso	121	122	43	–	–	–
Lamborghini[a]	318	550	355	276	201	105
Maserati[b]	557	738	571	201	195	292
De Tomaso	2,718	–	196	235	147	128
Total	5,557	3,182	2,601	2,049	1,970	2,323
FRANCE						
Alpine[c]	1,481	1,307	969	1,114	1,048	1,353
Matra-Simca	2,159	4,228	11,264	7,338	7,376	12,094
Total	3,640	5,535	12,233	8,452	8,424	13,447

a   Now owned by a Swiss company
b   Owned by GEPI
c   Associate company of Renault

stable in character, arising as it does from a minority group with an interest in a particular type of car rather than a high income level. This second type of demand — for what we might describe as a small sports car — is therefore both income and price elastic. The manufacturer must operate in a price-sensitive sector of the market where considerations of price and quality mean that only a highly specialist model can generate enough sales to enable a small firm to operate profitably. Morgan, for example, have produced a largely unchanged style of product since the 1930s, when the firm became the only source of 'traditional' metal-bodied sports cars. Panther began in the 1970s with replicas of pre-war 'classic' models, modified to meet the standards of motoring in the 1970s. In each case, the firm has been able to secure a highly particularised and closely defined marketing niche, offering a unique product to a small but enthusiastic group of consumers, most of whom are prepared to wait for delivery, but not all of whom necessarily have unlimited funds available with which to indulge their particular tastes.

As we have seen, not all of the smaller producers can rely solely on cost-plus pricing, particularly those whose products are aimed principally at the quality car market, as opposed to the luxury segment where competitive pressures make demand price-sensitive. A distinctive product is vital, certainly, but in the quality car segment the manufacturer must be able to overcome the major cost disadvantages which are the inevitable result of low output and unavoidably high tooling costs (compared with the volume manufacturer). Disadvantages can be minimised by restricting the range of output (Rover, for example, concentrated for some time on one body and two engines) and by longer model runs, i.e. producing the same basic model for a much longer period than a volume producer would, thus spreading at least some of the tooling costs. One other factor which can help smaller manufacturers is the extent to which they buy in components. Reliant, for example, uses a Ford engine in the Scimitar, while Jensen used either a Chrysler or a Lotus engine – even Lotus used to fit a Ford engine. TVR used Ford engines, Morgans are equipped with BL and Ford engines, Bristols with a modified Chrysler engine, Panther with either BL or Vauxhall engines and so on. Most, if not all, of the bought-in components are manufactured internally by the mass producers themselves whose scale economies are passed on to the smaller manufacturer. In some respects, small-scale firms in the UK depend for their survival on the existence of a highly developed and remarkably efficient components industry, from which they are able to purchase components and supplies which they could not hope to manufacture themselves.

Export sales are summarised in Table 9.2. Rolls-Royce and Jensen were the principal exporters in 1975, for most of the manufacturers (with the exception of Aston-Martin and Panther), the US is the major export market, although Rolls-Royce sales are evenly distributed world-wide, aggregating more than £25 million in export sales in 1975.

TABLE 9.2

Car Exports of Small Producers in 1975

	Europe	America	Asia	Africa	Oceania	Total
Rolls-Royce	403	1,143	232	21	51	1,850
Reliant	–	–	–	–	3	3
Jensen	128	1,370	20	3	23	1,544
Lotus	58	139	43	1	2	264
Aston Martin	5	6	7	–	1	19
Panther	24	16	7	3	0	50

We have seen that there are, in general, three distinct groupings into which the smaller manufacturers can be divided; and that in order to improve or strengthen their rather marginal position, these producers can adopt a number of strategies to minimise the burdensome cost disadvantages incurred in small-scale car production. Let us turn, now, to an examination of some of the specialist manufacturers themselves.

Rolls-Royce

With full order books, a reputation − deserved or otherwise − for quality and one of the most highly distinctive product ranges in the market, Rolls-Royce is the most successful of the small UK producers. In 1975 the company exported 60 per cent of its output, dropping to 56 per cent in 1976. Although the company is heavily export-orientated, it has a healthy volume of sales in the domestic market − worth over £30 million in 1976. If the UK market were to collapse, Rolls-Royce *could* continue to function as a viable concern, but the company would certainly find life much less tolerable in the absence of a domestic market. Quite how an otherwise shaky UK market can support a continuing demand for a car that is double or very nearly treble the price of an average family house − let alone the price of the average family car − is an intriguing puzzle. Tradition and snobbery of the type peculiar to the UK certainly play their part, but there may be other more mundane explanations for the phenomenon. For example, the vast number of international concerns with prestige offices and/or headquarters in London certainly account in part for the fact that London has a high density of Rolls-Royces per capita.

Reliant

Reliant, who also manufacture the ubiquitous three-wheeler, now concentrates on production of two types of car, both with fibre-glass bodies. The smaller car − the Kitten − lacks the refinement of mass produced small cars, confirming the old adage that a small-scale producer simply cannot spread the costs of a full-scale research and development programme over a small production run without threatening the product's chances of a success in the cost-conscious volume market. In 1976, only 2,043 Kittens were produced, more than half of them as estate models. The Reliant Scimitar, on the other hand, has been much more successful; the company accurately identified (and quickly filled) a marketing gap for a 2 + 2 estate coupe, although major manufacturers have now introduced rival models, which could jeopardise the long-term future of the product.

However, Reliant's future is not as depressing as it might appear. Possibilities exist for further scale economies in the production of the three-wheeler and the Kitten, and Reliant have been quick to grasp the importance of buying in components: the Scimitar uses many Ford components. Reliant's capacity is strictly limited. The Kitten has, at best, soaked up some of the excess but Reliant is wary of over-extending itself. To compensate for lack of production facilities the company has diversified into the sale of systems abroad. Reliant has already established a production plant for a Turkish car firm and has now undertaken a similar operation for a three-wheeler taxi plant in Indonesia. All in all, however, Reliant's future is not uniformly rosy.[1] The company must find further capital to finance improvements on the two cars already in production; but a new model development programme might be a prior condition for any significant increase in the company's export sales. Any major sales drive might have to be curtailed or at least tailored to suit Reliant's limited capacity, but the company's present dependence on domestic sales could be over cautious, given that markets overseas offer stronger and much more attractive possibilities in the longer run.

Lotus

Originally, Lotus were renowned for small sports cars, including the mid-engined Europa, but in the mid-1970s the company moved up-market with an attractive new range of considerable appeal. Sadly, the move coincided with the oil crisis, and sales slumped dramatically (see Table 9.1). Although the company has had some success in generating export sales, these have never matched the performance of Rolls-Royce, either in volume or revenue: roughly 50 per cent of the 1975 output was allocated to overseas markets, but the percentage had fallen to less than 33 per cent in the following year. Export performance in 1977 may improve, however, largely as a result of the whims and caprices of the movie-going public — a Lotus featured prominently in the James Bond film released in 1977/8, and there has been a noticeable upswing in Lotus sales subsequently, particularly in the US market; however, as Aston Martin found out, such marketing images are short lived.

Lotus seem to have now cured their reliability and other problems, but having developed their new range of cars are left with surplus engineering and development capacity.

News of a major specialist manufacturer (De Loreon) which with the aid of Government funds will produce a sports car in Northern Ireland arrived too late to incorporate into the text. However, this development is discussed in Chapter 16.

Although De Loreon must be a competitor to Lotus, the willingness of the new company to ask Lotus to help engineer and develop the prototype for production, must be a relief for Lotus. As well as providing a direct link-up for the two companies, the resulting extra cash from the link-up will help reduce the overhead burden of the Lotus design team. It is a pity that De Loreon could not go further and use the Lotus engine rather than the Douvrin V6 engine.

Unlike Jensen, Lotus has decided to produce their own two-litre engine. This may prove to have been a costly mistake: development costs have been high, and the new engine received a mixed reception in the motoring press, which commented on poor reliability and high servicing costs. Although a four-

---

1. Although Reliant produced promising interim profit figures in 1978, the car operations were still reporting losses. Reliant hope that a reorganisation of their operations will generate profits for its ailing car operations, although as the main text points out more than a reorganisation may be necessary. However Reliant is luckier than most since it does not completely rely on its car side.

cylinder engine has sufficient power, it lacks the refinement and the low-speed torque of the larger engines fitted into competitors' cars. The argument against this is the potential savings in fuel consumption in the Lotus engine, but this may not be sufficient to outweigh the disadvantages. If the powertrain problems can be resolved, however, Lotus should survive. Like Reliant, Lotus uses a glass fibre body, but it has been far more successful in creating a new range of models with modern styling, generally considered to be competitive in most details.

Jensen

In the past, Jensen's reputation rested on the two Austin-Healey sports models produced by the company for BMC in the 1950s and 1960s. The company was in an almost perpetual state of financial crisis, undergoing frequent changes in ownership. Following the closure of the Healey line, Jensen's fortunes improved with the launch of the new Interceptor series, which on the whole was a qualified success. To compensate for the dropping of the Austin-Healey by BL, Jensen brought out a medium sports range – the Jensen-Healey – which did reasonably well in the US. But by 1975 the company was once again in the throes of what was a terminal financial crisis (although one can never be sure that the firm may not be resurrected at some future date). Jensen were consequently placed in the hands of the receiver in 1976.

TVR

TVR from the start has functioned as a small producer of sports cars with a now-famous shape, usually with Ford-based engines (which if turbo charged are cheap compared to the available competition). A successful export drive drew more than 50 per cent of total output overseas in 1976. Production has always been geared to fewer than ten units a week, and at this level, production remains sensitive to demand and can be controlled accordingly. As a very small producer with a highly distinctive product, TVR should continue to function profitably.

Morgan

The distinctive Morgan product is marketed as an exercise in motoring nostalgia, with a strong appeal to sports car enthusiasts (cf. the Panther marketing approach below). The company now produces only to order, with a waiting list measured in years rather than months. Most of the Morgan components are bought in, from Leyland and Ford. Morgan, unlike Panther, gradually slipped into this niche by failing to update its products. Panther, on the other hand, actively went out to design a product consistent with motoring nostalgia.

Aston-Martin

Aston-Martin, like Jaguar, is one of the famous racing names – a strong motoring pedigree. For some years, engineering prowess elsewhere in the David

Brown group kept the car division afloat, but Aston-Martin cars were eventually forced to go it alone. If the company survives, it will do so only on the strength of its export sales. In 1976, 66 per cent of output was allocated for export. A strengthened US marketing strategy promises well for healthy export sales.

Bristol

Like TVR, Bristol manufactures an expensive product, based on a modified Chrysler engine. Production is strictly limited; cars are produced only on receipt of a firm order, and the waiting list is long, suggesting that Bristol's prospects are good.

Panther

Panther is also in the business of marketing nostalgia, producing historical replicas modified to satisfy modern criteria of comfort and performance. The top end of the Panther range (the J72 and the de Ville) use BL (Jaguar) engines, with Vauxhall running gear in the medium range Puma. Like Bristol and Morgan, the company produce only to order, and at the top end of their range, the cars are probably the most expensive in the world. A very high percentage of the Panther output is exported which effectively insulates the company from any downturns in the UK economy.

Others

The companies we have chosen to discuss have been more or less permanent features of the UK motor industry for some time, but there are a host of others – Caterham cars, Fairthorpe, Ginetta, et al – some entering, some abandoning and some remaining in the market to become permanent features (though at very small volumes). Rapid changes in the fortunes of these smaller firms makes it difficult to discuss their various strengths and weaknesses.

Assessment

The most important small/specialist manufacturer is unquestionably Rolls-Royce, whose main competitors are drawn primarily from the ranks of other West European producers, such as Mercedes, BMW, etc. Rolls-Royce, however, is alone in producing only two single models in the top price range, for which it would seem that a steady demand exists. The future for Rolls-Royce seems relatively assured. The company produces rather more than 3,000 vehicles per year and may soon expand this to 5,000. Total revenue per year is well in excess of £100 million – ample for the company's research and development needs. Even if the home market collapsed, export sales would enable the company to continue production although any development plans might have to be curtailed, and the company would find it difficult to produce new models, a vital element in any unashamedly expensive marketing bias.

Similarly, the future for the 'replica' producers – principally, Morgan and

Panther — would seem to be relatively assured. The demand is demonstrably there, although the market is obviously seriously limited. If no other manufacturer is drawn into the market, Panther and Morgan should prosper.

The fast-sports-car manufacturers who rely heavily on the UK market are faced with eventual collapse, merger or takeover. The fact that TVR and Aston-Martin have survived this long is not far short of a miracle. To survive much longer they will have to expand export sales, particularly to North America, but to do so they will have to improve the competitiveness of their product — which in simple terms means finding and spending more money on product design and drawing on reserves of ingenuity they simply may not possess. The fast sports car market is already highly competitive, split between the Italians, the Germans (with Porsche and the upmarket, 'quality' divisions of BMW and Mercedes) and the French. Lotus has a distinctive product, but what of the others? To the buyer in the US, what obvious advantages would an Aston-Martin have over a BMW 633, or an equivalent Mercedes model, or even a Jaguar? Obviously, BMW, Mercedes and BL could all afford to spend far more on model improvement and design innovation than any of the smaller producers. How, then, can they expect to compete directly?

Reliant has now diversified, but some of its models have lost their competitive edge. The other small producers may seek a distinctive product design or a marketing strength to prolong their life, but the question still remains: what advantage does the small manufacturer have? With no economies of sale available to them and as other major manufacturers move up market, the future for the small manufacturer must look uninvitingly bleak. Obviously, the major manufacturers cannot hope to meet all of the varieties of demand in a greatly diversified market, nor are they geared to manufacture those models which cannot be produced economically in sufficient quantity. These are the gaps which firms like Rolls-Royce, Morgan and Panther are logically equipped to fill, but in the fast sports (or quality) market, open season has been declared as the major manufacturers move in. Name and tradition alone will no longer guarantee sales, where no other obvious advantages (and a number of major disadvantages) exist. Those fast-sports car manufacturers who buy-in components may have a cost advantage over those who manufacture such components themselves. Smaller producers who can tailor production to firm orders — and build up a substantial waiting list in the process — could have an inbuilt advantage, in that as soon as orders drop, suggesting that something is wrong, remedial action can be taken in time to maintain volume throughput of production. A massive export order could prolong the life of an otherwise endangered small firm, but the possibility of such an order would be remote. In the conclusion (see Chapter 18) we discuss a number of recommendations which have been suggested in order to protect the smaller manufacturer. As a breed, they should not vanish, but their numbers could be greatly diminished.

234

SECTION THREE

COMMERCIAL
VEHICLES

INTRODUCTION TO SECTION THREE

In this section, the commercial vehicle sector of the UK motor industry is analysed. As well as the four major manufacturers, BL, Ford, GM (Bedford) and Chrysler, there are a number of smaller manufacturers who are important in the heavier sectors of the market. Leyland's original strength obviously lay in the manufacture of commercial vehicles but since then its energies have been directed to the expansion which culminated in the formation of BL in 1968. Although one can be far more optimistic with the commercial vehicle sector than with cars, the future is not without its difficulties. As well as commercial vehicles, the trailer and bus sectors of the industry are also explicitly taken into account.

This section comprises three chapters. The first chapter incorporates material primarily from Garel Rhys and the background and structure of the industry. The second chapter has sections which were written by both Krish Bhaskar and Garel Rhys and provides an analysis of the UK market, the major US owned manufacturers and Leyland Vehicles (formerly Leyland Bus and Truck Division). The final chapter deals with other sectors of the Commercial Vehicle industry and was compiled primarily by Garel Rhys.

CHAPTER 10

BACKGROUND AND GENERAL STRUCTURE
OF COMMERCIAL VEHICLES

INTRODUCTION

In the immediate post-war period the producers of commercial vehicles were split into two quite distinct groups: mass producers and specialists. The first sector consisted of firms mass producing fairly standardised products which in turn could be divided into three categories: car derived vans, medium sized vans and pick-ups, and trucks of over one ton capacity but generally of less than five tons capacity. The other sector was populated by specialist and heavy vehicle builders. Not all the specialists made maximum size trucks and

Table 10.1

Commercial Vehicle Output (1947)

Firm	No. produced (approx)	Market Share %
Mass Producers		
Nuffield	21,200	13.6
Austin	22,300	14.3
Ford	36,000	22.9
Bedford	32,000	20.3
Rootes	12,500	7.9
Others	5,000	4.3
	129,000	83.3
Specialist Producers		
Leyland	3,400	2.2
AEC[a] (ACV)	4,500	2.9
Albion	2,000	1.3
Dennis	1,400	0.9
Thornycroft	1,600	1.0
Scammell	1,100	0.7
Guy	3,750	2.4
Others	8.200	5.3
TOTAL	25,950	16.7

a.   Including Maudslay and Crossley bought in 1948.
Source: PEP, 'Motor Vehicles', p26, London 1949.

some concentrated on making light- and medium-weight vehicles, and until 1953 such firms were not in direct competition with the mass producers The early 1950s saw the start of the process whereby the mass producers moved up the weight scale to produce larger and larger vehicles. As a result, many specialists making light- and medium-weight trucks, such as Guy and Vulcan, met increased pressure from the cheaper mass-produced trucks made by the car firms. As the size and nature of this sub-market was conducive to larger output volumes the specialist batch-producers had no market imperfections available to protect them from more efficient concerns. Consequently, a number of firms either left the industry completely or merged their activities with other firms. The remainder tried to concentrate on heavier products but there they came up against competition from the well-established heavy vehicle makers such as Foden, ERF, Atkinson, AEC and Leyland. Indeed, of the medium-weight makers, only Dodge and Seddon were able to achieve long-term viability, initially by concentrating on well-made medium-heavy vehicles and then by making heavier types: Dodge's output of 1,700 vehicles in 1950 grew to 6,500 by 1962 and to 13,000 by 1964, when the 7,000 8 tonners produced gave Dodge market leadership in that sector.[1]

Leyland Motors, one of the specialist firms of 1945, grew rapidly in the post-war period. Expansion − mainly by acquisition rather than unitary growth − began with the purchase of West Yorkshire Foundries in 1945. In 1953 Leyland bought the medium-weight vehicle maker Albion and the heavy specialist Scammell in 1955 to complement its own range of medium-heavy to heavy trucks. Associated Commercial Vehicles, which had bought Maudslay and Crossley in 1948 and Thorneycroft in 1962 was itself acquired by Leyland in 1962. Meanwhile, Jaguar cars acquired Daimler cars and commercial vehicles in 1960, and purchased the truck maker Guy Motors in 1961, to gain almost total control of the Midlands heavy vehicle sector. In 1966 Jaguar joined forces with BMC in British Motor Holdings, which in 1968 merged with Leyland to form British Leyland, the largest vehicle manufacturer in the UK, with substantial interests in all sectors of the CV industry. A series of share exchanges between 1965 and 1969 gave Leyland first a 25 per cent and then a 50 per cent holding in the state-owned bus maker Bristol Commercial Vehicles and in 1969 the National Bus Company and Leyland announced the establishment of a jointly owned subsidiary, Leyland National, to make buses in a new purpose built plant.

In 1948, the heavy vehicle makers which came under Leyland's common ownership in 1968 had capacity of about 18,000 units. In 1954 this had become 22,500 and had increased to about 30,000 by 1968. Therefore in unit terms neither the growth of Leyland Motors nor of BLMC in 1968, was as spectacular as a cursory look at the output attributed to Leyland alone would suggest. The increase in production from 3,500 in 1948 to 25,000 in 1968 was in fact in terms of Leyland's own capacity, i.e. excluding 'acquired' capacity, a growth from 3,500 to 12,000. The growth of Leyland was based upon a philosophy of making better use of other people's capacity rather than

---

1. 'The British Commercial Vehicle Industry, 1945-1966', by D.G. Rhys. Unpublished Thesis (Birmingham University).

TABLE 10.2

Growth of Leyland Motors' Capacity

1948		1954		1967	1968
Leyland	3,500	Leyland	8,000	Leyland ⎫	⎫
Others:				Albion ⎬ 15,000	
ACV	4,500	Albion	2,000	Scammell ⎭	⎬
Albion	2,000		10,000		
Scammell	1,100			Thornycroft ⎫	
Thornycroft	1,600	ACV	5,000	ACV ⎬ 10,000	⎭
Guy	3,750	Scammell, Guy, etc.	7,500	25,000	25,000
Daimler	250				
				Guy ⎫	2,600
				Daimler ⎭	
				Bristol	750
					28,350

a belief in unitary growth. This may have constrained the UK's total heavy vehicle making capacity: slow growth and long waiting lists were the order of the day for the independent producers for most of the 1960s.

Although the mass producers threatened the medium-weight specialists as early as the mid-1950s[1] it was not until 1975 that Bedford and Ford were able to offer maximum weight vehicles. Between 1955 and 1965 the independent specialists prospered, left alone in their sub-market. However, waiting lists and the need to use larger vehicles on Continental hauls meant that in the late 1960s heavy trucks imported initially from other EFTA countries, mainly Sweden, appeared on UK roads. The flow of imports continued between 1970 and 1977, joined by the mass producers attracted by the high profit margins earned in this sector of the market. However, because of a limit to the size of the heavy vehicle market, the nature of the product demanded and the production techniques required, mass production of heavy vehicles has not proved practical. 'Quantity' production is the order of the day but it remains to be seen whether the cost reductions emanating from such out-

1. The mass producers having dealt with many of the 3-5 ton specialists in the 1930s.

put facilities are sufficient to offset the quality bestowed by the bespoke and batch production of the remaining UK specialists.

Following the purchase of Atkinson by Seddon in 1971 and then International Harvester's purchase of the merged group in 1974, only ERF and Foden remain as heavy vehicle making independents. However, Seddon Atkinson, Dennis, Shelvoke and Drewry, plus Metro-Cammell on the bus side, remain as small firms, admittedly as subsidiaries within larger groupings, to compete with much larger producers. Indeed, one concern, Richardson Brothers in the West Midlands, showed signs in the mid-1970s of trying to enter the industry by making 1,000 vehicles a year, illustrating that even in the 1970s barriers to entry in a major part of the CV industry are not insurmountable.[1] Perhaps even more remarkably the Metro-Cammell company, a Vicker's subsidiary, albeit by using the former British Leyland workforce freed when the Daimler bus plant was changed over to engine making for Jaguar, had in 1977 a potential capacity of 4,000 a year. If this capacity were utilised, the company could displace British Leyland from market leadership in the heavy duty bus sector. In addition, Dennis having re-entered the bus market in 1977 announced a planned installed capacity for 1981 of 800 chassis a year.

THE COMMERCIAL VEHICLE INDUSTRY: GENERAL STRUCTURE AND PERFORMANCE

While the UK car industry has become small scale even in European terms, the CV industry has maintained its size as one of the largest in Europe and is still a major force in world export markets, although the industry has undergone a considerable change in structure during the post-war period.

In 1950 there were some 40 separate CV producers in the UK, each one of some significance in the bus and truck market. By 1978 ten competitors remained, four of which – Ford, GM (Bedford), British Leyland and Chrysler – accounted for about 98 per cent of total production. However, in the heaviest vehicle class of 28 tons and above the specialist firms still have 30 per cent of sales, while in the 24-ton plus 'rigid' market Foden's eight-wheelers have around 37 per cent of the market, just behind Leyland's 40 per cent. It is in this heavy vehicle sector, and in the market, for buses and highly specialised 'environmental' vehicles – refuse collectors, fire-engines, etc. – that the small firm survives.

Many of the firms competing in 1950 concentrated on the light- and medium-weight sectors. Consequently when the mass producers such as Bedford began to move up the weight scale, utilising their efficient low unit cost manufacturing techniques to the full, the smaller producers could not justify the price premiums they needed to stay viable through a commensurate difference in quality. The result was sufficient financial embarrassment for firms either to leave the industry completely or to be absorbed by other, mainly heavy vehicle, producers.

1. A pre-publication comment pointed out that this statement overstates the case. Indeed as commented elsewhere in the book, substantial economies of scale do exist in the lighter segment of the CV market.

In the immediate post-war period three specialist firms achieved a larger than average size: Leyland Motors, Associated Commercial Vehicles and Jaguar (Daimler-Guy). In addition, Chrysler's long established subsidiary at Kew had facilities to make over 5,000 chassis a year. The first three firms absorbed other makers and then merged amongst themselves, all eventually coming under the umbrella of BLMC. At the same time as BLMC's creation Ford completed the reorganisation of its CV activities. This was done to such good effect that by 1970 the company had improved its position in the market for medium-weight vehicles, moving from a poor third to contest first place with the traditional market leader, Bedford. Ford's advance, based upon new ranges of trucks, vans and buses backed up by an improved sales and service network, was mirrored by the decline of BMC. BMC's replacement of its FK range by the unreliable FJ, plus the opening of the new Scottish Bathgate plant filled with old machinery from the Midlands, adversely affected the company's penetration of the medium truck market in the period 1965-7. Bathgate's problem was not one of location but the failure of its output to gain customer acceptance. Following the creation of BLMC, Leyland Motors improved quality control and productive equipment at the plant to such an extent that by 1975, it had become one of BLMC's most profitable centres. Chrysler (Commer, Karrier, Dodge) and Bedford maintained their market shares over the period 1965-75 at around 12 per cent and 29 per cent respectively. Ford doubled its share over the period 1960-75 to produce a see-saw struggle for market leadership in the 3.5 to 16 tons gross weight medium sector with GM's Bedford subsidiary.

Although the creation of BLMC partly restored fortunes in the medium weight market, the traditional market leadership of BMC in the medium van sector was destroyed by Ford's 'Transit' introduced in 1965. Indeed with improved models from Bedford, in the 1970s BLMC slipped further to contest, often unsuccessfully, a poor third place with Chrysler's Commer subsidiary, which held 16 per cent of the market compared with Ford's 30 per cent. Ford dominates the market for larger 2.5 to 3.5 tons gross vans with 66 per cent of sales, compared with 25 per cent and 6 per cent by Bedford and Leyland respectively. Only in the car-derivative CV market did the BMC-type products hold their own: in all other CV sectors the company suffered far more serious set-backs than it experienced on the car side between 1967-75.

The concentration of managerial and financial resources at BLMC on the reconstruction of the car divisions fortunes led to the neglect of the 'Truck and Bus Division' (which, apart from Bathgate consisted of Leyland Motors and Jaguar CV operations) and BLMC's strong initial position in heavy CVs was eroded. Much needed investment in plant expansion and modernisation, and in new products, was sacrificed to expenditure on the less profitable car side.[1] This allied to conservative investment policies by the specialists, meant that the excess demand for heavy CVs, significant since 1964, became acute between 1970 and 1974. This state of affairs increased imports so that by 1974 Sweden's Volvo had 19 per cent of the 28-ton gross market, to BLMC's 23 per cent, ERF's 13 per cent, Foden's 6 per cent and Seddon-Atkinson's 12 per cent. In 1974 the total import share of the heavy CV market was 34 per cent, with an

---

1.   See below for output and capacity figures.

import share of 46 per cent for vehicles suitable for use at over 32 tons.

Encouragingly, the UK makers have responded to the import challenge: whereas in 1972 the specialist producers in the UK heavy CV industry had combined capacity of 7,000 chassis a year, by 1976 this had increased to around 18,000. In addition, good quality products such as Leyland's 'Marathon' truck were coming onto the market at a rate of 2,000 units a year. Despite the temporary phasing out of truck manufacture at British Leyland's Guy plant at Wolverhampton, with a loss of some 2,000 units a year, there has been considerable expansion in UK heavy CV production facilities between 1971/7.[1] This increased availability, allied to a downturn in the market, produced a significant drop in import penetration in 1975. Indeed, although imports increased in 1976 there was no headlong growth as on the car side.

On the bus side, and as developed below, BLMC's monopoly of heavy duty bus chassis-making plus a small long-term growth in demand for double deckers, aggravated by a short-term boom created by the 'Bus Grant' scheme, has given an opportunity for new entrants. Volvo's Scottish based Ailsa subsidiary, and the British Metro-Cammell company from Birmingham had already made significant inroads, while Foden and Dennis hoped to follow them. Therefore even in 1975-8 it was possible to enter the motor industry and to serve a central and important market, as long as activities were confined largely to the assembly side, avoiding capital intensive component manufacture.

As we have seen (Chapter 2) vehicle manufacture consists of four main functions: foundry work to produce castings; forging and machining; steel press work; and final assembly. Of these, assembly has the lowest optimum output level measured on an annual basis. The large capital investment required to establish special purpose, high speed equipment means that operations such as cab making and major component manufacture is only efficiently undertaken — and therefore profitable in a competitive industry — when very large volumes can be made and sold. Many quite large continental heavy vehicle makers have been over capitalised for the scale of operation undertaken. On the other hand, the UK industry has evolved a highly efficient structure which involves even the larger firms in buying-out a high proportion of requirements and a specialised heavy vehicle sector which concentrates mainly on pure assembly, any manufacturing being done by techniques appropriate to low annual output volumes. As a result even large-scale manufacturers have bought out items such as gearboxes and axles from even larger-scale component makers, while the small scale specialists have been able to enjoy external economies of scale.[2]

By keeping their assembly operations at a high degree of efficiency, the small firms have survived and prospered by being able to purchase diesel engines, axles, gearboxes, cabs as well as the usual bought-out items such as electrical equipment, from large scale suppliers who themselves incur the cost and risk of high capital investment in manufacturing equipment. On the assembly side, ERF, for example, recently reduced the time for engine install-

1. In mid-1977 it was announced that a substantial increase in Leyland maximum weight vehicle capacity from 9,000 units a year to 20,000 units a year was to be undertaken by 1981 under the Ryder reconstruction.
2. See below for the development of this point.

ation from four hours to ten minutes. A small assembler in engaging in cab making will utilise glass-fibre where tooling costs are *one-fiftieth* of those needed for a pressed steel cab. However, as glass-fibre material and other direct costs are greater at output levels between 25,000 and 30,000 a year, steel is then more economic; but for lower volumes glass-fibre is the more efficient technique, a lesson fully absorbed by British producers. Most small UK CV makers tend towards pure assembly with little in-house manufacture. As long as sufficient external economies are obtained for cost-plus pricing to be viable in a competitive environment, the break-even output levels are normally a very small proportion of total capacity, fixed costs being so low.

Although the motor industry and large-scale output appear to be synonymous it would be wrong to suppose that the small-scale CV specialists are at risk in competing with larger firms in the small market for heavy vehicles. In fact, the large-scale Continental makers often produce engines and cabs at lower output levels, but with higher costs than British specialists such as Perkins or Motor Panels. Therefore, by concentrating on the small-scale assembly of premium products utilising bought-out components made in large numbers, the likes of ERF and Seddon-Atkinson have found themselves in a prosperous position. Foden is the most 'manufacturing-orientated' of the specialists, but by using simple equipment, it has managed to keep prices within 5 per cent or so of the assemblers', a premium the customer has willingly paid to obtain a fully bespoke product. Even so, the company's expansion plans are based for the most part on pure assembly activities, with a weekly capacity in 1975/76 for the assembly of 120 units and the manufacture of 12 chassis a week. Despite the greater commitment to manufacturing, Foden has tended to generate the highest level of profits in absolute terms, although because pure assembly needs less capital, ERF earned 25 per cent on capital to Foden's 15 per cent over the period 1970-75.

In the period 1970-74, BLMC's Truck and Bus Division produced some forty times as many vehicles as, say, ERF, by the prosperity of the small heavy

TABLE 10.3

Pre-Tax Profits (£'000)

	Seddon	Atkinson	ERF	Foden	BLMC (Truck & Bus) Leyland Vehicles Ltd estimated
1970	817	404	735	1,086	8,000
1971	840	783	915	1,295	8,000
1972	367		483	752	6,000
1973	781		921	1,144	9,000
1974	N/A		930	231	6,000
1975	N/A		634	946	27,000
1976	N/A		(−118)	(−1,020)	43,000 [a]
1977	N/A		1,700	1,740	27,000

a. 15 month period.

245

vehicle specialists is shown by their higher relative profitability. In terms of profits the small-scale specialists have been able to co-exist with larger firms. Indeed, the sale of Seddon-Atkinson to International Harvester was perhaps another case of the UK selling its seed corn as no pressing economic reason was apparent for the transaction, as distinct from short-term financial factors, except a possible need to speed up new product development to a rate which spent resources at a faster pace than internal funds could be generated. However, alternative means of raising capital, other than merger, are available to a good risk company.

RECOVERY AND NEW ENTRANTS IN THE TRUCK MARKET

After the mass producers spread their activities up the weight scale into the market served by specialist producers, Dennis Brothers of Guildford, one of the market leaders in the pre-war CV industry, found business increasingly difficult and by the late 1960s was making heavy losses. Indeed, by 1973 a loss of £1 million was made on a turnover of about £4.5 million.[1] The Hestair group, which bought Dennis in 1972, identified the company's strengths and weaknesses: truck production ceased and efforts concentrated on fire engines, municipal vehicles of all sorts and airport tenders. As a result, output of 14-15 completed vehicles a week in 1975-6 equalled the scaled-down capacity, earning a profit of £1½ million on a £15 million turnover, and exporting over 50 per cent of total output, when ERF and Foden were losing money for the first time. The reaction to this was a plan to expand capacity to 27 vehicles a week, probably 1,100 a year by early 1978. In addition, in 1977 the company re-entered the bus market after a gap of 10 years. The intention was not to compete head-on with the market leader Leyland, but to seek out and fill a market niche where there was a call for an alternative approach in design. The identification of a set of characteristics not conferred by any other product and the willingness to innovate are reasons enough to explain the survival of small firms. Add to this the ability to find enough slots in the market, and the flexibility of a small firm, and it is difficult to see why the heavy CV industry should not contain small scale but significant enterprises. In 1975-6 the £8 million earned by Dennis overseas covered 33 1/3 per cent of the UK's import bill for heavier commercial vehicles. Similarly, Foden exported 25 per cent of its £23 million turnover, in 1975. Only if such concerns tried to over-standardise their products, or found the market turning against non-standardised vehicles would their role end.

In the mid 1970s, Richardson Brothers in the West Midlands planned to enter the heavy CV market to tap the queue forming for UK products. A planned output level of 1,000 units a year was anticipated. This illustrates clearly that by utilising the supply infra-structure of the existing heavy CV firms, a firm can still contemplate entering the mainstream of truck assembly.[2]

1. In 1972 a profit of £139,000 on sales of £7 million was achieved.
2. A pre-publication comment pointed out that this case may have been overstated. The comment in the text refers to the heavy CV segment and we think it a reasonable statement in the light of the scale economies benefited from the component manufacturers.

On the car side, new entry can only be contemplated on the fringes of the market, not as in this case at the centre of a heavy goods vehicle market already served by established quantity producers. Similarly Magirus Deutz in the North-West and Volvo in Scotland have established truck assembly plants in the UK. A new company, Stonefield Vehicles, in which the Scottish Development Agency has a 49 per cent holding, commenced production in 1978 with all the planned production of 500 units already sold, mostly overseas. The company makes four-wheel drive vehicles with engines − from Chrysler or Ford − and transmission equipment (from Ferguson of Coventry) bought out. By 1981, planned output will reach 3,000 vehicles a year, and the product competes directly with Mercedes, Volvo and Steyr-Puch of Austria. The strengths and variety of the UK component supply industry in providing the CV makers with cabs, axles, transmissions, engines and gearboxes (all normally in-house activities on the Continent) confers sufficient external economies to allow small-scale assemblers to price profitably at levels which are competitive with prices charged by quantity assemblers. A similar state of affairs exists in the USA, where small-scale assembly operations by firms such as Kenworth, Peterbilt and Oshkosh among others, are supported by specialist makers of major components. Therefore, to compare the assembly volumes of, say, ERF, Seddon Atkinson or Dennis with those of Leyland, Mercedes or Iveco is to miss the advantages enjoyed by these firms from buying from firms with the output levels achieved by Rolls-Royce Diesel, Perkins, Eaton, Kirkstall and so on.

In conclusion, a number of points are apparent. The UK is the non-American CV manufacturing sector for the medium weight trucks made by the US multinationals. The facilities owned by these firms, and by BLMC, use high volume low unit cost techniques which gave the industry a significant competitive edge over the less efficiently organised Continental makers, who needed time to bring their facilities and product ranges to a position where unit costs could be controlled. In short the reorganisation of a great deal of the German CV industry under the Mercedes umbrella, the formation of the Fiat dominated Iveco concern covering facilities in France, Italy and Germany, the fusing of Saviem and Berliet under a government-sponsored plan to restructure the French CV industry may be all considered as reactions in the face of the potential superiority of UK CV firms. This potential could not be realised in the European market because our comparative advantage in CV production was frustrated by the UK Government's meek acceptance of the exclusion of CV trade from tariff reductions. The exclusion of CVs from the 'Kennedy Round' of tariff reductions was a result of UK competitiveness, as indeed was the creation of the 'Club of Four'[1] to make a common vehicle. On the other hand, the very success of the UK facilities of the multinationals has rebounded in that Ford, instead of expanding its capacity in the UK to make its new heavy truck range, is turning to under-utilised Dutch facilities, while there is concern that Bedford, to make room for the production of its heavy weight trucks, will transfer medium weight production to the Continent.[2] Already Chrysler completes its CV range in the UK by importing French vans and Spanish heavy

1. Consisting of Volvo, Saviem, DAF and Magirus Deutz.
2. A pre-publication comment points out that there are no plans (as yet) for this.

trucks. Nevertheless, in the heavy sector BLMC is of sufficient size and efficiency, despite past under-investment, to compete on equal terms with other major heavy truck makers. What was required by the late 1970s was extra bus and heavy truck making capacity and capacity for the manufacture of spare parts. With good management, the small scale UK CV makers could continue to prosper as the assembly 'tip' of a strongly based commercial vehicle component-making pyramid. The short-term financial problems which faced Foden in 1974-5 were, it must be remembered, the results of the effects of inflation on the working capital of a firm in the middle of capital expansion and *not* the manifestation of a long-term malaise. This was recognised by the City which, in July 1975 launched a rescue plan for the company, taking Foden off the Department of Industry's 'lame duck' list. Indeed, recovery was such that Foden was able to counter a Rolls-Royce takeover bid in 1977 with some ease. This illustrates that a small, efficiently run firm can survive in competition with larger firms by meeting the specific needs of a small specialised market: a market in 1977-8 of perhaps 20,000 heavy trucks and buses. As UK manufacturing facilities are capable of meeting most of this, many importers in

TABLE 10.4
BLMC Weekly Output (1975)

Leyland (Lancashire)	150 chassis [e]	AEC	115 chassis
Albion (Glasgow)	100 "	Bristol	16 chassis
Bathgate	470 trucks	Leyland-National	22 chassis
Guy	370 tractors		
	45 chassis		
Scammell	40 "		

Specialist Capacity (Annual 1978)

ERF	5,000	Bristol	1,300 [b]
Seddon-Atkinson	5,000	Leyland-National	2,000 [b]
Foden	5,500 [a]	Ailsa (Volvo)	300
Dennis	1,100	Metro-Cammell	500 [c]

Mass Producers Annual Capacity (Approximate) 1978

	Car Derivative CVs [d]	Medium Vans	Trucks		Heavy
			Light	Medium (24 tons+)	
Ford	40,000	45,000		70,000	2,000
Chrysler	–	15,000	5,000	5,000	–
Bedford	25,000	40,000	30,000	40,000	6,000
BLMC	50,000	30,000		35,000	16,000
BLMC (Land Rover)	55,000				

a. With slight modifications *single shift* capacity could be increased to 7,000. This assumes a 46-week year.
b. Associate Companies of BLMC.
c. With a minimum of investment, plus greater employment, this could be raised to 4,000 a year.
d. Capacity depends on car/car-derivative output mix.
e. By 1981, this could approach 500 chassis a week.

the middle of costly investment incurred in trying to break into the UK could find their position seriously at risk and be provoked into starting a price war. Paradoxically, the small producers with their very high bought-out content,[1] by enjoying great flexibility in their cost structure if output volumes fell, could find survival easier than many large firms.

THE SURVIVAL OF THE SMALL FIRM

In July 1969 the Bolton Committee was established to examine the role of small firms in the national economy, the facilities available to such firms, and the problems confronting them. In November 1971 the Report was published. It was to be expected that after decades of industrial mergers and the emergence of the multinational corporation one of the Report's main findings was that the small firm sector was in decline in terms of its share of economic activity. It is noteworthy, as seen above, that within the commercial vehicle sector in 1947 the specialised firms accounted for 16.7 per cent of output compared with 11 per cent in 1954, Leyland-AEC accounting for at least 6 per cent in both years. In 1977 the independent specialists accounted for under 2 per cent of output. The Committee put forward eight main functions which were fulfilled by the small firm, and these varied little from those outlined in traditional economics textbooks. For example, in some industries the optimum size of the production units or sales outlets is small, and the small firm is often the most efficient form of business organisation, or again, small firms, which can flourish in a limited or specialised market, add greatly to the variety of products and services offered to the consumers.

In manufacturing industry the Bolton Committee defined a small firm as one having fewer than 200 employees. By this criterion there is no such thing as a small firm in the heavy commercial vehicle industry. What this illustrates is that the output volumes, physical capacity and financial resources, stemming from and tied up in the motor industry are so large that even a relatively small-scale vehicle producer would be regarded as a large firm in any other industry.

TABLE 10.5

Turnover of the Small Heavy CV Manufacturer

	1972 £ million	1976 £ million
Seddon Group	16.6[a]	42.4
ERF	11.7	19.1
Foden	12.98	22.9
Dennis	4.00	15.0

a. Figures for Atkinson-Seddon

1. Foden purchased 86% of parts and components by value from outside the company.

It is worth putting the size of the small-scale heavy commercial vehicle producers in perspective, and it is also worth noting that within the Motor Trades sector the Bolton Committee defines a small firm as one with a turnover of under £100,000 a year. The various turnover figures in the heavy commercial vehicle industry in 1972 and 1976 are as shown in Table 10.5.

Table 10.6 puts these figures into direct perspective with those for various car firms:

TABLE 10.6

Turnover of the Small Car Manufacturer

	1972 £ million	1976 £ million
Lotus Group	4.4	5.64
Reliant	13.1	–
Rolls-Royce Motors	38.3	78.5
(Cars Division Only)	18.6	43.0
British Leyland	1,281.0	2,892.3
GKN	623.2	1,501.2

Rolls-Royce Motors is clearly a small-scale car producer but capitalised at £38.4 million and with a turnover in 1971 of £38 million the company is large enough to be included amongst the UK's largest 300 firms. However, if we take the Bolton Committee's wider definition of a small firm as one which has a relatively small share of the market within which it competes, is managed by its owners or part-owners in a personalised way, and is also independent, then a number of heavy commercial vehicle producers qualify as small-scale firms. Even Dennis Motors, purchased by the Hestair Group in 1972, and Shelvoke and Drewry, a part of the Butterfield-Harvey Group can be included, as the groups themselves concentrate primarily on supplying the heavy transport vehicle sector and the market for specialised vehicles such as refuse collectors and fire engines. Within its sub-market the Dennis-Hestair merger meant that the combined companies had over 80 per cent of the fire-engine market, 75 per cent of road-sweepers, 36 per cent of refuse collectors, and 70 per cent of sludge gulper sales. In other words, the importance of specialist producers cannot be derived simply by looking at their output volumes, and the rest of this section is devoted to analysing the significance of the small-scale and medium-sized firms in the heavy vehicle sector.

Only a tiny fraction of British car output is supplied by small-scale firms. Similarly, in the case of commercial vehicle production, *except* in the market for heavy trucks and buses, where the small firm holds a very important place. So, although independent firms specialising in the production of large custom-built vehicles account for less than 2 per cent of total British production, in the market for vehicles weighing between 14 and 25 imperial tons gross these firms account for 10 per cent of output while above 26 tons they account for over 36 per cent of total production.

In a world of large-scale mass production there still exists a place for small firms. If the total market is small or such that great attention must be paid to quality, variety and detail, and if firms enjoy great customer goodwill, and there is a need for flexibility in decision-making, then the market facing the small firm may be sufficient to support efficient small producers but too small to attract firms geared-up for large-scale mass production. The demand for single items or for small batches is often best satisfied by small flexible firms rather than those tooled-up with expensive specialised equipment which is only efficiently used when making standardised products in large numbers.

These factors explain the survival of small-scale commercial vehicle builders but they also indicate why smallness has not ensured the survival of such firms: if the market grows large enough to become attractive to the mass producers then the specialists' position can be put in danger. Indeed between 1945 and 1977 the number of small British commercial vehicle builders fell from 30 to 6. However, one of the 30 was Leyland Motors which, by efficiently producing trucks and buses, increased its financial strength sufficiently to purchase eight of its rivals by 1968.

As touched upon above a number of factors explained this process. The growth of Leyland only partly explains the fall in the number of small-scale specialists as other factors were involved. Small CV firms can be divided between those mainly *assembling* parts and components purchased from outside suppliers, and those *manufacturing* a high proportion of their requirements. As a manufacturer spends considerable sums of money on machinery, the cost of which is fixed no matter what the level of output, a fall in demand would be more serious than for the assembler which can quickly reduce costs by reducing its orders to its suppliers. However, both the assemblers and manufacturers of lighter heavy vehicles came under increasing pressure from the mass producers between 1945 and 1955. An increase in demand for such vehicles attracted the larger firms by making mass production worthwhile and they estimated that they could make products comparable to those of the specialists but at a lower cost and price. As a result firms like Bedford invaded the lighter end of the heavy vehicle market. The custom-building manufacturers and assemblers could not profitably match the prices charged by such firms and left the industry or concentrated on even heavier vehicles, a sector of the market not yet large enough to attract the mass producers. As the CVs made by mass producers and specialists in the lighter end of the heavy vehicle market were similar in all respects, the 25 per cent cost advantage given by mass production meant that the specialists could not compete. So the CV market is not necessarily conducive to the survival of the small firm.

Since the mid-1950s the mass producers have introduced even larger vehicles to try to tap the steadily expanding demand for very heavy CVs.[1] However, throughout the late 1960s and early 1970s the mass producers were not able to produce very heavy vehicles which the operator found comparable to those made by British Leyland or the specialists. With the import of vehicles

1. This demand is based upon the increased use of road vehicles and because the larger the CV the larger its net carrying capacity and the lower the operating costs per ton mile. E.g. a quarter-ton van costs about 80p per ton mile to operate, a 16-ton truck about 1.8p and a 32-ton vehicle about 1.4 pence over their representative mileages.

by Chrysler from Spain, and new designs introduced by Ford and GM in 1975, the mass producers have tried again. However, by the late 1970s the general conclusion must be that despite making very heavy vehicles the mass producers have not found it easy to repeat their previous success in the medium-weight sector.

The mass producers were attracted into the heaviest side of the market by the full order books, the growing output, and good profits earned by most CV specialists. Between 1965 and 1971 the British economy was stagnant; this had an immediate effect on the mass producers of cars and CVs, with low profits, and indeed losses, becoming usual. However, it was not until 1972 that the heavy vehicle producers experienced a downturn in business. This was because operators continued to replace smaller vehicles by more efficient larger ones, often on a two for three basis. So while the mass producers in general sold fewer vehicles the smaller CV specialists continued to do well. Largely because of the relatively conservative investment policies followed by the small producers, and a fear that orders might disappear overnight if trading conditions in the operating field deteriorated, waiting lists for heavy CVs became usual. This allowed Swedish firms, which enjoyed tariff-free trade under EFTA, to build up sales in the UK, but the British mass producers still did not find it easy to take advantage of this excess demand for heavy vehicles.

Such are the exacting operating requirements which heavy CVs must meet that mass producers are faced with a dilemma; either to produce a vehicle using many components common to those used in lighter types, or to use components produced on a small scale tailor-made for the heaviest vehicles. If the second approach is followed then the firm, despite its size, is unable to enjoy economies of scale.[1] In reality, until 1975 the British mass producers compromised by installing, in a basically standard vehicle, specialised components such as heavy duty diesel engines, axles and gearboxes purchased from outside, specialist suppliers. Consequently the 'bought-out' content of heavy vehicles made by the large-scale producers is higher than for lighter models. In short, an acceptable heavy vehicle must meet stringent standards, requiring a method of construction which makes it impossible for such vehicles to be entirely mass produced. The limited size of the market simply reinforces this point. So, although the 32-ton vehicles made by mass producers before 1975 cost about £1,000 less than vehicles of similar size made by the specialists, operators willingly paid the difference to purchase vehicles which proved cheaper in the long run and had the attributes required. Many operators fail to see in the mass produced CVs a satisfactory alternative to the custom-built products of the specialist producers and the way these products fulfil their tasks.

Despite the influx of imports and the new competition from the mass producers, the specialists are still in a strong position in the industry. Although Leyland and Foden experienced some short-time working in early 1972, by the end of that year these firms and the other main heavy vehicle specialists — ERF, Bristol, Seddon-Atkinson — were experiencing full order books once

1. A firm producing products in large numbers can install production methods which reduce the unit costs of production. Clearly a large firm producing products in small production runs cannot enjoy such cost reductions.

again. Although waiting lists for heavy vehicles have been endemic, only as late as 1959-64, 1968-70 and again in 1973-4 have major rounds of investment to increase capacity been undertaken by the small firms. As late as 1972 the typical capacity of the specialist firms was just over 2,000 units a year, although the amalgamation of two specialists,[1] Seddon and Atkinson in 1970 created an enterprise with a capacity of 5,000 units a year.[2] It may be argued that given the strength in demand for heavy vehicles investment policies have been too cautious, and the growth of container traffic and trans-European haulage as well as general economic growth could only have increased this demand. Despite public concern concerning heavier lorries in the UK — although such vehicles would be no bigger than existing ones — the eventual use of 40-ton or even 44-ton gross vehicles would give the expertise of the small-scale specialist an opportunity to produce such vehicles. So if vehicles become larger and as more operators find it profitable to use larger units, then the specialists' market could grow. In addition, as long as the long-run costs of operating custom-built vehicles can be shown to be lower than those for mass produced types, the growth in the market need not mean dominance by larger firms — firms which may be able to offer rather lower initial costs.

The slump in economic activity in 1974-5 was a severe blow for the specialist makers but much larger firms such as DAF in Holland and Berliet in France were equally affected. Foden's position was aggravated by the company being in the middle of an expensive expansion programme.[3] However, by 1977

TABLE 10.7

UK Market Shares 1975-6
(over 28-tons class)

	%
ERF	13
Volvo	25
British Leyland:	
Leyland	
Guy	
Albion	20
AEC	
Scammell	
Foden	7[a]
Seddon Atkinson	17
Other British and	
other imports	18
	100

a.   35% of 24 ton–28 ton rigid class.

1.   The costs of disruptions due to an expansion programme made Atkinson the prey of a number of bidders attracted by the low share price.
2.   British Leyland's heavy vehicle capacity is around 35,000 a year.
3.   Eighth Report from the Expenditure Committee, Trade and Industry Sub-Committee 1975-1976, Public Expenditure on Chrysler UK Ltd, p.15.

all the UK specialists were displaying healthy balance sheets. The problems faced by such firms were not those of a moribund firm in the middle of a long-term decline, but those generated by an unusually deep recession forcing demand and therefore output below the break-even point. ERF's position was aggravated by the Price Commission's refusal to permit price increases allowed to other UK and foreign firms, so that by late 1975 ERF prices were some £200–£300 below the competition. This gap was closed with the introduction of a new 'B' series truck range at the end of the year. The severity of the slump can be gauged by the semi-trailer output figures produced in Table 12.1. However, the specialist makers, with new truck ranges introduced in 1975-7, appear at present to be set fair to keep their impressive share of the market.

Consequently, the troubles of 1975-6 in the specialist side of the business do not indicate any long-term malaise, especially given the efficiency of the back-up suppliers.

THE SMALLER FIRMS' FUTURE

The techniques needed to produce vehicles with the long term operating life and low maintenance costs required by operators precludes mass production methods. The size and nature of the market, and the need for detailed assembly and custom-building, suggests that a mass producer would under-utilise his expensive equipment both because the throughput was small and because of the need to stop and reset machinery. This would make the mass producer's costs prohibitive. If only small numbers are needed, then it is cheaper in terms of material and tooling costs to make cabs and bodies in fibre glass rather than steel, and more economic to use simple machinery than high speed automated equipment. The small British firms use these techniques and at the same time call upon one of the most efficient heavy commercial vehicle equipment sectors in the world. Firms specialising in making parts and components pass on economies of scale to the vehicle producers. As diesel engines cost around £3,000, CV gearboxes £2,000 and axles £800, any small percentage saving in production costs has a considerable monetary effect. In the UK, firms such as Perkins, Gardner, Rolls-Royce, Cummins and Dorman specialise in making diesel engines, therefore the small-scale vehicle firms can avoid expensive investment in equipment which they could not fully utilise anyway. Axles are made by firms such as Eaton and Kirkstall Forge, while even British Leyland found that its output was not large enough to allow it to produce as cheaply as the axle specialist North American Rockwell. As well as selling its Maudslay plant to Rockwell, Leyland sold its heavy transmission and gearbox plant to Eaton in 1972 for the same reason.[1] In short, the specialist makers enjoy competitive sources of supply which produce components cheaper than they could themselves. Where it does manufacture items then the small producer of CVs uses the techniques most appropriate to its scale of operation instead of using more complex but more expensive

1. Although some economies of scale were involved one suspects that British Leyland's main motive for these sales was a desperate attempt to cobble together capital to invest in the ailing car business. Without this need it is doubtful whether such key component capacity would have been sold.

methods better suited to the mass production of cars and CVs. Unlike cars, most heavy CVs are made in a chassis form only, the vehicle's body being added later. In the UK over 400 firms specialise in bodybuilding for goods vehicles and buses, which gives the customer a choice and frees the CV maker from having to invest in a highly specialised and complex sector which needs its own expertise.

Where bus production is concerned, the mass producers such as Bedford and Ford are the market leaders in the lighter end of the market. By using many components common to their mass produced trucks, these firms are able to supply a vehicle which fully meets the operator's requirements but at a cost of production and price which greatly undercuts those of British Leyland and the small specialist. Some operators, mainly those running large fleets, require heavier and more durable vehicles able to withstand the rigours of regular use. Although it is not economic to mass produce such vehicles, mainly because of the detail needed in manufacture and partly because of the size of the market, quantity production is possible. In this sector of the market British Leyland and its associate companies, Bristol and Leyland-National, dominate the market. Leyland's quantity production techniques — a compromise between custom-building and mass production — are appropriate as the heavy bus customer is willing to accept a partly standardised product. Leyland's dominance stems partly from this fact. As many customers require large batches of identical vehicles — which allows production to be highly mechanised — a larger firm has a cost advantage as it is able to spread its fixed costs more widely. In addition, many other bus-making firms were purchased by other manufacturers, often as an incidental to a larger transaction, and eventually these larger groupings were themselves absorbed by Leyland. Firms such as Bristol, Seddon and Metro-Cammell have shown that even in the 1970s a relatively small firm can compete successfully in the bus market, either by concentrating on a few standard models or by giving the customer something different at a price he is prepared to pay. Leyland-National mass produces a standard bus in a highly mechanised and automated tailor-made plant and plans to increase production up to the factory's ideal capacity of over 2,000 a year. However, neither this output target, nor the cost and price levels achieved, put existing bus-building techniques in jeopardy, partly because mass production techniques are only used at the final assembly stage with output being insufficient to justify such methods in the production of many of the parts or components, and partly because the market place demands a variety which it is prepared to pay for. So, only if the market for standardised buses increases to over 5,000 a year would the more conventionally made large bus be substantially undercut in price.

The conclusion must be that as long as the cost premium incurred by specialised CV makers does not more than offset the lifetime operating cost savings stemming from the use of their products, then the mass producer will be unable to force the small firm out of business. This, together with the steady growth in the demand for heavy CVs should ensure a good future for the specialist producer. Indeed, the Swedish firm Volvo has established small-scale production facilities for trucks and buses in the UK. Unlike the enterprises making lighter vehicles, the existing small firms make a product which cannot be duplicated efficiently and profitably by mass producers. As a pointer to the future and as an indication of the British specialist producers' resolve to meet the threatened influx of imports following our entry into the EEC — a reaction to increased Swedish penetration of the market — Foden plans announced in 1973 to increase output by 50 per cent, meant a target of 100 vehicles a week by 1977-78. The continual increase in demand for the heaviest type of CV — reinforced, as in 1973, by rapid cyclical upsurge in demand about the upward trend — first allowed Swedish firms Volvo and Saab-Scania to establish themselves in the UK market, and then attracted other importers. As an EFTA partner Sweden could export duty free to the UK after July 1968, an opportunity eagerly grasped by her heavy CV makers. The success of their marketing effort was shown by the fact that as early as 1972 Volvo sold 2,200 vehicles in the UK and accounted for 18 per cent of the UK heavy vehicle market for types of 28-tons gross and above, compared with Seddon-Atkinson's share of just over 20 per cent. The other Swedish firm Scania sold almost 1,000 chassis over the same period. This foreign penetration was a function of the excess demand for British CVs and, in particular, the Swedish firm's ability to supply the right product perfected by their long experience of making very heavy vehicles for transcontinental haulage. Perhaps the importance of quality, but also the ability to give quicker delivery, was illustrated by Newport Corporation's resolve to spend £160,000 on ten Metro-Scania double deckers instead of £130,000 on British Leyland models on the basis of the lower maintenance costs experienced in the operation of Swedish-based vehicles already owned.[1] However, the small British firms and the medium-sized operations covered by British Leyland's Truck and Bus Division became alerted to the fact that extra capacity and new models were needed to stem the tide of Swedish imports and to combat the late entrants from the EEC such as Mercedes-Benz, DAF, Iveco and MAN. Although there was some evidence in the mid-1970s that some British operators were switching their orders back to British suppliers. UK market share still dropped and this is further analysed in the next chapter. It would appear, therefore, that the small British firms and indeed the medium-sized enterprises, such as Volvo, Scania and Leyland Vehicles will survive in the face of competition from much larger producers, such as Ford, Bedford, Iveco and Mercedes-Benz, by being able to satsify the peculiar needs of the heavy vehicle operator at a price economic to both producer and operator.[2]

Our attention is now turned to a more depressing in-depth analysis of the UK market and major UK manufacturers.

1. A pre-publication comment pointed out that in this instance the double-decker went out of production after the Newport order and that there are not many other examples. Nevertheless we still believe that quick delivery can be a significant factor on occasions.
2. For a fuller account of the economies of the commercial vehicle industry, see Chapter 12 and 'Heavy Commercial Vehicles: The Survival of the Small Firm, by D.G. Rhys in the *Journal of Industrial Economics,* July 1972, published by Basil Blackwell, Oxford.

CHAPTER 11

THE UK COMMERCIAL VEHICLE MARKET
AND THE WEST EUROPEAN MANUFACTURERS

INTRODUCTION

In this chapter a more detailed analysis of the UK CV market is undertaken together with a detailed breakdown of the major European manufacturers, and in particular the four major UK manufacturers. The chapter is also concerned with the 'home market goes European' theme. However, there is one distinction between the content of this and the previous chapter concerning the strength of the UK CV industry in facing up to a more aggressive European, Japanese and even Soviet Block exchange.

ANALYSIS OF MARKET

Most European car makers produce CVs, the exceptions being BMW, Seat and, to all intents and purposes, Alfa Romeo. In addition, Peugeot-Citroen only make car derivatives and light-medium panel vans and pick-ups. In the 1980s VW will extend its range through joint ventures with MAN, the remaining medium-sized German CV maker. In addition, Volvo's DAF car subsidiary only makes car derivative vans, while the multinational operations of Chrysler in France and Ford and GM in Germany and Belgium only make car derivatives or at best panel vans like the Ford Transit or Opel Blitz.[1] The only mass producers of cars engaged in heavy CV production are British Leyland, Fiat (Iveco) and Renault (Saviem-Berliet) plus Ford, Bedford and Chrysler Spain. However, the European heavy vehicle market leader is the specialist car and CV firm, Daimler-Benz.[2] The smallest of the front rank firms is Volvo, a position which would have been dramatically changed if the proposed merger with Saab in 1977 had occurred as the combined group had a capacity for heavy CVs of some 50,000 units a year, second only to Daimler-Benz. This would have left British Leyland as the smallest of the front rank firms, with a heavy vehicle capacity over twice the size of the three medium-sized firms, Saab-Scania, MAN of West Germany and DAF, which in turn are twice the size of the leading small-scale enterprises ERF, Foden and Seddon-Atkinson.[3] However, in the early 1980s Leyland's Truck and Bus Division, following a £50 million[4] expansion, will have a heavy vehicle capacity of 20,000 trucks

1. This model was discontinued in 1975, but the Opel car derivative vans are still made.
2. Its rise to European market leadership with a capacity for all types of CV of 250,000 units a year, compared with Ford's 200,000, was only partly due to its purchase of Henschel's 75,000 units capacity.
3. On the other hand, if Foden, ERF, Metro-Cammell and Dennis were brought together in a holding company structure with Rolls-Royce Motors and various independent component makers, a substantial enterprise would be created. Whether this would give further advantage to those stemming from existing external economies is a moot point however.
4. £20 million in Bathgate and Glasgow, and £32 million at Leyland in Lancashire.

plus its leading position in bus making, which will keep the company in the front rank for all types of CV including heavy vehicles. The combined capacity of International Harvester owned and associated firms, namely Seddon and DAF, is around 20,000 units, which is close to the Volvo figure. As well as these producers there are even smaller concerns such as Dennis and Shelvoke and Drewry in the UK, Saurer-Berna with plants in Switzerland and Austria, Steyr of Austria, Faun and Kaeble of West Germany. The Leyland associate Pegaso of Spain is on a par with Seddon-Atkinson in size and is as integrated as many larger firms. Hino, a leading Japanese producer of CVs has a facility owned by an Irish licensee, while Mack of the USA has a presence in Holland. Additionally, there are a number of bus making specialists such as Setra and Kassbohrer of West Germany, Aerfer and Viberti in Italy, Metro-Cammell in the UK.

Table 11.1 shows the total market size and market shares of the major West European manufacturers, although the truck market segment (the heavy CV part of the industry) is distorted by the sale of light and medium vans. For example in 1975, 1.3 million CVs were made and 931,000 sold in Western Europe with some 360,000 exported. Of those CVs registered domestically, 230,000 were car derivatives, 427,000 were small trucks and medium vans (e.g. panel vans), and the remaining 274,000 were trucks and heavy CVs. Consequently VW, Renault and Peugeot-Citroen are not as large in the CV market as their market share would suggest. Renault though now comprises both its own company (Saviem) and Citroen's former subsidiary Berliet, which makes Renault a formidable CV producer.

FIGURE 11.1

UK Market Shares and Import Penetration

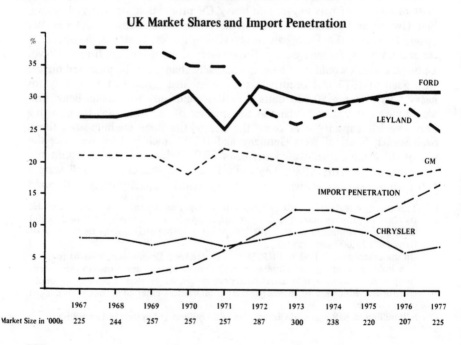

TABLE 11.1

Western European Market Shares

	1975	1976	1977
Market Shares in %			
VW	10.6	10.5	10.2
Daimler-Benz	10.7	10.9	10.5
Renault (including Berliet)	12.2	15.0	14.1
Fiat	8.7	8.7	9.4
Leyland	8.0	6.4	5.9
GM/Bedford	6.4	5.6	6.2
Peugeot-Citroen	11.2	11.3	11.1
Japanese	1.9	2.5	3.0
Others	16.7	16.2	16.1
Market Size in 000s	931	1102	1156
Industry Segments in %			
Light (e.g. car derived vans)	24.7	15.4	24.5
Medium (e.g. vans and small trucks)	45.9	45.8	47.4
Heavy (e.g. trucks, artics)	29.4	28.8	28.1

UK Market Size and Shares

In Figure 11.1 the UK market size, import penetration and market shares of the four major UK manufacturers are shown. The most marked change in market shares has been Leyland; its share has dropped from 38 per cent in the late 1960's to 25 per cent in 1977, although the post-Ryder rescue saw a short lived recovery. As with cars Ford's performance has been more consistent with market share stabilising at around 31 per cent. GM's subsidiary Bedford has also been fairly consisten at just under 20 per cent. Chrysler's share increased during the early 1970's as sales of small imported vehicles from Chrysler France were successfully introduced into the UK market. The 1975 crisis and the closure of part of the CV operation brought about a consequent drop in market share for Chrysler, even though effective assembly capacity was in fact not reduced.

Domestic sales and the import penetration percentage are also shown. In the late 1960s and 1970-1, Leyland had clear market dominance which it has now conceded to Ford. More importantly, import penetration has risen from a negligible level in the late 1960s to around 14 per cent in 1973 and 1974. A reduction in 1975 seemed to raise false expectations since import penetration once again increased in 1976 and 1977.

If production or domestic sales have been mildly disappointing, exports have been the success story of the industry. Leyland's poor domestic record, for example, is offset by its steady improvement in its exports. Bedford also has had high exports in line with the UK company being GM's European CV manufacturer.

Imports in the car-derived van and other van market segments have been increasing (see Table 11.4) partly due to a successful Japanese attack on these market segments. Import shares of rigid trucks have traditionally been low but a significant share is now being taken by importers. It is, however, in the heavy sector that import penetration is highest and we will consider this topic separately.

TABLE 11.2

UK Exports of CVs in '000s

	1972	1973	1974	1975	1976
GM (Bedford)	31	46	54	53	45
Chrysler	4	6	6	5	5
Ford	39	74	57	71	72
Leyland	67	67	63	77	81
TOTAL	141	197	182	204	208

It would be wrong to analyse the CV market as consisting of one more or less uniform market. Unlike cars, CVs can be broadly split into car derived vans, small trucks and vans, and the heavier trucks and CVs. The market shares of each sector are shown in Table 11.3. The most conspicuous change has been the increase in the 'heavy' CV market segment whilst the two lighter market segments have suffered a decline. Such a tendency is consistent with the increased Europeanisation of the UK CV market and the enhanced UK motorway network. West Germany's 'heavy' segment tends to be about 40 per cent of the total market while the French proportion tends to be significantly lower at 20 per cent. The UK market could be expected to stabilise at or near the European average 'heavy' market segment which is just under 30 per cent. (See Table 11.1.)

An analysis of the light and medium van segments of the total market shows up an interesting drive by Moskovitch in the early 1970s to capture a

TABLE 11.3

Industry Segments of UK Market

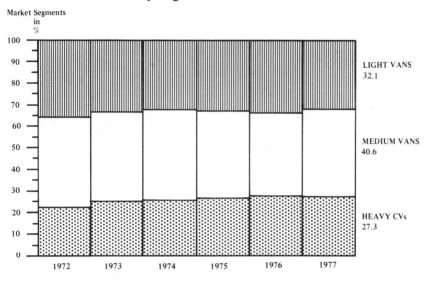

significant share of the 'light market'. After an initial success, sales have declined, but the threat of a reintroduction must still exist. However, Chrysler France supplied most if not all of Chrysler's car derived vans. VW was another importer who 'peaked' in the early 1970s with 12 per cent of the 'medium' segment of the UK market. Since then VW too have found that sales and share have declined. A surprising feature of the lighter segment is that Leyland's market share in these segments has held up, despite the absence of a competitive product line. Ford's share of the market has also been maintained illustrating the highly professional style of management in that competitiveness is maintained in every market segment that Ford chooses to be in. A rather different story unfolds with regard to both Chrysler and GM (Bedford) whose shares have both declined. Import penetration has increased markedly in the lighter segment where a major Japanese sales drive started to occur in 1977 and early 1978. There is also some evidence that this challenge will spill over into the 'medium' segment.

Heavy CV Segment

It is in the heaviest segment (e.g. tractor units for articulated CVs) that import penetration is highest. Figure 11.2 shows that import penetration has been the most serious and established in the 'heavy' CV segment, rising to some 23 per cent of the market. To date the main importers have been primarily West European, although some Soviet Bloc manufacturers and two Japanese firms (Hino and Mitsubishi) may impose an even greater threat to an already poor situation. Even more disastrous as it is this market segment which forms the backbone of

TABLE 11.4

Industry Share of Non-heavy UK CV Market in %

	1972	1973	1974	1975	1976	1977
INDUSTRY SHARE OF:						
(a) Light Vans in %						
Leyland	37.4	34.0	39.1	44.4	38.3	32.0
Ford	29.7	31.0	27.5	24.7	28.4	26.5
GM (Bedford)	21.5	20.9	19.2	20.8	18.8	25.2
Chrysler	5.8	7.1	9.9	7.1	5.0	5.7
Imports	4.6	7.0	4.3	3.0	9.5	10.6
(b) Medium Vans in %						
Leyland	20.6	19.0	19.0	22.0	24.2	22.5
Ford	37.7	33.3	36.1	38.3	40.3	39.7
GM(Bedford)	19.2	19.2	18.5	16.1	14.6	14.6
Chrysler	9.0	11.1	11.1	10.2	6.5	5.8
Imports	13.5	17.4	15.3	13.4	14.4	17.4

the sales of Leyland Vehicles Ltd (formerly BL Bus and Truck Division). Despite a strong mid-range of vehicles, Leyland's market share of this segment has systematically fallen. Chrysler's market share has also dropped following reorganisation of CV facilities after the 1975 rescue. As argued earlier the smaller UK manufacturers have been able to hold their own, although the period 1974-6 saw some decline in share. Table 11.5 shows the tremendous increase in all manufacturers with the exception of Scania. The indigenous UK manufacturers are unlikely to be able to repel these importers since they have now found marketing gaps in the UK suppliers and solid distribution networks have been built which will ensure a significant share of the market. The type of marketing niche which many of the importers concentrate on is reliability, minimum maintenance, minimum 'downtime',[1] high torque engines which do not require constant changing of gears and which can therefore lead to lower fuel consumption, and so on. On present evidence it is now no longer a question of whether the UK manufacturers can reverse the trend in the heavy CV segment; instead it is even questionable whether a further decline in the market shares of the UK manufacturers can be prevented.

PRODUCTION

In figure 11.3, production is shown separately for the major UK manufacturers. Production of CVs declined in 1972 and has since remained at a lower level. Whilst by 1976 Ford and the smaller manufacturers had made a recovery, Chrysler, after its reorganisation, had a more compact set of production

1. An important factor in an articulated vehicle costing around £35,000.

FIGURE 11.2

Industry Share of Heavy CV Market in %

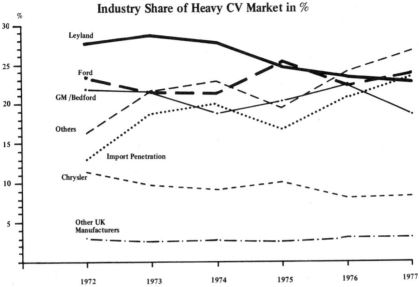

TABLE 11.5

Heavy UK Sales by Selected Importers

	1973	1974	1975	1976	1977
Tied Imports					
Ford (Holland)	–	–	–	245	281
Chrysler (Spain)	–	–	–	176	61
Other Imports					
DAF	407	688	559	969	1,431
Fiat	1	255	399	654	1,148
Saviem	–	–	–	17	189
MAN	–	143	272	312	330
Magirus Deutz	–	–	158	303	448
Mercedes-Benz	1,226	1,239	967	1,290	1,652
Scania	1,332	1,093	723	803	885
Volvo	2,492	2,615	2,241	2,815	2,815
Roman[a]	–	–	–	61	178

a. Romanian (– MAN vehicle made under licence).

facilities. Although the Maidstone plant was closed, the rationalisation of CV operations increased efficiency and overall capacity has in effect not been reduced. However, neither Leyland nor Bedford showed signs of recovery.

No doubt in the case of Leyland despite record exports, the decline in the home market share coupled with production interruptions has made for lower overall production.

FIGURE 11.3

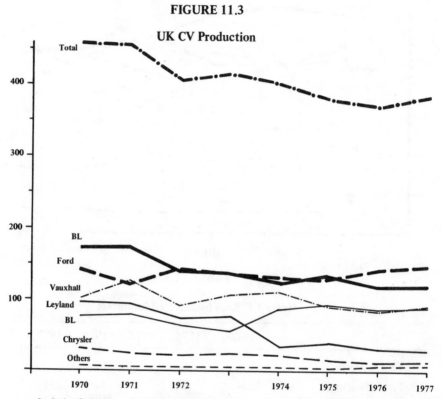

a. Includes Land Rovers which do not fall under the category of estate cars up to 1973, thereafter all Land Rovers are shown under Cars. The element of Land Rover production included under Leyland Vehicles was 39,000 vehices in 1972 and 36,500 in 1973.

Chrysler's CV operations in the UK are now centred around Dunstable and Luton. Chrysler's policy seems to be to import light vans from its French factories and some heavy CVs from its Spanish plant. Ford's CV operations are fairly scattered. The main assembly plants are Langley in Slough (medium CV assembly) and Southampton (Transit vans and truck cabs). In addition there are a number of smaller plants specialising in CV manufacture; Swansea (axles and heavy CVs), Leamington (truck and tractor transmissions), and Basildon (tractors); transmissions units also come from Halewood and engines from Dagenham. Heavy CVs are however imported from Holland and there are truck assembly facilities in Belgium. GM designated Vauxhall as its CV producer for the whole of West Europe (and much of the rest of the world outside the US), while Opel was made to concentrate on the highly profitable production of cars. At Luton, Vauxhall assemble the Bedford HA and CF vans, whilst the heavier truck and bus assembly is concentrated at Dunstable. Leyland's plants as at 1975 are shown in Table 11.6 although additional investment has mainly taken place at Bathgate and Leyland, and a certain amount of rationalisation has already taken place — for example the Albion plant has been turned into a component plant with vehicle assembly being phased out.

TABLE 11.6

Leyland's Plants as at 1975

Plant	Old Marque associated with plant	Location	No of employees	Product
Leyland	Leyland	Leyland in Lancashire	11,000	Machine shops, spares, alternators, truck assembly
Bathgate	BMC	Edinburgh	5,000	Light truck assembly and tractors.
Albion	Albion	Glasgow	2,000	Truck & component assembly.
Southall	AEC	Southall, Middlesex.	3,000	Heavy trucks & buses.
Wolverhampton	Guy	Wolverhampton	700	Heavy trucks
Watford	Scammell	Watford Middlesex.	1,000	Heavy truck & special equipment assembly.
Park Royal	Park Royal Vehicles		800	Buses, body building
CH	Roe		300	Body building.
Eastern Coachworks	ECW	Lowestoft	900	Body building.
Bristol	Bristol Commercial Vehicles		500	Bus chassis assembly
Leyland National	Leyland National	Workington	400	Integral single deck bus assembly.

US Multinationals

Ford seems to be going from strength to strength in the CV market as in the car market: the company actually seems to be able to achieve higher productivity levels. Following the rationalisation of its UK CV operations, Chrysler's market share has deteriorated to what maybe a new lower equilibrium level. GM's

265

performance has been consistent rather than startling. However, Opel (GM's German subsidiary) has been grumbling about Vauxhall's delivery times, reliability and model policy. GM has also developed links on several fronts behind the Iron Curtain. It is not inconceivable that GM may start to import CVs from the Communist Bloc rather than from the UK. Certainly if Bedford is to serve Europe with CVs, it must become a more dynamic CV operator.

Leyland

In Table 11.7 production by various different marques of Leyland is shown and is surprisingly small. It must, however, be remembered that the Truck and Bus Division sells much higher priced products. Nevertheless, Leyland's CV division is in terms of volume[1] a small company, but comparatively large when compared with the European specialist CV producers. Only Daimler-Benz truly dominates Leyland in every respect. However, in Chapter 3 we noted that Leyland had the widest range of CVs (as it does in cars) yet hardly the volume with which to produce a competitive product.

According to Leyland's internal newspaper[2] the fact that Leyland has been unable to match the sales efforts of its competitors has led to a fall in market share.[3] The classic loss of vehicle syndrome which so badly affected the car division is also found in Leyland Vehicles. Just under 1,600 vehicles were lost due to internal disputes whilst further disruption was caused by suppliers. The critical analysis went further:

> Manufacturing efficiency was lower than levels which were achieved in the past and targeted improvements in new machines were not achieved. In 1977, the division achieved 69% of its production programme, a short-fall which represents the loss of customers, spares sales and repeat orders to competitors, and a serious dent to profitability. This, of course, means borrowing more heavily to financing investment programmes (*Financial Times*, 10.2.78).

Shades of BL Cars?

To put it bluntly Leyland has a number of weaknesses. As with cars productivity is low and the reputation for reliability, durability and quality not good. Plant and equipment is rapidly ageing; and as with cars there is a notable absence of both engineering and managerial resources. Moreover the product range requires development: at the moment it is too extensive and is least competitive at the top end of the range whilst the Japanese competition is likely ultimately to erode the lower end of the market.

---

1. Around 40,000 vehicles capacity per year (excluding light vans produced by BL cars and Land Rovers). Land Rover production has been around 50,000 to 60,000 per year and derived vans production has been around 40,000 per year and light van (Sherpa) production has been around 20,000 per year.
2. As reported in the *Financial Times*, 10.2.78.
3. Where the market for Leyland Truck and Bus is defined as all trucks, artics and some of the heavier vans.

TABLE 11.7

Detailed CV Production Figures for BL

	1975	1976	1977
BL Cars			
Car-derived vans	41,015	22,589	38,340
Vans (less than 3½ tons GVW)	11,287	16,614	19,967
Land-Rovers (not included under cars)[a]	38,523	35,932	29,761
Mini-buses	915	1,240	1,634
	91,740	87,375	89,702
Leyland Vehicles			
Rigids			
Leyland Scotland	17,717	13,716	15,464
Guy	303	101	21
AEC	1,282	451	270
Albion	6,956	5,150	4,576
Leyland	3,479	3,291	1,620
Scammel	444	509	486
	30,181	23,218	22,437
Artics			
Leyland Scotland	435	143	104
Guy	613	376	312
AEC	1,270	1,256	1,327
Albion	790	509	425
Leyland	641	764	1,289
Scammel	354	321	172
	4,103	3,369	3,629
Buses			
Guy	602	490	334
AEC	651	963	547
Albion	1,290	500	721
Leyland	4,490	4,259	2,534
	7,033	6,212	4,136
TOTAL CV production Truck and Bus division	41,317	32,799	30,202
a. Land-Rovers (included under cars)	14,158	12,582	11,848
Range Rovers	10,585	9,552	9.696

In other words Leyland is suffering from the same ailments which have afflicted the Car Division — with three exceptions. First, the problems are not yet quite as severe as with the Car Division. Secondly, the Truck and Bus Division can still generate profits and a healthy cash flow which can be ploughed back in the form of new capital investment. Thirdly, Leyland has several marketing advantages; the marque Leyland is well known; Leyland has a strong position in some of the less developed countries (notably Africa); and in general Leyland, with the exception of West Europe, has a strong CV dealer network. However, Leyland must be careful not to let complacency set in; there are still very challenging and very real problems ahead.

Leyland's Strategy

Leyland do appear to have a coherent plan. First a new simplified model programme is already well advanced and seems fairly logical, and it should be completed by the early 1980s. A new heavy truck range soon to be announced will ultimately replace the Lynx, Bison, Buffalo, Octopus, Marathon, Routeman and Crusader series. Replacements for the medium range of trucks — namely the Boxer, Mastiff, Chieftain, Clydesdale and Reiver series — must follow before long, while a replacement for the lighter weight EA, FG and Terrier series is obviously a long-term goal.

Secondly the rationalisation of the numerous manufacturing processes seems well advanced and seems to indicate two large assembly sites; Leyland in Lancashire (heavier CVs), Bathgate in Scotland (lighter CVs, tractors and powertrain) with a number of smaller plants; Wolverhampton (the old Guy factory — very heavy CVs and buses), Southall (buses), Scammell (off-road specialist vehicles), Albion (powertrain), and others. The bus model range will be integrated so that it will heavily revolve around planned CV models in order to rationalise the combined product range.

Third the capital investment plans for Leyland Vehicles are relatively large (over £300 million between 1978-83[1]) and should put Leyland into a competitive position, though some West European manufacturers such as Daimler Benz have been known to spend several times this amount. However, given sufficient opportunities to utilise the economies of scale supplied by the extensive component industry, these funds should be sufficient to make Leyland competitive in its mid-range and the top end of its models.

If Leyland does succeed then it may be able to re-establish itself with around one quarter of the heavy CV market. Table 11.8 shows a possible projection of the UK heavy CV market and Leyland's sales. The conditions for this relatively modest achievement are further discussed in the conclusion of the book.

1. The Ryder Plan envisaged about £346m of capital investment in the Truck and Bus Division. The new plan increases the planned capital investment to over £400m since the 1975 rescue. These figures do not include capital investment in Land-Rovers, car-derived vans or the Sherpa van.

TABLE 11.8

Possible Optimistic Projection of Leyland's Sales

in '000s

	1976	1980	1985	1990
Market size ('000)	207	280	320	350
Heavy segment in %	27	27	27	26
Heavy market size ('000s)	57	76	86	91
Leyland's UK share in %	23.2	23	25	26
Leyland's domestic sales ('000s)	13	17	22	24
Leyland's exports ('000s)	13	17	25	30
Leyland's total sales ('000s)	26	34	47	54

The UK Industry in a European Context

In 1975, the UK CV industry produced and exported more than any other European CV industry and its large positive contribution to the balance of payments was maintained. Despite problems on the car side, the four UK mass producers appear to be more viable as CV makers (see Table 11.9).

However, this rosy picture is in some respects misleading for whilst output between 1960 and 1965 stagnated and fluctuated between a record 466,000 in 1969 and 381,000 in 1975, France and Italy doubled production, while Japan's output increased from 316,000 in 1960 to 2.37 million in 1975. However, German output rose more slowly, reaching a peak of 314,000 in 1970, producing 278,000 in 1975 – this reflects the strong bias of official West German transport policy towards railways and the need for firms like Daimler-Benz to export to survive.[1] Similar stagnation in the UK faced with growth abroad is evident from the export figures. Between 1960 and 1975 UK CV exports rose only 11 per cent, compared with 88 per cent in France, 53 per cent in Germany, 200 per cent in Sweden, while Italy, starting from a low base, increased overseas by 71 per cent. Since 1975 whilst most other European countries have substantially increased their production, only the UK and Sweden have achieved a marginal rate of growth (see Table 11.9).

Because of the importance of the mass producers (particularly Ford and Bedford) the UK is almost as significant a producer of medium to heavy vehicles as West Germany; in the heavy vehicle category, however, the UK in 1975 was only the seventh largest producer, behind all the countries in Table

1. Not all West German car-based CVs are included in the figures, thereby under estimating total CV output.

269

TABLE 11.9

Output and Sales (CVs) (.000s)

New registrations	1974	1975	1976	1977
West Germany:				
Output	260	278	321	314
Imports	18	22	26	29
Exports	174	178	206	189
New registrations	108	109	137	138
France:				
Output	376	315	423	415
Imports	54	42	92	96
Exports	142	137	144	148
New registrations	253	206	293	298
UK:				
Output	403	381	372	386
Imports	40	26	27	37
Exports	161	180	188	192
New registrations	242	225	215	231
Italy:				
Output	142	110	119	143
Imports	31	20	55	57
Exports	48	45	49	70
New registrations	101	75	90	112
Sweden:				
Output	42	50	51	52
Imports	13	15	20	12
Exports	34	40	42	41
New registrations	17	17	19	20

11.10, plus Holland and Spain. In terms of individual producers, the UK's importance in the 6 ton + market does not ensure that its producers are particularly well placed. Indeed, because of a more highly concentrated industry, where Daimler-Benz faces internal competition from MAN and the German arm of Iveco (Magirus Deutz) the former is a clear European leader. West Germany's strength in CVs is due largely to the strength of Daimler-Benz. In 1975 it had 24 per cent of the European truck market producing the largest total of CVs, despite a weakness in the mass market for medium vans. In the over 6 ton sector, the firm made over 100,000 vehicles, compared with 60,000 by Iveco, its nearest rival. In the 15 tons + sector the figures were 58,000 to 38,000.

TABLE 11.10

Production by Weight Category (1975)

Gross Vehicle Weight:	6 tonnes and over	15 tonnes and over
UK	128,000	40,000[a][b]
West Germany	145,000 [a]	80,000
France	46,000 [a]	30,000
Italy	35,000 [a]	23,000 [c]
Sweden	45,000 [a]	40,000 [a]

a. Estimate
b. Over 14 tonnes
c. Over 12 tonnes

Iveco, which is 80 per cent owned by Fiat, also incorporates the Fiat subsidiaries of Unic in France and OM and Lancia in Italy, as well as the German concern Magirus Deutz. Having come together in 1975, Iveco aimed to complete the integration of production by the end of 1977 and to offer an integrated world range, plus Magirus's involvement in the Club of Four, by the early 1980s. Only the separate air-cooled Magirus diesel engines and the conventional Fiat units will escape this process of standardisation. The combine employs 50,000 workers spread through 16 plants and hoped to make 120,000 vehicles in 1977 with a worldwide output of 180,000 by 1980.

Although a wide range of vehicles helps to establish and maintain a good dealer network, Volvo and Saab Scania has shown that concentration on a heavy vehicle range is no handicap in this respect. However, as regards British Leyland's assault on the European market, laid down in the Ryder plan, the lack of a good dealer chain, which has proved a handicap in the past, requires attention. ERF's aim in increasing the export ratio from 15 per cent to 30 per cent of output is based upon a selective assault on the European market, a policy previously successfully pursued by Volvo. Ford is improving its network with considerable success, and they and Bedford have successfully increased van sales. However, sales of UK trucks are starting from a low base, mainly because UK Construction and Use Regulations did not encourage the development of European type vehicles, and actively discouraged the use on British roads of maximum size European lorries capable of around 38 tons gross, the UK limit being 32 tons. As a result, the Europeans in 1975 were able to take

58 per cent of the UK market in 28 ton vehicles, compared with only 16 per cent for whole 16 ton class as UK operators continued to re-equip with maximum size vehicles for use in the UK and on the Continent, where they would be supported by adequate sales and service facilities. The UK makers have in the period 1975-7 introduced a new generation of European size vehicles, but, although some success in import saving is detectable, the UK firms must impress Continental operators that their products are fully competitive with European types. On the UK firms' success in this regard depends the success of the industry's penetration of the European heavy vehicle market. However, in terms of being able to supply a complete range of vehicles covering all aspects of the market, four of the seven firms capable of doing this are British based, although Chrysler's heaviest vehicles are made in Spain, the others being Mercedes, Iveco and Renault (Saviem-Berliet). With a comprehensive range plus a range of new vehicles the UK industry could prove as successful in penetrating the European market (perhaps initially on a selective basis) as it has been in making sales to the Third World, or indeed, in protecting all but the heaviest sector of the home market from imports, where in any event sales of imported heavy vehicles were for the most part caused by excess demand and waiting lists for UK products between 1964 and 1971 rather than any shortcomings in the product.

International Co-operation

As very few specialist CV suppliers exist on the Continent (with the exception of the German ZF and Swedish Voith transmission makers) Continental makers have for a decade or so been co-operating closely in order to try to spread costs and internalise the external economies enjoyed by the British. This is done either by straightforward inter-firm transactions or by the setting-up of jointly owned subsidiaries. In order to combat the advantages enjoyed by the UK mass producers in the medium CV range, Saviem, Volvo, Magirus Deutz and DAF formed the 'Club of Four'[1] to design, produce and buy components for a common range of 6 to 13 ton trucks which none of the four firms had successfully made and marketed before. In late 1974 the first two trucks, from DAF and Saviem, were announced. The common components for the two vehicles were produced on tools jointly owned by the European Truck Design consortium and the vehicles in which they are incorporated were to be marketed by each of the four partners under their own names and through their own sales outlets. In addition, each member was free to sell trucks wherever it chose. However, for each truck sold, the individual member company paid a fee to the central ETD group to help amortise costs. The links between Saviem and Berliet, DAF and International Harvester, and the purchase of Magirus Deutz by Fiat-dominated Iveco had in no way altered the basis of the Club. However, the size of these groups may subsequently persuade some 'club' members to go it alone in this area of business.

Saviem has had a long established two-way link with MAN for components and sales, the French company exchanging lighter vehicle items for heavy-duty

1. After the initial agreement, the group design office was established near Paris in 1972.

equipment. Saviem is also linked with Fiat and Alfa Romeo in the joint development and manufacture of small h.p. diesel engines. In turn, MAN (whose vehicles are also made under licence in Romania) produces axles and some engine blocks jointly with Daimler-Benz and joint production of 6–12 ton trucks with VW is possible, thereby rectifying the company's exclusion from the Club of Four, VW, who are already quite strong in lighter CVs, would then join the select band of mass producers in the heavy CV market.

The two European leaders, Mercedes and Iveco, already linked with other firms, took steps in 1976 towards their own co-operative venture – the manufacture of automatic gearboxes.[1] Volvo and Saab-Scania's plan for a merger in 1977 may have proved abortive but technical links can be expected to develop. British Leyland has strong links with Pegaso in Spain while Ford buys Saviem-Berliet cabs for its heaviest vehicles. Seddon-Atkinson is linked to DAF via International Harvester, while Foden and Faun have manufacturing and marketing links. In short, apart from ERF and, until 1977, Scania, all major European truck manufacturers had links with other firms. Further developments along such lines by the CV manufacturers can be expected to continue.

The underlying currents are clear. The smaller manufacturers, at present committed to high in-house production, like Volvo, Scania, DAF, MAN and perhaps even Saviem-Berliet, will continue to seek partnerships and even the big companies will prefer joint ventures where they feel that going alone cannot achieve the necessary economies of scale to remain competitive or where risks are higher : the manufacture of automatic gearboxes, for example, is largely a hedge against future buying trends which may or may not develop in Europe as they have in the USA. Ford and Bedford, with the strength of the parent companies behind them, can stay alone on most projects, but even here the bought-out content of Ford's heaviest trucks is amongst the highest in the European CV industry, being on a par with ERF. British Leyland, on the evidence of its sale of axle and transmission facilities to Rockwell and Eaton, could equally find it beneficial to co-operate with competitors to cut costs. However, it and Chrysler have the alternative of buying out from the British CV supply infrastructure.

Clearly, it is possible that Continental firms could come to rely increasingly on suppliers as the UK and US industry does. In the land of giant motor industry corporations, the US CV industry finds room for a large number of medium and small makers such as White, Mack, Kenworth, Peterbilt and so on. Like the UK specialists they are able to control costs below levels which belie their smallness, by purchasing on an industry wide basis. To use a car analogy: by buying from such sources, Kenworth is to GMC what Buick is to Chevrolet, and not as Rolls-Royce is to Chevrolet, which a comparison of final assembly capacity might suggest. Ford, a giant in the USA, follows this policy with its super-heavy Transcontinental range made in Amsterdam. This vehicle's Ford 'content' is almost confined to the added value of final assembly costs. Seemingly many Continental makers regard this form of production as a handicap, perhaps because of fears concerning precise specifications, delivery and quality

---

1. This proposal was being examined by the West German Cartel office in 1978.

control.[1] However, the in-house policy of many Continental firms has presented them with ruinously high unit costs; consequently, their sceptism of Ford's policy must be treated with reserve. Notwithstanding their viewpoint, a number of UK and US component firms are keeping a watching brief on new marketing possibilities.

One area of concern of more significance for the car side but of oblique interest to the CV sector, concerns the possible take-off in demand for diesel-engined cars. Already, Mercedes Benz's total car output is typically around 40 per cent diesel powered. Peugeot and Opel are also well established in this field and have recently been joined by VW.[2] Significantly, VW's thrust is at the private motorist while the other firms have catered for the taxi, hire car and general business-use market. In the UK, the application of diesel power to products catering for the above markets is almost totally confined to the 'London-type' BL-Carbodies taxi cab, which uses either BL or Perkins diesels, while ordinary saloon car taxis and hire cars in the UK are petrol-engine powered, unlike their Continental counterparts. As small diesels normally share the same basic configurations as similar size petrol units they can be made with the same tooling and on the same production lines. Consequently, the scale involved suggests that production by the vehicle makers would be a practical proposition. On the other hand, some makers may judge that what extra expenditure is required in establishing production facilities would not be justified by potential sales, so in this case a specialist source of supply would be useful. The UK's lethargy in this field is not due to a lack of the right products but the failure to juxtapose suitable but available car models and existing small diesels. Technical opinion insists that the BL 1.8 litre diesel is a potential market leader in car usage while Ford also produce 2 litre units in the UK, although these may need development to complete the transfer from van to car successfully. In addition, Perkins has small units available which have found a considerable market in car use.[3] Initially, Ford decided to use Peugeot diesels in their diesel cars but BL can provide an in-house product. Vauxhall can call upon Opel's facilities while Chrysler could purchase from other car firms, possibly by cementing its existing inter-firm trading links with VW, for example, or by buying out from a specialist producer such as Perkins or possible new contenders such as GEC or Hawker Siddley: the latter having considerable diesel engine interests apart from Gardner. Consequently, the car and CV industries can fill the gap in UK diesel car making, but it is likely that Ford's entrants will be German made cars with French diesels with only BL supplying an all UK effort. However, firms such as Perkins, Weyburn and Lucas are fully cognisant of possibilities in this field and are more than likely to become major contributors in satisfying any substantial growth in consumer demand for diesel cars.

1. However, between 1973-6 the UK component industry worked closely with the vehicle makers to produce as luxurious and well-sprung vehicles as the continentals and often producing more reliable, longer lasting and economical products.
2. Saviem (Renault), Fiat and Alfa Romeo's joint project in light diesels could also have car applications.
3. In late 1977 Perkins announced an expansion at its Peterborough works to produce a new 2-litre diesel engine at the rate of 90,000 a year. The engine is aimed at the van, light truck and car market and was due to appear in late 1978.

Future Developments in Europe

Rationalisation of the supply side does not overcome a problem of general over-capacity in relation to demand, in conditions of slow and patchy growth. CV demand is a function of (i) a strong economy (i.e. a high and growing GDP); (ii) government transport and environmental policies (e.g. Britain's refusal to allow vehicles of more than 32 tons gross, compared with Continental weights of 38-52 tonnes – while despite the lower GDP the UK industry is larger than the West German where home demand is constrained by a rail-biased transport policy); (iii) running costs, such as fuel, or the effects of labour legislation on matters like permitted driving hours.

The amount of goods traffic will grow as Gross Domestic Product grows,[1] but the demand for CVs may not be proportional. For instance, carrying capacity may increase but the number of vehicles could fall as the average lorry size increases. On the other hand, if lorries become bigger either on average or absolutely, then entry to cities may be banned with trans-shipment to smaller vehicles at motorway 'marshalling yards' being necessary. Depending on which influence is the stronger the number of CVs could increase less or more than proportionately with GDP.

Certainly the trend during the last decade has been towards larger lorries, which in turn has benefited firms specialising in their manufacture. Since the maximum UK weight limit increased from 24 tons to 32 tons in 1964 there has obviously been a move to increased size. Furthermore since 1964 there has been an increase in the number of heavy lorries weighing over 28 tons. For instance, in 1975 11,000 such vehicles were registered increasing the total stock in use to 66,700, or just under 12½ per cent of the total number of goods vehicles. In 1976 over 12,000 such CVs were registered – over 21 per cent of the year's total registrations. Furthermore, over 7,000 of these were designed to carry more than 32 tons. Clearly, therefore, the market available to the heavy vehicle makers, and notably the specialists, is growing. Indeed, if the maximum weight limits in the UK are increased to 38/40 tonnes then an increased surge in business is likely. However, this demonstrates that the commercial interests of CV manufacturers could conflict with prevailing social interests as a 40 tonne vehicle with 5 axles would do 136 per cent more road damage than a similar 32 ton truck, while fully laden it would do the road damage to equivalent of 80,000 cars.[2]

The future export market is likely to be more competitive, for whilst the Middle East and Third World's demand for transport increases insatiably, so will the number of rail building projects and the number of CV producers seeking business. The Japanese are strong competitors, while the Russians will be a more significant force when the Kama river truck plant built with Western technology begins to operate at its planned low cost output levels of 150,000

1. Car demand studies see car ownership approaching some limit in terms of cars per head. However, if GDP grows without limit then theoretically there is no limit to the growth of goods traffic. This is obviously absurd as new distribution patterns limiting total traffic can be expected. Therefore, no infinite demand for lorries (or lorry drivers) can be expected.
2. Source: Department of Transport.

trucks and 250,000 diesel engines a year. However, the expertise of UK firms in dealing with such markets, coupled with its range of 4 x 4 vehicles (e.g. Land-Rover), plus the well appointed sales and service network, generally means that the CV export effort has been more firmly based than the car one. Therefore, the UK should continue to be well represented in the fastest growing CV markets[1] — although these markets may become protected and/or increasingly competitive in the future.

The attack on Europe will be more difficult, as the sales and service facilities have yet to be established in force, and must then be fully utilised by winning sales from well entrenched competitors ready to cut prices to maintain sales and to avoid the horrors of too much excess capacity. (This can only be done when the new heavy range of CVs is introduced.) It would not be beneficial to the UK's long-term interests on the CV side if British Leyland's attention was too much directed to the European CV market to the detriment of protecting its position or increasing sales in its traditional market place outside Europe. Here the size of the cake is increasing but in Europe BL would be mainly faced with carving out a larger slice from a slow growing confectionery.

Clearly, competition will intensify, and one manifestation of this will be to see CV import penetrations in Europe becoming more comparable with car levels, except in the UK where the comparatively stronger CV industry is unlikely to let as much of the CV market slip to overseas suppliers as it did between 1969-77 on the car side. The major firms should be able to withstand the competitive blast, with Renault and BL having government backing, Ford and Bedford having strong parents, and Mercedes and Iveco having internal strength. MAN linked to VW would be in a much stronger position as would DAF as a subsidiary, rather than an associate, of International Harvester. Volvo and Scania are well entrenched in their non-tariff protected home market, and the latter has the added advantage of being fortified by Saab-Scania group sales and defence contracts. As the groupings enlarge and none give way, the stage is set for bouts of cut-throat competition such as that followed by desperate importers in the UK in 1976 when the new UK vehicles halted the tide of imports into the slow growing market. Indeed, the small firms, such as ERF or Foden, by being able to cut factor inputs to the bone in a slump could trim production and ride a storm better than many larger firms with huge overhead commitments. If overseas competition is 'unfair' then State help to smaller firms would be quite justified. That is, if foreign governments, rich parent companies or copious defence orders are keeping CV firms afloat then it would be a gross misallocation of resources to allow the market mechanism to operate only upon small UK specialists. The theory of the 'Second Best' tells us that optimality is closer approximated if one distortion is met with another. Consequently, the European Commission has a real responsibility to see to it that marketing is orderly and based upon commerciality in its fullest sense.

1. Recent controversy over a possible BL 'Slush Fund' might hamper the company's efforts in certain markets in the future.

STRENGTH OF UK

The small UK CV specialists whose future viability is often discounted because of their smallness are not as small as they seem : a large supply infrastructure operating at output levels often more than commensurate with those reached by the major CV producers can pass on significant economies to the UK specialist makers. On the Continent, small firms exist in a self-sufficient vacuum, but that is not the case in the UK. Indeed, the suppliers provide strength all round, both to the large UK CV makers selling abroad and to the export drive in their own right. The success of UK firms in holding import penetration below the car figure is ample demonstration of the acceptability of UK CVs. Indeed, imports are largely the result of excess demand for British vehicles, a fact that may provoke new entry by British entrepreneurs to the industry, again utilising the supply infrastructure. Further strength is conferred by the UK being the centre of the non-American CV activities of Ford, GMC and Chrysler, although the latter's main super-heavy commitment is at present in Spain. However, Chrysler could find it beneficial to use the supply infrastructure in the way Ford has to build fully competitive super-heavy CVs in the UK. The US component makers are also basing their operations in the UK, with Cummins exporting 92 per cent of output and Rockwell's intention to export 50 per cent by 1980. The rescue of BL, although made necessary by shortcomings on the car side, has profound implications on the CV side. Since 1976 there has been no call to cross-subsidise car activities by milking the CV operations of much needed funds. This policy had begun to destroy the very strength upon which the transferred funds were being generated, with the result that BL has to catch up on lost time to restore to the CV operations their previous comparative advantage. However, the UK industry has seen major new developments, such as the electric truck and bus developments of Lucas and Chloride often in conjunction with the likes of BL or Seddon-Atkinson. Furthermore, despite the low growth of the UK economy the road bias of the transport system has produced Europe's largest home market, even larger than Europe's strongest economy, West Germany. Even considering the larger size of German vehicles and the larger number of such vehicles made, the UK market's demand for road vehicles carrying capacity is commensurate. There are no *prima facie* reasons to suggest that the UK CV industry should not continue to develop and maintain its position in a highly competitive market, although much uncertainty would be removed if UK makers knew what design parameters and maximum weights they could expect in the UK and the European Community in the period up to 1985.[1] Although in the UK there is a relatively large home market, exports have stagnated since 1964. Quite clearly the lack of export growth considering the strength of the industry is reprehensible although relatively the performance is still markedly better than that of the car sector. The poor European dealer network is a serious

1. This depends on national governments agreeing to implement, and the Community being able to establish, common axle and maximum weights.

problem but it is imperative that whilst attending to this, the industry's marketing strength elsewhere should not be jeopardised. Finally, the UK CV industry, like the motor industry generally, often obtains its economies of scale by purchasing from giant suppliers. Many continental firms have become more self-sufficient mainly because this was the only way to control component costs when no major suppliers existed, and not necessarily because it was the optimum organisational arrangement. Consequently, moves towards greater vertical or horizontal integration must be judged strictly on the particular merits of the case, and cannot be regarded as *ipso facto* a good thing.

A Possible Projection

In Chapter 8 a projection of UK car production was made. A similar but more tentative projection is now made for UK CV production. Since the CV market has been subject to wider swings during recent times, the UK CV market is more difficult to predict. In addition many of the assumptions are arbitrary. Nevertheless a sample possible projection of the UK CV market size and UK production is summarised in Table 11.11.

The scenario embodied in Table 11.11 is a reasonably optimistic one for Leyland — that is Leyland meets its targets as set out in Table 11.8. Ford remains market leader, particularly due to its strong lower range of CVs. Pressure from importers finally cause the market share of Ford and Leyland to wane. GM meanwhile fights a more successful campaign which includes revisions to its model range right across the board. Chrysler's market share only slightly deteriorates. Import penetration from both the Japanese and the Soviet Bloc increase steadily, with major successes of the Japanese being at the lower end of the market, whilst the Soviet Bloc's strength is in the medium segment. All in all this scenario is favourable but the same caveat must be made as with that on Leyland's performance; such success can only occur within the context of an industrial policy coupled with permissive and associative government action. This is further discussed in the conclusion of the book.

CONCLUSION

The Japanese are bound to take a significant share of the smaller end of the CV market. Potential purchasers require a reliable commodity at a competitive price and if details of trim are not important, the Japanese product scores over the equivalent Leyland product.[1] West European manufacturers now dominate the heaviest segment of the truck market, and are likely to retain and even increase their grip on this section of the market. Leyland is being squeezed from both ends of the market and as yet has not been successful in countering the new aggressive competition. Even Vauxhall has not been performing well in the truck segment, it will have to be provided by Ford — and there is evidence that Ford will take up the challenge.

The message to Leyland must surely be that the next few years are to be of tremendous importance. New product development not of the 'we know

1. i.e. the quality adjusted Leyland price is too high.

278

TABLE 11.11

Possible Projection for UK Production

	1976	1980	1985	1990
UK Market ('000s)	207	280	320	350
Market Share %				
Leyland	29	27	26	25
Ford	31	30	28	28
GM/Vauxhall	18	19	19	19
Chrysler	6	7	6	5
Import Penetration	14	16	19	21
UK Sales by major manufacturers ('000s)	154	227	246	263
UK Sales by minor manufacturers ('000s)	10	11	12	13
Exports	208	220	230	220
Vauxhall	45	50	55	50
Chrysler	5	5	5	5
Leyland	81	90	100	100
Ford	72	75	70	65
Total Production	372	458	488	496

best' variety but aimed at competing with the equivalent European product is essential. Leyland has the scale and components infrastructure to be competitive. The next few years will be crucial.

CHAPTER 12

OTHER SECTORS OF THE COMMERCIAL
VEHICLE INDUSTRY

INTRODUCTION

Although the previous chapter discusses the CV manufacturers directly, there are three other important sectors of the CV industry. First there is the trailer making industry; just about every tractor unit of an articulated lorry will at some point 'tow' a trailer. We therefore begin by analysing this particular and highly specialised industry which has often (and the UK is no exception) been neglected. Second there were in 1975 about 20,000 buses produced in Western Europe. Even within the UK new contenders have recently been attracted into the industry to challenge the traditional market leader – Leyland Vehicles. Finally our attention is turned to one of the factors that provides the UK CV industry with a fighting chance of survival as a major industry. Namely the CV manufacturing process is more assembly oriented than that of cars. To survive it is of paramount importance that there exists an efficient CV component supplying industry. A common theme in all three sections is the takeover by US companies of viable albeit small companies. One cannot help wishing that some equivalent of the NEB might have existed in order at least to provide an alternative purchaser to some of the US multinationals.

UK TRAILER-MAKING INDUSTRY

The UK trailer-making industry consists of some 55 producers about 25 of which produce large trailers and semi-trailers, such as platforms and tankers, suitable for use with medium and heavy lorries. Of these 25 firms, three account for around 80 per cent of the market. The demand for semi-trailers for use with motive units increased significantly from 1964, when revisions to the Construction and Use regulations allowed articulated vehicles to be used at 32-ton gross weight compared with 26 tons for rigids. Prior to 1964, the economics of trailer operation was based upon the possibility of greater util-isation of expensive motive units; subsequently artics had a clear payload advantage which led to a boom in demand. Recently, 30-ton rigid vehicles have been authorised but the interim has seen the artic demonstrate its efficiency and flexibility to such good extent that a strong and growing demand is assured. In 1968, regulations were altered to allow the carriage of 40-foot containers on British roads, which required the use of artics, while the amend-ments, in 1970, to the legislation applying to draw-bar trailers, also favoured the trailer makers. However, the 32-ton weight limit has tended to constrain the advantages of using road trains: in 1974 only about 1,000 large trailers for carrying 10 tons plus were made, compared with perhaps ten times as many semi-trailers.

The structure and structural changes within the industry are not independ-ent of the size of the total market, a market which has displayed considerable growth since 1964, and a resilience during the difficult trading conditions of the last few years including a catastrophic collapse in the market in 1975.[1] This is best illustrated by the sales of semi-trailers shown in Table 12.1.

TABLE 12.1

Sales of Semi-Trailers

	Export	Home	Total
1963	671	8,376	9,047
1964	865	11,436	12,301
1969	1,225	24,093	25,318
1973	2,820	19,117	21,937
1974	3,587	15,086	18,673
1975	7,400	3,440	10,840
1976	7,529	5,451	13,030

In 1966 three firms — York, Boden and Crane Fruehauf — shared 50 per cent of the market. In 1968 Crane Fruehauf purchased Boden to become clear market leader, and reinforced this by taking over the UK marketing of Highway and Multiwheeler trailers. By 1976 the company held 45 per cent of the market for trailers compared with 25 per cent held by second place York and 15 per cent by Cravens-Tasker in third place. However, in 1976 York bought Carrimore and in 1977, Scammell, increasing its market share to 35 per cent. US trailer makers have had long experience in making large trailers in considerable volume and this expertise is utilised in the UK. For instance, both Crane and York have transatlantic links, while Peak belongs to the US Pullman concern. Crane trailers of Norfolk concluded an agreement in 1961 with Fruehauf, a US concern producing 30 per cent of the Western world's trailers, giving the latter a one-third equity stake in Crane Fruehauf.[2] York is 75 per cent owned by a Toronto parent company.

In much the same way as heavy commercial vehicle builders have their products bodied by outside specialists, no vehicle maker in the UK, apart from Scammell, was significantly involved in trailer making. The pre-war demand for trailers was tiny and by the time it reached significant levels in the mid-1960s the 'know-how' and expertise was firmly in the hands of the specialists. Except for marketing economies there are no advantages in integrating vehicle and trailer making. The former is a larger-scale activity needing expensive capital equipment to make complicated products: trailers still remain simple, labour-intensive products. In addition customers regard the motive unit and trailer as two distinct products with different replacement

1. For instance, in 1975 Crane Fruehauf's profits fell from £1.9m to £111,000.
2. In late 1976, the US Corporation made a bid for all the Crane equity which was vigorously contested. In view of the extra financial strength to be placed behind a concern claiming 50 per cent of the UK market in 1976, the bid was referred to the Monopolies Commission. Interestingly, the more clear-cut case of increased monopoly power, that of York buying Scammell, was not referred to the Commission.

cycles, and wish to exercise the widest choice in determining which trailer best meets the operating needs.

Until 1977 British Leyland had an involvement in trailer making which stemmed from its Scammell Trailers subsidiary, latterly sited in a new East Midland factory organisationally separated from its historic home at Scammell Lorries, Watford. Scammell was a well established trailer maker, being Europe's largest in the 1930s, mainly due to winning contracts to supply the railways with mechanical horses. Prior to 1964 Scammell, dominating the medium-sized trailer market, was the largest producer in a limited market of some 8,000 trailers a year. The demand for heavier trailers saw Scammell overtaken by other firms, but the creation of Scammell Trailers in 1974, as a separate BL subsidiary, was an attempt by the company to make a determined bid to gain more of the market. The failure to utilise capacity sufficiently was admitted by the sale to York in 1977. In 1975 Scammell was probably the fourth largest maker behind John Brown's Cravens-Tasker Homalloy concern which then had 10 per cent penetration. Tasker also manufactured US Freightmaster vans under licence, and the US involvement in the UK industry was further strengthened in 1974 when Peak Trailers, which had 5 per cent of the market, was purchased by Trailer SA, a French subsidiary of the Pullman Corporation. With four concerns holding about 95 per cent of the market the remaining twenty or so firms interested in the heavy haulage sector are obviously much smaller in scale in terms of output. However, by concentrating on a specialised niche in the already specialised trailer market, some firms are able to achieve efficient output volumes by dominating particular sub-markets: Alcan's Freight Banallack dominates the UK refrigerated van sector with 50 per cent penetration; Dyson and King lead, and largely confine their activities to the specialised market for ultra-heavy trailers of up to 200 tons gross. Nevertheless, firms such as Merriworth and M and G are able to compete with much larger firms in the main freight carriage markets, while others such as Murfitt and Neville prosper in specialised markets for car transporters, bulk carriers and tippers. The trailer industry has clear market leaders, but there are a whole host of smaller firms to ensure a highly competitive industry. Size is not a sufficient condition for prosperity, as the financial collapse in 1974 of France's leading trailer maker, Titan, illustrated.

Competition between trailer makers is intense with rather small profit margins, illustrating the failure of the dominant firm(s) to impose price leadership. Consequently, profitable production depends upon either a large turnover or low overheads to spread fixed costs. As a result the trailer industry has tended to polarise itself around two types of producer: those which are large in relation to the market; and the very small operations.[1] The vulnerable firms are those with between 3 per cent and 5 per cent of the market, producing significantly less than the market leaders but having invested more heavily than the very small firms in capital intensive methods which may be under-utilised because of a demand constraint. Consequently, because of competition and the ease of entry, firms continually leave and enter the industry: perhaps 15 firms have ceased trailer making since 1970 to be partly replaced by half a

1. Some of the small trailer makers are part of a larger grouping: for instance, M and G belong to J. and J. Dyson while Ferguson Tankers is a Wadham Stringer company.

dozen new entrants; of the 150 container manufacturers registered in 1966 only a dozen substantial firms remained in 1975. The squeeze on the medium- and small-sized firms is illustrated by Crane Fruehauf's and York's combined market share of 50 per cent in 1966, which increased to 70 per cent by 1975 and 75 per cent by 1977. Quite significant firms such as Thompson left the industry and others forged new links.

The survival of so many firms and the continuing ease of entry is due to the nature of the product and the absence of really significant scale economies, except at very high outputs of standardised units. Unlike the lorry maker's need for expensive capital equipment to make power trains, the trailer maker produces a relatively simple product. Trailer SA's expenditure of £200,000 to purchase the assets of Peak, was sufficient to enter the trailer industry with 5 per cent of the market; in contrast, in 1974 Foden spent £5 million on a new truck assembly hall. The nature of the product and the availability of bought-out components obviate the need for large capital expenditures. Consequently, in 1976-7 Trailer Systems with a capacity of 400 units entered the industry solely in order to attack the export market while Tidd, with a capacity of 1,000 units entered by using new materials and technology to offer a different product to those made by established firms.

The running gear – axles, wheels, suspension – account for 60 per cent by value of a trailer and these items are normally bought-out. Almost all axles are made by Rubery Owen, although York is self-sufficient and Eaton supply some. Wheels are made by GKN and Rubery Owen; rubber suspensions by North Derbyshire Engineering and Metalastik and air suspensions by Hands Neway. The highly competitive nature of trailer making was highlighted by an occurrence at the beginning of the present decade when York established its own axle making capacity after Rubery Owen introduced its own trailers. Evidently, York was not prepared to buy from a direct competitor although other trailer makers buy avidly from them. Only York, and to a lesser extent its new Scammell subsidiary, and Crane Fruehauf, are vertically integrated to any extent, making their own chassis when other producers buy fabricated sections from Dorman Long or Rubery Owen. The smaller firms bow to economic reality and buy out, often from Rubery Owen whose importance to the trailer industry is noteworthy.

The growth trend in trailer demand between 1964 and 1975 induced firms such as Cranes and Scammell to expand capacity and others to enter the industry. The small capital amounts needed, the availability of outside suppliers, the existence of many non-franchise trailer dealers and the basic simplicity of the product reducing the impact of 'know-how' as an entry barrier meant that no substantial barriers to entry existed. However, it may become more difficult for the industry to continue to support the same number of firms as at present. The need to keep costs and prices down has induced both the vehicle operator and the trailer maker to accept greater standardisation. This has allowed some firms to introduce flow lines which has put pressure on firms trying to compete in making standardised products by bespoke methods. The more standardised the market becomes the more difficult it will be for small firms, albeit with tiny overheads, to compete. As in many other industries the small firms will survive to serve small specialised markets where economies of scale do not exist. What does help the position of the smaller firms is their enjoyment of external scale economies conferred by outside specialist suppliers: this has allowed the half dozen trailer makers producing 500-1,000 units a year to compete with York and Crane, making 400 and 1,000 units a month respectively.

During the 1960s there existed in Europe a large potential market for British trailer firms as their products were both cheaper, and lighter than Continental units. However, a 22 per cent tariff barrier, untouched by the Kennedy Round, excluded British direct exports. The small volume of road freight traffic between the UK and the Continent plus the different Construction and Use regulations, meant the emergence of distinct types of trailer, each suited to its own environment. However, after 1964 the large UK trailer demand was increasingly met by standardised, often mass produced, units. Continental trailers, having sacrificed payload and low production costs to bulk, gave UK trailer makers a chance to enter the market: low price and new European-type trailers meant a Continental boom in demand for British units in 1974-5. Indeed with the slump in home demand the export ratio in 1975 for trailers and semi-trailers was almost 67 per cent.

The structure of the UK trailer industry has affected the European sales drive. For instance, Crane Fruehauf's former US associate and now owner already has manufacturing capacity in France, West Germany and Holland. In France it is number two in the market and market leader in Germany. Consequently, Crane was excluded by the terms of their Fruehauf links from these markets. York and the other firms are not limited in this way, although the smaller firms would find it difficult to finance a concerted sales drive and might find licensed production the best policy. It would be wrong, however, to over-emphasise Europe, as the major growth markets are Africa and the Middle East, where the simple rugged UK products could have marketing advantages.

Over the period 1964 to 1973 the export percentage for semi-trailers remained around 5 per cent, although that for trailers was over 30 per cent. Since 1973 Continental demand for UK trailers has increased substantially, with the export percentage for semi-trailers growing rapidly from 32 per cent in 1975 to 38 per cent in 1976. With Crane Fruehauf excluded from the EEC, York accounted for 50 per cent of total exports, selling 46 per cent of its output overseas, including 90 per cent of its Carrimore subsidiary's output. Merriworth's exports in 1976 were about 26 per cent of output compared with 2½ per cent in 1972; Dyson exported 80 per cent of output but by following a risk spreading policy only 7 per cent was destined for Europe. Taskers, exporting 26 per cent of output, combine production and marketing economies by shipping standardised chassis overseas for local specialised bodies to be fitted. The establishment of plants or licensing arrangements within the EEC is another aspect of the trailer industry's sales drive. The trailer makers have been quicker off the mark than the heavy truck makers in availing themselves of the new marketing opportunities in Europe. In turn this has given opportunities to the component makers, first in establishing spares and service facilities and then in selling original equipment to Continental trailer makers. Indeed smaller trailer makers have been well to the fore in the export drive with M and G exporting 60 per cent of output, while Trailer Systems exported

100 per cent of production.

The UK trailer industry has a structure which reflects efficient production: either due to large-scale output or to the purchase of low cost bought-out parts. Consequently a large number of firms of widely differing size are able to prosper and to give the customer a competitive choice. Competition has led to product improvement, keen prices and efficient sales and service networks. In turn this has put the industry in a useful position to penetrate overseas markets with a range of tailor-made products and good back-up from component makers. The main organisational danger is the pressure from US interests for UK affiliates to avoid certain, perhaps lucrative, markets. Consequently the reduced independence of the Crane company following the 1976-7 contested takeover, which resulted in the company falling under US control is of great significance here.

Conclusion

The Fruehauf takeover of Crane allied to the other giant US firm Pullman's ownership of Peak and the Canadian percentage of York put 80 per cent of UK trailer making capacity in North American hands — far more than the albeit substantial US stakes in diesel engines, cars and CVs. Surprisingly the York takeover of Carrimore and Scammell which increased penetration from 25 per cent to 35 per cent was not referred to the Monopolies Commission. As it is, Pullman is likely to want to increase its UK market penetration and therefore to act very aggressively.

The trend in the trailer industry is to larger size but as initial capital outlay is not prohibitive, new entrants still appear. Consequently, if a firm has a good idea, and because hauliers have such diverse wants, a small firm can both enter and survive. The age of the entrepeneur is not yet over in the trailer sector. Although smaller firms may specialise and increase their sophistication, larger firms through diversification can present them with competition in their specialised niches. However too much diversification destroys the economies to be reaped from scale which require a certain standardisation of output. Therefore, smaller firms can expect to meet closer competition from larger firms but not to lose all their specialities. However, problems of a different sort face another major part of the CV industry, that of bus production.

BUS MAKING: AN INDUSTRY IN FLUX

Since 1968 the stability of the bus making industry has been affected by shortages of vehicles and spare parts. Leyland, as the dominant firm, with a virtual monopoly of double-decker production since 1968, has been unable to keep pace with demand. Because of a dislike of Leyland's monopoly and because of demand exceeding supply, bus operators have encouraged new entrants both by inducing them to enter the industry in the first place, as in the case of Ailsa-Volvo, and by being ready to patronise other entrants attracted by the conditions of excess demand, such as Metro-Scania. Although demand for 'heavy-weight' buses, able to withstand the requirements of intensive urban and inter-urban use, is very strong, an examination of the market facing the bus user appears to suggest that bus makers might face longer term problems of excess capacity.

The Bus Makers' Environment

Consequent to the post-war boom in bus travel, British bus makers have been supplying a declining total market: the decline in stage carriage operation more than offsetting the growth elsewhere. Bus trips on stage services fell from nearly 11.8 billion in 1964 to 7.7 billion in 1974, resulting in many services becoming uneconomic. The decline was not arrested by increased central and local government subsidies to bus operators from £85 million in 1973-4 to over £200 million in 1975-6. The general picture is one of a decline in bus and coach travel by an average of some 2 per cent a year in passenger miles, and 4 per cent in the numbers of passengers, between 1965 and 1975: despite a slight growth in usage in 1974. The prime causative factor here has been the doubling of car ownership between 1962 and 1972. The Department of the Environment's 'low' estimate of a 38 per cent increase in car usage between 1975-85 is not seen as being inconsistent with a 20 per cent fall in bus patronage over the same period, although, as the DOE's 'Transport Policy: A Consultative Document' puts it, restrictions on car usage and bus priority schemes 'will tend to limit the effects of increasing car ownership in some areas'. As well as the adverse effect of income growth on bus travel, there has also been the influence of increased relative prices: fares have increased by 94 per cent and the general price index by 81 per cent between 1970 and 1975, although, as the price elasticity coefficient is around 0.3, revenues have been increased by the increased fares.

Nevertheless, the effects on the bus makers have not been proportional to those felt by operators. Stage carriage work may have fallen but growth has occurred in the field of express services, contract and private hire. In addition the volume of bus services provided has not fallen commensurably with the decline in ridership. In urban areas between 1970 and 1974 bus services have been maintained at a consistent level, although in rural areas the National Bus Company's stage services fell by 7 per cent. So despite the fall in patronage, the maintenance of most services and the growth in some sectors has meant that, discounting the post-war boom in bus travel and the need to catch up on replacement, the annual registration of buses and coaches between 1952 and 1967 increased steadily.

1968: The Beginning of Excess Demand

This steady market was disturbed in 1968 when the then Ministry of Transport was empowered to make 25 per cent cash grants to bus operators towards the cost of buying new buses of approved types. The aim of the scheme was two-fold: first to increase the efficiency and profitability of bus operators by encouraging them prematurely to replace fleets with buses more suitable to one man operation; secondly, to foster the purchase of more standardised buses, thereby allowing manufacturers to tool up for longer, lower cost production runs.

As the scheme was to end in 1976 operators started to bunch their orders so that demand increased significantly above trend. Waiting lists appeared for all types of bus but especially modern double-deckers. Only about 7,000 of the 36,000 double-deckers existing in 1968 were suitable for one-man operation, so to allow operators to extend one-man operation to their double-decker fleet by 1976, a productive capacity of some 5,000 vehicles a year would have been needed. Table 12.2 illustrates the problem.

Throughout the post-war period, capacity allocated to double-decker production was never much more than 3,000 a year, and throughout the 1960s with the appearance of high capacity single-deckers the demand for double-deckers fell from a domestic peak of 2,700 in 1962 to 1,665 by 1967. As capacity continued to be switched to other uses, and as operators faced long delivery dates, the 1970 output figure reflected total available capacity. Excess demand led to queues, rationing and price increases. Traditional suppliers, unsure of the longevity of the excess demand, were loathe to install new capacity. Indeed it was only in 1974, some three years after the Department of the Environment's announcement in 1971 of the continuation of the grant scheme — now risen to 50 per cent, until at least 1980 — that BLMC found time to turn from its car troubles to proclaim a projected increase in capacity.

Although the extension of the grant scheme reduced the peak in demand, operators were guaranteed long-term help in buying vehicles, and manufacturers could anticipate a decade of strong demand. Another factor clouding the issue between 1968 and 1971 was the need for operators to catch up on replacement postponed because of the uncertainty engendered by the 1968 Transport Act. In essence, the grant scheme was a well-intentioned measure which, in fact, disturbed market forces to such an extent that both the operator and bus maker were put under great pressure.

The Emergence of Monopoly Supply

By attrition, merger and association the 15 or so firms making heavy duty buses in the early post-war period had, by 1968, been reduced to just the British Leyland Motor Corporation and its associates. This, together with

TABLE 12.2

UK Bus Production

	Double-Decker	Single-Decker
1960	2,222	7,842
1968	1,264	7,804
1970	1,673	10,584
1974	1,891	13,604
1975	2,441	14,048
1976	2,415	10,085
1977 (first 6 months)	972	3,830

Source: SMMT

associate companies, was the only example of a true domestic monopolist in the British motor industry. Although Bristol Commercial Vehicles had been owned by the State since 1948, by 1969 BLMC had increased the 25 per cent stake bought in 1965 to 50 per cent. In July 1969 another joint venture with the National Bus Company was announced involving the construction of the Leyland National plant to produce up to 2,000 standardised single-deckers a year. Directly or indirectly, British Leyland dominated heavy duty bus chassis manufacture. Competition had been lively and beneficial in the bus market, especially that between Leyland and Daimler in the 1960s, and in order to secure alternative supplies, operators have always shown themselves willing to purchase from various companies, even at premium prices. The danger of monopoly and the readiness of operators to insure themselves against exploitation, led to several 'new' entrants as early as the period 1968-70. Seddon, Ford and Bedford were for the first time able to make significant inroads into the main markets for stage carriage vehicles, and the Anglo-Swedish Metro-Scania venture produced a brand new entrant.

New Entrants

The initial boom in demand caused mainly by the Grant Scheme had only slightly moderated by 1971. Continued excess demand grew to bizarre proportions in 1973-5, after a loss of double-decker chassis production caused by the 1973 Gardner strike and disruption caused by the transfer of Fleetline production from Coventry to Leyland. The continued strong demand, the concern shown by the Passenger Transport Executives, the local authorities, the Scottish Bus Group, and Independents at the appearance of monopoly, meant that during the period 1968-76 the market was ready to support a new source of supply, even at premium prices. However, it is clear that many of the new entrants have been attracted for different reasons.

Existing firms such as Seddon, Ford and Bedford, who traditionally made lighter bus chassis, together with Metro-Scania,[1] were attracted into the market in the period 1968-70 by the excess demand existing for all types of stage carriages. The original Metro-Scania, the latter predominantly British Metro-politan Mark II, and Dennis double-deckers were mainly a response to the huge shortfall of BL double-decker production in 1973, although Metro's plans had been well advanced. The Scottish Bus Group is on record as saying that it had tried to break the near-monopoly of British Leyland by encouraging other builders, principally Seddon for single-deckers and the Alexander-Ailsa-Volvo for double-deckers. (The latter can be used with other bodywork; the vehicle's design is strongly differentiated from other products by deliberately avoiding a rear engine.) When it appeared that BL, first with the Leyland National and then with the B15 double-decker, was going to concentrate on integral vehicles, perhaps leaving no work for independent bodybuilders, the latter took action. Metro-Cammell's involvement with the Metro-Scania and the later Metro-politan Mark II and Alexander with Ailsa-Volvo, are cases in point: in

1. This was a joint venture between the Laird Group's subsidiary Metro-Cammell-Weyman (MCW), a Midland based bodybuilder, and the Swedish company Saab-Scania. Subsequently, MCW branched out on its own as a substantial bus maker.

addition, the initiative for the Foden double-deck chassis came from Northern Counties, the Lancashire based bodybuilders. Dennis appears to be the most independent venture; plans indicate an intention to make a premium priced product in small numbers and already a Midland local authority has bought a pre-production batch. In all instances the new entrants are firms traditionally operating in the bus or heavy vehicle industry. The Ailsa vehicle is 90 per cent British, only the Volvo engine being imported; the Mark I Metropolitan double-decker made by Metro-Cammell had a 70 per cent UK content, the Mark II being almost all British: both ventures have relied heavily for their success on the know-how of an established bus bodybuilder.

The Position of British Leyland

Since 1968 when the way was opened to the one-man operation of double-deckers, the manufacturing side has attempted to find ways of forecasting and levelling out the cyclical nature of the revived demand for double-deckers. When BLMC was phasing down Daimler, AEC and Guy bus production, it hoped to compensate with the Leyland National. However, the market moved against single-deckers and the latter's output has never approached productive capacity. As BL's capacity growth was not directed at meeting the increase in demand for double-deckers, new entrants were attracted by the excess of demand over supply. However, the signs are that BL will soon substantially increase its bus, including double-decker, production.

The nationalised firm's current double-decker bus making capacity of 2,000 a year is likely to increase by over 25 per cent. The new B15 Leyland Titan with integral construction is as much a bodybuilding job as anything else, and its manufacture at two of BL's bodybuilding plants at Leeds and Park Royal as well as at AEC Southall, would be sensible: especially when considering Park Royal's experience in this field. In view of the DOE's estimate of a fall in bus usage the limited net expansion of 3,000 double-deckers in 1976, falls back to between 2,000 and 2,500 a year over the period 1977-90, but with a severe trough of 2,000 to 1,750 a year between 1981 and 1984.

If BL's capacity is increased to 2,500 (although phasing out some current models and turning the capacity over to truck or single-decker production could reduce this) and with a minimum contribution of 100 vehicles a year from Ailsa, 250 from Metropolitan and additional output from Foden and Dennis, BL is forecasting excess capacity between 1977 and 1987. Indeed, by 1983 this could be as high as 1,000 units, although exports would halve this. In the short term BL might be aiming at supplying the trend level of demand, leaving the new entrants to cater for the margins of demand. The main danger of this is that the new entrants could build up considerable customer goodwill and establish such a foothold that BL is left with less long-term business than anticipated.

The value of the Bus Grant Scheme was to have been reduced in real terms after 1976-77, but the 1977 White Paper announced that subject to cash limits, its value would be maintained until 1980-1 and then gradually phased-out by 1985.

290

Conclusion

The phasing-down, although easing the adjustment needed when the scheme is abolished in 1985, can still place manufacturers in an invidious position: either people at the end of the queue would have to pay full prices after 1980-1 or a system of rationing would have to be worked out with the operators. Such a position may induce operators to come closer together to co-ordinate needs and to avoid the troughs in demand, especially that predicted for the early 1980s: indeed, a gradual, rather than a sudden, phase out of the bus grant could help here. Additional potential new entrants exist, including a Bedford double-decker, the Public Transport Executives and London Transport: but any manufacture by the latter two groups is likely to be undertaken jointly with an existing bus maker. Unlike the mass producing car and CV industries, entry to the bus making industry is not prohibitively expensive or difficult. However, new entrants could only become significant if BL lost a sizeable part of its market. This is unlikely in view of the new product development and the customer loyalty the company enjoys : the large customers have extensive workshops geared to servicing BL products, use large fleets of BL products and have a workforce well versed in handling them. To retain this goodwill, BL must take account of the customers' needs and resist the temptation to *act* as a monopolist by a 'we know best' or 'take it or leave it' policy. To this extent new competitors would be no bad thing in keeping BL competitive.

It must be remembered that the choice facing West European bus operators is potentially very wide, with an excess of 20 separate suppliers, the largest of which are listed below (Table 12.3). Leyland's traditional strength has been in the bus and truck field which is reflected in its domestic and overseas business : in the latter case rugged chassis for the Third World supplement more sophisticated domestic models. As the car making activities are not now appropriating all investment funds, BL's strength on the Truck and Bus side should be reinforced. However, the position of the small firm should not be discounted, with Dennis making two related but distinct models for home and overseas markets. The invigorating and dynamic nature of competition is illustrated by that company's motivations and objectives. The aim was to avoid playing the large producers at their own game on their own ground, in the belief that there was a good market for an alternative approach in design. Firms do not have to be big to be successful, particularly if the small firm is clever and finds the right niches in the market place. Smallness brings the advantage of flexibility, Dennis for one being able to accommodate the whims and fancies of customers without difficulty. In essence, however, the CV makers in the UK depend in no small measure on the strength of the infrastructure supporting vehicle assembly.

THE CV INDUSTRY INFRASTRUCTURE

The CV industry has its own particular supply network. Most of the car suppliers are used, but in addition, there are a number of separate firms and

TABLE 12.3

Major European Bus Makers (estimated annual capacity)

Daimler-Benz	10,000	Bedford		3,500
Leyland	6,500	MAN		2,000
Iveco	5,000	Ford		2,000
Saviem-Berliet	3,000	Volvo		5,000
Kassbohrer	1,250	Scania		2,000
		Metropolitan	(4,000 potential capacity)	
		Dennis	(800 units planned capacity)	

separate divisions of car component firms unique to the CV sector, e.g. GKN's Kirkstall Forge subsidiary. Engine suppliers such as Perkins, Gardner, Cummins, Rolls-Royce and Dorman, gearbox producers such as Turner-Dana, David Brown, transmission makers such as Eaton, axle makers such as GKN and Rockwell, cab, frame and body makers all combine to provide a strong infra-structure on which both large and small bus and truck makers depend. The UK CV industry is almost unique in the strength of its infrastructure – a basic reason why the multinational firms continue to use the UK as their main non-US manufacturing and assembly base. The products of the various CV makers, particularly the specialists', are varied enough to meet customer requirements very closely. This consequently improves the efficiency of the transport services provided by the operators of such vehicles; it is often the case over-seas that the smaller specialist infrastructure tends to impose companies' designs on the operator. Only the USA has a similar structure but there the peculiar operating regulations and conditions produce vehicle designs which are specifically American and are not always as acceptable to a world-wide clientele as some European products. In the UK, demand for product variety is met by a number of bodybuilders, trailer- and tanker-makers and produces a highly competitive market for the buyer to exploit. UK truck and bus body-builders also service a number of foreign markets by producing purpose-built kits for local assembly. This, together with the manufacture of special heavy duty bus chassis has given firms like British Leyland a strong hold on the Third World bus market. Similarly, by meeting the needs of rugged operating con-ditions, Dennis is a market leader in many markets for fire-engines and mun-icipal vehicles. The infrastructure conferring this advantage is worthy of more detailed analysis.

The CV Industry's Suppliers

Both car and CV industries provide examples of vertical disintegration with many parts, materials and components 'bought out'. Although in the late 1960s the bought-out content of a mass produced car was greater than that of a mass produced CV, by 1977 the position had reversed. This indicated that the cost competitiveness of outside suppliers had increased relative to in-house sources, or that new designs had new specifications which included compo-nentry not made in-house or that external costs had been controlled more than internal costs. Evidence from the CV mass producers does not suggest that the third factor was of significance. The specialist CV makers, like the specialist car makers, tend to be highly dependent on outside suppliers. Traditional 'manufacturers' such as Foden are building two vehicle ranges, one with about 70% bought-out content and one with something like 40% bought-out. In both cases there has been increased use of outside suppliers in recent years, so that Foden's position is now closer to the traditional 'assemblers' ERF and Seddon-Atkinson. Some suppliers operate on an industry-wide basis, such as Rubery Owen, while others have to compete with the more highly integrated CV makers. In the field of electrical equipment, tyres, wheels, front suspension assemblies, castings, brakes and forgings, the CV market is largely supplied by the same firms supplying items for car production, although some differences exist. It is in the area of axles, transmissions, diesel engines, gearboxes, cabs and bodybuilding that a really separate supply infrastructure can be detected.

In the chapter on components, comment is made concerning the virtual monopoly of Lucas subsidiaries in the field of diesel engine injector equipment, and the significant share of the European and world market supplied by the company. Indeed, Leyland in 1967 broke Lucas's monopoly in heavy duty alternators and starter motors by making its own Butec brand under American conferred licence. The underlying factor here was dispute over the quality and reliability of supply of the products made by the market leader. In 1976 British Leyland established SU-Butec in order to rationalise the organisation of its component making and marketing. However, for the most part electrical equipment is supplied by the same firms which supply the car side, although some unique products are involved.

Although Automotive Products and Lucas-Girling dominate the car brake market, the air brakes used in heavy CVs — trucks and buses — are mainly the product of Clayton Dewandre[1] and Bendix Westinghouse. Indeed the former is a major force in the supply of componentry to the CV industry. Wheels and tyres are purchased from the same firms as supply the car sector, with the addition of Rubery Owen as a maker of wheels. Indeed, the market sharing arrangement between GKN Sankey and Dunlop, whereby the former would concentrate on CVs and the latter on the car and car-derivative CV side, allowed Rubery Owen to strengthen its position in response to buyers' demands motivated by a dislike of a potential monopoly. However, this is a case of a supplier peculiar to the CV industry. Significantly, there are some bought-out items which are peculiar to the CV sector, including gearboxes, diesel engines, axles, transmissions and chassis frames from outside sources. Engines are bought from four main outside suppliers: Perkins, Cummins, Rolls-Royce and Gardner. [2]A fifth, Dorman, has been unable to break into the

1. In 1977 this enterprise was absorbed by US interests.
2. In 1976 Rolls-Royce bought a 16.7% shareholding in Gardner which in turn owned 8.5% of ERF's equity. In 1977, overtures by Rolls-Royce aimed at absorbing Gardner were frustrated by a £14 million agreed cash bid from Hawker Siddley. This company was eager to find outlets for the funds obtained from selling its aerospace interests to the State. In the event the UK was left with two firms in a situation where a Rolls-Royce-Gardner merger would have left one. Furthermore, the £2.8 million Rolls-Royce received for its Gardner shares gave it the necessary working capital to develop its diesel engine range.

automotive field despite claims to have a competitive product. By the end of the decade, Perkins expect to have a capacity of 1 million engines a year world-wide with a facility for producing 320,000 in the UK. By comparison, Mercedes-Benz, the largest in-house builder on the continent will probably make less than 200,000 units, illustrating the external economies enjoyed by Perkins customers. Although on a smaller scale, the other diesel specialists save vehicle assemblers from having to tool up to produce engines in smaller volumes than those achieved by industry wide suppliers.

North American interests are prominent in diesel engine manufacture through Cummins and Perkins; the same is true of heavy duty axles, gear-boxes and transmissions. The US Dana Corporation, owner of the Brown Brothers car accessory company, in 1978 bought a majority stake in the gearbox maker, Turner of Wolverhampton, and has built a Soma Europe Transmission plant at Leamington, in which it has a 33 per cent holding. Eaton, already strong in axle, transmission and gearbox manufacture, strengthened its position by purchasing the Thornycroft heavy gearbox concern from British Leyland in 1972 for £5 million. In the same year, British Leyland sold its Maudslay axle plant to North American Rockwell for £4.5 million, the same buyer purchasing the pressings division of Clarke-Chapman-John Thompson of Wolverhampton for £3.6 million. This plant made axle housings and truck frames for the CV makers, hence the 'retaliatory' interest of Eaton in the Rubery Owen facilities for axle housings displayed in 1977. Consequently, Rockwell, the world's largest maker of heavy-duty axles and brakes for CVs, became a major force in the European axle business almost overnight, and provided intense competition for the British heavy-duty axle maker Salisbury – Kirkstall Forge (GKN) as well as Eaton, Primrose and Rubery Owen – already linked to Rockwell through a jointly owned company making trailer axles. It is significant that a producer the size of British Leyland, which oper-ated Maudslay at a profit, stated that the Rockwell expertise was such that it could buy parts cheaper from Maudslay than retain the business themselves. This was partly because Leyland CVs, already cross subsidising the volume car business, could ill afford the amount of research and development involved in axle making. Whether the company would have been as ready to sell off the 'seed corn' in the post-Ryder world of greater financial plenty, is, however, a moot point. Nevertheless, the cost cutting advantages of buying from special-ists do appear to be significant in heavy CV output.

TABLE 12.4
Relative Engine Costs

Capacity (engines per year)	1,000	2,000	5,000	100,000
Index of total costs (1967)	112	105	100	80

The magnitude of the cost saving involved in producing major components in large annual volume, and consequently the cost penalties avoided by such firms as Dennis making under 1,000 vehicles a year and Foden and ERF making under 5,000 in 1977 is shown in Table 12.4[1] from an example taken from the diesel engine sector.

The same source indicates that an increase in output from 5,000 to 10,000 a year reduces costs by 3 per cent and a further 1 per cent cost saving occurs at 15,000 units. However, this under-estimates the total cost reduction as increased output is derived from shift working with all other unit costs assumed to be constant. These admittedly tentative results do indicate the cost reductions derived from higher production, although some of the saving is not from economies of scale *per se* but from a mechanistic spreading of overheads. Although the above example refers to diesel engines, the same type of picture could be drawn from the specialised heavy-duty gearboxes made on expensive equipment, used in CVs. Traditionally, firms such as Bristol, Daimler, Guy, Foden and Dennis supplied most, if not all, of their gearbox and transmission needs but increasingly these firms, as well as the rest of British Leyland, Ford, Bedford and other specialists are turning to outside sources of supply. In the even more specialised world of heavy duty automatic gearboxes, recent developments are illustrative of the pressures facing CV makers. At present the use of these units in Europe, unlike in the USA, is limited, partly because they cost up to £4,200 each — about £1,500 more than a manual unit. However, if the market grows the unpreparedness of European vehicle makers could give the US suppliers a clear field — GM's Allison subsidiary already makes some 20,000 units a year. The European response to this possibility has been to form a company jointly owned by Daimler-Benz and Iveco, to develop, produce and market automatic gearboxes for large CVs. In 1977, the bus market was the only European market of size for these units, with Mercedes and Fiat already making a few hundred each, as did British Leyland. However, the aim of the joint company was to win further scale economies which gives scope to reduce price and to further increase demand. Even so, both Mercedes and Iveco were contemplating approaching more gearbox makers to join the combine in order to produce at least 4,000 units a year (GKN has developed a derivative under licence) thereby reducing the American firms' cost advantage per unit from an overwhelming 20 per cent or so to a more manageable 10 per cent or so. However, if the US producers enter the European market directly and retain most of their cost advantage then specialist CV makers buying from the Americans would enjoy lower costs than those large CV makers who attempt to produce automatic gearboxes 'in-house', albeit in a joint-subsidiary which is able to offer some 'external' economies to the parent firm.

TABLE 12.5

Estimated UK Diesel Engine Capacity (1978) of Specialists

Gardner	5,500 units per year
Rolls-Royce	7,000 units per year
Cummins	35,000 units per year
Perkins	320,000 units per year

1. 'Economies of Scale in Manufacturing Industry', C.F. Pratten, University of Cambridge, Department of Applied Economics, *Occasional Papers:* 28, Ch.18, pp. 180-83.

Although Gardner's and Rolls-Royce's capacity is little more than that of ERF, Foden or Seddon-Atkinson, the specialised nature of the power units made means that none of these CV firms would be able to provide a market for much more than a thousand or so units. Therefore, the specialist engine makers are able to provide a range of engines tailor-made for precise conditions and usage and yet achieve output levels, by supplying more than one CV assembler, well in excess of what each CV firm could attain if each attempted to make 'in-house' engines. Bristol, Daimler, Metropolitan and Dennis buses also use Gardner units, the total output of these CV makers ranging from a few dozen to around 750. Consequently, the large and small engine makers are able to give the vehicle assemblers external economies of scale, whilst producing engines tailor-made to precise requirements. Units made in larger volume, although of lower first cost, are often of inferior cost effectiveness. Indeed, the larger firms' attempts to make similar units often require the use of separate production lines where unit costs are similar to those incurred by the likes of Gardner or Rolls-Royce.

In 1977, Rolls-Royce's attempt to combine its diesel engine interests with those of Gardner in order to provide funds for a future common range were overtaken by Hawker Siddley's purchase of the latter. This insures the future individually of Rolls-Royce and Gardner products, as Hawker Siddley required expertise in this area to fill a gap in its product range. In the event, Hawker's cash which purchased Gardner and Rolls-Royce's stake in that company provided funds for both firms to develop their products.

The future is bright for diesel engine makers. The total world diesel market for cars and CVs in 1976 was about 4.0 million units, by 1985 it is expected to grow to between 7 and 8½ million units − depending on the expansion of diesel powered cars. In 1976, Perkins was the world market leader, selling 511,000 automotive-type units, while all other UK-based producers, including the engine-making vehicle producers, experienced excess demand. The pursuit of greater thermal efficiency in the face of rising oil prices is likely to continue. Consequently, the 70 per cent of UK CVs of below 6 tons gross which were made with petrol engines in 1975 could fall to 50 per cent in 1978, and with penetration beyond the medium van sector into the car derivative market, to 80 per cent by the early 1980s. As much of the growth will probably be in the lighter end of the market, the main beneficiaries are likely to be Perkins and the in-house makers, but the steady growth in the vehicle stock and in the demand for heavy vehicles will help the other specialists considerably.

However, the disturbing ease with which well-run major UK component makers, occupying key positions in the CV and car supply infrastructure, can end up in overseas, particularly US, hands must be critically considered. A short case study is sufficient here. Weyburn Engineering is a motor industry component firm with a speciality in making diesel engine camshafts. In 1972 a profit of £129,000 was made, but the following year, having come under the control of two efficiency orientated entrepreneurs, profits increased to £415,000 and because of spectacular commercial success profits for 1976 reached £2.87 million. By curing some of Ford's supply difficulties, Weyburn became one of its major suppliers while the reliable delivery and low cost of their products provoked Chrysler into considering pulling out of their own camshaft production, as Weyburn had diversified into petrol engine camshaft production as well. Indeed, the company had bought Hartman Camshafts from Lucas, their main UK competitor, for £165,000; they purchased British Leyland's entire Australian Camshaft line for £100,000 and transferred it to the UK; acquired Sheffield Blackstock Engineering truck and trailer component facilities from the receivers for £400,000, and bought Camshaft Specialities of Michigan and Ewalt-Bartel in West Germany. Consequently, between 1973 and 1976 Weyburn became the dominant producer of camshafts in the UK but in 1977 it was sold to the Carborundum Corporation of the USA, in order to facilitate growth overseas, especially in the USA. Although it may be argued that no UK company had made a bid, the point remains that having quickly made itself the dominant firm in a sub-sector of the market, this dominance had been transferred to US control for no better reason than that an unrefusable offer had been made. It must be seriously considered whether or not this transfer of ownership of valuable resources is a desirable occurrence where successful UK firms are concerned. This problem is likely to reoccur with increased interest in the European component sector being shown by transatlantic firms.

The UK CV supply industry also contains specialist axle and frame makers. In addition to those already mentioned are Moss Gears, York Trailers, Unipower, Foden and a number of other producers. Indeed, some of these firms, as well as the likes of Reynolds-Boughton are active in the field of converting two-axle vehicles into three-axle CVs, or to turn two-wheel drive CVs into four-wheel drive. In view of Leyland's decision to sell its heavy axle interests to Rockwell and discounting their need for capital, it is clear that substantial economies can be made when CV firms buy from such specialists. Chassis frames are in the main bought-out from the market leaders Rubery Owen, Thompson (Rockwell) and Dorman Long; indeed, so slight is the involvement of the CV firms in this field, that this is an area of maximum dependency on outside suppliers.

Due to the tremendous expense involved in purchasing press tools and the resources needed to design an efficient welded steel cab, many firms buy out from specialists. Motor Panels (Rubery Owen) supply a basic design to a number of firms, including Dennis, Foden, Unipower and Shelvoke and Drewry, while British Leyland purchase from Sankeys (GKN). Chrysler UK purchase from both these sources. However, with a planned individual volume at the end of the decade of some 7,500 units a year, the likes of ERF and Seddon-Atkinson have deemed it worthwhile to tool up to make their own metal cabs, although the former are using an ingenious design, utilising a great deal of plastic, and made on low volume equipment[1] used to capacity.

In the complex world of the CV bodybuilder, the typical size of firm on the truck side is small in relation to the market, about 450 firms supplying a market of some 150,000 units provided by 'servicing' the home sales of chassis-cab units by the vehicle makers. On the bus side, the typical size of firm in relation to the market size is medium to large, as here relatively standardised,

---

1. For a full account of this sector, see *The Motor Industry: An Economic Survey*, D. G. Rhys, Chapter 4.

or at least batched, runs are possible. The double-decker market of some 2,500 units is catered for by Alexander, Willowbrook, Park Royal-Roe (a BL-NBC company), MCW, Northern Counties and East Lancashire. The single-decker bus market is served by the same firms plus Duple, Plaxton and Marshall, while the coach market is the virtual preserve of Duple and Plaxton. A relatively new development in the UK is the aforementioned production of integral construction vehicles by Leyland and MCW for the home market, although in the light of consumer preference, both are producing conventional vehicles as well.

The CV Makers and the Specialist Suppliers

At this juncture it is worth pointing out that all the mass producers are to a lesser or greater degree dependent on the suppliers peculiar to the CV industry. Chrysler UK buys out all its diesel engine requirements, whilst the largest Ford vehicles use Cummins units. Indeed, even Bedford (GM) 'buys out' its Detroit Diesel engine components (from the US), assembling the engines at Dunstable.[1] British Leyland offers a wide range of engine options in its larger trucks and buses. Similarly, in the case of axles, frames and transmissions, large and small CV makers find it beneficial to buy out. The Industrial Strategy Working Group on Diesel Engines (1976-7) tentatively estimated that over the next decade the demand for diesel engines of less than 500 bhp, the area of the UK industry's greatest strength, could double, as much due to the increased demand for construction and related equipment as to CV demand, or indeed, car demand. The efficiency of the UK industry puts it in a position to obtain a disproportionate amount of this growth as long as serious supply bottlenecks in the casting sector are overcome. Whether this would provoke vertical integration by diesel engine makers into iron foundering remains to be seen, but it does illustrate the need to protect the complex infrastructure which makes up the motor industry. Many vehicle makers, highly dependent on bought-out major components, have suffered from the supply bottlenecks experienced by the suppliers of these components, with the result that some orders have perforce been placed with overseas suppliers. A quite different issue is that, although prevented in 1977 from absorbing Foden, Rolls-Royce may figure in future moves to create a vertically integrated group, including some other component makers and various independent CV assemblers.

---

1. Similarly, Seddon-Atkinson buys International Harvester engines from Germany, but its large vehicles range uses Cummins, Rolls-Royce and Gardner units.

298

SECTION FOUR

OTHER SECTORS OF

THE MOTOR INDUSTRY

— The Components Industry

— Marketing Policy

— Problems Facing the Retail Motor Trader

INTRODUCTION TO SECTION FOUR

This section starts with an analysis by Garel Rhys of the component sector of the UK motor industry. The components sector has received good press and publicity recently and is an area of strength. Even so, warning clouds are appearing on the horizon. Chapter 14 then looks at the marketing policies and strategies of the big four UK manufacturers. Obviously, an important element in marketing policy is the distribution system adopted by any company. BL's distribution philosophy on its car side has been highly controversial and this is also discussed in Chapter 14. Chapter 15 analyses the problems facing the motor retailers, who form an exceedingly large and significant area of the motor industry but who have by and large failed to move with the times. Chapter 15 looks at various remedies.

302

CHAPTER 13

THE COMPONENTS SECTOR

British car makers indicate that some 55 per cent of the total ex-works cost of their products is made up of bought-out parts, materials and components. Consequently, the large mass producers of cars largely confine their manufacturing activities to sub-assembly and final assembly work and the machining of various major components. As a result the supplier takes on a very important role, and the efficient and continuous operation of even the smallest of the 2,000 firms involved is crucial to the motor industry's well-being.

Although the major car manufacturer increases the risk of dislocation by becoming dependent on outside sources of supply, a number of countervailing factors exist to explain such behaviour. A car maker may be loathe to become involved with an unfamiliar area of technology; he may not have (or may not wish to tie up) the capital needed to establish component-making facilities; many parts are too small a proportion of costs to be worth the trouble of making; the optimum size of plant needed for the production of certain components may be of such magnitude that if all economies of scale are to be reaped just one or two firms would be able to meet the needs of an entire industry.

The car industry's suppliers are of two types : the raw material producers, e.g. steel, aluminium, paint and textiles; and the 'sub-contractors' making components and accessories. It would not be realistic to include the first group in the motor industry as the products they supply are indistinguishable, for the most part, from those sold to other customers. On the other hand, the 'sub-contractors' are engaged in making items which in most instances only have a motor industry application. This is not to say that such suppliers do not manufacture other products for other industries, but that their automotive activities and facilities are closely identified with the needs and fortunes of the vehicle makers. Consequently, although 70 per cent of all special steels and 65 per cent of sheet steel sold in the UK are bought by the motor industry, the nature of the product is not unique to the vehicle industry. This is not true of the output of many iron or steel foundries and forges, nor of the makers of, say, brakes, wheels and carburettors.

THE EMPLOYMENT SIGNIFICANCE OF THE COMPONENT SECTOR[1]

The Department of Employment's Minimum List Heading 381 within its Standard Industrial Classification is the nearest one gets to an official definition of the motor industry. However, a degree of arbitrariness is involved here. For instance, a highly integrated car manufacturer with its own castings, forgings, drop stampings, rubber and electrical component-making facilities would have these included in Minimum List Heading (MLH) 381, whereas firms

---

1. One is sometimes tempted to use the term component *industry*, but as the products are so heterogeneous — from light bulbs to iron engine blocks — their only point of similarity is in supplying the vehicle makers. Therefore, 'sector' may be a more appropriate term.

such as GKN, Birmid-Qualcast and Lucas, with between 40 per cent and 70 per cent of their activities geared to the automotive market, would not. To the typical MLH 381 employment total of around 500,000 (achieved in 1970-77) should be added some 100,000 workers employed solely on motor industry 'sub-contracting' under other MLHs. This does not include workers whose jobs are geared to the supply of raw materials.[1] Of this 600,000, some 340,000 are employed by the vehicle firms themselves, some in making part and components, with 260,000 in the independent component sector. Those engaged in supplying the *car* industry alone has been put at 205,000[2] or some 1 per cent of the total UK workforce. On the basis of previous analysis of the 'impact effect' of the *motor* industry on employment,[3] that is including the suppliers to MLH 381, the total job significance would in fact be some 37 per cent greater than 260,000 and after the application of a multiplier of 1.2 per cent[4] the total job importance of the component sector would be 427,000 or 1.9 per cent of the total workforce.

BASIC STRUCTURE

As the ex-works price of a car is largely made up of bought-out items the efficiency of the car makers is dependent on their suppliers' efficiency, both in terms of costs and in output continuity. Raw material supply is typically concentrated in few hands, but some 2,000 separate organisations are involved in producing often no more than a fraction of 1 per cent of a car's ex-works cost. Nevertheless, the large number of small firms are still very important, many being capable of bringing car assembly to a halt.

About 50 per cent of the bought-out content by value of UK cars[5] (a proportion which can vary between 50 per cent and 70 per cent)[6] is accounted for by ten firms or so. The largest suppliers include Associated Engineering, Lucas, GKN, Automotive Products, Birmid-Qualcast, Chloride, Pilkington-Triplex, Smiths and the rubber companies, Dunlop-Pirelli, Goodyear and Firestone. In addition, there are large-medium firms such as Rubery Owen, Wilmot Breeden, Armstrong Patents and Associated Engineering's close competitor Sheepridge Engineering among others. However, it would appear that the first four firms mentioned above, plus Dunlop, are the Big Five of the component sector, having a total turnover from automotive sales in excess of that of Vauxhall or Chrysler UK.

Unlike the US penetration of the UK car industry where some 50 per cent of capacity is in American hands, the component sector is largely UK owned. Indeed, apart from the tyre companies Firestone and Goodyear, the Americans have not absorbed any of the largest enterprises. However, US penetration is increasing. In the UK the US-owned firms of Eaton and Rockwell (both

1. D.G. Rhys, 'Employment, Efficiency and Labour Relations in the British Motor Industry', *Industrial Relations Journal*, Summer 1974, Vol. 5, No.2.
2. 'The Future of the British Car Industry', CPRS, 1975, p.11.
3. Fourteenth Report from the Expenditure Committee, Trade and Industry Sub-Committee, HC-617 of 1974-5, *The Motor Vehicle Industry*, pp. 15-16.
4. Eighth Report from the Expenditure Committee, Trade and Industry Sub-Committee, *Public Expenditure on Chrysler UK Ltd*, pp. 79-80.
5. *The Motor Vehicle Industry*, p.17.
6. CPRS, p.76.

producing axles), Cummins diesel engines, TRW valves and steering gear, and Bendix brakes have been long established and may be joined by other concerns, such as International Telephone and Telegraph (ITT). However, only in automatic transmissions (Borg-Warner) and CV axles does a North American influence predominate, although adding the Canadian-owned Perkins diesel engine operation to those carried out by Cummins, Ford and GM places a great deal of the UK's diesel engine capacity in overseas hands. Although European based companies such as Solex—Zenith and Michelin have significant markets in the UK, British companies have been even more aggressive in their penetration of the European market.

Although it can be argued that there is no car component industry as such, with suppliers being found covering various types of manufacturing activity and with the proportion of their output sold to car assemblers varying from negligible to 100 per cent,[1] the fact that some 46 per cent of suppliers have over 50 per cent of their employment geared to the car industry's needs makes such an assertion open to qualification. At the very least there is a components 'sector' highly dependent on supplying the car makers and market but separate from them in terms of ownership.

IMPORTANCE OF THE COMPONENT SECTOR

The job significance of component making has been alluded to above and amounts to some quarter of a million direct jobs. A West Midlands survey[2] put the region's first round dependency on the *car* industry in mid-1975 at 9 per cent of all employees, or 203,000, of which 103,400 were in component suppliers. A previous study which covered the *motor vehicle* industry put total first round dependence in the West Midlands at 327,000 or 16 per cent of the total employed,[3] and as it is believed that the West Midlands employ 50 per cent of the total numbers employed in component making, then a national employment of some 330,000 is implied.[4] However, as the methodology of this former study was in some ways suspect, with no account being taken of double counting and greater capital intensity and productivity in the component side, it is believed that an employment of over 260,000 in the independent component sector is realistic.

As the total significance of the component sector is some 43 per cent of the motor industry's total and given the past history of greater productivity and profits, it might be hypothesised that the component sector accounted for 50 per cent of the 6 per cent investment in plant, machinery and vehicles which is the motor industry's share in the total invested by the British manufacturing sector between 1971 and 1973.

During the first eleven months of 1976, the component sector combined to display one of the most bullish performances within the motor industry,

1. *Component Suppliers to the Car Industry in the West Midlands Region,* DOI, March 1976, Paras. 22-5.
2. Ibid., DOI, para 10.
3. *The Motor Vehicle Industry,* para. 43.
4. That it is assumed that about 50% of the 327,000 were in component making.

in terms of the contribution to the motor industry's larger trade balance (see Table 13.1).

TABLE 13.1

Contribution to the Motor Industry's Trade Balance in 1976

		Imports £m	% Change	Exports £m	% change on previous year
Cars		886	72	582	19
CVs	Heavy	99	32	396	24
	Light	24	60	152	39
Components, parts and accessories		551	42	1,502 [a]	31
Other products		110	22	595	12
Total		1,670	54	3,227	25

a. It must be remembered that some 40 per cent of this total is accounted for by the car makers themselves. Therefore, much of the UK's components exports reflect creditably on the vehicle makers. This merely underlines the fact that component making does not exist in a vacuum within a self contained sector.

Table 13.2 shows that the behaviour of the balance of trade in cars and components illustrates the crucial importance of the latter in maintaining a significant total net positive contribution to the UK's export performance, although the car firms are responsible for much of this themselves.

TABLE 13.2

Balance of Trade in Cars and Components in £'s million

	1970	1971	1972	1973	1974	1975	1976
Balance of trade in cars	243	182	18	-24	50	-30	-304
Balance of trade in components, parts, etc.	327	360	344	374	395	650	951

As the UK car makers are so dependent upon outside suppliers, their total costs are highly dependent upon the efficiency and competitive pricing of the latter. UK component makers continue to be highly competitive and cost advantages of up to 27 per cent have been reported.[1] On the other hand, quality and continuity of supply has been questioned, and as this can lead to a need to hold larger stocks there is a consequent increase in working capital commitments which in turn reduces the advantages conferred by the low first cost: an advantage which in 1978 was as much as 30 per cent for some items. Nevertheless, in terms of employment, investment, export performance and basic efficiency the component sector is a highly significant element in the motor industry in particular and the economy in general. It is imperative that this position be maintained and that growing overseas competition be successfully met.

MARKET SHARES

We have already commented on the identity of the largest component makers and on the fact that despite the existence of some 2,000 firms, about 50 per cent of the value of bought-out content is accounted for by some ten firms. In trying to evaluate the competitiveness of such firms it is instructive to analyse the amount of invigorating competition they do or do not experience.

GKN's proportion of the ex-works price of a car at 5½ per cent, of a medium-sized commercial vehicle at 4½ per cent and a large truck or bus at about 6½ per cent is about the upper limit contributed by any outside supplier. Figures supplied by the other largest firms suggest that their total aggregate contribution to the ex-works price of a car amounts to about 30 per cent of the total. In the case of heavy CVs the contribution of another set of significant suppliers, for instance making diesel engines, axles and gearboxes, puts the contribution of the twenty largest suppliers at about 60-65 per cent of total ex-works costs. However, not only are such firms well represented in the cost profiles of the final product, they also dominate the markets in which they operate. Such dominance could, *if unconstrained*, be used to exercise monopoly power. Table 13.3 gives the 1970 supply position facing the car makers.[2]

The market share of figures given in Table 13.3 *include* competition from the vehicle makers, therefore a market share of 55 per cent could indicate, say, 90 per cent for bought-out items. It is clear that the 1970 figures and those estimated for 1976 indicate a number of instances of single firm dominance. The list in Table 13.3 is not exhaustive − GKN, for example, make 80 per cent of axle shafts − nor does it illustrate how in many markets perhaps no more than five firms will control almost 100 per cent of sales. Breaking down the figures into sub-sections can also reveal the real dominance of a particular firm. For instance, it has been estimated[3] that Lucas has 95 per cent of the starter market, 80-85 per cent of lamps and horns, 50 per cent of new batteries and 18 per cent of replacements and 50 per cent of car and CV brakes. In the market for diesel fuel injection pumps Lucas have an effective monopoly in the UK, with perhaps 25 per cent of world sales, and aims for 33 1/3 per cent of a market that is forecast to grow by 10 per cent a year up to 1985. Conversely, a firm like Associated Engineering although dominant meets competition from the consid-

---

1. *'The Future of the British Car Industry'* CPRS Report, p.76.
2. *The Economist,* 11 July 1970.
3. *Sunday Times,* 14 November 1976, p.63.

TABLE 13.3

Market Shares of Component Suppliers

Product	Supplier	Market Share (%) 1970	Market Share (%) 1976 Estimate
Sheet steel	British Steel Corp.	100.0	75
Glass	Pilkington	99.9	75
Clutches	Automotive Products	80.0	90
Electrical equipment	Lucas	75.0	80
Door locks	Wilmot Breeden	70.75	70
PVC, etc.	ICI	70.0	70
Pistons	Associated Engineering	60.0	75
Sparking plugs	Champion	60.0	75
Transmission equipment	GKN	60.0	75
Forgings	GKN	60.0	55
Batteries	Chloride	50.0	45
Tyres	Dunlop	50.0	30
Castings	Birmid-Qualcast	50.0	55
Brakes	Automotive Products	50.0	50
	Lucas	45.0	45
Carburettors	Zenith	35.0	35
Paints	Berger	30.0	n.a.
	Courtaulds	30.0	n.a.

erable enterprise, Sheepbridge Engineering, in four of the five classes of goods it makes, and from GKN in two, including the one not covered by Sheepbridge. Therefore, potential major competition can also exist where overall dominance is indicated.

EUROPEAN MARKET SHARES

Given the enlargement of the home market from that of the UK to that of the European Community, dominance of UK sales must be looked at in the context of the European market. Of the firms covered in the 1976 West Midlands survey, two-thirds made zero exports and of the remainder 60 per cent exported less than 10 per cent of total output.[1] It would appear that given the desire of car makers to minimise the length of their lines of communication the best way to break into foreign markets is to establish overseas manufacturing facilities rather than export direct. Already the firms carrying the burden of the UK component sector's export drive are doing this. Lucas has overseas operations in France, Germany, Australia, India (49 per cent owned) and a joint venture with Automotive Products in South Africa. Lucas' position in diesel injection pumps has been alluded to and its dominance of UK markets illustrated but in Europe the company is second in size to West Germany's Bosch in automotive electrics and electronics. Again, although Lucas has 18 per cent of the Continental

1. *Component Suppliers to the Car Industry in the West Midlands Region,* DOI, March 1976, paras 22-5.

market for commercial vehicle brakes, until 1973 the German market has been monopolised by the American company ITT's Alfred Teves subsidiary. In the market for air brakes, Lucas competes with German firms and Clayton Dewandre from the UK as well as the US Westinghouse concern.

GKN, which is probably the largest engineering component maker in Europe, owns 60 per cent of UniCardan, a German maker of universal joints and propeller shafts. If the company's 1976 bid to absorb the German company Sachs — the country's largest clutch maker — had been successful, GKN's West German turnover from automotive interests would have exceeded its UK's. A further by-product of this would have been the invigoration of GKN's UK clutch interests which had less than 10 per cent of the market in the face of dominance by Automotive Products.

It appears then that, although dominant UK makers face substantial competition in the European market, the British firms are taking steps to spread their home dominance within a European context. Lucas has acquired majority stakes in the French companies Ducellier and Rotor-Diesel, in Italy's Cavello and in Spain. GKN is increasing its grip on Germany. Associated Engineering, already Europe's largest piston maker, has plants in France, Italy and Germany. Wilmot Breeden is well established in France as a market leader while Armstrong Patents, a rival to Sachs in the shock absorber field, is building a French plant. Such firms are committed to a European approach to the component industry. Furthermore, German-based operations could well overshadow British interests during the next decade as Germany has Europe's largest and strongest car-making industry with better growth prospects than the British. In future, the British component-making international and multinational companies will rank all their operations on equal terms when investment decisions have to be made, which could result in most growth being in overseas centres of production.

REASONS FOR THE INDUSTRY'S IMPORTANCE

The long-established UK engineering tradition meant that from the early days of motor car production, outside specialists were available. In the 1920s and 1930s, these specialists were encouraged to increase production, especially by Morris and Standard. Consequently, few items can be made by UK-based car makers at the same volume or unit costs as Lucas, GKN, Birmid, Automotive Products or Associated Engineering can achieve. The British car industry, except for Ford, is almost unique in its dependence on outside suppliers for castings and forgings, normally an in-house activity abroad. Therefore, the vulnerability of continental component makers is a function of size. The British car industry's structure has tended to foster larger concerns than in the rest of the European Community, as UK car firms have made less in-house. The big continental car firms are the centre for clusters of smallish component firms, often in the hands of one family and therefore amenable to takeover by a large, perhaps British, concern.[1] So although the Continental competition to

1. *Financial Times,* 8 December 1975, p.10.

UK component-makers has increased there seems little doubt that the efficiency of British firms will allow them to make further inroads into foreign markets. This, together with a tradition of exporting which stems from the post-war export drive and the need to back up cars exported in kit form, has made the UK component industry more export minded than their Continental rivals. Indeed, only Bosch and Ferodo have become truly pan-European in the way the leading British component makers have, although as we note below, US-owned firms are actively following a policy of European expansion. Indeed, Alfred Teves has opened facilities in the UK and has obtained original equipment orders from UK firms eager to dual source at the expense of Automotive Products and Lucas.

In conclusion, it is worth noting that the high bought-out content of firms such as Chrysler and Vauxhall has enabled them to take advantage of external economies of scale which to a degree offset the disadvantages they suffered as a result of their comparatively small size when compared with the other car firms competing in the mass market.[1] However, it is important to enquire whether the dominance of many component makers in the markets for their products led to monopoly pricing which appropriated much of the mark-up open to the car, or final product, makers.

PROFITABILITY

The close nature of the links between component makers and vehicle assemblers is such that firms such as GKN felt that, generally speaking, the component manufacturer was an extension of the production capacity of the assembler.[2]

TABLE 13.4

% Return on Shareholders Funds

	(Average 1970-3)		
Chrysler UK	−9.6%		
Vauxhall	−8.4%	Dunlop Holdings	5.4%
British Leyland	5.6%		
Ford UK	5.9%		
		Lucas Industries	6.7%
		GKN	7.2%
Automotive Products	13.5%	Associated Engineering	9.3%
Birmid-Qualcast	13.5%	Smiths Industries	12.2%
Chloride Group	14.04%		

Source: CPRS, pp.63-77

1. It is worth adding here that these smaller firms benefit because of the throughput other, often larger, firms give the component makers. Therefore, if BL's volume car division closed, the quality cars and trucks would have to pay a far higher, perhaps prohibitive price for components. Therefore the closure of a major part of BL could, via such indirect effects, turn the profitable specialists into loss makers.
2. *Motor Vehicle Industry*, para. 51.

Indeed, such firms would be very seriously affected if one of the big four UK producers went out of business. If Chrysler UK were to disappear, it has been estimated that, after allowance is made for extra business made by the remaining car firms, 18,000 jobs in vehicles making and 31,000 jobs in the supplying industries would be lost, of which some 40 per cent would be in component making.[1] On the same basis, the loss of 170,000 British Leyland jobs[2] could destroy some 100,000 component making job opportunities. Clearly the component makers could be expected to seek out new markets vigorously, so perhaps the above relationship is an over-estimate of job loss, but despite this qualification the close integration across the market place of the activities of vehicle makers and component manufacturers means that their fortunes are closely linked.[3] In the event, the component maker has been more profitable than the car maker (see Table 13.4).

However, in view of the fact that many overseas car firms earned 10% or more on shareholders' funds, the profitability of some of the major UK component makers may be judged as barely adequate. Given that firms such as Dunlop and Lucas have a large part of their business in the more profitable and much more stable and predictable replacement market, profits on original equipment must be alarmingly small. In order to meet the likely increase in overseas competition, UK component firms must be prosperous enough to ensure that new products and new facilities are sufficiently forthcoming to strengthen their international competitiveness. The past profitability of some firms from their UK facilities may not be sufficient for this need, hence the move to overseas investment in more lucrative markets. So, although the component sector's greater profitability may be due to the existence of monopoly in certain areas, there appears to be little indication of monopoly profits *per se*. A further inspection of financial performance seems to reinforce this view (see Table 13.5).

Although most firms are profitable, real pockets of financial distress occurred as some firms lost money while few of the profitable firms were consistently able to put in double figure performances. Clearly, from the raw figures, little evidence of monopoly profit is discernible. However, the fact that the sector tended to be profitable at all whilst the car assemblers were in considerable financial difficulties over the same years might still be taken to mean that some marketing power was exercised or that the component makers, by looking to their own interests, placed the car firms in difficulties as regards adequate supply volumes.

PROFITS AND MARKET POWER

It must be remembered that with profit maximising behaviour, with no cost plus pricing regimes, economic theory[4] indicates that with given costs then

1. *Public Expenditure on Chrysler UK*, paras. 159-60.
2. *British Leyland: the Next Decade* (The Ryder Report), HMSO, 1975, para. 3.2, p.14.
3. Indeed, it would not be at all far fetched to have envisaged a consortium of component makers attempting to keep British Leyland's volume car business afloat in the absence of a State rescue.
4. See, for instance, *Economic Analysis and Industrial Structure* by D. Needham, chap. 8; Holt, Reinhardt and Winston, New York, 1969.

TABLE 13.5
Profitability in the Component Industry

	Profit as a % of total assets	
	1972/3	1974/5
Cummins Engines	3.0	18.0
Bendix Westinghouse	3.8	16.1
Clayton Dewandre	9.4	11.3
Armstrong Equipment	12.9	11.2
Atherton Bros. Ltd.	29.5	10.8
L. Gardner & Sons Ltd	22.2	8.7
Tristy Draper	8.0	7.2
Burman & Sons	16.5	6.6
Wipac	13.6	5.6
Zenith	6.3	5.5
Rubery Owen	(3.0)	(4.6)
Wilmot Breeden	14.0	3.3
Kirkstall Forge (GKN)	(3.5)	2.8
Borg-Warner	(1.6)	(1.1)
Clear Hooters	12.1	(2.1)
Concentric Pumps	9.3	(2.2)
Cam Gears	11.6	9.0

price, output and total profits will be the same whether a firm is integrated or not. Only the distribution of profits between different stages will be affected.[1] On the other hand if vertical dis-integration results in cost savings which increase with the scale of output, then profit maximising output increases and price is lower. Therefore, without full cost pricing, the exercise of monopoly power at one stage in the production process leaves combined firm profits, and final price, unchanged whether production is integrated or not. However, if the supplier earns profits and the car maker loses money, but the entire operation is profitable, then vertical integration would be beneficial to the car firm. In short, given the overall rate of return on capital, only if one stage in manufacture is earning abnormal profits would integration be worthwhile.

Some component makers do have virtual monopolies in certain sub-markets, such as GKN in making prop shafts and joints, but for the most part either in-house or foreign competition is present. Lucas has tended to experience more competition and deny being in a position of monopoly. (The Expenditure Committee, Paragraph 50, 1974-5.) Be this as it may, it is clear

1.   This point is not always fully appreciated. One motor industry chief stated that cost plus pricing is not a feature of car making, but he still asserted that turning separate stages of his organisation into profit would increase total costs and lead to an increase in the price of the final product.

that UK component firms do enjoy positions of dominance and Lucas's 95 per cent share of the starter motor trade is but one example of many. At the same time given the cushioning effect of the steady market for replacement parts which many component makers enjoy, the rates of return earned by these firms do not suggest that abnormal profits are being earned. Indeed, given the higher returns earned by foreign car firms, it is unlikely that the zero profits earned by some UK car firms and the albeit small profits earned by component makers is a sign of the latter using monopoly power to push all the effects of the recession onto the former — in terms of the European motor industry the UK component sector's returns are not exceptional. Consequently, the rate of return earned by component makers does not suggest that they are appropriating by market power all the available profits to be earned from car making. The car makers' low profits are due to quite separate factors largely internal to them. This is not to deny that an integrated firm could not at least share their profits over car and component making. However, as the profits at the component stage are not repeated at the assembly stage, the overall rate of return would be so low as to put the entire enterprise in jeopardy. Cross-subsidisation is more often than not the road to financial embarrassment.

The completely opposite view, that many component makers are subject to quasi-integration with vehicle makers[1] because their freedom of action is constrained by monopolistic power, is also an over-statement. It is true that more than one component maker sees his activities as an extension of those of vehicle builders,[2] but to the extent that the component maker is dependent on the car makers[3] in many cases the car maker is dependent on the component firm.[4] Countervailing power is often the order of the day, while in addition, component makers supply a number of major customers, the very feature which has allowed such firms to grow to a size which confers external economies on car makers. Few items could be made elsewhere at the same volume cost and therefore efficiency as they are by the component producers. Quasi-vertical integration is more correctly described as vertical dis-integration — in an industry which is normally more highly integrated — but with very close across-market contacts.

It does appear that the large component makers produce their own independent forecasts of vehicle demand and the success or otherwise of individual models. The sector is of the opinion that its estimates are superior to those of the car makers, and that errors are minimal. The failure of the car makers to realise their more optimistic forecasts may be a sign of wishful thinking, or inferior forecasting competence, but it could also be due to a self-fulfilling ordinance. If component makers gear up to supply x number of orders, but the car men could have made $x + 10$ per cent, the car makers are constrained by the component makers supply schedules. To this extent, the component makers cannot be wrong. However, it is unlikely that this could be a long-run feature given the close inter-company links and discussions

1. K.J. Blois, 'Vertical Quasi-Integration', *The Journal of Industrial Economics*, July 1972, Vol. XX, No.3.
2. *The Motor Vehicle Industry*, para 51.
3. Ibid., para. 72.
4. Ibid., paras. 48-51.

between vehicle and component makers, and the long-term possibility of developing new sources of supply in the face of continued lack of co-operation by component makers.[1] From company data it appears that on average the value added per employee in the component sector as compared with that in vehicle assembly has been some 10 per cent higher over the period 1971 to 1975. Given also that returns on capital were some five percentage points above the car makers' performance, it might be justifiable to assume that the superior financial performance of the component makers was a result of superior efficiency. However, as value added is partly a function of sales *price*, such an indicator is by no means conclusive proof of superior efficiency. Even so, the international competitiveness of the industry and the relatively low rates of return on capital suggest that component makers function competitively and are more productive and efficient than the generality of UK car makers. The industry perhaps cannot afford to be anything else in view of the intensified overseas competition.

OVERSEAS COMPETITION

Direct investment by North American companies, beginning with Perkins and Cummins in diesel engines in the 1950s, has been followed by further involvements by US firms. The most significant presence is in heavy CV componentry, where Eaton is a market leader in axles, and Dana is highly involved in transmission production. Obviously, US tyre firms such as Firestone and Goodyear have been well established for some time, being largely responsible for reducing Dunlop's market penetration of over 50 per cent in the mid-1960s to some 30 per cent, as they carved out 35 per cent between them. Similarly, Borg-Warner is a major force in the automatic transmissions and overdrive field but its almost total dominance of the market in 1960 has been more than halved by in-house manufacture by GM and Ford, as well as new competition from Automotive Products. Indeed, a number of other car firms, including Rolls-Royce, buy from GM, or Ford, rather than Borg-Warner.

Apart from these firms, a major investment wave aimed at car component manufacture in general has occurred during the last decade. Between 1967 and 1977, ITT has established a $ 1 billion turnover in Europe through the purchase of going concerns, including Alfred Teves, possibly the largest brake maker in Europe and the world leader in disc brakes. Of similar magnitude is the TRW involvement in Europe, which includes dominance of the steering gear industry in the UK (Cam Gears) and West Germany (Ehrenreich). A third US firm, Bendix Westinghouse, is a substantial competitor in the air brakes trade, a trade which has also seen American Standard via its successful bid for Clayton Dewandre as a recent entrant. To these firms must be added the highly efficient component subsidiaries of GM (AC Delco) and Ford (Autolite) both of which engage in inter-firm trading. To US firms involved in analysing ways and means of participating in the growing and lucrative European business in parts and

---

1.　Indeed, firms such as GKN and Associated Engineering, with less replacement-parts business, would not find it in their long-term interests to weaken the market competitiveness of their customers.

components, the existence of many small family concerns, especially on the continent, may appear as tempting entry points. Consequently, the UK industry must expect increased US competition via Europe-based subsidiaries invigorated by injections of US capital and know-how. Indeed, many of the large independent component makers supplying the CV market in the UK are US-owned, and successful attempts by transatlantic interests to buy firms such as Crane-Fruehauf or Clayton Dewandre – the latter very important in the CV brake market – only reinforces this position. Not only will continental firms act as springboards for US entrants to the market, but the glass makers of Belgium and Italy are already making inroads to the UK original equipment market, while established giants such as Bosch and Ferodo can be expected to seek out similar business. However, as indicated above, the largest UK component makers are taking tactical and strategic steps to protect not only their UK business but to spread their market leadership to the Common Market as well. Such a policy may have repercussions for the UK's export performance in components not wholly beneficial to the British economy.

EXPORTS

This possibility is worrying because of the contribution of parts, components and accessories to the motor industry's export drive. It must be appreciated that because of the export of non-countable CKD car kits, spare parts and inter-firm trading, the car makers themselves account for over 40 per cent of the export value of this sector. Nonetheless, the contribution of the independent component makers is still considerable. Questions of quality and continuity of supply may lead overseas car makers to insist that really large-scale business with the UK component sector would require the latter to establish more and more production facilities within those car firms' home markets. However, the lower prices charged by UK firms have induced many buyers to overcome their reticence, and indeed the ex-works price of cars made by the quality conscious Swedish concern of Volvo reflects a 20-25 per cent UK content.[1] Furthermore, many mass producers, such as Fiat,[2] VW and various Japanese concerns have, or are displaying an intention to purchase considerable volumes from UK sources. Clearly, Europe could become a common market for components in the way it has long been for cars.

The need to back-up car exports, the multinational approach of US and UK companies, the desire of many car makers to spread risks by dual sourcing, the drive to lower costs generally, inducing car firms to participate in the 'replacements' market throughout Europe, all add up to marketing strategies based upon European-wide supply and demand conditions. At this stage the indications are that the UK component sector is winning an increasing share of world markets.

In particular sectors UK firms are world leaders: GKN in forgings and transmission parts; Associated Engineering in engine components such as pistons, rings and cylinder heads; Lucas in electrical equipment and brakes;

1.   Expenditure Committee, *The Motor Vehicle Industry*, para. 59.
2.   *The Motor Industry News Digest*, SMMT, November 1976.

Automotive Products in clutches; Burman and Sons in steering gears; Dunlop in tyres and safety wheels; Rubery Owen in truck frames and rear axles. The component makers attract foreign vehicle makers not only because prices are very competitive, but because of the technical excellence of the products. In addition, the UK component sector has a much larger presence in Europe than Europeans have in the UK, especially in terms of plants and marketing operations. In addition, the component sector has a considerable presence in Japan, but mainly through the licensing of local manufacture. Multi-sourcing by vehicle makers, as a hedge against supply interruption by one supplier, helps UK exports but, at the same time, provides a threat to the component firms' home market production. However, so far these firms have successfully defended their home territory, perhaps because so few foreign suppliers can offer sufficiently competitive prices. Nevertheless, although the import content of motor vehicle industry output is only about 7 per cent this is gaining, as is the trend towards the assembly of vehicles such as the Ford Fiesta, Chrysler Alpine, and Vauxhall Cavalier and Chevette which are almost 50 per cent, by value, imported.[1] This type of multinationalism, can only be expected to develop further. Consequently, the independent suppliers must endeavour to gain original equipment orders overseas partly to maintain their UK position.

ONUS FOR EXPORTS

Impressive, though the component sector's record is, as so often in UK industry at large, the main export burden falls on but a few firms. If we accept that 2,000 firms supply the vehicle industry[2] (and that 600 of these are highly dependent on the vehicle industry)[3] then on the basis of a sample survey,[4] where only about 13 per cent of all firms exported more than 10 per cent of output, only some 260 firms were significant exporters. Indeed, two thirds exported no part of their production at all.

From these figures it is not surprising that the component sector as a whole was pessimistic as regards increasing exports, as it would appear that most firms cannot be bothered with this type of business. At the other end of the scale, the same sample survey indicated that the major exporters judged that the best way to increase foreign sales was by direct investment overseas. If this indeed proved to be the case, then the income and employment generating potential of the component sector will, in part, be transferred overseas to the detriment of the domestic economy. This is not to suggest that component firms should not act in a way that protects their own interests, but it does illustrate that greater dynamism is required in the UK car assembly industry in particular and the economy generally in order to make UK investment as attractive as overseas investment for the component makers. The benefits

---

1. A pre-publication comment pointed out that Chevette import content in 1978 had been reduced to only 12½ per cent and that the Cavalier import content was falling with the build-up of UK production.
2. *The Motor Vehicle Industry*, para. 45.
3. *Financial Times*, p.22, 19 October 1976.
4. *Component Suppliers to the Car Industry: The West Midlands Region*, paras. 22-5.

derived from a growing market are shown by the performance of the diesel engine makers in the motor industry.

DIESEL ENGINES

The UK motor industry is noteworthy in that it contains a substantial sector specialising in the independent manufacture of diesel engines. The thermal efficiency of these engines, compared with petrol units,[1] has meant that with the long-term increases in petrol prices (recently reinforced by soaring oil prices), there has been, in 1973-7, a boom in diesel engine demand. Internal estimates by the motor industry put the annual growth over the next decade of all types of internal combustion engine at 1½–2 per cent per annum, compared with 10 per cent per annum for diesels alone. Lucas dominates the UK market for diesel fuel injection pumps and plans to increase its share of the world market from 25 per cent to 33 1/3 per cent over the period 1977-85 during which the total market will have doubled in size. This would increase earnings from this source from about £100 million in 1976 to about £280 million by 1985 in 1976 prices. Such growth is a function of increased CV output in Eastern Europe and the developing countries plus the switch from petrol to diesel engines in small trucks. If the substantial growth in demand for diesel cars, which some people expect, does take place, expansion would be even greater. Lucas's investment is put in perspective when it is realised that £35 million is involved. This compares with an investment by Perkins over the period 1976-8 of some £30m to increase the manufacture of completed diesel engines by some 33 1/3 per cent.

Of the independent diesel makers, Cummins and Perkins are North American owned. Nevertheless, the latter's activities are based on the UK while the former sources European supplies from its British plants. The diesel engine sector's strength led it to being singled out as a growth leader by official circles and in 1976 investments worth £46m qualified for aid under the advanced profits scheme operated by the Department of Industry. The National Enterprise Board could find this sector an attractive one to help in terms of financing the investment needed to meet the generally forecast diesel engine demand boom. Indeed the growth of this sector of the major component industry has highlighted bottlenecks within the motor industry infrastructure.

BOTTLENECKS

Allusion was made above to component firms making their own demand forecasts and how this could have led to supply difficulties for vehicle makers. These difficulties may have been due to planned output levels of component firms under-utilising capacity but more serious long-term bottlenecks where there is insufficient investment and supply could also be a problem. In 1976 the diesel engine industry worked at 80 per cent capacity but it appears that above 90 per cent capacity, supply constraints, involving materials and components, are a problem. A shortage of capacity for making cylinder heads and

---

1.   Diesels are about 25 per cent cheaper per mile to run in terms of fuel costs.

blocks may be a feature of the difficulty,[1] while diesel makers are becoming dependent on German supplies of crankshafts. A further shortage of pistons and rings has also occurred. This illustrates why the Department of Industry has given special aid not only to diesel makers but also to the iron foundry and machine tool sector in order to increase capacity with efficient facilities.

The parts famine, which became evident with the UK motor industry whenever a final product is being made at near capacity, is of long duration. In early 1974 Perkins Diesel engines instigated a world-wide hunt to try to gather enough grey iron castings. As a result, whereas in 1970 only 3 per cent of the material content of a Perkin's engine was imported, by 1975 this had reached 30 per cent. At any stage in the motor industry's production process a smooth inward flow of parts is critical to company efficiency. The infrastructure of an efficient components industry only exists as a result of a large number of companies making considerable investment. An insidious effect of long-term under-investment in a number of companies is to put the entire motor industry out of balance, with relatively small bottlenecks leading to magnified and considerable losses of output and earning power. Any failure to make up any under-investment might require vertical mergers, involvement of the NEB or outright nationalisation to rectify. Although some major component makers may have been loathe to accept the car firms' sales forecasts, long-term bottlenecks caused by under-investment are more likely to be found in medium and small firms as these are more susceptible to cash-flow problems. Such a decline by key medium-sized component makers clearly threatens the present size and future stability, leave alone growth, of the motor industry as a whole.

PROBLEMS OF THE MEDIUM-SIZED FIRMS

The particular investment problems facing medium-sized firms have already been noted. Insufficient capital and inadequate forecasting techniques add up to a general inability or refusal to invest. In the latter case investment is not undertaken until demand pressures are experienced, when it is too late from the point of view of the firms dependent on the slothful investor. In addition, it is evident that few medium or small firms bother to export and that for the most part 'the exporters tended to be the larger firms'.[3] However, such firms do well in the 'accessories' market.

MARKET SEGMENTS

Although the component sector has been described as an entity, the firms involved can be active in one or more of three quite distinctive sectors: the markets for original and replacement parts, plus the ill defined market for accessories. The replacement market is huge; within a total car stock of some 14 million vehicles nearly 8 million replacement exhausts alone were bought in 1976. Therefore, although GKN is mainly dependent on the original parts

1. *The Motor Vehicle Industry*, para.92.
2. *Component Suppliers to the Car Industry, The West Midlands Region*, paras.26-8.
3. *Component Suppliers to the Car Industry, The West Midlands Region*, para.22.

market other large component makers supplied anything between 55 per cent and 70 per cent of their turnover to the replacement sector. One confidential estimate put the accessories market at £160m a year, broken down into (i) engine maintenance (ii) products aimed at car 'after care' and (iii) products used to embellish the car. As car makers add more items as standard, the size of the third category declines, but as more stripped down cars such as the Escort 'Popular' appear a countervailing tendency occurs. The accessories market is the preserve of small to medium firms, although the giants do participate. However, the thrust of their activities is the original and replacement parts business. Table 13.6 gives an estimate, on a European basis, of the size and growth of the replacement market.

TABLE 13.6

Replacement Market (Millions of Units)

	1975	1980
Exhaust systems	27.5	33.0
Shock absorbers	32.5	46.0
Brake sets	54.0	71.0
Lamp bulbs	330.0	395.0
Spark plugs	295.0	335.0
Batteries	20.5	23.5
Tyres	85.5	95.0

Source: Frost & Sullivan Survey, 1977.

RESEARCH

Part of the reason for the success of the components sector lies in the technical excellence of many of its products, which is a compelling addition to the price advantage experienced by the industry. To maintain this position a flow of innovations in the field of injector pumps, brakes, fuel economy, weight saving are ready, or nearly ready, to come in to the market place.

DEVELOPMENTS AND PROSPECTS

(i)   Vehicle Makers' Co-operation

The larger production runs experienced by the large component makers are attracting many overseas vehicles makers and are, indeed, making a number question whether their bought-in content is too high. In short, significant cost savings could be made by switching sources from in-house to a major, often British, independent supplier. On the other hand, some car makers are making a determined effort to break in to the profitable replacements market or to persuade other car makers to purchase from them. Furthermore, the growing trend to joint manufacturing on the part of car and CV makers could be a considerable threat to some sectors of component supply. For instance,

Mercedes and Iveco in 1976 established a joint company to produce and market automatic gearboxes for big trucks, posing a threat to specialist producers. The logic of these joint ventures in the car field is to establish joint facilities for making engines and transmissions in order to gain maximum scale economies, and also to pool resources to generate the levels of funds needed for research, development and investment. The question is really where the car makers will stop; for instance, the establishment of automatic transmission plants by Ford and GM proved a heavy blow to Borg-Warner. If the car makers extended their joint facilities many other component makers would be placed under pressure.

Against this the component makers offer car firms a real alternative source of supply for key parts. In addition the suppliers are creating larger and more powerful organisations and finally, they have a considerable depth of technical ability which cannot be easily duplicated. Such factors imply that the component makers will not be easily dislodged from their place within the motor industry. Furthermore, it is difficult to get away from the volume-to-cost relationship: one component maker reported that by being able to substitute fully automatic for semi-automatic equipment operating at 10 per cent the volume of the former, direct labour costs were reduced 47 per cent. In many instances it is only the industry-wide supplier that achieves the volume necessary for such cost savings.

(ii) Increased Integration

As firms establish overseas manufacturing facilities, as their products become accepted as original equipment on a European-wide basis, and as US component makers attempt to carve out a place for themselves in the market, the European component sector will become more of an integrated entity. As many European suppliers are small-scale, even family concerns, they could easily fall prey to increased competition. Indeed, as European cars become increasingly similar 'under the skin' only the larger firms will benefit as they alone have the production potential to meet such orders in bulk and thereby pass on to the customer the economies of scale he seeks. Along the way, larger firms will pick up technical excellence which is contained, but perhaps under-developed, in the small firms they acquire. For instance, GKN, through its Sach's interests in clutches,[1] could invigorate its Laycock subsidiary in the UK which has been unable to loosen Automotive Products grip from 90 per cent of the market.

(iii) General Prospects

Clearly the development of a common market in components means that greater competition is going to be felt by the UK component sector. To face the type of pressure already experienced by the car makers the component makers international competitiveness must be preserved and strengthened. This may involve overseas investment, but given the size of the UK car stock a substantial home market exists which is sufficient to give efficient pro-

1.   GKN has a major 25 per cent holding in the West German firm.

duction runs for some producers. As anything from 55 per cent to 70 per cent of the costs of a car are bought out, the competitiveness of the UK component industry in comparison with overseas suppliers is of great advantage to the car makers. Unfortunately problems of quality and reliability exist which must be overcome before the full benefits of this advantage can be realised. Again the extent to which the development of new materials, new types of car and motive power, and their introduction are dependent upon responses from the component sector, the long-term competitiveness of the entire car and CV industry is crucially tied up with the efficiency of the major suppliers. Deficient supply sectors would prove disastrous to the long-term developments of the industry. Already shortages in machine tool capacity have provoked the need for Government help via the Department of Industry during the period 1976-7, so that the critical needs of vehicle and diesel engine makers could be met.

Failure to keep in step with the needs of the other sectors of the motor industry would lead to increased import penetration. So while some component makers increase exports and substitute for imports by making parts for imported cars, other gaps would appear leaving imports to fill them. With motor car manufacture becoming increasingly multinational and with products being single sourced — as in the case of Ford Fiesta with engine blocks made at Dagenham, axles at Bordeaux, and stampings at Saarlouis — the import content of 6.74 per cent identified for UK cars in 1970 is likely to increase. Indeed, the Fiesta has an almost 50 per cent import content by value. Any weakness on the part of the component industry would increase the import content of bought-out parts as well. Another area of concern is that of production equipment. The increase in the import proportion of the total of machine tools bought in the UK from 12 per cent in 1963 to 48 per cent in 1974, explains government concern and assistance, including the purchases of Alfred Herbert by the NEB for £25 million in 1975.

Until 1970, most import content consisted of materials but the 1970s has seen intra-firm importing of cars as well as parts by the multinationals together with some penetration by overseas component makers, especially in glass and sheet steel supplies, where the car makers have dual sources in order to overcome supply interruptions in the UK. Indeed, between 1969-75 Perkins increased the import content of materials from 3 per cent to 30 per cent, mainly because of supply difficulties in the UK. Consequently, it does seem that imports are a function of long-term supply difficulties either due to capacity constraints or short-term delays, or to production interruptions all leading to dual sourcing. If the quality and reliability problems of supply for components are not checked and solved then the costs of increased working capital needed for stand-by stocks and the costs of interrupted production, costs which may be saved by buying foreign, will reduce the 'total' cost of imported parts below the UK level. This will mean a new overseas supplier. Such an eventuality can be prevented only by realism on the part of all those involved in the efficient manufacture of components, including greater responsibility on the part of the workforce. The UK component industry is a European leader in its field, but this position needs to be protected at home by a willingness to invest in new plants and products, and to maintain the continuity of production of the right quality. If these conditions are met there appears little reason why the embryonic attack on the European market should not become a full-scale onslaught leading to European leadership for the component sector's leading firms. However, it must be remembered that small production runs of cars and power trains in the UK must lead to the small-scale production of parts and components *somewhere* in the manufacturing chain. For instance, although a manufacturer of cars may use the same basic engine over a wide range of models, the variations to that engine would require a variety of piston types and sizes. Consequently, the large model runs of identical cars on the Continent give these car makers an advantage it is difficult to overcome by buying out.

THE UK COMPONENT MAKERS AND THE US MARKET

Due to legislative requirements concerning safety and fuel efficiency, the trend in the US car industry is towards smaller European-type vehicles often embodying European-type technology. Indeed, by the mid-1980s many in Detroit expect 25 per cent of all US car production to be front wheel drive. Therefore, a technological convergence between the US and European, and indeed Japanese, motor industries is likely. In turn, this gives European component makers an opportunity to make significant inroads into the US market: already the Chrysler L car of 1978 has GKN transaxles and Burman and Cam Gears steering from the UK, while Automotive Products has become a clutch supplier to American Motors.

The main European push can be expected in the areas where they have the greatest technological advantage over US suppliers. Roughly speaking this appears to mean: transaxles (GKN); forgings (GKN and Birmid Qualcast); Diesel engines (Perkins) and engine equipment (CAV-Lucas, Bosch, Associated Engineering); electrical components (Lucas, Bosch); steering (Cam Gears, Burman) and braking systems (Girling-Lucas, Teves-ITT). From the above, UK firms can be expected to be well to the forefront, with only some German-based firms being of sufficient size and efficiency to offer an alternative source of supply.

Given some success in breaking into the US market in a signficant way, the European suppliers will have to judge whether direct exporting or the purchase of US-based productive capacity would best serve their marketing and production interests. As already seen, US-owned companies have entered the European component market by direct investment either through acquisition or by unitary growth. The US offers a source of low cost capital, a proven record in controlling inflation, an efficient work force, and marketing advantages. These factors seem to have persuaded GKN, Associated Engineering and Lucas into buying US capacity, a move already undertaken by Bosch and reinforced by taking a 10 per cent shareholding in Borg-Warner. In addition Dunlop and Chloride are already in the USA, the latter being already the fifth largest US dry-cell battery maker.

To cover the growth of both European and US markets, and to offset slumps in one by gains in the other, US companies such as Eaton, ITT, TRW, Rockwell, Bendix, Dana and Cummins are represented in both. European firms are showing the same multinational tendencies for the same reason, and partly as a defensive move to attack the US firms in their own market. Therefore, the US move to European-sized cars and European-style technology gives the European, and especially UK firm, an opportunity to enter the market which should not be missed. Nevertheless, some of the first moves have been made by North American owned firms, such as Teves, Perkins and TRW, but the UK producers look set to emulate them. After all the trend towards small diesels in the USA provides Lucas and Bosch (of West Germany) with great opportunities as the technology involved is difficult to master with most of it protected by strong patents.

The UK component firms do appear to be able to compete with the US multinationals in their field, but to maintain their position the British firms must avail themselves of the opportunities for increased efficiency and financial strength which would be presented by a significant penetration of the US market. After all, the US component firms can bring their considerable resources to bear to swiftly develop suitable products which in turn can be readily marketed in Europe. Consequently, to avoid a long-term threat to their general position, the UK producers could find it in their best interests to take up the challenge to enter the US market. If this is achieved, and allied to the considerable strength enjoyed by the UK suppliers in the European market, the component industry can but remain a major feature of the motor industry in particular and the UK economy in general.

ADDENDUM TO CHAPTER 13

Garel Rhys has analysed the main problems facing the components industry. This short addendum simply comments on some of these problems in the light of recent events. Import penetration within the component industry suddenly rose in 1977 by over 70 per cent and will probably contine to rise in the future, though by smaller amounts. The reasons behind the deterioration in market share in 1977 are discussed below. One of the most important reasons is that US multinationals, following their integrated European production policies, have directly imported components from overseas.[1] As with cars, a second reason is the rash of strikes that have affected the UK components industry.[2] These strikes have had a dramatic effect on the components industry. When BL starts to look elsewhere for components during a strike by one of the component manufacturers, it has been economically desirable (quantity discounts) to sign long-term contracts for a minimum of one year.[3] A fourth reason is based upon the rising import penetration in both the car and CV markets. Foreign vehicles as they grow old give rise to a market for replacement parts. Since many of the vehicles have to be serviced through the manufacturer's franchise, it is not unnatural that parts will be used which were manufactured in their country of origin.

1. I.e. by importing cars such as the Ford Fiesta, Vauxhall Cavalier, Chrysler Alpine.
2. Such as the long dispute involving the Lucas toolmakers which occurred in 1977.
3. Bosch, Cibie, Ducellier have all taken advantage of this type of selling strategy.

The industrial relations problem might be temporary —a period of frustration for the skilled engineering workers whose pay differential has been eroded. Moreover the import of components through tied imports of vehicles is not disturbing as there should be a compensating export of components in tied exports — eventually, if not at this particular point in time. However, the industry is probably resigned to a newer and higher level of import penetration caused primarily by larger imports of vehicle parts of foreign manufacturers and the multi-sourcing policy by the manufacturers.

The situation must be put into perspective. The value of exports is still twice as great as imports[1] although the export balance of trade may either remain static or decline. One of the reasons for the growth in the favourable balance of trade is that the larger UK companies have been aggressively seeking their own export markets, particularly in Europe. It is believed that half the profits for some companies are coming from overseas. BL's spare parts division[2] (Unipart is the trade name) has also launched itself successfully since the Ryder Report. In 1977, it is estimated that the division had a UK turnover of £200 million and about £100 million in exports.

Despite an estimated imported car replacement market of around £350 million in 1977, out of a total market of £1,600 million, UK component manufacturers have been reluctant to tool up for some of the more complex items. As the total stock of imported cars increases (now over 3 million vehicles) then the UK manufacturers will manufacture an entire range of components for the imported vehicle. Surprisingly one of the most go-ahead companies with respect to this is BL parts division which has extended its range to include most imported cars. Initially BL will buy the majority of this new range from the country of origin, although ultimately plans are afoot to start manufacture in the UK. The growth of BL's spare parts division to some extent affects the remainder of the industry. This is particularly true in respect of the new range of parts for imported cars where BL is competing head on with its suppliers who are also waiting to reach the point where tooling can be seriously considered, and who (unlike BL) have not taken advantage of the possibility of importing and selling under their own brandname.

BL parts division in the 1977/78 reorganisation comes under the BL Cars umbrella. Since the parts division is profitable it should help to balance the less profitable car production operators.[1]

---

1. In 1977 exports rose by 22 per cent to £1.64 billion whilst imports rose by 43 per cent in 1976 and 66 per cent in 1977 representing £756 million worth of goods. The balance of trade fell from £890 million in 1976 to £884 million in 1977.
2. Since the latest BL reorganisation BL parts division now comes under the BL Cars division but has retained some autonomy within its new structure.
3. Although if the profits are reported separately, as they are intended to be under Edwardes new profit centres, it will be possible to ascertain how much money the parts division is making.

CHAPTER 14

MARKETING POLICIES

INTRODUCTION

Although we have already referred to various aspects of marketing policy in earlier chapters, we feel it would be expedient at this point to draw these marketing strands together.

Marketing policy is a much misunderstood, maligned and hidden aspect of applied economics. Economic theory is usually concerned with price and output decisions, although advertising has been explicitly incorporated into a demand curve. Hence the usual demand curve

$Q = f(P)$

where Q = quantity demand

P = price

has been modified to include advertising

$Q = f(P,A)$

where A = advertising expenditures

But marketing is concerned with more than just the incorporation of advertising. The design of the product, the market segment at which the product is aimed, the product qualities emphasised in advertising campaigns, the method of distribution are all important.

Marketing must include an analysis of the market in terms of its maturity, wealth, requirements, tastes and so on, *and* in terms of the range of products currently being sold in the market place. Pricing policy is only one of a number of important factors. Product design and characteristics are also significant. To illustrate this take, for example, a basic product — the ballpoint pen. Ballpoint pens vary from the cheap functional plastic pens to expensive gold plated pens. Both perform the job well. The more expensive pen may write with greater ease, but the increase in price (say from 7p to £15) cannot be justified purely on these grounds. The price mark-up is gained by emphasising the prestigious nature of the object, the precision engineering which went into the product in order to make it function better, the elegance of design, and so on.

Different markets are amenable to the emphasis of different product characteristics. Continuing with the ballpoint pen analogy, we might attempt to analyse what characteristics we would emphasise for an 'up market' pen in the UK, West German, Italian and French markets if we were to introduce an expensive pen. West Germany would probably be susceptible to the precision engineering and durability emphasis — i.e. the product is basically a better functional object than its much cheaper rivals. In Italy the romantic influence would dictate emphasising the elegance of the product. In France the sophistication and brilliance of design would probably be useful features to

325

stress. The traditional nature of the UK would mean that the prestigious nature of the product and the precious materials contained therein would make the product acceptable both as a present or an indication that success had been achieved.

Such influences can be applied to cars. Mercedes often appear as being a better but still functional car, whilst the Italian luxury car is more exotic and practical (e.g. Ferrari, Lamborghini). The French luxury car has much technical sophistication built into it (e.g. Citroen). The British luxury car on the other hand is a prestigious object, often made with wooden dashboards, etc. The differences between tastes in different markets should never be underestimated. Ford in Europe have, for example, developed the Fiesta to be a central, almost commonplace car, taking between 4 per cent to 6 per cent of the market (implying 330,000 to 500,000 cars): whilst the same car in the US would be doing well if it achieved a 1 per cent market share (100,000 cars).

Obviously, a product may have all the desirable ingredients of all markets. But it is important to emphasise those characteristics which are most likely to lead to sales in a particular market.

Principal marketing decisions therefore include the type of model produced, the range of model variants based on the model, the options to be included as standard and those which are to be marketed as optional extras, pricing, advertising, future model development, and the method of distribution which includes the numbers and type of retail outlets.

On a historical note, it must be remembered that GM and Ford (US) took over Vauxhall and Ford in the UK, followed by the gradual Chrysler (US) takeover at Rootes, which began in 1964 and was completed in 1973. In 1968, meanwhile, British Leyland was created. The decades of the 1960s and particularly the 1970s saw the development of new and radically different marketing strategies, as manufacturers realised that a single product could be marketed in a variety of marketing modes, distinguishing one model from another through a series of subtle styling changes.

CARS

The current European product policy has now been well formulated. While Ford has focused on an integrated European policy, GM retains two distinct policy ranges — one for the UK and one for the rest of Europe. In the long run, GM will merge the two to produce a single policy range using styling variations to maximise regional marketing advantages. The Vauxhall brand name will be retained despite the fact that in operational terms Vauxhall will be absorbed by the larger Opel car operation. Chrysler, meanwhile, have opted for a variation on the single European model theme, tailoring more conventionally engineered products for manufacture and sale in the UK and producing the more sophisticated Simca range on the continent. (Although it is conceivable that Chrysler may be modifying its policy more towards a Ford-like integrated range following continued losses in the UK.) BL are to concentrate on a 'unified range' covering all seven of the basic market segments (see Chapter 3), although the continued success of the specialist BL sports models in the US could prolong the pro-US specialist marketing bias.

Historical Context

Vauxhall's models were principally aimed at the mass market with an emphasis on the larger market, although the introduction of the Viva extended their marketing activities into the small to light car segment. Chrysler, on the other hand, inherited a number of Rootes brand names: Hillman, Humber, Sunbeam and Singer had been acquired by Rootes itself in the course of earlier mergers or takeovers, while the Minx, Super Snipe, Rapier and Hawk model names covered a wide cross-section of the market, ranging from the small/volume segment (Hillman Minx) through to the quality/luxury segment (Humber), with Sunbeam sales accommodating the specialist sports model market. Since then, Chrysler's US parent company has redirected the activities of Chrysler UK into sales of volume cars, using minor product differentiation to distinguish older model names from each other.

Like Chrysler, BL acquired a stable of model names — Austin, Morris, Standard-Triumph, Rover, Jaguar, MG, Riley, Wolseley, Vanden Plas, etc. — all associated with formerly independent companies. With the formation of BMC, Morris and Austin, the two principals, continued to operate as more or less independent concerns: Morris concentrated on production of the Morris Minor and Oxford, while Austin manufactured the A35, A40 and A50/55 models. The Mini and the 1100 series were launched under the new corporate image of badge engineering (the 'and-while-we're-about-it' syndrome) — with an Austin and a Morris variant and more luxurious Riley and Wolseley Mini and 1100 models. Working on the assumption that no one can have too much of a good thing, MG and Vanden Plas both developed 1100 models. Having developed the Farina styled medium car, badge engineering worked success-fully in maintaining and exploiting the goodwill each name or marque engen-dered. Meanwhile, Standard-Triumph launched a new Herald series and even-tually after the takeover by Leyland spawned an entirely new model range which was to form the basis for the Dolomite series. This burst of activity in the volume car market was matched by a similar proliferation at the quality end of the range. Jaguar — once a stolidly one-model company — launched the successful smaller model, the MK2 series, while Rover — which already had a multi-model range — chose to concentrate on the Rover 2000 (P6) series and the ageing 3-litre series. Austin and Wolseley retained their quality ranges, with the A110, the Westminster, the old Princess.

With the formation of British Leyland in 1968, a new strategy was out-lined — one which has been roundly criticised but which was unquestionably a brilliant innovative departure. The problem that faced BL was that it had three companies which made volume cars: Austin, Morris and Triumph. For volume cars two parallel product lines were to be developed, partly in response to the needs of the vast and extremely complex set of distribution networks already in existence and partly in order to maximise market share. The philo-sophy is shown dramatically in Figure 14.1. Both Austin and Morris were to 'market' Minis, while at the same time Austin manufactured the more sophisticated Allegro and Morris produced the Marina, essentially a larger version of an updated Morris Minor. Meanwhile Austin, Morris and Wolseley acquired badge-engineered versions of the 1800/2200 series. In the normal

327

(and uninterrupted) course of events, Riley and Wolseley variants of the Allegro would probably have been evolved, in addition to the Vanden Plas Allegro, but one vital detail had been omitted from the overall marketing strategy: no arrangements had been made for a direct replacement or substitute series for the 1100/1300 series at the bottom of the small or light car market.[1] Although BL probably decided to ditch the twin parallel product line philosophy fairly soon after the merger, its ramifications still survive. As well as the two parallel product lines, the other companies were to concentrate on specialist products. The Triumph range had already been identified as a quality product, an approach which culminated in the development of the Dolomite Sprint with its pretentions to rivalry with BMW. Both Triumph and Rover produced a 2000 range, with the Triumph marketed as a larger/executive car and the Rover as a smaller but more powerful model, with its 3500cc engine, carrying it into the luxury segment. The familiar Jaguar model retained its hegemony in the luxury car market while sacrificing its niche in the small/fast/ luxury car segment to the emergent Dolomite and Rover 3500 (P6) models: with Daimler and Vanden Plas, Jaguar had also moved towards the development of the badge-engineered model.

The Ryder Plan was more or less an overlay, superimposed on the existing BL marketing strategy and using sound financial principles to justify reducing the seven-segment range to five segments. Prior to the Ryder Plan, one might have expected to see the gaps at the bottom end of the market filled by Austin or Morris models (a possible product plan is shown in Figure 14.1).

The 18/22/Princess series had been reformulated in accordance with the concept of badge engineering and the top end of the market was covered by the new Rover SD1 (2300/2600/3500). The Rover SD2 − conceived as a small, fast quality car and designed to compete with the smaller BMW cars, was dropped in favour of a more streamlined five-car approach: the new Mini series, the LC10 medium car series; the larger (Princess-type) car;[2] the Rover large/executive series; and the luxury Jaguar range. In the financial and economic climate prevailing at the time of the Report, it is difficult to imagine what else Ryder might have recommended, when considerations of scale economies were uppermost, but the Ryder Plan failed to recognise that marketing strategies based on artificially created product differentiation could increase market share. The responsibility for the now legendary (and disastrous) fall in BL's marketing strategy at the time of the plan, must to some extent rest on the Ryder Report's failure to appreciate this despite the high (short term) cost penalties involved in a strategy of that sort. BL's former strategy resembled GM's 'divisional' approach in many respects, but with one important exception − unlike GM, BL did not try to maximise economies of scale by using common componentry. Although BL operates at a much smaller volume than the US multinational the company had reached the point where it could have implemented a GM approach with great success. This however, was not to be one of the conditions of the Ryder Plan.

1. Although the Allegro and Marina were supposed to be replacements but in practice catered for a different and larger market segment.
2. Although as shown in Figure 14.1 the Princess replacement would aim to capture part of the upper medium car segment.

FIGURE 14.1

Analysis of BL's Model Policy for Cars

	Mini	Small	Light	Medium	Large	Executive	Luxury
Up to 1976							
Morris	Mini						
Austin	Mini						
Riley/Wolseley)			Allegro	Marina	18/22 Princess		
Vanden Plas)			versions of		18/22 Princess		
Triumph			the Allegro	Dolomite		Dolomite sprint	
Rover						2000 series (P6)	
Jaguar							XJ6
Post 1978 Developments	Mini	New Mini (LC8)	New smaller car (LC10)	Marina	Princess replacement	New Dolomite	XJ series (modified)
					Princess replacement	New Rover Rover replacement	Jaguar replacement
The 1985 Ryder model Strategy	New Mini	New small to medium car			Princess replacement to cover medium to large segment		

329

Ford, of course, has always developed a single range of cars covering a wide segment of the market, acquiring a less characteristic 'sports' veneer with the Lotus-Cortina and RS series. The major Ford marketing success, however, came with the creation of the E-series (Executive), subsequently metamorphised into the Ghia series on the (apparently correct) assumption that with the addition of conspicuously luxurious accessories and the use of a larger engine, a car can virtually double in price without jeopardising its showroom appeal. This approach carries the various economies of scale/financial considerations arguments to that logical conclusion – always assuming that the customer is prepared to pay the price.

In happier times, both Chrysler and BL produced sports cars – but now only BL remains active in that particular specialist market, with the TR and MG ranges. Vauxhall and Ford are apparently content to restrict their activities to the production of sporting saloon derivatives. As we saw in Chapter 6, GM are now committed to the development of a saloon derived sports model, while Ford may not continue to develop the Capri as a separate model. Having abandoned a separate sports range, Chrysler UK worked on a sports version of the Arrow range (the Sunbeam Alpine/Rapier) but discontinued production in the 1976 financial crisis. BL resolutely clings to a parallel sports car range with the smaller Triumph and MG models (the Spitfire and the Midget) and the larger TR6/7 and MGB sports cars. The Stag was marketed as a single line, although rumours of a mid-engined Rover sports model suggest that the company ran out of either cash or engineering resources or that Jaguar made a successful bid to protect its E-type market. Although no other major UK firms actually *manufacture* sports cars, Chrysler imports the partly Chrysler-built Bagheera S and Vauxhall supplies mechanical components for the Panther's Lima range (see Chapter 9).

PRICING POLICY

The company pricing policies and price band widths (at April 1978) are shown in Figure 14.2. Ford has the most logical price band width, running from £2,200 almost without interruption to a top price of over £7,000. GM has good coverage at the lower end of the market with the parallel Opel and Vauxhall ranges, but virtually nothing in the £6,000 bandwidth,[1] although BL's Rover 2300 and 2600, and the new GM model range help to fill this gap. Chrysler ignores the top end of the range completely, while BL – with the Dolomite – has a wide spread, although there is a gap between the Dolomite Sprint and the Rover 2300. The cancelled SD2 would have covered this segment.

With a high import penetration figure, it may be thought that prices are set by international comparisons and that there is little scope for price cutting *per se* – profit margins in Europe being too small, especially in the smaller car segments. But this is not entirely true. Motor vehicles are not a homogenous product. For example, a car has a number of characteristics which

---

1. Plans to import the Senator and Monza in late 1978 may remedy this and even extend the range beyond this limit.

include: equipment (see Table 14.1), performance, economy, packaging, supervision, roadholding, handling, body style, and so on. Each manufacturer's product is differentiated from another by having a different combination of the above characteristics.

FIGURE 14.2

Pricing Spider: The Price Band Width of Models (at end April 1978)

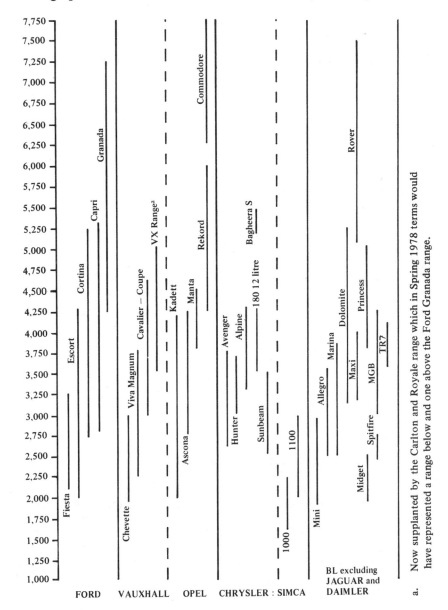

TABLE 14.1

Representative List of Equipment

Interior

Seat valences, front armrests, rear centre armrests, headrests, pockets, interior lights, map reading light, rear courtesy light, boot light, engine compartment light, carpets, glove box light, special steering wheel, flick wipe, scuff plate, wood door cappings, level of trim, handbrake gaiter, headlining, trip recorder, brake failure warning light, oil pressure gauge, ammeter, air vents, heating controls, n speed blower, facia finish, handbrake warning light, side window demist, rear compartment heating, adjustable steering column, seat belt warning light, driver's seat height adjustment, electrically heated driving seat, gear lever knob, tool kit, seat belt mounted on seat frame, concealed inertia reel, door opening warning lights, self-levelling ride, cigar lighter, central locking, electric windows, clock, radio, stereo cassette, day/night mirror, intermittent wipe (variable or non vairable), air conditioning, and so on.

Exterior

Bodyside moulding, beltrail moulding, bright bonnet moulding, wheelarch moulding, windshield/backlight moulding, black/bright window frames, drip rails, quarter bumper pads, wrap-round bumper pads, tape-stripe, exhaust trim, bright rocker applique, grill, spoiler, wheel trim, paint finish, ignition system, dampers, horn, bonnet and boot locks, special springs, mudflaps, diagnostic socket, side turn indicator, bumper inserts, black back panel, bonnet/ boot gas strut, lockable fuel cap, electric fan, wheelarch liners, mudflaps, day side lights, safety bumpers, adjustable headlamp, rear fog lamps, front fog lamps, tinted glass, laminated glass, vinyl roof, sliding roof, halogen headlamps, over-riders, special wheels, power steering, automatic transmission, overdrive, 5 speed gearbox, power antenna, door mirrors, headlamp wash/wipe, engine type, and so on.

A change in product differentiation can cause results that appear contradictory. For example, in Figure 14.3, the curve DD shows a demand curve for a given level of product characteristics and advertising expenditure. Suppose that the product characteristics are so improved that the demand curve shifts to the right. It is possible for both price and quantity to increase. Hence, although price is important, the product characteristics are to some extent even more important.

FIGURE 14.3
Marketing Policy and Shifts in the Demand Curve

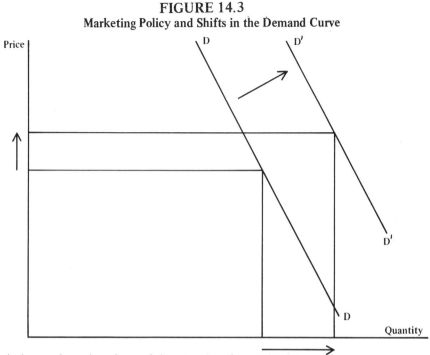

An increase in product characteristics can cause an increase in price
and quantity by shifting the demand curve to the right.

As discussed in Chapter 5, academic studies have shown that the price
elasticity of demand is high. This and other marketing considerations are
discussed within the context of a statistical framework in Appendix 14.1 at
the end of this chapter. However, academic studies may have failed to ascertain
the actual prices of cars, because the advertised retail price of a car may not
in reality be the actual price. For example, it is considered by manufacturers
to be inappropriate to announce price reductions across model lines. A preferred way of actually reducing prices to to 'incentivise' the model by giving
a special deal to the dealer for a set period, which may be backed up by an
extensive advertising campaign (e.g. Superdeal). Alternatively, additional
extras may be fitted 'free' to products which are sold at the same price —
the so-called *white* sale. Both ways have the advantage that prices can simply
be increased by phasing out the special scheme without changing published
prices and without the public being fully aware of such changes. Different
prices can, in any case, be hidden by higher dealer margins.

Brand loyalty is another aspect of marketing. If consumers can be made
sufficiently satisfied with their current product that they would not wish to
change readily, the price elasticity may become inelastic for small price changes.

A more pragmatic approach adopted by manufacturers usually analyses
price elasticity by market segment. In general, higher price elasticities are
assumed to occur with small car buyers who are assumed to be more price
constrained (otherwise they would buy a larger car). In any particular price

change situation, it appears[1] that a 1 per cent reduction in price leads to around a 3 per cent or more increase in demand at the bottom end of the market, whilst the elasticity reduces from -3 down to as low as -1 at the top end of the market.

Most importantly, prices must have been perceived to have changed by the customer. A price change from £3,991 to £3,900 may have no effect, whilst an additional price cut to £3,890 may have a dramatic effect.

Young and Hood[2] argue that Chrysler have apparently pursued a long-term pricing policy of undercutting competitors although increased sales do not appear to have compensated for lower unit profits. In fact, their case is over-stated and probably only applies to the period 1970-5. A margin of £50 to £100 makes very little difference to the consumer if he can be persuaded that a slightly more expensive product is a better buy, therefore we would hesitate before suggesting that price alone determines choice; other product charac-teristics are important. Styling, newness of model, performance (i.e. top speed and acceleration), fuel consumption, cost of servicing and repairs, roadholding and handling, interior fittings, seating, instrumentation, gadgetry, roominess, fuel tank capacity, turning circle, the 'feel' of a car (a highly subjective con-sideration, this), accessories supplied as standard fittings, price and reliability all affect (and determine to varying degrees) the consumer's final choice. By emphasising attributes *other* than price, Chrysler's competitors have balanced Chrysler's undercut pricing. An illustration of this effect is portrayed in Figure 14.3.

A manufacturer will in general charge for a particular piece of equipment. A list of equipment is given in Table 14.1. Any particular series in a model will have a range of equipment. This range of equipment can be priced item by item. Hence the cost of equipment difference can be as much as £1,000. In Table 14.2 an analysis is made of eight cars in comparison with BL's Princess. On an analysis of sheer equipment, BL's Princess HLS can command an extra price of £245 over the Volvo 244DL to cover the additional equipment.

Rational manufacturers within Europe set their pricing policies in two dis-tinctive ways. First there is the target competitor pricing strategy. This may con-sist of a manufacturer choosing a competitor's model as a target. Suppose we are attempting to price a product identical to the Audi 100 GLS. We may then choose the Princess HLS as our target. Then, by analysing all the features and equipment on our model, a target price may be arrived at after allowing for all the product differences. In Table 14.2, it can be seen that the Audi 100GLS has a deficiency of £20 in equipment. On the other hand, we may decide that our hypothetical model is worth £1,000 more than the target because of rival appearance, performance, economy and better reliability. We would then charge an extra £980 (£1,000 − £20) over the target price as given by the Princess HLS. Such a pricing strategy will probably be followed by European manufacturers, who are relatively minor in any particular country or market. A variation on the target price theme is to choose several models as targets and to try to price in between the targets. There is some evidence to support the hypothesis that both Chrysler and Vauxhall usually follow prices set by Ford

1. On the basis of confidential interviews.
2. *Chrysler UK, A Corporation in Transition*, Stephen Young and Neil Hood, Preger, New York, 1977.

TABLE 14.2
Value of Equipment Differences as compared with BL's Princess HLS
(Summer 1977 prices)

	Vauxhall 2300GLS	Peugeot 504GL	Audi 100GLS	Volvo 244DL	Citroen CX2400	BMW 518	Renault 30TS	Ford Granada 3.0,GL
	£	£	£	£	£	£	£	£
Radio	0	100	-70	-100	-50	-100	-100	0
Clock	0	0	0	0	0	-20	0	0
Headrests	0	+30	+30	+30	+30	+30	0	+30
Halogen headlights	0	+15	0	0	0	+15	+15	0
Door mirrors	0	-5	+10	-10	-5	-5	-5	+10
Fog lights	+40	0	+60	+20	0	+15	0	40
Laminated windscreen	0	+45	+45	+45	+45	+45	+45	0
Tinted glass	0	-45	0	-35	-35	-35	0	-35
Intermittent wire	0	+10	+10	0	0	+15	+15	0
Two cigar lighters	-5	-5	-5	-5	-5	-5	-5	-5
Electric windows	0	0	0	0	+100	0	+100	0
Central locking	0	0	0	0	0	0	0	+80
Tachometer	+10	0	+10	0	+10	0	+10	+10
Centre console	0	0	0	0	0	0	+10	0
Power steering	0	-150	-150	-150	0	-150	0	-150
Sliding roof	0	+120	0	0	0	0	0	+120
Tyre differences	0	-30	-30	-30	-10	-30	-30	-30
Seat belt differences	0	0	-25	+40	0	0	0	0
Overriders	0	-10	-5	0	-5	0	-5	-10
Vinyl roof	0	-50	-50	-50	-50	-50	-50	0
Sports roadwheels	0	0	0	0	0	0	0	+45
Cloth trim	0	0	0	0	0	0	-15	0
Underbody treatment	0	-15	0	0	0	0	0	-15
Metallic point	+40	0	0	0	0	0	0	0
Trim halogen driving lamps	+30	0	0	0	0	0	0	0
Headlamp wash	0	0	+40	0	0	0	0	0
	+115	-220	-20	-245	+25	-275	+65	+10

and BL in the UK – although there are exceptions to this rule.

The second approach is to fix prices without explicit reference to the competition. The motor industry works from the axiomatic approach that its volume is fixed by plant capacity. Therefore, in order to maximise profits, prices must be charged to clear its capacity. What this approach entails is that each manufacturer has, in essence, a demand curve for each product, based on its product characteristics and market appeal (which includes styling). If a given quantity is to be sold, then a price can be fixed accordingly. Changes in that price will affect the quantity sold. In some cases, this would dictate extremely high prices. Such prices might arouse general public or Government hostility, both of which would probably be regarded as constraints on pricing strategy. The reader may be surprised at why public hostility may be a constraint, but most volume car manufacturers would not wish to gain a reputation for having an unfair pricing policy.[1] Obviously, a Government may be able to influence prices through the Price Commission but new model prices have not been subject to prior review and the definition of what constitutes a new model is vague. Such a price leadership approach can only be adopted where the range of products is competitive, and where a manufacturer has a major share of a market.

An optimal pricing policy therefore requires two distinctive stages. In Figure 14.4 the short run average cost curve of a manufacturer is shown to be at Q^* — i.e. capacity. Thereafter, a small amount of extra capacity can only be attained by incurring overtime at high labour rates. Maximum profits are attained at the point where marginal costs are equal to marginal revenue. In Figure 14.4(a) the point at which profits are maximised is below capacity. Profits could be further increased if the demand curve could be shifted to the right. It was shown earlier that the demand curve *can* be shifted to the right by improving the product (e.g. adding 'extras'). Unfortunately, as well as shifting the demand curve to the right, the additional 'extras' cost money. Supposing that £1 of extras actually had a marginal cost of £1. The optimal output would not change, although the price charged would be higher. Another way to approach the problem is to analyse the demand and marginal revenue curves as being net of the average and marginal costs respectively. Hence, in the example where the extras cost £1, the demand curve shifts out but is shifted back to its original position having been *adjusted* by the additional costs. Fortunately, these so-called 'extras' are highly profitable. Table 14.3 shows the large amount of marginal profit that can be made from 'extras'. Therefore, a manufacturer, by fitting and charging for these 'extras', can move the cost adjusted demand curve to the right. Thus, not only can profits be maximised on a base model (i.e. without many 'extras'), but by adding (or subtracting) 'extras', the demand curve can be shifted so as to maximise profits at capacity output.

Extras are not the only means a manufacturer has of shifting a demand curve. The demand curve can also be shifted to the right through visual styling changes, etc, although this may incur certain fixed design and development costs. Given that a demand curve can be manoeuvred to the right, then profits are globally maximised at the point where marginal costs cut marginal revenue at point Q^* — the point of maximum output. It is this manipulation of the demand curve which is so critical in marketing terms and more often than not

---

1. Such a reputation might induce a reduction in long-run demand.

ignored in micro-economic theory.

In practice, if a manufacturer fixed its price above its competitors,[1] two things would happen. First customers would be lost through the lowering in demands as dictated by the demand curve. Secondly, customer loyalty would, over a longer period, gradually be eroded. The combined effect would be a long run *shift* in demand. So, in practice it is counter-productive for a firm to set its prices too high. Profits are usually maximised when practical capacity output is sold at the highest price the market will bear. A manufacturer whose price is below the average may gradually win orders by tempting those consumers who do not have brand loyalty. In effect, what this implies is that Sweezy's kinked demand[2] curve may operate in reverse for those manufacturers who are not market leaders. Figure 14.5 demonstrates the kinked curve. Above the target price, demand is less elastic, whilst below it, demand is relatively elastic as new customers are 'pinched' from other manufacturers. Such a relationship would only hold to a small extent and probably with lags. It would however be difficult empirically to prove its existence since the effect would be small and difficult to distinguish.

An example of the use of this kink are the aggressive pricing policies of manufacturers attempting to buy into a market. Some of the Japanese and Communist Bloc manufacturers have in the past priced below the competitive target equivalent, in order to increase market share quickly. Exchange rate changes and the automatic adjustment to those changes can also cause some peculiar pricing quirks.

Other Factors

In the pricing decisions for a model, several factors must be taken into account. First, the bodystyle and series mix. Initially the Rover was announced as a single product which was later expanded to a 3 model range. Ford market their Granada with a choice of saloon or estate, each with a choice of five series: low,[3] L, GL, S and Ghia. Secondly, there is the range of equipment to be offered on each model, and the range of equipment differences between models. Obviously, the higher series models must make a considerably greater contribution to profits, since the basic material and labour charges are the same, yet up to several thousands of pounds of extras may have been fitted at a large mark-up (see Table 14.3). Sometimes the full product value of a particular range will not be charged if market share is weak and competitive considerations dictate such a move.

A model range must also be carefully balanced. Ford, for example, found that the cheaper Consul product detracted from the quality image of the Granada range. Hence the series was dropped. This step has been taken one step further by in effect dropping the low series Granada. Certain products are only offered with a certain range of engines or gearbox option in order to

1. Bearing in mind differences in equipment, styling, performance, economy, ride, etc.
2. P.M. Sweezy, 'Demand Under Conditions of Oligopoly', *Journal of Political Economy*, 1939.
3. i.e. No.L, GL, S or Ghia designation.

FIGURE 14.4

Shifting the Demand Curve by Changing Product Characteristics so as to Maximise Short Run Profits[a]

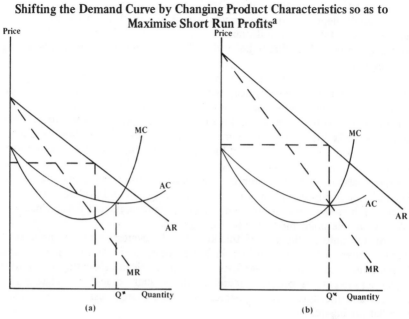

(a)

(b)

a. Purists will note that the MR curve is not drawn accurately – the MR curve should dissect the distance between the AR curve and the axis.

TABLE 14.3

Typical Prices and Costs of Equipment

	Variable Cost £	Price Charged £
6 cylinder engine	150	200
Central locking	40	80
Sliding roof	50	120
Tinted glass	10	35
Power steering	60	150
Vinyl roof	20	50
Metallic paint	10	25
Headlamp wash	10	35
Remote control mirror	5	15
Head restraints	10	30
Inertia rear seat belts	20	30
Electric windows	60	170
Leather trim	160	260
Air conditioning	180	400
Power antenna	10	25

FIGURE 14.5

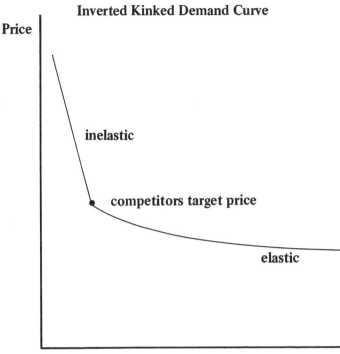

Inverted Kinked Demand Curve

enhance the image of the product.

An important change in the UK market may be the joining of the Executive and the large car market segments. In the 1960s, there was a niche between the medium 1½ litre mass produced cars and the large 3 litre car, which was filled by the so-called Executive cars. However, such cars as Cortina 2.3 litre, Renault 20TS, Peugeot 504, Princess HLS, Opel Rekord have, to some extent, filled this gap. Meanwhile, the traditionally large cars (e.g. Ford Granada, Opel Senator), whilst currently being placed in the Executive class, are moving up market and are firmly pointing towards the luxury segment.

Interestingly enough, price wars *do* occur — but in a rather unexpected way. Ford, for example, had priced the Mk1 Granada to compete with BL's Princess. The Granada won very few sales from the Princess and the UK profitability of the series was low. As a result, the new Mk2 Granada was moved into a higher price category, with the marketing emphasis on a well made product and styling. In order to produce a competitive rival to the Princess, the cheaper Cortina 2.0 and 2.3 was positioned up market to compete head-on with the higher series Princess. The policy was confined to the UK.[1] In

---

1. No repositioning of the Granada series occurred in the German market place where the Granada was losing out from its more stylish competitors (Audi 100 series, BMW, Opel's larger models etc).

Europe, GM and VW were actively competing in the same segment as the Granada, whereas in the UK there was little direct competition in that particular category. BL's Princess will probably follow the Granada up market, in a slightly revised and repriced version, probably featuring the new Rover 2300 or 2600 engines.

ADVERTISING

Figure 14.6 graphs some recent (and very revealing) figures for market shares of press and TV car advertising. From 1970 onwards, advertising expenditure by certain foreign manufacturers increased dramatically at a time when UK producers could not meet demand — a point evidently not lost on the importers, who were quick to grasp the marketing opportunities and establish a firmer foothold in the UK.

In part the loss in advertising market share may have been caused by the lack of new models (advertising revenues rise sharply with new model launches) or the lack of cars to sell. Whatever the reason, the decline in advertising market share went hand in hand with an actual decline in market share. Although this might suggest a simple remedy to falling sales, BL's increased advertising revenues in 1974 and 1975 failed to improve the company's market share, due to the intervention of other factors.

In line with other oligopolies, advertising has often been used by the car manufacturers as a much more aggressive marketing tool. Young and Hood point out that in 1970, Vauxhall spent £5 per car sold on press and TV advertising for the Viva, compared with BL's and Ford's £2 and Chrysler's £7 per unit sale. Chrysler's advertising expenditure on the Avenger dropped to £4 per car in 1974, while Vauxhall and Leyland (launching the Allegro) increased advertising to £9 per unit sale.

Media attitudes have an important effect in determining the level and the scope of advertising, and advertising itself can be used to change the image of a company's product. Ford's products, for example, have not in the past enjoyed a particularly strong reputation for engineering or innovation, nor have they gained high levels of 'social acceptibility', but Ford is now moving to correct this, particularly through heavy stress whether true or not on engineering[1] in current marketing strategies for product publicity. GM, in the aftermath of the Opel-Vauxhall integration, has yet to decide on its media attitudes and priorities, although it will probably follow Ford's lead in this respect. Chrysler, meanwhile, received excellent coverage and more than a modicum of praise for the Alpine range, when the new car won the Car of the Year award in 1976. Both GM and Chrysler will presumably wish to stress the 'worldwide' breadth of their models, while GM may introduce some regional publicity variations. Although BL's Rover also won an award, BL could not benefit from this because of serious supply constraints.

WARRANTY

The Warranty/Guarantee offered is another feature of an aggressive marketing

---

1. As discussed in Chapter 6 this does not mean technical innovation but simply a competitive European product.

policy. In the 1960s and early in the 1970s, the standard warranty was issued for 12 months or 12,000 miles, whichever came first. However, in periods of depression, one aspect of aggressive marketing is to offer extended warranties. Hence, in 1967/8 and the middle 1970s, most manufacturers improved their warranties. However, it was the latter depression which saw the greatest competition in this area. Towards the end of 1975, Chrysler extended its guarantee to unlimited mileage, with a further undertaking to replace without charge certain worn out (rather than simply defective) parts within a specified period. On the Imp, Chrysler also offered free servicing for one year. A week after this arrangement had been announced, BL retaliated with a master marketing stroke — Supercover — which followed a sales drive on old models called Superdeal. Supercover offered to cover the cost of replacing major components

FIGURE 14.6

Market Share of Press and TV Advertising Expenditure on Cars (in per cent)

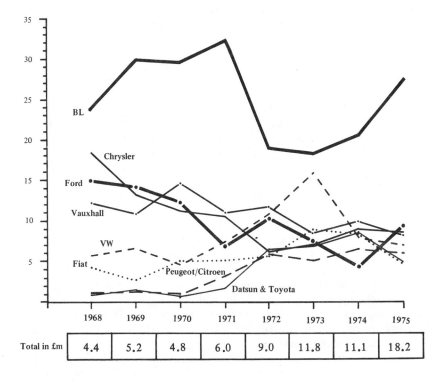

| Total in £m | 4.4 | 5.2 | 4.8 | 6.0 | 9.0 | 11.8 | 11.1 | 18.2 |

Source: MEAL, Media Expenditure Analysis Ltd

341

for a second year (again with no mileage limitations), and incorporating AA cover as a further incentive. Shortly after, Ford and Vauxhall fell into line with unlimited mileage clauses, but only for the first year.

Judging from the US market, however, it would seem that once the market recovers, manufacturers will be anxious to return to the more restricted warranty provisions of a 12 month/unlimited mileage condition – a move which, at present, would have to be dictated by BL. Until BL decide to abandon Supercover, it will remain a powerful marketing weapon.

FUTURE MODEL POLICY

In Chapter 6 we confirmed that the model strategies of the three US multi-nationals are now well established. Figure 14.7 shows the possible *future* model strategy for the Big Three. If our assumptions are correct, Ford will integrate the Cortina and Granada ranges further, possibly merging them into a single range covering the medium, large and executive market segments, while the company concentrates on developing a range of technically sophisticated Fiesta and Escort models. The new Escort (codenamed Erika) will be front-wheel drive with independent rear suspension and featuring an overhead camshaft engine, (to be made at Bridgend). The Capri, in future, will probably be produced as a variant of one of the saloons.

GM will continue to produce a Vauxhall 'range' (using minor styling features to distinguish it from other GM products) while Opel will dominate the upper end of GM's market. With the new 'S' car – which may or may not be marketed under both Opel and Vauxhall brand names – GM will then have a basic five-model European line up, with sporting derivatives of its medium and large saloons. Front-wheel drive and an overhead camshaft with an aluminium head will probably feature as a technical improvement in the 'S' car and 'T' car (Chevette/Kadett) replacement, although suspension will be more conventional. At the top end of the market, there could be a marginal increase in the number of GM cars imported into Europe from the US. As US-made Cadillacs and Buicks are downgraded in size they could become more acceptable at the top end of the European market.

Chrysler's basic range will involve a series of technically advanced front wheel drive cars based on the new Horizon C2, which is to be produced world-wide. The Sunbeam and the conventional Avenger will stay in production in order to tap Chrysler's marketing advantages acquired through selling basic cars to less developed countries and as fleet sales. Recent events indicate that Chrysler may have changed direction[1] and may try to establish a more uniform range, although a major capital investment programme will be necessary to move away from its current line-up of UK produced models (Sunbeam, Avenger and, in smaller numbers, the Hunter). However Ryton is geared up to assembling KD kits from Poissey and this trend will undoubtedly continue. Chrysler's extreme weakness at the top end of the model spectrum is also bound to be remedied.

1. How Chrysler might integrate its models with those of Peugeot-Citroen is discussed in Chapter 17.

FIGURE 14.7

Future Model Strategy of US Multinationals

Manufacturer/Car Segment	Ford	Vauxhall	GM Opel	GM (US) Brandnames	Chrysler Conventional Engineering	Chrysler Modern Engineering
Mini	—	—	—	—	—	—
Small	Fiesta	S Car	S Car	—	Sunbeam	new Simca 1100
Light	Escort	Chevette	Kadett	—	new Avenger	C2 (Horizon)
Medium	Cortina	Cavalier	Ascona	—	Arrow range	Alpine (C6)
Large	Cortina Granada	Carlton	Reckord	—	—	C9
Executive	Granada	Royale	Senator	Buick, etc.	—	C9
Luxury	—	—	Monza?	Buick, Cadillac, etc.	—	C9
Sporting	Escort/Cortina derivations	Cavalier coupe	Manta (Ascona derivative) Monza (Senator derivative)	—	—	Borgheera S Alpine derivative

One feature in common with all US multinationals is that, in marketing terms, they will attempt to cover the basic seven car market segments, although one bodystyle may attempt to cover more than one market segment. Put another way, segments such as the Executive and Luxury cars, will be covered by variants of the other segments. There are clear signs of such phenomena occurring in the US, where the Cadillac, GM's prestigious division, has produced a luxury 'intermediate' (medium) car. Similarly in Europe, one can expect Executive and even Luxury variants of the medium and large segments. At the largest end, there will probably develop an ultra-large segment. From the point of view of the US multinationals, this segment might be satisfied by US built imports.

BL's future model policy is more difficult to predict. Had the Ryder strategy been continued in its original form, the company would have produced five basic models (see above, p.329). A contraction along the lines suggested in Chapter 7 could involve a number of different model strategies, most of which are outlined in Figure 14.8 (a). Adopting our preferred strategy, we give a possible model policy outcome in Figure 14.8 (b), which would involve the current Ryder model plans for the volume division, extending the model range towards the executive market segment. The specialist division would then be based in the Rover and Jaguar range, using common components where possible; the bottom end of the Rover range could move towards the large car segment. To balance the range successfully, a smaller quality car might be necessary — possibly a small Rover — which could extend into the medium car market but priced at well above the volume product range. An approach of this sort would, we envisage, maximise the marketing advantages of BL's quality range. The MG sports models might be attached to the volume division, while the brandname itself could be appended to the quality division, using badge engineering to distinguish certain volume cars and retaining a specialist range in the quality division.

The major distinction between the Ryder marketing strategy and our preferred strategy is that the latter would enable the specialist division to exploit (and capitalise upon) its existing reputation. The volume division could then concentrate on production of 'bread-and-butter' models with greater opportunities to look for gaps in the market and search for ways of filling them.

BL's new Corporate Plan under Michael Edwardes, will probably not greatly change the five car line-up proposed by the Ryder plan (new Mini, LC 10, Princess replacement, Rover, Jaguar). This is something of a disappointment, although four wheel drive and other special products are to be strengthened. As stated earlier, luxury versions of smaller cars are being developed and have kept BMW extremely busy. At the moment, the marketing strategy for Jaguar Rover Triumph seems to be to produce two large cars. A smaller, but specialist, product is certainly needed to fill the gap.

A further criticism can be levelled at BL's sports car policy. At the moment, there are five distinct ranges: Midget, Spitfire, MGB, TR7 and Stag. Including the E-type the total range was part of BL's marketing strength within the North American market. However, the Ryder plan envisaged a two sports car range: the Lynx (replacement Stag)[1] and a smaller sports car which may have been based on the TR7. Two of BL's strengths are the sports car brand names and the US franchise network. In order to retain these two advantages,

1.   Now cancelled under the new 1978 Corporate Plan.

FIGURE 14.8

Possible Model Strategies for BL

ALTERNATIVE	Mini	Small	Light	Medium	Large	Executive	Luxury
(a) As presented in Chapter 7							
1. Modified Ryder	old Mini	new Mini		LC10 range	Princess replacement	Rover	Jaguar
2. The proposed new middle car range dropped in favour of upgraded Allegro	old Mini	new Mini		upgraded Allegro	Princess replaceement	Rover	Jaguar
3. Uses upgraded old Mini	upgraded old Mini			upgraded Allegro	Princess replacement	Rover	Jaguar
4. Uses old Mini	old Mini			upgraded Allegro	Princess replacement	Rover	Jaguar
5. Restricted range – quality cars only				upgraded Allegro	Princess replacement	Rover	Jaguar
6. Specialist range only			SD2 derivative		Princess replacement	Rover	Jaguar
(b) Preferred strategy							
Volume	Mini	LC8	LC10	Marina	Princess replacement		
Specialist			SD2 derivative			Rover	Jaguar

a sports car range must be produced. It would seem logical to produce a range of sports cars based on the common componentry of new and existing car products. In this way, the only unique investment would be some £10 to £25 million for body design and pressings. With BL's strategy, something more than a VW Sirocco could be created out of common componentry; for example, the 5 speed 77mm gearbox could be used coupled to a variety of engines (the new 0 series, the Rover 2300/2600 series, the V8 etc.). BL would probably argue that it is all very well but they can only add the 'jam to their product range once they have developed the bread and butter'. A valid argument, but one which implies losing the above two strengths currently alluded to. If BL does not have the engineering resources to develop their sports car range, they must simply contract out such development. Recently, doubt has been cast on whether the TR7 and XJS are suitable products for the US market; BL's reputation is for something more traditional. Such concern makes it even more imperative that BL rectifies its sports car model policy.

In Chapter 7, it was also suggested that the Maxi be developed into a smaller Range Rover that could compete against the Chrysler Rancho. Although it seems that plans are well advanced for expanding and redesigning the Land Rover, it is a pity that an equivalent and parallel development could not take place for converting the Maxi into a recreational vehicle. Again, BL's limited development potential rules such a possibility out of court.

On the volume side, the Mini and the facelifted Marina (which almost certainly will include mechanical changes to improve ride and roadholding) will probably soldier on for some time to come. The revised new Mini (LC8) will fall in the Fiesta type class, whilst the LC10 will fill in the light car segment. The revised Princess will probably remain where it is, if the Marina is to be continued or (and more likely) made to cover the medium market directly and will therefore replace the Marina, although like the Cortina, will extend to the Executive market segment.

Conclusion to Car Marketing Strategies

The three US multinationals have all based their future European marketing strategies on the cardinal virtues of product development[1] and a comprehensive model range stretching from the small to the executive car segments. Most model ranges will develop a 'Ford-type' price bandwidth, within which the highest priced models will cost significantly more than basic models. Reaction has set in against the implications of the Ryder strategy: although scale economies will be maximised in BL (through common componentry), marketing activities will aim for a broader spectrum, maximising traditional marketing philosophies.

CVs

CV marketing is less frivolous — in concept and approach — than car marketing: CVs are regarded as strictly functional in character; the market for them is small (in comparison with the car market) and potential buyers are neces-

---

1. Which has to conform to the European norm.

sarily better informed. Figure 14.9 gives the model policy at the bottom end of the market for the four major UK manufacturers. All of them produce a car-derived van; BL and GM offer car-derived vans in the two sizes. Until recently, only BL offered a four-wheel drive vehicle, but Chrysler has developed the Chrysler Rancho (a variant of the Simca 1100) as a cheap 'utility' vehicle. In line with the Ryder Plan, BL will pursue an aggressive marketing campaign for both the Land-Rover and the Range Rover. The Land-Rover's reputation as a sluggish performer could be greatly enhanced with the installation of the V8 Rover engine.

All four manufacturers also market panel van/lightweight trucks, BL with two models, the rest with a series covering the market. The mobile caravan — the European equivalent of the US 'recreational' vehicle — also falls into this category. As yet, none of the major UK producers unlike VW have entered the caravanette/mobile home market directly, although a number of them supply chassis or basic models to the specialist manufacturers (see Table 14.4).

Figure 14.10 gives the model policies of the four major UK manufacturers in the light to heavy truck market. As we noted in Chapter 3, BL is the only major European manufacturer with a complete across-the-board range, although the range is too complex and is now ageing. Ford and GM (Bedford) produce the widest if not the most complete range (the latter in line with GM's European policy) while Dodge (Chrysler) also have a fair coverage of the market. Somewhat belatedly, Bedford, Ford and BL have all entered the heavy end of the market, but only BL has a foothold in the premium built truck segment, although Ford and GM have both developed new products aimed at this section of the market. In summary, in the past, Leyland's apparent neglect of its truck division allowed Ford and Bedford to acquire market leadership in the light-weight truck sector. Leyland's revitalised light-weight range is now being marketed as a high performance model range and should increase BL's market share at this end of the CV market.

Future marketing strategies will focus on the panel van segment, for which Ford are rumoured to be preparing a new and more versatile Transit range. Chrysler's marketing strategy is at present unclear, in the wake of the 1976 reorganisation, but a new light truck is imminent, while Ford and GM must be gearing up for a head-on marketing collision in the lightweight truck market.

BL's future model policy (for CV's) might consist of:[1]

(a) A new heavy truck range which is imminent. Over the next three years, the range should be simplified to consist of a central core of 3 series.

(b) The light/medium truck range above 6.5 tonnes could be renewed and simplified by using versions of the heavy truck cab and refining existing chassis units. This would occur once the heavy truck range had been primarily implemented and may be based on a 2 series model, although options could extend the coverage throughout the medium truck range.

(c) Leyland might sell a competitive bought-out light truck in the UK to assist franchise holders; such an arrangement could form part of a collaboration venture.

1. See for example, Sunday Times, 24.9.78

FIGURE 14.9

Model Policy at the Bottom End of the Truck Market

	Car Derived Vans	Four-Wheel Drive Vehicles	Panel Vans	Trucks (lightweight)
BL	Mini Van Marina	Land-Rover Range Rover	Sherpa	EA FG
GM	HA Series Some Opel derivatives Chevanne		CF/Blitz[a] Series	TJ Series
Ford	Escort		Transit Series	A Series
Chrysler	Simca variant	Simca 1100	PB Series Spanish Panel Series	Walk Thru

a. Blitz now only used on Bedfords sold in Germany.

TABLE 14.4

Motor Caravans

Motor Caravan Manufacturer	Using Models from				
	Other	BL	GM Bedford (Vauxhall)	Ford	Dodge (Chrysler)
Autosleeper		✓	✓	✓	✓
Bariban	Mercedes Benz				
Canterbury			✓	✓	✓
Carawagon	Renault	✓			
CI Autohomes		✓		✓	
Danbury	Toyota				
Denon	VW				
Dormobile	VW		✓		
Endrust		✓			
European		✓	✓	✓	
Motorhomes International	Fiat, VW	✓	✓	✓	
Newlander	Toyota	✓	✓	✓	
Nimhys				✓	
Richard Holdsworth	VW	✓	✓	✓	✓
Suntrekker		✓	✓	✓	
Toreors		✓	✓	✓	
Wilsons		✓			

DISTRIBUTION NETWORKS

BL, who has traditionally had the larger domestic market share, has always had the largest distribution network. BL has now reduced its number of retail outlets from nearly 6,000 in 1968 to less than 2,300 at present, whilst the Ryder plan envisaged for a further reduction in number to fewer than 2,000. Since the Edwardes reorganisation, it is likely that BL will now defer a further reduction in its distribution network; in fact there are clear signs that BL will actively attempt to maintain its network at its current levels, although a Ryder type reorganisation might remain as a longer term aim. Ford has also

FIGURE 14.10

Model Policy of Light to Heavy Segment of Truck Market

Segments Manufacturers	PRODUCTION				VOLUME PRODUCTION		PREMIUM BUILT
	Lightweight Trucks				Medium Weight Trucks	Heavy Trucks	
	3½-6 tons	6-16 tons	16-22 tons	22+ tons			
BL	FG	Terrier-Boxer-Mastiff			Chieftan Clydesdale Reiver series	Lynx-Bison -Buffalo Series Mercury- Marshall- Mammoth Series	Routeman Marathon Crusader
GMa (Bedford)	TJ TK	TK	TK		TM	TM	
Dodge	Walk-thru Kerrier Bantam	Commando	Commando		Dodge 500 K Range (Spain)	11/382 (Spain)	
(Chrysler)							
Ford	A series	D series	D series		D series	Transcontinental	

a. Some of the lighter trucks are marketed in Germany under the Opel Blitz badge.

'rationalised' its dealer network, which now comprises some 1,200 outlets. Chrysler and Vauxhall, too, have shed dealers as their respective market shares declined. Apart from the fall in the number of franchised outlets, the overall number of dealerships has also fallen. In 1974, there were 11,000 sales outlets; this had dropped to fewer than 9,400 in early 1977. In the CV sector, all of the UK manufacturers have rationalised their dealer networks, particularly BL and Vauxhall.

Overall, the greatest drop in the number of sales outlets has occurred in BL's distribution network, which inevitably raises the question of whether this fall is in any way responsible for BL's worsening performance. Dealers who were actually *dropped* by BL are potential recruits to an importer's rival network; the CPRS estimate that about one third of the 'disenfranchised' BL dealers took on import franchises subsequently. In a survey of 300 dealers dropped or shelved by the various UK manufacturers, the CPRS found that 35 per cent obtained an import franchise, 15 per cent switched to another manufacturer and 50 per cent either left the motor trade altogether or are no longer franchised. In this respect, BL's rationalisation (and the reduction in number of sales outlets by the other UK manufacturers) certainly did nothing to hinder foreign manufacturers in their efforts to build up distribution networks. Importers now account for nearly 50 per cent of all retail outlets.

If we now examine the dealer network in terms of the size of retail outlets, it seems that Ford is pursuing a strategy of increased sales volume through a smaller number of larger outlets. Ford's unit sales (see Table 14.5) are also relatively large. BL's below par CV sales per outlet are partly distorted by the greater number of heavier vehicles sold. Within the Leyland network Jaguar and Daimler retailers recorded fewer sales per outlet (between thirty and forty units per outlet) while the Rover/Triumph and Austin/Morris figures recovered from around 80 and 91 units respectively in 1970 to 122 and 128 respectively in 1974. Figures for non-Jaguar/Daimler dealers are now even higher.

Generally speaking, there are two principal methods of organising a distribution network. In the 'single-tier' system, dealers are supplied direct from the factory. In the multi-tiered system, a pool of main dealers or distributors work through a series of smaller distributorships to supply dealers. The distributor's function in this case is to finance and hold a stock of cars and a complementary stock of spares and parts, with which to supply dealers. The distributor could expect to receive an additional discount on retail sales. In a multi-tiered system, moreover, the dealer himself need not finance a stock of cars or parts, thereby acting more as an agent than a retailer proper. The system fails, however, if a distributor is unable to maintain adequate stocks or neglects to offer advice and guidance to the individual dealers — in which case the dealer, who has no direct access to the manufacturer, is left more or less high and dry. During the BL car shortage, in the early 1970s, distributors were liable to allocate the lion's share of their car stock to themselves, often 'starving' dealers in the process. Allowing for this weakness, the multi-tiered system does have certain advantages: left to their own devices, very few dealers would be able to maintain even minimal stocks of the necessary parts and spares.

FIGURE 14.11

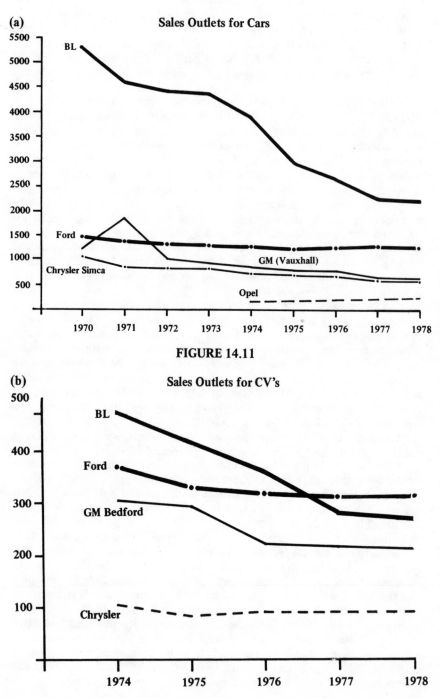

(a) Sales Outlets for Cars

BL

Ford

Chrysler Simca

GM (Vauxhall)

Opel

1970 1971 1972 1973 1974 1975 1976 1977 1978

FIGURE 14.11

(b) Sales Outlets for CV's

BL

Ford

GM Bedford

Chrysler

1974 1975 1976 1977 1978

352

TABLE 14.5

Sales per Outlet in 1977

	Number of Dealers	Average Sales per Outlet
a) Cars and light vans		
BL	2,250	143
Ford	1,260	302
Chrysler/Simca (cars only)	612	137
Chrysler/Simca (vans only)	477	11
GM (Vauxhall)	783	221
Opel	210	82
b) Other CVs		
BL	279	50
Ford	305	97
Chrysler	96	53
GM (Bedford)	216	75

Although Ford's distribution network (see Table 14.6) is dominated by the main dealers and distributors, it is nevertheless essentially a two-tier system. By the end of 1976, Chrysler had started to implement a direct dealer scheme: all Chrysler dealers are now considered to be direct dealers. GM have adopted

TABLE 14.6

Dealer Networks as at 1st January 1978 of the US Multinationals in the UK

	Main Dealers or Distributors	Retail Dealers	Direct Dealers	Total
Ford				
Cars	395	865		1,260
CVs	140	165		305
Chrysler/Simca				
Cars		170	442	612
Light Vans		28	449	477
Other CVs	87	9		96
GM (Vauxhall & Bedford)				
Cars			624	624
CVs			216	216
GM (Opel)				
Cars			210	210

Source: Franchise Networks, Sewell PIU, June 1978 with author's modifications.

the same policy for their Vauxhall dealer network, which has now been re-organised into a single-tier direct dealer system covering all 624 car franchise dealers.

Figures for total dealerships in either of the two tiers of the BL network have not been released. Table 14.7 (a) gives the 1974-5 totals of the two tier system which are the most recent firm figures available. Assuming that most of the dealers who have been dropped from the scheme since that time were smaller retail outlets, one can estimate the number of dealers still in operation in later years (see Tables 14.7 (b) and (c)). The Ryder Plan envisaged a reduction in the number of UK distributors to about 200 who would in turn supply roughly 600 retail outlets, with a further 1,000 direct dealerships – giving a total of approximately 1,800 sales outlets. By 1980, the reorganisation should be complete. Assuming a UK market of around 1.6 million cars and a domestic market share of over 30 per cent, this would yield a sales per outlet figure commensurate with the levels reached by Ford (i.e. around 300 cars per outlet).

In many respects, the Leyland philosophy is fairly logical. Prior to 1968, BL's dealer coverage was dangerously uneven. In some areas, the company was – if anything – over-represented with too many dealers carrying only a single model range (i.e. Jaguar, Rover Triumph, Austin or Morris). Table 14.8, for example, gives the number of BL outlets and their franchises in the Bristol area in 1975. Obviously, not all of the garages listed could be expected to carry the entire BL range, but those dealers able to market, say, both Austin and Morris models would be in a highly competitive position. BL's declared intention was to reduce overlap and wastage and to compact their dealer network into a smaller number of relatively large dealerships. Furthermore, there are a number of areas where BL is at the moment *under*-represented, and where the company might wish to create new dealerships. The CV dealer network has been similarly rationalised. Numbers have now fallen to roughly Ford and Vauxhall levels: any further contraction must be ruled out.

Dealers themselves have expressed mixed feelings about the Leyland moves. Of the 1,000 direct dealerships which the company expects to create, we estimate that roughly 400 will be drawn from the ranks of the distributors, while a further 400 will be upgraded from their existing retail status and the remaining 200 will be entirely new franchises. The retailers involved are obviously pleased with their newly acquired dealer status although some have expressed concern over the additional finance involved. The distributors – who have, in effect, been downgraded – are less enthusiastic about the change-over, arguing that their past loyalties have gone unrewarded and that they have tied up money in stocks for nothing. It might be argued that if the two-tier system had functioned more efficiently, the reorganisation would have been unnecessary. Although some dealers could lose money as a result, the direct dealer strategy would seem to be a sensible development.

If one of the contraction alternatives discussed in Chapter 7 is adopted, there could be a further reduction in the number of dealers. Table 14.9 gives a summary of a computer model built on various assumptions concerning market size and share and the number of cars sold per outlet (312 per outlet in 1980, and 350 per outlet in 1985 for *non* Jaguar/Daimler dealers; 50 cars

TABLE 14.7

BL's UK Distribution Networks for Cars

		Main Dealers or Distributors	Other Retail Outlets	Direct Dealers	Total
a)	As at 31st December 1974				
	Austin-Morris	363	2,292		2,655
	Rover/Triumph/Land-Rover	163	644		807
	Jaguar/Daimler	98	305		403
		624	3,241		3,865
b)	Estimated as at 31st December 1976				
	All brandnames	600	1,900		2,500
c)	Estimated as at 31st December 1977				
	All brandnames	580	1,670		2,250
d)	Ryder plan to be completed by 1980 (but now postponed)	200	600	1,000	1,800

per Jaguar/Daimler outlet). The results are not optimistic, but they do suggest that many dealers might be forced to leave the BL franchise if the company follows further along the Ford path without at the same time improving its market share. Radical reorganisation might even lead to a reversal of the present distribution strategy. If this were the case, the first four alternatives would involve only a minor drop in the number of dealers. In the two alternatives remaining, the number of dealers would probably not fall much below 1,000.

In our preferred strategy — separating the volume and specialist divisions — the question of distribution is left rather open. A return to the fully-fledged multi-tier system is unlikely. Distribution strategy might remain unchanged or could be marginally expanded to encompass the 1,800 dealers already targeted with a number of additional direct dealers affiliated to *either* the volume *or* the specialist division. Following Edwardes new plans with a concentration on short-run factors, any further reorganisation of the dealer network is likely to be postponed until the 1980's when new models come on stream.

Distribution Overseas

The US multinationals, with global distribution systems and good coverage throughout Europe, are adequately represented in the UK. As the CPRS report observed, this in itself presents a major potential strength for the UK industry, since creating a dealer network is both time conusming and expensive. BL's

TABLE 14.8

BL's Franchises in the Bristol Area circa 1975

Company	Austin	Morris	Rover	Triumph	Jaguar	Daimler	Land Rover	CV's
Company (abbrev.)								
Berkely Vale		✓						
Cannocks		✓						
Central		✓						
Clist and Rattle 1	✓							
Clist and Rattle 2		✓						
Cash and Son	✓		✓	✓				
Dutton-Forshaw		✓	D	D	✓	✓	D	
Harris		✓						
Henlys 1	D							
Henlys 2	✓							
Henlys 3	D		✓	✓	D	D	✓	
Henlys 4	✓							
Holdens	✓		✓	✓			✓	✓
JO-Bet		✓						
S O Kingiott	✓							
Lex Mead	✓	D	✓	✓	✓	✓	✓	
Lex Motor	✓	D						✓
Lex Tillaton								D
MWM			✓	✓			✓	✓
Pensford	✓							
Quality Cars		✓						
Regal	✓							
Shins		✓						
TT Motors	✓							
Tiley		✓						
Ubley		✓						
White Tree	✓							
Williams	✓	✓						

D = Franchise Distributor

coverage in Europe is poor: BL networks in Denmark, the Netherlands and Portugal are strong enough to be reasonably competitive, but elsewhere distribution is deficient in both number of outlets and quality of dealers. BL has only half as many outlets in Germany as its main import competitors. Average sales per dealer are less than one-fifth that of the Ford dealers. The French network is only just below full strength numerically, but many of the dealers are too small.

356

TABLE 14.9

Numbers of BL's Cars Dealers Under Various Alternatives

Option	Description	Domestic Market Share %	NUMBER OF DEALERS	
			1980 Market = 1.6 million cars	1985 Market = 1.7 million cars
1	Modified Ryder Plan	30%	1,653 – 1,961	1,791 – 2,117
2	As per 1 but using upgraded Allegro	25%	1,423 – 1,679	1,547 – 1,819
3	Curtailment of investment in vehicles at lower end of range	23%	1,330 – 1,566	1,449 – 1,691
4	Mini replacement abandoned in favour of minor changes to existing car	21%	1,238 – 1,453	1,352 – 1,580
5	Controlled withdrawal from volume cars	16%	1,007 – 1,171	1,107 – 1,281
6	Rapid withdrawal from volume cars	10%	730 – 833	814 – 923

NB The option numbers of the alternatives refer to those given in Chapter 7 (Table 7.11). Under Michael Edwardes' new regime an attempt will be made to maintain the number of dealers at its current level (2,250).

One of the problems in building up the dealer network within Europe hinges upon the poor reputation of BL's volume products. Although a better reputation is enjoyed by specialist cars, they are generally sold, in common with volume products, by the poorer dealer. A way round this problem, would be to joint franchise them or develop exclusive franchises for specialised products. Since dealers selling volume cars can only be retained by also selling specialist cars, either of the above two strategies would lead to a deterioration in volume car sales. The only course open to BL is to improve its volume cars and dealer network simultaneously, or alternatively, to drop volume cars.

In the major North American market, BL has made strenuous efforts to improve its distribution network, halving the number of outlets (now just under 700) while encouraging more of the remaining dealers to carry the full BL export range. As a result, sales per outlet have doubled although they still compare unfavourably with other European producers selling in the US market. The dealers themselves have found it difficult to overcome the major problems of erratic or non-existent supply — a factor which has contributed in large measure to BL's loss of international market share.

The problem with the North American market is that legislative requirements make product development costs expensive. In addition, increased competition from the Japanese and from US manufacturers, who are actively 'downsizing' their innovations, are making conditions difficult for the US dealer network. In fact, sales are dependent upon the MGB and the less successful TR7. The MGB is an old product line and one that BL may discontinue. If this happened, BL would be certain to lose its profitable dealer network.

On the CV side, Leyland's distribution overseas is generally good, although European representation is still very much below par — an omission highlighted by the Ryder Report. Although the position can and will be greatly improved, a fully adequate CV distribution network will take some time to establish and is partly dependent upon the introduction and proving of the new range of trucks.

CONCLUSION

The three US multinationals have now developed well-defined marketing strategies, most of them based on the assumption that competition in the immediate future will centre on an aggressive model policy rather than a price war. BL, meanwhile, is pursuing the Ryder policy line on marketing, in which the Supercover strategy is a more positive approach, although the marketing policy overall has been weakened by decisions on model policy and distribution. Although *ceteris paribus* plans for the new distribution network are logical in objective and implementation, the loss of market share incurred in shedding dealers has not been fully appreciated or understood in terms of the Ryder Report. Sooner or later the distribution network would have to be rationalised. In normal circumstances one might expect BL to have waited until it had a stronger model policy before undertaking any major restructuring in its distribution/dealer network. As it is, over a third of the disenfranchised

BL dealers have transferred their spurned allegiances to foreign competitors. In doing so, they are selling a stronger volume product range than BL can hope to have for some years to come. This strategy has now been reversed and BL is now hanging on to all its cherished dealers. Of course, if the proposed merger between Citroen-Peugeot and Chrysler goes ahead, on the basis of the group's current strategy there will be a certain amount of autonomy for the new management of Chrysler. Exactly how much autonomy is still unclear. Despite claims to the contrary some rationalisation of the dealer network is inevitable.

APPENDIX 14.1

A STATISTICAL ANALYSIS OF MARKETING CONSIDERATIONS

This appendix attempts to summarise the results of statistical analysis on various marketing considerations.

A recent discussion by Cubbin and Leech[1] illustrates the more quantitative factors involved in marketing. The authors attempted to quantify the sensitivity of consumers demand for cars to a whole series of factors. The estimates were derived using cross section data on sales and the rate of change of sales between 1974 and 1975, (using sample data for one year).

Their theoretical model was specified in terms of the demand for a particular model being a function of a number of marketing variables, viz:

$$Q_i = f(P_i, X_i, A_i, M) \hspace{3cm} 14.1$$

where Q_i is the demand for model i

P_i is the price of model i

X_i = a list of attributes of the model or conditions surrounding its sale

A_i = the extent to which the model is advertised

M = total size of market

In equation 14.2, the term X_iB can be viewed as the predicted level of price for model i and $(P_i - X_iB)$ is the actual level of P_i minus its predicted level X_iB, which can be given by the residual from the regression of P on X. Difference in running costs can be allowed for by regressing these other costs on the set of characteristics and using the residual as a measure of the relative running costs of the model in question. The variable M was ignored because the study only considered a single time period (i.e. fixed M). The problem with the model in 14.1 is that the list of attributes (X) is potentially so large that the number of degrees of freedom becomes small. The solution to this problem was to use a single variable, quantity-adjusted price[2] instead of taking price and a list of attributes as the explanatory variables. Equation 14.1 can then be transformed to:

1. *Import Penetration in the UK Passenger Car Market: A Cross Section Study* by J. Cubbin and D. Leech, *Applied Economics* December 1978.
2. *'Quality Change and Pricing Behaviour in the UK Car Industry, 1956-1968'* by K.G. Cowling and J.S. Cubbin, *Economica*, 42, 1975, pp. 43-58.

$$Q_i = g \, [(P_i - X_i\beta), X_i^o, A_i] \hspace{4cm} 14.2$$

where X^o is a subject of the characteristics of X which is sufficient to define the market segment of each model

        $X_i\beta$ the average price one would expect to pay for model i with the particular set of characteristics X_i

        P_i is the actual price of model i

        $(P-X\beta)$ is the quality-adjusted price of each model

        β is the estimated coefficient obtained by regressing price on the X characteristic for the sample of cars offered for sale. NB the coefficient β_j represents the extra price asked on average for one extra unit of characteristic j.

Table A14.1 shows the averages of the explanatory variables. The data was split up into a British produced models only and imported models only — the latter being subdivided into a 'SMMT' sample and a *'Motoring Which?'* sample.[1] The actual demand equation estimated was (invector format):

$$\log Q_i = \beta_0 + \beta_1 \log P_i + \beta_2 MPG_i + \beta_3 IG_i + \beta_4 A_i + \beta_5 \log ND$$
$$+ \beta_6 Di + \beta_7 AOR_i + \beta_8 NV_i + \beta_9 G_i + \beta_{10} E_i + error.$$

where:

Q	=	quantity
P	=	price
MPG	=	miles per gallon
IG	=	insurance group
A	=	advertising expenditure
ND	=	number of dealers
D	=	delivery date
AOR	=	average number of days per year spent off the road in a garage for repairs
NV	=	number of variants of the same model
G	=	guarantee
E	=	number of extras

In addition a variable dealing with 'the number of years since a model has been introduced' was incorporated into the equation in a number of different ways.

The regression results produced an estimate of price elasticity between -2 and -5. Not surprisingly, MPG, as a measure for final economy, was significant, while insurance groups appeared not to have any perceptible effect in explaining short term changes in 1974/75 but was significant in the longer run

---

1.   The 'SMMT' sample contains data relating to those popular saloons for which new registration figures were available. The *Motoring Which?* sample contains all British models in the 'SMMT' sample but a subset of the imported sample. (*Motoring Which?* provided the reliability data.)

TABLE A14.1

Averages of Explanatory Variables

	British Models	Imported Models	
		"SMMT" sample	"Which?" sample
Delivery (weeks)	3.5	3.8	3.6
Guarantee (months)	12	9.2	8.6
Yrs. Intro.	6.8	4.9	5.3
Range	7.9	4.3	4.9
Ins. Group[a]	-0.14	0.0004	-0.22
MPG[a]	0.37	-0.17	0.51
log price[a]	0.04	-0.01	0.0001
No. of dealers	1315	282	316
Advertising (£000's)	403	106	142
No. of extras	3.4	3.5	3.3
Av. off Road (days per year)	2.9	–	1.4

Source: Cubbin and Leech, *op. cit.*

a. Denotes quality adjusted variables which are measured as the residual from the regression of the variable on quality characteristics.

level of sales.

Of the five quality variables (delivery, reliability, product range, guarantee period, numbers of extras), delivery was statistically insignificant. A surprising result, due probably to the choice of date period in which there was substantial excess capacity, and a time in which the extent of lost production through strikes were small. Cubbin and Leech take a slightly different view and maintain that it puts the 'recent publicity about the importance of lost production through strikes into proper perspective'.[1]

However, the proverbial problem that has been experienced by, for example, BL, is excess supply of certain models and long delivery times of other models.

Both 'guarantee' and 'numbers of extras' were also insignificant. The fourth quality variable, 'Average number of days off the road', is a measure of reliability and was statistically significant. 'Product range' was also significant.

Of the remaining variables, the size of the distribution network and advertising were both highly significant. Cubbin and Leech had mixed feelings about the explanatory variable 'Years introduced'. This variable was included to test the hypothesis that consumers prefer newer models − a theory advanced by the CPRS as a reason for the success of Japanese cars. The author's conclusion was that the age of a model is not a serious factor. However, this result is clearly at odds with certain volume models (e.g. Volkswagen's recovery was due to the introduction of new models.)[2] The statistical insignificance may be due to high order multicollinearity or to the fact that 'years introduced' acts as a proxy variable for the model's reputation.

Cubbin and Leech then produced an interesting analysis of the policy implications for firms selling to the UK car market. The profitability of a quality variation was made possible by examining the first-order condition for profit maximisation with respect to a quality characteristic, Z:

$$ \mu_z \left[\frac{P - MC}{P} \right] = \frac{1}{P} \frac{\delta AC}{Z} \qquad\qquad 14.3 $$

where P   is the price of output
MC   is the marginal cost
$\frac{\delta AC}{\delta Z}$ is the effect on average cost of a unit change in Z

$$ Z = \frac{Q}{Z} \cdot \frac{1}{Q} $$

which is the proportional increase in sales when Z is increased one unit.

The results of their policy conclusions are shown in Table A14.2. It is, for example, worth improving delivery dates by one week if this increases costs by more than ½ per cent of the selling price. Reliability and insurance groups seem to be particularly important. However, the conclusion about delivery dates has already been criticised. The insurance groups conclusion is puzzling. Perhaps this variable is picking up the effects of improving safety and reducing the cost of spares, which may result in a cheaper insurance rating.

1. A pre-publication comment by Cubbin and Leech points out that one reason why delivery date is insignificant may be that *What Car* figures (on which the delivery date was based) may be misleading. Another reason maybe that it is in prestige cars where the problem is greatest, and these were not included in Cubbin and Leech's sample.

2. A pre-publication comment by Cubbin and Leech argues that it is the purpose of statistical analysis to check this sort of generalisation. They agree however, that older models may not be able to easily incorporate technical advances which may lead to more desirable characteristics or provide better value for money.

The authors concluded that profitability may be increased by increased expenditure on advertising. Assuming the objective of profit maximisation and an import penetration of 35 per cent, they felt that an optimal advertising expenditure for UK manufacturers as a whole was 4 per cent of sales revenue.

The final conclusion of the paper noted that the variable's which had been most important in recent changes in market share were: fuel, economy, price, advertising and reliability. Of these the change that would be most likely to be profitable appeared to be the improvement of reliability.

TABLE A14.2

Values of the Increase in Average Cost it Would Be Worth Incurring in Order to Generate Extra Sales

Change in quality proposed	Increase in cost as a percentage of price to manufacturer that would lead to break even
1. Improve delivery date by one week	0.6%
2. Increase guarantee period by one month	0.75%
3. Reduce agerage age of model by one year	0.1%
4. Get car into next insurance group down	4.9%
5. Improve fuel economy by 1 MPG	0.1%
6. Provide the typical extras as an option rather than 'built in'	0.75%
7. Increase reliability so as to reduce the average number of days off the road by one	3.1%

NB This table should be regarded as illustrative and giving orders of magnitude only, especially in view of the non-significance of some of the coefficients. The table assumes a price-cost margin of 12 per cent which is not substantially altered by the proposed quality change and that firms do not collude to restrict quality improvements.

CHAPTER 15

PROBLEMS FACING THE RETAIL MOTOR TRADER

It is often forgotten that a significant proportion of the UK motor industry is taken up with the retail side. Whether vehicles and parts are manufactured in the UK or imported, they must still be sold through retail outlets, which in themselves are a major source of employment in the UK. Problems affecting the UK manufacturers have inevitable repercussions for the retailers quite apart from the difficulties peculiar to the retail trade itself.

It must be remembered that roughly 450,000 people are employed directly in the business of selling, repairing and maintaining vehicles, while the number of these employed in related (if non-specific) retail activities is on the increase as more outlets are drawn into the supply of vehicle parts and accessories. On the whole, the retail industry is largely unaffected by the question of import penetration, since vehicles must be sold and maintained wherever they come from. Proprietors of many of the more successful garages were quick to see the advantages to be gained in switching from a domestic manufacturer to an importer, earning themselves fortunes in the process. Elsewhere, garages specialising in the supply of parts and accessories or exploiting certain closely defined marketing gaps appear to have done well. But the fact remains that the retail side of the motor industry in the UK is facing mounting pressure at the moment. In this chapter we examine these pressures and consider a number of possibilities for new developments within the industry.

FUNCTIONS OF A RETAILER

The retailer is expected to perform a number of diverse functions, involving new vehicle sales, used vehicle sales (often conducted as two quite separate operations), sales of spare parts and accessories, vehicle maintenance, servicing and repair, and forecourt services. Any one of these functions can be affected in a particular way by changes in the economic climate. A slower rate of growth in the new vehicle market, for example, might persuade a retailer to concentrate more of his resources on sales of used vehicles. Similarly, the health of the UK manufacturers will critically affect the choice of franchise — a choice which has bedevilled many motor traders in the last few years, and which we will discuss later in the chapter.

Used vehicle sales (shown in Figure 15.1) have been running at almost twice the level of new vehicles sales for a number of years. In 1976, total after-sales vehicles parts replacement trade was estimated at around £1,500 million. Table 15.1(a) gives a breakdown of approximate market segments in 1976; specific sales volumes are listed in Table 15.1(b), giving some indication of the size of the parts market. Although new vehicles have the highest turnover, sales of used cars and parts are not far behind, and may soon catch up if there is little growth in new vehicles sales.

STRUCTURE OF THE INDUSTRY

Traditionally, the retail industry is based on the franchised garage. Although the specialist retailers (selling exhausts, tyres or batteries, for example), super and hypermarkets have now acquired a substantial share of the retail side of the UK motor industry, the franchised garage still dominates the retail side of the UK motor industry, but there have been major changes within this sector. The number of UK car dealers has fallen dramatically in the last few years, from well over 14,000 in the 1960s, to around 9,000 in 1978, with a similar decline in the number of CV dealers (see Table 14.2). The number of garages holding importer franchises steadily increased during the late 1960s and early 1970s. By 1973, the retail networks were substantially complete. Figure 15.2 illustrates the change in the number of dealers by principal manufacturing bloc. Overall, the number of West European (non-UK) dealers dropped marginally between 1973 and 1976; the DAF car dealership network was wound up[1] and the BMW, Fiat, Mercedes, VW and Saab networks were slightly reduced in size. Citroen, Peugeot, Renault and Volvo, on the other hand, managed to increase the size of their dealer networks. East European dealer franchises declined, but there has been phenomenal and continuing growth in the number of dealers offering Japanese models.

The number of West European dealers will probably decline further, as the various networks retrench, although this will to some extent depend on the fate of the various manufacturers, a problem we will return to later in the chapter. Some contraction is almost certain to occur in the Peugeot and Citroen networks, and possibly in the Saab/Volvo network, should their merger finally come off. The number of East European model outlets should grow as the Lada/Moskovitch network expands. The Japanese dealer network is apparently still in the process of expanding and could grow further with the addition of separate Subaru and Daihatsu networks, although both of the companies involved are in fact part of the Nissan (Datsun) and Toyota groups, respectively.

On the CV side, the decline in the number of UK manufacturers' franchises has not been so dramatic. At the moment, UK producers selling in the medium-to heavy-weight truck sector only, face competition from West European manufacturers, most of whom have expanded their retail networks in the last few years. During the 1980s, one can expect to see a growing number of CV imports from Japan and Eastern Europe, which would certainly involve the creation of new and probably distinct CV franchises.

The present structure of the various car retail networks is shown in Table 15.3, giving the average number of sales per dealer for each of the manufacturers. Ford lead the field with the highest volume of retail sales per outlet, followed at some distance by Datsun. Generally, other importers show relatively poor average sales per outlet, with the exception of Fiat, Renault and VW.

---

1.   Following the takeover of DAF cars by Volvo.

FIGURE 15.1

Used Vehicle Sales

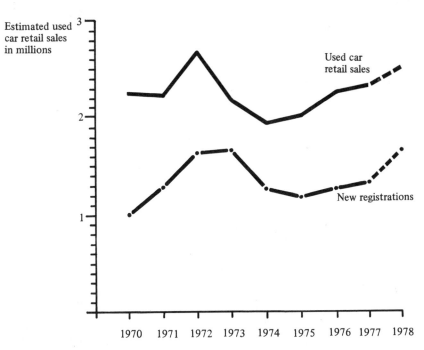

Source: Glass's Guide

NB According to the Motor Agent's Association's monthly statistical review about 2.8 million used cars changed hands each year in the UK.

Table 15.4 gives the number of outlets and average sales per outlet for the CV market. Predictably, CV sales volumes are much lower than car sales, with Volvo, Ford, GM and Seddon/Atkinson well ahead of the rest of the field in average sales per outlet.[1] In general terms, importers show a much lower average number of sales per outlet than the UK manufacturers – a pleasing, if solitary, exception to the usual rule!

When we considered the drastic reorganisation of British Leyland's dealer network in the previous chapter, some of the conclusions seemed to suggest that there was no direct relationship between the health of the particular manufacturer (perhaps measured in market shares) and the number of retail

---

1. Some manufacturers however either sell direct from the factory or have their own sales depots which are not included in the figures embodied in Table 15.4.

TABLE 15.1

a)   After Sales Parts Market for 1976

Segment	Size (£ million)
Tyres	450
Batteries	105
Electrics/lighting	150
Exhaust systems	75
Engine parts	120
Filters	60
Brakes	75
Cooling systems	150
Bodywork	150
Accessories	165

b)   Specific Sales Volumes for 1976

Segment	Size (£ million)
In car entertainment	35
Wing mirrors	15
Auto-books	10
Shock absorbers	12
Polishes	29
'Extra lamps'	10
Fastmoving service lines (e.g. plugs, filters)	200
Car care accessories (e.g. chemicals etc.)	85
Bolt-on 'goodies'	62

Source: Parts and Accessory Marketing Statistics, Sewell's Profit Information Unit

outlets. However, the ratio of retail outlets to market shares in the UK for the years 1974, and 1976 is shown in Table 15.5, giving a clear indication that the number of dealers is inextricably linked with the size of the domestic market share — a correlation coefficient between the two of .92.[1] There are, of course, a few notable exceptions: Fiat, Mercedes-Benz, Skoda, Toyota, VW and a lone UK producer — Vauxhall — all slightly reduced the size of their various dealer networks while increasing their respective market shares. Renault, on the other hand, expanded its dealer network but failed to increase its share of the domestic market. Vauxhall's apparent success is a little misleading. The company's market share had in fact fallen. An uncompetitive model range left Vauxhall grossly over-endowed with dealers when compared with the 7 to 8 per cent market share achieved, but by 1976 the success of the new Chevette and Cavalier models had reversed the trend.

1.   The equivalent correlation coefficient of CV dealers is smaller, and that for heavy CVs smaller still (about .7).

TABLE 15.2

UK Car Outlets

	1967	1969	1973	1976	1977	1980 forecast	1985 forecast
BL	6,700[a]	5,500[a]	4,500[a]	2,600[a]	2,250[a]	2,000[b]	1,900[b]
Chrysler	2,725	1,749	822	646	612	600	500
Ford	1,682	1,609	1,280	1,242	1,260	1,300	1,250
Vauxhall	1,400	1,298	912	783	624	650	650
	12,507	10,156	7,541	5,178	4,746	4,550	4,300
Other UK			500	168[a]	100[a]	150	120
Importers	N/A	N/A	3,729	4,172	4,391	4,750	4,700
Total dealers			11,270	9,518	9,237	9,450	9,120

a. Estimated
b. Forecast as under old Ryder Plans, the new Edwardes plan may see little change over the 1978 dealership levels implying some switching dealers away from BL and some new BL dealerships being created. Ryder Plan may then be implemented in mid to late 1980s and might even be scrapped altogether.

NB 1980 and 1985 assumes Chrysler UK and BL remain in current form. If the proposed Chrysler/Citroen-Peugeot merger goes ahead some 200+ dealers may be shed.

FIGURE 15.2

Recent Trends in the UK Car Outlets

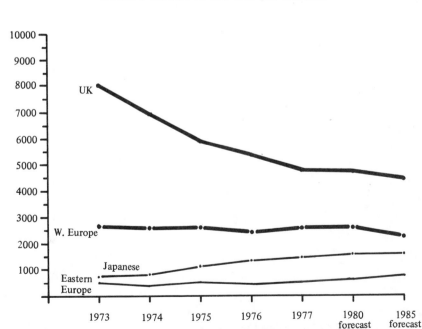

TABLE 15.3

British Car Networks

	Car Networks as at 1 January 1977	Average Sales per Outlet in 1976
BL	2500 (estimated)	154
Chrysler Cars	646	134
Light Vans	465	11
Ford	1242	296
GM (Vauxhall)	632	172
Lotus	25	22
Reliant	75	13
Rolls- Royce	75	19
	5195	182
Alfa Romeo	106	84
BMW	141	61
Citroen	208	103
Colt	192	36
Datsun	360	213
Diat	333	153
Honda	243	60
Lada/Moskovitch	150	62
Mazda	231	53
Mercedes Benz	92	63
Opel	185	86
Peugeot	180	99
Polski-Fiat	80	27
Porsche	18	18
Renault	382	153
Saab	198	33
Skoda	270	35
Toyota	252	86
VW/Audi	341	140
Volvo	210	107
	4145	102

Source: Sewell's Profit Information Unit

TABLE 15.4

British CV Networks

	CV Networks as at January 1 1977	Average Sales per Outlet in 1976 (selected light vans)
Vauxhall (Bedford)	221	76
Chrysler UK	92	51
Foden	21	47
Ford	306	83
BL	357	35
Seddon/Atkinson	35	76
	1032	64
MAN	29	13
DAF	21	46
Fiat	25	26
Magirus Deutz	23	20
Mercedes Benz	33	42
Saviem	17	9
Scania	24	33
Volvo	28	95
	200	45

Source: Sewell's Profit Information Unit

N.B. Some manufacturers have their own sales depots or sell direct from the factory.

Choice of Manufacturer

Viewed from another perspective, the fortunes of a particular manufacturer are a source of constant concern for the dealer. A weak manufacturer may be unable to produce a competitive range, thus relinquishing a share of the domestic market, which will, in turn, mean fewer sales for the dealer. Or the manufacturer may choose to reduce the size of the dealer network. Dealers must take both possibilities into consideration when assessing the strength of a producer and the possible or probable weaknesses.

European manufacturers share a number of common problems. For example, although the North American and West European markets are of roughly comparable size, the US market supports only three major manufacturers, while the West European market is divided up amongst *fourteen* indigenous producers.[1] Table 15.6 itemises this and the many other problems already discussed (see Chapter 4 and *passim*). The Japanese producers may also experience difficulties. There is a growing resistance in Europe to the idea of unlimited Japanese exports to the West without some sort of reciprocal agreement on Western sales in Japan. Some of the newer producers — the South Koreans, the Communist Bloc manufacturers and the newly independent South American firms — could present a more attractive proposition to the troubled dealer looking for a more profitable franchise.

TABLE 15.5

Relationship between Dealers and Market Shares

	Number of Dealers			Market Shares		
	1974	1977	Change %	1974%	1977%	Change %
BL	3,865	2,500	-35.3	32.7	27.4	-16.2
Chrysler	737	646	-12.4	10.8	6.5	-40.5
Ford	1,258	1,242	-1.3	29,6	25.3	-14.6
Vauxhall	862	632	-26.7	7.3	9.1	24.7
Alfa-Romeo	77	106	37.7	0.3	0.6	93.6
BMW	150	141	- 6	0.5	0.7	40.2
Citroen	168	208	23.8	1.3	1.6	28.5
Colt	0	192	—	0	0.5	—
Datsun	292	360	23.3	4.6	5.4	15.7
Fiat	351	333	-5.1	3.4	3.8	10.0
Honda	129	243	88.4	0.3	1.0	305.0
Mazda	158	231	46.2	0.6	0.8	30.6
Mercedes Benz	96	92	-4.2	0.4	0.5	28.7
Opel	170	185	8.8	0.7	1.2	86.2
Peugeot	172	180	4.7	1.0	1.4	36.3
Polski-Fiat	0	80	—	0	0.1	140.0
Renault	360	382	6.1	4.5	4.4	-1.8
Saab	229	198	-13.5	0.6	0.5	-6.3
Skoda	320	270	-15.6	0.5	0.7	47.0
Toyota	254	252	-0.8	1.2	1.7	47.3
VW/Audi	355	341	-3.9	3.1	3.4	11.3
Volvo	190	210	10.5	1.4	1.8	29.7

1.   Although this is not to say that the US figure is the optimum for European conditions.

At the moment however, most of the franchises in the UK are West European, and we will therefore examine them in greater detail.

Excess capacity, high cost structures and lack of resources demand a fundamental change in the structure of the West European motor industry. The dictates of scale economies suggest that a viable West European motor industry might consist of four or five major manufacturers with a joint capacity for at least two million cars and a significant CV capacity, with room for perhaps one or two smaller-scale or specialist producers. Traditional solutions to the problems of a fragmented industry involve either allowing inefficient manufacturers to collapse or encouraging mergers to form larger, more integrated units. European governments, on the whole, have been anxious to maintain existing levels of employment and have therefore preferred state aid to rescue ailing firms: British Leyland, VW, Peugeot-Citroen, BMW and Volvo have all been bailed out to a greater or lesser extent. There is very little likelihood that any national government would now be prepared (or could afford) to countenance the collapse of a major industrial concern. The alternative merger strategy has been pursued principally along nationalistic lines, although possibilities for further mergers are now strictly limited, as it would seem that most of the possible permutations have been exhausted. The proposed Chrysler link-up with Peugeot-Citroen may however, set a new precedent for multinational mergers within Europe.

New solutions to the problem have emerged. There is growing enthusiasm for the concept of more or less continuous government support for the industry, for which British Leyland and Alfa-Romeo have established a conspicuous precedent. A second possibility involves the use of a functional merger approach, whereby several independent manufacturers agree on joint development and/or production of a major component (i.e. the Peugeot-Volvo-Renault agreement on joint production of the Douvrin engine range) or co-operate in the marketing of each other's products. To date, functional mergers have not been entirely successful. The Club of Four project, to develop jointly a medium weight truck for example, has more or less foundered in a morass of conflicting interests. Of the four participants – Daf, Saviem, Magirus-Deutz and Volvo – Magirus-Deutz joined the Iveco (Fiat) group, while Daf relinquished part ownership of its CV operation to the International Harvester concern. Saviem (Renault) meanwhile merged with the Citroen CV division, Berliet, who were already producing a medium weight truck range! Similarly, the Douvrin engine has been criticised as a 'committee' engine, jack of all trades, master of none, and making very little in the way of a contribution to the particular needs and objectives of the various companies concerned. Nevertheless, a number of strong links between manufacturers already exist, and there is no evidence to suggest that they will be severed in the immediate future. Manufacturers, after all, share a common concern and face the same problems. They must be prepared to co-operate, particularly in the development and production of powertrain, axles and suspension systems.

Apart from across-the-board integration of the industry as a whole, there are possibilities for further effective rationalisation *within* many of the existing companies. Components used by a number of different firms, for example, could be manufactured by one producer on a scale large enough to supply

TABLE 15.6

Problems Facing the European Manufacturer

Problem	Explanation
Increased import penetration	Cheap new producers (e.g. Communist Bloc Countries)
Reduced exports	Traditional market coming under attack from new producers
Increased competitive pressure	The result of slower growth in addition to the two factors above. Effect will be to reduce profitability
Labour problems	Shorter week, increased living standards, less boring work, coupled with the union activity to prevent the export of assembly capacity aborad
Insufficient scale to compete effectively	A superficial comparison with the US motor industry would lead to between 3 and 4 European manufacturers
Government controls	Ultimate effect will be costly
Lower level of automation compared with Japanese or US rivals	Massive capital expenditure required
New technology	Again, high capital expenditure required

several companies at a lower cost than if they were to produce the same component themselves. In this way, each firm would then benefit from the economies of scale achieved without actually entering into a fully-fledged merger agreement. This arrangement has in fact operated for some years in the UK, enabling many of the smaller producers (particularly the CV producers) to survive when they might otherwise have collapsed.

In reality, however, vertical integration will probably increase rather than diminish. Many of the car manufacturers have been looking greedily at the profits made by the components industry, and it would not be altogether surprising if the car firms sought to extend their domain into more component manufacture in the hope of grabbing a slice of the component-makers' profits. In France and Germany this move into component production is already under way.

Table 15.7 suggests a possible scenario of eventualities — excluding functional mergers — categorised by type of solution Table 15.8 examines each company on a country-by-country basis. Both these tables incorporate fairly pessimistic projections for European specialist manufacturers. Daimler-Benz

TABLE 15.7

Future Scenarios

Type of Solution	Company	Comment
Propping up of firm by means of Government cash aid	Chrysler (Europe)	Next depression coupled with stylistic obsolescence of new models. Parts of UK plant will still require Government assistance notwithstanding the merger with Peugeot-Citroen
	Fiat	After a bout of industrial unrest coupled to a depressed Italian economy.
	Peugeot-Citroen	Lack of rationalisation and/or insufficient funds to carry out further rationalisation – Chrysler (Europe) may be more than the management can handle.
	Volkswagen	Public institution argument, most unlikely though.
	Volvo	Norwegian deal collapsed, but technical link-up with VW and Porsche may help.
	Saab	A possibility
Mopping up of smaller firms	UK small car producers	Unsympathetic current Government, foreign concerns seeking top end may be tempted, though unlikely.
	UK small CV manufacturers	Between now and 1985 – extremely likely, although there will always be room for a few small independent manufacturers.
	Porsche	Change in technology will provide a capital expenditure hurdle which may mean takeover, possible candidate is VW.
	MAN	Possible link to VW
	BMW	At the moment would complement VW. BMW will only merge when forced to from financial considerations which may not occur.
	Saab-Scania Volvo	Despite the recent abortive merger a long term possibility is the merger of the two firms coupled with government cash aid.
Larger Mergers (Nationalistic Lines)	VW-MAN-BMW-Daimler-Benz	Commented on above
	Peugeot-Citroen-Chrysler	See Chapter 17
	BMW-Daimler-Benz	Unlikely – too close a product
	Volvo-Saab	Likely as discussed above
	Renault-Peugeot-Citroen-Chrysler	A logical long term development for the French motor industry
	Fiat-Alfa Romeo	Alfa Romeo too small to be viable on its own. Some political pressure for nationalisation at moment. Probably a longer term development.

has been the most consistent profitable European manufacturer. Other European companies will attempt to emulate Daimler-Benz's strategy thereby securing some of Daimler-Benz's profits. Whilst Daimler-Benz may be able to withstand such an onslaught some specialist manufacturers might have to be content with smaller profits or may take ill-advised retaliatory action which could be unprofitable. Either way the future must be less certain.

Rationalisation of Distribution Networks

Further concentration of the French industry (Peugeot-Citroen and Chrysler plus the further long term possibility of Renault) will mean some rationalisation of dealer networks. This could also occur in the event of a Volvo-Saab merger. Possible mergers in the West German industry, however, are less likely to involve a substantial reorganisation of the respective retail outlets. A merger between Fiat and Alfa-Romeo would certainly involve a major reorganisation, but the possibility of such a merger at the moment is remote. The effect of alternative plans on the future organisation of the BL network has already been discussed in the preceding chapter.

Multi-franchise

Far more so now than in the past, the motor dealer must keep a close eye on his supplier, and be prepared to switch franchises if necessary. One possibility could be the development of the multi-franchise. If this were coupled with a swing to smaller, more basic cars in times of depression — a feature of the saturated market and one lesson, at least, to be learned from the US market — the optimal strategy would certainly be a dual franchise, whereby a single dealer could offer a range of cheap, basic imports and/or quality product. With only one possible franchise available, a dealer would be advised to choose a manufacturer offering a wide range of products.

Other Retail Operations

As a vehicle market matures, so new vehicle sales become relatively less important than the other functions of a retail motor outlet. Used car sales, parts, accessories and servicing are all growth areas, yet the motor trader — by and large — has not responded well to this shift in emphasis, preferring to operate, Canute-like, in a more traditional manner. The traders' sins of omission have granted free access to the lucrative motor market to other forms of retail organisation, all of whom have been quick to benefit from the changing conditions. In the remainder of this chapter we examine the problems and challenges now facing the motor dealer.

MARKETING PROBLEMS FOR THE RETAILER
Do-It-Yourself

The growing interest in DIY has obviously affected the retailer's earnings. Roughly 16.5 per cent of the total £1,500 million parts market is accounted

TABLE 15.8

Country by Country Projection

Country	Company	Projected Action	Comment
UK	GM(Vauxhall)	Becomes assembly plant of Opel on its car side	UK has benefit of Bedford which is GM's European CV company
	Ford		Continues current coherent strategy
	Chrysler	1) Possible future contraction 2) Further Government aid (with Japanese takeover of most inefficient plants)	Likely late 1980s, notwithstanding the Peugeot-Citroen takeover.
	British Leyland	Ryder report put into action: If BL loses market share (down to the 14-22%) then BL will become a non-volume producer	Some sections will be profitable, others may achieve 'Concorde' status
	Smaller CV Manufacturers	Mopped up by larger foreign manufacturers	
	Smaller Car Manufacturers	Small amount of mopping up for others, closures	Highly dependent on US market for survival. Ability to finance the necessary changes in technology required to meet successively more stringent US regulations is questionable
France	Renault	Small expansion	Renault's objective is to break-even rather than make profits
	Peugeot-Citroen	1) Will require finance 2) May be rationalised with Renault	Peugeot has traditionally always had close links with Renault
	Chrysler	May survive whilst Chrysler (UK) collapses or contracts	Long term future not good. French Government more likely to support Peugeot-Citroen than Chrysler
Sweden	Volvo Saab	Declining market, large capital expenditure requirements will force parents companies to a) merge b) get Government backing	Daf operations will be a continuing problem, though Norwegian finance has provided Volvo with a breathing space
Spain	Seat	If anything expansion may occur	Has taken over BL's old Authi plant
West Germany	VW	Will survive. Possible major partner in merger with some of below. Possibility of State finance in emergency	US plant may not be such an ideal solution to dwindling US exports problem — caused partly by Japanese competition
	Daimler-Benz	Likely to survive as independent yet merger should not be ruled out	Spending £1.3b on investment in cars before 1980. Most profitable European company. Attempts by other companies to emulate Daimler-Benz may cause problems
	BMW	In theory merger or collapse likely. In practice BMW still extremely profitable	Seems unlikely now but it is a fairly logical conclusion for the 1980s+. One mistake could easily sap profits
	MAN	Merger with VW or Daimler-Benz	VW most likely
	Porsche	Continued independence or merger with VW	
Italy	Alfa Romeo		Continued substantial drain on Government
	Fiat	1) State takeover	Logical long term development
		2) State aid	Likely at some point. Fiat is almost a national institution. Ultimately if this occurs, Alfa Romeo and Fiat (cars & CVs) might merge

for by DIY purchases, and the share is much higher in certain market segments. Forty per cent of the fast-moving service line parts, 49 per cent of the bolt-on 'goodies' and 87 per cent of car accessories are supplied to the DIY market. DIY suppliers have also changed. In 1970, approximately 80 per cent of DIY needs were met by garage outlets. By 1976, however, this share had plummeted to around 9 per cent. DIY car servicing has increased in every market sector, but particularly in the higher income groups, where real incomes have been particularly hard hit in recent years, although skilled manual workers and blue collar workers still comprise the major DIY market.

As the costs of labour-intensive garage servicing continue to rise, growth in DIY will be commensurate, but garages should make every effort to adopt to the changing requirements of the consumer by supplying parts and advice, and — where appropriate — the use of specialist tools not otherwise available to the 'home' mechanic. The decline in the number of private car owners who are prepared to pay for garage servicing may be offset by increased use of garaging and servicing facilities by business users, who could be less inclined to employ their own mechanics. Loss of trade to the DIY enthusiasts may be compensated for by increased business usage.

The Specialist and Non-traditional Retail Outlet

The franchised dealer and the garage proprietor have both seen their trade eroded by the proliferation of supermarkets and high street shops selling spare parts, the specialist tyre retailers and the exhaust, suspension, brake and electrical/in-car-entertainment centres or specialists. Mobile services — engine tuning and windscreen replacement, for example — are also taking a growing proportion of the market. Table 15.9 confirms this move away from the traditional source, in sales of one particular commodity. In general, the specialist retailer has been a principal beneficiary in this transition, although the motoring supermarkets have had the highest rate of growth.

Specialist retailers have already seen one period of considerable expansion, first with tyre retailers, then exhaust systems, then electrical specialists and so on. Their success depends partly on having a uniform and easily manageable stock, offering a rapid, while-you-wait service unhampered by long checking-in procedures at job reception and occasionally providing a cheaper alternative to garage servicing. Garages can meet this threat in one of four ways. First, they can develop specialist units — alongside the more conventional garage workshop — in which normal reception procedures can be circumvented for those repairs requiring only the use of the specialist unit. A more interesting alternative to this species of head-on competition could involve offering a maintenance contract covering all items on a car — the sort of contract already used by manufacturers of other consumer durables such as refrigerators. On the whole, garage owners have shown very little initiative on this front. Few proprietors are interested in discussing the possibility of a maintenance contract, and yet it could prove their salvation. Contracts might, for example, be offered with the option of a substitute hire car if the owners vehicle is off the road for any length of time. Workshop managers can be relied upon to point out that 'problem' vehicles would generate losses under such a scheme. But they should be set against the much higher number of perfectly normal,

TABLE 15.9

Proportion of Battery Sales

	1960	**1976**
Garage	85%	19%
Tyre/battery specialist	5%	42%
Accessory shop	2%	8%
Filling station	5%	15%
Supermarket	1%	12%
Other (e.g. mail order)	2%	4%

Source: Parts and Accessory Marketing Statistics, Sewell Profit Information Unit.

untroublesome vehicles whose routine maintenance could be carried out well within the contract cost, generating normal mark-up and a margin to cover the additional costs of less straightforward servicing and repair. Once a garage acquired a sufficient number of maintenance contracts to cover overheads, additional cash business could be generated by pricing at a very much cheaper marginal cost basis (i.e. parts cost plus minimal mark up).

A third possibility for at least deflecting the specialist outlets' challenge would involve omitting job reception altogether and building up a personal relationship between mechanics and customers through direct contact between the two, although the positive results of such an arrangement are less assured.

Finally, a garage could offer a more flexible service, offering a mobile workshop facility wherever possible or by relocating in office and public car parks and therefore offering a 'while-you-wait' variation on the drive-in drive-out theme. Parts could be supplied from a central depot although higher distribution costs would have to be met by the customer — who might be prepared to pay for the sake of convenience. Alternatively servicing of 'private' cars could be made more attractive through the provision of mobile servicing units, capable of carrying out work at people's homes.

Supermarkets and multiple stores pose a more direct threat. At the moment, they concentrate on the profitable fast turnover of items constantly in demand. Parts for which demand is sluggish or unpredictable can still be stocked manageably — and profitably — by a garage, but as interchangeability of parts increases, the supermarkets and stores will find it even easier to hold wider and more comprehensive stocks. Garages could react to this by stressing their expertise and by offering a wider range of parts themselves. The garage, after all, has one enormous marketing advantage, in that it can offer specialist advice, ensuring that the customer buys the right part or parts in the correct quantity. Where space allows, a shop counter display of parts and replacements would compete effectively — and directly — with the renegade supermarkets and multiple stores.

Both garages and supermarkets, however, will probably have to face intense competition from the growth of multi-franchise hypermarkets, incorporating a workshop, a parts centre, a discount centre and so on. Canada, the US and Sweden have all seen similar developments, after initial resistance from manufacturers, and the UK will probably follow suit. Garages are not necessarily excluded from a development of this sort: it might be possible to lease workshop facilities on the hypermarket site, or enter into a form of partnership agreement.

The final challenge comes from the growth in high-volume low-profit discount centres handling a limited range of car parts and a more comprehensive selection of 'in-car entertainment' products. Only the larger garage chains will have enough purchasing power and a sufficiently wide choice of locations to compete in this field.

OTHER FACTORS OF CHANGE

We have now discussed the specific marketing problems which a dealer must contend with, but there are a host of other factors and difficulties which he must now take into account.

Franchise Networks

We have already discussed what seems to be a commitment, on the part of manufacturers, to eliminate wholesalers and form a single-tier retail network. With BL's changeover to this marketing approach, direct dealerships will become the norm. Importers' networks are now more or less complete, and as UK manufacturers reduce their franchises in line with more realistic market shares, a service vacuum will be created, producing a demand for local service facilities for new car customers.

New Car Showrooms

Large, prestigious new-car showrooms must give way to changing market conditions, as new cars account for a diminishing proportion of total sales and as greater emphasis is placed on the car as a functional means of transportation. The high opportunity cost of land will also militate against the traditional concept of a new-car showroom.

There seem to be three distinct tendencies. First, smaller, new-car showrooms will more usually be incorporated into office blocks and shopping precincts, proving more convenient for (and more accessible to) the business community. Showrooms could also be relocated on industrial estates and factory sites. Not exactly a door to door sales pitch, but at least a more convenient and more visible shop window. Increasingly, showrooms will also handle contract hire, leasing and short-term car hire. Secondly, hypermarkets will extend their product range to cover all related products within the motor trade. Thirdly, and probably as a direct result of the rising cost of land, new car supermarkets will be created in low-cost, low density land areas. Garages will face increasing pressure to stock other non-related products in their new-car showrooms – possibly caravans or other leisure products, such as power boats. The sale of 'in-car entertainment' systems could also be extended to showroom sales, given adequate purchasing power.

Forecourts

A trend towards petrol company ownership (diversifying on-site parts sales and vehicle servicing) is already well-established, with the large to medium size garage groups – Dorado, Blue Star, Heron, Kennings, Pond, Henleys, Lex, etc. – accounting for most of the remaining ownership. Again, there will be something of a three-pronged development. First, new sites will be located in areas of high-volume throughput, to justify inclusion in an integrated property development. This should encourage the growth of new forecourts situated close to hypermarkets, supermarkets and other integrated shopping and property developments. Secondly, lower volume service stations will have to switch to self-service delivery or possibly unattended service to overcome labour problems and avoid high labour costs. Thirdly, in all but the highest volume stations, efforts will be made to offer a much wider range of goods, sales of which would help to justify the high opportunity cost of land. In urban areas, a range of consumer durables, parts, accessories and even food might be stocked. In rural areas, snack bars and restaurants might be necessary possibly using some form of speciality franchise in the style of the ubiquitous Wimpy Bar.

Figure 15.3 illustrates some of these trends. The total number of retail petrol outlets has reduced from 37,501 in 1970 to 29,347 in 1977. The number of sites now owned by oil companies remained static during the 1970s but bearing in mind that the total number of sites has fallen, the proportion owned by oil companies has significantly increased to about 30 per cent of the total. Self-service sites have also increased to 15 per cent of the total. The trend is therefore to a smaller number of self-service, oil company owned petrol sites.

Used Vehicle Markets

The used vehicle market is about to undergo a radical transformation. At the moment its outlets can be grouped into three more or less distinct categories: the smart used car salesrooms, mimicking the new-car showroom; the middle of the road used car trader, with a showroom and vestiges of the new-car sales approach; and the back street used car salesmen. In the US, used cars are displayed and sold with a far higher degree of professionalism and much more sophisticated techniques, and as the market moves closer to saturation in the 1980s and 1990s, so used car sales will assume a greater significance in the UK, requiring an entirely new marketing approach.

One possibility would be the development of large out-of-town used car supermarkets, with a resident AA/RAC testing centre. Cheap land, a large display of cars on or near a motorway, a tightening of consumer safeguards – all point towards a development of this sort, whereby the consumer can be assured of a 'fair' buy and a vehicle in roadworthy condition.

Hire Car Market/Leasing

The large car hire firms have captured a significant proportion of the market, but it is possible that they have neared their saturation level. Local car hire firms can still expect to see considerable growth in the volume of local trade.

Further growth is also possible in longer-term hire contracts or leasing arrangements, possibly coupled with maintenance contracts agreed on for the duration of the hire or lease period. Businesses facing liquidity problems might find contract hire preferable to the option of tying up large amounts of capital in car purchase and a number of professional people might similarly prefer a leasing arrangement to outright purchase. Private motorists who in the past might have purchased a second car as a hedge against immobility, might in future reconsider the advantages of short-term hire.

FIGURE 15.3

Decline in Retail Petrol Outlets

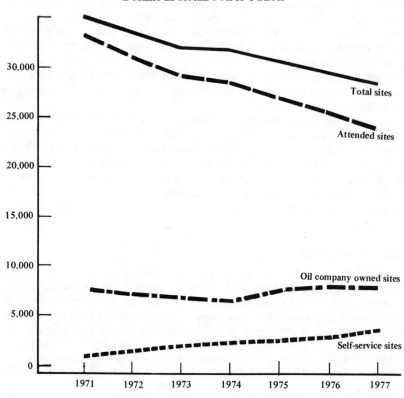

Source: *Franchise Networks*, Sewell PIU

The importance of leasing must not be underestimated. Euroeconomics[1] in their analysis of the French market for 1977 came to the preliminary conclusion that leasing acted as a 'supercharger'. to demand; by increasing demand between 5—10 per cent more than might otherwise have been expected.

1.   'The European Car Industry Review 1978-82' *Euroeconomics* Eurofinance 1978.

Bodyshops

Escalating accident and insurance costs — and the problems of lay supervision of costly body repair work — could provoke a radical change in body shops. New materials — plastics, ceramics — will mean heavy investment penalties, and this factor, coupled with demands for greater consumer protection, could mean that the smaller panel and paint shops are forced to cease trading. Larger, centralised bodyshops handling work from a wide area could become more common, possibly working under the supervision of an on-site controller (i.e. MOT inspectors) to ensure compliance with safety regulations and controls.

Service Workshops

Service workshops have already run into difficulties with adverse publicity and rising service costs but their real problems have more to do with attracting the skilled mechanics needed and then persuading them to spend part of their time on purely routine tasks. With land at a premium, suitable sites are usually overpriced, which can add to the problems, but possibilities for further growth have not been exhausted. One obvious possibility is the development of a flow-line workshop[1] specialising in pre-delivery inspection, voucher servicing and other routine operations. Locality servicing in small workshops sited near business or parking areas and industrial estates is a further possibility, although the servicing facilities of existing garages could be revamped and streamlined to cope with changing consumer demands.

CONCLUSION

The traditional motor trader has failed to move with the times and in so doing he has lost a share of his market. Unless the motor trader adapts himself to the changes taking place at the moment, this process will be bound to continue. The great advantage of the motor trader is his specialist knowledge and the depth of coverage. But the motor trader has not exploited these. For example if someone's car is off the road waiting for delivery of a spare part, this may necessitate hiring another car. In these circumstances the motorist may be willing to pay a very high mark-up (far in excess of current norms) in order to have his vehicle on the road — thereby saving hire fees, etc. If another car is not hired then there may be inconcenience and so on.

With a great deal of change taking place with manufacturers and now greater uncertainty about certain manufacturers, motor traders must be careful about their franchise. As a body they must surely try to persuade manufacturers of the merits of multi-franchise outlets.

One thing is certain — the troubles of the motor trader will continue. The uncertain times ahead do not look good for this traditional industry. Yet if the opportunities that do exist are fully exploited, there is clear evidence that such action will be rewarded in high profits.

---

1. Sufficient throughput is essential if this technique is to realise its full profitability.

384

SECTION FIVE

CONCLUSION

INTRODUCTION TO SECTION FIVE

Originally Section Five was going to have only two chapters; one dealing with a summary of the various conclusions reached in the earlier sections and the other focusing on the policy issues involved. It was my intention not to finalise the conclusion until the very last moment. Sure enough, the advent of the Peugeot-Citroen purchase of Chrysler's European operations has necessitated the addition of a hastily written separate chapter in which the ramifications of this news are assessed.

Chapter 16 begins by summarising the main conclusions of the book. Where appropriate a certain amount of new material is added to bring those conclusions up-to-date. Briefly of the three sectors of the motor industry, the car sector is in the most serious difficulties. Both the CV and the components sectors give rise to a note of cautious optimism. However there are signs that even in these sectors there are tendencies which if they persist may cause some alarm.

Chapter 17 attempts an appraisal of the Peugeot-Citroen takeover bid for Chrysler's European operations. Some of the earlier conclusions are modified by this development. However at the moment the merger is still ill-defined. There are many options open to all parties and this complicates any comprehensive analysis. There are good points and bad points to the merger, however it is probably too early to pass a definitive judgment on the marriage. It certainly should not force BL into a hastily conceived and ill-matched partnership.

Finally Chapter 18 focuses on policy issues. Within the European motor industry, natural forces are not being allowed to operate. For this reason I believe the Government must carry out an interventionist policy. If it does not then the ramifications to the UK's industrial structure could be enormous. Any interventionist policy must be conducted within the framework of an industrial strategy. To form such a strategy clear guidelines and objectives must be set. At the moment recent policy whilst being supportive of the motor industry consists of a set of reactions to short-term crises. If this continues then it is highly likely that the industry's decline will persist. There is however still time to act and there are some sectors which, with the right encouragement could be successful on an international level.

For my own part I would like to see the decline stopped and the UK motor industry re-established as a major world producer. I desperately hope and pray that BL will succeed. In case it does not the UK is fortunate in being tied into Ford and perhaps Peugeot-Citroen. While the latter is an unknown entity Ford has proved itself as a significant and consistent part of the UK and European industry. Everything possible should be done to nurture Ford. Encouragement should also be given to Peugeot-Citroen should they take over Chrysler and GM.

The biggest stumbling block with the UK motor industry is the low productivity and poor quality of work found almost without exception among the motor vehicle manufacturers. This tendency must be rectified. A number of suggestions are provided throughout this section for dealing with this problem. Frankly I doubt whether any of the suggestions will be politically acceptable. This is a pity for the one thing that is certain to cause the downfall of the whole industry is the continued reputation for low productivity and poor workmanship by the UK labour force.

Although Garel Rhys has provided contributions elsewhere in this book (see the preface), the conclusion is more personal. The responsibility for the conclusions rest solely with myself.

CHAPTER 16

SUMMARY AND OVERVIEW

In dealing with a subject as complex as the motor industry, a summary of the main points is essential if the reader is to thread his or her way through the maze of fact, opinion and conflicting theory which we have attempted to assess in earlier chapters.

There is a problem in so doing in that the motor industry is fast changing shape. Already the news about the Peugeot-Citroen takeover of Chrysler has made parts of this book out of date. So much so that the discussion of Chrysler/Peugeot-Citroen is deferred until Chapter 17.

SECTION 1

In Chapter 1, for example, we noted that UK manufacturers had been at the receiving end of a plethora of reports, critiques and policy programmes offering advice (occasionally conflicting) on what the manufacturers and policy-makers should do to salvage/revitalise/transform the UK motor industry.Any efforts to carry out policy changes, however, were hampered by the determination of successive Labour and Conservative governments to use the motor industry as a tool for regulating the economy – an important point which we shall return to in the final chapter.

Chapter 2 isolated two important factors which must be taken into account in any consideration of the motor industry. The first concerned the importance of achieving economies of scale in production. We saw that if a single manufacturer is to remain competitive, it must be in a position to produce a minimum number of cars – something in the region of 1 million units assembled from common components. Falling below this level incurs significant cost penalties, but these must be put into a closely-defined context. BL's failure to achieve suitable scale economies, for example, is due partly to poor productivity, rather than lack of physical capacity – *BL has enough difficulties utilising existing physical capacity leave alone an enlarged capacity.* The second point dealt with in the Chapter concerned the importance of the UK motor industry to the UK economy. Allowing a suitable multiplier, the UK motor industry provides jobs for approximately 10 per cent [1] of the total working population – a figure which excludes employment totals on the retail side. The effect on employment of any sudden major closures in the motor industry is obviously an important consideration, but it is not the only one. The UK motor industry still has a substantial balance of payments surplus. If all manufacturing in the UK motor industry ceased, the current positive net balance of some £1,000 million would be replaced by a negative net balance – in 1978 terms – of

---

1. 1.25 million less 0.45 million engaged in retailing = 0.8 million. A multiplier of 3, to include supply industries (steel, boxes, components, timber, glass, plastic, foam, etc), yields a figure of 2.4 million.

£10,000+ million, which would include an £8,000+ million import bill.[1] Not, surely, the sort of change that any government would be prepared to countenance?

Chapter 3 provided an overview of the motor industry and reiterated some of the principal conclusions reached in various government reports on the problems of the industry-

1. Excess capacity
2. Too many (outdated) models
3. Too many plants
4. Over-manning
5. Low productivity
6. Inadequate capital investment
7. Poor product quality, durability and reliability
8. Some evidence of poor distribution and inept marketing.

Some of these criticisms must now be qualified, in the light of subsequent events. The problem of excess capacity, for example, seems insignificant in comparison with the problem of making the best use of existing resources — correctly identified by the CPRS report, amongst others, as a question of low productivity. But poor productivity is, in turn, a short-term difficulty which must not be allowed to obscure the longer-term problems identified in Chapter 4, where these and other contentious issues were discussed. Unit working, for example, was shown to be an inappropriate solution to the particular problems of the UK industry. Continued use of large plants in existing locations was not in itself seen as a necessary and sufficient condition for achieving scale economies, with the possible exception of pressing and power-train operations. In other respects we noted that there was no particular advantage to be gained from concentrating assembly work in one or two plants. In administrative terms, we offered a modified endorsement of the Edwardes plan to divide BL into new organisational units offering better lines of communication and a chance to exercise greater control with few if any cost penalties, although we suggested that further changes might be needed before BL's organisational structure reached an equilibrium.

A number of alternative structures were proposed, although it was noted in passing that volume car production in Western Europe as a whole might eventually cease to be the desired objective as manufacturers in low labour-cost

1.   The figures in the text are based on assumptions, and estimates are given below:

	Imports £m	Exports £m	Total £m
Cars (1.6m x £2,500 =)	4,000	1,000	5,000
CVs (.26m x £4,500 =)	1,170	650	1,830
Components	2,500	1,800	3,300
Other motor products	500	700	1,200
	8,170	4,150	11,330

areas entered the market and high-cost, high-technology Western manufacturers found that their volume products were no longer price-competitive.

Of more immediate importance, Chapter 4 discussed the various causes of low productivity. The villains of the piece are variously singled out as inadequate capital investment and what must appear to outsiders as an incompetent and lazy workforce. The controversy about the cause and effect continues to rage, but it was noted in Chapter 4 that a combination of both factors contributed in their own ways to low productivity. Chapter 4 pointed out that, on the one hand, piecemeal improvements in plant and equipment were not enough; on the other hand, large-scale capital investment in new and more efficient plant is not a sufficient condition for achieving improved productivity, a point sadly borne out by events at the new Rover plant at Solihull. But at the same time, the point was made that BL's investment plans are disturbingly modest when examined in an international context, particularly when one remembers just how far the company has fallen behind and how much lost ground it must now recover if it is to remain competitive. The inescapable conclusion must be that the problem of poor productivity simply has to be dealt with on all fronts. Apportioning blame is a particularly fruitless exercise. Inadequate remedies, in my opinion, are only marginally more useful than no remedies at all — a point returned to several times in the course of the book.

SECTION 2: CARS

The car sector is understandably the most troubled sector of the motor industry, but it is tempting to spend rather too much time analysing those troubles, when in fact a closer look at other sectors may be more rewarding.

Notwithstanding the Peugeot-Citroen takeover of Chrysler UK (discussion of which is left to the next chapter), the problems of the existing UK company remain substantially unchanged. References to Chrysler UK now imply a reference to the UK plants of the larger Peugeot based group.

Of the multinationals involved in volume car production in the UK, Chrysler UK was and GM is following Ford's example in integrating their operations on a European-wide basis — a change which on the whole could benefit the UK. Of the Big Three, GM and Ford are now reassuringly buoyant, while Chrysler's position has strengthened somewhat since the 1975 rescue. Which leaves BL, the only major domestically-owned firm, still floundering and still facing an uncertain future. Can it catch up with its rivals or will it continue the downward slide? Section 2, devoted exclusively to cars, looked at these and many other questions concerning volume car production in the UK, and at the dilemma now confronting the policy-makers, and the choices open to them.

Demand

Chapter 5 considered first of all the problem of anticipating levels of demand in the immediate future and in the longer term. It was argued that during the 1980s UK car registrations would meet and possibly exceed record levels; continued growth would not be sustained, although in the absence of a major depression, new car registrations could remain high, as the business buyer represents such a high proportion of total demand in the UK that the domestic market is (and will probably continue to be) less sensitive to economic fluctuations than markets elsewhere.

On the export front, Chapter 5 stressed that the UK could continue to export to Western Europe and the US, although sales in the latter market would be critically dependent on (1) 'captive' imports from US multinationals overseas and (2) on the continued attraction of BL's sports models.

[*Recent events:* In fact, new car and CV registrations in 1978 have exceeded all expectations, even the most optimistic ones, demonstrating beyond doubt that vehicle demand (and car demand, in particular) is still buoyant. An increase in the number of company leasing arrangements may have contributed to this upswing but the private buyer has also played an important part in boosting total demand. For the first time in a number of years, real disposable income increased (whilst car prices have not risen so quickly) – a proportion of this must have been transmitted to new car registrations. The arguments in Chapter 5 in favour of a recovery in car demand have been largely substantiated.]

The UK Manufacturers

If demand is buoyant, the supply picture is rather less enthralling. The UK industry has now been overtaken by Italy and lies in fourth place in a European ranking. The motor industry in the UK is not merely stagnating – it appears to be in decline. Production hovers at early 1960s levels at a time when all other major producers have managed to expand production dramatically. Five factors in particular (some of them already familiar) have contributed to this poor performance:

1. Low productivity (the result of poor industrial relations, discontinuity of internal and external supply, slower work-pace and over-manning).
2. Insufficient capital investment.
3. Organisational/structural weaknesses, making it difficult to achieve maximum potential economies of scale.
4. Irresponsible and sometimes hostile government attitudes towards the motor industry.
5. Poorer quality of work by the labour force; Ford finds its non-UK plants achieve better workmanship as does BL with its Seneffe plant.

Low productivity, it seems, is endemic in the UK motor industry. While some companies (not only Ford) argue that their investment record is good, it remains true that, isolated exceptions notwithstanding, the UK industry as a whole *has* suffered from under-investment. Ford, again, have integrated their production and model policy on a European basis, but Chrysler, GM and BL have been slow to follow Ford's obviously sensible example – and have missed scale economies as a result. And on the question of government attitudes, there can be no doubt that positive government action has been conspicuous by its absence in successive Labour and Conservative administrations. Past Labour governments in particular seem to have regarded the car as a dispensable luxury consumer durable, preferring to accord a higher priority to necessary consumer goods, welfare services and the like. The recent Labour government,[1] however, seems on the whole to have a rather more favourable attitude to the motor industry in general and has actively promoted a healthier economic and political climate for the car producers.[2] In this one respect (with the exception of the sanctions threat against Ford in Autumn 1978) it seems that the government is now providing the leadership and support that the industry so desperately needed and failed to get in the past.

BL

The difficulties facing the UK motor industry in general have affected BL in particular to an extreme degree. Poor industrial relations and inadequate capital investment have now become acute problems for the company. BL has not yet been able to reorganise its operations in order to obtain maximum potential economies of scale, as its facilities are too dispersed and the supply patterns for parts and components too complex. There is now at least a faint glimmer of hope that the company's fortunes could change for the better, a prospect discussed at length in Chapters 7 and 11.

A few popular misconceptions remain, however. In broad outline, the Ryder plan was logical and well-conceived. Its major flaw was the provision that investment capital should be withheld pending satisfactory industrial relations — a point more fully explored in Chapter 7. Other critics felt that the investment requirements were excessive: in fact, Ryder's proposed £2.8 billion is modest in international terms. Evidence to this effect is provided in Chapter 4. It was also felt that splitting BL Cars into an Austin Morris division, and a Jaguar Rover Triumph division would incur diseconomies of scale, although the discussion in Chapters 3, 4 and 7 shows that the new organisational structure could in fact improve communications and tighten control without sacrificing economies of scale.

In general, we would support the actions and the management style of Michael Edwardes, but it must be remembered that BL is still desperately short of management resources and skills. Edwardes' newly appointed management team may alleviate this shortage but it has not removed it altogether.[3] There are similar shortages in both systems and engineering divisions (including model development and product engineering departments) which helps to explain the unusually long gestation period that new or updated BL models appear to need. The scarcity of technical resources and manpower is particularly damaging at a time when BL's model policy (with some exceptions) is dangerously outdated and uncompetitive. But BL's greatest weakness — in the eyes of the government and the general public — has been its chronic inability to meet successive production targets.

BL's new management team have been desperately trying to remedy these various deficiencies. In view of our comments on the need for investment,

1. Perhaps partly due to the Lib-Lab pact.
2. Although the government's threat of sanctions against Ford must be deemed highly irresponsible; it was argued in Section 2 that Ford may consider placing any expansion of European assembly capacity in the UK.
3. Even the long run survival of the current team is in doubt since Michael Edwardes is only on *secondment* from the Chloride Group.

they are to be congratulated for finally securing at least some of the much-needed finance and for their efforts to rationalise production in accordance with the Ryder plans. Moreover, by concentrating on short-term measures — pending the arrival of new BL models in the 1980s — the company has at least managed to make better use of some of its resources. Production in the new Solihull car plant is up, and the 'O' and 'OHC 6' series engines are now in production and will presumably be extended.[1] Other technical improvements are in hand; the Mini is to remain in production; and, finally, the UK distribution network has been given the sort of high priority so badly needed if it was to survive.

There have been some disappointments. One of BL's few remaining strengths is its US franchise network, a major outlet for the MG and TR models. Chapter 5 came to the conclusion that UK exports to the US would be in the region of 100,000 units per year. But BL have failed to capitalise on this advantage, and are apparently set on running down their sports car programme — their one real strength in the US market. If BL is unwilling to meet the US demand for a distinctive sports model, another producer will all too quickly step in to fill the gap — and BL can write off for good another one of its strengths. It could be that this is a classic example of a conflict of interests between BL's profitability instincts and a more general balance of payments criteria. If this is indeed the case, there is a strong argument for some form of government subsidy to underwrite BL's sports car programme — if only to preserve its balance of payments contribution.

The second disappointment concerns the viability of Jaguar Rover Triumph as a separate unit. The current projected line-up involves Jaguar, Rover and a sports car range, plus the continuation of the ageing Dolomite. This range alone is simply inadequate, but there is ample evidence that a gap exists in the European markets for an up-market quality car, smaller than the present Rover models — a gap which the proposed Jaguar Rover Triumph division is not yet equipped to fill. Chapters 7 and 14 suggested that one solution might be the reintroduction of the SD2: revitalising and improving the existing Dolomite would be a poor second-best.

Overall, two scenarios were provided in Chapter 8, both spelling problems for BL Cars until the firm reaches a state of equilibrium in the mid-1980s. Scenario One envisaged a struggling firm, but one which managed to maintain its market share and remain a major car manufacturer. Scenario Two was an eventually rationalised and diminished company with a much smaller market share. The next few years will be critical for BL Cars. If Scenario One is to come about, much good faith will be needed — from everyone associated with the company, including management, politicians, dealers and customers. No doubt whatever is finally decided, public debate will continue to rage.

Even if Scenario Two is the eventual outcome, all is not lost from the UK point of view. In this event, it would still be possible to export high-value cars while importing cheaper volume cars. Redundancies would be inevitable but some employment at least would be maintained. At the moment, indeed, it

1. The 77mm gearbox is also being utilised more fully (i.e. in the TR7, Rover, Jaguar and presumably, other models soon). The four wheel drive programme is rapidly being expanded and implemented.

seems that Scenario Two is the more likely outcome for BL, unless the present model policy is drastically revised and revitalised. But this, in turn, could prove difficult unless the existing shortages in technical resources and manpower are overcome.[1] There are a number of possible reasons for this deficiency, namely:

1. BL is not at the moment prepared (or able) to pay salaries high enough to attract top-calibre engineering staff. Pay policy constraints should be lifted and BL should — as a matter of urgency — increase salaries accordingly in order to attract highly qualified personnel. Alternatively, the company could contract the services of 'outside' personnel.
2. Until recently, BL literally had no money with which to recruit additional engineering personnel. The new equity injection has now eased this situation.
3. In general, the UK is suffering from a chronic (and, by now, well-documented) shortage of suitably qualified engineers. Logically, BL should consider setting up a jointly-sponsored BL/NEB training institute or at least encourage the development of new tertiary education training courses, to remedy the problem in the long term. As a stop-gap measure, it might be possible to make use of contract services, although unions are violently opposed to any such move. It should be possible to convince them otherwise.

In Chapter 7 a number of recommendations were made. Table 16.1 lists most of these, with the exception of specific model policy changes. We leave a fuller discussion of policy implications to Chapter 18, although at this point it should be noted that the multi-sourcing of internally-manufactured components could be achieved by expanding capacity of BL's Seneffe plant in Belgium — although such a policy may not meet the government's employment or balance of payment's objectives. The possibility of BL undertaking a joint venture with its car operations is discussed later in this chapter.

[Recent Events: At the moment, BL's market share is falling. In 1978 it declined to 24 per cent — mainly due to flagging sales in the Jaguar Rover Triumph division. Production in any event fell short of the planned BL targets by some 10 to 15 per cent, but in fact these targets were sadly pessimistic. BL anticipated a market size of 1.5 million cars, though in reality, the market was 1.6 million.

Partly as per original plans and partly as a consequence of the production shortfall, a further 7,000 redundancies[2] will be aimed for in 1979, and probably a similar number for 1980. Total employment in BL cars should be slimmed to about 120,000 by the end of 1979. The switch of the TR7 from Speke went smoothly and the development of the TR7 into a family of sports cars should be seen in 1979 (convertible and a V8).

1. BL has only 240 engineers per product line compared with 800 in Ford of Europe and Ford has a smaller product line and much greater rationalisation in componentry. Michael Edwardes has gone on record as saying that the engineering shortage was 'just as serious a limitation on long-term success as industrial disputes are in the short-term'. (Financial Times, 10.11.78)
2. There was a net loss of 6,000 jobs in 1978 through natural wastage.

TABLE 16.1

Summary of Some of the Recommendations Made in Relation to BL Cars

Recommendations	Effect	Cost to BL	Cost to UK and UK Government	Likelihood of Success
Multi-sourcing of component manufacture	More continuous production through less supply interruptions	*External multi-sourcing.* None. The extra competition could even be advantageous in keeping prices down.	*External* Greater import of components and less employment in the components industry.	*External* Moderate to good.
		Internal multi-sourcing. Not so feasible with powertrain manufacture.	*Internal* Some £200 million extra capital investment.	*Internal* Good, see rider below.
Increased Capacity (1 assembly plant and 1 powertrain plant)	More continuous production through targets being greater than actual demand.	1. *Greater capital expenditure* a. Assuming that there is some saving in the re-building, re-furbishing and re-equipment of older plants, then total cost may be around £400 million. b. Assuming no savings elsewhere, then total cost could be £600 million.	Greater Government aid necessary for BL.	Good unless the labour force begins to co-operate industrial action between different plants.

TABLE 16.1 (Cont.)

Recommendations	Effect	Cost to BL	Cost to UK and UK Government	Likelihood of Success
		2. *Increased recurrent costs.* Greater labour costs, raw material costs, and finance costs borne on higher capital invest-ment and greater working capital.		
Smaller plants	Better industrial relations	£100–200 million	More finance for BL	Good after initial labour unrest.
Automation of repetitive jobs	Less boredom on a shop floor, greater flexibility in production and cheaper model changes (which only require a new computer programme).	£500–£1,000 million	More finance for BL and Government may have to administer the project	Good after initial unrest. Labour would, however, still be the vital link in certain places and could halt production.

BL seems to have been promised more money than the £450 million equity injection received in 1978. So far arrangements have been authorised for the provision of a further £400 million (mostly for 1979). However, BL did withhold some investment as a result of industrial disputes in 1978. This is not a return to a Ryder strategy but must be seen in the context of a new tougher attitude to industrial disruption — with the emphasis on gaining specific agreement designed to improve productivity. For example contractors have been withdrawn from the site at Solihull where work had started on the first £30 million phase of the £280 million project. The bargain that was eventually struck was an undertaking from the workers to operate a double shift system. Progress has been made towards parity pay in late 1978, this together with new productivity deals and a buoyant market for profitable components and spare parts sales suggest that there is some hope for improved output and greater profitability in the near future].

Ford

Ford occupies a particularly important place in the UK motor industry. It is now the major supplier and an important employer and investor. In fact, Ford's investment plans are only marginally below those of BL, with a £250 million capital investment in the Bridgend engine plant, a further £160 million at Halewood and additional investment at Dagenham. The UK cannot afford to disregard the activities of this energetic multinational. If BL should fail as a volume car manufacturer, Ford alone would be in a position to stem the rising import tide. For this reason the company must receive encouragement from the government — and particular efforts must be made to counter the industrial problems peculiar to the UK, if the company is to be persuaded to expand operations here rather than move elsewhere. It was therefore surprising to witness the Government actually proposing to implement the sanctions threat against Ford in 1978.

The nine week old strike at Ford in the autumn of 1978 ended in a 17 per cent wage deal which was deemed to be outside the 5 per cent phase four pay policy. With rumours that the strike cost Ford some £400 million the Government decided to impose sanctions but quickly backed down. It is interesting to note the effect of the Ford strike on its European operations. The Saarlouis (whose powertrain is sourced from the UK) and Amsterdam plants suffered relatively quickly (between 4-6 weeks) whilst Valencia managed to soldier on until the eighth week although Cologne and Ghenk carried on, but at reduced levels. Alternative suppliers of some components managed to keep production running longer than was imagined by the UK strikers who implemented the blockade. Nevertheless the strike has affected European sales by some 100,000+ vehicles and nudged Ford from the position of European market leader.

Since it was argued in Section Two that Ford was already short of European capacity prior to the strike, and that the UK may have been in line for an expansion of assembly facilities, the threat of sanctions may have persuaded Ford management to look elsewhere, and there have been reports of talks by Ford, with Austria, France and the Soviet Union. Sanctions were the last action the UK Government should have threatened Ford with, if employment was an objective (although the effects of a pay explosion may increase unemployment, there were clear signs that the 5 per cent policy would be breached regardless of the Ford settlement).

In this respect, Ford's problems are certainly less acute than BL's, but the performance at Ford's UK plants is poor in relation to Ford plants elsewhere in Europe — and the gap is widening, as non-UK plants increase productivity and improve quality while the UK operation marks time, with little or no improvement. Production bottlenecks have checked Ford's progress towards a 30 per cent UK market share, but their model policy would seem to be bang on target, with a front-wheel drive Escort replacement in the pipeline and a successful marketing adjustment for the Granada (now outselling BL's Rover). Further changes are expected in the Capri range, which could disappear altogether, to be replaced by an imported, US-made Mustang-Capri — a *quid pro quo* for UK Fiesta exports to the US which could make a great deal of economic sense in the longer term.[1]

GM

Vauxhall is now firmly established as part of the Opel Car operation, but as we saw, full use of UK capacity will depend on a number of factors, notably labour costs and industrial relations. GM certainly needs extra capacity somewhere in Europe, and it could be found in the UK if the company can make better use of its existing UK capacity.

We have already noted that Vauxhall's loss of autonomy could have negative consequences for the UK industry. GM's German subsidiary might be used to source the UK with powertrain and components, for example, although this is thought unlikely in view of the fact that six of GM's nine[2] European component plants are now in the UK. Certainly *without* the Opel tie-in, Vauxhall would very probably be producing fewer cars. If the choice lies between producing 90,000 cars with 80 per cent local content and 160,000 cars with, say, 50 per cent local content, the latter choice offers greater employment and balance of payments benefits to the UK, assuming that the difference in car volumes would be made good by increased imports in the former case.

In sum, the integration of GM's European car operations will probably benefit the UK. There are already signs that GM is trying to make better use of existing UK capacity. Most of the small and medium-size GM models will probably be made in the UK, although production of the up-market Senator and Monza models is expected to remain in Germany. However, as the UK sources a number of world markets, it probably produces rather more than Vauxhall's total UK sales.

At the moment, Opel imports account for between 1 and 2 per cent of the UK market, and Vauxhall should be able to export some cars to Europe — but the Opel-Vauxhall trade balance should be watched carefully. Of rather more immediate concern is any future shift in GM's Europe-US policy.

At the time of writing, the GM (US) concern has successfully downsized

1. Although the Fiesta will not be recognised in computing Ford's US fuel consumption figures, exports of US made cars to Europe might change attitudes.
2. The non-UK plants include two in France and one in the Irish Republic.

its cars and produced a more 'European' feel – so much so that fears have been expressed over the possibility that GM will eventually export cars from the US to Europe in significant volumes. I am not convinced that such an outcome is either desirable or necessary. GM's position *vis-a-vis* anti-trust sanctions in the US could make further sales expansion there extremely difficult, and it has been argued that GM's wish to reduce US sales but maintain existing production levels makes the export of US-manufactured cars inevitable, but both arguments ignore the fact that there is *still* some room for further growth within the US. The European market is currently growing faster than the US market, and GM could well choose to install additional capacity in Europe, using any excess European capacity to manufacture cars for export to the US – using different brand names in the process to avert the threat of anti-trust sanctions in the US. In any event, there is some doubt as to whether GM has sufficient spare US capacity to export cars to Europe in any significant quantity, except at the top end of the luxury market segment and the specialist ranges. GM (Europe) is a highly profitable operation, overall, and there is no sound reason why the US parent should wish to damage that profitability in return for a marginal improvement to its sales in the US.

[Recent Events: In general, I have been optimistic about GM's performance and some readers could argue that this optimism is unjustified, given the slight fall in GM's market share in 1978. In fact, I would still contend that GM has considerable marketing strength within the UK, although the company failed to anticipate the increase in the size of the UK market and were as a result caught short on the supply side.[1] In response, Cavalier production has been switched to the UK with phenomenal speed – and double shift working at Luton in the spring of 1978 helped to boost GM's market share to 13.5 per cent. Ellesmere Port has been modified to cope with the launch of the UK-Opel Rekord and Senator variants (Carlton and Royale) and the company has announced plans for an expansion of the dealer network. Plans are underway for construction of a new, £15 million component plant near Belfast and a new £10 million parts centre at Milton Keynes.[2] All of this must surely underline GM's determination to increase its UK market share and to continue and expand its manufacturing operations in the UK. Opel (GM's West German subsidiary) once again had a record year in 1978 for both production and domestic demand. Opel plants were operating at full capacity in 1978 and the DM5 billion five year plan currently envisages no new major assembly plants. The bulk of its investment has been channelled into rationalising and eliminating bottlenecks at existing plants. This may be good news for the UK in that production at the Vauxhall plants will be increased before new European assembly capacity is installed. Vauxhall also announced a profit in 1978 (of £2 million) for the first time since 1971.]

1. Although shortage on the supply side may have been a reason, rumours indicate that GM, in part, blame the recently reorganised distribution system (now a reduced single tier system). GM may very well expand its distribution network in the near future.
2. Although GM's first non US battery plant costing $55 million is to be placed in Sarreguemines, France.

FIGURE 16.1

Capacity Utilisation in the UK Car Industry

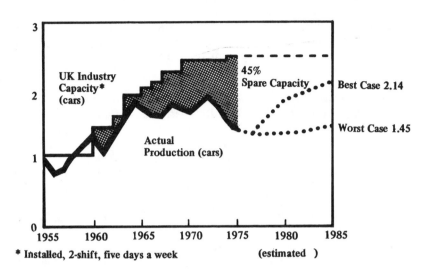

Source: CPRS Report, *The Future of the British Car Industry*,
HMSO, London, 1975.

Chrysler

Discussion of the Chrysler takeover by the Peugeot-Citroen group is deferred until the next chapter. Much of the analysis of Chrysler UK is still relevant. The UK plants are now part of a larger group and the success of those plants must crucially depend on their integration into the Peugeot group. Doubt was placed on the ability of Chrysler (Europe) to actually achieve the economies of scale to maintain Chrysler as a competitive volume car producer in Europe. The UK plants may now be merged with what has become the largest European car producer. Whether the Peugeot group will want to utilise Chrysler's UK plants and whether the plants can be integrated to achieve the necessary scale economies are questions we return to in Chapter 17.

[Recent Events: Chrysler UK is expected to make much higher losses in 1978 than anticipated. Rumours of a loss of around £11 million for Chrysler Europe as a whole have been reported. On the UK front, poor productivity and a deteriorating situation in Iran has cut production for the Iran order. Meanwhile George Turnball (back from Hyundai in Korea and Iran National) has become chairman of Chrysler UK with a restructured Board.]

Production

In Chapter 8 it was noted that UK production would only catch up with the early 1970 peak by the mid-1980s, unless the UK plants owned by the three multinationals are used to a greater extent to supply European demand. From the mid-1980s on, UK production should exceed 70 per cent of installed capacity and, in the absence of industrial unrest, should also be reasonably profitable. There would certainly be no need to *reduce* capacity — as recommended by the CPRS Report — unless the UK government at some point wished to contract the motor industry. This policy decision is discussed in Chapter 18. With some encouragement for the multinationals, and assuming better productivity, then actual production figures should be near the top end of the range shown in Figure 16.1.

One interesting conclusion reached in Chapter 8 was that production totals would not be significantly affected by BL's performance (improved or reduced outputs) as any vacuum left by BL would be partially filled by an increase in GM, Ford and Chrysler UK production. But this point does not apply to employment levels. Scenario Two, for example, envisaged an increase in sales by the multinationals, implying an increase in the volume of 'captive' imports which in turn could have an adverse effect on employment in the UK components industry. In Scenario Two, moreover, BL will move steadily down towards the bottom of the suggested range, as the company gradually withdraws from volume car production.

These, then, are points to be remembered in assessing future production levels — but we also examined some of the reasons for current UK production lagging so far behind in European terms. Some of the conclusions reached can, be summarised by comparing the data shown in Table 16.2. Excluding the UK, the European norm apparently involves producing between one quarter and one half in excess of domestic consumption. Japan exports twice as much as its own domestic market, whereas the US cannot meet total domestic needs from its own output. In the UK, production is roughly equal to consumption. If the UK had followed the European pattern more closely, the 1.3 million 1976 production total would have been increased to between 1.5 million and 1.9 million cars. Why is it that the UK cannot match its European competitors in production? One of the major reasons must be — as we concluded in Section 2 — the poor industrial relations record in the UK, which taken in its broadest sense, must also remain a question of over-manning and a generally slower workpace.

Smaller Manufacturers

We saw in Chapter 9 that with the exception of Rolls Royce, many of the smaller independent manufacturers are extremely vulnerable, given that they are by definition unable to benefit from the cost advantages conferred by economies of scale and must therefore rely on meeting demand in those marketing gaps not filled by the larger manufacturer. With the establishment of the new De Lorean plant in Ireland, competition in this sector will almost certainly become even fiercer, but we are convinced that it would be possible to secure the future of some of the smaller firms as part of an integrated plan for the whole of the UK car industry. This is discussed in Chapter 18.

[Recent Events: The link-up between Lotus (now backed by American Express

TABLE 16.2

Production and New Car Registrations for Selected Countries

	Production in millions			New Car Registrations in millions		
	1976	1977	1978	1976	1977	1978
UK	1.3	1.3	1.2	1.3	1.3	1.6
France	3.0	3.1	3.1	1.9	1.9	1.9
West Germany	3.5	3.8	3.9	2.3	2.6	2.7
Italy	1.5	1.4	1.5	1.2	1.2	1.2
Spain	.8	1.0	1.0	.6	.7	.6
Japan	5.0	5.4	5.6	2.5	2.5	2.6[a]
USA	8.5	9.2	9.4	9.8	10.8	11.3

a. Estimated

finance) and De Lorean looks interesting. With Lotus engineering know-how, the marketing flair of John De Lorean and government finance, the De Lorean project looks promising. Co-operation between De Lorean and Lotus is interesting since they may have been close competitors. The stage may well be set for a formalisation of that co-operation at some future date.]

Import Penetration
Import penetration rose from 43 per cent in 1977 to nearly 50 per cent in 1978, largely due to a loss of market share for BL and GM, and increased imports by BL, Ford and GM. The Japanese exercised some restraint, but still increased total sales substantially and market share was slightly up. Any further change will depend to a considerable extent on the ability of UK firms to increase production in line with the recovery in demand. BL and Chrysler have managed to up production in the first half of 1978, although Ford and GM have not yet managed to improve their position. Total production will probably show an improvement on 1977 figures, although the size of that improvement will depend on future production interruptions.

SECTION 3: COMMERCIAL VEHICLES
The UK CV industry can at least boast a number of strengths: (1) the sourcing of GM and Ford (European) CV production in the UK; (2) the component supply infrastructure; (3) the trailer and bus sectors; and (4) the number of small specialist firms who have correctly identified consumer preference. These strengths should begin to pay important dividends in the immediate future, as the UK CV industry emerges as a major force at the heavier end of the CV market. Until now, progress has been slower than it perhaps should have been, partly because of cautious policies in expanding final assembly capacity and partly because BL's traditional strength in the CV market has been dissipated in order to subsidise car operations. The outcome was inevitable: a shortage of supply coupled with a failure to keep abreast of the needs and changing patterns of demand in the market place. By 1981, these problems should have been dealt with, but in the interim period foreign manufacturers

have found it all too easy to gain a foothold in the UK, while UK products in turn have been conspicuously absent from the European heavy vehicle market.

The UK industry has an extensive marketing task on its hands if it is to recover lost ground and strengthen its position on the continent, but it would indeed be a mistake to concentrate all energies on fighting for a share in an already crowded market, at the expense of the UK position in less developed markets which might offer a greater potential for major growth in road transport. The process of either vertical or horizontal integration in the European CV industry is far from complete. As larger and larger groups fight for survival, the market is likely to become even more competitive, and will have to face the additional threats of Japanese and East European competition and wider legislation to control and even divert new and existing haulage traffic to other forms of transport. At the moment, the heavy segments of the UK CV industry (where scale economies are less important) are in a relatively strong position, and there is no immediate need to enter into co-operative ventures with other vehicle makers either within or across frontiers – although such ventures should not be completely ruled out. However, in the larger panel van and light truck segment – where economies of scale are more crucial – BL (the weakest of the four major UK producers) might well be involved in a merger or some form of link-up with European firms, particularly at the bottom end of the Leyland range.

It is therefore likely that if rumours[1] of a link-up between Leyland Vehicles and another European manufacturer are true, it might occur at the bottom end of the Leyland range (where economies are greatest) or in the area of engines, gearboxes, axles and so forth.[2]

Overall, the structure and performance of the UK industry indicates that it may survive these various challenges, despite an indifferent showing in recent years. The commercial vehicle divisions of Ford, GM and Chrysler have been fairly thoroughly integrated as part of the European CV operation for some time – much more so, in fact, than the car divisions – and in all three cases the European CV operation has been centred on the UK, which is a source of considerable strength. The two areas of potential difficulty concern future problems with BL and the possibility of Japanese manufacture in the UK, which would benefit the UK as a whole but could damage other UK CV manufacturers.[3]

BL

Leyland Vehicles has a large product range, particularly strong in the mid-range (see Chapters 3, 11 and 14). Leyland Vehicles' weaknesses as a CV company, however, are similar to the weaknesses which have affected the car operation although they are by no means so acute. Leyland Vehicles, as with BL Cars, suffers from low productivity, poor reliability and a shortage of technical resources and facilities. Recent managerial changes suggest that

1. See, for example, the Financial Times of 22.6.78, and the Sunday Times of 24.9.78.
2. As discussed in Chapter 12, it is quite common for CV manufacturers to buy in major components from the CV component supply industry.
3. Mitsubishi hope to assemble heavy trucks in South Wales, while an importer in Northern Ireland wants to assemble large Hino (Astrum) trucks in Manchester.

the CV management is still not functioning satisfactorily. Lack of technical resources means that BL will have to rely on the UK component supply industry for some time to come.

Another external factor which has affected Leyland Vehicles in the last few years has been the fierce competition from European and Japanese manufacturers. The Japanese in particular have already made significant inroads into the European market and they have yet to exploit all of the potential marketing gaps. The Communist Bloc countries have constructed highly sophisticated, superbly equipped CV plants — often with the help of West European manufacturers such as GM and Daimler Benz — and are waiting in the wings, eager to snatch at the first opportunity to break into the lucrative European market. Within Western Europe, as shown in Figure 16.2, there have been a series of defensive mergers and co-operative ventures, any one of which could produce a dramatic shift in the balance of market power. Given these changes, there has been a certain amount of speculation in recent years on a possible BL joint venture, but what form this would take is still uncertain. Three possibilities seem most likely:

1. Complete merger with another European manufacturer.
2. Joint development (and possible common production) of certain components/models, with another European manufacturer.
3. A 'franchise' of some sort, in which Leyland Vehicles marketed another manufacturer's products.

A strong argument could be made for a complete merger: Leyland Vehicles' world truck market[1] could reach 2.2 million by 1985, rising to 2.5 million plus in 1990 as demand in less developed countries picks up. The market is therefore only modest. Potential economies of scale could only be found at the lighter end of the market and in component manufacture — and then only if the European industry was further rationalised. If this is so, Leyland Vehicles might see fit to merge with another producer sooner rather than later, in order to share development costs. In countering this argument we must remember the point raised in Section 3 that scale economies were relatively unimportant since body building and vehicle assembly form only a very small part of total value-added. Expensive items such as powertrain and axles can already be produced in quantity by the existing component supply infrastructure, which means that any further cost saving to be achieved through merger would be of only marginal importance.

The second possibility — joint development — has too few successful precedents to recommend it. The Douvrin engine, jointly developed by Volvo, Renault and Peugeot, has been only a qualified success. Too many compromises between conflicting aims have been made, and the loss of autonomy and prestige involved in a joint venture of this sort do not augur well. The Club of Four project experienced different problems. The difficulties do not necessarily outweigh potential benefits. If successful, joint ventures promise a high return, but it seems that a successful formula for co-operation has yet to be found.

A joint marketing arrangement would perhaps offer a better chance of success, although it involves a loss of marketing 'face' unless suitable reciprocal

---

1. Excluding car derived vans and light panel vans (e.g. Sherpa, Transit, etc).

FIGURE 16.2

Link-ups within the European CV Manufacturing Industry

Figures show commercial vehicle production
(except for buses) for 1977, (000s)

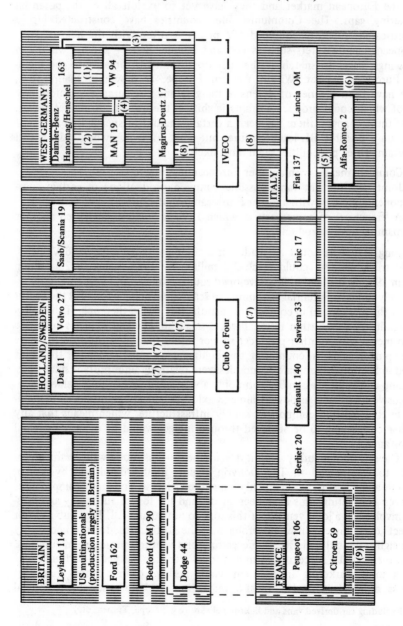

Adapted from Daimler-Benz

FIGURE 16.2 (cont.)

Key to European CV Relationships

(1)　VW and Daimler-Benz each own 50% of a research and development organisation DAG.

(2)　MAN and Daimler-Benz collaborate in truck manufacturing and marketing. There is a joint venture for the production of common components for heavy vehicles (MTU).

(3)　Daimler-Benz and IVECO are principal partners in a joint venture to produce automatic transmission (ATU). Other partners may include Volvo and ZF. The venture is currently being investigated by the West German cartel office.

(4)　MAN and VW are preparing to jointly produce 5-9 tonne trucks.

(5)　Fiat, Alfa-Romeo and Saviem each own one third of a light vehicle diesel engine plant in Sicily (SOFIM).

(6)　Peugeot-Citroen and Fiat have joined forces to build a $280m plant for making 80,000 light vans a year in Italy's South.

(7)　Saviem, DAF, Volvo are all part of the 'Club of Four'. Each company uses its own chassis and components but share a common cab design.

(8)　IVECO is 80% owned by Fiat and 20% owned by KHD, which used to own Magirus-Deutz. IVECO consists of Magirus-Deutz, and Fiat's former subsidiaries UNIC, Lancia, OM and Fiat (CVs).

(9)　Chrysler (Europe) and Peugeot-Citroen merger.

NB:　Other link-ups include: Audi-NSU's (VW) assembly of Porsche 924 and the manufacture of its powertrain; Fiat's 50% ownership of Ferrari; the Renault/Peugeot/Volvo co-operation in the Douvrin engine (FSM); Audi-NSU's (VW) and Citroen each have a 50% stake in Comotor. *BL's absence of any European link is rather remarkable.*

arrangements can be made, whereby both parties to the agreement can extend their model ranges by filling gaps in their own ranges with suitable products from their partner's range. The benefits are mixed: dealers and fleet customers would find the arrangement to their advantage but prestige might be damaged in the process and it would certainly involve giving extra profits to an erstwhile competitor. A strategy of this sort would certainly help BL, but it would be of little benefit to the UK.

The possibilities of joint ventures with cars is more remote. The sharing of a body is almost impossible, which simply leaves components. The trouble is that the number of European manufacturers who have suitable components *and* who would wish to be associated with an ailing UK competitor in this way are limited. However, even with cars the possibilities for joint ventures on powertrain developments exist and whilst being less likely should not be ruled out of court.

With news of the proposed Peugeot-Citroen takeover of Chrysler's European operations come fears for BL. The new group may swamp BL with greater resources and even a fairly large dealer network in the UK. This has led to speculation of a greater urgency in BL's search for joint ventures. Some informed comment believes that it is now imperative that some collaboration occurs even with the car division. For example one informed comment was:

'In this world of big battalions Leyland simply cannot go on alone,' one senior Director said.

'No one is talking about a full merger on the Peugeot-Chrysler scale. But there is a strong opinion that Leyland will have to seek urgently a full co-operative agreement on joint model development, sharing of component manufacture, assembly and marketing. The favoured candidate is a Japanese firm, especially Datsun.' (Observer 13.8.78)

Of course Datsun (Nissan) is not the only company that is rumoured to be thinking of collaboration with BL. For some time Renault has been associated in this role.[1]

Another comment was:

'Both IVECO, the Fiat-controlled consortium and MAN of West Germany are said to have looked over Leyland Vehicles and said: "No thanks".' (Financial Times 5.12.78)

The Peugeot-Citroen takeover makes joint ventures in the car division more desirable from BL's point of view, however it also narrows the choice. We return to an examination of BL's possible European partners in the next chapter.

[Recent Events: SP Industries and Leyland Vehicles have been reorganised. The successful Coventry Climax, Alvis and Self-Changing Gears are being added to Leyland Vehicles to form a new company. BL Commercial Vehicles (Ashok and Ennore in India, Leyland Nigeria and interests in Iran are also included in the new group). It is rumoured that Aveling Barford and Prestcold will be hived off and sold. Meanwhile Leyland Vehicles has not had a good year and will return a loss for 1978 — mainly due to industrial disruption. A quote by Roger Eglin aptly summarises the effect of this news:

'Leyland's plunge into losses has shattered the widely held belief that even if the car business is teetering on the edge of disaster, truck and bus is still as strong as ever, the rock which has anchored the rest of the group for so many years.' (Sunday Times 24.9.78)

Meanwhile Leyland Vehicles have had a number of changes in management and a £58 million investment cut-back (mainly at Bathgate where several ultimatums failed to produce a return to work by machinists and where production has been running at 65 per cent of its planned levels). BL also plans to close its Southall plant at a cost of about 2,500 jobs.]

Import Penetration

Import penetration is still rising in the CV sector — from 13.4 per cent in 1977 to nearly 22 per cent in 1978. The increase suggests that the CV market is not necessarily as robust as is generally assumed. Toyota, Mazda, Datsun and VW all made a particularly strong impact on the van and pick-up sector,

1. See for example the Financial Times of 12.8.78

while Ford increased its imports of car-derived vans (1 per cent of the total market).The UK manaufacturers' share has continued to drop, with GM and Ford recording the largest loss of share. Ford imported nearly 4,000 vehicles from Spain in 1978.

SECTION 4: COMPONENTS

The UK components industry has the efficiency and the energy to maintain its already strong position and even to use the opportunities presented by a wider European market to expand and prosper — although one or two shadows loom on the horizon.

One point emerged particularly strongly: the components industry does not function in splendid isolation; it depends on the large volume of orders received from UK vehicle-makers. Without these orders, it would be impossible to maintain present production volumes: the unit production costs which allow them to price so competitively would vanish. While the UK components industry is larger and generally stronger than its European equivalent[1] — and can offer corresponding price advantages because of this — it does not necessarily follow that European buyers will look to the UK for competitive component pricing. European firms are characteristically wary of relying too heavily on sources liable to industrial unrest and supply irregularities, which are the two features most commonly associated with industry in the UK, in whatever shape or form. The extra business obtained from European firms may all too often be supplied from factories located on the European mainland.

As UK component manufacturers seek to improve and extend their coverage in Europe — by siting overseas if necessary — foreign investors can be expected to purchase component firms in the UK. Where CV componentry is concerned, we have already seen the extent to which many of the major specialist suppliers are US-owned. The trend is unmistakably towards an increased US involvement in the future. Takeovers of this sort, allied to aggressive marketing, will certainly threaten the hegemony of the giant UK producers. This underlines the fact that even though a small number of firms dominate particular sectors of component supply, the wider component market has remained highly competitive. Pricing is keen, customers exercise considerable countervailing power, competition and competitive pressure is intense and the restraints on non-competitive behaviour are enormous. Potential competition from large European firms merely adds an extra dimension to the market situation.

Rumours of a possible merger between ERF (run by Peter Foden) and Fodens have not as yet been confirmed. Whilst ERF plans a £10 million expansion (which it can only just afford), Fodens already have plenty of room for expansion. However, there are no indications that the two branches of the Foden family will join forces.

More interesting is the possibility of a Welsh assembly plant for Mitsubishi. Such a plant has not as yet been given a definite go-ahead by the govern-

---

1. Due to the historical influences which shaped the peculiar structure of the UK motor industry.

ment. Although a Mitsubishi CV plant will create new jobs, the government might be fearful of its effects on Leyland Vehicles.

Furthermore, many of the components sold by the UK motor industry are made by the car and truck producers themselves, and are therefore heir to the same problems. The component sector proper displays certain weaknesses of its own, production bottlenecks for example, or a certain lack of enthusiasm for any significant export trade in some quarters of the industry.

Even so, the component sector is a major source of strength in the UK economy. All indications suggest that this position will be maintained as the sector flexes new muscles in the European motor industry at large. There is plenty of evidence to suggest that component manufacturers and the small specialist vehicle makers are fighting hard to retain their technological lead as well as exploiting opportunities for existing products, but they may have further adjustments to make as patterns or distribution and buying policies change.[1] European buyers are prepared to shop around to get the best price/quality mix and to ensure alternative sources of supply. In turn, the component makers themselves have sought orders for a wide variety of manufacturers. The European components industry has seen a number of take-overs, mergers and cross-shareholdings, as manufacturers seek to gain additional capacity and to eliminate competitors, but the impetus for further rationalisation is probably spent, judging from the abortive GKN merger with Sachs and the Lucas link with Ducellier.

The increasing tendency for less developed countries to have their own motor industry including some form of assembly operations puts the UK in a strong position to take advantage of this growth. The European norm of a vertically integrated business may not be able or willing to offer as competitive a product as the largely independent UK components industry. If the search for greater economies of scale leads to worldwide common components, then this too could help the UK industry.

Unfortunately, import penetration of motor components is increasing: in 1978 imports rose by over 20 per cent compared with a much lower rise in export sales. This can be partly accounted for by the change in attitude of the major UK vehicle manufacturers, who have begun to follow the European example in shopping around. As the US multinationals integrate their production on a European basis, there has also been a tendency to import components from established overseas sources for assembly in UK plants, which gives an additional boost to the import bill. And finally, the number of foreign-made cars has generated a not unexpected demand for replacement parts — most of which must be imported.

---

1. In terms of new technology, it is of consequence that the UK has the world's only mature and viable electric vehicle industry with firms such as Crompton Parkinson, Smiths and Harbilt supplying road vehicles for commercial use. In addition, Lucas and Chloride, with some US involvement, are co-operating with chassis makers to try to extend the market for battery electric vehicles. Therefore, the component industry and small specialist vehicle makers are endeavouring to remain at the forefront of technology as well as exploiting opportunities for their existing products and productive capacity.

One other worrying feature must be taken into account. The major motor vehicle manufacturers may well wish to extend the principle of greater rationalisation to the new territories of component supply. Vertical expansion is obviously appealing, as it offers improved security of supply and the chance of higher profit margins. There are signs that even BL Components and Parts have started to play the game by these new rules. If the trend continues it could affect an otherwise fairly rosy future for the UK components industry. Firms hoping to survive would be well advised to keep a close watch on the market place, and on the activities of the motor vehicle manufacturers.

[Recent Events: BL's expansion into component supply may not continue as there are clear signs that BL are making sensible decisions. Quotations, for example, are being sought from outside suppliers as an alternative to producing components in-house. (For example axles for Land-Rovers, whose production is to be doubled, and engines in general for trucks). BL has reorganised its engines marketing operations (to be known as Austin Morris Power Systems) and intends to increase engine sales to a wide range of automotive, marine and industrial applications (increasing revenue from £4 million in 1977 to £12 million by the early 1980's). The new division will actively sell to some of the smaller car manufacturers thereby beginning the restructuring process suggested in Chapter 18.]

CONCLUSION

Nearly everyone concerned with the UK motor industry was caught on the hop by the unexpected recovery in demand, but it came as no surprise, in the event that supply could not keep pace with demand. Ford, GM and Chrysler UK are all performing as expected, although BL's performance has been a little disappointing. Overall, there is room for cautious optimism in some sectors of the UK motor industry, but the problems identified earlier in the book still exist and must still be dealt with. Meanwhile, the UK balance of payments continued to deteriorate in 1978.[1] This deterioration poses some interesting policy issues for the UK Government. For example, it is by no means obvious whether the downward trend of the UK car producers should be halted. This and other problems are analysed in Chapter 18. Whatever the policy issues involved, no UK motor vehicle manufacturer can afford to rest on its laurels, particularly when facing the renewed challenge in the fiercely competitive European market. There can be little doubt that international competitive pressures played a major part in Chrysler's decision to sell its European subsidiary.

---

1. The balance of payments for all items connected with the motor industry fell in 1978 from £1,331 million to £776 million.

412

CHAPTER 17

The Peugeot-Citroen-Chrysler Affair

INTRODUCTION

Although at the moment the air is thick with news of the proposed Peugeot-Citroen take-over of Chrysler's European operations (henceforth PCC), it is far too early to conclude that the deal will actually go ahead. The proposed merger does not, in any case, envisage that Peugeot will take full control of Chrysler Europe until 1981. So the short-run for Chrysler must follow plans laid down by the current Chrysler management. It is the longer run that will be affected and this accords well with the conclusion given in Section 2, in which short-run prospects were more promising than the long-run prospects of viability.

Since no agreement is going to be finalised quickly, and the timescale between 1978 and 1981, when Peugeot takes full control, is fairly long, there is plenty of time for pressure to be exerted for the terms of the deal to be changed or even for the deal to be called off.

These pressures include the UK Government, the French Government, the UK trade unions and labour force, and second thoughts by Peugeot-Citroen. The UK Government naturally wishes to protect its investment and would desperately like to preserve employment at Linwood. The French Government may be worried about the implications of the merger on Renault. A secondary fear may be that, if PCC proves to be too big a cherry for Peugeot to chew, then it may have to come to the rescue of the new group, a task which may include pumping money into UK and Spanish plants – a prospect close to an anathema to the fiercely nationalistic French attitude.

For the UK Government, resistance will come in the form of fear that parts of Chrysler's UK operations will not find a place in the new PCC group – a fear that is explored later. Chrysler's UK labour force may also be worried. For, although they managed to "train" Chrysler's management into reduced expectations of productivity, it may be more difficult to do the same to the new Peugeot management. Similarly, the new management may fail to understand why threats and warnings have little effect on the labour force. Repeated threats by the old Chrysler management have made the labour force immune to such warnings.

The solution of placing a government nominated director to protect the investment of UK public funds may not be satisfactory from a Peugeot standpoint. After all, Peugeot is paying some £220 million for Chrysler's European operations and it is certain to have to cough up further funds for investment in the UK (if the UK plants are to be retained). Why should the Peugeot management readily yield control to external forces?

There are, therefore, problems in the proposed merger. A lot more discussion, negotiations, and agreement have yet to be conducted before the proposed merger will become a certainty. The proposed Volvo-Saab merger won universal support and approval, yet Saab-Scania's employees managed to effectively kill (or, maybe, only postpone) the merger. Similarly, the concept of a PCC has a long way to go before it becomes a reality.

To hedge against such an eventuality, an assessment of Chrysler UK without

PCC merger is provided in Appendix 17.1. Since very little information has been provided about Peugeot-Citroen, a statistical appendix is provided in Appendix 17.2. As well as information on Peugeot-Citroen, production information on the other major European companies is provided. In Appendix 17.3, a brief analysis of the effect on dealers is undertaken.

Peugeot-Citroen

Before the Peugeot-Citroen merger in 1975, Peugeot ranked behind BL, VW, all of the US multinationals, Renault and Fiat in terms of capacity and sales. In the last three years, Peugeot has become the largest European manufacturer and may be close to challenging Daimler-Benz to the number one position in terms of sales revenue. As well as the Citroen and possible Chrysler mergers, Peugeot has other joint ventures. There is the joint engine project with Renault and Volvo[1], and Peugeot-Citroen and Fiat have recently agreed to join forces to build a $280m plant for making 80,000 light vans a year in Southern Italy. In addition, Citroen and VW are joint owners of Comotor, which is a design and research project.

Although Peugeot-Citroen may now become the largest European manufacturer, it has inherited a dispersed set of manufacturing facilities and an immensely complex pattern of sourcing. To reap full economies of scale will be a mammoth undertaking. Parallels with the formation of BL in 1968 may be made.

Peugeot-Citroen has an enormous task ahead of it. This task would be made easier if a certain amount of rationalisation was performed. Surgery of the most troublesome and least profitable operations may occur.

We now turn our attention to an investigation of why Peugeot-Citroen and the French motor industry in general has done so well in the past few years.

What motivated Chrysler (US) to sell?

Chrysler is the weakest of the US big three multinationals. It has made losses in 1974 and 1975, modest profits in 1976 and 1977, and, with US market shares slipping from more than 16% to 12%, is expected to turn in another loss in 1978, of some $205 million. Because of US Federal legislation, Chrysler must undertake a massive capital investment of some $7.5 billion if the company is to remain an effective force in the US motor industry. The difference between what Chrysler (US) needs to spend and what it will be able to raise has been estimated to be about $1.5 billion by 1980-1. Some of this deficiency has been borrowed but the company is already highly geared. The PCC deal means that Chrysler (US) receives $200 million in cash (and $230 million in shares) and, at the same time, has divested itself of some $400 million of debt. Profitability of its European operations has not been spectacular, and its UK operations have been a significant drain on cash. Some estimates put the $430 million as high as the equivalent of around 12 years of its European earnings. The signals emanating from Chrysler (US) show that it has had enough, and that if it does not want to keep ownership of Chrysler France, it is even less likely to

---

1. The Douvrin (FSM) engine project.

want to keep Chrysler UK. This point has ramifications in the later analysis.

THE FRENCH INDUSTRY

To understand why Peugeot-Citroen has done so well, one must enquire into the health of the French motor industry. France's period of phenomenal growth has occurred primarily since 1968. Since the 1950s, West Germany has been the largest car producer and the producer with the fastest growth. However, this growth started to tail off in 1969 and by the boom period of the early 1970s, the West German industry almost stagnated. Why? The reason was partly due to the revaluation of the German Mark, which appreciated by 87 per cent *vis-a-vis* the French Franc, and by 95 per cent against the US Dollar between 1968 and 1978. Meanwhile, the French Franc devalued by some 46 per cent against the German Mark. Taking the favourable effect on the import price of a French passenger car entering West Germany, and the unfavourable price of a German car entering France, the combined movement amounts to some 133 per cent over the ten year period. Over half of this change occurred since 1976. Small wonder that the French were able to expand — to some extent at the expense of West Germany.

Figures 17.1 and 17.2 illustrate the rapid rise of the French industry compared with other European countries.

The Peugeot background

Having enquired into the French motor industry in general, our attention is now focused on Peugeot in particular. Up to about 1975, Peugeot was a small well run car manufacturer with a reputation for solid but rather unexciting engineering. The company was very much a large specialist manufacturer rather than a small, volume manufacturer. Production was below that of BL. Peugeot's rejuvenation has been attributed to M. Jean-Paul Parayre, who used to be a civil servant with special responsibilities for the motor industry, and who now heads the Peugeot-Citroen group. It was perhaps his time as a technocrat that decided Parayre to rationalise the European motor industry, and certainly all the evidence suggests that Peugeot-Citroen will become a pan-European force.

Parayre joined Peugeot when the Peugeot-Citroen merger took place. "... his arrival and that of a £115m state loan to help cement the marriage with Citroen are not considered a total coincidence" (Financial Times, 12.8.78). The philosophy behind the Peugeot-Citroen merger was to allow Citroen managerial independence whilst the group retained financial control.

Before the AMC (the ailing US firm) and Renault link-up was announced, there had been much speculation that Peugeot-Citroen would take over AMC. Some commentators believe that when that deal fell through, Peugeot-Citroen then started to look at other partners and the choice came naturally to Chrysler. The French government must have been supportive of this move. De Gaulle reluctantly let a US multinational take over Simca. This may be remedied, for, if the merger goes through, the French industry will again be in totally French hands.

Peugeot-Citroen's operating results are shown in Table 17.1. In Table 17.1

FIGURE 17.1

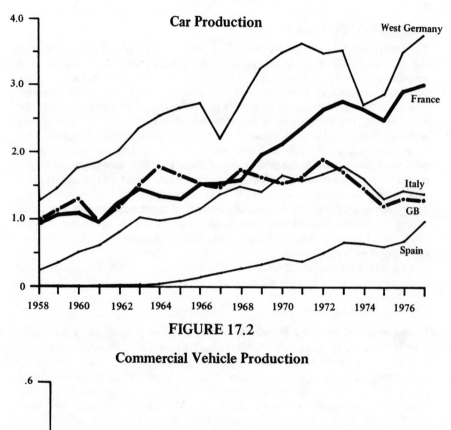

Car Production

FIGURE 17.2

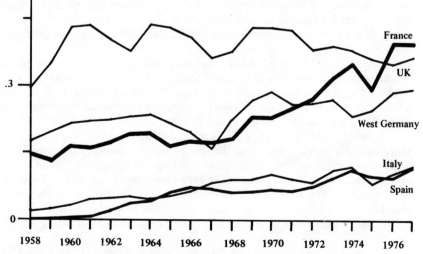

Commercial Vehicle Production

(a), production and market share figures are provided and they demonstrate that the company is improving its position within the French market and industry.

TABLE 17.1

Peugeot-Citroen's Operating Results

(a) Production, Sales and Labour Force	1976	1977
Production (in '000 of vehicles)	1,438	1,518
Share of French production %	42.3	43.3
French sales (in '000 of vehicles)	727	757
French market share %	33.8	34.3
Export (in '000 of vehicles)	670	760
Share of French exports %	40.7	43.0
Labour force ('000)	177	185

(b) Financial Summary	1976 £m	1977 £m
Sales	4,125	4,927
Profit before interest	466	540
Interest (net)	67	86
Profit before tax	399	454
Tax	174	178
Profits after interest and tax	225	276
Retained earnings	168	147
Investment	238	458
(of which capital investment)	216	390
Internally generated funds	408	454

The financial summary in Table 17.1 (b) highlights just how quickly Peugeot-Citroen recovered from Citroen's liquidity crisis in 1974. Profits were large and the healthy internally generated cash flow was primarily used to undertake new capital investment.

Peugeot-Citroen was so confident that by 1978 it was even able to pay off its £115m state loan. The reason for the repayment of the loan ahead of schedule was probably political expediency rather than surplus cash,[1] since the Left were making political capital out of the state loan (a present to the Peugeot family).

'The take-over would give Chrysler a 15 per cent stake, the second largest, in the new *menage-a-trois*, provided for by an increase in capital to FFr 794m. The Peugeot family, which directly and indirectly has some 48 per cent of the current Peugeot-Citroen combine, would hold about 42 per cent. The Michelin tyre empire, which once controlled Citroen, would have between 6 and 7 per cent, the rest being distributed among minor shareholders including the Caises des Depots.

Thus, looming behind the earnest features of M. Parayre, the Protestant hierarchy of the Peugeots is anything but extinct. The 11-man supervisory board includes three Peugeots — Roland, the president; Bertrand and Antoine. Pierre is one of the managing triumvirate,[2] having played, it is said, a key role in the Chrysler deal.

Peugeot has managed to keep clear of much of the labour trouble that has plagued other European motor companies. Its strike record is better than Renault's, although Renault workers are better paid; Renault being anchored in more populous regions, strongly politicised and with a big immigrant percentage in its labour force. Peugeot is happier in its provincial stronghold. Sochaux is as much a company town as Volkwagen's Wolfsburg.

The paternalistic tradition now covers all the group's 184,000 employees. Housing and social activities are well looked after. Workers have company shares, as they do at Renault, and receive holiday credits and early-

---

1. Cash for the group in 1977 was fairly tight, necessitating a new long term loan of £256 million. Peugeot-Citroen's reconstructed sources and application of funds statement for 1977 was:

Sources	£m	
Profits (net of exceptional items, taxes, dividends and other distributions)	233	
Depreciation	203	
	436	
Increase in long term loans	256	
Sales of assets	28	
New equity (participating scheme)	28	
Other	12	814
Applications		
Investment	458	
Repayment of long term loans	169	629
Change in Working Capital		
Increase in stocks	190	
Increase in debtors and short-term loans	327	
Decrease/(Increase) in current liabilities	(332)	
Decrease/(Increase) in bank overdraft	(17)	
Other	17	185

2. The triumvirate is composed of Pierre Peugeot, Jean-Paul Parayre and Gerard de Pins.

retirement facilities, if they clock in regularly. "The characteristic of Peugeot which makes it different is that in spite of its growth and size it has remained a family business", says an executive. "This is not only in terms of ownership, but also in terms of camaraderie and friendship among the people who work there."

The other side of the coin is that Peugeot has a reputation for worker surveillance. Other unionists claim the company pays its labour leaders, and Peugeot-Citroen is the stronghold of one of Europe's most Right-Wing unions, the CSL, whose record of industrial action seems to consist in beating up Reds.' (Financial Times, 12.8.78)

As an aside, the PCC management will find the atmosphere at UK plants completely alien from what they have been used to in France. The open hostility between the shop floor and management will be a novel experience. Some would argue that a significant proportion of the fault lies with management, but Frank Page's comment succinctly puts the opposite view :

' "The real poser is how to make a bunch of employees work when they don't really believe there is any need to work, because the government will always look after them if they don't", one ex-Chrysler man told me.'
(Observer 13.8.78)

The Citroen Angle

Citroen had always been a rather schizophrenic car company with a reputation for models at the top and bottom end. There was very little in between. Either you bought a 2CV or Dyane or you bought a technically brilliant piece of sophisticated engineering which in itself was expensive to produce and may have given rise to large warranty claims.

Citroen ran into trouble at the end of 1974, when a new factory was opened and a new range of models were launched just before the oil crisis. The effect of the oil crisis was a move towards the smaller car. In this sector Citroen was singularly ill-equipped, with only the 2CV and its derivatives. Although the fall in CX and GS sales was made up by increased sales of 2CV and Dyane, profitability suffered since the mark-up on the bottom end of the range was small.

With the bankers worried, the Government, under Parayre's influence perhaps, decided to reorganise the French industry. With the help of Parayre and a one billion FF loan (£115m) Peugeot, predominantly a car firm, took over Citroen, whilst Berliet, Citroen's CV subsidiary, was linked to Renault's CV subsidiary, Saviem. Peugeot-Citroen concentrated on exercising financial control by reducing stocks, improving the packaging on the Citroen cars, and boosting sales.

Rationalisation between the two groups was kept to a minimum as there was insufficient time to do much else. Reorganising the basic weakness of the small car segment, Peugeot-Citroen created the Citroen LN, by dropping a Citroen engine and transmission into a Peugeot 104 body. Later in 1978

Citroen will unveil a new car called the Visa, which is a more carefully planned model than the LN with distinctive Citroen features but nevertheless based firmly on the Peugeot 104 model range.

The Peugeot rescue of Citroen was a painless affair. Citroen, apart from one or two weaknesses, had a sound product range – albeit strong in the upper segments. However, a combination of the oil crisis, "debugging" new models, and problems with a new factory meant that Citroen needed a breathing space. Peugeot gave Citroen their breathing space and has been able to rectify one or two other weaknesses – such as the lack of a competitive small car. However, if there had been anything more fundamentally wrong with Citroen, then it is unlikely that Peugeot would have been able to restore Citroen to profitability so effortless or so quickly.

POSSIBILITIES OF THE MERGER

There is one possibility that is unlikely to occur and that is the complete collapse of all negotiations. With the nationalistic French government behind them the very minimum that will be achieved is the merger between Peugeot-Citroen and Chrysler France. A list of alternatives which may be ranked in order of desirability from Peugeot-Citroen's point of view can be analysed.

Granted that Chrysler France is the number one prize (and this would probably include Chrysler Spain) then the next most important asset is Chrysler UK's Dodge plants, which have recently been extended and modernised. The next most attractive plant must be Ryton, which assembles kits sent from France. The Stoke and Dublin plants would be the next most desirable, and might provide some continuity with the Iran order[1]. At the bottom of the list of desirability comes Linwood.

For each of these possibilities there is the additional complication of the various responses by Chrysler (US). The reason for the complete take-over not going ahead would be resistance by the UK parties concerned (government and trades unions). In this event, Chrysler might feel quite free to re-negotiate its position. Specifically, it has three possibilities :

> complete withdrawal
> partial withdrawal
> maintains existing UK presence.

For each of the above, the existing arrangement with the UK government may be maintained, it may be scrapped and a new agreement negotiated, or all agreements may be cancelled with no new ones being created.

The range of possibilities is therefore fairly large. We will now consider each participant in turn (Peugeot-Citroen, Chrysler US and the UK government) in order to narrow this range of possibilities.

Peugeot-Citroen

In order to see which alternatives Peugeot-Citroen would be most happy with, let us analyse the pros and cons of the deal for Peugeot-Citroen. Advantages include:

1. See Chapter 6 for a discussion of the Iran order.

1. Given rationalisation and the greater commonality of body panels, power-train and other parts, maximum economies of scale (about 2 million cars per year) should be available to the new group. This could give PCC a cost advantage of between 0-5% over its nearest competitors. However, it would take some time to reorganise production and models in order to reap the full advantage.

   However, maximum economies of scale could be achieved by just merging with Chrysler France and Chrysler Spain. There is no necessity to bring the UK plants in to achieve full cost advantages.

2. Peugeot-Citroen has almost no interest in the CV field. By taking over Chrysler, Peugeot-Citroen inherit a fairly strong and well-organised CV operation. The UK produces the light and medium range trucks, whilst Spain produces the heavier range of CVs.

   This advantage augurs well for the take over of Chrysler UK, since the major part of Chrysler's CV set-up is situated in the UK.

3. Chrysler remains a 15% shareholder of the new PCC group which may be allowed to use the Chrysler North American dealer network. In any case, the model programmes of the old Chrysler (Europe) will be very much linked in to the global model programme of Chrysler.

4. Chrysler's European network of dealers will, after suitable rationalisation, enable PCC to strengthen those areas where its dealer network is weak. It also provides the PCC group with a ready-made CV dealer network through-out Europe. This in itself must be invaluable. BL is finding it a difficult, expensive and lengthy process to build up a CV network which will not be nearly as comprehensive as Chrysler's.

5. Both Chrysler Europe and Peugeot have been very active in selling to the Middle East. Peugeot is due to start selling 305 kits to Iran in the near future. With the formation of PCC there will be a certain continuity, since Chrysler UK has been, and will continue to be, a major supplier to Iran.

Chrysler (US)

Any alternative which left Chrysler (US) with just the cash sapping UK operation would be clearly undesirable. Chrysler (US) wants out for the best reason in the world — to save itself. Any action that left it with either extra debt (Chrysler must reduce its debt burden so that it can borrow new, badly needed finance in the US) or the possibility of requiring scarce cash resources must defeat Chrysler's objective.

The UK Government

Although no clearly stated objectives have been issued, an ideal solution would be for all the Chrysler UK plants to employ the existing labour force, not only without making losses but generating sufficient profits to ensure that the future model programme is fully competitive — in other words, to secure long

421

run viability. Unfortunately, on the present evidence, this ideal situation is a long way from the truth. In short, the Chrysler UK plant exhibits the characteristics endemic of the UK motor vehicle manufacturing industry : low productivity, sometimes an indifferent standard of workmanship and so on. The Ryton plant is also operating below capacity. Unless production increases, the car operations are marginal.

Merger of Chrysler's UK plant with BL has been ruled out in the past because BL has enough to do without the added complication of Chrysler's plants. The Chrysler solution was a sensible one, although there was always the doubt about Chrysler Europe's long term prospects. The possibility of a Japanese manufacturer to take-over, for example, the Linwood plant, may also be attractive. Although this may remain a possibility, astute Japanese businessmen would probably prefer to use either a plant with a better productivity record than Linwood or a greenfield site built to their own specifications. Nationalisation of the Chrysler UK group *per se* would not be feasible since the Chrysler UK operation is far too small to be viable on its own. The PCC venture looks attractive, and, on the face of it, seems the only option open to the Government. The Government's fears may be translated into a hypothetical example. If production was to be expanded and if unemployment is an election issue in France, the UK and Spain, then all three countries might be tempted to "bribe" the PCC group with promises of aid, in order to attract additional production and employment to their country. Whether the UK government would be willing to enter into this poker game is irrelevant. The PCC group, with the lion's share of capacity in France[1], and very much a nationalistic concern[2], will surely be swayed by the protestations of the French government. In the last analysis, the French government, if their displeasure was incurred, could, by being awkward, do more harm to the PCC group than any other government.

From the UK government's point of view, it must have two central fears. First the new PCC group may close down some of the plants which are surplus to their requirements. Second, the danger that the PCC group's main focus of interest and principal operations are in France, so that UK interests are peripheral and, indeed, may even be regarded as a marginal appendage.

Whether these fears will reach fruition or not depend on the prospects of the new group.

PROSPECTS FOR THE PCC GROUP

The prospects for the group depends on a number of factors. First, whether the Peugeot management can successfully integrate the group and can assimilate Chrysler Europe without too much disturbance to itself. Secondly, what the likely demand and supply prospects would be for an integrated PCC group. These questions are tackled in turn.

1. France, UK and Spain have respective capacities of 2, 0.4 and 0.2 million vehicles per year.
2. Evidence of this can be seen in Peugeot-Citroen's annual accounts for 1977 : "Dans la Division Automobile, au contraire, il a ete cree pres de 6,600 emplois nouveaux en 1977, *presque tous en France,* alors que les problems du chomage, se trouvaient *au premier rang des preoccupations nationales".* (p.37)

Can Peugeot form an integrated PCC?

As suggested earlier, the Citroen situation was not too serious; all the company needed was a breathing space. Chrysler Europe is a rather different kettle of fish. Certainly, Chrysler UK has been running into serious difficulties and the Chrysler Spanish operation is still marginal. Overall, Chrysler Europe has a large number of plants and a complex sourcing pattern with one of the UK plants operating under capacity. Peugeot-Citroen have never been a company which has been particularly good at integrating components and plants. This is particularly true for Peugeot. Many of the models require different parts, rather than drawing from one integrated range. The new PCC group will probably start with more than 14 engines (compared to Ford's basic four engines). The model policy looks even more complicated.

Table 17.2 shows the model ranges of the new group. In the light and medium sector, there will be five principal models (Peugeot 305, Citroen GS and Visa, Chrysler Alpine, Chrysler Horizon) and the Chrysler Avenger (which surely must cease production soon?). In comparison, Ford have just two models covering this area, the Taunus/Cortina and the Escort.

There can be no doubt that the group has an enormous range of components and models. To be competitive with its nearest rival, Ford, a vast amount of rationalisation must occur. If it does not, then PCC will not receive the benefits which the size of the group should confer in terms of scale.

The ability of the PCC to rationalise is more worrying since Peugeot's role in reorganising Peugeot-Citroen was limited. With Citroen, the chairman, finance director and about 16 key Peugeot-based personnel were sent into Citroen and then left virtually on their own. This and the Citroen LN (based on the Peugeot 104) was all that was necessary. With Chrysler Europe, there is no shortage of models overall, and the simple replacement of management is unlikely to yield the benefits that it did with Citroen.

The PCC philosophy will be to keep three sets of distribution networks, maintain three ranges of models and names, and provide the management of the three groups with a certain amount of autonomy and flexibility. To do this with the size of diversity of interests within PCC may mean that certain conflicts in model policy will never be resolved.[1] Money will be spent on fighting among themselves. Duplications of models has certain marketing advantages, but a group of PCC's size still cannot afford to have three entirely independent model programmes. Evidence of rationalisation in the Peugeot-Citroen company can be seen with the Citroen LN and Citroen Visa. Will loyal Citroen buyers still be so loyal when Citroen has substantially Peugeot-based models? This remains to be seen. With Chrysler, the Alpine (C6), and Horizon (C2) have just been launched and must survive for a number of years. Given that Chrysler will also be making the Horizon in the US, a long life for this product (and its replacements) is assured. The UK Government would not be too pleased to see the Sunbeam dropped. The Simca 1100 replacement and the C9 (180/2 litre

---

1. The same argument could apply to GM (US), but despite four model ranges and divisions, the company manages to resolve all conflicts. On the other hand, however, it has been organised in this way for some time, and procedures and mechanisms exist to iron out all conflicts.

TABLE 17.2

PCC Model Range 1978 +

MANUFACTURER	Mini	Small	Light	Medium	Large	Executive	Luxury
PEUGEOT		104	204	305	504	604	⟶
CITROEN	2CV	LN	VISA	GS	⟵	CX	⟶
CHRYSLER							
– Current		1100	Horizon (C2)	Alpine (C6)	180/2 Litre		
		Sunbeam	Avenger				
– Future		1100 replacement			C9a		

a.   Possibly fitted with the Douvrin engine.

replacement) could be dropped. However, by the time Peugeot takes full control, both of these new models will have been launched.

An additional problem is that, given an optimal assembly plant size of between 200,000 and 400,000 cars a year, the Ryton, Linwood, Madrid (Chrysler), and Citroen's Spanish Plant are probably too small to be efficient.

What are the market prospects for the group?

The total capacity of the group is fairly complicated to assess. The European capacity of Chrysler has already been discussed. The capacity of Peugeot-Citroen can be demonstrated by looking at their total world-wide production. Table 17.3 shows production and assembly outside France. Table 17.4 shows production broken down into category of vehicle. Capacity of Peugeot-Citroen must be over 1.6 million and with Chrysler Europe, total European capacity of PCC is assumed to be around 2.6 million cars and car derived vans and some 30,000 non-car derived vans and trucks, plus a share of the 80,000 trucks planned in the Fiat link-up.

A range of estimates are provided in Table 17.5 for total demand for the group. These figures are illustrative and have been devised so that the bottom of the range is 2 million cars. This has been done because if total demand fell below 2 million, it is likely that the PCC group would be forced into making some closures. Peugeot in particular has been a very active exporter – particularly in Africa. The combined PCC group would also be able to cover the US market if Chrysler (US) was willing to let the group use its dealer network. However, assuming that the market share of the group falls to 17% and exports remain at their current level, then a central forecast for 1980 and 1985 is 2.17 and 2.32 million cars respectively. Thus, in the medium term, unless there is a major slump in demand, it is unlikely that sales will fall below their current levels. Consequently, no drastic surgery will be necessary. On the other hand, there is either none or only a small shortage of capacity abroad, so that it is unlikely that production would be switched to the UK.

The collapse of Austin-Morris or the whole of BL Cars could affect this conclusion. If the new PCC group was prepared to try to fill part of the vacuum left by BL, then its UK plants could be kept fully utilised in supplying the UK and meeting existing export commitments.

THE NATURE OF MARGINALITY OF CHRYSLER UK

From the previous section we have seen that in the short run and medium run, it is unlikely that production would be switched to the UK by PCC. If market share fell below 17% of the European sales or demand slumped, then it is even possible that production may be switched away from UK. However, on balance, the *status quo* for the short and medium runs will probably be maintained. The long run prospects are considerably brighter.

This analysis does not mean that PCC will make no closures. If production in UK plants remains at or around current levels, historical evidence seems to indicate that Chrysler UK is at best marginal. Figure 17.3 shows the profitability of Chrysler plotted against volume sales. Despite the 1975 rescue,

TABLE 17.3.

Production and Assembly
outside France

1977

Peugeot	'000s	Citroen	
Argentina	20	Belgium	53
Chile	2	Spain	142
Nigeria	24	Portugal	8
South Africa	15	Argentina	14
Malaya	1		279

TABLE 17.4
Category of Production

	1977
Citroen	'000s
Assembled in France	541
Assembled elsewhere	100
Countable KD kits	95
Non-countable KD kits	68
	804
Peugeot	
Assembled in France	724
Countable KD kits	58
Non-countable KD kits	27
	809

Chrysler UK is still marginal.

What of the future? If the 1975 rescue had been successful, then Chrysler would have generated at best moderate profits in the medium run which by the mid-1980s would have begun to deteriorate. Table 17.6 provides some sample forecasts for the Chrysler rescue. Unless PCC can undertake drastic rationalisation (which might prune European market share) then the profits indicated in Table 17.6 are probably a reasonable estimate of what earnings PCC in the short run and medium run can expect from Chrysler's UK plants.

One factor that will tend to reinforce the conclusion of marginality, is the low productivity of Chrysler UK. Citroen worldwide, in 1977, achieved a productivity level of over 13 cars per employee per year. Peugeot achieve a level in excess of 12 cars per employee per year. Chrysler UK in total achieved about 8-9 cars per employee per year (bearing in mind that Alpines are built from French parts). Chrysler's productivity figures are, however, good when compared with BL's current level of 6 cars per employee per year.

TABLE 17.5

Prospects for PCC Cars

	1977	1980	1985	1990
European Market in millions	9.9	10.7	11.6	12.7
European Market Share in .%	17.7	16-19	15-19	14-19
European Sales in millions	1.75	1.7-2.0	1.7-2.2	1.8-2.4
Non-European Sales in millions	0.35	0.3-0.4	0.3-0.4	0.2-0.4
Total Demand in millions	2.1	2.0-2.4	2.0-2.6	2.0-2.8

A direct comparison can be made between Ryton's quality of workmanship and Chrysler's Poissy plant in France, both of which produce the Alpine. Ryton compares favourably.

"Even the French acknowledge that the quality of the Ryton Alpines is good."[1]

"Ryton and Stoke labour relations and productivity have been very good since the Government agreement, and the quality of parts they are turning out is excellent."[1]   (Financial Times, 18.8.78)

The same cannot be said of Linwood (see Appendix 17.1). Some allowance can be made for recent disruptions such as the introduction of the Avenger (which used to be produced at Ryton) and new Sunbeam models, the installation of a new paint shop, the reintroduction of second shift working and other detailed changes. Notwithstanding this, there can be no doubt that productivity and quality of workmanship is poorer than PCC's French plants.

The overall effect is that PCC will find the Chrysler UK plants not quite up to scratch but at least within spitting distance of the European norm.

ANALYSIS OF PCC MERGER

From Peugeot-Citroen's point of view, the merger provides the capacity and the means to be a major European and worldwide motor company. PCC's UK plants would, during the short or medium run, probably remain marginal unless BL withdraw from volume cars — an assumption which would indicate that BL moved towards the bottom end of Scenario Two. If this does happen, then plant closures whilst not being particularly likely, cannot be entirely ruled out.

The possibilities if the PCC merger do not go through are essentially limited. One rumour currently circulating implies that Chrysler also tried to sell its European operations to VW and Nissan before Peugeot-Citroen. The fact that neither Nissan nor VW were sufficiently interested underlines just how few options are now left open for the UK government.

1.   An interview by John Elliott with Don Lander, Chrysler's Vice-President in charge of international operations and former managing director of Chrysler UK. Of course, these statements may have been a marketing exercise but other evidence collaborates these statements.

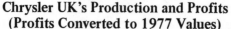

FIGURE 17.3

Chrysler UK's Production and Profits
(Profits Converted to 1977 Values)

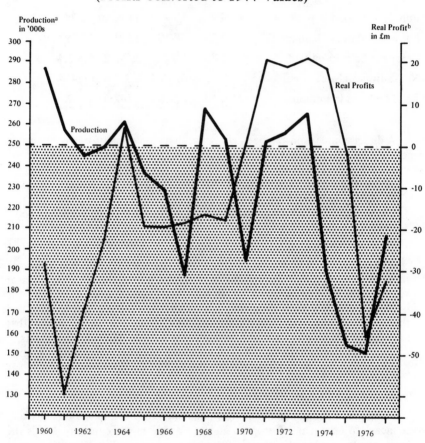

a. UK production of cars and CVs in thousands.
b. Net profit after tax and extraordinary items but before Government grants and
    converted to 1977 values using the retail price index, in £ million.

A full list of options is provided in Table 17.7. It is assumed that whatever
happens, PCC will want to take over Chrysler France and Spain and at least
some of the UK operations.

There are two major strategies concerning the complete or partial merger
of Chrysler UK into PCC. Either way the UK Government would be well advised
to encourage PCC to switch production to the UK. As is discussed in the next
chapter, aid to Chrysler UK in the past has been a surprisingly cheap form of
job creation.

TABLE 17.6
Projections of Chrysler U.K.[a]

Alternative Production Assumptions[b] (built up units in '000's)	1978	1980	1982	1985
A	163	183	185	194
B	188	210	211	222
C	229	255	255	270
Sales Revenue [c] (£ million)				
A	482	524	504	522
B	531	577	556	580
C	610	668	665	671
Net Profit [d] (£ million)				
(i) Chrysler UK on its own				
A	-12	6	-12	-19
B	- 7	7	0	3
C	3	29	17	14
(ii) Chrysler UK integrated into Chrysler Europe but no integration into remainder of PCC				
A	-12	8	- 3	3
B	- 3	17	10	14
C	3	29	17	21
(iii) Full model and production integration of Chrysler UK into PCC				
A	-12	8	1	6
B	- 3	21	20	25
C	3	35	33	40

Notes
a. These projections were contained in evidence as Minutes of Evidence taken before the Trade and Industry sub-committee, eighth report of the Expenditure Committee, Public Expenditure on Chrysler UK, T171. A financial simulation model was used to generate the projections and details of the model can be found in the report. (Allowances have been made for inflation.)
b. In addition to these built-up units there are a number of bits and parts which are supplied to Iran but whose value tails off and is negligible by 1982.
c. In 1978 terms.
d. After interest and depreciation but before tax in 1978 terms.

TABLE 17.7

Possible Strategies for Chrysler UK

Strategy	UK Government Action	Potential Long Run Viability	Actual Long Run Viability	Other Comments
1. Complete PCC merger	Encourage UK production by aid and threats.	Excellent	Depends on ability of PCC to rationalise	French interests put first?
2. Partial PCC merger	Encourage UK production by aid	Good for remaining plants	Good as remaining UK plants must be tied into PCC model policy	French interests put first? Loss of employment and negative effect on components industry and Balance of Payments
3. Of the remaining plants, one of the following could be carried out :				
a) Interest another European manufacturer	Encourage by aid	Good	Depends on sales of European manufacturers.	Possibilities are limited.
b) Interest a Japanese manufacturer	Encourage by aid	Excellent	Excellent	Unlikely

In the event of a partial withdrawal of PCC from the UK, the question arises as to what to do. An interesting alternative would be to persuade a

430

TABLE 17.7 (cont.)

Possible Strategies for Chrysler UK

Strategy	UK Government Action	Potential Long Run Viability	Actual Long Run Viability	Other Comments
c) Merge with BL	Make this a condition of further aid	Good	Depends on BL managing to sort out its problems. (see text)	A real possibility had BL Cars made more progress. Chrysler UK has some short-run advantages which dovetails nicely into BL's weaknesses.
d) Takeover UK plants to allow breathing space until options (a), (b) or (c) could be undertaken or, if all else fails, alternative projects providing employment integrated.	Heavier administrative burden for UK government. Temporary ownership could be through NEB, or a BP type solution.	Unviable as a separate entity on its own ultimately depends on one of the above.		Worthy of serious consideration.

Japanese manufacturer to come to the rescue suitably encouraged by massive aid and use the UK as a base for export into Europe. The aid could be given on the promise that a certain percentage of UK components would have to be used in the assembly of each UK car.

AN ALTERNATIVE TO PCC

A possible alternative to the PCC merger is some form of short-term holding operation combined with the long run possibility of merger with BL.[1] In effect, this proposal is to buy Chrysler UK from Chrysler, probably for a nominal sum.[2] Part of the agreement would be to continue production of the Alpine (C6) which would still be sourced from France until 1980, the substitution of the Horizon (Chrysler's worldwide C2 car) for the Avenger, and the introduction of the C9 (the top end of Chrysler's range). Part of the deal would be the sharing of Chrysler's European distribution chain.[3] In order to ensure that Chrysler (US) remains friendly to its old UK plants, the purchase price could be paid in stages over a number of years.

The Sunbeam would not be produced in France or Spain, whilst the C6 would be shared with Chrysler (US) and PCC. The C2, C6 and C9 would have to be sourced from France for a period of time until UK plants could be geared up to source these cars.

Eventual merger with BL could be arranged. What are the benefits of such a proposal? As well as UK ownership and control, Chrysler UK at the moment has a number of strengths which dovetail nicely into BL's weaknesses. These are:

1. BL is short of good small and medium saloons. This proposal envisages that this gap would be filled by versions of the Sunbeam, C2 and C6. If the Sunbeam and the LC8 (new mini) conflicted and I am not sure they will, then the Sunbeam can be dropped in favour of the LC8 and the spare capacity used by building more old Minis.

2. BL is chronically short of technical and engineering resources. Chrysler's European design centre is situated in the UK at Whitley. Its excellence has been demonstrated by the C6 (Alpine) being voted "car of the year" in 1976 and by the phenomenal speed in which they were able to develop the Sunbeam. This centre would be a most valuable asset for a joint BL and Chrysler UK operation.

3. Extra capacity is automatically provided. If BL's recalcitrant work force continues to be a problem, closures of BL plants could occur without endangering the whole of the BL Cars operation.

4. The use of all or part of Chrysler's European distribution network would be most valuable. BL has not managed to acquire a good dealer network. In the UK extra dealers with access to a larger range of models (Chrysler plus BL) could help to stop the erosion of BL's market share.

1. The PCC group would then consist of Peugeot-Citroen and Chrysler France and Spain. Chrysler UK would temporarily form an independent unit.
2. Say £25 million plus the cancellation of all debts (amounting to some £65 million).
3. Either each dealer could handle PCC, Chrysler UK and BL vehicles, or the distribution network could be split. The PCC group would however, oppose BL using Chrysler's European outlets and this might be something of a problem.

5. A joint BL/Chrysler UK would have a total capacity of about 1.5 million cars[1] and some 80,000 CVs. This would make BL a very large and strong CV producer and a car producer of about the same size as Renault, VW and Fiat. With the deficiencies of the models cured in the short tun, this provides BL with a breathing space to develop good long run models.

EFFECT ON BL

Assuming that the PCC merger does proceed, then this must have a longer term effect on BL. In particular, it underlines the dilemma of whether to contract into a smaller and more specialist manufacturer or whether to find a European partner and together attempt to become a fully competitive manufacturer.[2] In the latter event, one might ask the question — with whom shall BL merge? Table 17.8 provides a list of companies and a comments for cars and CVs.

With cars, the best partners from BL's point of view would be Renault, VW or GM. GM (US) is so profitable that it does not need to enter into links with other manufacturers. Neither would it particularly wish to take over a problem organisation like BL. If it wants expansion, GM has the necessary resources to do it from scratch. VW is more interesting. High labour costs has made German production expensive. On the other hand, with the new US plant coming into operation, another move abroad may be difficult to justify to its trade unions, especially merging with a problem company like BL.

This leaves Renault, BL's strengths in its models dovetails nicely with the good small and medium ranges of both VW and Renault. Renault, however, is government owned and has also had many more trades union problems than Peugeot-Citroen. Would the trade unions or the French Government wish to help BL? The answer is yes, if there seemed a reasonable benefit for Renault. It may just be that the new PCC grouping will be considered sufficient reason.

On the CV side there are many more possibilities for the reasons outlined in the previous chapter, namely Leyland Vehicles is a much more healthy operation with a number of strengths that BL Cars does not possess. Certainly a number of manufacturers could see potential long run benefits of a merger. Renault's CV operations are running at a loss and this may cause the company to review its position. On the other hand, the company is undertaking a reorganisation of the Renault, Berliet and Saviem divisions. VW is another possibility. Its strengths in the lighter van and truck segments would be enhanced by BL's medium and heavy CV range. However, here again, the movement of VW and MAN towards a partnership might deter VW. Fiat too has been a major expansionist force. The creation of IVECO must be completed and a new partnership with Peugeot-Citroen has just been agreed. Any future partnerships seem relatively unlikely. One of the Japanese manufacturers might think otherwise. The launching of a major European sales drive may be contingent on some link-up with a European manufacturer. BL, with a viable medium and heavy CV range, might look like a good proposition. GM is

1. Including car derived vans.
2. A quick look at Table A17.1 and A17.2 in Appendix 17 should convince the reader that BL is neither big nor small in a European context.

TABLE 17.8

Who Will BL Merge With?

Manufacturer	Cars		CV's	
	Probability of Merger	Reason	Probability of Merger	Reason
Renault	Medium	BL's top end fits in nicely with Renault's bottom end. Renault may feel pinch of the new PCC merger. Problems may be encountered with the French trade unions and Government.	Medium	Renault has just launched itself into a giant reorganisation of its CV division (which includes Berliet and Saviem).
SAAB/Volvo	Low	Too small, no bottom end for BL.	Low-medium	Strength of Swedish companies lies at the heavy end. BL already has new models planned.
GM	Low-medium	Needs extra capacity but doesn't need BL's problems. Can easily afford to build new plants elsewhere.	Low-medium	See comment under 'Cars'.
Ford	Low	No motivation	Low	No motivation
VW	Medium	BL's top end fits in better with VW's bottom range. BUT what's in it for VW?	Medium-high	In the absence of the VW/MAN link-up, BL's medium and heavy CV range would have dovetailed nicely into VW's light van range.
Fiat	Low	Fiat has enough troubles of its own and is more likely to fully take over SEAT	Low-medium	Fiat has been an expansionist force in the CV field in the past – may be content to stay put at the moment.

TABLE 17.8 (cont.)

Who Will BL Merge With?

Manufacturer	Cars		CVs	
	Probability of Merger	Reason	Probability of Merger	Reason
Daimler-Benz	Low	Daimler-Benz is not interested in volume cars. Doing well enough in any case.	Low	No CV deficiency.
BMW	Low	BMW does not produce volume cars and the extra capacity of BL would more than swamp BMW.	Low	No CV range
Nissan/Toyota/ Mitsubishi	Medium	The Japanese must start assembling in Europe soon. BL, however, has too many problems and is too large to be absorbed by the Japanese. Some form of licensing agreement may work but the Japanese would be terrified that the reputation of BL produced Japanese cars would be poor.	Medium-high	Japanese sales have not really gained a tight grip on the European market apart from some of the smaller countries. Link-up with Leyland Vehicles would provide an interesting possibility particularly at the bottom end of the CV range.

unlikely to link-up for reasons previously enumerated. Volvo and Saab have strengths in the top end of the CV range, whilst BL would prefer a partnership where there was a strong light van and truck range.

CONCLUSION

As it stands, the PCC merger for the UK offers the prospect of long term viability but very little change in prospects over the short and medium terms. Indeed, there is a small but real possibility that PCC will not wish to continue with all of Chrysler UK's plants. However, it will take some time before all the negotiations are concluded and all the details worked out. Even then, changes in plans and modifications to the organisational structures are bound to occur in response to a dynamically evolving environment. An alternative solution was proferred and should be born in mind during the next chapter.

APPENDIX 17.1

Chrysler UK – A Pre-Merger Conclusion

> This appendix was primarily written before the PCC merger was announced. Doubt has already been cast as to the likely outcome of the PCC negotiations. This appendix may be useful in the event of a collapse in negotiations.

If Chrysler had persisted with its parallel model programme of conventional and modern engineering and failed to win new substantial export orders, then Chrysler would have faced a bleak future. However, Chrysler's integration has had an about-face (see Chapter 6). The Ryton plant is to continue to link into the French model programme and Linwood is to continue with the UK models (Avenger and Sunbeam). In Chapter 6, some doubt was cast as to whether Chrysler's integration of its UK plants into Europe has been sufficient. Too much should not be made of this. If Chrysler rationalised its model policy, fully integrated its European operations and geared up its UK distribution network, then Chrysler (just) has the necessary scale to achieve long run viability. But it will have to follow an aggressive strategy with some long term expansion. Obviously, if Scenario Two in relation to BL occurs, then Chrysler will be in a stronger position.

The short run prognosis for Chrysler is fairly good. To explain why this is so, the terms[1] of the 1975 rescue must be examined. Over the period 1976-9, a £55 million *loan* to be used in capital investment in plant, equipment and models was to be given to Chrysler by the UK Government. In addition, a medium term loan of £35 million, to be raised in the private banking sector,

---

1. The Expenditure Committee Report, *Public Expenditure on Chrysler UK Ltd,* Eighth Reports from the Expenditure Committee Session 1975-6, HMSO, London, 1976, p.93.

was to be guaranteed. The Government, in addition, was committed to providing up to £72.5 million in the period 1976-9 (up to £50 million in 1976, up to £10 million in 1977, up to £7.5 million in 1978 and up to £5 million in 1979).[1]

Chrysler's optional policy (in order to maximise its shareholders wealth) would be, though this is probably a hypothetical situation, to ensure that the company achieved the lion's share of the Government aid. This would be achieved by varying the various arbitrary accounting procedures in such a way as to gain some — for to take all might arouse suspicion — of the Government's grant towards losses.[2]

Once a second model is introduced into Ryton and production is increased, thereby improving the capacity utilisation of the plant, then the short run financial viability of Chrysler is ensured. Pre-tax profits should be in the region of £10-£25 million (see Table 17.6 in the main chapter).

As for long term viability, some doubt must be placed on current evidence for Chrysler (Europe) to actually achieve the necessary scale economies. Even if Chrysler UK was fully integrated into Chrysler (Europe) it would be one of the smallest major European producers. As Chapter 6 pointed out, Chrysler's locations within Europe are not ideal

The longer run crisis situation for Chrysler will occur when its models need revitalising, coupled with either a depression and/or extensive industrial unrest. In this situation, with Ryton firmly tied into the French model programme, the big question-mark must be over Linwood and the maintenance of the Stoke plant at its existing capacity.

Adverse publicity about Chrysler UK's industrial unrest just before the announcement of the possibility of the merger is clearly due to a combination of a wary management, who must have known "something was up" and a similarly sensitive work force. Hence, the following quote probably sums up the feelings.

"Another stoppage of this nature, even over a short period of time would obviously be disastrous for this factory", Mr Jimmy Livingstone, the TGWU convenor, said after the paint shop vote "We can't go on producing at only 80 per cent of the target figures, we recognise that. But this dispute could have been settled by negotiation. If the management go about any future negotiations in the ham-fisted way they did in the paint shop issue, then we are in for trouble. Industrial relations in this plant have got to be sorted out."

Industrial relations at Coventry, the very heart of the Chrysler UK operation, also appear to have turned sour. "Had the company wanted to recreate the sort of crisis atmosphere among the work force that preceded its financial collapse in 1975 they could not have made a better job of it". says Mr Bill Lapworth, a senior Midlands official of the TGWU based at Coventry.

1. By 1978 Chrysler had received £51.5 million in Government grants and £30 million in loans. Chrysler is eligible for a further £25 million in loans and may qualify for up to £12.4 million in grants.
2. The amounts paid so far have been

	1976	1977	1978 (estimated)
Loss £m	43	21	4
Government contribution £m	41½	10	2

Morale is low and rumours rife about the company's plans for the UK. Mr Lapworth places responsibility firmly upon management and maintains that the fund of good will that the state-supported company could command has been "frittered away, particularly in recent weeks".

(Financial Times, 7.8.78)

Far from solving Chrysler UK's problems, the PCC merger has now focused attention on them.

APPENDIX 17.2

Statistical Appendix on Peugeot-Citroen and
Other European Manufacturers

This appendix consists of five tables :

Table	Data
A 17.1	European car production by manufacturer
A 17.2	European CV production by manufacturer
A 17.3	Peugeot-Citroen production by model
A 17.4	Peugeot-Citroen sales by geographical region
A 17.5	European Production of CVs by Weight

In tables A 17.1 and A 17.2 there is a certain element of double counting. Some kits are recorded as production both in France, and in Spain. The total production figures shown in Table A 17.3 for Peugeot-Citroen include all built-up and complete KD kits from France. There are however some smaller kits whose value slips through unrecorded unless the Spanish production is shown. CV production is predominantly car derived vans and this fact can be picked out from Table A 17.3. The distribution of sales round the world can be seen from Table A 17.4. Apart from Europe, Peugeot-Citroen's sales are strong in Africa. Table A 17.5 shows production by CV weight for the major European CV manufacturers. From this it can be seen that the PCC group will still be a comparatively small CV manufacturer, but that BL's production strength (apart from Land-Rovers) is in the medium to heavy range.

TABLE A 17.1

European Car Production by Manufacturer ('000's)

	1973	1974	1975	1976	1977
PCC group					
Citroen (France)	607	531	548	614	667
Citroen (Spain)	52	70	93	109	108
Peugeot (France)	656	596	564	656	676
Chrysler (France)	498	385	383	483	477
Chrysler (UK)	265	262	227	145	169
Chrysler (Spain)	87	76	67	82	96
(N.B. includes a certain element of double counting)	2,165	1,920	1,882	2,089	2,193
Renault group					
Renault (France)	1,101	1,174	1,042	1,218	1,259
Renault (Spain)	166	167	193	202	224
	1,267	1,341	1,235	1,420	1,483
Ford					
Ford (UK)	453	384	330	383	407
Ford (West Germany)	456	286	413	487	543
Ford (Belgium)	241	139	182	285	306
Ford (Spain)	–	–	–	18	213
	1,150	809	925	1,173	1,468
GM					
Opel (West Germany and Belgium)	868	578	657	919	922
Vauxhall (UK)	138	137	99	109	93
	1,006	715	756	1,028	1,015
VW group (West Germany)	1,774	1,436	1,255	1,463	1,596
BL (UK and Belgium)	876	739	605	688	651
Fiat (Italy)	1,559	1,360	1,125	1,257	1,201
Seat (Spain)	359	361	329	342	347
Fiat and Seat	1,918	1,721	1,454	1,599	1,548
BMW (West German)	196	185	217	268	285
Daimler-Benz (West Germany)	332	340	350	378	409
Alfa-Romeo (Italy)	205	208	190	201	201

TABLE A 17.2

European CV Production by Manufacturers ('000's)

	1972	1973	1974	1975	1976	1977
PCC group						
Citroen (France)	62	67	66	50	65	69
Citroen (Spain)	16	21	22	18	23	33
Peugeot (France)	66	77	93	80	103	106
Chrysler (France)	–	28	24	25	28	29
Chrysler (UK)	25	26	25	19	14	16
Chrysler (Spain)	5	7	9	7	5	5
(N.B. includes an element of double counting	174	226	239	199	238	258
Renault group						
Renault (France)	106	108	118	87	147	140
Saviem (France)	33	37	40	35	41	35
Berliet (France)	22	23	25	24	24	20
Fasa (Spain)	12	16	17	13	11	13
	173	184	200	159	223	208
Fiat group						
Clive (France)	9	10	10	14	16	17
Magirus-Deutz (West Germany)	12	11	14	18	23	10
OM (Italy)	18	26	30	24	21	22
Fiat (Italy)	85	104	108	83	95	73
Autobianchi (Italy)	1	1	1	1	1	1
	125	152	163	140	156	131
Seat	3	3	3	3	4	6
Fiat and Seat	128	155	166	143	160	137
Daimler Benz group (West Germany)	103	117	125	145	180	174
VW-MAN						
VW (West Germany)	195	187	134	136	94	94
MAN (West German)	14	16	16	16	19	21
	209	203	150	152	113	115
Volvo (Sweden)	18	21	23	31	30	30
Saab-Scania (Sweden)	15	16	18	19	21	22
DAF (Netherlands)	12	13	12	10	N/A	N/A
BL (UK)	140	137	125	133	120	120
Ford (UK)	144	137	151	129	142	148
GM group						
Beford (UK)	91	112	107	91	86	92
Opel (West Germany)	6	6	5	2	3	3
	97	118	112	93	89	95

TABLE A 17.3

Peugeot-Citroen's Production by Model ('000's)

	1972	1973	1974	1975	1976	1977
Peugeot						
104	17	102	138	115	156	190
204	164	128	104	96	50	–
304	145	169	96	93	137	160
305	–	–	–	–	–	10
404	104	96	101	65	73	74
504	185	207	216	242	274	293
604	–	–	–	10	36	25
J7	24	31	32	23	33	30
	639	733	689	644	759	782
Citroen						
2CV	165	158	190	137	156	150
Dyane-Mehan	106	90	124	108	110	103
LN	–	–	–	–	5	65
Ami	81	91	59	50	41	35
GS	197	223	172	190	232	248
CX	–	–	12	97	112	113
D series	92	97	40	1	–	–
H	4	3	16	9	12	10
C35	20	19	3	7	11	12
	665	681	616	599	679	736

TABLE A 17.4

Peugeot-Citroen Sales by Geographical Region ('000's)

	1972	1973	1974	1975	1976	1977
Peugeot-Citroen						
France	716	811	658	636	743	759
EEC	310	375	394	359	367	397
Other European Countries	142	89	109	79	126	157
Africa	65	82	129	93	107	131
N. America	16	13	19	21	16	21
Asia and Oceania	34	41	73	52	41	36
Diplomatic	12	13	14	13	13	18
	1,295	1,424	1,296	1,253	1,413	1,519

TABLE A 17.5

European Production of CVs by Weight Broken Down into Weight Segment for 1976
('000s)

CV Segment	PCC (estimate)	BL Austin-Morris	BL Land-Rover	BL Leyland Vehicles	Ford	GM	Daimler Benz[c]	VW and MAN[d]	IVECO	Renault Berliet Saviem
0-2 tonnes and car-derived vans	115[a]	52[a]	39[a]	1[a]	64[a]	40[b]	6	64	11	87
<6 tonnes	47	—	—	3	3	6	52	72	58	23
6-12 tonnes	4	—	—	11	17	33	39	1	17	6
>12 tonnes	5	—	—	15	22	10	50	11	38	21
Artics	4	—	—	4	3	1	15	3	7	6
Buses	1	1	—	8	22	4	13	2	8	3
TOTAL	176	53	39	40 {133}	131	93	175	153	131	146

a. Figures calculated on the basis of < 3½ tonnes
b. Includes 1,662 CVs made in West Germany.
c. Excludes 50K trucks and 11K buses assembled abroad; includes Hanomag-Henschel.
d. Excluding assembly abroad.

APPENDIX 17.3

Effect on PCC Merger on Dealers

This appendix deals with one salient feature of the merger as yet undiscussed —

the effect of the merger on the UK distribution network. At the moment, Peugeot-Citroen are providing assurances that all three distribution networks will remain intact. Table A 17.6 shows the size of the three networks.

Before the merger, Peugeot was looking for some 30 or 40 additional dealers whilst Citroen wanted to build up its dealership towards 300. Up to now, Peugeot and Citroen maintained distribution and marketing operations. The philosophy being that neither company would have been able to have achieved the same level of sales and market penetration if they had worked as one entity.

With a current market share of some 10-11% combined with the expansion of the Peugeot and Citroen network, this would imply that the PCC group will have around 1,200 dealers, which is just under the number Ford has. With a market size of 1.7 million and a market share of 11%, the PCC group will have a UK sales level of 187,000 cars. It would be feasible to maintain a base of around 1,000 dealers, if the dealer network had grown up with few locational conflicts. However, the problems that were seen in Chapter 14 (Table 14.8) might occur with PCC — too many PCC dealers crowding a particular location. Some contraction in the number of dealers must occur as a result of the merger. Apart from locational conflicts, there is also a large model range with many conflicts. No one distribution network can offer all the benefits of all three marques. Chrysler lacks a top end of the range, and Citroen has certain weaknesses in its mid-range. Only Peugeot can offer a fully comprehensive range, but its products lack the "luxury" feel of the Citroens. Sooner or later, some dealers may wish to "pollinate" their range with the other PCC marque names. Moreover, if the Chrysler UK operations are to be closed down then this may have ramifications for the Chrysler UK dealers. In fact, the extent of the dealer rationalisation may be directly related to the extent of the rationalisation of the new group. A guesstimate of the dealer network would involve a total of no higher than 1,000 and probably somewhere between 800-900, although this would be by no means a lower limit.

TABLE A 17.6

UK Dealer Network for PCC

	CARS		CVs	
	Total Outlets in 1978	Sales per outlet for 1977	Total Outlets in 1977	Sales per outlet for 1977
Chrysler/Simca	—	—	96	53
Cars	612[a]	137	—	—
Light vans	477[a]	11	—	—
Peugeot	226[b]	113	—	—
Citroen	234[c]	115		

a 1977 figures   b 201 dealers in 1977   c 234 dealers in 1977

CHAPTER 18

POLICY ISSUES

INTRODUCTION

Throughout this book a number of observations and recommendations have been made and certain conclusions have been reached. These are now brought together in a systematic attempt to itemise all policy considerations, but this chapter also breaks new ground in discussing some fundamental policy issues — such as *where* is the motor industry going?

POLICY OBJECTIVES

Whenever policy is discussed, a sharp and very real distinction arises between policy for the UK government and policy for the motor vehicle manufacturer. A private company will seek to maximise profits, for example, and in order to achieve this certain unprofitable products may be eliminated. This in turn could lead to a restriction of manufacturing capabilities for the firm in question, which the firm itself might find acceptable but which could well be contrary to the interests of the UK government. In simple terms, this highlights the dichotomy (and the conflict) between policies which are judged to be in the best interest of a firm and policies which accord with government priorities.

It seems to me that the true nature of this distinction has not yet been brought home to UK governments. On the one hand, the government is seriously concerned with levels of employment. On the other hand, BL has been given a remit by the NEB not to boost or maintain employment levels but to become a profitable, self-financing concern operating in accordance with traditional commercial criteria. There are many instances in which BL's actions may be correct in the context of its own commercial objectives, but they could still be counter-productive in terms of a wider UK context.

Long-Run Plans versus Short-Run Crisis Actions

Government action to date has been primarily 'event' or crisis-orientated. Action is only taken in response to short-run phenomena, usually of a critical nature. The need to find effective and immediate solutions to pressing problems has obscured if not obliterated long-term objectives, particularly in the case of BL. What should now be determined— as a matter of urgency — is just what sort of motor industry is to be established in the UK, and how that industry is to be run.

In Europe, firms such as Renault and Alfa-Romeo have set aside orthodox commercial criteria and operate within much broader constraints: Renault, for example, is expected only to 'break even', and to make some contribution towards the balance of payments and the problem of employment. It may be impossible for weaker firms in the U.K., still profit-oriented, to compete with healthier industries in Europe which do not have to respond to commercial, profit-making criteria.

Industrial Strategy

The problem of reconciling long-term and short-term objectives is also a direct result of the absence of any coherent industrial strategy for the UK motor industry, whereby all short-term measures were undertaken with a view to achieving a set of long-term planning objectives covering all aspects of the motor industry. At the moment, the industry has no planning horizons and no framework within which plans and decisions can be made. If the component makers who now supply BL had taken the government at its word, for example, they would have had to change their plans every few months in the last few years. What the industry needs now is policy continuity and consistency, so that investment can anticipate requirements with greater confidence. BL must be revitalised as a matter of urgency. And if redundancies are inevitable, new job opportunities must be created to take up the surplus labour.

At the moment, the government provides financial support in one form or another for each of the four major companies in the UK, without apparent regard for the fact that all four are in direct competition with one another. A viable industrial stategy could foster a level of competition within a national policy framework that is to the benefit of the UK as a whole rather than in the interests of individual companies.

One warning note must be sounded. If an industrial strategy is to work at all, it must set out long-term objectives which are acceptable to all major political parties and which are regarded as sacrosanct by them. Long-run objectives endorsed by one party and shelved by its successor are of no use at all. Politicians must recognise that it is no longer in the country's interests to make political capital out of the motor industry.

WHAT SORT OF INDUSTRY?

With the formal specification of longer run objectives, what options are open to the government in relation to the motor industry?

At the risk of gross oversimplification, the list of long-term choices governing the type of industry can be reduced to three alternatives :

1.   Contraction State

The industry is reduced in size and scope, producing only a proportion of the total domestic requirement but with a margin for export trade. BL would follow Scenario Two, discussed at length in earlier chapters, and would gradually drift towards the bottom end of the range envisaged in the scenario. A contraction state of this sort is extremely stable : once reached, it would be virtually impossible to reverse the process. The reason for this is that the smaller size of the industry implies cost penalties through loss of scale economies. To re-expand in order to achieve those economies would require an astronomical investment over a broad spectrum of industries and a subsidy until the industry had grown to a competitive[1] size.

2.   Status Quo or Existing State

The industry remains at about the same size. BL would then follow Scenario One or possibly the top end of Scenario Two, although as the latter is

---

1. See Chapter 14 for a discussion of what competitive means. A technically inferior product could still be competitive by being sold at a reduced price. However, without a subsidy, a natural limit on price reductions is set by the vehicle's marginal production costs.

unstable there would be a strong tendency to drift down. For reasons which will be more fully explained later, this state is inherently unstable, in that success breeds expansion whilst failure could lead to contraction.

Within the volume car and CV market, the ability of any individual manufacturer to alter demand through pricing is limited — especially at the bottom end of the market. Motor vehicles in general are becoming much more of a perfect market.[1] Within this market, either a manufacturer's product is competitive or it is not. If it is not, then demand will switch to a competitive brand and sales will decline. On the other hand if the company produces a competitive product then sales are only limited by capacity and marketing considerations.

3. Enhanced State

The industry is expanded, in which case BL would have to expand beyond Scenario One. Not all of the additional production would (or could) be exported initially, so that domestic demand would have to be stimulated artificially (through the removal of HP restrictions, for example, and/or the slackening of tax allowances on leasing arrangements).

Illustrative production figures for the three different states are shown in Table 18.1.

TABLE 18.1

Effect of Alternative States of the UK Motor Production (in millions)
Illustrative Ranges

	Current Level 1978	Enhanced State	Existing State mid — 1980's	Contraction State
Cars	1.3 – 1.4	1.8 – 2.5	1.5 – 1.8	1.2 – 1.5
CV's	.4	.5 – .6	.3 – .4	.2 – .3

Contraction is most likely to occur on the car side, particularly if BL's performance falls at the bottom of the Scenario Two range and the US. multinationals fail to take up a significant amount of the slack left by BL. The existing-state strategy has few ramifications for Ford, GM and Peugeot, as they are operating in accordance with pan-European objectives. There are two ways in which BL could also find an equilibrium position. First, BL could develop a distinctive product that did not compete directly with the larger European manufacturers. Secondly, BL could merge with another manufacturer or could undertake joint ventures with another firm, although this latter arrangement would be more likely with CV's than with cars. Given that most of the major European motor manufacturers are in the process of augmenting or extending their ranges, BL might be reduced to looking for gaps in a market where none existed. Many European firms are already producing up-market models in direct competition with the Jaguar/Rover/Triumph product.

1. The industry is still described as being oligopolistic, and Sweezy's kinked demand curve was described in Chapter 14.

Joint ventures, on the other hand, seem to be strictly temporary in character. Any benefits arising from cooperation with another firm would probably be insufficient to ensure the survival of BL Cars in its present form.

Expansion of the UK industry would involve major changes, and might seem ill-conceived in view of the eventual certain exhaustion of world oil reserves. However, there will always be a demand for motor vehicles – although the power source may switch from oil-fueled engines to an alternative energy source. The TASS[1] expansion plan (growth to 1.5 million cars capacity) for BL offers one possibility in this direction, although it could only be implemented on a longer timescale – which would mean not until after the 1980's.

One possibility would be to notionally divide the industry into distinct car and CV operations. This would allow the adoption of policy measures designed to promote expansion within the CV assembly and component manufacturers, whilst having a more neutral effect on the car sector. All policy measures affecting the car sector would remain neutral until sufficient information had been collected, or became available, about the chances of remedying the sector's weaknesses.

At the moment the government appears to be following the line of least resistance in letting major sores fester and using piecemeal remedies to ease the pain. The problem with maintaining the status quo is that it is inherently unstable. For example, if the short-term solutions for BL fail, then BL will accelerate into an ungraceful decline, which in turn may set the industry as a whole on course for contraction[2]. Once the industry has contracted, re-expansion would be virtually impossible, particularly for BL. The signs are very clearly there : the government must now decide to take positive, long-term action, and it must make a firm commitment to determine the future welfare of the industry.

RANKING THE POLICY OBJECTIVES

For the UK government, three important economic objectives must be considered in determining policy. First, the employment implications of any policy must be taken as a critical variable. Secondly, the effect of any policy on the balance of payments must be fully understood and accepted. And, finally, the amount of government expenditure needed to implement policy must be carefully evaluated. In non-economic terms, the government must decide what the general public (and the electorate in particular) will find acceptable. It is assumed that the government's highest priority is to discover a cost-effective means of promoting employment, followed by cost-effective action to make a favourable contribution towards the balance of payments.

The first point to note about the government's policy objectives is that even with BL the two sets of objectives may conflict. If BL is to be self-financing, for example, there may be employment and balance of payments implications which run contrary to the UK government's own objectives.

1. *"Collapse or Growth: An Alternative to Edwardes"*, issued by the Technical, Administrative and Supervisory Section (TASS) in 1978.
2. The decline of BL will mean fewer scale economies for the component manufacturers and suppliers to the motor industry. This in turn may mean high material costs for the whole industry.

At the moment, the above priority structure is purely speculative as there is no other information available relating to longer term objectives. Any positive action taken thus far has, in fact, been in response to crises in the industry and has involved short-term remedies only. A closer look at government action to date is now taken.

SHORT-RUN ACTION

Thus far, the UK government has made two decisive but largely unplanned forays into the motor industry battlefield — both in 1975. The BL rescue culminated in the Ryder Plan which, despite modifications, is still with us. The Ryder proposals were to cost the government £1,400 million. The second rescue — Chrysler — was to cost a maximum of £163 million. In either case, was the price too high?

The government was severely criticised in both cases, but in my opinion, the decision to intervene was substantially correct, for reasons explained below. Quite apart from the fact that the cost of both operations was exceedingly modest by international standards, it must be remembered that a complete closure, in either case, would have had a dramatic effect on unemployment and would also have involved even higher costs to the government.

There are two types of costs associated with increased unemployment. First the government will have to pay transfer payments to the newly unemployed. Secondly, generous financial inducements have to be made to attract firms to invest and thereby create jobs. A calculation is now made of the government money saved by the BL and Chrysler rescues.

Taking investment aid first, two recent examples of recipients of such aid are Ford and De Lorean. Ford are to receive roughly £100 million in various aid payments, in order to employ some 2,500 people at the new Bridgend plant, (approaching £40,000 in aid per new job created). New jobs created at the De Lorean plant will cost between £25,000 – £50,000 each. A useful rule of thumb often used in planning is that each new job created costs an average of about £20,000 in government aid — although in both examples cited the actual figure is substantially higher.

The Chrysler rescue saved approximately 17,000 jobs. If we assume that the government tried to attract *new* investment — at the rate of £20,000 per job — then a Chrysler replacement might have cost up to £340 million in aid, to which redundancy fund refunds, social security payments and subsequent revenue loss must then be added. According to the Expenditure Committee Report[1], it is reasonable to assume that 55,000[2] people might have lost their jobs as the direct or indirect result of a Chrysler closure and that they would have remained unemployed for about one year. The total cost to the government would then have been £10 million[3] for redundancy fund repayments and £60 million[3] in revenue loss. If those 55,000 people are still unemployed for a

1. *Public Expenditure on Chrysler UK Ltd,* Eighth Report from the Expenditure Committee, Session 1975-6, HMSO, London 1976.
2. Consisting of 17,000 employees directly employed by Chrysler and 38,000 employees indirectly employed in the components industry.
3. Ibid, see page 18. Figures provided are in 1975 terms and are therefore an underestimate in current money values.

second year, revenue loss would remain constant, with some reduction in Social Security payment costs – to, say, £48 million . The first-year cost would therefore have been £150 million, with the cost in second and subsequent years (if all 55,000 remain unemployed) falling marginally to £128 million. These figures make the Chrysler rescue, which only cost up to £163 million spread over a number of years, positively cheap.

Similarly, if Austin Morris were to collapse, 80,000 people would lose their jobs as a direct result of closure: the figure rises to a total of roughly 250,000 unemployed if unemployment as an indirect result of closure is taken into account. The cost of attracting new industry would amount to £1,600 million in government aid plus a further £682 million[1] in redundancy payments, Social Security benefits and revenue losses in the first year, falling to £582 million[1] in the second and subsequent years. It would seem that the money now being used to keep Austin Morris going is not as ill-advised as critics of BL make out.

This theme is returned to later for it gives rise to the notion that an industry should be supported no matter how uncompetitive it is – a dangerous conclusion since efficiency can only be judged by the success in achieving government objectives.

Against this, it has been argued that intervention of this sort provides an artificial subsidy for the UK motor industry, making it difficult for industry in general to channel resources into those sectors where the UK can more justly claim to be an efficient producer and to enjoy a comparative advantage.

The discussion at the beginning of this chapter[2] however, highlighted the fact that natural market forces do not operate in Europe. Both France and Italy have been subjected to a highly interventionist regime, and even West Germany has been tainted by "unnatural" forces.

LONG-TERM CONSIDERATIONS

With this justification of short-term government rescue measures in mind, we can now examine the effect of longer-term action on employment and balance of payments – the most significant policy variables. Employment considerations are tackled first, using the car manufacturers as an illustration.

Employment

Employment in the motor industry is very much akin to a pyramid. A small number of assembly workers represent the apex of the pyramid whilst at the bottom of the pyramid there is a much larger number of workers in ancillary, components and other industries (steel, glass, rubber etc.) which provide the necessary inputs for the manufacture of a motor vehicle. What this implies is that assembly operations are highly geared: a small change at the top of the pyramid has a much larger effect on the base of the pyramid. However the total effect on employment is larger still since any change in employment will

---

1. Figures calculated in proportion to the Chrysler figures. Figures provided are in 1975 values and therefore, are an underestimate in current values.
2. See also Chapters 14, 16 and 17.

affect the spending power in an economy which in turn has a multiplier effect through the whole economy. Every job lost at the assembly end of the motor industry gives rise to a further indirect loss of between one to three jobs. A useful planning rule is that one redundant assembly worker creates two other redundancies.

Figure 18.1 reproduces a much modified CPRS diagram[1] on the number of workers needed to produce the requisite number of cars. In fact the reduction in the labour force of some 55,000 has not taken place : currently, some 192,000 are employed to produce roughly 1.4 million cars.[2]

The CPRS estimated that in 1975, productivity norms on the continent would be ten cars per employee per year and that during the next ten years this would rise to twelve cars per employee per year. The CPRS report clearly showed the need for a substantial reduction in employment – something that has never happened. Assuming that it really is infeasible to reduce employment by very much, the existing labour force[3] could be employed and with gradually improving productivity could fulfill the Scenario One central forecast. Unfortunately by the time the UK has achieved a level of ten, continental manufacturers will have increased their productivity levels to twelve plus cars[4] per employee per year in an attempt to try to stay with the Japanese.

Certainly if UK labour could achieve the performance indicated in the dark shaded area, then the gap between UK and European norms will have closed. Fortunately the UK does not require parity with European productivity levels in order to be competitive, since UK labour costs are comparatively cheap – as shown in Figure 18.2. Although comparatively cheap labour is an important UK asset, this advantage is more than offset by low productivity. The UK average is shown in Figure 18.1, BL's productivity is only half that of European firms, and is less than one third of current Japanese productivity levels.[5]

Nevertheless, cheap labour costs could be used to attract new investment into the UK. If productivity could also be improved, then the cost/performance ratio of UK labour would be unbeatable. At the moment, however, the UK is not competitive because of the poorer productivity levels. It is worthwhile repeating the warnings of the CPRS.[6]

"The CPRS considers that any car company which is able to compete in the difficult market environment of the next decade must *at a minimum* achieve present continental levels by 1985. Failure to do so will entail

---

1. *The Future of the British Car Industry,* by the Central Policy Review Staff, HMSO, London 1975, p.112.
2. A rough calculation would be BL with 125,000 employees with a productivity level of six cars per employee per year. Ford, GM and Chrysler could be assumed to have a productivity level of ten with employment figures of 40,000, 12,000 and 15,000 respectively.
3. With some sectional changes – i.e. BL reduces whilst Ford increases its labour force.
4. Citroen already has a productivity level in excess of thirteen.
5. 1977 Japanese production figures were 8.5 million vehicles (5.4 million cars) and employment figures were 653,000 in the motor vehicle manufacturing industry. Assuming half are employed in the production of cars yields a productivity level of 16.6 cars per employee per year.
6. CPRS Report, op. cit., p.112.

FIGURE 18.1

Employment by UK Car Manufacturers

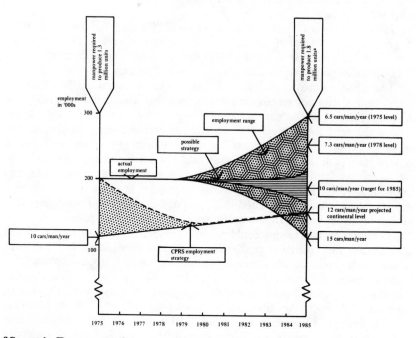

ª Scenario Two assumed

substantial and continuing losses ..."

Employment levels in the motor industry are certainly far too high. They would fall if the industry contracted, or the situation could improve if the UK labour force worked as hard and for as long as its European equivalent, or if automation was extensively used to perform boring and repetitive jobs. Employment however is a delicate political issue. BL, for example, currently employs over 125,000 people in the car division to produce some 800,000 vehicles. In Europe, fewer than 80,000 employees would be needed for the same task. If BL productivity rose in line with current European trends over the next few years, BL would need only 67,000 employees to produce one million vehicles (using a productivity level of fifteen cars per employee per year). If BL is to stand a fair chance of functioning as a viable unit in the long run its work force will have to be fairly drastically cut. The less cost effective BL is, the less attractive it must become as a means of maintaining employment. *Other projects could offer more promising returns from the government's point of view, offering a greater chance of success at a lower cost.* Certainly, maintaining employment at existing levels could threaten the jobs of everyone in the industry – a point which the unions in particular are reluctant to accept.

The union negotiators could argue that employment – in these terms at

452

FIGURE 18.2

Comparative Cost of UK Labour

Per capita labour costs (thousands of US dollars)

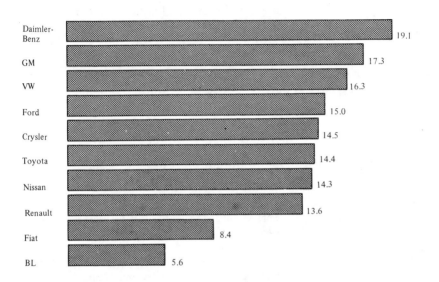

Daimler-Benz	19.1
GM	17.3
VW	16.3
Ford	15.0
Crysler	14.5
Toyota	14.4
Nissan	14.3
Renault	13.6
Fiat	8.4
BL	5.6

Source: The Motor Industry of Japan, published by Toyota, 1977

least — should be maintained at any cost as a major government objective. The government might not agree. If the government wastes money on maintaining inefficient forms of production, then money that might more usefully be spent in increasing employment elsewhere is not available. A sharp distinction must be drawn between manufacturing an unprofitable but efficiently-made product and maintaining production of a good that is no longer profitable because of overmanning. The UK economy as a whole stands to benefit if excess labour is released and the money thus saved is used to finance an efficiently-made product (which might at least make some contribution to the balance of payments), and which in turn will provide employment.

The process of shedding excess labour could be made marginally more palatable by phasing it over a longer period of time than a sudden mass redundancy, and by active government efforts to promote alternative employment. Although the car sector is used throughout as an example, the situation in the CV sector is broadly similar. The employment implications for the whole motor industry are now examined.

Taking the three scenarios outlined earlier, Table 18.2 gives current employment and a range of possible future levels. Two points are immediately clear. First, there can be no doubt that intervention gives the government

TABLE 18.2

Effect of Alternative States of the UK Motor Industry on Employment (in '000s)

Illustrative Point Estimates

	Current Level (1978)	Enhanced State	Existing State	Contraction State
			mid 1980's	
The UK big four	275	250	215	180
Other under MLH 281	200	200	170	140
	475	450	385	320
Other suppliers and components sector	300	300	255	215
Total UK employment	775	750	640	535

NB   Other sectors of the UK would also be indirectly affected by the three alternative "states" of the motor industry. If the car sector declined whilst the CV sector thrived, about 30% of the UK big four plus other manufacturers under MLH 281 are accounted for by CV employment and a guesstimate in the other sectors would put employment at about 20%.

enormous leeway in maintaining employment. Secondly, even if both Chrysler and BL continue, total employment in the industry must fall. Even if the industry expands, employment levels in BL must still fall although levels in the industry as a whole could remain more or less unchanged. In this case there could be a regional adjustment as employment moved away from those areas formerly dominated by BL as a major employer of assembly labour. A similar shift could also occur in the components industry.

Balance of Payments

On the balance of payments front, the UK motor industry is rapidly assuming the character of a disaster area: there is a substantial payments deficit on cars, and positive balances on components, CV's and other motor products are in real terms rapidly dwindling — as shown in Table 18.3. Although the government may not attach much importance to the deterioration in the motor industry balance of trade, the downward trend places a very severe strain on the UK economy as a whole : if current trends continue, the motor industry will in fact represent a net drain on the balance of payments. Some of these trends which have started cannot be stopped. For example the increasing import penetration during the 1970's means there is a large stock of imported cars which may in turn mean an increase (after a suitable delay[1]) in imported components.

Table 18.4 illustrates possible balance of payments contributions that could arise under the three different states described earlier. At best further

1. To allow the components to wear out.

TABLE 18.3

UK Motor Industry Contribution to Balance of Payments

	1970	1973	1976	1977	1978 estimated
Balance of Payments Contributed by:	£m	£m	£m	£m	£m
Cars	170	-132	-253	-572	-800
Commercial Vehicles	166	160	425	442	350
Components	350	478	890	884	950
Other Motor Products	180	231	468	558	500
Net Balance in all motor products	866	737	1529	1312	1000
Net Balance in all motor products in real terms (in 1978 values)	2350	1562	1860	1430	1000

decline in the motor industry could mean a worsening of the UK balance of payments position by some £2 billion – £4 billion. North Sea oil – the national cure-all – might cushion a blow of these dimensions for a decade or two, but it can only be expected to act as a temporary buffer. When North Sea oil is exhausted, what then?

POLICY MEASURES

Divorcing ourselves from the more fundamental questions relating to policy, there are a number of short run policy measures which may be relevant for the crises-ridden UK motor industry. These actions include measures designed to:–

1. provide a stable economic environment
2. tackle the low productivity problem
3. help manufacturers to automate
4. attract foreign manufacturers in the UK
5. protect the domestic industry
6. re-structure the industry

The first policy measure relating to the stability of the economic environment facing the motor industry is essential – a pre-condition before any other measure can happen. Others are of a far more speculative nature.

Stable Economic Environment

It has already been pointed out that there is a clear need for a stable domestic level of demand. The adverse effects of the frequent changes in HP regulations and tax rates are illustrated in Figure 18.3. Each change in tax or HP has usually had a marked effect on new car sales. The Government must also seek to

455

prevent sudden and sharp boosts of demand. The large increase in demand in 1971 caught the industry unawares. Supply could only respond after a considerable time lag, during which imports filled the vacuum and thereby captured a sizeable share of the market.

From now on, the Government must perhaps take more positive steps to stabilise demand. Demand should be encouraged if it falls much below current levels and held back if the increase transpires to be greater than the available supply by the UK manufacturers.

A stable economic environment also includes such aspects of economic policy as the pay policy. This has very severe ramifications, for an industry which has a record of poor industrial relations requires the flexibility of changing rates which might violate a pay code.[1]

Central to the question of stability of demand is the proper understanding of the nature of demand. Given that a much larger share of the market is taken by business, the government must be careful not to disturb any tax allowances or other regulations relating to the business buyer.

Another important influence on demand is the general government attitude to cars and CV's. If the recent anti-car feeling that has been exhibited by some local authorities[2] were duplicated on a national scale, then this could significantly affect demand and in turn have repercussions for the motor industry.

Part of the action the government must take to ensure a stable economic environment is an active road building programme. This should be at least sufficient to remove the worst types of congestion which may deter car ownership.

Low Productivity

Whatever happens to the UK motor industry, a central question is, will the industry improve the near legendary low rate of productivity and lack of continuity of production? To some extent higher productivity can only be achieved by purchasing it. For whatever alternative measure is considered, a common theme among all of them is that they cost money. Some of these measures are listed in Table 18.5. The simplest way of purchasing it is to pay much higher wages[3] to the labour force and hope that this has the desired effect. But there is no guarantee or evidence to suppose that it will. Other ways of increasing productivity are to ensure continuity of supply through the multi-sourcing of externally purchased and internally made components or, to ensure that the market place receives a continuous supply is, to build up finished goods stocks. BL has always found great difficulty in doing this. A less

---

1. As aptly demonstrated by the Ford strike in Autumn 1978.
2. For example, the labour controlled G.L.C. of the mid 1970's. Cars were actively discouraged from use by actions planned to remove car parking facilities and increase congestion.
3. Rewards in the motor industry have fallen in the 1970's. In MLH 381 (vehicles), the average weekly earnings of full time men manual workers as a percentage of average for all industries was:-

Year	1950	1960	1970	1977
Index	115.7	116.8	115.6	103.7

Source: *Employment Gazette*

TABLE 18.4

Effect of Alternative States of the UK Motor Industry on the Balance of Payments
(In £ million)

Illustrative Point Estimates

	Current Level 1978	Enhanced State	Existing State	Contraction State
	(estimated)	in mid 1980's (1978 values)		
Cars				
Exports	1,000	1,500	1,000	600
Imports	1,800	1,200	2,200	2,600
	-800	300	-1,200	-2,000
CV's				
Exports	600	750	650	400
Imports	250	250	400	500
	350	500	250	-100
Components				
Exports	1,850	1,800	2,000	1,500
Imports	900	1,500	2,000	2,500
	950	300	0	-1,000
Other motor products				
Exports	700	700	600	500
Imports	200	250	500	500
	500	450	100	0
TOTAL EFFECT	1,000	1,550	-1,000	-3,100

satisfactory way is to build up raw material stocks. It is, of course, necessary to have buffer stocks sufficient to cover most normal eventualities and the shorter strikes.

However, to utilise raw material stocks implies that no production problems will arise in the final assembly stage. A finished good does not have the same gauntlet to run of industrial disruption spreading to the final assembly stage. Even if no strikes occur, a sudden increase in demand cannot be

457

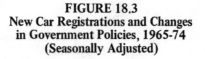

FIGURE 18.3
New Car Registrations and Changes
in Government Policies, 1965-74
(Seasonally Adjusted)

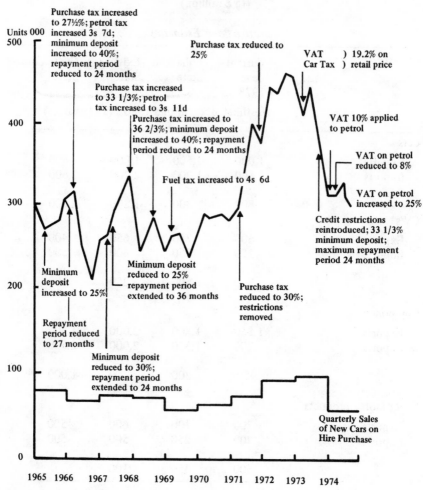

Source: SMMT

satisfied since the conversion of the raw materials into finished goods stock cannot in all probability be speeded up. Whereas with large finished goods stock, an under-estimation of demand can be satisfied through the depletion of the finished goods stock.

Another way of attempting to satisfy demand is to install additional capacity on the basis that to produce x cars you plan to produce $1\frac{1}{3}x$ and assume that industrial action will always lose $\frac{1}{3}x$ of the firm's planned production. Notice that in periods of smooth production, finished goods stocks will rise. This means that to some extent the increased capacity and the greater

458

TABLE 18.5

Some Suggestions for Dealing with Low Productivity

ACTION	COMMENT
1. Higher Wages	Relative earnings have fallen in the motor industry, but the restoration of these earnings will not guarantee higher productivity; historically higher wages have not been synonymous with better productivity.
2. Multi-Sourcing	See Table 16.1
3. Greater Stocks	Some strikes of longer duration will always defeat stock build ups. More relevant for finished goods stocks.
4. Additional Capacity	See Table 16.1
5. Smaller Plant Sizes	See Tables 16.1 and 18.8
6. Higher Level of Automation	See Table 16.1 and subsequently in Chapter 16
7. Direct Assault on Labour Relations	Difficult to implement (e.g. security motivation, loyalty etc.)

finished goods stock policies are complimentary.

A further method of improving productivity is to reduce industrial unrest by improving communications. It was argued in Chapter 7 that this could be

TABLE 18.6

Proportion of Establishments and of Employment in Establishments that were not Affected by Stoppages in Manufacturing Industries

	1971	1975	Average 1971-75
Percentage of establishments not affected by stoppages	98.1	98.1	97.7
Percentage of total employment in unaffected establishments employing			
11-99 employees	99.4	99.4	99.3
100-199 employees	97.3	97.5	96.8
200-499 employees	94.8	94.6	93.0
500-999 employees	86.5	86.9	83.4
1,000 or more employees	59.7	42.2	51.1
Percentage of total employment in all unaffected establishments	83.1	77.7	79.5

Source: *Employment Gazette,* January 1978

achieved by having smaller plant sizes (up to, say, 10,000 employees). To support this argument, Table 18.6 demonstrates that a very high proportion of manufacturing plants were free from industrial stoppages. In general the smaller the establishment the lesser the chance of a stoppage. The problem is a concentration of stoppages in a relatively small number of establishments. In my opinion communications and plant size are very important in minimising industrial unrest.

At BL cars it was advocated that a combination of ideas may be beneficial. These included splitting assembly up into smaller plants, increasing capacity by so doing, increasing the extent of multi-sourcing and building-up stocks. We defer a discussion of higher levels of automation and turn instead to those actions which may be classified as a direct assault on labour relations.

A Question of Attitude

The CPRS were correct in identifying one of the principal component of poor industrial relations as being the result of "trench warfare attitudes".

Part of the blame for poor industrial relations must be laid at the door of management — it takes two to make a fight. It takes time however to change such attitudes. As the CPRS Report said[1]:

"The CPRS considers that three major changes in attitude must take place. First, management must recognise the importance of giving workpeople a greater understanding of the central issues which determine their firms' success or failure and their ability to provide a secure livelihood for their employees. For example, they must make available and discuss with stewards and full-time union officials information on the precise details of financial and marketing performance and encourage them to visit continental plants to review manning levels and work practices. Second, the unions must recognise their critical role in improving the three factors of productivity, quality and continuity of production. For example, shop stewards must recognise that in the short run excess manning may preserve the jobs of a few, but in the long run it threatens the jobs of everyone in the plant and they must bring home to those they represent that disputes which stop the line for short periods are cumulatively just as serious as major disputes over wages. Third, both unions and management should work to combat the influence of politically-motivated extremists out to wreck the industry."

Brave words, but they have either fallen on deaf ears, or have proved impossible to implement. One of these actions, that of visiting continental plants, has been carried out. It was argued that BL Cars' productivity was half that of its continental rivals yet this admission by representatives of the labour force had very little effect.

One proposal that has been put forward to create the right attitude is to guarantee a weekly wage which could be paid. This would provide a safety guard against loss of earnings through strikes by component manufacturers or other sectors of the company.

As the CPRS Report indicated.[2]

1. *The Future of the British Car Industry*, by the CPRS, HMSO, London 1975, pp 131-2.
2. CPRS Report, *op. cit.*, page 135.

"*The insecurity of employment and of income* in the motor industry is one of the most critical factors in souring industrial relations in the industry. Fluctuations in the level of employment due to fluctuations in demand are inevitable. If the workforce required to man an efficient and viable industry is not provided with adequate security of employment and income, comparable to that provided for workers on the continent by a combination of company and government lay-off schemes, then industrial relations can never be expected to be put on a satisfactory basis. The CPRS sees it as essential, as part of the programme of achieving higher productivity and better continuity of production, for the Government and the companies jointly to devise and negotiate improved lay-off pay provisions."

Certainly, an industrial strategy would attempt to provide long-term stability of employment. Something which is extremely uncertain at the moment.

A counter-view would argue against security. Since the "Welfare State" has become a major part of the lives of some people, job security has no meaning. If another job cannot be found (and perhaps even if it can), then the myriad of payments in existence will ensure that the individual and his family will not starve. This attitude can lead to a lack of motivation and breeds the concept that the state owes an individual a decent standard of living, regardless of that individual's contribution to the state.

I am not qualified to judge which attitude is most relevant, but it seems that there is a certain amount of evidence of *both* influences. Certainly long run guarantees may not be possible, but a stable and consistent policy would help. At the same time something ought to be done about the "couldn't care less about jobs" attitude through training and re-education. At a young age people should be informed that greater effort produces greater rewards even within the context of a Welfare State.

There are two ways of trying to motivate people through increased rewards. First differentials have been eroded and the restoration of pay differentials could help to redress one of BL's weaknesses — the shortage of technical and engineering resources. Table 18.7 shows how low differentials between manual and non-manuals became in 1974, although by 1977, the differentials had been partially restored. Nevertheless even this differential of 21.8% represents only some £16-01 which after tax is only £11 per week.[1]

The second way of improving productivity through the mercenary motive is to introduce some sort of incentive scheme, which provides some incentive to work harder. Under BL's old piece rate system, the higher the productivity the higher the pay. Now this production incentive has gone, its replacement — measured day working — cannot be affected by any one individual's efforts, and there is less incentive to work harder at the individual level. A great deal of thought must go into reworking an incentive scheme. However, even some of the best incentive schemes are counter productive and there can be no guarantee that this will work. It may even be appropriate for a partial return to a piece rate system. A piece rate system is inappropriate for assembly

---

1. It may of course be argued that the distinction between manual and non-manual work is no guide to effort or skills. In the above analysis the assumption is that it was such a guide.

operations, but it is possible to have group bonus schemes for a particular assembly line, production process or even plant. This method of incentives has been adopted in Europe and the incentive payment has been up to 15% of the total pay. BL is currently holding negotiations with the unions for some type of incentive scheme. Because there are many strikes by component manufacturers or other sectors of the company, it may help to create the right attitude if a guaranteed weekly wage could be paid.

What else can be done to foster better labour relations? Loyalty to a manufacturer would help and this may be achieved in a number of ways. For example one way is good internal public relations. Another way may be to reduce labour turnover rates where they are high[1]. This may be accomplished by paying according to a salary scale in which there may be annual increments for length of service. Those plants with good industrial relations' records could be rewarded by being given the prospect of greater job security[2].

Another suggestion which would be extremely beneficial is to train all management in the art of tact, diplomacy and *practical* labour relations. Similarly a process of indoctrination to the labour force, of the benefits of high productivity and good workmanship may be initially "laughed out of court", but if implemented carefully and tactfully might help to change attitudes.

Having looked at some of the cures so far, it may in the final analysis, prove extremely difficult to motivate people into putting effort into boring and repetitive tasks and where work conditions are often unpleasant and noisy.

Level of Automation

Whatever action is taken, nothing can really change the fact that certain repetitive tasks are boring and soul destroying, especially for an individual who has had a substantial education. The only long term solution is to automate such jobs by the means of computerised robotic equipment. The labour force would then concentrate on trouble shooting, rectification work and the reprogramming of the machines to cope with a new model mix, changes to models or entirely new models. An additional advantage being that no unique investment for model changes has to be made except for software development costs. This radical solution was discussed in Chapter 7 (see also Table 18.8).

TABLE 18.7

Differentials

Differentials between non-manual males and full-time manual males based on average weekly earnings in all industries.

Year	1960	1965	1970	1974	1977
Differential as a percentage	31.5	30.3	28.8	11.9	21.8

Source: *Employment Gazette,* May 1978.

1. Although the reported rates do not indicate that the motor vehicle manufacturing industry is particularly bad for labour turnover.
2. BL's Abingdon plant is a case in point.

Such a dramatic change would have to be developed by the UK Government and would probably be beneficial to Ford as well as BL. A separate team of production engineers tied to the project may be necessary to implement the new production technology.

The drawback with such a policy is a lower level of employment.[1] But one can ask the question of whether a routine repetitive manual task is the kind of job which UK labour wishes to perform in the long-run. The job satisfaction of such a task must be low and perhaps this is one of the fundamental reasons why the UK motor industry has low productivity. In other countries in Europe, the worst assembly jobs are performed by immigrants or people who have left the country-side in search of jobs. In the UK, the assembly plant is very often manned by the traditional and indigenous motor industry worker.

Someone has to perform the worst jobs[2] and it is here that industrial unrest probably finds a good breeding ground. What little motivation there is may be marginal between the prospect of a job or no job coupled with social security payments. The long-run answer must surely be to automate the worst tasks. Should the process of automation be carried further?

The arguments for automation

Computerised robotic equipment[3] (see Chapter 7 and Table 18.8) has the following advantages :

1. ideal for reptitive tasks.
2. do not require as "clean" environmental conditions as humans.
3. easy to reprogramme to cope for model changes or a changing mix of models[4]
4. does not need breaks.
5. can achieve a better consistency of work.
6. in most applications (e.g. fine tolerances) can achieve a better quality than humans.
7. may be faster.
8. does not go on strike

The two principal arguments against automation are cost and employment implications. The cost argument can be partially rejected through the higher level of overall productivity and the lower costs incurred for model changes.[5] The employment argument is more serious. In mitigation, two points can be made. First, if productivity does not improve, employment in the motor industry will decline. Therefore, if the choice is some jobs plus automation,

1. One plant where automation could be implemented without loss of jobs is Ryton, which is facilitised for 40,000 Alpines with a work force of under 3,000. By automating some of the operations and a modest increase in the workforce, the plant should be able to body-build and assemble between 2 to 4 times as many cars.
2. Certain jobs in welding, paint boothes, pressing and some final assembly work.
3. Probably controlled by micro-processor.
4. A central computer can instruct the separate micro-processers which model they are about to receive and therefore which programme to use. This distributed processing network would provide a very high degree of flexibility. If a micro-processor was to malfunction, the central computer could take over operation of the equipment, or could stop or slow down the line.
5. In a conventional plant, a new model may mean that several transfer lines have to be moved, new pieces of equipment tailor-made to various work-stations, and so forth. For robotic equipment, it simply means reprogramming the micro-processor.

TABLE 18.8

Fiat's Robotic Technology

Plants and production processes

"Considerable activity is reported in the introduction of highly-automated technological systems in the various phases of production. The following is a list of the major innovations during the course of the year.

Pressing technologies

"An increasing number of presses were equipped with automatic traverse systems: 30% of the lines is now mechanized. A system for feeding sheet steel automatically to front presses has been introduced.

Bodywork technologies

"Assembly of body-shells.
The assembly line of the "Ritmo" model at the Rivalta plant has been equipped with a "Robogate" system, with the result that the assembly of body-shells is now almost entirely automatic.

"The installation is controlled by a computer which supervises the flow of robocarriers — the battery-driven vehicles on which the body shells are located.

"The "Robogate" is a big step forward in production line flexibility because it can be easily switched from one version to the other of the same model. It also contributes to the improvement of the working environment, in addition to representing a saving in investments (because the same installation can be used for the assembly of different models and production costs can be spread over a wider range of vehicles).

"Body painting.
In the course of 1977, the Rivalta and Cassino plants were equipped with their first body painting robots featuring "anthropomorphic" arms, which means that their position can be changed automatically according to the body type to be painted. These robots, which can be programmed to switch immediately to a different body colour, will in due course be installed at Miraflori, too.

"Europe's first powder-painting system went into operation at Termini Imerese, resulting in a considerable improvement in the working environment (the new process has done away with solvents) and greater body resistance to corrosion (on account of the use of powders).

Mechanical technologies

"The Florence plant adopted a new process for the hardening of "Ritmo" axle-shafts; while an integrated electronically-controlled system was introduced on the 128 and Ritmo engine crankcase lines. Robots feeding heavy components to mechanical processing machine tools are now in operation at both Mirafiori and Rivalta."

Source: *Fiat's Annual Accounts*, 1977.

or no jobs, the former alternative may be preferable.

The second argument uses the pyramid employment concept. Why should 80,000 Austin-Morris workers, by continuing their anti-social practices, lose their own jobs and, indirectly, the jobs of another 150,000 workers.[1] The steel workers, who would be made redundant as a result[2], might have preferred, say 30 to 40,000 Austin Morris workers to have lost their jobs through automation rather than having the job prospects of a much larger group destroyed.

It is unfortunate that of all the proposals, automation is potentially the most politically sensitive. It is a feasible way of catching up and over taking the European norm in one step, rather than several steps. BL particularly has an advantage, since so much equipment will in any case be replaced over the next few years. To those politicians who regard such proposals as an anathema, a previous question must be re-stated. Is a boring, repetitive manual operation in unpleasant conditions, the type of job that they would envisage for their constituents over the next decade or so?

This point can be brought home by quoting from an article in the Financial Times[3] on industrial relations problems at Chrysler's Linwood plant :

"It also seems that the threat of closure has lost its effect on the work force, which has become immune to the dire warnings about the future. Turnover of labour in the plant is high. Many other workers see their time doing boring and repetitive tasks on the assembly line as anyway limited – a period to earn good money whilst looking for more interesting jobs elsewhere. Plant loyalty is hardly likely to be strong among this type of employee."

Planning mistakes

Planning in the past has been based largely on false estimates of the improvement in industrial relations. Unfortunately, no significant improvement has occurred. Planning in the future must be firmly based on continuing industrial relations problems. Any improvement will take a long time and may not even improve with 'shock' redundancies being announced. Ultimately, given that BL is in the public sector, one would hope that both labour and management would find a way of working in closer harmony to preserve the UK's only major indigenous car manufacturer.

Foreign Manufacturers

To hedge against a future problem with BL, or simply in order to expand jobs in the motor industry, it is useful to start negotiations to attract a Japanese manufacturer to either take over in the event of a future collapse of UK plants, or to set up an additional assembly plant, or to use a discarded BL plant, such as Speke in Liverpool. Such negotiations will take many years. Unquestionably, the Japanese will soon need European assembly plants. If a Japanese manufacturer can be tempted to come, the UK will then be locked into exports to Europe. A Japanese manufacturer will require tempting with a carrot and stick

1. And may be several times that amount when all the multiplier effects have worked through the economy.
2. This may be as high as one in six.
3. Financial Times, 7-8-78.

approach. The carrot should be Government aid; the stick would be loss of UK trade through some form of effective protectionism. Government aid might be provided on the basis that a high proportion of all output must be exported.

Assuming that BL's Austin Morris division does contract and that no Japanese manufacturer can be persuaded to come to the UK, then it may be possible for BL to utilise some of the capacity by building Japanese cars under licence.

Import Controls

Obviously, with BL's market share falling, any Government might think of introducing import controls. How this would work with the multinationals remains to be seen. Presumably, their captive imports would be excluded from any import control. The particular form of control would probably be import quotas. In theory, this could be useful in giving BL the necessary breathing space until its new model programmes could be implemented. In practice, it would simply allow industrial relations problems to cause car shortages. Such shortages would provide a ready market for non-UK built vehicles sold by the multinationals.

In the final analysis, the only way the UK car industry can recover is to produce competitive models. If one removes the incentive to produce such models then the loss will become a substantial drain on the UK balance of payments. Only by allowing BL's and the multinationals' products to become internationally competitive will the UK industry have a chance of long-term survival.

Nevertheless, a degree of protection may be necessary to allow BL to retrench its position over the next two years or so. Obviously, any form of protection carries with it enormous risks of retaliatory action. Consequently, the current informal agreement with the Japanese would have been brilliant if it had worked. At the moment, it is only partially successful but, nevertheless, this measure of partial protectionism is beneficial and should be retained against the Japanese and, in time, used against other cheap importers.

As predicted, the problem has been that, during this period of protectionism, BL Cars have been unable to produce the goods. The gap in demand has been made up by increased sales of the European multinationals and the US multinationals. Ford, for example, in order to meet demand, has had to increase the percentage of UK sales that have been supplied from abroad from one quarter in 1977 to nearly one third[1] in 1978. More startling is that this percentage was as low as 8.9% in 1976. So the principal beneficiaries during this period of protectionism has been, not BL, but its European rivals. The success of any protection crucially depends on UK productivity, which in 1978 showed little or no sign of an improvement.

Restructuring the industry

In this section, a plan is put forward involving BL Cars and some of the smaller manufacturers. However, with the exclusion of BL, the remaining three major manufacturers are all multinationals, so, not surprisingly, this section concen-

---

1. Figures taken for the first seven months of 1978.

trates on the one UK controlled company.

The first way that the government can help to restructure the motor industry (and it is the top of the pyramid that is worst off) is to revitalise some of the smaller specialist producers. The smaller producer makes a valuable contribution to the industry for the following reasons:

1. UK manufactured components are often used.
2. Industrial relations and productivity are good (for a specialist producer).
3. Plants are small and can be scattered around the country.
4. The specialist producer has an excellent export record.
5. UK marque names (Aston-Martin, ERF, Foden, Lotus, Jensen, Healey, Morgan, Panther, Reliant, Rolls Royce, Seddon-Atkinson, TVR, etc.) are world famous and, unlike the UK's larger manufacturers, have an enviable reputation for quality.
6. Closure of a plant employing a few hundred people is not such a major headache as with a larger plant.
7. Subsidies, if required, are fairly cheap in terms of job creation programmes, and requests for additional funds can be viewed in relation to the success of the venture and alternative employment prospects in the area.

For these reasons, a good case could be made for the support of the small specialist manufacturers in both the car and the CV field. A strategy is suggested below which applies primarily to cars. Essentially, by using parts of the BL organisation, smaller manufacturers can achieve some of the economies of scale open to BL. For example, Rolls-Royce bodies are made by BL, Morgan buys the Rover V8 engine, and so on. What is suggested below is a formalisation of this process into a national structure.

Integrated Car Plan

This strategy attempts to form a rational basis for BL Cars, the components industry and some of the smaller manufacturers. The plan assumes that there is a separate BL Components Division and an International Division, although most of the exports in some markets would be handled by Austin/Morris or Jaguar, Rover Triumph. BL's Components Division would then be free to supply BL's assembly divisions as well as some of the smaller manufacturers. To some extent, the Components Division would compete in certain areas head-on with some of the private component manufacturing companies. Similarly, BL's assembly operations could use the International Division for certain export markets whilst marketing themselves direct in other markets. The smaller manufacturers could also use BL's International Division to market their products in certain international markets. A small manufacturer might come into the scheme on providing a slice of 'equity' through the NEB mechanism or a much more informal commercial arrangement may be made. A schematic diagram of this approach is shown in Figure 18.4.

The car divisions would be free to purchase components from either the BL Component Division or the private sector component companies. This would provide an incentive to only go into those areas where there is a comparative cost advantage. The BL components industry would be free to manufacture components for other companies, whilst the car divisions might choose not to

467

market their cars through BL's International Division in some markets. Finally, BL's International Division should also be allowed some autonomy, though this is fraught with more difficulties. And, in certain markets and in certain products, the International Division might market another manufacturer's products (as it is currently doing in Canada).

The benefits for each division is that it has autonomy and can exercise a degree of influence on its supplier and export marketing division, since there are alternatives to using either. Smaller manufacturers would benefit from economies of scale in component manufacture and in export marketing. Of course, if some of the decisions made by the autonomous groups are seen not to be beneficial for the group as a whole, central group management could dictate a solution to a particular division. Otherwise, this scheme will permit a longer run solution to the small manufacturer and provide BL's car operations with the necessary motivation and incentives.

The biggest single advantage of this scheme is that it offers a high degree of flexibility, a high level of motivation and provides an incentive within their smaller (but still large in absolute terms) autonomous units.

A similar sort of plan can be made for Leyland Vehicles, the private components companies, the specialist CV producers and BL's International Division.

Other Restructuring

Dealing with cars first, any further restructuring of the industry must depend on the Government's long-term objectives. An expansionary policy would require a major effort to persuade Ford and GM to increase their UK based production. If the PCC venture goes through, then pressure could be exerted on the new group. As for BL, after a period of retrenchment, a modest expansion should be undertaken in order to bring BL up to a cost-effective size. If the PCC merger does not go through to the Government's satisfaction, then a viable alternative would be to take over Chrysler UK and, ultimately, merge it with BL. Chrysler's model policy and engineering centre at Whitley are two vital assets that would help to overcome two of BL Cars' weaknesses.

A policy geared towards contraction would envisage the decline of BL Cars into Scenario Two and below. Eventually, by the 1990s, the UK would be one of the smallest car producing nations, ahead of Scandinavia and the Netherlands, but behind the rest of Europe, Brazil, and so on. There would be severe repercussions on the components and other industries.

The status quo strategy places the UK on either Scenario One or Two. Both GM and Ford should still be encouraged to move production to the UK. The merger of Chrysler UK and Peugeot-Citroen could still take place, although there must be some rationalisation leading to redundancies, and it is this prospect which may deter further evaluation. Of course, that prospect is still with us if the PCC merger is cancelled.

On the CV front, every encouragement should be given to Leyland Vehicles as there is every chance that BL can become a competitive CV manufacturer. Ford and GM should be encouraged to expand UK CV production. If the PCC merger goes ahead, then the transfer of CV production to France should be discouraged.

FIGURE 18.4

Possible Integrated Strategy for UK Motor Industry

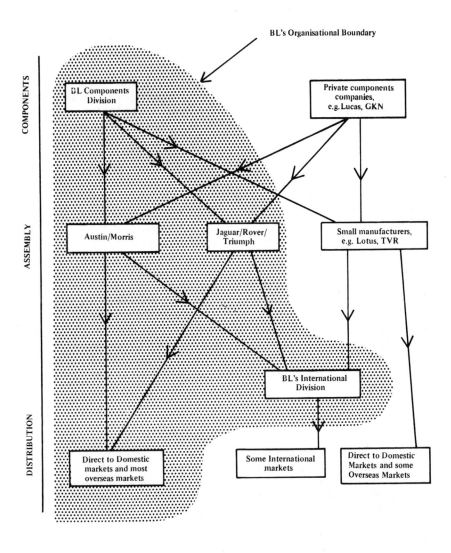

GOVERNMENT ACTION IN RELATION TO SPECIFIC MANUFACTURERS

A brief look is now taken with respect to each of the manufacturers. However, it is impossible to make any definite proposals in the absence of a clear statement of Government objectives.

BL

One course of action which is vital is that the UK Government helps in every way possible to make good the deficit in technical resources and facilities and endeavours to provide support for improving attitudes between the shop-floor and management. The Government must also resolve conflicts between its own objectives and those of BL. For example, BL's policy, if asked to be self-financing, would be to rationalise production and concentrate on those products which are most profitable. This factor might persuade BL to expand the Seneffe plant as a hedge against low productivity in its UK plants.

From a purely theoretical point of view, BL, at some time, must ask whether it wishes to become a company that can keep pace with VW, Ford, Fiat, Renault, Peugeot-Citroen, GM etc? But BL is too small at the moment to compete with these giants which, with the exception of GM, are producing nearly twice as many cars as BL. If BL wanted to compete, then it would have to expand production to the 1.5 million mark that was recommended by TASS.

The alternative is to be like Daimler-Benz or BMW. Both produce substantially fewer cars than BL does at the moment but the comparison is certainly not that straightforward. However, if production in 1978 is around 750,000 units and further plant closures[1] limit this to 650,000, of which half is exported then by the 1980s, BL will have, by default, contracted into Scenario Two. This is not a prediction but purely an illustration of what might happen if the Government, management and the labour force were content to leave things as they are.

From an analysis in the previous chapter, the benefits of a successful merger are great. An unsuccessful merger, however, could leave BL worse off than when it started. European co-operation, if it does go ahead, must be carefully worked out and planned. At the moment, the most likely contender for European co-operation must be Renault. Success is not necessarily ensured and there are parts of Renault (CV operations) which have been in difficulties. Let us hope that such co-operation does not follow the example of another Anglo-French project — that of Concorde.

Ford and GM

Ford, like GM, are probably motivated by profit. However, Ford, unlike GM, rely heavily on the UK for powertrain and other components, and Ford are the top selling car manufacturer within the UK. It is the latter fact that probably limits what Ford can do, both in the eyes of the public and of the Government. Certainly Ford have more to lose in the UK and more to gain. Ford have announced quite a considerable investment in the UK. One of the conclusions from Chapter 8 was that Ford may possibly choose the UK to install additional capacity.

From the policy making point of view, there are two issues. First, how can Ford increase productivity and improve the quality of workmanship? Second, what factors would be helpful in persuading Ford to install further additional capacity in the UK? The answers to these questions are relevant to both Ford

---

1. e.g. Canley could be switched from Vehicle assembly to component manufacture.

and GM.

Ford could automate routine operations and it might do so if it could be guaranteed that, for example, Halewood would subsequently operate at a higher capacity. But this is expensive. An almost fully automatic welding line costs around £90 million. But to automate the UK, and only the UK, causes some problems. Ford would have to support two production engineering teams : one for the automated UK system and one for everywhere else. Space restrictions may mitigate against too radical a change. Therefore, a Government supported and/or backed programme to increase automation within Ford might be the only way Ford would be willing to unilaterally automate its processes in one country.

For Ford to increase capacity within the UK it needs, amongst other things, the right economic environment, a stable demand for UK products, a supportive Government and generous investment grants. Most of the above are present in the UK at the current time.[1] The one ingredient that is lacking is the basic motivation of the labour force, which is partly to blame for low productivity and poor workmanship. Whilst low productivity can be partially overcome by the lower cost of UK labour, there is little that Ford can do to compensate for poor workmanship. Ford do not, however, find that all UK labour suffers from the same problem; to date, Ford have been pleased with the performance of their Welsh plants.

Chrysler

In the previous chapter a list of alternatives was provided and discussed. It is too soon to know whether the merger will come off and, if it does, exactly what form it will take. Realistically, whatever is decided now, the real decisions will only be taken over the next few years. The merger of BL with Chrysler UK in the longer term is a strategy which has an intuitive appeal, despite complex organisational and administrative problems. Closure of Chrysler UK plants seems blatantly unjust when their productivity record is better than BL's, and the other alternative of attracting a foreign manufacturer seems remote.

SUMMARY

The law of comparative advantage usually operates to encourage countries to specialise in those industries or services which operate more efficiently than the same industries elsewhere — those areas, in short, for which countries enjoy a comparative advantage. In general, efficiency implies satisfying two conditions: cheap material and/or labour; and economies of scale.

In the UK motor industry, Ford, Chrysler (under the Peugeot-Citroen banner) and GM are all in a position to achieve the necessary economies of scale, but the apparent advantage of lower labour costs is obliterated by poor productivity and by the industrial stalemate which it creates. Only the components sector can manufacture competitive products in spite of the recurrent industrial interruptions. BL is hampered by an inadequate product range and poor cost-effectiveness — largely the result of a failure to take advan-

1.   Although the recent strike by Ford's unions against the 5 per cent pay limit may be argued to amount to unsupportive action by the UK government.

tage of low labour costs, [1] old plant and equipment and insufficient scale economies. The deteriorating balance of payments position in the motor industry and
the widening gap between productivity levels in the UK and Europe are unmis-
takable symptoms of a general decline in the motor industry.

Some readers might feel that too sharp a distinction has been made between
the enhanced state and the existing state, but if the industry is to expand
successfully, it must do so in accordance with the conditions established in
the European market. Half measures are a virtual guarantee of failure.

It was noted earlier that failure to take positive action, thus allowing
natural market forces to operate, would lead to the eventual certain decline of
all sectors of the UK motor industry — particularly BL volume cars and the
component manufacturers. It has been calculated that every job lost in the
motor industry proper generates a further indirect loss of two more jobs in
ancillary industries, which suggests that the employment implications alone
could have significant repercussions, particularly when allied to a worsening balance of payments. The argument that natural market forces should be allowed
free play has already been considered, and that resources should be channelled
elsewhere, but it should be remembered that the timescales involved before
equilibrium can be restored are so large that a basic level of government intervention is inevitable in any case — both as a temporary measure to boost
employment in the interim period, and as a means of providing new investment.

CONCLUSION

The UK motor industry has survived the oil crisis despite (rather than because
of) irresponsible government action over a number of years. The UK still has
some strengths which may provide the wherewithal to overcome its weaknesses.
It is not too late for the motor industry to fully recover. The French CV
industry has shown signs of weakness with import penetration figures of over
30%. Yet Renault, and perhaps the new PCC group, are reorganising the
industry with active government approval. Similarly it is not too late for the
UK — especially as the industry still has many strengths despite some
conspicuous weaknesses.

Government intervention within the framework of a rational policy could
be beneficial to the industry. The weakest point in the industry is cars and help
in this sector is badly needed. There are, however, no easy solutions. The CV
and components sectors, notwithstanding evidence of some problems, are in
good shape to face up to the 1980s, providing the domestic market is still a
major producer of components and parts.

Provided the industry is handled with care and despite a deteriorating
situation, there is now some room for cautious optimism.

---

1. The lower wage rate of UK labour being offset by low productivity.